The Marine Corps and
the State Department

The Marine Corps and the State Department

*Enduring Partners in
United States Foreign Policy,
1798–2007*

Leo J. Daugherty III

McFarland & Company, Inc., Publishers

Jefferson, North Carolina, and London

LIBRARY OF CONGRESS CATALOGUING-IN-PUBLICATION DATA

Daugherty, Leo J.
The Marine Corps and the State Department :
enduring partners in United States foreign policy,
1798–2007 / Leo J. Daugherty III.
p.   cm.
Includes bibliographical references and index.

ISBN 978-0-7864-3796-2
softcover : 50# alkaline paper ∞

1. United States. Marine Corps Embassy Security Group — History.
2. United States. Marine Corps — Foreign service — History.
3. United States. Dept. of State — Buildings — Security measures — History.
4. Embassy buildings — Security measures — United States — History.
5. Diplomatic and consular service — United States — History.
6. United States — Foreign relations.   I. Title.
VE23.D35 2009   327.73 — dc22   2008049097

British Library cataloguing data are available

On the Cover: The Marine detachment defending the home
of U.S. Consul Caborne at Matautu Point, Apia, Samoa in
April 1899, (USMC Photo); seal of the United States Marine Corps,
Wikipedia; World map ©2008 Shutterstock.

Manufactured in the United States of America

*McFarland & Company, Inc., Publishers
Box 611, Jefferson, North Carolina 28640
www.mcfarlandpub.com*

To all Marines who have stood watch over a troubled world
at Post One in the past, the present and in years yet to come

Acknowledgments

Writing history is the work of many, not just one. Such is the case with the writing of this book. Throughout there have been many individuals who made this project possible. Above all others, however, Lieutenant Colonel David W. Berkman, USMC, who was the executive officer of Marine Security Guard Battalion (1998–2000) located at Quantico, Va., Captains P.J. Smith and J.P. Valencia, as well as Mr. Fred Graboske, the head of Archives, History and Museums Division, HQMC, deserve special mention: Lieutenant Colonel Berkman, for the interest he expressed in seeking a historian to write a history of Marine Security Guard Battalion; Mr. Graboske, for kindly suggesting this author's name to Lieutenant Colonel Berkman as one who might be interested in writing a history of the Marine Security Guard Battalion.

The initial three-week period of combing through the archives at Marine Security Guard Battalion and assistance of several individuals involved with the Marine Corps' mission with the State Department contributed to the writing of this history. Thanks also goes out to Captains W.J. Gibbons and R.L. Nichols at Marine Security Guard Battalion for their outstanding support as well as that of their staffs, which was crucial in the completion of this study, and for that I am very grateful. Mr. Graboske was very helpful in providing command chronologies and a copy of the diary of Private Oscar J. Upham, USMC, which covered the period of the Boxer Rebellion and the subsequent relief of the International Legation Compound (June–September 1900) by the Allied Relief Expedition. Mr. Graboske put the author in touch with Private Upham's heirs, who in turn kindly granted permission to use portions of the diary in this manuscript. He has also been a great mentor and teacher, and for that I will be forever grateful.

Also deserving of mention are the following Marines from Marine Security Guard Battalion: Colonels William E. Rizzio, Boyette S. Hasty, D.S. Burgess, David W. Hurley, and David J. Head; Lieutenants Colonel Mary "Ginger" Jaycocks (Ret.), David W. Berkman, Stephen F. Kirkpatrick, A.R. Strauss, and F.D. Baker; Sergeants Major R.M. Biggs, J.M. Wertjes, Jimmie Brown, and Paul J. Nugent, Jr.; Majors Anthony R. Herlihy, Timothy L. Sullivan, K.C. Dugan, M.E. Sayegh, L.D. Volger, and P.R. Devore; Lieutenant Commander V.M. Huertas, MSC, USN; Captains Sarah Tragor and Morgan O'Byrne; CWO2 J.A. Pcola; Master Sergeant Josh Schenkler, First Sergeants Daniel P. Brown (deceased) and Maria Marty; Gunnery Sergeants Clayton L. Niles, Edward J. Burke, J.R. Boudreaux, J.L. Procopio, Richard K. Prather, and B. Jackson; Staff Sergeants Gilliland Rodriguez, Cory B. Knox, R.J. Edwards, and C.D. Dawkins; Sergeants Edwin Arce, Jr., C.D. Bell, Kiandra Hardware, M.D. Kindley, C.A. Joseph, Paul A. Schuster (now SSgt.), L.M. (Miller) Taetsch, Erick Cortes, and R.L. Daniels; Corporals E.A. Santosabrue, J.L. Reeder, J.T.D. Collie, A.W. Harriman, L.E. Bacon, and W. Jones; and Lance Corporals Michael J. Mehay, Courtney Hammond, and P.J. Saueur. Also worthy of mention is Mr. Alfred J. Verrier, retired State Department diplomatic courier.

I would finally like to thank the countless number of Marines stationed at the Marine Security Guard Battalion during the past five years. Their assistance and support proved crucial during my research trips to Marshall Hall, the home of Marine Security Guard School at Quantico, Va. Thanks also goes out to John Konicki and Lloyd Miller of the U.S. Department of State, and to their assistants, Sergeant Alejandra Medina and Corporal Agustin C. Pulido, both of whom greatly assisted in typing and collating while awaiting posting. Mr. Konicki is an instructor at the Marine Security Guard School. Mr. Miller, who served as an instructor at the Marine Security Guard School, was a detachment commander in Islamabad, Pakistan, in November 1979, and later became chief instructor with the Marine Security Guard Battalion School until his retirement in the spring of 2004.

I would like to say a special thanks to the individuals I work with on a daily basis at the U.S. Army Accessions Command, Fort Monroe, Va.: Lieutenant General Dennis D. Cavin, former commanding general, U.S. Army Accessions Command; his successors, Lieutenant Generals Robert L. Van Antwerp, Michael D. Rochelle and Lieutenant General Benjamin C. Freakley; Major General Jeffrey A. Arnold; Brigadier Generals B.P. Lennox and Dennis E. Rogers; Colonels Harry "Critz" Hardy, Paul Reoyo, Colonel Dennis Krings, Kevin Schwedo, Fred Keinle, Carol Smith, David E. Glover, Anthony Crutchfield, and Michael S. McGurk; Lieutenant Colonels Pete Badioan, Eugene Vecerra, Roy Brown, Terry Love, Joseph Allred, Daniel Dillon, M.G. Williams, Karen Whitman, and Paul Dulchinos; Majors Walter T. Caro, Emory Phlegar, David J. Horan, Robert Gonzalez, Dennis Daniels, Daryl Darden, and James T. Orr; Captains Angela Hildebrant, D.P. Mcoy, and Stanley Olsen; CWO4 R. Gambino; Command Sergeants Major Perry L. Roberts and Dennis E. King, Master Sergeant T.D. Keeling, Sergeants First Class Robert White, M.F. Menapace, M.I. Mounce, B.E. Scott, Craig Johnson, and Kitrona Rice; Staff Sergeants Jose Pagan and Jadore Scovell; Sergeants Kareem Terrell and Angelo Cisneros; Patrick McAndrews, Ed Maddie, Fay Allen, Carolyn Reynolds, Bonnie Morelen, Agnes Pettyjohn, Leslie Bulger, Rick Hartline, Art Coumbe, Mike Swisher, Robert O. Burns, Charles Wilson, Gary J. Lewis, Max Padilla, Tom Brooks, Captain Scott M. Smiley, Roger Yelverton, John Char, Eugene Adams, Diane Moses, Bill Copeland, Melody Taylor, Levi "Chip" Martin, Vic Powers, Ben King, Mrs. Cathy Meadows, Keli Slusher; Ms. Nikki Barry, Ms. Judi Stephenson, Greg Burget, B.J. Hewitt, and to the soldiers and civilians at Army Accessions Command I work with on a day-to-day basis.

To the staff at the History and Museums Division located at the Marine Corps Historical Center, Washington Navy Yard, particularly my commanding officers, Colonels Dennis Mroczkowski, Nicholas E. Reynolds, and R. Bonadonna; Lieutenant Colonel William L. Naehle; Colonel Jon T. Hoffman; Colonel Charles Cureton, who gratefully assisted this author through his vast knowledge of Marine uniforms; Mr. Robert Acqualina, Ms. Annette Amerman and Shelia Grambling of the Reference Section; Miss Evelyn Englander, Librarian; Al Croft, and his son Alex Croft, Mrs. Joyce Conyers Hudson, Ms. Judy Petsch, Jay Rhodes, and Miss Christine Laba, all of the Archives Section. Thanks also goes out to Mr. Trevor Plante of the National Archives in Washington, D.C., for his tireless assistance in the location of documents relating to Marine Legation Guards in China, Haiti, and Nicaragua. Miss Belinda Kelly of the Marine Corps Archives, Marine Corps University, Quantico, Va., deserves mention and thanks for my requests concerning material from the Lieutenants General James C. Breckinridge, USMC, and Pedro A. del Valle Papers. Thanks also goes out to Mrs. Nancy Lee Hoffman, deputy editor, and Jason Monroe of *Leatherneck* magazine; Ronald Lund, Jr., and Mrs. Bonnie J. Martin, all of the Marine Corps Association, for their assistance and friendship over the years.

To my academic advisors at Ohio State University, in particular Professors Allan R. Millett (Colonel, USMC Ret.); Alam Payind, David Stebenne , John F. Guilmartin (Lieutenant Colonel, USAF, Ret.); Williamson Murray (Lieutenant Colonel, USAF Ret.); Samuel Chu, and Michael Hogan. Also to my colleagues and friends at Ohio State University, including Mary Lynn Kiaz, M.D., Pamela Dull, M.D., Bradley Welling, M.D., and his two very special assistants, Mrs. Brenda Adkins and Mrs. Mary French; (Major) Christopher Ives; Jay Agan; Alexander Lassner; Mrs. Beth Russell; Miss Sujen T. Fung, supervisor of circulation, Mr. Don McCoy and Loretta Smith of the Stacks Department, all at the Main Libraries at Ohio State University; and Mrs. Lori Schleeter, assistant librarian at Ohio State University, Lima Campus. Both Miss Fung and Mrs. Schleeter oftentimes went out of their way to request books and other hard-to-find monographs through inter-library loans; to Dr. Allison Gilmore, chair of the History Department and a former supervisor; Dr. Michael Cunningham, academic vice president; Mrs. Melody Vermillion, Dr. Wayne Kaufman, Mrs. Jenny Burget, Jim Kerr, Mike Shipper, Dr. Javad Abdalkhani, Dr. Philip Rothmaler, and Dr. Phillip Heath, all at Ohio State University, Lima, for their advice and friendship while I was an instructor there.

I would like to thank Ms. Sara Allen, Ms. Belinda Boyd, Ms. Chantel Gray, and Mr. Justin Frasure for their hard work in assisting Dr. Smith-Daugherty with the indexing.

Also, thanks is extended to Professor Katherine A. Reist, chair and professor of history at the University of Pittsburgh, Johnstown, Pa., who read and commented on the chapter dealing with the Marines in China. Special appreciation goes out to two very special colleagues, Professor Doris T. Chang, who holds a Ph.D. in East Asian history, and Ms. Lisa Pillow, librarian at the University of Illinois (Chicago). Also, Christopher Reed, associate professor of Chinese history at Ohio State University. Both Ms. Chang and Professor Reed were particularly very helpful in the identification of sources on China in the nineteenth and twentieth centuries that proved helpful in preparation of my chapters on the involvement of the Marines in China during those years. Ms. Chang, who is presently assistant professor of women's studies at Wichita State University, spent many hours with the author discussing Chinese and Taiwanese history and nationalism during the early twentieth century. Likewise, the same can go out to a very special person and friend, Miss Lisa Pillow, formerly the reference librarian with the Black Studies Department at Ohio State University's main library. Miss Pillow, who now works at the University of Illinois, Chicago, was very kind in pointing out sources on the various African tribes along the Ivory Coast that the Marines and bluejackets oftentimes dealt with during the mid-nineteenth century. Lisa's knowledge of African American history was much appreciated. Finally, I would like to express my deepest gratitude to Miss Patti Hinson of the Mariners' Museum Library in Newport News, Va. Miss Hinson provided this author with a much-needed copy of the map of Lieutenant Presley N. O'Bannon's march across North Africa.

I would like to make special mention of my parents, Leo Jr. and Frances H. Daugherty, my sister Terry (Daugherty) Boehm, and my beautiful wife, Dr. Rhonda L. Smith-Daugherty. It has been their encouragement and support throughout the years that have allowed this author to become the historian that he is today. To my father, a sergeant in the Marine Corps, who has been my role model in shaping my Marine Corps career and life, as well as to my mother and sister, who never stopped encouraging my academic and military endeavors. Finally, to my wife Rhonda, whose encouragement, scholarship, and friendship have brought forth much sunshine to my life and enthusiasm to my writing and pursuit of scholarship, I want to say a big thanks.

Table of Contents

Preface

From its formation in 1775, the United States Marine Corps developed a close working relationship with the diplomatic service of the Continental Congress and later, in 1798, with the newly created United States Department of State. This relationship continues today as Marines provide security for many U.S. embassies and consulates worldwide. This history deals with the close working partnership between the Foreign Service and the Marine Corps that began in 1775, when Marine detachments accompanied U.S. diplomatic representatives to the French Royal Court in 1778. Since then, Marines have worked closely with the State Department during the Barbary Wars (1798–1815), the opening of the Middle Kingdom of China in 1836, and the signing of the executive order by President Theodore Roosevelt which formally established a Marine Legation Guard in that same country in January 1905. During the first two decades of the 20th century, Marines became even more involved in the security of consulates and later embassies in such places as Peking, Shanghai, Tientsin, Paris, London, and St. Petersburg.

This study examines the unique relationship between the U.S. Marine Corps and the State Department from 1798 through 2007, and how it evolved from providing ship's detachments for diplomatic missions abroad to guarding U.S. embassies and consulates worldwide. As is illustrated throughout the text, the Marines and the Department of State have had a long partnership that has proven critical in the execution of U.S. foreign policy since the earliest days of the Republic.

This partnership continues today as Marines provide security for many U.S. embassies and consulates worldwide. The basis for the close working partnership between the State Department and the Marine Corps centered upon the signing of the original Memorandum of Agreement between the State Department and Department of the Navy in 1948, when it was agreed that Marines would provide internal security in the protection of classified material and diplomatic personnel at U.S. embassies and consulates worldwide. With the signing of the Memorandum of Agreement between the Department of State and Marine Corps, the partnership forged between the two agencies solidified, as Marines spread out across the globe in order to defend and deter against attacks on American diplomatic personnel and provide security against external and internal compromise for classified information. Indeed, the Memorandum of Agreement recognized the unique abilities and history of the Marine Corps and its role as a naval security and expeditionary force, as well as its close association with the Department of State since its beginnings.

More importantly, this book attempts to illustrate the evolving nature of the relationship and missions of the Marines when in service of the Department of State. In fact, as the missions of the expeditionary battalions that preceded them changed during the first half of the 20th century, so have the current missions of Marine embassy guards. Since the signing of the original Memorandum of Agreement in 1948, embassy duty itself has evolved into one of the most important functions performed by Marines outside of the more traditional role of providing expeditionary forces in readiness. Even as the threats faced by Marines guarding consulates and embassies in such places as China, Africa, and the Middle East during the past two centuries have changed, the mission of Marine embassy guards has essentially remained the same. In sum, while the uniforms of the Marines who landed as part of naval landing parties in the late 18th, 19th and 20th centuries have changed from blue to camouflaged digital utilities, the mission of Marines standing watch in the many embassies and consulates remains constant. The Marines who stand guard over diplomatic posts worldwide today are truly the descendants of Marines who accompanied the many diplomatic missions of two centuries ago. As the events of the post–9/11 world have demonstrated, these young Marines, in fact, are oftentimes the sole line of defense in a troubled and unstable world. It is to these Marines that this book is dedicated.

Acronyms and Abbreviations

AESF: Amphibious Evacuation Security Force
AFPFL: Anti-Fascist People's Freedom League
AFRC: Armed Forces Ruling Committee
AMCITS: American Citizens
ANGLICO: Air Naval Gunfire Liaison Company
ARG: Amphibious Ready Group
ARVN: Army of the Republic of Vietnam
ASL: Army of Southern Lebanon
ATM: Anti-terrorism Marine
BCT: Battalion Combat Team
BEQ: Bachelor Enlisted Quarters
BLT: Battalion Landing Team
Bn.: Battalion
CBIRF: Chemical and Biological Incidence Response Force
COMISH: U.S. Military Mission in the Congo
CONUS: Continental United States
CPI: Communist Party of India
CS: Tear gas (chlorobenzylidenemalononitrile)
CVA: Aircraft Carrier
CWO: Chief Warrant Officer
DAO: Defense Attaché Office
DCM: Deputy Chief of Missions
DC/S: Deputy Chief of Staff
DET or Det.: detachment
DOD: Department of Defense
DOS: Department of State
ECC: Evacuation Control Center
ELA: Revolutionary Popular Struggle (Greece)
EOD: Explosive Ordnance Disposal
EOKA-B: National Organization of Cypriot Fighters
ESG: Expeditionary Strike Group
FAST: Fleet Anti-terrorist Security Team
FBIS: Foreign Broadcast Information Services
FCE: Forward Command Element
FMLN: Farabundo Martí National Liberation Front
4th MEB (AT): 4th Marine Expeditionary Brigade (Anti-Terrorism)
HMM: Marine Medium Helicopter Squadron

HQMC: Headquarters Marine Corps
INPFL: Independent National Patriotic Front of Liberia
ISMT: Indoor Simulator Marksmanship Trainer
JRA: Japanese Red Army
KLM: Swedish Airlines
LAAW: Light Anti-armor Weapon
LCDR: Lieutenant Commander
LCM: Landing Craft Mechanized
LCU: Landing Craft Utility
LST: Landing Ship, tank
LURD: Liberians United for Reconciliation and Democracy
LZ: Landing Zone
MAB: Marine Amphibious Brigade? 305
MACV: Military Assistance Command, Vietnam
MAF: Marine Amphibious Force
MAU: Marine Amphibious Unit
MCCDC: Marine Corps Combat Development Center
MCESC: Marine Corps Embassy Security Command
MCESGC: Marine Corps Embassy Security Guard Command
MCI: Marine Corps Institute
MCRD: Marine Corps Recruit Depot
MCSF: Marine Corps Security Force battalion
MCU: Marine Corps University
MEB: Marine Expeditionary Brigade
MEF: Marine Expeditionary Forces
MEU Marine Expeditionary Unit
MEU (SOC): Marine Expeditionary Unit (Special Operations Capable)
MOS: Military Occupation Specialty
MOA: Memorandum of Agreement
MPD: Military Personnel Division
MSC: Military Sealift Command
MSG: Marine Security Guard
MSGDET: Marine Security Guard Detachment
NBC: Nuclear, Biological and Chemical
NCOIC: Noncommissioned Officer in Charge
NEO: Non-combatant Evacuation Operation
NPFL National Patriotic Front of Liberia
NVA: North Vietnamese Army
NVGs: Night Vision Goggles
PDF: Panamanian Defense Force
PFLP: Popular Front for the Liberation of Palestine
PLO: Palestinian Liberation Organization
PRC: People's Republic of China
PRD: Dominican Revolutionary Party
PSU: Personal Security Unit
PT: Physical Training
REACT: Reaction Teams
ROK: Republic of Korea
RPG: Rocket Propelled Grenade

RSO: Regional Security Office or Officer
RVN: Republic of Vietnam
SEAL: Sea, Air and Land
SEATO: South East Asian Treaty Organization
SNCO: Staff Noncommissioned Officer
SNOIC or SNCOIC: Staff Noncommissioned Officer in Charge
SSGT or SSgt.: Staff Sergeant
SSD: Special Security Detail
TO/E: Tables of Organization/Equipment
URNG: Guatemalan National Revolutionary Unity Group
USA: United States Army
USAID: United States Agency in International Development
USDAO: United States Defense Attaché Office
USDEL, FPJMT: U.S. Delegation, Four-Party Joint Military Team
USIA: United States Information Agency
USIS: United States Information Service
USLO: United States Liaison Office
USMC: United States Marine Corps
USN: United States Navy
USOM: United States Operation Mission
USSAG: United States Support Activities Group
VC: Viet Cong
WO: Warrant Officer
XO: Executive Officer

CHAPTER 1

Origins of a Mission, 1798–1900

For nearly two and a half centuries the history of the United States Marine Corps and the U.S. Department of State has been intertwined, and is a story of continuous service together whether on land or at sea, at home and abroad. Marines have guarded embassies, consulates, and acted as security forces for diplomatic missions since the Quasi-War with France (1798–1801) and Lieutenant Presley O'Bannon's celebrated assault on Derne in 1805 up through the Boxer Rebellion in China in 1900. In fact, since the U.S. Department of State's permanent establishment in July 1798, the United States Marine Corps has had a close working relationship with the agency.

Throughout the 19th century, Marines along with Navy bluejackets accompanied both diplomatic representatives and naval officers ashore to foreign countries as a naval security force in such places as Haiti, China, Japan, and Korea. Oftentimes, as was the case in China in 1856 and Korea in 1871, leathernecks landed to protect U.S. diplomatic and civilian personnel, defend consulates or, as was the case during the 19th and early 20th centuries, storm fortresses manned by government-sponsored insurgents determined to prevent foreigners from entering their country. The Marine detachments aboard naval vessels oftentimes were the only means of defense in what many times proved to be a hostile and strange environment. Led either by officers or veteran noncommissioned officers, these Marine detachments were at the forefront of U.S. diplomacy during the 19th and early 20th centuries. They also set the precedent followed by Marine Security Guards today.

The Early Republic, 1798–1854

The first recorded assistance rendered by Marines to the fledgling Department of State took place in March 1799, when a detachment commanded by First Lieutenant Anthony Gale[1] accompanied the American Consul General Edward Stevens to Cape Francois (Cap Haitien) to establish diplomatic relations with the Haitian rebel leader Toussaint L'Ouverture. The primary goal of the diplomatic mission was to win the "good opinion of his people." Instructed by the first secretary of the navy, Benjamin Stoddert, to "hover about [Haitian waters] for a day or two to give Doctor Stevens an opportunity to influence Toussaint to invite you in, in which case it might be useful," the Marines not only served as a security force guarding the consul general, but openly assisted Toussaint in his struggle with rival leader Rigaud by providing him with arms and munitions as well as naval gunfire.[2] Rigaud had made a common practice of murdering and committing other outrages against shipwrecked American sailors, to which Toussaint had objected most strenuously. In commending the Marines in one of his official dispatches to the State and Navy departments, Mr. Stevens praised the "steadiness and smart actions" of the Marines, particularly those aboard the USS *Experiment* commanded by Second Lieutenant Nathan Sheredine in driving off Riguad's forces during one of their assaults against the Americans.[3]

During the last months of the Quasi-War with France (1798–1801), Marines aboard the USS *United States* rendered assistance as a security force to the State Department when a detachment accompanied U.S. envoys to France in order to secure a peace treaty with the French Revolutionary Council known as the Directory. The leathernecks, commanded by Captain Franklin Wharton[4] and First Lieutenant John Darley, provided shipboard security for the diplomats and accompanied the envoys that carried the peace treaty ashore once they reached the continent in 1801.[5]

Shores of Tripoli, 1803–1805

At the completion of their mission, the Marine detachment from the USS *United States* joined the U.S. Mediterranean Squadron then sailing off the coast of North Africa. Here, the leathernecks performed one of the most spectacular renderings of assistance to the U.S. Department of State during the years of the early Republic. When the ruling pasha of Tripoli, Yusuf Karamanli, seized the Tripolitian throne after murdering his older brother and taking hostage the family of his successor, Hamet, who had first fled to Tunis and finally Egypt, Hamet called upon the United States Navy's Mediterranean Squadron to assist him in regaining his throne. Yusuf became the de facto bashaw of Tripoli and continued to exact tribute from the foreign powers plying the waters of the Mediterranean. In order to emphasize his sovereignty and dissatisfaction with the United

The uniform of a Marine enlisted man in 1805 (courtesy Lt. Col. Charles H. Cureton, USMCR).

First Lieutenant Presley Neville O'Bannon, USMC, 1801–1807, was with William Eaton on the march from Alexandria, Egypt, to Derne, Tripoli, in 1805. After a fight with the Barbary pirates, O'Bannon's force of Marines, sailors, and Arab mercenaries captured the fort on April 27, 1805, and raised the American flag over foreign soil for the first time (courtesy U.S. Marine Corps).

States in the amount of tribute they paid to "sail" the waters of the Mediterranean unmolested, the bashaw on 14 May 1801 ordered the flagstaff of the U.S. Consulate cut down even as President Thomas Jefferson ordered a squadron of warships under the command of Commodore Dale to the Mediterranean "to show the flag." Commodore Dale's squadron likewise carried a "present of $10,000" to be paid to the bashaw as tribute even while the president

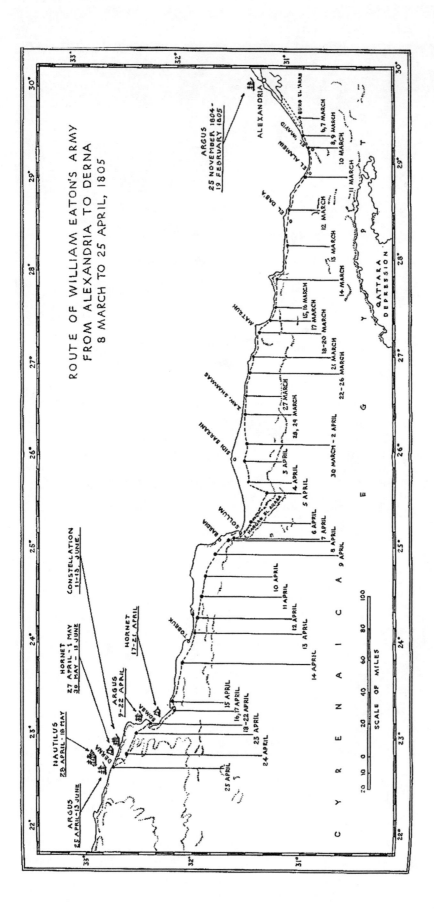

Map 1. Lieutenant Presley O'Bannon's march across the Libyan desert to Derne, Tripoli, in April 1805.

sought a means to end this form of piracy. Dale's squadron remained on station in the Mediterranean for three years.[6]

On 31 October 1803, one of the U.S. ships, the USS *Philadelphia*, ended up too close to the shore and went aground. The bashaw's forces captured the *Philadelphia's* entire crew, including forty-five Marines (one officer and forty-four enlisted men) and imprisoned them, demanding that an additional tribute be paid for their release.[7] In a daring raid that next February (1804), a combined force of sailors and Marines under the command of Lieutenant Stephen Decatur of the U.S. Navy forced their way past the bashaw's men and set the *Philadelphia* on fire.

It was during the summer of 1804 that Mr. William Eaton, a former U.S. Army officer who had been an acting "Navy agent" for several of the Barbary states and U.S. Consul at Tunis, conceived an idea to free the Americans being held prisoner, restore Hamet to his rightful throne, and end the paying of tribute to Yusuf and the other Barbary states. Eaton planned to launch a daring combined land and water attack on the bashaw's stronghold at Tripoli. Part of his plan called for a force of Marines to lead the assault, and he requested from the local U.S. naval commander, Commodore Barron, 100 Marines. In his message to Secretary of the Navy Smith, Consul Eaton wrote, "Those provinces in our possession will cut off from the enemy and turn into our own channel a source of provisions, and will open a free intercourse with the interior of the country. I have requested of the commodore for this purpose one hundred stand of arms, with cartridges and two field pieces, with trains and ammunition; *and also a detachment of one hundred Marines, if necessary, to lead a coup de main*"[8] (emphasis Eaton's). The commodore refused Eaton's request, fearing that he lacked the authority to provide such a force for such a mission absent explicit orders from the

The uniform of a Marine officer with the Mameluke sword presented to 1st Lieutenant O'Bannon by the ruler of Tripoli in recognition of his seizure of Derne. In honor of O'Bannon's gallantry, the Mameluke sword is worn by all Marine officers (courtesy Lt. Col. Charles H. Cureton, USMCR).

Navy Department. Commodore Barron did, however, provide Eaton with passage on the USS *Argus* to search for Hamet and restore him to the throne. On board the *Argus* was Marine Lieutenant Presley O'Bannon, Midshipman George Mann and seven Marines.

Consul General Eaton's force began its march across the Libyan desert toward Derne on 3 March 1805. His force included footmen, camel drivers, mercenaries, and nine Americans of whom eight were Marines (O'Bannon, a Marine sergeant, and six privates).[9] As Eaton's force proceeded westward, it kept as close to the sea and its provision ships as was possible until it finally reached the port of Bonda near Derne on 14 April 1805. Here, Eaton's force was augmented by the remainder of the Marine detachment aboard the *Argus* as well as those from the USS *Hornet* that Lieutenant O'Bannon quickly added to his own small detachment. Joined also by the USS *Nautilus,* Eaton's combined force prepared to assault Yusuf's fortress at Derne. Prior to the assault on Derne, Consul Eaton initiated one more attempt at diplomacy to win the release of the American captives and Hamet's throne back from the bashaw. Eaton's terms of "amity" to Yusuf were answered with a simple though straight-forward message: "My head or yours." With that reply Eaton prepared his forces for an assault on Derne.

Prior to Eaton's last attempt at diplomacy to win the freedom of the captives, the *Nautilus* and *Hornet* positioned themselves offshore to provide fire support for any assault that might be launched. After negotiations failed to resolve the outstanding issues between Yusuf and Eaton's forces, the two ships pounded the fortress of Derne with cannon fire. Meanwhile, Lieutenant O'Bannon's force of Marines, Greeks and Arabs commenced a landward attack on 26 March 1805. After nearly two hours of bitter, oftentimes vicious hand-to-hand fighting the Marines succeeded in seizing the fortress of Derne. In the midst of the fighting, the Marines managed to plant the American flag over the fortress, the first time the Stars and Stripes "flew over the fortress of the old world." As tradition has it, Lieutenant O'Bannon managed to climb on a rampart overlooking the city and plant the Stars and Stripes. After repelling two savage counterattacks by Yusuf's broken though not beaten forces, the Marines held their ground and beat back the attacks. In a final spirited bayonet charge the Marines drove off Yusuf's forces and restored Hamet to his rightful throne. In gratitude for this service by the Marines, the rightful bashaw of Tripoli presented to O'Bannon a jewel-encrusted sword carried by the Mamelukes of Egypt. Constructed of a fine curved blade and topped off by a "Mameluke" hilt, this sword became, with only a brief interruption (1859–78), the one exclusively worn by Marine officers.[10]

Actions Ashore in the Western Hemisphere, 1817–1821

Throughout the first two decades of the nineteenth century, Marines served ashore and afloat in the suppression of the slave trade (banned in 1804) on the coast of Africa and in the War of 1812 against Great Britain (1812–15). Marine detachments aboard the various frigates of the sailing Navy likewise escorted diplomats and landed on occasion to protect American citizens against local uprisings and prevent depredations against them. In the Western Hemisphere, Marines and Navy bluejackets landed to fight pirates or extract American citizens from such countries as Puerto Rico or Haiti (Hispaniola).

One such landing took place in Haiti in July 1817 when the ruler of southern Haiti, Petion, forced the American consul general living there to leave the island. The State Department sought to re-establish relations with this insurgent leader and the ruler of northern Haiti, General Christophe, and thus dispatched an envoy, a Mr. Tyler, to Haiti. To accompany Mr.

Tyler was a squadron under the command of Lieutenant Commander Charles N. Morris, USN, and a force of forty-seven Marines. While Petion received Mr. Tyler and Commander Morris and welcomed an opportunity for de facto recognition by the United States, Christophe refused to receive Tyler's mission, citing its lack of proper authority. Christophe maintained that Tyler's instructions were "not in due form," and thus caused the mission to fail. Commander Morris recalled in his memoirs in later years that even though the mission failed to produce tangible results insofar as the establishment of diplomatic relations with Christophe, the trip to Hispaniolan waters nonetheless proved indispensable in the collection of intelligence on Haiti, its people, and the current state of affairs there.[11] This information on Haiti was used in 1821 when Marines aboard the USS *Ontario* returned to Haitian waters in order to evacuate what few U.S. diplomats and civilians remained in this revolution-wracked country.[12]

In keeping with its close working relationship with the State Department, the U.S. Navy often transported American diplomats to their various consular posts on its warships. The Marine detachments on board these ships carried out special duties such as armed escorts for the diplomats. In fact, "this duty for many years was a very frequent one."[13] For instance, "In 1818 the *Peacock* carried a Minister to Europe, Second Lieutenant George Bethune, being her Marine Officer. The Franklin sailed from Annapolis on November 19, 1817, taking out Mr. Richard Rush and his Suite on his Embassy to England. Her Marine officer was First Lieutenant Benjamin Richardson."[14]

On 23 April 1818, the secretary of the Navy informed Lieutenant Colonel Commandant Franklin Wharton that the USS *Guerriere* would carry "a Minister of the United States to the Court of St. Petersburg in Russia," and that was to provide an appropriate guard for this mission. Lieutenant Colonel Wharton assigned First Lieutenant Lyman Kellogg and Second Lieutenant Thomas Stanhope English as the detachment's commanding and executive officers, respectively, as well as fifty-three Marines. Three corporals were placed in direct command of the enlisted Marines. Prior to the start of the diplomatic mission, the lieutenant colonel commandant informed Commodore Thomas MacDonough, the commanding officer of the *Guerriere*, that pursuant to his request a suitable detachment of Marines had been selected to accompany the minister, though due to a shortage of Marine officers only First Lieutenant Kellogg would be available for this mission. In 1819, a Marine detachment under the command of Second Lieutenant Joseph C. Hall escorted the newly appointed minister to Spain, Mr. Forsyth, to Cadiz.[15]

Early Contacts with China and Japan, 1836–1854

By the beginning of the 19th century, American merchants and traders had established a profitable business with the Middle Kingdom of China. Clipper ships from harbors such as Boston and Philadelphia traded tea, tobacco, and other goods for fine silks and spices with Chinese and European businessmen living in China and Korea. While the United States established its first diplomatic relations with China in 1842, American warships had already had contact with this part of Asia as early as 1835. Hoping to establish diplomatic contacts with Japan as well as China and the rest of Southeast Asia, President Andrew Jackson dispatched Mr. Edmund Roberts to the Far East in order to negotiate treaties with Cochin China (Vietnam), Siam (Thailand), and Muscat (Oman). President Jackson also authorized Roberts to undertake a separate mission to Japan "if he found the prospect favorable."[16] The USS *Peacock*, commanded by Captain David Geisinger, USN, set sail from Boston in March of 1832.

During his visit, Mr. Roberts negotiated a treaty of friendship and commerce with China, Siam, and Cochin China. Accompanying Mr. Roberts ashore was the *Peacock's* Marine detachment, commanded by Second Lieutenant H.W. Fowler.[17] Having returned to Washington, D.C., in the summer of 1834, Mr. Roberts once again set sail for the Orient, this time hoping to visit and establish relations with Japan. Unfortunately, Roberts died in China before setting sail for Japan. Commodore Edmund P. Kennedy, who commanded the U.S. East India Squadron, abandoned the mission, for he had no instructions to proceed forward if something were to happen to Consul Roberts.

The United States nonetheless did not give up its attempt to negotiate a treaty with Japan. Depredations against shipwrecked American sailors as well as those of other countries by Japanese officials prompted Washington to continue its efforts at negotiating a treaty with the emperor. President John Tyler appointed Mr. Caleb Cushing as the first "commissioner" to China, and instructed him to negotiate what became the first treaty between the United States and China. Cushing had hoped to induce the Japanese to sign a similar treaty, and thereby informed Secretary of State John C. Calhoun of his intentions. In response to Cushing project, President Tyler gave Cushing full diplomatic power to negotiate with Japanese authorities on behalf of the United States. Accompanying Mr. Cushing to China were the warships of the U.S. East India Squadron, commanded by Commodore Foxhall A. Parker, USN. Mr. Cushing, who traveled on board the USS *Brandywine*, landed on Macao on 27 February 1844. Aboard the *Brandywine* was the ship's Marine detachment, commanded by First Lieutenant Archibald Gillespie, who accompanied Cushing ashore and established a Marine guard around the minister's residence.

On 15 April 1845, Secretary of State James Buchanan wrote to Cushing's successor, Mr. Alexander H. Everett, and instructed him to negotiate with the Japanese a commercial treaty. After setting sail aboard the USS *Columbus*, Mr. Everett became seriously ill. He therefore granted Navy Commodore James Biddle plenipotentiary powers to negotiate with the Japanese. The Navy Department had anticipated such a possibility and directed Commodore Biddle in his orders to "persevere in the design, yet not in such a manner as to excite a hostile feeling, or a distrust of the government of the United States.[18] The *Columbus* and the USS *Vincennes* arrived off Macao on 5 January 1846 and sailed to the Chusan Islands off the southeast coast of China. In early July Commodore Biddle decided to proceed to Japan. Writing to Secretary of the Navy George Bancroft, Biddle informed the secretary, "As your instructions direct me to ascertain if the ports of Japan are accessible, I proceeded to upon leaving the coast of China towards the coast of Japan." On 20 July 1846, as Marines and sailors half a world away hoisted the first American flags over Monterrey during the Mexican-American War, the *Columbus* and *Vincennes* sailed into Yedo Bay in their quest to establish diplomatic and commercial relations with the Japanese.

Even before the *Columbus* and *Vincennes* dropped anchor, a Japanese officer along with a Dutch interpreter boarded the *Columbus* and asked Biddle what was "my object in coming to Japan." Biddle informed the Japanese officer that he "came as a friend" and sought only to inquire whether Japanese ports, like the Chinese ports, were open to foreign trade, and if not could a treaty be negotiated whereby American vessels could enter Japanese ports for the purpose of trading.[19] As the Japanese pondered Biddle's request, all sorts of military and civilian boats surrounded the American warships. Japanese officials denied Biddle or any of his crew permission to land. They raised objections to the passage of the ships' boats of between the two American vessels. Japanese military representatives also insisted that the Americans turn over all of their armaments, including muskets, swords, knives, and cannon, as it was the custom of foreigners to do when entering Japanese ports. Biddle refused this request as well and sternly replied that it "was impossible for us to do so."

Biddle sought intervention by the emperor himself and therefore addressed a letter to him. The Commodore included copies of the treaties of commerce negotiated with the Chinese that he felt might convince the mikado to open Japanese ports to foreign ships. Commodore Biddle waited six days for the emperor to reply. After he sent a terse note to the governor of Yedo inquiring as to the status of his request, the emperor's reply came. The note, which arrived on 27 February 1846, delivered by an eight-man royal delegation, reiterated Japan's refusal to trade with the United States and stated that "the Japanese would only trade with the Chinese and the Dutch." Furthermore, the reply stated, "It won't be allowed that America make a treaty with Japan or trade with her, as the same is not allowed any other nation." The Emperor ended his note with the words "you must depart as quickly as possible and not come any more in Japan."[20] The emissaries then with a veiled threat re-emphasized what the emperor had written: "The Emperor positively refuses the permission you desire ... and [he] earnestly advises you to depart immediately and to consult your own safety by not appearing again upon our coast."

Biddle, however, was not to be deterred. Instead he attempted to board the junk carrying the emissaries in order to receive the letter from the emperor. When Commodore Biddle set foot on board the Japanese boat, a Japanese official struck the American naval officer so hard that he was thrown back into his whaleboat. While the Japanese apologized for this unfortunate occurrence, the Marine detachment aboard the *Columbus* commanded by First Lieutenant Nathaniel Sheafe Waldron and Second Lieutenant John C. Cash readied their weapons and prepared to defend the commodore. The other Marine detachment aboard the *Vincennes*, led by Orderly Sergeant Henry Larimer, likewise prepared for possible action which, of course, never occurred, as Biddle tactfully withdrew and ordered the squadron to set sail for the United States.[21]

One last attempt to establish relations with Japan prior to Commodore Matthew C. Perry's historic visit occurred in 1849 when Commander James Glynn, commander of the USS *Preble* and on orders from Commodore David Geisinger, set sail for Nagasaki, Japan, to retrieve several shipwrecked American sailors. On board the *Preble* was a Marine detachment commanded by Orderly Sergeant John Culp. While en route to Nagasaki the *Preble* visited Napa, in the Lew Chew Islands, and became the first American warship to visit these islands. After reaching Nagasaki, Commander Glynn demanded the release of the shipwrecked Americans. Without hesitation the Japanese quickly handed over the imprisoned Americans. Shortly thereafter the U.S. warship pulled anchor and headed for Honolulu, Hawaii, on 20 May 1849. Commander Glynn was the first American who was able to induce the Japanese to "yield to foreign demands."[22] Commander Glynn's success in retrieving the shipwrecked Americans "greatly aroused public interest in Japan." Captain Glynn likewise aroused the interest of President Millard Fillmore in a letter he had written[23] shortly after his return to the United States in the spring of 1851.

With the end of the Mexican War (1846–48) and the expansion of the territorial United States there were increased demands for an expansion of trade into the Pacific. In early May 1851, Commodore John H. Aulick, who was preparing to assume command of the East India Squadron, proposed in a letter to Secretary of State Daniel Webster that as a sign of goodwill toward Japan, the United States should return several Japanese sailors who had been picked up at sea by an American vessel and taken to San Francisco. Aulick wrote that this might serve as a step toward the establishment of commercial relations with Japan. Secretary of State Webster brought this request to the attention of President Fillmore, who, after discussing Aulick's idea with his cabinet, "decided to establish a mission to Japan and to entrust it to Commodore Aulick, who was made an envoy of the United States and empowered to negotiate a treaty with the Japanese on 30 May 1851. Secretary of State Webster furnished Commander Aulick with a letter signed by President Millard Fillmore dated 10 May 1851 addressed to the Japanese emperor. Webster informed Aulick that he was to deliver the letter to "such of his [the emperor's] high officers as he may appoint," and that he had full diplomatic powers to negotiate such a treaty.

The Marines and Commodore Perry's Mission to Japan, 1851–54

As Commodore Matthew Calbraith Perry[24] prepared his squadron for its journey to the Far East, Brigadier General Commandant Archibald Henderson likewise began to prepare the Marine detachments that would accompany the commodore on his historic voyage. To lead the detachment of Marines, the brigadier general commandant selected Major Jacob Zeilin, due to the "importance and interest" of the Japanese Expedition, and because such a mission, Henderson concluded, "required officers of ability and experience." General Henderson believed that Major Zeilin (who became brigadier general commandant of the Marine Corps in 1864) was "well adapted for that service."[25]

Prior to their departure for the Far East, the Marines selected for this mission trained at the Marine Barracks, Washington, D.C., oftentimes in "the yard before the East Front of the Capitol," in front of the citizens of that city. In their brand new uniforms the leathernecks "presented a most lively scene" as noncommissioned officers marched and counter-marched the men in columns of twos and fours, and they conducted endless and repetitive drills in the manual of arms and practiced firing their muskets. While the Marines drilled, the Marine Band played delightful tunes for the accompanying crowds that gathered to watch them.

On 24 March 1852 Secretary of the Navy Graham formally ordered Commodore Perry to take command of the East India Squadron. The squadron at the time consisted of the USS *Susquehanna*, USS *Plymouth* and USS *Saratoga*, to which the Navy added the USS *Mississippi*, USS *Princeton*, and the stores ship USS *Supply*. In the fall of 1852, the Navy Department added the USS *Vermont*, USS *Macedonian*, USS *Allegheny*, USS *Vandalia*, and the USS *Southhampton*. The *Mississippi* served as Perry's flagship and set sail from New York Harbor destined for Annapolis, Maryland. At Annapolis, the *Mississippi* was to join with the *Princeton* prior to setting sail for the Far East. Boiler problems prevented the *Princeton* from sailing, however, and the Navy Department replaced her with the USS *Powhatan*. After a visit by President Fillmore and Navy Secretary Kennedy, the *Mississippi* headed first for Norfolk and then across the South Atlantic, where she visited Madiera, St. Helena, the Cape of Good Hope, Mauritius, Ceylon, and Singapore before her arrival at the port of Hong Kong, China, on 6 April 1853. The squadron rendezvoused at the port of Shanghai and received final instructions from the United States' consul general to China. Commodore Perry's squadron, including its force of Marines, set sail for the Lew Chew Islands, where it dropped anchor on 26 May 1853 on the island of Okinawa. Only the *Plymouth* with its Marine detachment remained behind in Shanghai to protect the American diplomatic staff if the need arose.

On Okinawa, as the prince regent to the emperor and his cortege met with Commodore Perry, Major Zeilin and members of his staff who accompanied Perry ashore requested permission to find a suitable level place where he could drill his Marines.[26] On 30 May 1853,

Major Zeilin, four of his officers, four crewmembers of the *Susquehanna* (where Zeilin and his Marines had been stationed), and four Chinese went ashore to explore the island on orders from Commodore Perry. While Major Zeilin and his staff explored the area for a suitable drill field, the prince regent and his retinue met with Commodore Perry and discussed through interpreters the place for the next official meeting between the United States and Japan. The two parties agreed that Perry's return visit would take place at the Palace of Shuri. Precisely at 9 a.m. on the morning of 6 June 1853, whaleboats carrying the Navy blue jackets and Major Zeilin's Marines came ashore. Major Zeilin and the other officers of the squadron formed their respective detachments into two facing columns as Commodore Perry's barge arrived on shore. Shortly thereafter, Major Zeilin, who had ordered his Marines to fix bayonets, shouted, "Present arms" as the commodore, his flag officers and staff walked up and down the ranks of sailors and Marines to inspect them. The two companies of Marines, in their dress blue coats and white trousers, then formed behind the commodore (who had been provided with a sedan chair) and headed toward the meeting with the Japanese prince regent at the Shuri Castle. Accompanying the leathernecks was the band of the *Mississippi* and two guns from the *Susquehanna*. Not knowing what to expect once ashore, the Marines carried six rounds of ball cartridges in their ammunition pouches. In his description of the initial landing on Okinawa, Commodore Perry later wrote, "I cannot conceive of a more beautiful pageant."[27] The procession of Marines, bluejackets and musicians included several Japanese officials who had wished to minimize the Americans' contacts with the peoples of Lew Chew. To denote their rank these officials wore yellow caps. Upon reaching the gate to the Shuri Palace the Americans were met by the regent and three consular officials known as "pe-chings."[28]

The regent and other Japanese officials remained wary of these foreigners. Perry noted in his journal that the regent and his court appeared agitated when they saw the Marines and sailors approach the palace grounds with their muskets and swords. After Perry assured the regent that no harm was meant and that no sailor or Marine would enter the gate with their arms, his group gave a great sigh of relief. After a banquet that included many toasts of saki held in his honor the commodore delivered President Fillmore's note to the regent. The commodore informed him that the note was to be sent to the emperor and that it expressed the desire to establish relations with Japan. The regent and the pe-chings took the note and assured Perry that it would be delivered to the emperor for his decision. Perry informed them that they would return in several months for a reply. After several more visits with Japanese officials on Okinawa and at Napa in the Lew Chews, as well as a rendezvous with its stores ship *Supply,* and renting a coaling station from the islanders, Perry's force returned to Chinese waters in late July 1853.

Commodore Perry's fleet returned on 1 August 1853 to Hong Kong, where he awaited the emperor's reply to President Fillmore's letter. While in Hong Kong, the Taiping Rebellion broke out in China. It required assistance from the various foreign navies, including Marines and bluejackets from the East India Squadron docked in Hong Kong and Shanghai. After the arrival of the French, British, and Russian fleets to Chinese waters, as well as a rumored visit of a Russian squadron to the port of Nagasaki, Japan, Perry decided to set sail for Japanese waters. He pulled anchor in January 1854 and once again headed for the Lew Chews. Meanwhile, it had been agreed upon by the Japanese to meet with the Americans at a place of their choosing, which turned out to be, after some diplomatic wrangling, the port of Yokohama. Commodore Perry's squadron arrived off Yokohama 4 March for the meeting with the representatives of the emperor set for 8 March 1854.

On the eve of the first meeting between Perry and the Japanese commissioners, the com-

The landing of Commodore Oliver Perry and officers and men of the U.S. squadron. Along with the sailors was a contingent of Marines who met with Imperial Japanese commissioners at Yokohama, Japan, on March 8, 1854 (courtesy U.S. Marine Corps).

modore's staff officer issued an order which stated that "on the first landing of the Commodore to meet the Japanese Commissioners he will be escorted by all the Marines of the Squadron, who can be spared from duty and that Major Zeilin will make all the necessary arrangements ... all boat guns to be mounted and ammunition in boats." At 11:30 a.m. on 8 March 1854, Commodore Perry, his staff of Navy and Marine Corps officers and his escort "consisting of about five hundred Officers, Seamen, and Marines, fully armed, embarked in twenty-seven barges, in command of Commander Buchanan," headed for the shore where a large tent had been erected that housed the Japanese officials sent to greet the Americans.[29] Perry's force of five hundred men landed and the Japanese officials watched in amazement as the foreigners marched from the shore line in perfect order. One observer described the landing:

> When the escort had landed, the Marines were drawn up in a hollow square, leaving a wide open space between them, while the naval officers remained in a group at the wharf. The Commodore on landing from the Powhatan "was received by the group of officers, who, falling into a line, followed him. The bands now struck up a lively tune, and the Marines, whose orderly ranks in complete military appointment, with their blue and white uniforms, and glistening bayonets, made quite a martial and effective show, presented arms as the Commodore, followed in procession by his immediate staff proceeded up the shore.[30]

The first order of business between Perry and the Japanese commissioners was the burial of Private Robert Williams, a Marine who had died on 6 March 1854 aboard the *Missis-*

sippi. Commodore Perry sought permission to bury Private Williams on Japanese soil. At first the Japanese informed Perry that it was forbidden that any foreigner be buried on Japanese soil. After some convincing on the part of the commodore they consented to the request. On the following day, with an honor guard of Marines, seamen, and Japanese soldiers as well as a Navy chaplain and a Buddhist priest (supplied by the Japanese), Private Williams, was laid to rest in a special cemetery for foreigners near Yokohama. Shortly thereafter, the Japanese constructed a bamboo hut over the grave of Private Williams as was customary in the Buddhist ceremony for the dead. The Japanese likewise placed a guard next to the grave for a short time to honor the memory of Private Williams, who became the first American serviceman to be interred on Japanese soil.[31]

On March 9, Perry's expedition once again came ashore, this time to present to the emperor's representatives the gifts that were carried in the holds of the various U.S. warships. In order to insure the safety of the Americans and Japanese, Henry B. Adams, commander of the fleet, issued General Order No. 16 dated 14 March 1854. It directed that

> a Marine officer be sent on shore every day at the building adjoining Yokohama where the Engineers and Mechanics of the Squadron are employed. He will be attended by four orderlies wearing side-arms, & his duty will be to prevent any intrusion by the officers or men into the new building, or the houses of the people; to see that the work going on is not neglected nor the persons employed at it, allowed to wander away from the vicinity. Strict orders must be given that the men are not to leave the boat when they land. A disregard of this order will not be overlooked. The order forbidding intercourse with the shore, or the admittance of the Japanese on board the ships for any purpose whatever, unless by permission of the Commodore is to be strictly observed."[32]

The day before (13 March 1854), Major Zeilin had issued his own order that directed Captain William B. Slack and a company of Marines to stand guard over the presents to be given to the emperor of Japan by the president of the United States.

On 24 March 1854, Commodore Perry and his staff went ashore at Yokohama as guests of the Japanese, who had ordered a large reception in honor of the American naval officers, including all of the Marine officers. After the dinner Captain Robert Tansill and a company of Marines "were put through their various evolutions, drills, and etc." This martial display impressed the Japanese commissioners, who commented on the "soldierly air and excellent discipline of the men."[33] The Japanese likewise put on a display of their own martial arts with a troupe of Sumo wrestlers, who greatly impressed the Marines by their size and discipline.[34]

Brigadier General Jacob Zeilin, USMC, seventh commandant of the Marine Corps, June 10, 1864, to October 31, 1876. Then-Major Zeilin commanded the detachment of Marines sent ashore during Oliver Perry's historic visit to Japan in March 1854 (courtesy U.S. Marine Corps).

After a dinner aboard the *Powhatan*, Perry's flagship, on March 27, the Americans and Japanese commenced the business of negotiating a treaty dealing with the establishment of diplomatic relations and the protection of Americans while on Japanese soil when conducting business. After a final banquet on 31 March 1854, held in a great reception hall in Kanagawa, Japan, American and Japanese representatives signed the Treaty of Peace, Commerce, and Navigation which, besides establishing peace and friendship between the two countries, opened the ports of Shimoda and Hokadate to American ships. The treaty also led to the establishment of full diplomatic relations between the United States and Japan. The Japanese likewise dictated that the port of Shimoda was to be the seat of the U.S. Consulate. Furthermore, the United States agreed that while in Japan, Americans were subject to "just and amenable laws." The United States likewise granted Japan most-favored nation status insofar as trade and commerce were concerned. The Treaty of Peace, Commerce, and Navigation established "the territorial limits of where Americans were permitted while on Japanese soil, and that ratification of the treaties was to take place within eighteen months of the date the treaty had been agreed upon."[35] After the signing of the treaty, Commodore Perry entrusted the delivery of the treaty to Washington, D.C., to Commander Henry B. Adams of the USS *Saratoga*. Accompanying Commander Adams was Major Zeilin, who had been transferred to that same ship while Perry conferred with Japanese officials. While Major Zeilin headed home with the treaty between the United States and Japan, Captain William B. Slack proceeded to China on board the USS *Mississippi*. Captain Slack's Marine detachment had been ordered there in order to protect the U.S. nationals caught up in the ongoing Taiping Rebellion.[36]

By terms of the treaty negotiated by Commodore Perry, the United States and Japan exchanged diplomatic representatives. The first American appointed consul general to Japan was Mr. Townshend Harris. After a journey that lasted one hundred forty-nine days, Mr. Harris arrived in the Far East in January 1856 when, after a further delay of seventy-nine days, he was transported by the USS *San Jacinto* to first Singapore and later Hong Kong before arriving in Shimoda, Japan, on 21 August 1856. After his arrival in Japanese waters, and accompanied ashore by Captain Bell of the *San Jacinto* and its ten-man Marine detachment, commanded by Second Lieutenant Henry B. Tyler, Mr. Townshend Harris set foot on Japanese soil and presented his diplomatic credentials to officials of the shogun.[37] Throughout the remainder of 1856 and 1857, Marines of the *San Jacinto* came ashore and conducted drills and guarded the consulate and its grounds. In his annual report to the Secretary of the Navy, Commodore Armstrong wrote on 4 September 1856 that "the American flag was flying on the Consular Flag Staff on shore." Elevated from American consul general to minister resident of the United States to Japan, Mr. Harris moved the consulate from Shimoda to Kanawaga into a former Buddhist shrine known as the Shin Shiu Temple ('Shrine of Virtue and Happiness'). At Kanagawa, the Marines from the USS *Mississippi*, USS *James Fenimore Cooper* and USS *Saginaw* provided security amid the threats of murder, assassination attempts, and other acts of violence that erupted in 1859 directed against foreigners.[38]

In 1860 the United States and Japan exchanged the first diplomatic missions with the arrival of the first U.S. minister to Japan. The Japanese, however, were unable to send their representatives due to their lack of modern ships. Japanese officials asked the U.S. minister if it were possible that a U.S. warship could transport the first Japanese delegation to Washington, D.C., a request that was immediately approved. On 13 February 1860 the USS *Powhatan* left Yedo Bay carrying aboard it the first Japanese diplomatic mission to the United States.

Detailed to guard the emperor's representatives was a detachment of Marines commanded by Captain Algernon S. Taylor, who was responsible for their "comfort and safety." The Marine detachment provided security for the Japanese diplomats until their arrival in Washington, D.C., on 14 May of that same year.[39] On their return trip to Japan, the Japanese diplomats were accompanied by First Lieutenant Israel Greene and Second Lieutenant George Butler along with the Marine detachment aboard the USS *Niagara*, which provided security for the envoys until they reached Shimoda, Japan, in November of that same year.

At the conclusion of the American Civil War in 1865, Marines once again resumed their peacetime functions that included providing security for consular and diplomatic officials. Two of the more notable occurrences took place when the Marine guards assigned to the USS *Shenandoah* and *Wyoming* provided security for Mr. Van Valkenburg, the American minister to Japan, during his visit with the shogun at Osaka in May of that year. On 19 January 1868, during the civil war that took place in Japan prior to the restoration of the Meiji Emperor (1868), a Marine guard was assigned to the American minister's residence at Yokohama, Japan. Second Lieutenant John C. Morgan and four enlisted Marines remained assigned to guard the American minister until 26 September. This was one of the first long-term Marine guard assignments in support of the Foreign Service.[40]

The detachment of Marines "presents arms" as the Japanese delegation arrives in Yokohama, Japan, on March 8, 1854 (courtesy Lt. Col. Charles H. Cureton, USMCR).

The Marines and China, 1854–1866

Since 1835 the Marine Corps has been at the forefront of the United States' diplomatic relations with China. Indeed, the first Marine involvement in the 'Middle Kingdom' occurred as early as 1835 when the U.S. East India Squadron made its base along the Chinese port city of Hong Kong. When the United States opened full diplomatic relations with China in 1842, Mr. Caleb Cushing, the first U.S. minister to China, established the U.S. Consulate two years later (1844) in the port city of Macao.[41] A squad of Marines from the USS *Brandywine* led by a veteran noncommissioned officer accompanied Mr. Cushing and remained ashore for the next two months to provide security. The decision to send the Marines ashore had been designed to impress upon the Chinese the importance that the United States attached to its relations with that country.[42]

After an American killed a Chinese merchant, rioting shortly thereafter broke out among the inhabitants of the city of Whampoa, who demanded the handing over of the culprit, who had taken refuge in an American factory. When the occupants of the factory refused to comply with the mob's demand, Mr. Cushing requested that a landing party of bluejackets and Marines be sent ashore from the USS *Brandywine* and USS *St. Louis,* in order to protect American lives and property in Whampoa, and around the U.S. diplomatic compound. On 19 June 1844, a force of Marines and forty-four sailors landed, armed with muskets and cutlasses, and headed toward the factory in order to disperse the crowd and restore order. After the restoration of order and arrest of the individual accused of murder, the sailors returned to their respective ships on June 21. The leathernecks remained ashore for another month to provide security for the consulate and its surrounding grounds.[43] During Commodore Perry's historic voyage to Japan, Marines stood off the coast of China aboard ships of the U.S. Navy's East India Squadron to safeguard the lives of American consular officials and citizens living in Hong Kong and Shanghai.

When fighting broke out between the British and Chinese in the second of what were called the "Opium Wars" in October 1856, the U.S. consul to Canton, China, Mr. Oliver H. Perry, requested a force of bluejackets and Marines to protect the interests of the United States. Assigned to this force were eighteen enlisted Marines from the USS *Portsmouth* (Commander Andrew H. Foote, USN), led by Second Lieutenant William H. Kirkland, and sixty-four sailors (four naval officers and sixty enlisted men). With his force of Marines and bluejackets as well as a field howitzer, Second Lieutenant Kirkland headed for Canton. As this force landed in Canton on the morning of 22 October 1856, another force of leathernecks and bluejackets, from the USS *Levant* commanded by Second Lieutenant Henry B. Tyler, proceeded toward Canton where to join forces with the Marines and sailors from the *Portsmouth*. By 14 November 1856 the force of Marines and sailors ashore had grown with the addition of twenty-eight more Marines from the frigate USS *San Jacinto* led by Captain John D. Simms. Overall command of the force ashore, which had now grown to 150 sailors and Marines, had now passed to Commander Foote, who was the senior American officer ashore. On November 16 the Marines and sailors re-embarked aboard the USS *Levant,* where they remained off of Canton in case they were needed ashore. As the Marines and sailors came aboard the *Levant,* Chinese pirates who had occupied a series of forts in the Canton River fired on the boat carrying the commander. Commodore Foote, with approval of Mr. Perry, ordered the force of Marines, commanded by Captain Simms, as well as the Navy bluejackets, to ready an assault on the enemy's barrier fortresses that had fired on the flag of the United States.

Even as Commodore Armstrong's force prepared for an assault against the barrier he attempted several meetings with Yeh, the governor of Canton, to try to peacefully remove the bandits from the barrier forts. Unfortunately, however, the governor replied that he was powerless to enter into negotiations with them. This in turn prompted the commodore to ready his forces for the assault on the fortresses. Commander Foote's assault force was augmented by the steamer *Williamette* and steam tug *Kum Fa.* The storming party consisted of "two hundred and eighty seven persons, Officers, Seamen and Marines, with four howitzers," commanded by Commander Foote.

The bandits did not wait, however, for the Americans to assault. They launched a furious fusillade aimed at the *Portsmouth,* which damaged her rigging and penetrated the frame of her stern. This Chinese fire also wounded a Marine aboard the *Portsmouth.* The American ship fired 230 shells of her own at the fortresses, which soon ceased all fire. Commander Foote, now in overall command of the fort due to Commodore Armstrong's illness, planned to launch a combined attack.

From the 18th through the early morning hours of November 20, the American ships in the Canton River pounded the forts with howitzer and cannon fire until the commander gave the order to "land the landing force." At 0630 the assault force embarked in ship's boats and headed for shore.[44] The combined force of Marines and sailors, backed up by the renewed fire of the *Portsmouth*'s howitzers and cannons, landed unopposed at 0850 and stormed the first fortress. The Marines and bluejackets were able to force their way into the fortress, where they soon encountered a determined and savage enemy. In the battle that ensued, the Americans drove away from the forts the Chinese bandits, who left many dead and wounded inside the fortress. The Marines and sailors then repelled two subsequent counterattacks that left scores of Chinese dead or wounded. After the withdrawal of the remnants of the last enemy attack, the Marines ran up the Stars and Stripes over the first fort's battered ramparts.

The Marines and bluejackets returned to their respective ships and prepared for the next day's assault. Early on the morning of November 21, the Marines and sailors of the landing force embarked once again in the ships' boats and, towed by the steam tug *Kumfa,* moved upstream toward their next objective. American guns from the offshore ships once opened up with a deadly barrage of cannon fire in support of the landing. As this was taking place, the Chinese likewise opened up with a deadly cannonade aimed at the ship's boats carrying the assault troops. In one instance, a 68-pound shot knifed through one of the American boats, killing three bluejackets and wounding five others. While the Chinese fire proved frightening in its volume and ferocity, it was nonetheless inaccurate and scattered. Once the Marines and bluejackets aboard, reached the shore, Captain Simms led his assault force across a waist-deep swamp and over granite walls. While a Chinese force that numbered just over a thousand troops stood barely outside the range of the howitzers landed by Simms' force, Marine Corporal William McDougal of the *Levant* ran from cover and planted the Stars and Stripes on the adjacent parapet.[45]

Once the second fort had fallen Commander Foote ordered Captain Simms' force to clear the Chinese from the river bank so that his boats would not be caught in a crossfire during the last phase of the operation, which was an attack on Napier Island. Staying close to the river's embankment, they soon came upon a Chinese artillery battery of seven guns. The leathernecks caught the Chinese by surprise. After a brief though heavy exchange of musket fire the Chinese fled as Simms' Marines spiked the enemy guns. Simms then moved his force to the top of the embankment and opened fire in order to silence the third of the Chinese fortresses. Simms' Marines then returned to the *Levant* to prepare for the third and final assault against the barrier fort on the Canton side of the Whampoa River.[46]

The capture of the third fort enabled Simms to use the position to cover his third and final assault against the center fort. This fort proved the easiest, though at the time of the assault on them the morning of November 21, Simms did not know this, as his force once again embarked in their whaleboats and headed in assault formation to their objective. As was the case with the other forts, Simms' Marines prepared for a furious and bloody fight. As the ships offshore and cannons emplaced in the captured forts pounded the center fort, a deadly silence soon descended over the objective, as the Chinese apparently had decided to hold their fire until the last moment. As the Marines approached the walls of fortress, there was still no reply from the Chinese inside. Supported by ships and howitzers firing grapeshot, the Marines disembarked with their muskets and swords ready, but failed to encounter any enemy fire. Once inside the fortress, the Marines discovered that the Chinese had fled but had managed to plant a cannon set to go off, aimed at the assaulting boats. Upon seeing the smoldering powder train, the Marines quickly snuffed it out and raised the American flag in order to signal the offshore ships that the fourth and final fort had been silenced.[47] By 2:30 p.m. on the afternoon of 22 November, all four of the barrier forts were in the hands of the Americans — thanks in large part to the efforts and efficiency of the leathernecks and sailors who stormed these forts.

The efficiency of the Marines' and bluejackets' fire could be seen in the scores of dead and wounded Chinese left behind, as well as the number of enemy guns destroyed or spiked as the forts were captured. As for American losses, the assault force of 300 Marines and sailors incurred six dead (all bluejackets) and twenty wounded (six of the wounded being Marines).[48] To prevent the forts from again being occupied by a hostile force, the Marines and sailors returned to them and throughout the next two weeks systematically leveled them and left not one wall standing. Even more important was the resultant diplomatic success that came shortly thereafter on 16 November from the governor of Canton, who expressed his deepest apologies for the attacks against the American ships. With the assistance of Captain Simms' Marines and the force of bluejackets, Commander Foote had avenged this insult to the American flag and made certain that the Chinese at Canton would "behave in the future."[49] The Marines and sailors were not done in Chinese waters, however, as attacks against Americans and other foreigners continued to occur as the remnants of the Taiping Rebellion once again necessitated the presence of an American force.

During the late spring and early summer of 1866 certain warlords still made forays into imperial territory and committed diverse depredations of rape and murder and harassed innocent Chinese as well as foreigners that oftentimes became caught up in the violence. One such attack occurred against the American Consul at New Chwang, Mr. Francis P. Knight, who was attacked and molested by the followers of a local bandit leader named "Sword Rack Hoo." Rear Admiral Henry H. Bell, commanding officer of the U.S. Asiatic Squadron, sent Commander Robert Townsend and the USS *Washusett* to the area in order to arrest and punish Sword Rack Hoo and his followers.

Commander Townsend arrived off New Chwang by the middle of June 1866 and immediately sent a platoon of fifty bluejackets and Marines ashore to capture Sword Rack Hoo. After securing the cooperation of the local Chinese officials, the force, commanded by Navy Lieutenant John W. Philips, went ashore, and after an exhaustive search captured Sword Rack Hoo and several of his followers. Eventually Sword Rack Hoo and his captured followers were placed on trial and punished for their crimes. In compliance with local Chinese officials, the Marines and sailors stood guard over the bandit leader and his men each day during the length of the trials.[50]

The Marines performed one more mission that year for the U.S. State Department in Chinese waters, as guards for the American consulate general, Mr. William H. Seward, and his interpreter, Mr. Jenkins. Both men proceeded to Chinkiang on board the USS *Washusett* to meet with American consular and Chinese officials there. When Mr. Seward's party reached Chinkiang, the Marines and sailors provided an escort to insure their security while ashore.[51]

Japan and Korea, 1868–1896

After the establishment of full diplomatic relations between the United States and Japan, Japanese officials invited the U.S. minister, Mr. Van Valkenburgh, to meet with the Shogun, who was the nominal ruler of Japan at Osaka.[52] Prior to his visit Mr. Valkenburgh requested that the commander of the East Asian Squadron, Rear Admiral Bell, accompany him. On 1 May 1867 the Marine detachments from the USS *Hartford*, USS *Shenandoah* and USS *Wyoming* escorted the minister and Admiral Bell to the Shogun's palace, where they were given the customary diplomatic honors.

The end of the shogunate and restoration of the Mikado resulted in the outbreak of civil war in Japan. Some of this fighting spilled over into the foreign settlements that in turn caused the landing of U.S. Marines on several occasions in order to protect American lives and property. Eventually, the troops of the Mikado forced the shogun to abdicate and flee Osaka. Shortly thereafter, the shogun found protection from the U.S. fleet lying offshore; he was given protection by a detachment of Marines and bluejackets from the USS *Iroquois* until he transferred to one of his own warships on 1 February 1868.

The violence ashore continued unabated. Several foreign ambassadors sought protection from the *Iroquois* and its complement of Marines. Meanwhile, the troops loyal to the restored Mikado stormed the foreign settlement area on 4 February, wounding one bluejacket from the USS *Oneida* in the attack. The violence against the foreign diplomats forced the assembled squadrons to land their troops and sailors in order to organize a joint defense of the foreign settlement area. Among this international force were Marines and sailors who remained ashore until 8 February in defense of the international compound. Despite assurances from the mikado to the various foreign governments that their residences would be safe, the naval commanders from France, England, Italy, Prussia, and the United States met in Yokohama, at the request of the diplomatic officials of their respective countries, "in conference to find a means in which to better defend their respective interests and the foreign settlement."[53] They agreed that each naval commander would land a certain naval force ashore that would remain ashore until they decided that the violence had subsided to the degree that such forces were no longer necessary.

This plan was implemented by all of the above-mentioned countries, including the United States, which, upon the suggestion of Mr. Valkenburgh, landed a detachment of twenty-five Marines and bluejackets from the USS *Monocacy* and USS *Iroquois*. This force, commanded by Navy Lieutenant G.F.B. Glidden, remained ashore from 4 April to 12 May 1868. A month later, on 12 June, Marines from the *Iroquois* landed once again in the port of Yokohama to prevent the departure of a Japanese warship in violation of the agreed upon neutrality between the United States and Japan. One Marine officer and two enlisted Marines remained ashore until the next day, when they retuned to their ship, while a separate Marine guard maintained security at the American minister's residence from 19 January to 25 September. This force, led by Second Lieutenant John C. Morgan and four enlisted Marines, returned to the USS *Piscataqua* after successfully completing their assignment on the 26 September.[54]

A similar situation prevailed on the waters and shores on the Korean peninsula. Mr. Frederick F. Low, the U.S. minister to China was instructed by the State Department to arrange a "convention with Corean [sic] authorities for the protection of American citizens."[55] To carry out the negotiations with Korean authorities Mr. Low instructed Admiral John Rodgers to proceed to Korea, where he was to undertake negotiations with representatives of the Korean government. When Korean rebels attacked an American survey team working on the Salee River, both Mr. Low and Admiral Rodgers decided that this "outrage be explained" and that an apology be immediately forthcoming by Korean authorities. When there was no reply from the Koreans, so American officials planned on assault on the forts and citadel from which the rebels had fired upon the Americans.

On 10 June 1871, the USS *Monocacy* and USS *Palos,* along with four steam launches that carried a battalion of Marines led by Captain McLane Tilton, as well as a brigade of bluejackets accompanied by seven field guns and led by Captain Homer C. Blake of the Navy, captain of the USS *Alaska,* headed up the Salee River. As the force proceeded along the Salee, it came under intense fire from the forts along the banks of the river. Within seconds the guns of the *Monocacy* and *Palos* opened up on the enemy forts and quickly silenced them. As the naval gunfire continued, Captain Tilton's Marines, who had been aboard steam launches ready to land, were cast loose and headed to shore.

Captain Tilton's Marines landed amid heavy enemy fire in some of the most difficult terrain due to the steep banks and the deep, soft mud and scrub brush, which impeded their ability to concentrate their fire coming from the redoubt on their right flank. The naval brigade followed shortly thereafter as Captain Tilton's Marines silenced the enemy musket fire. In a combined assault of Marines and bluejackets, the Korean rebels abandoned their guns and fled out the rear of the fort. The American force then entered the fort, spiked the guns and dismantled the walls of the fortress.[56] On the morning of 11 June, Tilton's force advanced toward the second line of enemy fortifications, which the Marines and bluejackets found abandoned. The Americans quickly dismantled the fortifications and then prepared for the main assault on the main enemy fortification called the citadel.

The citadel was built upon a hill overlooking a ravine and had been constructed to resist just such an attack, with walls that ran continuous with hardly a break in them. Fortunately, the Marines and sailors had the services of the *Monocacy*'s and *Palos'* guns, which blasted holes in the citadel's walls and permitted the Marines and sailors to rapidly enter despite the heavy musket fire. Fighting inside the citadel was intense as the leathernecks and bluejackets fought it out with the Koreans, sometimes hand-to-hand with muskets that were used as clubs, bayonets, swords, and knives in an unyielding, no giving of quarter with none expected struggle. Only when the last Korean defender fell dead did the fighting inside the citadel end. As the citadel fell to the Marines, two leathernecks, Private Hugh Purvis of the *Colorado* Marine detachment and Corporal Charles Brown of the *Alaska,* captured the enemy's yellow cotton flag with its large Chinese cabalistic character in its center. As the citadel's defenders fought to the death, the remaining rebels realized that the fight was over and shortly thereafter fled from the last of the still-occupied forts. This signaled the end of the fighting. In his after-action report of the fight on Salee River, Commander A.L. Kimberly noted that "Captain Tilton and his Marines had the honor of ... first landing and [were] the last in leaving the shore." He also mentioned that Captain Tilton's Marine battalion was the first in leading the advance on the march, in entering the forts, and in acting as skirmishers. Commander Kim-

Marines storm Fort Cho'oji jin on the Salee River near Seoul, Korea, in 1871 (courtesy U.S. Marine Corps).

berly specifically noted the "steadiness and discipline" of the Marines in their march toward the citadel and other enemy fortifications, and that how they were "looked to with confidence in case of difficulty, their whole behaviour [*sic*] on the march and in the assault it was not misplaced."[57]

The combined Marine-Navy assault on the citadel did not bring an end to the need for Marines in Korea. In 1888, rebels once again began to menace foreign residents, necessitating an American naval presence. The USS *Essex*, under the command of Commander Theodore F. Jewell, at anchor in the harbor of Chemulpo (today known as Inchon) responded to the request from the U.S. minister there to send a detachment of Marines ashore in order to guard the U.S. Consulate. Commander Jewell answered in the affirmative by sending First Lieutenant Robert D. Wainwright and twelve men from the *Essex* as well as a force of thirteen sailors ashore. They marched to Seoul twenty-five miles away and reported to the U.S. minister as a guard for the consulate and its grounds. The Marines and sailors remained ashore until 30 June, at which time they returned to the *Essex*.[58]

Toward the end of the 19th century, Marines landed in Korea on two more occasions (1894 and 1896) in order to protect American citizens and diplomatic officials. The first instance was during the Sino-Japanese War of 1894–95, when Japanese troops seized Seoul in June 1894,[59] which in turn compelled the American minister to Seoul to request a detachment of Marines and bluejackets to protect the consulate. Landing from the USS *Baltimore* was Captain George F. Elliott[60] and a 21-man Marine detachment which made a night march from the port of Chemulpo starting on 24 June 1894 and arrived in Seoul the next day. Captain Elliott's Marine detachment remained in Seoul until 26 September 1894, when it was relieved by an eighteen-man detachment of Marines from the USS *Concord* on 26 September. This force in turn was replaced by a detachment of Marines from the USS *Charleston* commanded by First Lieutenant B.S. Neumann on 2 November 1894. This practice continued for the next year, as succeeding ships of the Asiatic Squadron sent detachments of Marines ashore in rotation in order to defend the U.S. Legation in Seoul. This practice continued until 1896, when it was briefly discontinued. Marines re-established the Legation Guard in 1904 when a 100-man Marine detachment under the command of Captain Arthur J. Matthews arrived from the Philippine Islands in Seoul, where they assumed the role as the legation's security force.[61]

Landings on Formosa in 1867

Upon the receipt of orders from Rear Admiral Henry F. Bell, commander-in-chief of the U.S. Asiatic Squadron, Commander John C. Febiger, commanding officer of the USS *Ashuelot,* responded to a request for assistance from both the American minister in Peking and Mr. Charles Carroll, the British consul. Commander Febirger was ordered to proceed to the southeastern tip of the island of Formosa (modern day Taiwan) to investigate the rumors that the captain, his wife, and the crew of the American ship *Rover* had been murdered by members of the Botansha tribe (one of the aboriginal tribes on Formosa). The lone survivor of this massacre was a Chinese sailor who made his way back to the mainland to inform authorities. Upon his arrival in Amoy, China, Commander Febiger, Consul Carroll and American Consul General General C.W. LeGendre, attempted unsuccessfully to communicate with the Tokitok, the chief of the Botanshas. Ultimately, the failure to communicate with Tokitok forced Commander Freibeger to order a punitive expedition ashore comprised of Marines and sailors.[62] On the afternoon of 13 June 1867 a force of forty-three Marines led by Captain James Forney and one hundred thirty-five bluejackets came ashore at Takow and proceeded inland. As the landing force headed toward the hills, the Formosans opened fire from concealed positions. Within several minutes the Americans were hit from all sides as the aborigines conducted a series of successful hit-and-run raids. By 4 o'clock that afternoon, the Americans, battered by the enemy and beaten by the intense heat, were forced to retire to their ships. Meanwhile, Lieutenant Commander Mackenzie, who had been wounded in an ambush prior to the order to retreat and incurred a mortal wound to his chest from enemy fire during an ambush, died before returning to the *Asheulot* as the Marines and sailors carried him to the rear for treatment.[63] After much difficulty General LeGendre was able to negotiate a treaty with Tokitok, who agreed to not commit any more outrages against shipwrecked seamen.[64] After retiring to their ship, the Marines and bluejackets set sail for their base in Hong Kong.

Leathernecks and Slavers on Africa's West Coast, 1835–1868

As Marines and sailors landed to protect consulates and diplomatic officials in China and Japan, other Marine detachments stormed ashore to safeguard American diplomats and interests on the Isthmus in Central and South America as well as on Africa's tumultuous west coast. Throughout the first half of the 19th century, Marine detachments aboard the various ships of the U.S. Navy's Mediterranean Squadron landed on Africa's west coast to protect American lives and property as well as to enforce the ban on the African slave trade.[65]

The first of these landings occurred in 1843 after the murder of two American ship's captains by natives from the Sinoe and Berribe tribes in Liberia and Ivory Coast, respectively. In response to these and other outrages against Americans, as well as the continued illegal smuggling of slaves on board ships bound for the southern United States, the American government called upon four ships from its Mediterranean Squadron commanded by Commodore Matthew C. Perry. This squadron consisted of the USS *Decatur*, USS *Macedonian*, USS *Porpoise*, and USS *Saratoga*. Each of these ships had a Marine detachment, with the exception of the USS *Porpoise*, led by First Lieutenant Jabez C. Rich and Second Lieutenant Isaac T. Doughty. Leaving New York in the early fall of 1843, Commodore Perry's squadron (minus the *Porpoise*, which had been sent on a separate clandestine mission disguised as a merchantman), arrived off Sinoe (Liberia) on 27 November 1843 and prepared to exact revenge on the Sinoese. Early in the morning hours of 29 November 1843, Commodore Perry embarked his force of seventy-five Marines and sailors in whaleboats and landed in Monrovia. Here, the commodore met with Mr. Joseph Jenkins Roberts,[66] governor of Liberia, in the Methodist church to discuss the circumstances surrounding the murder of the Americans on board the *Mary Carver*.

Commodore Perry surmised that it was not the Sinoese but the Berribe tribes from the neighboring state of the Ivory Coast that had precipitated the murder of the crew and captain of the *Mary Carver*. Commodore Perry's force set sail to exact a punishment on the offending tribes and shortly after arriving there ordered the destruction of the villages. During December, Commodore Perry and his squadron sailed up and down the coastline of Liberia in a show of force to settle the matter of the killings of the Americans and to conduct negotiations with the various African tribes. On each occasion Marines landed in order to protect both the commodore and Mr. Roberts, who accompanied Perry as an interpreter. In early December 1843, Marines and bluejackets landed on two separate occasions and returned fire against the natives as they attempted to return to their respective ships after having conducted military operations ashore. Commodore Perry had rightfully suspected that the African king, Crack'O, had planned an ambush against the Marines and bluejackets since he had been implicated in the killing of the American crew of the merchant ship *Mary Carver*. Commodore Perry, in foiling the king's ambush, set out to provide a sharp reminder that the Americans held the "upper hand in such negotiations!"[67] In short, the Berribe tribes discovered that the Marines and bluejackets meant business.

In 1860, the Marine detachment aboard the sloop USS *Marion* landed at the port of Kabenda in Kissembo upon the orders of the *Marion*'s commanding officer, Commander Thomas Brent, after consultations with American diplomatic officials in Tunis. The Marines and sailors landed in order to protect American lives and property against the warring Portuguese merchants. The detachment landed on the morning of 3 March 1860 along with a British landing party from *HMS Falcon* and remained there for a few hours before returning to its ship. Their mission completed ashore, the leathernecks and bluejackets re-embarked aboard the *Marion* later that afternoon.

The Landing at Alexandria, Egypt, 1873

After riots in the port city of Alexandria, Egypt, killed and wounded over two hundred of the city's European inhabitants, both the British and French fleets that had arrived on 11 June 1882 in response to the violence prepared a powerful answer to the rioters. Shortly thereafter, an American squadron, commanded by Rear Admiral J.W.A. Nicholson, arrived at Alexandria on 27 June 1882 and offered the forces under his command to assist in the evacuation of the frightened civilians. After the evacuation of the Europeans took place, the decks of the flagship USS *Lancaster*, as well as the other vessels in the squadron, soon became a refuge for the hundreds of European citizens fleeing the violence ashore. After a meeting between the American, British, and French naval commanders, it was decided that a powerful response would be made to the insurgents ashore. The westerners also believed that a military occupation of the city would be necessary to quell the violence. On 14 June, a detachment of naval artillery, under Lieutenant Commander Goodrich, as well as force of sixty-nine bluejackets, two Gatling guns, and a detachment of Marines, came ashore from the U.S. squadron to assist in the restoration of order. The Marine detachment, led by Captain Henry C. Cochrane, consisted of Lieutenants F.L. Denny and L.W.T. "Tony" Waller, and sixty enlisted Marines. The Marines and bluejackets were given the mission to put out the many fires, stop the pillaging and looting, and protect the American and other foreign consulates near the Grand Square of Mehemt Ali. In order to protect the American consular officials, the leathernecks quickly established a guard at the American consulate. With the consulate as their base, the Marines then fanned out throughout the city and established a series of continuous patrols. The presence of the Marines was immediately felt, as they were, according to a history of the landing, "the first troops to reach the centre of the city."[68] The Marines remained ashore until Admiral Nicholson ordered them withdrawn on June 18. A six-man consulate guard led by Lieutenant Denny remained ashore, however, until 24 June. The smartness and professionalism of the Marines won the praise of many during this affair. The British ambassador, Lord Charles Beresford, told a reporter from the *London Times* that "without the assistance of the American Marines he would have been unable to discharge the numerous duties of suppressing fires, preventing looting, burying the dead, and clearing the streets." In a follow up to his statement to the *London Times*, Lord Beresford, on 24 October 1882, sent Lieutenant Denny a personal note of thanks for the services of the Marines under his command during the riots in Alexandria. The note read in part: "It gives me great pleasure to testify to your very valuable services and true courage during those irksome, terrible days after the bombardment of Alexandria. I can confidently say that without the services of American troops order could not have been restored, and the great fires in the city subdued. To Lieutenant Hutchins, and you, and your smart, faithful force great credit is due.... I have represented these facts to my government.... /s/ Charles Beresford."[69]

Unrest in the Western Hemisphere, 1817–1900

Marine detachments aboard ships of the South Atlantic Squadron conducted similar operations off the coasts of Central and South America during the 19th century. As early as February 1817, the Marine detachment aboard the USS *Ontario* provided security for the newly appointed American commissioner to Chile. Originally commanded by First Lieutenant John Harris,[70] the *Ontario*'s sixteen–Marine detachment was led by Sergeant Edward McFadian. After its arrival at Valparaiso, Chile, in January 1818, the *Ontario* remained in Chilean waters until June of that same year before it sailed around Cape Horn and proceeded to the Northwest Coast near the Columbia River, where it took possession of Fort George (Astoria) from the British as part of the terms of the Treaty of Ghent (December 1814) that ended the War of 1812 with Great Britain.[71]

When Commodore Oliver Hazard Perry was ordered by the secretary of the Navy to undertake negotiations with the representatives of the Venezuelan government, a Marine detachment accompanied the naval hero up the Orinoco River three hundred miles to Angosture. The Marine detachment from Perry's flagship, the USS *John Adams*, was led by First Lieutenant Henry E. Dix, while Sergeant Samuel Townshend led the detachment aboard the USS *Nonsuch*.[72] Unable to negotiate the shallow waters of the Orinoco, the *John Adams* remained in deep water while Perry transferred his flag to the *Nonsuch* and proceeded up the river, where he met with the representatives of the Venezuelan government in an effort to resolve past problems over indemnities claimed by both governments. At the conclusion of negotiations Perry contracted malaria and shortly thereafter died. Both Marines and bluejackets served as an honor guard as they transported Perry's body to Lapeyrouse Cemetery, Port of Spain, Trinidad, where it was laid to rest. In December 1826 Perry's body was exhumed and re-interred at Newport, Rhode Island.[73]

Later on, the Marines, led by Lieutenant Lawrence Kearney, accompanied the USS *Enterprise* to Omoa in the Bay of Honduras as a security force, in order to protect an American agent sent there to negotiate with a group of pirates who had seized the American merchant vessel *Retrieve*, murdered its captain and imprisoned its crew. After a show of force by the *Enterprise* the Spanish governor relented and released the vessel and the turned over the perpetrators of this crime to the Americans. The American force then transported the ringleader back to the United States where he was later killed in a public execution held in the middle of the East River near New York City.

Prior to the war between the United States and Mexico (1846–48), Marine First Lieutenant Archibald H. Gillespie had been assigned as a special agent of the State Department and as an executive agent of the president of the United States, James K. Polk. Lieutenant Gillespie met with Secretary of State James Buchanan and President Polk and was instructed to give coded messages to the U.S. Consul in Monterey, Mexico, Mr. Thomas O. Larkin, Captain John C. Fremont, U.S. Army, and Commander John D. Sloat, U.S. Navy. While the subject of the messages remains unknown to this day, it is apparent that they were related to the impending war with Mexico and the separation of California from the Mexican Empire.[74]

Reaching the west coast, Lieutenant Gillespie made his way to Mexico City traveling as a businessman. After having been delayed due to a revolution in California, he delivered his messages first to Commander Sloat, whose Pacific Squadron had recently arrived off the coast-line (March 1846), then to Consul Larkin in Monterey (17 April 1846), and finally on 7 May 1846 to Captain Fremont, who had been encamped by the Klamath Lake near the Cascade Mountain ranges in south-central Oregon. After delivering his messages from the president and secretary of state, Gillespie remained with Captain Fremont, where he and the Army captain engaged in clandestine activities designed to separate California from Mexico.[75]

In 1858, the Marines attached to the Brazil Squadron were sent ashore at Montevideo, Uruguay, which had been wracked by revolution and political unrest since 1855, in order to protect American lives and interests. On 2 January 1858, French Forrest, commanding officer of the USS *St. Lawrence*, ordered ashore the Marine detachment led by Brevet Major John G. Reynolds in order to protect the American Consulate there. In a joint operation with British Marines, who had been landed to protect British interests, Major Reynolds' detachment secured the area around the U.S. Consulate and customs house until 27 January 1858, when it re-embarked aboard the *St. Lawrence*.[76]

Another area that proved to become all too familiar to Marines and bluejackets was Mexican waters. In June of 1870, the United States consul at Mazatlan, Mexico, had received a message from his counterpart in Guaymas, Mexico, that a mercenary army aboard the steamer *Forward*, flying the flag of San Salvador, had forced him into providing coal and other supplies as they made their way to Panama. While in Guaymas, these mercenaries had committed a series of robberies, rapes, and other outrages against the local populace. The American consul therefore requested that an American naval force be sent to punish these mercenaries. W.W. Low, commander of the USS *Mohican*, set sail for the Mexican coastal town. While underway, Commander Low discovered that the *Forward* was at anchor in the Gulf of California. In a brief engagement shortly after arriving near Mazatlan, Commander Low captured the *Forward* and ordered her destruction, which was accomplished in short order by Navy Lieutenant Brownson and combined detachment of Marines and bluejackets. Singled out for exceptional conduct in the performance of their duties against the pirates were First Sergeant Philip Moore and Corporal F. Moulton of the *Mohican*'s Marine detachment.[77]

On the Isthmus, 1853–1899

The Isthmus in Central America had long been an area coveted by Americans. Slave owners had hoped one day to make the former Spanish colonies slave states while others, such as Tennessean William Walker, had hoped to carve out their own empires amid the political chaos and disorder that characterized the history of the region for nearly a century and a half after the collapse of Spanish rule. Along with the commencement of the California Gold Rush (1848–50) came the idea to build an isthmian canal from the Gulf of Mexico to the Pacific. The desire to build a canal across Nicaragua (and later Panama) drew the United States into the revolutionary turmoil that characterized much of Central America during the middle to late 19th and 20th centuries.

The first landings by U.S. Marines in support of U.S. foreign policy in Nicaragua occurred on 11 March 1853, when Commander George N. Hollins from the sloop USS *Cyane* landed his Marine detachment at Punta Arenas to protect the property of the American Steamship Company. The *Cyane*'s Marines, led by Orderly Sergeant James E. Thompson, remained ashore for three days before they were withdrawn. Several months later, insurrectionists seized

Mr. Borland, the newly appointed U.S. minister to Nicaragua, and prevented him from leaving the country. After being absent from the waters off Greytown, Commander Hollins arrived aboard the USS *Cyane* and he demanded an apology from the de facto government for this assault on the U.S. minister. The authorities made no reply, which in turn prompted Commander Hollins to issue a public proclamation that "unless his demand was met, he would land his Marines and if necessary, bombard the town."[78] With no reply forthcoming from the Nicaraguan authorities, Commander Hollins ordered Marine Lieutenants Fauntleroy and Pickering and a combined force of bluejackets and Marines under Orderly Sergeant Thompson to prepare to land. About 1 o'clock in the afternoon, Hollins ordered the landing force ashore, where they seized muskets, ammunition, swords, and several field pieces before returning to the *Cyane*.

After still not having received an apology, Commander Hollins ordered a bombardment of the town that commenced the next morning. Commander Hollins once again ordered the landing force ashore, where it once again destroyed not only arms and ammunition but also the town. By 17 March, Hollins believed that sufficient punishment had been meted out to the Nicaraguans and set sail for home. After the *Cyane*'s departure the Nicaraguan government submitted a demand for reparations for losses incurred as a result of the bombardment of Greytown. In rejecting the Nicaraguan claim, Secretary of State Marcy informed the Nicaraguan representatives that the damage done to American property, not to mention the affront to the American minister, all in the name of Nicaraguan nationalism justified the actions of the *Cyane*.

In 1894, Marines once again were part of a landing force. Mr. B.B. Seat requested a Marine detachment be sent ashore to protect American interests in Bluefields. A detachment of Marines from the USS *Marblehead* under the command of First Lieutenant Franklin J. Moses, as well as a company of bluejackets led by Navy Lieutenant Bowman, landed on 6 July and remained ashore until 7 August. The naval commander on the scene ordered reinforcements from the USS *Columbia* sent ashore on 31 July. Commander Charles O. Allibone assumed command of this combined force until all Marines and sailors were withdrawn on 7 August.

The next phase of Marine involvement in Nicaragua, which lasted until the final withdrawal of the leathernecks from that turbulent country, began in 1896 with the forced reelection of Jose Santos Zelaya, who continued ruling Nicaragua as a virtual dictator. Zelaya's attempt to hold on to power resulted in foreigners being again endangered. This time the threatened area was the port of Corinto. Here, the Nicaraguan commandant informed the U.S. Consul, Mr. Henry Palazio, that he was unable to assure the protection of all foreign nationals and it was advisable that a U.S. landing force be sent ashore in order to protect Americans and their property. The American Consul immediately communicated this to Commander Franklin Hanford of the USS *Alert*, who in turn ordered a combined landing force of bluejackets and Marines ashore, commanded by Navy Lieutenant Albert W. Dodd. The fifteen-man Marine detachment was led by First Sergeant Frederick W.M. Poppe. The entire force came ashore in the afternoon of 2 May and remained ashore until the 4th of that month.

Two years later the USS *Alert* returned to Corinto to once again restore order. Mr. Charles Holman, the American consul, ordered the flying of the American flag with the union downward, a signal that denoted imminent danger to the consulate and its residents. About 4 o'clock on the afternoon of 2 May, a force of fourteen Marines and nineteen sailors under the command of Lieutenant Harry A. Field came ashore from the *Alert*. On the following day, the

Nicaraguan commandant informed the Americans that he could guarantee the safety of all foreigners, with the result that the landing party was withdrawn.

On 24 February 1899, a similar landing occurred at Bluefields after the American vice-consul, Mr. F. Percy Scott, and Navy Commander Frederick M. Symonds, on board the USS *Marietta*, came ashore on the morning of 13 February to conduct a first-hand inspection of the living conditions. Navy Lieutenant Frederic B. Bassett, Jr., a detachment of Marines and sailors, numbering about 16 men, and a Colt automatic gun joined forces with a similar British detachment to guard foreign interests. After completing their mission, the American force returned to the *Marietta* by 7 o'clock in the evening of the 28 February.[79]

Unknown to Marines and State Department officials at the time, the landing on 24 February 1899 established the pattern for the next thirty-four years, as the Marines landed in Nicaragua three more times: first in 1910, 1912, and finally a major intervention that began in 1927 and lasted until 1933. More importantly, however, the interventions by the Marines convinced the Department of State that a permanent Marine legation guard would have to be established in order to safeguard both American diplomatic personnel and its interests in this turbulent country. As Marines landed in Nicaragua, other detachments of leathernecks and bluejackets conducted landing operations in other parts of the Spanish Main (the Northern coast of South America and along the Gulf of Mexico), particularly in Panama in 1860, and later in 1885.

In fact, Panama and Nicaragua were two countries that Marines and bluejackets became intimately familiar with over the next few decades as interest in the United States turned toward the construction of an isthmian canal. In response to revolutionary violence in July 1860 the American consul in Panama requested an American naval presence ashore. Commander David Porter arrived shortly thereafter aboard the USS *St. Mary's*. After the outbreak of shooting whereby several individuals were killed, the American consul requested that Porter land a portion of his force. In response to the consul's request, Commander Porter landed a combined force of sailors and Marines in order to protect not only American lives and property but to secure the rail station that had been threatened by the rebels. Landing on 27 September, the bluejackets and leathernecks (under the command of Lieutenant Edward M. Reynolds) remained ashore until relieved by a force of British marines on 7 October 1860.

In one of the largest displays of force to-date, a combined force of Marines and bluejackets landed in the port of Colon on the Isthmus of Panama on 12 April 1885, after a request by Mr. Robert K. Wright, the American consul general, to Navy Commander Lewis Clark, to provide a detachment of Marines and sailors to protect the property of the Panama Railroad Company as well as the consulate and American lives and property. At 6 p.m. on the evening of 12 April, Major Charles Heywood[80] and the First Battalion of Marines came ashore and marched immediately to the rail station. There the Marines and bluejackets took up defensive positions as well as the job if armed escort on board every train departing the station in order to keep the lines of communications opened with the interior of the country and Colon.[81]

During the next month and a half, the Marines under Major Heywood protected American lives and property and with the help of the bluejackets helped restore order until finally being withdrawn on 21 May 1885. In his report to the secretary of the Navy, the American consul general in Colon, Mr. Adamson, praised the "firm bearing, strict discipline, and splendid conduct of the Marines" under Major Heywood.[82] The consul general added in his report that this strict adherence to discipline and military bearing did much to allay the fears of the foreign residents living in Colon.

Even as the United States returned to more peaceful pursuits such as westward expansion and industrialization in the aftermath of the War Between the States, Marines and sailors found themselves on constant call from American ministers and consular officials in these oftentimes unstable and revolution-torn countries. As events in both Nicaragua and later China illustrated, Marines and bluejackets became the guarantors of both stability and order in an increasingly volatile political and social climate as the 19th century came to a close.

The Marines in China and on Samoa, 1894–1899

Starting in 1894 Marines and sailors of the Asiatic Squadron landed in China no less than nine times, with the longest period beginning in 1932. In fact, the events of the last six years in the 19th century on the Asian mainland served as a prelude to the chaos and political disorder that culminated in the United States' intervention and occupation three decades later (1927–1940). This intervention by Marines in particular laid the foundation for the establishment of not only a permanent Marine legation in the Middle Kingdom starting in 1905 but also for the Marine Security Guard program of today.

In 1894 China and Japan went to war over which power would control Korea and hence the Asian mainland. The Japanese seizure of Seoul, the capital of Korea, and its march on Peking forced the Western powers including the United States to send warships off the Chinese coast in order to protect its citizens and vital interests. The Navy Department instructed Rear Admiral Charles C. Carpenter, the commanding officer of the U.S. Asiatic Squadron, to "provide the utmost protection for American interests, due to the unsettled conditions and consequences of the war." After further Japanese successes against the Chinese forces, Admiral Carpenter was ordered in a cablegram to "place his Marine Guard at the disposal of the American Minister, Colonel Charles Denby, at Peking, to protect the Legation."[83]

In response to the chaos and apprehension that permeated the air in Peking and other major Chinese cities due to the advances of the Japanese Army near the Forbidden City, Admiral George Dewey ordered the *Baltimore* to Chefoo. The USS *Baltimore* arrived after a two-day voyage from Nagasaki, Japan, on 4 December. The Marines under the command of Captain George F. Elliott prepared for possible action ashore. Captain Elliott and his men transferred to the tug *Yiksang*, which proceeded to Taku. Landing at Taku, Elliott's Marines then boarded a train bound for Tientsin and after a two-hour, very cold journey (most of the Marines had only summer uniforms), arrived in Tientsin where the Marine captain reported to the commanding officer of the USS *Monocacy* at anchor in the river. Despite the edict from the Chinese emperor that foreign troops were forbidden to enter the "Forbidden City" (Peking), Captain Elliott readied his Marines for just such a move.[84] As Elliott readied his force for possible action the navies and marines of the other western powers shortly arrived in Tientsin, where they also readied for possible action against the Imperial Chinese troops as well as from anti-foreign sentiment that might arise.

Even as the threat of anti–Western violence subsided in and around the major Chinese cities of Peking, Shanghai, and Tientsin, the Sino-Japanese War continued unabated. Colonel Denby requested that in spite of the edict of the Chinese emperor forbidding foreign troops from entering the capital, the Marines should prepare to establish a guard at the U.S. Legation in Peking. Colonel Denby requested a meeting with Captain Elliott to ascertain the requirements of feeding and housing the Marines. After a harrowing journey through an estimated 25,000 Chinese troops and clogged rail lines, Captain Elliott arrived for his meeting with the U.S. minister. While Elliott was in Peking conferring with Denby, the Marine captain and Navy Paymaster Cowie served as his military attachés while the minister met with Chinese officials. During the meeting, Imperial Prince Lung requested that Denby act as an intermediary between the Chinese and Japanese in order to arrange a peace treaty and end the Sino-Japanese War. After peace had finally been restored between these two Asian nations the presence of the Marines (and other foreign troops) was deemed unnecessary, with the result that Captain Elliott's force of Marines returned to the *Baltimore* and other ships that had arrived in China in case of an emergency.

In 1898, the rise in anti-foreign sentiment once again resulted in the dispatch of a force of Marines to China. Rear Admiral Carpenter once again responded to a request from the U.S. minister to China, Mr. Edwin H. Conger, and dispatched a force of Marines to Peking for the explicit purpose of establishing a Marine legation guard at both the U.S. Legation in Peking and the U.S. Consulate in Tientsin. This view was upheld by the U.S. consul general in Tientsin, Mr. James W. Ragsdale, who shared in Minister Conger's apprehension as to the political uncertainty surrounding the removal of the Chinese emperor in favor of the empress dowager. Admiral George Dewey concurred with the minister's opinion and issued the necessary instructions for the guards to be sent to Peking and Tientsin.[85] Orders went out to the commanding officers of the USS *Baltimore*, USS *Boston*, and USS *Raleigh* that instructed them to furnish a certain number of Marines for a legation guard in Peking. On 4 November five Marines from the *Boston*, five Marines from the *Raleigh*, and eight from the *Baltimore* proceeded on orders to Peking, where they established the first legation guard made entirely of

The Marine detachment defending the home of U.S. Consul Caborne (on the porch) at Matautu Point, Apia, Samoa, in April 1899 (courtesy U.S. Marine Corps).

U.S. Marines. A week later, on 12 December 1898, the same three ships were instructed to provide a like number of Marines for the establishment of a legation guard at Tientsin. The Tientsin garrison was placed under the command of Lieutenant John Gibson, USN, of the *Boston*. Each Marine legation guard was provided with a full complement of equipment that included a Gatling gun as well as a generous supply of ammunition.[86] The Marine guard at the U.S. Legation in Peking, under the command of First Lieutenant Robert McM. Dutton, was, in fact, the first permanent legation guard to be established by the U.S. Department of State. The establishment of a Marine Guard in Peking also became the precedent upon which the Marine Embassy Guard program was built around after 1905 in China.[87]

As the Marines on guard in Peking and Tientsin observed the new year, there was little abatement of the anti-foreign sentiment that brought the Marines to China in the first place. In fact, senior American officials in China and Washington, D.C., believed that for the moment, the presence of the Marines provided a measure of stability and assurance to both the Americans and the Chinese. By the middle of March both State Department and legation officials believed that conditions in China had settled down to the point that the Marines were no longer required. Subsequently, on 15 March 1899, the legation and consular guards were withdrawn from their posts. Two days later, on 17 March, the Marine guards returned to their respective ships after having successfully completed a rather difficult though extremely important mission ashore.[88]

When political chaos from the natives on the island of Samoa threatened U.S. citizens residing there, American Consul General Mr. Harold M. Sewell requested a detachment of Marines and bluejackets from the commander of the USS *Nipsic* in order to protect them and the consulate. On 13 March 1899, a detachment of Marines and Navy bluejackets carrying their issued 9mm Lee rifles and wearing cartridge belts "bulging with ammunition" as well as toting a tripod-mounted Colt machine gun came ashore. The combined detachment led by Navy Lieutenant G.W. Brown and Marine First Lieutenant Constantine M. Perkins had been ordered to "proceed to the American Consulate within the capital of Apia."[89] The Marines and bluejackets were to remain there "indefinitely."

After arriving at the American Consulate (which was small house with a veranda) the Marines and sailors quickly took up positions in and around the structure. In actions resembling a modern day noncombatant evacuation (NEO), a squad of leathernecks and sailors escorted the American consul, his wife and son, and other American officials aboard the USS *Philadelphia*. As Marines set out to defend the consulate, they shortly thereafter came under attack by a band of rebels led by a claimant to the Samoan throne, Mata'afa Iosefo. Reinforcing the Americans was a force of British Royal Marines and sailors that had been ordered to "pursue the hostile natives into the interior, defeat or capture them and bring the troubled conditions to an end."[90] In a series of ferocious firefights, the Marines, bluejackets, and Royal Marines were able to fend off repeated attacks by Mata'afa's followers. Far from being the uncoordinated and poorly led attacks experienced by earlier landing parties on Samoa, Mata'afa's attacks were well-coordinated and expertly led, which caught both the Americans and British off guard. The attacks, however, were beaten back by the superior firepower and marksmanship of American and British landing parties. In one such attack, Sergeant Bruno A. Forester linked up with another pair of Marines led by Sergeant Michael J. McNally and Private Henry Hubert, all of whom fought a rearguard action in order to protect the rear and flanks of the combined American and British forces that had been surrounded by the natives. For this and other acts of bravery that day, Forester, McNally, and Hulbert were awarded the Medal of Honor for conduct that "was worthy of all praise and honor."[91] During the fighting, the United States lost two naval officers (Lieutenant Philip Lansdale and Ensign John Monaghan), two sailors, and one Marine. The Royal Marines and Navy suffered heavier casualties. After a punishing naval bombardment from the combined American and British fleets, Mata'afa agreed to make peace. Samoa was eventually partitioned between Germany, Great Britain, and the United States with Western Samoa (American Samoa) becoming independent in 1962.

Summary

Starting in 1798 up through the dawn of the 20th century, Marines and sailors had stood side-by-side in the defense of diplomats and consular agents tasked with carrying out U.S. foreign policy in an oftentimes dangerous and uncertain world. The flexibility and readiness of the Marine Corps to provide detachments that ranged from five to a hundred Marines offered the Department of State with a well-trained and disciplined security force. What is more important, however, is the fact that these Marine detachments were oftentimes the difference between success or failure of a diplomatic mission.

From the standpoint of manpower and mission accomplishment, the use of Marines as a diplomatic security force oftentimes fell to detachments led by veteran non-commissioned officers. This proved crucial in the training and discipline of Marines afloat and ashore in such places as Hispaniola, China, Japan, and Formosa during the 19th century. In fact, noncommissioned officers not only formed the backbone of the Marine Corps in general during this era, but specifically of the Marine Security Guard program. This use of noncommissioned officers served as the critical link between the use of Marine ship's detachments during the 19th century and the Marine Security Guard program of today.

CHAPTER 2

"Our Flag's Unfurled to Every Breeze": Marine Legation Guards from China to Nicaragua, 1900–1940

As the Marines departed China after the brief establishment of a legation guard in 1899, the seeds of rebellion had already been sown. The Manchu dynasty, led by the Empress Dowager T'zu-his, struggled to retain its hold on the throne and loosen the grip of foreign interests in China. In fact, China stood at the threshold of one of its most tumultuous centuries as a nation-state. As the United States and the rest of the foreign powers that had obtained concessions along China's eastern coast in the 1880s would soon discover, the winds of change sweeping over China would soon embroil it in this same revolutionary struggle.

This revolutionary fervor and political chaos not only affected China but also Nicaragua. As the United States turned its attention toward the completion of the inter-ocean canal across the Isthmus of Panama, American diplomats and businessmen became increasingly concerned over the stability of not only Panama but also its neighbors, of which Nicaragua was by far the most prominent. The continued political chaos in this Central American nation became a major concern in Washington, D.C., as well as in the banking houses of New York City. As Nicaragua slipped further and further into political disorder, President William Howard Taft and Secretary of State Philander C. Knox implemented what became known as "Dollar Diplomacy," whereby businessmen instead of Marines became the leading agents. Unfortunately, as events in Nicaragua culminated into a bloody civil war, the Marine Corps and U.S. Navy stood ready to intervene in what would become one of the longest occupations (1912–1933) in its institutional history.

U.S. Marines, Navy bluejackets, and soldiers played leading roles in the events that soon engulfed the United States during the first three decades of the twentieth century. Furthermore, as events in China during the Boxer Rebellion (June–September 1900) and Nicaragua (1912–25 and 1927–1933) demonstrated, Marines soon found themselves in the forefront of diplomatic and consulate security during this era. As Marines guarded legations and consulates and protected American and foreign citizens, the revolutionary tide that swept not only the Manchu dynasty from power also brought to power in Nicaragua the Somozas, one of the most powerful and authoritarian families ever to rule a country.

Winds of Change in China, 1899–1900

The winds of change that brought about the collapse of the Manchu dynasty date back to the rule of Emperor Kuang-hsu, who initiated a series of reforms inside the Chinese government and its bureaucracy in order to make it more efficient and responsive to the average Chinese peasant. Despite the popularity of the reforms initiated by the Emperor Kuang-hsu, the empress dowager, acting under pressure from her more conservative ministers, had the emperor (her nephew) arrested and imprisoned in the summer palace. Warned by the British and Japanese diplomats that they would not tolerate the murder of Kuang-hsu, nor the placing of the son of Prince Tuan (Tz'u-his's conservative minister) on the throne, the anti-reform movement soon took on a more virulent form of anti-foreign sentiment in the royal court. Indeed, the Ch'ing government "identified subversion with Westernization."[1] Even much more tolerant officials shared the belief held by the empress dowager that those "Chinese who adopted foreign ways were betraying the traditional political order." Finally, the average peasants, who were superstitious by nature, saw the series of natural calamities — including floods in the Yellow and Yangtze Valleys, droughts, and the inevitable famine starting in 1875 — as a result of the influx of foreigners into China's day-to-day affairs.

A severe flood occurred in the Shangtung Valley when the Yellow River overflowed its banks and destroyed over five thousand square miles of the northern plain. Bedeviled by highwaymen and profiteers and a central government that appeared corrupt and inefficient, the peasants soon formed their own village militias, relying primarily upon professional convoymen who were skilled in sword fighting and martial arts. Groups such as the "Red Lantern" (Hung-teng) openly trained in para-military drills that soon took on an increasingly anti-foreign tone as Chinese officials began to openly support them. In one instance, the governor of Shangtung openly encouraged members of the Small Sword Society to attack Christian missionaries, which in 1897 resulted in the murder of two German missionaries. In short, while Chinese officials saw these armed Chinese peasants as a potential means of driving out the foreigners, they also saw these same militias as a potential danger that could get out of hand if not properly controlled.

One such para-military group that took on an increasingly hostile anti-foreign tone was the one formed in Shangtung, where thousands of young men practiced "stylized exercises of Shaolin and Pa-kua boxing — exercises that were supposed to release their *ch'i* (pneuma) and invest them with strength so awesome that it repelled foreign bullets."[2] Taoist magicians believed that simple magic spells and formulas could reinforce the ability of these militiamen to block the foreigners' gun barrels. Eventually, these activities coalesced around the masters of martial arts in Shangtung. Here, professional boxers such as Chang Te-cheng "were selected by village youths to be their leaders." In turn, these charismatic leaders gathered a following that soon challenged the authority of the imperial government. The movement in Shangtung took on the name of one if its leaders, *I-ho ch'uan* or Righteous and Harmonious Fist, otherwise known by its Western name, the "Boxers."[3]

The goal of the Boxers was to not only drive the foreigners from Chinese soil but to force the Manchus from power. After the execution of Li Wen-ch'eng, the acknowledged leader of the Boxers, in November 1899, the provincial governor of Shangtung, Yu-hsien, who himself was anti-foreign, "believed that the Boxers could be turned to good use against the foreigners."[4] After negotiations with the boxing masters Yu-hsien was able to arrange an alliance between the Boxers and the imperial government. In return for their support against the foreigners, the Boxer leaders agreed to drop their anti–Manchu sentiment. For its part the imperial government recognized the Boxers as a regular militia band. In spite of the fact that the Boxers' claim to invincibility to firearms had been dismissed after the Imperial Army commander General Ch'eng Wen-ping put fifty Boxers against the wall and had them shot, Prince Tuan (the empress dowager's foreign minister) and the empress dowager wanted to "believe both that the Boxers were endowed with magical powers, and that they represented a popular force which would save the dynasty and drive out the foreigners." Despite the skepticism expressed by the empress dowager herself of the power of the Boxer movement, she nevertheless ignored these sentiments because she needed to feel that the dynasty had not lost popular support among the peasantry. The Empress Dowager Tz-u-hsi realized that they represented the patriotic feelings of the Chinese people. With her throne endangered from both foreigners and the Chinese themselves, the empress dowager had but little choice but to marshal the Boxer movement and use it to her advantage.

Throughout 1899 and to the early spring of 1900, the Boxers began a systematic campaign of assault and murder against the foreigners living in the Chinese countryside. By early June 1900 bands of Boxers began to enter the area surrounding Peking from the east. As the Boxers approached the Imperial City, anti-foreign riots broke out there and elsewhere along the coast. On June 11, 1900, rioters killed a Japanese diplomat while another mob set fire to several Christian churches in Peking and slaughtered the Western and Chinese worshippers inside. Fearing an attack on the legation quarters, British Ambassador Sir Claude MacDonald sent an urgent note to British Vice Admiral Edward Seymour requesting reinforcements for the now besieged legation compound.

The Marines and Defense of the Legation Compound

With conditions in Peking deteriorating rapidly, the American minister to China, Mr. Edwin H. Conger, requested that a detachment of Marines be sent to Peking as part of an international relief force then forming at the port of Taku, where it had landed on 31 May 1900.[5] Accordingly, a detachment of forty-eight Marines, under the command of Captains John T. "Handsome Jack" Myers and Newton T. Hall, landed at Taku from the USS *Oregon* and USS *Newark* and proceeded to Peking via Tientsin. One man from the USS *Oregon*'s Marine detachment, Private Oscar J. Upham, kept a meticulous diary of the events experienced by the Marines during the march to and siege in Peking.[6]

After receiving permission to send the Marine detachments via rail to Peking from local Chinese authorities, Captains Myers and Hall's formation set out first for the U.S. Consulate in Tientsin. After disembarking from the USS *Oregon* and USS *Newark* the leathernecks boarded steam launches which took them ashore in the late afternoon of 26 May 1900. Upham recalled that while aboard the *Oregon* the word came down to prepare for a landing operation. Three days later Rear Admiral Louis Kempff received Minister Conger's instructions to land the Marines at once and to proceed to Tientsin and await further orders before proceeding to Peking.[7] After a quick breakfast the Marines aboard the *Oregon* boarded whale and ship's boats and headed toward the beach. Later that afternoon the Marines from the USS *Newark* landed along with a battalion of Navy bluejackets, a Colt automatic gun, and a 3-inch field piece. After boarding the steamer *Morning Star* and joined by the bluejackets and leathernecks of the *Newark,* the combined force of Marines and sailors proceeded up the Pei Ho River to Tangu.

Shortly thereafter U.S. Marines and Navy bluejackets arrived in Tientsin in the English

U.S. Marines form a skirmish line near the residence of U.S. Minister to China Edwin H. Conger in Peking during the Boxer Rebellion in June 1900 (courtesy U.S. Marine Corps).

Concession area. Escorted to the American Consulate by a Chinese band and a large number of Europeans, the Marines and sailors quickly took up defensive positions along the walls of the British Concession. Joined by Admiral Kempff and two Marine officers, Marines and sailors quickly settled in and mounted a guard watch. The leathernecks and the bluejackets took turn standing guard prior to departing for Peking. Once in Tientsin, British soldiers shortly thereafter arrived to assist the Marines and bluejackets in defense of the two consulates.

On May 31, 1900, at approximately 11:45 A.M., Captain Myers passed the word to the Marines and bluejackets to be prepared to move out. After arriving at the train depot with full field packs and unslung rifles, the Marines commandeered a train made up of ammunition carriers, flatbeds hauling field pieces, and ten coaches to transport the troops, which Upham recalled "were made up of Americans, English, Russians, Japanese, Italians, Austrians, and French soldiers." After a non-eventful journey the international relief force arrived at the Peking train station about 6 P.M., disembarked once again and in heavy marching order proceeded to the legation quarters. As the Marines and bluejackets arrived at the U.S. Legation, Captain Myers ordered his Marines to "double time," as he thought the Chinese might close the huge doors in front of the legation compound and prevent the Americans from entering the grounds. Arriving in the U.S. Legation, the Marines and sailors enjoyed a welcome meal and took up positions in and around their assigned areas. The next day, June 1, 1900, the Marines and bluejackets established a rotating guard schedule. Meanwhile, Minister Conger requested that a detachment of ten Marines (a corporal and nine privates) be assigned to guard the American Mission, roughly 700 yards from the U.S. Legation. As Private Upham recalled, "Corporal Hunt and 9 privates were sent to the American Mission to guard it"[8] as the situation began to deteriorate as the Boxers made their way to the gates of the Forbidden City. By this time the Boxers were, according to Upham, "getting more bold every hour, as the Chinese soldiers sent out to guard the Foreign property are assisting the Boxers to loot the places."[9]

CHART 1. ROSTER OF THE PEKING LEGATION GUARD DURING THE BOXER REBELLION, JUNE–SEPTEMBER 1900

USS *Newark*	USS *Oregon*
Captain Newton K. Hall	Captain John T. Myers
Sergeant J. Fanning	Sergeant Walker
Private J.C. Ammann	Corporal Dahlgren
Private R.M. Barratt	Corporal Hunt
Private G. Brosi	Private Boydson
Private W.L. Carr	Private Butts
Private Dan Daly	Private Fischer
Private H.W. Davis	Private Greer
Private E.J. Donovan	Private Herter
Private W.F. Donovan	Private Hobbs
Private L.R. Gaiennie	Private Horton
Private H.C. Gallagher	Private Kehm
Private H. Gold	Private King
Private T.S. Hall	Private Moody
Private J. Kennedy	Private Moore
Private A.J Kuhn	Private Mueller
Private J.J Layin	Private O'Leary
Private J.C.E. Martin	Private Preston
Private J.H. Schroeder	Private Quinn
Private F. Silver	Private Scannell
Private F.J. Tinkler	Private Thomas
Private J.W. Tutcher	Private Turner
Private W. Zion	Private Upham, Oscar J.
Musician J.A. Murphy	Private White
	Private Young

U.S. Navy Bluejackets

Chief Machinists' Mate T. Peterson (USS *Newark*)

Colt Gun Crew	U.S. Navy Medical Corps
Gunner's Mate 1st Class J. Mitchell	Assistant Surgeon T.M. Lippitt
Seaman J. Sjorgeen	Hospital Apprentice R. Stanley
Seamen A. Westermark[10]	

In order to defend the Christian missionaries and Chinese civilians seeking protection from the Boxers and Imperial troops inside the American Mission compound, Captain Newton T. Hall, Corporal Dahlgren and nine privates arrived about 7 P.M. on the evening of June

11. Captain Hall's detachment made "every effort to protect the native Christians, who were being massacred by the Boxers."[11]

On June 13, German Marines killed ten Boxers as they attempted to enter the legation compound along the southern battery near the Tartar City Wall, in the rear of the German Legation. Meanwhile, Captain Hall and squad of four Marines came down to the base of the Tartar Wall's gate and relieved the Chinese keeper to prevent the key from falling into the hands of the Boxers or Imperial troops.

By now "the combined strength of the Legation Guard at the Legation Quarters was 21 officers and 429 enlisted men, with a moderate supply of ammunition," with no artillery.[12] Meanwhile, Major Littleton W.T. "Tony" Waller along with a battalion of 7 officers and 132 enlisted Marines left the Cavite Naval Station in the Philippines and landed at Taku on 18 June. Major Waller's unit was joined by the 30-man Marine detachment from the USS *Nashville*, and after landing at Taku proceeded to Tientsin upon the orders from Admiral Kempff, who feared that a massacre of the American consul and citizens by the Boxers was imminent.[13] While Waller's force of Marines marched toward Tientsin, violence in Peking once again shifted the scene of action to the legation compound, as the Boxers and a mob of Chinese demonstrators brutally murdered the German ambassador, Baron von Ketteler, two days later (20 June) as he approached the compound. The ambassador's personal secretary was critically wounded in the same attack. As the German sailors and marines attempted to retrieve the ambassador's body, the Boxers and Chinese civilians launched a furious assault against the legation. The siege was now underway, as the U.S. Marines and German marines and sailors repelled these attacks with a hail of gunfire.

Private Upham recalled the Boxers set fire to all shops selling foreign goods, burning a large area west of the Chin Mein (Main Gate) and destroying the front of the gate house used by the royal family. Private Upham wrote that the "Boxers are determined to exterminate everything Foreign."[14] The Marine private recalled one brutal episode that occurred on June 15 in which "Ten American Marines and twenty Russians from the Legation marched down to the Nom Tong or (South Church) and found some Boxers killing and torturing some Chinese Christians, our boys killed abut 50 and rescued 800 Christians many of them wounded, among the rescued was the blind mother of the Minister to France."[15] Upham wrote that upon his return from this particular mission the Marines and other foreign troops inside the legation compound received word that "Captain Bowman McCalla, USN and a force of foreign sailors and Marines were on their way from Tientsin to relieve us."

Despite the losses due to the accurate marksmanship of the U.S. Marines and other foreign troops inside the legation compound, the Boxers continued to attack the Westerners. The Boxers became, as Upham wrote, more daring in their attacks as they attempted to force their way past the defenders located at the Chin Mein gate. The Western troops inside the legation repeatedly turned back these attacks in a hail of gunfire.

By June 21, the Chinese Imperial troops had joined in the attack with the Boxers against the Westerners. On June 23, Imperial troops from Kansu under the command of the Moslem Chinese General Tung Fu-hsiang, whose hatred of the foreigners was as intense as that of the Boxers, launched a combined assault against the Russian Marines and sailors near the Tartar Wall.[16] In the action, the Boxers killed a German Marine whose body was recovered by an American Marine before it rolled off the roof of the Russian Bank building. By June 24, Captain Myers' force had established its position behind a barricade while the Germans established their positions behind that of the Marines in order to reinforce them in the case of a breakthrough. As Upham recorded, the fighting that particular day was most severe:

We'll they [the Boxers] are after us early this [day] at about 6.A.M. They opened up [on] us with their field piece and also advanced in numbers on Legation St. taking advantage of the ruins of the buildings burned yesterday. They planted these banners fifty ft. from our barricades on the house tops and opened a galling fire on us, we received orders to get our things together and be ready to move over to the British Legation as the report came in that the other legations were being abandoned we fell in and marched over to the British Legation.[17]

During this particular engagement the Chinese troops killed Marine Private Charles King as he looked around the corner of the bank at the British Legation. When the Germans abandoned their positions due to the heavy fire from the Boxers, Captain Myers boldly took his force away from its own positions and advanced down its wall within 500 feet of the Chien Mein gate, where another heavy battle erupted between the opposing armies. After a Chinese field piece wounded Private Kehm in the back with shrapnel, the Marines returned fire with their Colt guns. Blowing bugles, the Boxers made a quick dash for Captain Myers' Marines. Upham wrote that the Marines remained in their positions and let loose a terrific return fire, killing many of them before "they [the Boxers] took the hint to leave us alone." As Myers' force awaited the next assault they built a 4-foot barricade, which the U.S. Marines were assigned to defend at all costs. Surveying his position, Captain Myers found it to be too large to be defended by a platoon of Marines. The captain suggested to the British, Russians, and Germans that it "was necessary to reinforce them each day with small detachments of Russians, Germans, and English" troops.[18]

Determined to break through and enter the legation compound, the Boxers constructed a large tower in order to hurl stones and other projectiles against the defenders inside. The American Marines were once again called upon to neutralize the tower. In a spectacular combined night attack with the Italian troops, the leathernecks overcame a hail of Chinese bullets and destroyed the offending tower. Unfortunately, the Boxers managed to kill two more Marines and wound Myers in their assault.

In the assault against the towers launched in the early morning hours of July 3, Captain Myers and a mixed force of Marines, Royal Marines, and Russians killed, after a lengthy firefight, thirty Chinese. Private Upham recalled that the Marines launched the attack "yelling like Indians" as Privates Turner and Thomas led the assault. Eventually, as the British and Russian Marines poured a heavy concentrated fire on the Boxers, the Marines maneuvered around the main Chinese positions into their rear and forced the enemy to beat a hasty retreat. As the Chinese retreated a spear pierced Captain Myers' left leg while Private Turner was killed instantly when a bullet penetrated his skull as he charged forward. Private Thomas was likewise killed in the assault when an enemy round pierced his stomach.[19] After July 3, the Marines and allied troops settled into a routine of sniping and occasional Boxer and Chinese assaults that were becoming more and more sporadic as it became apparent to all that the forces inside the legation would hold out until relieved by a relief expedition. It was during this period that Private Dan Daly of the USS *Newark*'s Marine detachment won the first of two Medals of Honor as he covered a squad of Marines assigned to strengthen the defenses around eastern or Hata Mien gate.[20]

For the remainder of July and into early August 1900, the siege continued, though with less and less intensity. The empress dowager and her advisers squabbled among themselves and with the Boxers as to their next move when it became apparent that the resolve of the Westerners remained unshaken. On August 14, 1900, the first troops of the Allied Relief Expedition appeared outside the Tartar Wall. Leading this contingent of allied soldiers was a battalion of U.S. Marines led by Major William P. Biddle.[21] The "fifty-five" days at Peking were officially over as the Boxer movement quickly disintegrated and the Imperial troops withdrew into the palace grounds. Despite the arrival of the Marines and other allied soldiers, however, the fighting was not over.

During the final phase of the siege two companies of Major Biddle's force (which comprised a full regiment of 29 officers and 482 enlisted Marines)[22] fought it out with a combined Imperial Army–Boxer force along the Chien Mien gate along the Tartar Wall. After clearing the wall and surrounding area of enemy troops, the 2d Battalion of Marines maneuvered several field pieces and poured a heavy fire into Boxer positions. Marine riflemen meanwhile opened with a deadly barrage of their own against Imperial Chinese troops and within four days (15–18 August) had broken the grip of the last contingent of Chinese forces surrounding the legation. By 19 August the Marines controlled the entire west gate and were able to move into the legation settlement.

As for the actions prior to and after the breaking of the siege at the legation settlement, a smaller force of U.S. Marines and allied soldiers were able to clear Tientsin of Boxer and Chinese troops. Meanwhile the International Relief Expedition under British Vice Admiral Edward Seymour fought its way through the enemy and entered Peking on August 14. With the siege broken, the empress dowager and her advisors asked for an armistice. After nearly four months of intensive fighting the Boxer Rebellion was officially over.

The Marines counted their casualties. The vast majority consisted of heat prostration, dysentery, malaria, and poor rations, while inside the legation compound, where the bulk of the heavy fighting took place, combat with the Boxers resulted in eight U.S. Marines killed and eleven wounded.[23]

"A splendid job"

As for the performance of the Marines it was, according to Ambassador Conger, "splendid." In his report of the rebellion and siege in Peking, Ambassador Conger wrote Secretary of State John Hay:

> To our Marines fell the most difficult and dangerous portion of the defense by reason of our proximity to the great wall and the main city gate, over which the large guns were planted. Our legation, with the position which we held on the wall, was the key to the whole situation. This given up, all, including many Chinese Christians, would at once be driven into the British legation, and the congestion there increased by several hundred. The United States Marines acquitted themselves nobly. Twice were they driven from the wall, and once forced to abandon the legation, but each time, reinforced, immediately retook it, and with only a handful of men, aided by ten Russian sailors, and for a few days British Marines, held it to the last against several hundred Chinese, with at least three pieces of artillery. The bravest and most successful event of the whole siege was an attack led by Captain Myers, of our Marines, and 55 men — American, British, and Russian — which resulted in the capture of a formidable barricade on the wall, defended by several hundred Chinese soldiers, over 50 of whom were killed. Two United States Marines were killed and Captain Myers and a British Marine wounded. This made our position on the wall secure, and it was held to the last with the loss of only one other man. I cannot close this dispatch without gratefully mentioning the splendid service performed by the United States Marines, who arrived here on May 31, under the command of Captain Myers. The conduct won the admiration and gratitude of all, and I beg you to kindly communicate the facts to the Navy Department.[24]

Perhaps the most significant praise came from the missionaries themselves. In a letter to Minister Conger and forwarded to Major Biddle, Mr. Arthur E. Smith, who represented the

American missionaries in Peking, praised the "courage, fidelity and patriotism of the Marines, to whom we so largely owe our salvation."[25] Smith added that the Marines "by their bravery in holding an almost untenable position on the city wall in the face of overwhelming numbers, and in cooperating in driving the Chinese from a position of great strength, made all foreigners in Peking their debtors, and gained for themselves, an honorable name among the heroes of their country."[26]

The Marines under Major Biddle and Captain Myers remained in Peking until 28 September, when they were ordered either to their respective ships whence they came or to the Philippines. A similar order was given to all Army units except for a detachment that remained behind in Peking as a legation guard. This changed, however, in July 1905. After considerable correspondence passed between the State, War, and Navy Departments, President Theodore Roosevelt signed an executive order that authorized the substitution of U.S. Army's 9th Infantry Regiment then on duty at the U.S. Legation in China for Marines. In a memorandum signed at the president's summer home in Oyster Bay, New York, Mr. B.F. Barnes, Roosevelt's acting secretary, informed Mr. Alvey A. Adee, the acting secretary of state, that "the President directs that a Marine guard be substituted for a military [Army] guard at the Peking Legation."[27] Subsequently, orders were issued to the First Marine Brigade then stationed in the Philippines to "transfer a detachment consisting of Captain Henry Lee, First Lieutenant Thomas Holcomb, Jr., Second Lieutenant Edward P. Larned, and one hundred enlisted men" for duty at the U.S. Legation, Peking, China. This detachment sailed to China on board the Army transport *Logan*. The enlisted men selected for this assignment were required to have at least eighteen months left on their enlistment contract and were furnished with the navy ration and commutation. The Bureau of Medicine and Surgery provided the Marine detachment with one medical officer, one hospital steward, and one hospital apprentice first class along with a complete medical outfit.[28]

Outfitted with new equipment and uniforms (with the exception of the newly issued regulation full-dress and undress coats and caps which were sent to them later) by the Quartermaster's Department, located at League Island at the Philadelphia Navy Yard. In compliance with the change in the legation guard, the Army quartermaster transferred to the Marine Corps all of the furniture, military stores, Krag-Jorgensen ammunition "and other equipage at the barracks in Peking as might be of service to the Marine guard, reimbursement for the cost of such be made in the usual manner by the transfer of funds."[29] In a separate order, President Roosevelt appointed Captain Henry F. Leonard, USMC, as the U.S. Military Attaché to Peking. This was the first time that a Marine Corps officer had been appointed to such a post for duty at an U.S. Embassy.[30]

A Ready, Available Force

Despite the presence of a large embassy guard in Peking, continued revolutionary foment in China required the landing of Marines throughout the next two decades. Upon the abdication of the last Manchu ruler and proclamation of the Republic of China under Dr. Sun Yat-sen in February 1912, Marines remained off China's coast in order to lend assistance to the American diplomats residing in China.

When Chinese bandits attacked and molested American citizens living in and around the major cities of Tientsin and Shanghai, the commanding officers of the USS *Albany* and USS *Rainbow* landed their Marine detachments in order to guard several important cable

In an Executive Order issued by President Theodore Roosevelt in January 1905, Marines were given sole responsibility for the defense of U.S. Consulates and Missions in China. Here, two U.S. Marines stand guard at the entrance of the U.S. diplomatic compound in Shanghai during the 1920s (courtesy U.S. Marine Corps).

stations located throughout Shanghai on November 4, 1911. Navy Commander R H. Jackson of the USS *Albany* sent two 12-Marine detachments ashore to guard these facilities against marauding bandits. The Marines remained ashore until they were withdrawn on November 14, 1911.[31]

Marines landed in China on two more occasions prior to its full-scale intervention in May of 1922. In August of 1912 a company of leathernecks landed off of Kentucky Island near Shanghai under the command of Captain Thomas C. Turner to safeguard American lives and property. In a similar move the State Department requested that the Marine Legation Guard in Peking be increased to include an additional company of Marines. By the end of 1912, the Marine Legation Guard in Peking numbered 8 officers and 213 enlisted men.[32] Revolutionary violence once again resulted in the landing of a sizable Marine detachment from both the USS *Albany* and USS *Rainbow* on July 27, 1913.

Ships' Detachments and Horse Marines in China, 1922–1939

During the latter part of April 1922 political turmoil in China once again necessitated the landings of U.S. Marines in order to insure the protection of American lives and property. Commander Louis C. Richardson, commanding officer of the USS *Albany*, ordered a detachment of Marines under the command of Captain Charles H. Martin ashore on April 28, 1922. After reinforcement of the Marine Legation Guard in Peking, Captain Martin's force was withdrawn after a brief period ashore. Meanwhile, a battalion of Marines, under the command of Captain Roy C. Swink on board the USS *Huron*, landed at the port of Taku on May 5, 1922, and proceeded to Shanghai, where they remained until May 11. While in Shanghai, the Marines established a consular guard and disarmed the armies of the rival warlords that threatened the city and in particular the foreigners living in the city.[33] In fact, during the interwar era (1919–1937) Marines aboard the various ships of the U.S. Asiatic Fleet were landed periodically in order to reinforce the legation guards in Peking, Shanghai, and Tientsin.

Lieutenant General Edward A. Craig, who was a platoon commander at the time on board the USS *Huron* (1922–23), recalled one such landing when the rival Chinese armies were fighting outside the city, and they [U.S. State Department] were afraid that one army would retreat into the city; and Marines were landed in order to protect the foreign nationals there, together with the British Marines, Italian, Japanese, and so forth. And we stayed ashore protecting the settlement at that time about one month."[34] General Craig remembered while in Chefoo aboard the USS *Huron*, the order came down to "disembark ... in destroyers and proceed to Tientsin where we would take a train and go to Peking to reinforce the Legation Guard there, Chiang Tso-lin and Wu Pei-fu were battling in that area. Chiang Tso-lin was holding Peking, as I remember, and Wu Pei-fu's armies were coming up the railroads ... from a place called Shanhaikwan. "[35]

After a dangerous journey that took the Marines of the *Huron* through the lines of both rival warlords, the leathernecks reached Peking. Armed with their M1903 Springfield rifles, Browning Automatic Rifles (BAR's), 50,000 rounds of ammunition, and two heavy Browning Machine Guns, the Marines quickly established a defensive perimeter around the International Settlement. While in Peking the Marines had normal garrison duties of mounting guard duty and watches, as well as patrolling the entire length of the International Settlement. One of the main duties of the Marine Legation Guard in Peking was to disarm the Chinese troops that came into the International Settlement. As Craig recalled, "One time they

[Marines] disarmed so many that we had a pile 10 feet high of Mauser automatic pistols with the holster stocks."[36] Occasionally, the Marines alternated with the other legation guards from the foreign community and "rode shotgun" aboard the trains that carried western missionaries and diplomats and traversed the routes between Peking, Tientsin, and Shanghai. Craig stated that "each legation would furnish a guard," normally a 10 to 12 man detachment armed with rifles or BAR's. General Craig added that the Japanese oftentimes exceeded this number and instead provided a full platoon of some forty to fifty men. This caused some concern in the diplomatic community as the Western diplomats attempted to remain as neutral as possible in the fighting that had been ongoing since 1911. In March 1927, Marines landed in Shanghai as part of a full brigade, the 3d Brigade, under the command of Brigadier General Smedley D. Butler in order to bolster the defenses of the International Settlement. While the armies of Chiang Kai-shek's Nationalist forces battled the rival warlord armies of Chang Tso-lin and Wu Pei-fu during the mid to late 1920s, the Marines attached to the 3d Brigade patrolled the International Settlement on foot, horseback, and aboard specially converted flatbed trucks. The Marines also established defensive positions in order to prevent the fighting from spilling over into the legation area.

By far, however, it was the mounted detachment of Marines known as the 'Horse Marines' that provided both security and entertainment to the foreign and Chinese communities in Peking. Organized in 1907 to assist in crowd control and as mounted messengers to Americans living in the outlying villages and towns of Peking, the Horse Marines grew in both size and legend, riding their small though agile Mongolian ponies in sporting events (mainly polo playing) and military parades.[37] The Marines attached to the U.S. Legation in Peking (now part of the 4th Marine Regiment) remained there until the eve of the U.S. involvement in World War II. In November 1941, Headquarters Marine Corps received permission from a hesitant State Department to transfer the Marines at the end of November 1941 to the island of Corregidor in the Philippines. Many of the former Horse Marines later fought alongside U.S. Army and Filipino forces commanded by General Douglas MacArthur prior to their surrender in May 1942, when the Philippines fell to the invading Japanese.

Open warfare between the Japanese and Chinese in early 1932 prompted the State Department to once again request the presence of a force of soldiers and Marines to protect American citizens and interests. During the disturbances in 1932 in the International Settlement, the State Department requested the presence of a detachment of Marines from the USS *Houston* in Shanghai until they could be replaced by the U.S. Army's 31st Infantry. Later, when the 31st Infantry returned to the Philippines in June 1932, the commander in chief of the U.S. Asiatic Fleet recommended that the 4th Marines be brought up to full strength so that "it could effectively control the American sector of the International Settlement."[38] In time, Headquarters Marine Corps brought the 4th Marines up to full strength (a three battalion sized regiment) for a short while (19 December 1934). For the next few years, the majority of Marines in the 4th Regiment stood guard over the International Settlement while small detachments served aboard the U.S. Navy's gunboats that patrolled the Yangtze River from November 1933 until July 1935. Here, Marines protected the sailors and ships plying the waters from the bandits that frequently attacked.[39] The primary mission of the 4th Marines from mid–1935 to the end of November 1941 was to not only "thwart any Japanese attempt to change the status quo (by force) of the American sector," but also to keep Chiang Kai-shek's Nationalist forces from committing similar outrages against the foreigners. Under-manned and ill-equipped to fight off a major Japanese attack against the International Settlement, the U.S. government dispatched on September 19, 1937, the 2nd Marine Brigade, commanded by

"The Horse Marines" on parade inside the U.S. Diplomatic Compound in Peking, China, in 1937 (courtesy U.S. Marine Corps).

Brigadier General John C. Beaumont, to Shanghai, where it stood guard in the American sector of the International Settlement. As Marines such as Private (later Master Sergeant) Russell A. Bowers stood guard over the U.S. Embassy in Peking and U.S. Consulates in Shanghai and Tientsin, the situation became even more precarious as they watched the political and military situation in Asia deteriorate rapidly.[40] One of the Marines, Corporal William H. Chittenden, who served at the U.S. Embassy in Peking, recalled that the Japanese soldiers who occupied the Chinese capital regarded the Marines with much scorn, while the leathernecks likewise "held little respect for the Japanese."[41]

This situation persisted even as the United States and Japan drifted closer to war late in 1941. From the time Japan invaded China proper in October 1937 to the outbreak of World War II in Europe, the Marine positions became even more tenuous. Admiral Thomas C. Hart, the commander in chief of the Asiatic Fleet, recommended the withdrawal of the 4th Marines from Shanghai. While the bulk of the 4th Marines withdrew in November 1941, a detachment of Marine embassy guards remained on duty in Peking and Shanghai where they stood watch over a situation that deteriorated almost daily. In fact, the duties of these Marines became more precarious as each incident in China (and elsewhere in Asia) made it evident that war between the United States and Japan would occur sooner rather than later.

Marine Legation Duty, 1932–1941

The Marines who remained behind in China on duty in Beijing on legation duty spent the bulk of their time mounting guard duty. Surrounded by the walls of the "Forbidden City," the legation itself was self-contained and consisted of a post exchange, library, officers and enlisted quarters, a hospital, a motor pool, electrical plant, telephone exchange, and a water and ice plant. In Jonathan Hall located on the legation grounds was a gymnasium, a theater, a ballroom, bowling alley, and rented officers' quarters. The majority of the enlisted Marines lived in Beijing, as many were paid a subsidy besides their monthly pay that during the era of the Great Depression was considerable given the economic situation back in the United States. Both officers and enlisted men to a degree could live well off in China, a fact that made "China duty" not so onerous.[42]

By the terms of the 1904 Boxer Protocols that governed their duties in China, the Marines assigned to legation duty in either Beijing or in the International Settlement in Shanghai patrolled the grounds of the legation and in the case of Shanghai, the length of the American concession. In addition to their normal guard duties, Marines assigned to the American Embassy in Beijing likewise guarded a nine-man Marine-Navy detachment monitoring and decoding Japanese diplomatic and military messages as well noting the pattern of Japanese radio traffic from the Japanese Embassy next door to the American Embassy.[43]

War with Japan: 7–10 December 1941

For Chittenden and his fellow Marine embassy guards, the war against Japan started long before Pearl Harbor as the leathernecks maintained security at the U.S. Embassy in Peking amid the growing threat of war each day. When news reached the Marines in Peking of the Japanese attack on Pearl Harbor on the morning of December 8 (Peking time), 1941, Chittenden and the other Marine embassy guards began preparations for a possible siege of the embassy. At 0800 on the morning of December 8,[44] Consul General Richard Buttrick, the senior foreign service officer in Peking, received word that Japanese soldiers were "patrolling the streets" outside the U.S. Embassy, and had restricted the movement of Americans between the diplomatic and Marine compounds. Consul Buttrick likewise received word that War Plan WPL46 had been implemented, and ordered Colonel W.W. Ashurst's Marines to commence with the burning of all confidential codes and papers. At about 10:00 A.M. the Japanese army commander for the sector where the American Embassy was located issued an order that requested the disarming of the U.S. Marine Embassy guard. Similar actions were likewise taken in Tientsin and with the Marine train guards in Chinwangtao. As one observer noted, it was plainly evident that Colonel Ashurst "suffered the anguish of having to surrender his command [and was] heartbroken but steadfast ... this was a fearful blow to him."[45] The strain on Colonel Ashurst and his Marine embassy guards became evident when in a ceremony that turned over the grounds of he U.S. Embassy in Peking to the Japanese, the Marine bugler — who blew "Retreat" as other leathernecks lowered the Stars and Stripes, and stood at attention with their M1903 Springfield rifles in perfect formation — fought back tears that rolled down his cheeks as he blew the last call. When he finished his mournful notes, the bugler, who openly wept, took the bugle and crushed it on his knees in utter disgust of the forced surrender.

For Colonel Ashurst and his Marines, denied repatriation to the United States, the next few years as prisoners of war of the Japanese Army was the supreme test of endurance.

Many of them succumbed to the inhumane treatment of their Japanese captors. As Corporal Chittenden later recalled, the Marines who served in Peking and in North China "endured every kind of hardship throughout those long months ... disease, starvation, brutality, the humiliation of the situation and never knowing the honor of combat ... December 7th 2001 will mark 60 years from the day that 203 North China Marines began a new and special kind of duty.... The duty of serving three years and eight months under the bayonets of the Imperial Japanese Army.... We were the first American prisoners of war casualties of World War II."

Colonel William W. Ashurst, a Marine veteran from World War I and noted marksman, endured all of the hardships of captivity alongside his men. For his outstanding leadership in face of terrific adversity while a captive of the Japanese, Colonel Ashurst was awarded the Legion of Merit for his "skill, diplomacy and superior judgement in his dealings with the Japanese camp authorities," and for being "instrumental in lowering the mortality rate of the [Marine] internees" captured by the Japanese. Unfortunately, however, the long period of captivity adversely affected his health and he spent the remaining years of his life recovering from his ordeal as a prisoner of war.[46]

One of the most interesting events surrounding the Marine embassy guard in Peking during those last hectic days as war broke out between the United States and Japan was the disappearance of the bones of the recently discovered archeological treasure known worldwide as Peking Man. Entrusted to Colonel Ashurst's care, the Marine colonel assigned an eight-man Marine detachment to accompany the bones of Peking Man to a train bound for the Chinese coast, where they would then be placed on a ship headed for the United States. Japanese troops intercepted the train that contained Peking Man and accordingly, "the scientific treasure has been missing ever since." Reportedly, Colonel (later Brigadier General) Ashurst "was the last man known to have seen the yellowed treasure."

In spite of their surrender to Japanese forces, the Marine embassy guards who entered captivity on that fateful December day maintained their dignity and pride, much to the disdain of their captors, for almost four years. These same Marines demonstrated the qualities Marine security guards are still required to uphold. Corporal Chittenden and the Marines who stood guard in Peking, Tientsin, and Chingwangtao never forgot the standards and obligations demanded of them in times of war as well as in peace.

From the establishment of the first Marine Legation Guard in China in the mid–1850s to the withdrawal of the 4th Marine Regiment in November 1941, the leathernecks and sailors assigned to the "China Station" served as the most visible form of security to American diplomats and citizens living in China. In time, the Marines attached to consular and legation duty came to symbolize stability amidst the revolutionary chaos and turmoil that characterized China during the first half of the twentieth century. Either riding their Mongolian ponies or standing long hours of watch in the International Settlements of Shanghai, Tientsin, and Peking, the Marines of the Legation Guard lived up to the gallant precedent of those who preceded them during the Boxer Rebellion.

Revolutionaries, Bandoleros and Legation Guards: Marines in Nicaragua, 1912–1925

Revolutionary turmoil closer to home in Nicaragua necessitated the presence of a Marine expeditionary force in the summer of 1912 as competing political factions there fought each other and foreigners alike for political (and economic) control of the country. The objectives of President William Howard Taft and Secretary of State Philander C. Knox in Nicaragua were not only to protect U.S, citizens and property, but to provide support to a group of rebels led by Juan J. Estrada and their attempt to overthrow President Jose Santos Zelaya, whose presidency had been marked by corruption and inefficiency. After nearly a decade of rule, interrupted periodically by *coups d'état*, Nicaraguans who were tired of Zelaya's heavy-handed methods and foreign businessmen concerned over the seizure of their businesses and property conspired to overthrow Zelaya and replace him with Estrada in the summer of 1912. President Taft and Secretary of State Knox, convinced that Estrada's Conservative Party "represented the majority of the Nicaraguan people," severed diplomatic relations with the Zelaya government in the hope that his administration would be overthrown by a more friendly regime in Nicaragua.[47]

Accordingly, when Zelaya sought to calm the political waters by resigning with the appointment of Dr. Jose Madriz, another Liberal politician, the Taft administration withheld recognition, setting the stage for a full-fledged revolt by Estrada. When Estrada's revolt appeared to be in trouble, President Taft ordered several Marine detachments ashore that had been positioned off the west coast of Nicaragua as early as February 1910. The mission of these leathernecks was to guard American property and establish a "neutral zone." The Marine detachments from both the USS *Dubuque* and the *Paducah* under the command of Major Smedley D. Butler came ashore at Bluefields and established order. After some minor skirmishes with the Marines and forces of Estrada, the Liberal forces under Zelaya quickly evaporated as political infighting forced the president to flee to Mexico. Triumphantly, Estrada marched into Managua and assumed control of Nicaragua.[48]

Estrada's presidency proved to be only a respite from the political chaos that characterized Nicaraguan politics since 1899. Shortly after he gained power, Estrada's legitimacy was challenged by two men — Emiliano Chamorro and Luis Mena, both of whom questioned Estrada's commitment to the Conservative Party. Furthermore, the anger aroused among the Nicaraguan peasantry over the alleged affront to their sovereignty by the terms of the Dawson Agreement, which placed the United States in charge of the collection of Nicaragua's customs duties (in order to placate the foreign investors) further contributed to the country's continued instability.[49]

By the autumn of 1911, Nicaragua tottered on the brink of anarchy. As the United States sought to insure stability by forcing Estrada to resign, the various Nicaraguan political factions, which were virulently anti–United States though decidedly unable to unite, once again fought each other for control of the country. With Estrada gone, the Liberals under Benjamin Zeledon initiated hostilities by blowing up the Loma fort located in Managua. This in turn prompted the U.S. minister to Nicaragua, Mr. George T. Weitzel, to request the landing of a force of bluejackets and Marines in order to protect American lives and property.[50]

A detachment of bluejackets led by Navy Lieutenant James A. Campbell from the USS *Annapolis* established defensive positions outside the U.S. Legation in Managua on August 6, 1912. The next day, August 17, a combined detachment of sailors and Marines landed at Bluefields to protect American lives and property in and around the city. Meanwhile, on August 14, a battalion of 13 officers and 341 Marines under the command of Major Smedley D. Butler arrived on board the Army transport *Justin* from Panama and quickly established order ashore at Corinto. Major Butler's force was soon joined by a force of 19 Marines and 38 bluejackets under the command of Lieutenant Bradford Barnette, from the USS *Tacoma*. An additional 15 Marines led by 2nd Lieutenant Earle C. Long landed at Corinto from the

USS *Annapolis* to reconnoiter the railroad. Mr. Weitzel later reported that upon landing, the bluejackets and Marines boarded rail cars or filed into columns and headed (many Marines, in fact, rode the railroad) into Managua. As the U.S. minister reported, the situation in the capital and surrounding countryside continued to rapidly deteriorate as the

> ... bombardment of the city continued throughout the 11th, 12th, 13th, and 14th, with slight inter-missions and about 600 projectiles were fired into the residence portion of the city, according to the estimate of the Navy officers. One shell struck in the street directly in front of the Legation, and about 40 or 50 within dangerous proximity.... There were a hundred and thirty-two women and children killed and injured by shells and not one man. The last of the firing was heard at about 5 A.M. of August 14 and this proved to be a feint to cover the retreat.[51]

The Mr. Weitzel reported that while the sailors sent from the USS *Tacoma* and USS *Annapolis* were able to secure the grounds of the legation, the force was still "inadequate" to "afford protection for any length of time if the more serious fears felt by the general public had been realized." The U.S. minister added that as the shelling in Managua eventually died down, "Major Smedley D. Butler, U.S.M.C., arrived from Corinto (August 17, 1912) with his battalion of 350 marines from the Canal Zone (Panama) and was given a warm welcome by natives and foreigners alike." The minister reported to Secretary Knox that Major Butler "had moved his forces with remarkable rapidity and reached the capital at a most opportune time, for if he had arrived sooner he would have had difficulty perhaps in entering the city during the fighting." Mr. Weitzel also reported that "on the other hand if his coming had been delayed the railroad communication would have been cut and the relief work seriously hampered for a long time."[52]

As Butler's force set out from Managua into the surrounding to countryside to prevent further attacks by Luis Mena's forces,[53] Colonel Joseph H. Pendleton's 1st Provisional Marine Regiment arrived from the Canal Zone and came ashore at Corinto, where it quickly spread out throughout the country to hunt down and disarm the rebels.[54] Sergeant Frank F. Zissa described one such engagement with the rebels to his girlfriend, Miss Flora Huetter, in a let-ter dated October 9, 1912: "We have had several fights with the revolutionists of this revolu-tion-ridden country since my last writing. The first was about three weeks ago when a train with a battalion of Marines on board was on its way to ... Granada, the extreme end of the railroad.... This was a regular hot-bed for rebels as they had possession of everything, even the food supply, causing people to pay exorbitant prices for what they might want to buy."[55]

Sergeant Zissa recalled that one of the primary goals of the Marines during this peace-enforcing mission was to disarm the rebels. In the same letter, he told Huetter, "Upon reach-ing Granada, which is about 15 miles from Masaya, our men immediately proceeded to take possession of the town, disarm the rebels, take charge of the food supply and distribute among the needy. There was little trouble in taking the guns and such other firearms as the rebels carried, for the news of the damage that our guns can make had preceded the coming of the 400 Marines and they willingly turned everything over. There [was] over a carload of rifles taken."[56]

By mid–October, the Marines were able to restore order as the revolution led by Presi-dent Estrada fell apart. With the end of rebel resistance the greater part of Major Butler's force and Colonel Pendleton's 1st Provisional Regiment was withdrawn and sent back to Panama. Rebel leader Luis Mena and his son were likewise sent into exile by the United States to Panama.

As resistance in Nicaragua ended, the secretary of state, after considerable discussions between the U.S. Legation in Managua and the State and Navy Departments, agreed upon the creation of a legation guard in Managua comprised of Marines. On 9 December 1912, the senior U.S. Naval officer present recommended to the Navy Department that "if conditions in Nicaragua remain as at present, Marines ... be withdrawn about January 15, 1913, retaining at Managua 50 Marines, temporarily as Legation Guard, attached to the Station Ship at Corinto." On January 21, 1913, Lieutenant Colonel Charles C. Long reported to the secretary of the Navy, "on January 4, 1913, I received orders by cable for the formation of a detachment of four officers and 101 enlisted men to remain in Managua as a Legation Guard. On January 9, this detachment was formed with Captain Edward A. Greene, USMC, in command.[57]

The Marine Legation Guard was quartered in Camp de Marte, which was a Nicaraguan government reservation located on the southern edge of the city. The Marines themselves were housed in both tents and in a former barracks used by the Nicaraguan Army renovated by the Marines. Led by Captain Edward Greene, the Marine Legation Guard served as not only a force organized to protect the American Legation, but as reminder that the United States retained an active interest in political stability in Nicaragua and on the isthmus as a whole.

The Marine Legation Guard, 1913–1925

The departure of the 1st Provisional Regiment and Butler's battalion did not signal an end to the political in-fighting in Nicaragua. If anything it intensified as President Diaz's chosen successor, Emiliano Chamorro, and the Conservative Party used any and all means to remain in power for the next decade and a half. Unable to run himself, President Chamorro "stepped aside in favor of his old and feeble uncle, Diego Manuel Chamorro," who entered the presidency after a fraudulent election.[58]

Meanwhile, the Marines assigned to the legation guard continued to maintain an uneasy peace and served as a reminder that the United States remained committed to a politically stable Nicaragua. Despite its main assignment as a legation security force, the Marines attached to the U.S. Legation in Managua became identified as a force designed to preserve Conservative rule. In fact, in 1920, the Marine Legation Guard's commander at one point threatened to use the Marines under his command to prevent a *coup d'état* from occurring against the Conservative government.[59] This and other incidents prompted the State Department's decision to withdraw the guard in favor of a trained non-partisan constabulary. Through the efforts of Conservative President Bartolome Martinez, Nicaraguans in 1924 elected a joint Liberal-Conservative ticket of Juan Maria Sacasa and Carlos Solorzano that in turn prompted the State Department to continue its plan to withdraw the Marines from Nicaragua.[60]

Despite the desire of most Nicaraguan politicians (and U.S. State Department officials) that the Marine Legation Guard be removed, the new government of Juan Sacasa and Carlos Solorzano pressed the U.S. State Department to retain the legation guard. The Solorzano government feared that the constabulary, like the Army, might become partisan and serve as an instrument of political change and cause undue uneasiness in both foreign and domestic business circles in Nicaragua. In a memorandum to the American charge in Managua and forwarded to Secretary of State Charles Evans Hughes, President Solorzano wrote that withdrawal of the Marine Legation Guard would cause "(a) uneasiness [*desconfianza*] ... (b) a depression of bonds and depreciation of the currency ... (c) the obligation of the government to create without delay a standing army in expectations of possible disturbances or alterations of public order, an organization which would divert for its maintenance considerable sums of money which could be better employed in the development of resources or in the upkeep of public administration."[61]

In short, President Solorzano informed Secretary of State Hughes that it was undesirable to talk of withdrawing the Marines until a credible non-partisan native constabulary had been formed. The Nicaraguan leader emphasized that if the Marines were withdrawn hastily it would be next to impossible to train an efficient national guard. In his reply to the Nicaraguan foreign minister, Secretary of State Hughes emphasized the fact that the Nicaraguans had been informed fourteen months prior to the impending departure of the Marine Legation Guard and thus had sufficient time to train a credible national guard. In essence, Secretary Hughes informed President Solorzano that the U.S. would be fully "justified" in withdrawing the legation guard, as the Nicaraguans had been fully aware of Washington's plans.[62]

Eventually, the State Department and President Solorzano reached a compromise whereby the Marine Legation Guard would delay its impending withdrawal at the very latest by September 1, 1925, which by that time a credible native constabulary could be organized and sufficiently trained. Acting Secretary of State Joseph C. Grew outlined to the Nicaraguan foreign minister the plan to create a non-partisan national guard: "The Constabulary is to be armed, equipped, and trained as a military police force with the object of entirely replacing the existing national police, navy, and army of Nicaragua. This force is to be trained free from political influence as a national institution and used only to maintain peace, law, and order."[63] Acting Secretary of State Grew added, "In view of the desire of Nicaraguan Government that the United States lend its friendly cooperation in the formation of the Constabulary it is agreed that the officers and enlisted men of the Legation Guard, now stationed at Managua, will, until their withdrawal, voluntarily lend their service in its formation and training."[64] Despite the unenthusiastic support of the Nicaraguan government in the creation of such a force, the Marines labored under intense pressure in training the native constabulary and awaited a training mission from the United States. This training mission, headed by retired U.S. Army Major Calvin B. Carter, arrived in Nicaragua shortly thereafter to train a credible and non-partisan Nicaraguan national guard.[65]

After months of delay, due in large part to the problems associated with the organization of a credible native constabulary and arrival of a training mission from the United States, the Marine Legation Guard, commanded by Major Ralph E. Keyser, embarked aboard the Navy transport USS *Henderson* and set sail for the Navy Yard located at Norfolk, Virginia. After nearly twelve years, the Marines of the legation guard had maintained an uneasy peace amid the political unrest throughout Nicaragua.

The Marine Legation Guard Returns, 1926–1933

Despite the organization of a non-partisan native constabulary, Nicaragua's political scene remained chaotic. "Ultra-Conservative" Emiliano Chamorro launched a *coup* against the joint government of President Solorzano and Juan Sacasa, both of whom were "obliged" to leave the country as the Conservative army marched on Managua.[66] On January 16, 1926, with Solorzano and Sacasa gone, Chamorro's Conservative army entered the capital with the ultra–Conservative seizing power. As Nicaragua tottered on the brink of revolution, President Calvin C. Coolidge dispatched the USS *Cleveland* and landed its Marine detachment and force of bluejackets in order to protect American lives and property.

Meanwhile, in the jungles of eastern Nicaragua, the Liberal Army, led by General Jose Moncada, began to push the Conservative-led army back upon the port of Bluefields.

As the fighting soon spread throughout Nicaragua, the U.S. State Department was able to arrange a truce. On the day that the truce was set to expire (October 30, 1926), President Chamorro resigned. After considerable negotiations with the Nicaraguan political factions, all parties agreed upon the election of Adolfo Diaz until full-fledged supervised elections could be held in 1928. Despite the constitutionality of this arrangement, Diaz's government came under intense criticism at home and abroad as an illegal government installed by the United States. Even though this charge was unfounded, U.S. recognition of Diaz's government set the stage for a large-scale intervention by U.S. Marines and a brief return of a legation guard.[67]

As the U.S. State Department attempted to negotiate an end to Nicaragua's endless cycle of political upheavals, the warring parties continued to fight each other for control of the country. Eventually, President Coolidge's personal envoy, Henry L. Stimson, was able to arrange a peace treaty whereby elections were to be held under the supervision of a specially appointed electoral commission. By the terms of the Treaty of Tipitapa (May 1927), all of the Nicaraguan factions except one agreed to disarm and disband their armies under the watchful eyes of the U.S. Marines. The main opposition to this U.S.-brokered political arrangement came from one of the Liberal generals, Augusto Caesar Sandino, who vowed that he would not lay down his arms until the Marines were withdrawn permanently from Nicaragua. As the Marines spread throughout Nicaragua to disarm the various armies, Sandino's forces began a five-year insurgency against the Marines and the Marine-led and trained Nicaraguan constabulary.[68]

As the Marines of the 2d Brigade set about the task of disarming the various armies and chasing Sandino and his *bandoleros* throughout the jungles of Nicaragua, a Marine Legation Guard was re-established to protect the U.S. diplomatic mission in Managua. The Marine Legation Guard once again attempted to retain its neutrality as other leathernecks conducted combat patrols throughout Nicaragua. While in Nicaragua the primary mission of the Marines was to "maintain peace and provide for the security of the Nicaraguan Government and people."[69]

When an earthquake struck Managua on March 31, 1931, Marine General F.L. Bradman assumed control of the relief efforts. The Marines assigned to both the 2d Brigade and the legation guard enforced martial law, furnished guards for the city, helped to suppress the widespread looting that took place, and established many first aid and food centers.[70] As the Marines eventually restored law and order to Managua, the Marines continued to fight both fires and *bandoleros* who had hoped to take advantage of the lull in the fighting in the countryside, and had managed to advance largely undetected on the capital. In time, the Marines turned the vast majority of the relief effort over to U.S. Army and Navy engineers while they and the Nicaraguan Guardia resumed combat operations.

As the fighting against the guerrillas intensified during the last two years of the U.S. intervention, the Marines began to turn more and more of the war over to the Nicaraguan Guardia. With the election of Juan B. Sacasa as president of Nicaragua, U.S. President Herbert Hoover withdrew the Marines on January 1, 1933, including those attached to the re-established legation guard. With the withdrawal of the Marines from Nicaragua, the period of U.S. intervention in Latin America that started as early as 1903 ended quietly. The leathernecks marched up the gangplanks of the awaiting transports sent there to take them home.

Summary

The establishment of a Marine legation guard in both Peking and Managua came amid the seeds of revolutionary violence that shook both China and Nicaragua during the first three decades of the 20th century. During these three decades, the State Department had established Marine legation guards in Seoul, Korea (1904), the Dominican Republic (1915), China (1896), and Nicaragua (1912). In particular, the establishment of legation guards in China and Nicaragua served as a reminder that the United States remained capable of not only protecting the lives and property of its citizens and guard but able to back this determination with force.

Historically, the establishment of the legation guard in China had its origins in the U.S.-brokered Treaty of Shimonoseki (1896) that ended the Sino-Japanese War (1894–95), when the United States gained the right to establish a legation in Peking. As revolutionary violence periodically swept across the Chinese countryside, Marines took up the role as a legation security force. By the time of the outbreak of the Boxer Rebellion in June 1900, the leathernecks of the U.S. Asiatic fleet oftentimes landed to protect American diplomatic personnel in Peking, Taku, and Tientsin.[71] During the Boxer Rebellion, the leathernecks of the USS *Newark* and USS *Oregon* fought alongside their fellow marines and bluejackets from the other Western powers of Great Britain, Germany, Italy, Russia, and France and inadvertently created a new role for the Marine Corps as a embassy security force. Codified in President Theodore Roosevelt's July 1905 message to the secretary of state, Marine guards shortly thereafter became permanent fixtures in Peking, Teintsin, and later Shanghai. In time, the Marines of the Peking detachment, known as the "Horse Marines," soon established a colorful reputation amid the continued social and political upheavals characteristic of China during the 1920s and 1930s.

Unlike in China, the creation of a Marine Legation Guard in Nicaragua had the reverse effect, as the different political factions fought each other and the Americans for control of this Central American nation starting in 1912 and ending in 1933. Only after thousands had been killed, wounded or dispossessed of their homes and property did peace come to Nicaragua. Indeed, the intervention and establishment of the Marine Legation Guard in Managua met with a considerable amount of opposition both in Nicaragua and at home in the United States. The Marine Legation Guard was finally withdrawn only after the U.S. State Department saw the futility in the maintenance of a force that had become the very symbol of the 1912 intervention in Nicaragua. In fact, the Marine Legation Guard became the very symbol of a foreign policy that had been largely discredited as unworkable for goals that were largely unattainable.

Marines nevertheless laid the foundations for their role as embassy security during the first three decades of the 20th century. From the walls of the Chien Mein gate in Peking, China, to the steaming jungles and rivers of Nicaragua, the U.S. Marine Corps proudly demonstrated their country's "flag was unfurled to every breeze."

CHAPTER 3

Ashore and Afloat:
The Marines and Service with the
Department of State, 1904–1945

As the Marine Corps entered the 20th century, a new mission was born amid the revolutionary violence of China. This new mission was diplomatic security. For the Marine Corps and the United States, the modern era brought with it new challenges and responsibilities as it emerged to take its place among the world powers. As Marines experimented with their role as a naval expeditionary force on the beaches of Culebra, Puerto Rico, other detachments of leathernecks continued in their role as naval security forces, standing guard over navy yards, arsenals, legations and consulates. Little did Marine Corps and State Department officials realize one of the most important partnerships had been forged amid the violence of the Boxer Rebellion, one that would carry on into 20th and 21st centuries.

Prelude to Intervention: Marines in the Dominican Republic, 1903

When political unrest in the Dominican Republic threatened American lives and property, U.S. Consul General Campbell L. Maxwell requested from Commander William H. Turner of the USS *Atlanta* to land a force of Marines to guard the U.S. Consulate in Santo Domingo City. On April 1, 1903, First Lieutenant Richard G. McConnell and a detachment of twenty-five Marines landed in Santo Domingo City and set up a legation guard at the U.S. Consulate. Here, they protected the lives of both American and non–Americans against the revolutionaries. Lieutenant McConnell's detachment remained ashore until April 19, when it re-embarked aboard the *Atlanta*.[1]

A Most Unusual Mission: Marines in Abyssinia, 1903–1904

Far from the Middle Kingdom of China, the Marine detachments attached to the U.S. Navy's Mediterranean squadron participated in one of the most unusual diplomatic missions in its entire history, reminiscent of the Eaton Mission when Lieutenant Presley O'Bannon's leathernecks accompanied the Bashaw of Tripoli in 1805. In 1903, when the U.S. State Department announced its intention to establish diplomatic relations with Emperor Menelik II of Abyssinia, it dispatched Consul General Skinner to proceed to Addis Ababa in order to arrange a treaty of recognition and reciprocity between the two countries.[2] Accompanying Mr. Skinner was a force of nineteen Marines led by Captain George C. Thorpe and six Navy bluejackets commanded by Navy Lieutenant C.L. Hussey. The expedition proceeded inland toward Addis Ababa from Djibouti, and arrived at the town of Dire Dauos on 21 November 1903.

In the absence of rail or suitable roads, the Americans continued forward over scorching deserts and steep mountains toward Addis Ababa on mules and camels. After a difficult journey, oftentimes marked by mutinous native carriers and difficult terrain, the leathernecks safely delivered Consul Skinner to the Abyssinian capital. Informed by one of Emperor Menelik's confidants that the king had arranged a guard of honor for the approaching Americans, the Marines quickly put on their dress blue uniforms and continued toward the Abyssinian capital. As the Americans approached the city, the hills suddenly came alive as Menelik's warriors, adorned in their finest dress of leopard and lions' skins and armed with spears, suddenly arose out of nowhere to greet the strangers to the sounds of tom-toms and trumpets.[3] Mounted on fine Arabian horses and zebras, the warriors escorted the Americans to the emperor's palace, referred to as the *Gebi.*

Emperor Menelik, who had been impressed with the smartness and precision of this fine, small detachment of foreign soldiers, visited the leathernecks and bluejackets in their camp. Here, Captain Thorpe's men put on drills that, according to the Marine captain's report, "pleased him [the Emperor] greatly." Amidst the drills and parades, Consul General Skinner and the emperor held several meetings that concluded with an agreement to establish diplomatic relations between the two countries.

After both parties signed the treaties that brought recognition between the two countries, Emperor Menelik awarded each enlisted Marine the "Menelik Medal." The emperor presented Captain Thorpe and Lieutenant Hussey the coveted "Star of Ethiopia."[4] The Marines and sailors remained in Addis Ababa for two months before they set out for Djibouti on January 15, 1904, after which they returned home after having participated in one of the most interesting and perhaps the most exotic diplomatic missions Marines participated in up to that time.

The Marines and sailors were not finished with Africa, however, as the Moroccan bandit leader Raisouli kidnapped several foreigners as hostages. President Theodore Roosevelt, in response to this outrage, ordered a naval squadron to Moroccan waters to protect U.S. citizens and property. Arriving off Tangier in late May 1904, Rear Admiral French E. Chadwick met with the American Consul General Mr. Gummere and discussed the precarious situation ashore. Mr. Gummere, fearing further outrages by Raisouli, suggested that the situation "warranted the establishment of a suitable Marine guard at the Consulate," a suggestion with which Admiral Chadwick concurred.[5] Under the command of Captain John T. "Handsome Jack" Myers, the hero of the siege in Peking, the Marines assigned to the admiral's flagship, USS *Brooklyn,* landed in the afternoon hours of 30 May and remained ashore until the completion of their mission. On June 26, 1904, Myers' force re-embarked aboard the *Brooklyn.* While ashore, Captain Myers' force guarded the U.S. Consulate in Tangier, where it served as a powerful reminder that any attacks against American lives and property would be dealt with accordingly.

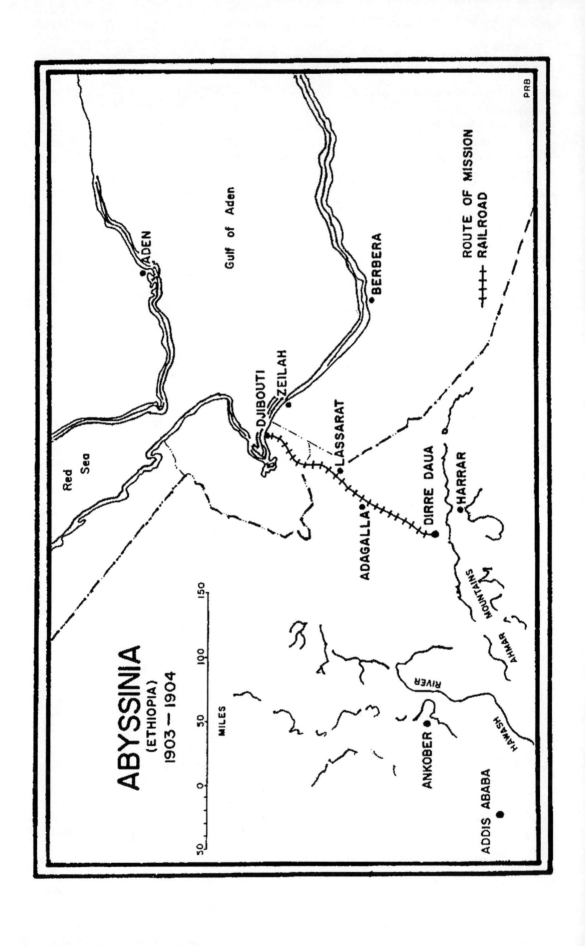

ABYSSINIA
(ETHIOPIA)
1903 – 1904

MILES

50   0   50   100   150

Red
Sea

Gulf of Aden

ADEN

BERBERA

ZEILAH

DJIBOUTI

LASSARAT

ADAGALLA

DIRRE DAUA

HARRAR

AHMAR
MOUNTAINS

RIVER

HAWASH

ANKOBER

ADDIS ABABA

ROUTE OF MISSION
RAILROAD

PRB

Attaché and Courier Duty During World War I, 1915–1919

When war broke out in Europe during the summer of 1914, President Woodrow Wilson asked Americans to be "neutral in spirit as well as in actions." Despite the nation's proclaimed neutrality, the war soon affected the United States and the Marine Corps. The U.S. embassies and confidential diplomatic mail were now placed in harm's way as the war spread throughout Europe during the summer of 1915.

In April 1916, Marine Major James Carson Breckinridge[6] was appointed as the assistant naval attaché to the U.S. Consulate located in Petrograd,[7] Russia, where he shortly gained a unique vantage point to the Russian Revolution and abdication of Czar Nicholas II by the Constitutional Democrats (Cadets) led by Alexander Kerensky. While serving as the naval attaché, Major Breckinridge sent back many letters to his family describing the events that literally "shook the world," as Russia went from one revolution to another in October 1917, and a left a lasting impression on Major Breckinridge.

Major Breckinridge (he was promoted to Lieutenant Colonel on August 29, 1916) arrived in Petrograd after a long trip across the United States, China and Siberia aboard the Trans-Siberian Railroad in early May 1916. In a letter to his mother dated 6 May

Lieutenant Colonel James Carson Breckinridge's passport while he served as the naval attaché at the U.S. embassies in Christiana, Norway, and Copenhagen, Sweden (J.C. Breckinridge Papers, U.S. Marine Corps University).

1916, Breckinridge described his arrival in Petrograd, his meeting with the U.S. Ambassador to Russia, Mr. David R. Francis, and with Tsar Nicholas II:

My Darling Mother:

Mr. Francis, the new ambassador, arrived several days ago, late at night of course, or rather early in the morning, it was about 3:15 A.M. The Embassy staff went bravely to meet him at 10:15 which was right & proper, but nobody had any idea when the train would arrive; it was reported at all sorts of hours, as being at all sorts of places, and as the hours dragged by the "Staff" thinned out. Only a few of the faithful were there at the finish, my gorgeous full dress uniform being the only dash of color in the party. I have seen nothing of the Ambassador, but I like him, I think he is a fine man, and there is room for such here. Our Embassy is a very plain mess. But things are beginning to clean up and straighten up already. I have hopes.... Today the Ambassador went to Tsarcoy Selo[8] to be presented, most of the staff accompanying him, including myself. It was most interesting, and I remembered all the time that I was only following where you and Father had so often been before; I did wish you were back here now. The Imperial station was at our service,

Opposite: **In 1903, U.S. Marines accompanied U.S. Consul General Mr. Skinner on a diplomatic mission to the towns of Dire-Daouah and Addis Ababa in Abyssinia (Ethiopia). The journey started in the port of Djibouti (French Somaliland) (courtesy U.S. Marine Corps).**

and we travelled in the Imperial train, which had the Trans Siberian and the Wabash between just seventeen days.... We arrived at the palace and were ushered through many handsome rooms to a waiting room. The Ambassador was received alone and was with the Emperor about half an hour, who proved himself to be of perfect poise and self possession.... If one can judge an Emperor in something less than ten minutes I would say that I agree with what you and Father said of him, he is a good man; he impressed me greatly.[9]

Lieutenant Colonel Breckinridge, who had lived in St. Petersburg with his parents before returning to the United States, offered insightful accounts of wartime Russia and of the revolution that soon engulfed that country in the spring of 1917. In a letter to his mother dated April 14, 1917, Lieutenant Colonel Breckinridge described the overthrow of the czar and his replacement with Alexander Kerensky[10]:

I heard of it in Kopenhagen [the revolution], and it was all over before I could have returned, had there been any need for me to return; so I missed the actual fighting, what there was of it. Not over 250 people were killed in all, most of them onlookers, trouble-makers and police; these last were the people hated and wanted to get rid of; all of them who were not killed were locked up, and will be sent to the front. They were a bad lot, thoroughly bad. The headquarters of the famous Secret Section (Othkranoe Otdearleyne) was utterly destroyed, all records being destroyed; all police officers and stations were destroyed, as was the High Court of Justice for political prisoners. All jails were opened and the fortress of Peter and Paul was emptied; those who had been banished to Siberia or abroad are at liberty to return, and are doing so. The train on which I came from Sweden was packed with returning refugees.

Breckinridge continued in painstaking detail on how the Russian Revolution occurred:

The revolution did not start as such. There was a demonstration on the Nevsky because people wanted black bread, and they wanted new and honest Ministers, and they wanted something very badly, but did not know what it was; They were desperately unhappy, but they had no idea of a revolution, or a change in government. Even at the last moment, had anybody in power been possessed of courage sense and honesty, it would have developed into nothing more serious than a few disorders. But, but, there was no such person; those who had one qualification had not the others. As usual, the Cossacks were ordered out to support the police, who had been doing their regular duties under these circumstances but the Cossacks not only did not fire on the people, who only cried out for bread, but laughed and joked with them, and the people cheered the Cossacks and called them friends. Then soldiers were ordered out to dispell the crowds, and they refused to fire. At last a detail of Police charged a crowd on the Littany, and the Cossacks fought the Police; and the crowds seeing that the Soldiers were with them did the rest; What were Police against soldiers and Cossacks? What took place on the corner of the Nevsky and Litteney at that second changed the Government of Russia. And the last Romanoff is now a prisoner at Tsarkoe Selo, alone with his thoughts and his guards. A few days ago he commanded his armies, from his Imperial Headquarters at Pskoff, and now he is allowed daily sugar and bread and bread tickets, and lives much as his one-time subjects live.

Lieutenant Colonel Breckinridge offered his own analysis of why Russian soldiers refused to fire on their own countrymen:

What induced the soldiers to refuse to fire, and eventually to fight the police was the fact that the Duma [the representative assembly] had been dissolved by the Emperor, and for the first time in history such an order had been disobeyed; the Duma knew what threatened Russia, and refused to dissolve; and sent the telegrams to the Emperor at Pskoff, begging to save his throne and the country.... Under it all lies a condition so rotten, so incompetent, so dishonest and utterly corrupt that even ancient Rome could not have been worse. The Ministers were all bad, everybody lied and grafted, no body trusted anybody, there was no unity of honorable purposes; the old Government had not one friend, not one regiment stood loyal to it, not one ship. It was bad, bad.[11]

Lieutenant Colonel Breckinridge remained in Petrograd until August of that same year before headquarters reassigned him to serve as the naval attaché for the U.S. embassies located at Christiana, Norway; Copenhagen, Denmark; and Stockholm, Sweden. He remained on this duty throughout the remainder of the World War until reassigned to serve as the commanding officer of the 15th Regiment, 2d Marine Brigade, then on expeditionary duty in the Dominican Republic. For his outstanding services as the U.S. naval attaché during the war, Headquarters Marine Corps awarded him the Navy Cross "for distinguished service in the line of his profession as Naval Attaché at Christiana and Stockholm, and for a time also at Copenhagen. At all of these posts of duty, the service of information established and conducted was of great value to the United States and allied Powers."[12]

Courier Duty

The United States formally entered World War I on April 6, 1917, "to make the world safe for democracy." The Marine Corps, which had numbered approximately 13,000 officers and men, quickly expanded to a force of some 75,000 by the time of the Armistice on November 11, 1918. During the war, two brigades of Marines (4th and 5th) served in France with the American Expeditionary Forces while other leathernecks served on expeditionary and sea duty. One of the most unique chapters of Marine Corps service during the World War occurred when the State Department requested a detail of Marines for assignment to duty as United States diplomatic couriers. The Marine assigned to courier duty worked with and under the direct supervision of the various U.S. ambassadors and ministers then stationed throughout Europe.

From the outbreak of the World War in August 1914 through 1917, all United States diplomatic mail and confidential dispatches had been transported from London and Paris to the other European capitals in a haphazard and insecure manner. With the possibility of diplomatic correspondence either not arriving at its intended destination or being compromised, the State Department with cooperation of the Navy Department and Headquarters Marine Corps arrived at a wartime expedient that called for the accompaniment of the sacks of diplomatic mail with an armed Marine guard in civilian clothes.

Coinciding with this desire to safeguard the diplomatic mails was a suggestion made by Leland Harrison, an official with the State Department, and Commander Edward McCauley, Jr., USN, from the Office of Naval Intelligence to the major general commandant of the Marine Corps that a Marine guard be assigned to protect the diplomatic mail. Brigadier General John A. Lejeune, an assistant to the commandant of the Marine Corps, responded to this obvious attempt to siphon off necessary manpower from the Marine Corps as headquarters prepared to send a contingent of Marines to France. In his letter to Harrison and McCauley, Lejeune asserted that while the Marine Corps would be willing to assign Marines to this duty, "It will be necessary, however, for your office to obtain the sanction of the secretary before we can take any action in regard to it."[13] On August 31, 1917, Secretary of State Robert Lansing made a formal request for Marine couriers to Secretary of the Navy Josephus Daniels. Secretary Lansing informed Daniels that it was highly desirable "of establishing a courier service to carry the Department's diplomatic pouches between Bergen, Norway, and Jassy, Roumania, via the Scandanavian capitals and Petrograd. It is believed that much of the delay now experienced in important and confidential official mail reaching its destination will thus be obviated."[14] Secretary Daniels responded enthusiastically to Secretary Lansing's request and informed him that he had communicated to the major general commandant the assignment of five Marines "for this work."[15]

Due to the sensitivity of the mission, Headquarters Marine Corps decided that only senior staff noncommissioned officers would be detailed to such duty. Among the first Marines selected for this duty were Gunnery Sergeants William O'Grady, Thomas Baisdon, George F. Kelly, Donald G. Oglesby, William R. Sands, First Sergeants Joseph J. Franklin and Michael Maloney, Quartermaster Sergeant Joseph A. Driscoll, and retired Sergeant Major Edward Rowland.[16]

According to Gunnery Sergeant William O'Grady, upon reporting to Headquarters Marine Corps, the Marines assigned to courier duty "received orders to pack and store away anything that savored of military uniform or equipment. The succeeding two weeks were spent in being outfitted with complete civilian gear, from trunks and handbags to loud four-in-hand ties."[17] In order to keep the Marines' mission and presence as much a secret as possible the State Department provided them with suits and other civilian attire. Likewise, the State Department stipulated that "any additional civilian clothing required by the men will be provided by the State Department while they are abroad, as well as any special equipment that may be needed in the discharge of their duties."[18]

CHART 2. CIVILIAN CLOTHES ISSUED TO MARINE COURIERS DURING WORLD WAR I

2 Suits	6 neckties
1 Overcoat	1 pair gloves
6 Shirts (Dress)	1 suitcase[19]
12 Collars	

After they were issued the proper civilian clothes, diplomatic passports and photographs as well as their commissions signed by Secretary of State Robert Lansing, the Marine assigned to courier duty met with Major General George Barnett, Commandant of the Marine Corps, who briefed them on their duties and responsibilities and what was expected of them. Before dismissing them, General Barnett wished the Marines "Godspeed" in their mission with the State Department. Departing from New York aboard the steam liner *New York*, the Marines arrived in England, where they reported to the U.S. Embassy located at Grosvenor Gardens. Here, the Marines were met by Mr. Sheldon L. Crosby, second secretary to the U.S. Embassy in London. Mr. Crosby would oversee the courier program for the next year and half of its existence. After receiving further instructions and their orders, the Marines set out to their respective destinations.

By far the most important and certainly the most dangerous assignment was that along the London-Scandanavia-Russia route, due to the intense allied negotiations over Russia's future role in the war effort after the seizure of power by the Bolsheviks. Assigned to this route were First Sergeant Joseph J. Franklin, Quartermaster Sergeant Joseph A. Driscoll, and Gunnery Sergeant William O'Grady.

Prior to his departure Gunnery Sergeant O'Grady spent the majority of his time getting the required visas from the Norwegian, Swedish, Danish, and Russian (Czarist) embassies as well as the time of departure of the boat train from London to Aberdeen, Scotland. Prior to his departure on the evening of November 21, 1917, Gunnery Sergeant O'Grady arrived at the U.S. Embassy in London to pick up the fourteen sacks of diplomatic mail and confidential dispatch bags he had been assigned to guard. Armed with a .45 caliber pistol, the sidearm issued to the couriers, and given the standard $5 per diem for meals, O'Grady collected the diplomatic mail and proceeded to the rail station, where he boarded a train heading north for Aberdeen, Scotland. Gunnery Sergeant O'Grady provided an accurate description of how the U.S. Embassy packed its mail:

> The evening of my departure (21 November) from London found me at the Embassy about 8 P.M. where I collected my mail sacks and confidential dispatch bags, about fourteen in number. The confidential dispatch bags were of a peculiarly British make. We adopted them from the style of the sack carried by the British King's messengers (the British Government equivalent of our diplomatic couriers). They were of a greenish colored canvas covered with large eyelet holes about the Size of a 25-cent piece. In the bottom of the sack was a long, cylindrical pocket, into which were placed three or four lead cylinders. The object of this arrangement was to ensure the bags' sinking when thrown overboard, in the event of the ship's being held up or hit by a German submarine.[20]

Arriving in Aberdeen the next day, Gunnery Sergeant O'Grady soon found himself in the company of the other Allied diplomatic couriers who traveled together in order to insure the safe passage and transfer of each other's diplomatic mail. Gunnery Sergeant O'Grady met up with Lieutenant Colonel James C. Breckinridge, then on duty as the U.S. naval attaché assigned to the U.S. Consulate in Christiana, Norway. After stowing the diplomatic pouches in a secured locker on board the *S.S. Vulture*, O'Grady kept the ultra confidential dispatches on his person "at all times." After arriving in Bergen, Norway, O'Grady remained there overnight before departing for Christiana, Norway, and then on to Stockholm, Sweden, where he met with the U.S. minister for further instructions. While in Stockholm, O'Grady had been instructed by the U.S. minister there to remain in Sweden for an "extra day or two ... as there were many alarming rumors regarding the situation in Finland and Russia," due in part to the Bolshevik seizure of power on November 7, 1917.[21] As O'Grady recalled, the situation in Russia had turned for the worse insofar as relations between the United States and Bolsheviks had been concerned. This turn was because:

> On the 7th November, Kerensky, who was at the head of the provisional Government that overthrew the Czar in March 1917, fled the capital. Petrograd, the Petrograd Council of Workmen and Soldiers, and the National Soviet, combined, named a new ministry and appointed as commissars of the people, Lenin as President, and Trotsky as Minister of Foreign Affairs.
>
> The situation had still further developed along unfavorable lines toward both the United States and British governments about the time of my arrival in Stockholm, and the feeling of the Bolshevik government toward representatives of either country was anything but cordial. This enterprise was caused by an underground suspicion that the British and American Red Cross organizations, then operating in Russia were secretly assisting the counter-revolutionary forces by feeding and clothing them, and encouraging them in their endeavor to reorganize their numbers. This suspicion was directed against all messengers, couriers, and other employees of the two governments.
>
> To complicate matters, the Finnish White Guards were just then starting a revolt against the Red Guards (Bolsheviks); and though the latter were still in complete control of Finland, the existing tension occasioned by these circumstances raised grave doubts as to the chance of my getting savely [*sic*] through to Petrograd.[22]

Despite the sporadic fighting that was still taking place in Petrograd and elsewhere in Russia, Gunnery Sergeant O'Grady and the British courier continued with their journey to the Russian capital. After a brief stop at Haparanda on the Swedish side of the Gulf of Finland, and awaited the train to take them into Petrograd. In Tornea, O'Grady and the British courier came upon a mixed group of former Imperial Russian Army officers and communist sailors who had been placed in charge of the town. Both O'Grady and Scales boarded a train at 7:30 P.M. on the evening of November 30, 1917, and set off for Petrograd. Upon the arrival in the town of Bielostov on the evening of December 1, 1917, Gunnery Sergeant O'Grady came face-to-face with members of the Red Guards when the rail car he and Major Scales were in was suddenly and inexplicably detached from the main train and pulled onto a railroad siding. There, the Russians detached the car and shortly thereafter boarded by three Red Guards with rifles and fixed bayonets. As O'Grady recalled, "several more guards, similarly armed, were stationed around the outside of our car." After being informed by a Red Guard that the passengers were confined to their compartments until further notice, O'Grady and Scales set down to discuss the unsettling events, which included the execution by the Bolshevik troops of ten Russian citizens from the town of Tammerafors. The next day the Red Guards escorted O'Grady and other passengers off the train to a nearby rail station where Soviet officials carefully looked over their passports. As O'Grady later wrote, "Our treatment all the way through this detention had been marked by courtesy on the part of Soviet officials."[23] After the situation in Bielostov had been resolved, the train car was re-attached to a train on 3 December and chugged toward Petrograd — an hour away. The two couriers arrived in Petrograd about 2 o'clock that afternoon and were met by representatives of the American and British embassies. O'Grady then "loaded all bags on one of the many droskys (Russian carriages) hanging around the station and, guided by an employee of the embassy, drove there to deliver my dispatches. After having done this and given the ambassador, Mr. David R. Francis, a full report on the Bolshevik incident, I went to the house of one of the employees [of the U.S. Embassy in Petrograd] and proceeded to make up for the enforced fast which I had undergone since leaving Tornea."[24] Eventually, Gunnery Sergeant O'Grady continued on to Jassy, Romania, where he delivered the diplomatic pouches entrusted to him to the U.S. minister there. On his return trip O'Grady accompanied the consul's wife and son back to Christiana, Norway, out of concern for their safety.

Gunnery Sergeant O'Grady recalled that upon his arrival back in Petrograd, he found the U.S. Embassy without proper security with only the diplomatic personnel themselves standing watch. After leaving Petrograd in April 1918, Gunnery Sergeant O'Grady remained on courier duty throughout the remainder of the World War. Toward the end of his duty as a courier he had been assigned to carry diplomatic pouches and "numerous sacks of war propaganda" destined for the U.S. Embassy at Archangel. As O'Grady recalled, "this trip proved to be one of the most interesting of my whole career as a diplomatic courier." In fact, as the violence throughout all of Russia increased, and food shortages occurred in Moscow and more importantly in Petrograd, Ambassador Francis became increasingly concerned over the lack of security at the embassy and for U.S. nationals living there.

In a letter dated November 24, 1917, Ambassador David R. Francis informed Secretary of State Lansing that the U.S. military attaché, Brigadier General W.V. Judson, U.S. Army, "independently advised that I permit two soldiers of the Litovski regiment to stand guard at the Embassy entrance as he had done at Military Mission. I think inadvisable to do so, consequently have had two Embassy employees on guard after 1 P.M., until which time the police officer sat in my apartment. My instruction to guard is not to fire on any one attempting forcible entrance but to advise me as I live in the Embassy. I should go to the entrance in such event and if necessary would dispatch messenger to Litovsk I barracks for guard. Such arrangements preferable to Bolshevik guard in whom have no confidence and do not know whom it would admit...."[25]

Due largely to his doubts over the use of Bolshevik Red Guards in protecting the U.S.

Embassy, Mr. Francis requested Secretary Lansing's permission to use the available Marine couriers as embassy guards, as the situation in and around the Russian capital became even more chaotic due to the violence and confusion caused by the October Revolution. Given the possibility of classified dispatches falling into the hands of enemy agents (German and Bolshevik), Secretary Lansing authorized the use of the Marine couriers as embassy guards. Subsequently, Quartermaster Sergeant Driscoll, Gunnery Sergeants O'Grady and Baisden, and a Marine named Christy, who had recently joined the program, were ordered to remain in Petrograd as guards for the embassy. In a note to the secretary of state, the U.S. ambassador to Petrograd noted, on 23 January 1918, "Marine couriers guarding tonight...."[26] Ambassador Francis later reported to Secretary of State Lansing, however, "the four Marines at first [were] displeased when I ordered them to remain in Petrograd." The ambassador added that due to the unreliability of the Russian guards, he had no other choice than "not to request any additional [Russian] guard for the Embassy; consequently, am attempting to protect it by its attaches. To-day, two members of the marine corps who were serving as couriers and were about to leave to-morrow morning were ordered by me to remain and to live in the Embassy. They remonstrated, but I was very emphatic — don't know at this writing whether they will remain or not. If they should go after my order to remain I shall cable the Department and demand that they be punished."[27]

Ambassador Francis reiterated his displeasure over the attitude of the Marine couriers and of their departure from Vologda, where the embassy and its staff had moved due to the turmoil in Petrograd in a letter to Secretary of State Lansing. In the letter, Ambassador Francis noted that the Marines would continue with their original mission to safeguard the diplomatic pouches that contained classified material destined for the U.S. Embassy in London:

> Vologda, March 17, 1918
>
> Sir:
>
> I have the honor to inform you that the marine couriers, Driscoll, Baisden, Sands, and Christy, whom I retained in Petrograd to guard the Embassy with your approval, will leave tomorrow for London via Murmansk and will take a pouch for the Department.
>
> These men have not served cheerfully nor efficiently; they were displeased when I ordered them to remain in Petrograd but I was positive and they did remain reluctantly. I am inclined to think that in addition to feeling that guard duty was beneath their dignity they had come to Russia poorly clad for the climate. The Embassy has been at Vologda since February 28th and has held a special train here to provide for an emergency should one arise. The marines have slept on the train and they have been maintained at the Embassy's expense, bills for which will be rendered in due course.
>
> I have cabled the Department today suggesting that couriers with our own pouches be sent direct from London to Murmansk and that I be advised by cable of their departure from London that I may wire our man at Murmansk of their coming and of our change in location in the event one should be made.
>
> We have had no pouch since your Number 198 which left Washington on or about December 18, 1917 — there must be at least twelve pouches for this Embassy at Stockholm.
>
> I have the honor to be, Sir,
>
> > Your Obedient Servant,
> > Hon. David R. Francis[28]

Despite their opposition to remaining in Petrograd, and being poorly clad for the harsh Russian winter, the Marines assigned to protect the Petrograd embassy nonetheless performed their job well until relieved in April 1918, when the U.S. Embassy relocated to Murmansk. As

Ambassador Francis noted, at the conclusion of this added security mission, the four Marines in Petrograd resumed their duties as diplomatic couriers.[29]

Sergeant Thomas Baisden recalled that prior to his assignment as an embassy guard in Petrograd, Ambassador Francis had received numerous bomb threats and feared for the safety of the embassy, the staff, and himself. As the Bolsheviks negotiated a separate peace with the Germans at Brest-Litovsk in January–February 1918, a move that effectively took Russia out of the World War, the leaders of France, Great Britain, Japan, China, and the United States ordered their diplomatic missions to begin preparations to evacuate Russia. In reference to the separate peace between the Bolsheviks and Germans, Ambassador Francis cabled Secretary Lansing:

> In my judgment terms of peace make Russia a German province with good prospects of becoming ally. I renew my recommendation for immediate possession of Vladivostok, Murmansk, Archangel. Allied mission chiefs remaining here for present. Japanese, Chinese, and American missions sending special train with some of their nationals and portions of their staff to Volgoda to-day to await orders. Wright, Armour, Johnston [Mr. Francis' private secretary]; also [with] marine couriers as anarchistic outbreaks possible.... Impossible to ascertain yet how far Soviet action will be approved in Russia. It may lead to civil war, Social Revolutionists declaring Constituent Assembly, be reconvened. I shall await further developments. Could only use my judgment in default of instructions. British and French have started via Murmansk, many colonists and most of military missions. Allied Ambassadors meeting at Embassy daily.[30]

After the break in relations between the United States and the Bolsheviks, Ambassador Francis ordered the evacuation of all diplomatic personnel from the embassy in Petrograd. In fact, fearful that the classified material at the U.S. Embassy would fall into the hands of the revolutionaries, Secretary Lansing ordered Ambassador Francis, via the U.S. minister to Sweden, Ira N. Morris, to "safeguard staff and archives from falling into enemy hands. Seals, codes, ciphers messages or translations should be taken with you or if this impossible should be burned and destroyed."[31]

As part of their security duties Sergeant Baisden and the three other Marines had been instructed by the ambassador to clear up the records. He recalled that this "was a big job; but after much work, we got things straightened out; and those records that could not be taken along with us were burned in the embassy courtyard."[32] After burning the material they could not carry, the Marines rejoined the other diplomats at the Finland Station and boarded a train bound for Murmansk. Sergeant Baisden recalled a humorous incident when the Chinese representatives made several attempts to occupy the U.S. section of a special diplomatic train set aside by the Bolsheviks for the Western diplomats. Sergeant Baisden stated that the reason for this odd behavior was because the Chinese did not have enough space for their rather large diplomatic mission. Baisden remembered that this occurred about a dozen times and proved to be a humorous annoyance amidst the ongoing chaos in Russia.[33]

Ambassador Francis was not the only one who desired to use Marines as embassy guards. In another instance, Admiral William S. Sims, Commander in Chief, U.S. Naval Forces, Europe, likewise requested that a detachment of Marines be assigned to the guard the U.S. legations in London and at The Hague. In a memorandum to Major General Commandant Barnett, Admiral Sims recommended that those Marines found unfit for courier duty remain in London for duty as legations guards. The admiral admitted that except for three Marines found to be unsuitable to continue their mission, the "marines who have been assigned duty here [as couriers] have behaved in an exemplary manner and have been a credit to the service and corps."[34]

The Marine courier program in Europe proved so successful that other U.S. ambassadors likewise made similar requests for Marine couriers. In addition to his request that Marines be assigned as embassy guards in London, Admiral Sims asked the major general commandant that a three-man Marine detachment be assigned to the U.S. consulate at The Hague. In his request of March 5, 1918, to Major General Commandant Barnett (which was approved several days later), the admiral wrote that the Marines "bring with them civilian clothes and that these men be highly trustworthy."[35] While many of these requests were in fact honored, Secretary Lansing rejected many out of hand as unnecessary. Other requests for Marine guards were likewise rejected out of hand by Major General Barnett and General John J. Pershing, commanding general of the American Expeditionary Forces,.

In fact, the major source of complaint over the drain on qualified Marine staff came from Marine field commanders in France and in the West Indies. Major General John A. Lejeune, who assumed command of the U.S. Army's 2d Infantry Division, American Expeditionary Forces, to which the 4th Marine Brigade had been attached, in September 1918, rejected any further requests for Marine noncommissioned officers for the courier program. General Lejeune cited the loss of these experienced veterans just at time when the 2d Division required their services. In a message to the major general commandant, Lejeune argued that all available Marines should be on duty with the 2d Division due to its high casualty rates.[36] The use of Marine couriers for diplomatic pouches and mail continued until December 1920, when Secretary Lansing no longer considered it necessary and ordered all Marines back to Quantico for further duty.[37] In all, Marines served throughout Western and Eastern Europe, China and Japan as well as in revolution-torn Russia and Mexico.

Intervention in Siberia, 1917–1918

Marine involvement with revolutionary Russia did not end with the end of the courier program. As Sergeant Baisden recounted, he and his fellow couriers ended their service in the city of Murmansk where the U.S. Embassy in Petrograd had been forced to re-locate in the wake of the cessation of relations between the United States and the new Soviet state. After moving to Murmansk, the United States along with its western allies (France and Great Britain) and Japan decided to come to the assistance of a contingent of former Czechoslovakian prisoners of war that had been fighting its way toward Allied lines in Siberia after the men had been released from a Russian prisoner of war camp when Russia withdrew from the World War in March 1918.

Fearing a possible counterattack by local Bolshevik forces (and former tsarist forces led by Admiral Kolchak), the U.S. consul general requested that Rear Admiral Austin A. Knight, USN, the commanding officer, U.S. Asiatic Fleet, provide a detachment of Marines in order to protect the U.S. Consulate in the port city of Vladivostok. After the USS *Brooklyn*'s[38] arrival in Vladivostok on March 1, 1918, Admiral Knight at first refused permission for the Marines to go ashore. The admiral remained concerned that the Marines and bluejackets would become involved in the heavy fighting then ongoing between the Bolsheviks and the Czechs. When Czechoslovak forces finally took the city of Vladivostok from the Bolsheviks, Admiral Knight gave the order for the Marines to go ashore. On the afternoon of June 29, 1918, the same day that the Czechs had succeeded in taking Vladivostok, a detachment of Marines led by Captain A.F. Howard and Navy bluejackets came ashore to protect the U.S. Consulate "and prevent any disorders in the immediate vicinity."[39]

As the log of the USS *Brooklyn* indicated, the primary function of the Marines ashore was to guard the U.S. Consulate:

June 29, 1918: 4:00 to 8:00 P.M. During the early part of this watch there was considerable firing on shore between the Czech soldiers and the Bolsheviki; during the engagement hand grenades, bombs, machine guns and rifles were used. At 5:25 [Second] Lieutenant [Conrad S.] Grove, USMC, one signal man and a detachment of thirty Marines were landed under arms to guard the American Consulate. At 6:00 the firing ceased, the Bolsheviki having been defeated, and the city became quiet.... At 7:35 the armed guard at the American Consulate was reduced to 8 Marines under the command of Captain A.F. Howard, USMC. At 7:40 about 30 of the Japanese armed patrol returned to their ship. At 7:55 Lieutenant Grove, USMC, and 30 Marines returned, having been relieved by Captain Howard's detachment. A squad of six Marine privates and two corporals under Second Lieutenant Conrad S. Grove left ship at midnight to form a Consulate Guard.

June 30, 1918: At 12:29 A.M. the armed patrol under the command of Captain A.F. Howard, USMC, returned aboard from the Consulate. At 4:00 A.M. Consulate guard under Captain Howard, USMC, 6 men and 2 petty officers left ship. At 4:20 relieved guard returned. At 7:48 Consulate Guard under Second Lieutenant Grove, USMC, left the ship, 8 men and 2 petty officers.... At 9:20 A.M. Consulate Guard under Captain Howard returned aboard.... At Noon, Consulate guard of 2 corporals and 8 privates left ship. Meridian to 4:00 P.M. Consulate guard of 8 Marines left, and relieved guard returned ... 4:00 to 8:00 P.M. Consulate Guard of 8 Marines left, and relieved guard returned. 8:00 P.M. to midnight. Consulate guard of 16 Marines left, and relieved guard returned.

Marines remained on duty at the U.S. Consulate in Vladivostok until they were withdrawn on August 24, 1918. In 1919, U.S. Marines once again landed in Siberia, this time at Tyutuke Bay, near the city of Vladivostok, to protect American interests as the Russian Revolution spread throughout that vast country. Captain Edgar B. Larimer of the USS *New Orleans* ordered First Lieutenant Leland S. Swindler and his thirty-one man Marine detachment ashore on July 30, 1919. This force remained in Tyutuke Bay until the next afternoon (1 August) when re-embarked aboard the *New Orleans*.[40]

Diplomatic Security Force at the Washington Naval Conference, 1921–1922

While Marine ships' detachments maintained security at the U.S. Naval Radio Station on Russian Island off Vladivostok, other leathernecks performed duty as a diplomatic security force during the Washington Naval Conference held between December 1921 and February 1922. The Washington Naval Conference on Limitations of Armament had been designed to establish a limit on the building of capital ships and naval armaments between the major world naval powers of Great Britain, the United States, Japan, Italy, France, and several lesser powers. The Marine detachment of 120 officers and enlisted men "protected the sanctity of the foreign delegations' special offices located on the ground floor of the Main Navy Building." Additionally, the "Marine Officer of the Day's desk controlled access to the delegates' offices."[41]

In addition to standing guard at the Washington Naval Conference, Marines also provided special detachments for international expositions such as the one in Rio de Janeiro in July 1922. General Lemuel C. Shepherd recalled that Headquarters Marine Corps had called for the formation of a special detachment in Philadelphia. The company, designated as the 83rd Company of the 6th Marines, were "specially selected Marines of good height," and were provided with specially tailored uniforms made at the Marine Corps Depot of Supplies located at the Philadelphia Navy Yard. This detachment set sail for the Exposition in Rio De Janeiro in July 1922.[42] The Marine Detachment arrived in Rio aboard the USS *Nevada,* one of two ships sent by the United States for the exposition. General Shepherd recalled that the Marines shortly thereafter set up camp "right in the center of Rio De Janeiro" and that it was

> a perfect place, an elipse [*sic*] in the park. Our tents fitted in there exactly. We had four platoons and a small headquarters company, a band, and a supply unit, bakery, and so forth. It made an ideal setup. We conducted a formal guard mounting and a parade every day. We marched through the city on various occasions and to the Exposition grounds which were nearby and paraded for various officials who visited there. It was an excellent public relations assignment and I think the Marine Corps gained a great deal of prestige from our presence in Rio.[43]

Thus, Marines performed not only security duty at home during the Washington Naval Conference but acted as "Ambassadors in Blue" during the 1922 Rio de Janeiro Exposition.

"A suitable Marine Guard"

After the withdrawal of the United States Marines guards and Navy communicators from Russian Island, Siberia, in February 1922, the United States broke off diplomatic relations with Soviet Union. This changed, however, on November 16, 1933, when President Franklin D. Roosevelt re-established relations with Soviet Russia. After the appointment of a career diplomat, Mr. William C. Bullitt, the U.S. State Department expressed a desire to detail five naval and Marine Corps officers as naval attachés at the newly established U.S. Embassy in Moscow. Due to a lack of funds, the Navy Department informed Secretary of State Cordell Hull that it could provide only one: Marine Captain David R. Nimmer (who was then on duty in the Office of Naval Intelligence). On 29 January 1934, the Navy Department appointed Captain Nimmer assistant naval attaché. Shortly after his appointment Captain Nimmer reported to the U.S Embassy in Moscow for duty.

The State Department made a similar request for a suitable Marine embassy guard. In response to the State Department's request, Headquarters Marine Corps appointed six non-commissioned officers for duty in Moscow as embassy guards. They arrived in Moscow on 1 March 1934 and quickly assumed their posts as an embassy security force. These Marines remained on duty in Moscow throughout the remainder of the 1930s, until the eve of the U.S. involvement in World War II.[44]

Appointment of Brigadier General John H. Russell as High Commissioner to Haiti, 1922–1929

One of the most interesting chapters in the history of the United States Marine Corps as "Ambassadors in Blue" occurred in February 1922, when President Warren G. Harding appointed Brigadier John H. Russell, then the commanding general of the U.S. Marine 1st Brigade in Haiti, the United States' high commissioner, with the commensurate rank of ambassador. As high commissioner, General Russell supervised and directed the implemen-

Brigadier General John H. Russell, USMC, appointed by President Warren G. Harding in 1922, served as United States high commissioner from 1922 to 1930 in Port-au-Prince, Haiti (courtesy U.S. Marine Corps).

tation of a massive public works program designed to improve the sanitation, education, and public health of the Haitians. As the U.S. high commissioner, General Russell likewise commanded the 1st Marine Brigade and Haitian Gendarmerie. Working with Haitian President Louis Borno, General Russell raised considerably the Haitian standard of living throughout the country. Also, General Russell had full authority vested in him to appoint members of the Marine Brigade or qualified civilians to assist in Haiti's rehabilitation. Secretary of State Charles Evans Hughes underscored this point in a letter to Secretary of the Navy Edwin H. Denby. In the letter, dated October 3, 1923, Secretary Hughes informed the Secretary of the Navy that "the President has recently expressed his approval of a suggestion made by this Department to the effect that the American High Commissioner at Port au Prince should be permitted to act in the President's name, without prior consultation with the Department of State, in presenting to the President of Haiti nominations of subordinate officials appointed under the Treaty."[45] Under General Russell's personal direction, "the American government sent two hundred American civilians to staff" the public works program implemented in Port au Prince and throughout Haiti by the Americans.[46]

After a series of devastating riots in Port au Prince and Cayes in December 1929, fueled primarily by the Haitian elite's anti–American hostility and worker unrest, President Herbert Hoover announced the start of a gradual withdrawal of the Marines from Latin America and the Caribbean.[47] As part of his pronounced "Good Neighbor Policy" Hoover ordered the *Haitianization* of that country's administrative infrastructure.

While disagreeing with the hasty withdrawal announced by Washington, General Russell nevertheless complied with Secretary of State Henry Stimson's order to turn over much of the country's day-to-day business to the Haitians.[48] In order to increase the pace of *Haitianization* and withdrawal of the leathernecks, Dr. Dana G. Munro, a skilled diplomat in the Latin American Division of the State Department, replaced General Russell as high commissioner in Port au Prince. Returning to the Marine Corps after an eight-year absence on extended duty, General Russell briefly assumed command of Marine Corps Base, San Diego, California, prior to becoming assistant to the commandant of the Marine Corps, who at the time was Major General Ben H. Fuller. In December 1933, General Russell became the sixteenth major general commandant of the Marine Corps (1934–1936). During his brief tenure as commandant, General Russell introduced a series of reforms that included promotion by selection and merit for officers as well as the continued organization of the Marine Corps into a naval expeditionary force, officially christened as the "Fleet Marine Force" on December 7, 1933.[49]

Colonel Pedro A. del Valle's Mission to Italy, 1935–1936

General Russell was not the only Marine officer during the interwar era to act as an American diplomatic representative. In early October 1935 Headquarters Marine Corps appointed Marine Colonel [later Lieutenant General] Pedro A. del Valle as the assistant naval attaché to the U.S. Embassy in Rome, Italy. After del Valle's arrival in Rome, the Italian government of Fascist dictator Benito Mussolini invited him to accompany the 4th Blackshirt Division to Ethiopia as a military observer during the Italian invasion of that African country. Colonel del Valle kept a meticulous diary of his experiences attached to the Italian Army in Ethiopia, which he later published in book form.[50] Del Valle's memoirs serve as one of the best accounts of the Italian Army during World War II. In recognition of his service with the Italian Army, Mussolini personally awarded del Valle the Order of the Crown of Italy (1936), East African Medal, Ethiopia (1936), and the Colonial Order of the Star of Italy (Cavaliere), Ethiopia (1936).

Embassy Guards at War in London During World War II, 1940–1946

Prior to the United States' entrance into the Second World War on 7 December 1941, Marines had already experienced live enemy fire as guards at the U.S. Embassy in London, England. While Marines of the 1st Provisional Brigade landed at Reykjavik, Iceland, in order to protect the northern approaches to the British Isles against a possible German assault, they were met at the docks by an advanced detail of leathernecks commanded by Marine Major Walter I. Jordan, whose ship, the USS *Maasdam*, had been torpedoed by a German subma-

MINISTERO DELLA GUERRA

S. M. il Re con suo Decreto in data del 12 novembre 1936 Anno **XV**.

Visto il Regio Decreto 4 Novembre 1932 Anno **XI** N. 1423;

Visto il Regio Decreto 24 Marzo 1936 Anno **XIV** N. 923;

Visto il Decreto Luogotenenziale 10 Febbraio 1918 N. 264;

Sulla proposta del Ministro Segretario di Stato per gli Affari della Guerra;

Ha sanzionato la concessione, fatta sul campo dalle sue preme autorità all'uopo delegate, della

Medaglia di Bronzo al valor militare, coll'annessovi soprassoldo di Lire cento annue al tenente colonnello di fanteria di Marina americana

Del Valle Pedro, Stati Uniti di America

Al seguito del comando di una grande unità italiana (colonna centrale «Frusci» muoveva te contro le forze abissine saldamente dislocate a difesa della direttice Harar-dal-Giggica, condivideva con lieto animo disagi e pericoli. Durante la cruenta battaglia di Biogol, per 22 ore consecutive sostava allo scoperto nella zona intensamente battuta dal fuoco avversario. Dimostrava la coscienza dell'onor militare e sereno, ragionato sprezzo del pericolo in combattimento. — Biogol — Hamantei — Sassabaneh Dagabur — Giggica, aprile — maggio 1936 - **XIV**.

Il Ministro Segretario di Stato per gli Affari della Guerra rilascia quindi il presente documento per attestare del conferito onorifico distintivo.

Roma, addì 20 gennaio 1937 Anno **XV**.

Registrato alla Corte dei Conti
addì 13 dicembre 1936 Anno XV
Registro N. 31 Guerra Foglio N. 266
f.to Cavallari

Il Ministro

R Mussolini

rine some 300 miles south of Iceland. These Marines, part of 60-man force, were en route from the Marine Barracks, Washington, D.C., to the U.S. Embassy at Grosvenor Square, in London, England. Jordan's 11-man Marine detachment had been ordered to "join forces with 48 other Marines, including three officers that included Captain John B. Hill and first Lieutenants Roy J. Batterton, Jr., and Joseph L. Atkins."[51] Eventually, the force consisted of 59 Marines and was designated as the Marine Detachment, American Embassy. Six months later, Headquarters Marine Corps augmented this force with additional Marines.

The size and organization of this first official embassy guard in Europe had already been agreed upon several months earlier by Major John C. McQueen at the request of Navy Admiral Robert L. Ghomerly, assistant chief of naval operations, who had been in London at the time. Major McQueen had been on another mission to observe and report back to Major General Commandant Thomas Holcomb on the British Royal Marine commandos. While in London, Major McQueen had expressed concern over the lack of security at the U.S. Embassy in London to the U.S. ambassador in London, Mr. John Winant. Impressed with the Marine major's keen observations, Mr. Winant made Major McQueen the embassy's security officer.

Once established at the U.S. Embassy in London, the Marines assigned to embassy duty there "became the reporting echelon for nearly all Marine personnel serving in Europe and Africa, including those on temporary duty and those attached to the OSS [Office of Strategic Services]."[52] In charge of the Marine detachment was Major Jordan, who held the simultaneous title of assistant naval attaché. Major Jordan was, however, the only Marine detachment officer to carry that title, as his successors — Captain Thomas J. Myers, First Lieutenant Alan Doubleday, and Captain Harry W. Edwards — were not so designated.[53]

Initially, the U.S. Marine detachment in London numbered four officers and fifty-five enlisted men. Prior to their assignment to London, each Marine who volunteered for this assignment was outfitted in with civilian clothes and given a government clothing allowance. Following standard U.S. policy prior to the commencement of the war, the Marines were instructed to travel in civilian clothes when en route to countries that were at war.[54]

As Lieutenant Colonel Edwards late wrote, "The mission of the London detachment was to provide security for the American Embassy and to furnish escorts for State Department couriers." Marine Sergeant John H. Allen, Jr., was assigned duty as Ambassador Winant's orderly. The Marine House was located within close proximity to the U.S. Embassy. Here, Marines established a mess, appointed an air raid precaution officer, and established a courier service after the arrival of several Harley-Davidson motorcycles. In early September 1940, the Marines attached to the U.S. Embassy in London soon found themselves in the middle of war zone as the German "blitz" against London began in earnest. Along with their British comrades the Marines served as air raid wardens and firemen for the U.S. Embassy.

When Admiral Harold R. Stark arrived in London to become commander, Naval Forces, Europe, the duties of the Marine Embassy Guard temporarily changed. The leathernecks moved to Rosneath, Scotland, in order to establish the Marine Barracks at the U.S. Navy Operating Base located there. The detachment at the U.S. Embassy in London was later re-established on January 21, 1943, and "resumed its original designation and duties." These duties included ensuring security for the naval headquarters, supplying orderlies for flag officers, operating a motorcycle and motor vehicle messenger service between the various military and

Opposite: **The Order of the Crown of Italy issued to Lieutenant General Pedro del Valle by Italian dictator Benito Mussolini while serving as U.S. naval attaché to Rome, Italy, in 1936 (Del Valle Papers, U.S. Marine Corps University Archives).**

Il tenente colonnello fant. M.

Del Valle Pedro

è autorizzato a fregiarsi della medaglia
commemorativa con gladio romano per le
operazioni militari in Africa Orientale.
(R. Decreto 27 aprile 1936-XIV N.° 1150)

Roma li 20 ottobre 1936 XIV

IL MINISTRO

Mussolini

LEVATE IN ALTO, LEGIONARI, LE INSEGNE,
IL FERRO E I CUORI A SALUTARE DOPO
QUINDICI SECOLI LA RIAPPARIZIONE DEL-
L'IMPERO SUI COLLI FATALI DI ROMA.

Mussolini

diplomatic offices, supplying escorts for the State Department couriers, and performing ceremonial duties as the situation required.[55] Marines remained at the U.S. Embassy in London until April 1946, when the detachment was deactivated.

Marine Diplomatic Couriers, 1943–1945

During World War II, veteran Marine noncommissioned officers once again served as diplomatic couriers for the Department of State. In a program reminiscent of the one used by the Department of State during World War I, Marines who had returned stateside for rest and or recuperation from wounds received in fighting the Japanese were recruited once again to serve as diplomatic couriers to guard State Department message traffic and other confidential materials sent to U.S. embassies and consulates abroad. Robert Kimball,[56] who served with the 1st Marine Division on Guadalcanal, in Finchaven, New Guinea, and at Cape Gloucester, on the island of New Britain in the Northern Solomons, had earned thirty-days leave back in the United States after having accumulated the necessary thirty points required. Once in the United States, Kimball traveled back to his home in nearby Ashton, Maryland. During a routine visit to Headquarters Marine Corps to inquire about an extension of his leave, Kimball was asked by a Marine major where he stood on the promotion list to gunnery sergeant. Dumbfounded, Kimball said he knew of no such list. After an inquiry, the Marine major called to another gunnery sergeant to check the promotion list and later informed Kimball that he was "number three on the list." The major then asked Kimball if he would like shore duty for six months assigned to Headquarters Marine Corps to replace another gunnery sergeant awaiting orders overseas.[57] Without thinking about it, Kimball said "Yes," and orders were immediately drawn up canceling orders which called for his deployment back to the Pacific theater of operations. While awaiting his replacement's transfer, Headquarters Marine Corps placed Kimball in charge of several security details prior to his assumption of his duties at Headquarters Marine Corps. Kimball served as an honor guard at Union Station in Washington, D.C., where he and his fellow Marines solemnly awaited the arrival of President Franklin D. Roosevelt's casket as it made its journey from Warm Springs, Georgia, to the nation's capital, then to Hyde Park, New York, for burial in April 1945. In the meantime, Kimball's promotion to gunnery sergeant came through from Marine Corps Headquarters.

Since his time as company gunnery sergeant of the Marine barracks had come to an end, Kimball remembered being called into the office of Colonel Donald J. Kendall, who asked the Marine gunnery sergeant if he would consider assignments that included a commission as a second lieutenant, assignment to the V-12 education program or, to a State Department program that utilized Marine staff noncommissioned officers as diplomatic couriers. Already familiar with the latter, Gunnery Sergeant Kimball, who had recently been married, talked the options over with his bride, Peggy, and the consensus that emerged was that diplomatic courier duty was the preferred option. Gunnery Sergeant Kimball admitted that the choice was not hard. "I was already familiar with what courier duty entailed such as ... traveling on the Pan American Clipper ships." Kimball admitted that courier duty was "really good duty ... staying in first class places and hotels, getting the best food ... [indeed] I thought I had

Opposite: **The Italian Medal of Bronze for Valor awarded to Lieutenant General Pedro del Valle, USMC, by Il Duce Benito Mussolini in 1936 (Del Valle Papers, U.S. Marine Corps University Archives).**

died and went to heaven."[58] Kimball recalled that it seemed rather "exotic" knowing that "I would be traveling, staying in good hotels, eating good food, and having a briefcase hand-cuffed to my wrist which I didn't even know what I was carrying." The Marine added that he had already talked to the guys that had been on courier duty and "it didn't seem to be all that dangerous.... it sure beat going back to the South Pacific!"

Gunnery Sergeant Kimball added that the Marine couriers, of whom there were sixteen, that he personally knew of during the war said that the duty was "just like being on vacation." After awaiting a lengthy Federal Bureau of Investigation and Secret Service background investigation, Gunnery Sergeant Kimball was assigned to the State Department as a diplomatic courier. Once deputized as an agent, State Department officials briefed the new Marine courier on the duties and procedures to be adhered to while traveling with diplomatic mail. This included discarding any identification with the Marine Corps (in Kimball's case his dog tags, his Marine identification card, and Marine Corps ring). Given a per diem rate while traveling, armed with a .38 caliber pistol, and dressed in a suit and clothes provided by the State Department, Kimball shortly thereafter embarked upon his first trip as a diplomatic courier to London, England, and Dublin, Ireland. Kimball recalled that the State Department gave him money in the form of a chit to go to Raleigh's, a men's clothing store in downtown Washington, D.C., where he purchased his clothes and a suit. Kimball emphasized that the suit was to be worn at all times, as the jacket covered his firearm.[59]

Kimball recalled that State Department officials, prior to his departure for overseas, placed special emphasis on how to sit on a train. Kimball recalled, "I was to sit with my back to the wall facing everybody, and that there would be an agent facing me as well as another agent sitting in the car behind me.... That I would always be met by an officer, a guard or State Department person, with proper identification, when I got to London or Ireland or any other destination." Kimball said that during the six months that he served on this program, "no one ever approached me or tried to take my briefcase from me."[60] Kimball remembered that besides the briefcase attached to his wrist, he also guarded pouches of diplomatic correspondence. The numbered pouches, similar to those used by the Marines during World War I, stood about four feet and were about 18 inches in diameter and were made of canvas. The Marine gunnery sergeant recalled that he normally guarded anywhere from two to five pouches.

Pictured here as a platoon sergeant, Gunnery Sergeant Robert E. Kimball served with the State Department as a diplomatic courier during 1945 (Robert E. Kimball Collection).

Gunnery Sergeant Kimball's passport issued by the U.S. State Department (Robert E. Kimball collection).

He was given fifty cents per pouch for the porters to load and unload them from the train. "Gunny" Kimball added that his main task "was to watch that brief case," though he always watched the porters load and unload the canvas pouches with one hand on the brief case and the other where his gun was located.[61]

Based in Washington, D.C., at 8th and "I," Gunnery Sergeant Kimball stated that he traveled the same route with little or no deviation: the Marine Barracks to the State Department, where he picked up the mail and his orders; then on to Union Station and from there to New York's Penn Station. At Penn Station, Kimball linked up with a diplomatic official and secured his .38 revolver, brief case and mail pouches in the mailroom vault. He then proceeded to the Hotel Taft, where he spent the night. There he called to verify his flight departure with Pan American and order a Cary Cadillac to pick him up the next morning and take him to Penn Station and then on to the Pan Am dock after he retrieved his .38, briefcase, and mail. He boarded the Pan American Clipper which flew him first to Ireland, then to Lisbon, Portugal, then on to Dakar down to Fisherman's Lake, Liberia, and from there across the South

Atlantic to Natal, Brazil, then to Bermuda and "finally home." Granted $6.00 per diem, Kimball was "authorized to travel by any feasible route and means. Travel by military aircraft is directed as essential in the war effort."[62] After delivering the mail sacks throughout his assigned route, Kimball returned to Headquarters Marine Corps (and home) and awaited new orders. Once home, Kimball said that he called in every morning to the main desk at 8th and "I" to see if he had a pending assignment. Gunnery Sergeant Kimball said that the longest period he ever waited for a new assignment was two weeks, while the shortest period was three days.[63]

When the phone rang, the procedure was always the same, he recalled. Starting in New York, upon leaving the hotel in the Carey Cadillac he had ordered, he then proceeded to Penn Station, where after agents from the State Department met up with him.

> I picked up my mail, briefcase, and revolver. I then went down to where the Pan American Clipper ship was on the dock and loaded everything on the ship. I then checked in with the passport and so forth and got a copy of the bill for the flight and took off for Ireland. We landed on the Shannon River and I was amazed at how it landed at night using radar. Radar was new then and I was amazed how effective it was. Being at night, I couldn't see a thing because it was dark but all of sudden we landed in the water ... on the Shannon River. After we landed, two guys from the Legation met up with me, as some mail was for them and so forth. I stayed overnight there and the next morning I caught a plane to London and had to go through the whole procedure over again. While in London, I stayed at the Reindeer Club....[64]

Kimball continued:

> The next morning, I flew on to Lisbon and there I usually met other couriers carrying mail to France or other points. Usually, from London to Lisbon I took the KLM. The only action that I heard that a Pan American clipper ship had was they landed on a bright sunny day, landed on the reflection of the water about twenty feet up and split the hull and sank. The courier drowned. That was the only casualty I heard of. And form there I went to Tangier, to Dakar, West Africa, and sometimes my duty took me to Horta, in the Azores.

Kimball stated that the trip over to London and Lisbon in those days was quite expensive, something in the order of $945 from New York to Foynes, Ireland. "You could just imagine what it is today," Kimball added.[65] As for interaction with the embassy staff, Gunnery Sergeant Kimball recalled that one time in Horta the embassy had a nice party, though for the most part these were rare, as he had very little if any contact with the embassy or diplomatic staff. The Marine courier said that the majority of people he dealt with were the agents sent to retrieve his mail and briefcase. While on courier duty, Gunnery Sergeant Kimball said that he never identified himself as a Marine, as he had only a State Department identification card and diplomatic passport. The Marine courier said that people, mostly in Ireland, oftentimes mistook him for a naval intelligence officer.

From the Azores, Kimball went to Bermuda and then home. Sometimes, Kimball remembered, "I went to Dakar, then on to Bolama,[66] and from there I went on to Fisherman's Lake, Liberia, a refueling station for the Pan American Clippers that then went over to Natal, Brazil." Kimball stated that he usually had mail going over to Brazil though Natal there was a three-hour stop to refuel before heading to Bermuda. He added, "Normally, the clipper ship would refuel there before heading northwest to Washington, D.C."

Kimball recalled that courier duty was very intriguing, as was the case in Lisbon, shortly after Germany surrendered in May 1945. The Marine gunnery sergeant, who was only twenty-four and a seasoned combat veteran, remembered one time while eating his dinner in a restaurant in Lisbon seeing two German Army officers in full uniform eating only a few tables away. Kimball said that it was a unique experience looking at these two individuals sitting and eating so nonchalantly clad in their uniforms as if they were in a café in Germany. Later, while on an extended stay at Fisherman's Lake, Liberia, on August 13, 1945, Kimball remembered how he and the other guests were notified of Japan's surrender. "You could imagine the feeling ... as the dinner bell mounted on a pole at the radio shack clanged out as someone shouted that Japan had just surrendered. We stayed up all night. I can't imagine where all the beer came from!"[67]

Gunnery Sergeant Kimball remained on courier duty until October 1945, when his assignment with the State Department ended. Despite the termination of the Marine courier program, Kimball's service, as well as that of the other Marine couriers who volunteered for this program, established the precedent that officials at the State Department later capitalized on in 1948 with the assignment of Marines as embassy security guards.

Ambassadors in Green

Even while the Marine detachment, American Embassy, London, provided security for U.S. diplomatic and military personnel there, other Marines served the State Department as couriers, ministers, ambassadors, and representatives. One of these officers was Colonel William A. Eddy, a distinguished Middle East scholar and Marine Reserve officer who served as an "an ambassador in green" during the closing months of World War II. Colonel Eddy, who was fluent in Arabic and had served previously as a Marine officer with the Office of Strategic Services (the forerunner to the Central Intelligence Agency), had accepted the appointment as the first U.S. minister to the Kingdom of Saudi Arabia in August 1944. Colonel Eddy, who resigned his commission in order to accept the ministerial position, remained in Riyadh until July 1946. During President Franklin D. Roosevelt's historic meeting with King Ibn Saud aboard the USS *Quincy* in February 1945, Colonel Eddy acted as an interpreter and translator for both heads of state.

The other top Marine officer to serve at the ambassador level was Lieutenant General (later General) Thomas Holcomb. General Holcomb, the corps' wartime commandant, who became the first U.S. minister to Johannesburg, South Africa, in March 1944, remained the U.S. ambassador there until his retirement in 1947. The press in Johannesburg praised Holcomb's professionalism and diplomatic skill as America's first ambassador to that country.[68]

Summary

From 1904 to 1946, Marines served on various diplomatic missions, starting with their missions to Abyssinia and Tunisia as naval security forces of both American diplomats and American consulates. This changed, however, during World War I, as Lieutenant Colonel James C. Breckinridge served as the U.S. naval attaché to Petrograd and Marine staff non-commissioned officers served as diplomatic couriers and embassy guards in Petrograd and Vladivostok during the tumultuous days of the Russian Revolution in 1917–1918. During the 1930s Marines comprised the first embassy guard detachment at the newly established U.S. Embassy in Moscow, in the former Union of Soviet Socialist Republics.

During the interwar era of the 1920s and 1930s, Marine officers found themselves assigned to a variety of duties and responsibilities. Brigadier General John H. Russell served as the U.S. High Commissioner to Haiti with the rank of ambassador. Colonel Pedro A. del Valle served as not only the assistant naval attaché to the U.S. Embassy in Rome but as a military observer to the Italian-Ethiopian War in 1936–37. There, Italian dictator Benito Mussolini recognized Colonel del Valle's bravery under fire and his skill as a military observer.

During World War II, Marines served for the first time in the U.S. Embassy at the Court of St. James in London, England. Here, they served as embassy security personnel, diplomatic couriers, and orderlies. Other Marines, most notably General Thomas Holcomb and Colonel William A. Eddy, served as ambassadors in South Africa and Saudi Arabia respectively. What is even more important, however, that it was during the dark days of the Russian Revolution and later World War II, Marines laid the basis for the modern day Marine Security Guard program.

In fact, as Marines guarded the diplomatic mail and acted as couriers during both World Wars, the precedent had been established for the use of Marine staff noncommissioned officers as detachment commanders. More important, however, was the recognition by the State Department that Marines, due to their training and assignments as a naval security force, were an ideal security force to guard U.S. embassies worldwide in an era of uncertainty and danger.

CHAPTER 4

A New Mission: Marine Embassy Security Guards and the Memorandum of Agreement, 1946–1954

The service performed by the Marines who served at the U.S. Embassy in London during World War II became the foundation for the Marine Security Guard program. In fact, the specific use of Marines as embassy security during the war set in motion a series of conversations between the State, War, and Navy Departments that led to the assignment of leathernecks to guard U.S. embassies worldwide. The State Department concluded that the Marines, because of their wide experience as a naval security force, were the logical choice to guard American embassies and consulates worldwide. State Department officials likewise concluded that given the onset of the Cold War with the Soviet Union and revolutionary foment in Asia, the Middle East and Africa, a more dependable and reliable military force was necessary to ensure security of embassies and diplomatic personnel worldwide.

A Trained and Ready Force

At the conclusion of World War II the Department of State re-examined the problem of providing adequate security for all U.S. embassies and consulates abroad. Prior to the war, the State Department relied upon the practice of hiring both American and foreign civilians in the host countries to guard its embassies and consulates. With the onset of the Cold War with the USSR in 1947, as well as the period of decolonization in the Middle East, Africa, and Asia in 1947, State Department officials believed that dependence on local guards was both an unsound and unsuitable practice that invited problems. State Department officials discovered that oftentimes these guards were unsuited for this type of work. Indeed, State Department officials "found the guard positions to attract only the old and the lazy, and that many of the American guards resided permanently in foreign countries and were married to aliens."[1] This situation prompted State Department security officials to look for a viable alternative to the problems concerning diplomatic security. In time, "it was only natural that thoughts should turn toward the establishment of a guard force which was young, alert, trained, and under strong discipline — in other words, a military force."[2]

In early 1947, the State Department made an informal request to the War Department (today Department of the Army) concerning the use of military guards at the various Foreign Service posts. While the War Department showed some interest in the proposal made by the

State Department, the drastic cuts in manpower and appropriations that came as a result of the post–World War II demobilization prompted the secretary of war to conclude that the proposal was infeasible. The State Department, however, renewed its request to the War Department on 8 September 1947 to provide suitable military personnel for Foreign Service duty. In order to make the offer acceptable to the secretary of war, the secretary of state informed his counterpart in the War Department that the State Department would relieve the War Department of any additional expenses. In fact, the general plan advanced by the State Department stipulated that the "War Department pay only costs of basic salaries, uniforms, and equipment and that the State Department pay costs of transportation, rentals, and cost of living."[3] While officials in diplomatic security believed that they could hire as many as three times the number of guards with the appropriations given to the War Department, they nonetheless believed that the War Department could offer potential volunteers worldwide travel and assist the Army in its recruiting effort.

Even before a committee of officials from both the State and War Departments met to discuss this matter, the legal adviser to the secretary of state informed Secretary of State George C. Marshall that, according to the terms under Section 562 of the Foreign Service Act of 1946, "the State Department could not enter into any agreement concerning guards with the War Department but that such action could be taken jointly with the Department of the Navy." Section 562 of the Foreign Service Act specified: "The Secretary of the Navy is authorized, upon request of the Secretary of the State, to assign enlisted men of the Navy and Marine Corps to serve as custodians under the supervision of the principal officer at an embassy, legation, or consulate."[4]

It became clear to all that the State and Navy Departments (including the Marine Corps) would now have to work together in order to organize and train an efficient security guard force. State and Navy Department officials likewise discovered that a precedent had, in fact, existed in the use of Marines as embassy security guards. Thus, the "provisions of Section 562 of the Foreign Service Act of 1946 actually served the purpose of renewing and re-invigorating an association which had long performed ably and well in the service of American interests abroad."[5]

The next step in the assignment of Marines as embassy security guards occurred in the discussions between the State and Navy Departments over the formal establishment of the Security Guard Program. With increased budgetary and staff restrictions already in place on the State Department's Foreign Service staff, there was increased pressure from both the State and Navy Departments to formalize an agreement between the two to identify the posts at which the leathernecks would serve as embassy guards. In April 1948, the commandant of the Marine Corps, General Clifton B. Cates, a veteran of service in World Wars I and II, as well as in China, agreed to Marine participation in the Embassy Guard Program provided that "no Marine would be assigned in areas primarily under Army jurisdiction, that Marines would be assigned directly to the Naval Attaché at each post, and that a fair difference be made up between the Marines' salary and the civilian guards' pay." After consultations with various areas in the State Department, Undersecretary of State Robert A. Lovett informed Secretary of the Navy John L. Sullivan on May 26, 1948, that Secretary of State Dean Acheson had approved the provisions of the memorandum of agreement between the two government agencies.

Several weeks later, on June 22, 1948, Secretary Lovett formally requested from the Navy Department that 300 Marines be assigned to Foreign Service duty as embassy guards. These first Marine embassy guards "were to be assigned for duty 'Abroad on Foreign Service' guard detachments." Assigned as members of the staff of the naval attachés, these first Marine security guards were administered and came under the authority of the Department of the Navy, while the State Department in turn agreed to pay for salary compensation, allowances, travel, and for civilian clothing, when necessary. After several more high-level discussions between the Navy and State Departments, Acting Secretary of the Navy John N. Brown authorized, on July 20, 1948, the assignment of the first 300 Marines to security guard duty. The Marines were then assigned to the field on the basis of the security needs of the posts in question.

Before any formal agreement had been made by the State and Navy Departments, the killing of the American Consul General at the U.S. Consulate in Jerusalem, in Jordan-controlled Palestine in May 1948, prompted the dispatch of a 20-man Marine detachment in order to guard the U.S. Consulate and diplomatic personnel from further terrorist attacks. Specifically assigned to protect the consulate in Jerusalem was a 12-man Marine detachment which the State Department reinforced with a further twenty-nine Marines in October 1948. Over the next few months, protestors wounded two Marines as they stood guard over the consulate in the disputed city.

The violence in the Middle East and Asia, as well as elsewhere in Europe and Africa, prompted President Harry S. Truman to approve a plan, on November 5, 1948, "whereby Marine detachments in civilian clothes could be assigned to posts when the Secretary of State should determine that circumstances warranted."[6]

This and other events worldwide demonstrated that security at U.S. embassies and consulates would, in fact, have to be increased as U.S. diplomats and facilities now became the focal point of violent protests and terrorist attacks. As the Marine Corps and State Department continued to negotiate the details of the assignment of Marines as embassy security guards, there still existed the requirement of a formal agreement between the two departments pertaining to the use of Marines at U.S. embassies and consulates. Further discussions were, in fact, held between the State and Navy Departments as well as the Marine Corps in August and September 1948 that resulted, on September 20, 1948, in the signing of an agreement that specified the duties to be performed by the Marines.

This agreement likewise outlined the chain of command in an embassy environment. Specific points of this *Tentative Agreement* included: (a) Marines were to be responsible to the chief of mission or principal officer of the Foreign Service post, through the senior marine commissioned or non-commissioned officer and the naval attaché, where assigned; (b) salaries were to be paid by the Marine Corps, but the State Department assumed the obligation for allowances when government facilities were not available; (c) Marines were to utilize government transportation when it was available but the State Department would arrange transportation when it was not[7]; (d) the State Department assumed full responsibility for the medical care of each Marines on post; (e) a clothing allowance of $300 was given to each Marine serving in temperate zones and those serving in tropical zones received $239; (f) finally, the specific assignment of individuals became the joint responsibility of the State Department and the Marine Corps, with the State Department charged with the development of the overall placement schedule. State Department budget officials estimated that by using Marines as security guards the U.S. government would save over $167,750[8] per year in salaries and other expenses had civilian guards been utilized in a similar role.

One major issue that remained a problem was whether Marines should serve in uniforms or in civilian clothes. The State Department and the Marine Corps agreed that Marines should serve in uniform whenever possible. Officials at the State Department asserted that there were certain instances when Marines should wear civilian clothes (such as in Cairo due to anti–American and anti–Western riots), in order to prevent the individual Marine from being singled out as a member of the U.S. military or a government official. President Truman, himself a former haberdasher (men's clothes salesman), approved the plan while the secretary of state was left to determine whether Marine detachments would be assigned to wear strictly civilian clothes. This policy regarding civilian clothes remains in effect at this writing with all Marine Security Guard personnel (both male and female Marines). The tendency in recent years has leaned more and more toward Marines wearing their service uniforms while on post in both embassies and consulates throughout the world.

After the Marine Corps and the State Department agreed on all of the above-mentioned points, State Department officials then queried the chiefs of missions in every U.S. Embassy abroad on whether or not they objected to the use of Marines as security guards. When it appeared that there were no objections, the next task of the State Department was to obtain permission from the host governments. With this final hurdle cleared, the Department of State on November 29, 1948, presented the secretary of the Navy with a draft copy of the Memorandum of Agreement. Signed by Secretary of the Navy John L. Sullivan and Undersecretary of State Robert Lovett on December 15, 1948, the memorandum of agreement became the basis for the subsequent use of Marines as embassy security guards.[9]

The Memorandum of Agreement of 1948

The importance attached to the Memorandum of Agreement (MOA) of 1948 cannot be understated, since it still serves as the basis for the Marine Security Guard program of today. In fact, since 1948, the original Memorandum of Agreement has evolved over time as the missions and roles of Marine security guards has changed. Despite these changes, however, the original memorandum signed between the State and Navy Departments has retained its original intent: protection of classified material and secondly, defense of U.S. embassies and consulates. Divided into eight specific sections, the Memorandum of Agreement of 1948 outlined in painstaking detail the obligations and responsibilities of both the Marine Corps and the Department of State. Covered in the original Memorandum of Agreement were issues over salaries, allowances, transportation, clothing requirements and tables, schedule for placement of personnel, instruction covering employment of Marines, Medical care, and finally, reimbursement procedures.[10] As for the actual Memorandum of Agreement the document outlined the rules and regulations regarding the employment of Marine Corps personnel and served as a guide for the enforcement of this agreement between the two government agencies.

As for salaries, Marines on embassy security guard duty were to receive their base pay and sea and foreign shore pay according to Marine Corps regulations concerning both sea and foreign shore duty. Allowances were also paid for quarters, subsistence, and travel expenses according to what the government called "per diem," or a fixed amount for subsistence while en route to and from a diplomatic post. This was one of the main points that caused some consternation between the State and Navy Departments. Eventually both sides reached a compromise whereby "the State Department agreed to assume the obligations for the payment of quarters and subsistence allowance when they are not furnished in kind." This would take place from the time the individual Marine reports to the Foreign Service establishment or at that point which he is considered officially detailed to the State Department."[11] For its part, the Navy Department agreed to pay the individual Marine "per diem in lieu of either actual or necessary expenses to members of the U.S. Navy and Marine Corps on duty outside the continental United States."

As for transportation, the Marine Corps agreed to "provide for the transportation to the point nearest and most convenient to the area in which the State Department desires to assign the individual." The Marine Corps likewise agreed to transport the Marine embassy guards to posts wherever possible. When this was not feasible, the State Department agreed to pay for and undertake the transportation of the individual Marine to his post.[12] Among the more important items covered were issues over clothing requirements, schedule and rotation of personnel, and instructions governing employment of Marines.

As for clothing requirements, the Memorandum of Agreement stated, "The Marine Corps will furnish shoes, underwear and socks in all cases and Marine Corps luggage unless otherwise specified." In the case of luggage the State Department agreed to furnish each individual Marine with civilian-type luggage if necessary. The Memorandum stated that "other clothing will be provided as stated below under the following four different conditions relating to uniforms." Specifically, the Memorandum stated:

(a) The Marine will wear his uniform at all times, in which case the Marine Corps will keep the individual adequately clothed.
(b) When wearing civilian clothes at all times, the Department of State agreed to furnish these civilian clothes.
(c) While required to wear their uniforms on post Marines were required to wear civilian clothes on liberty. The State Department agreed to pay for civilian clothes worn by Marines if deemed necessary.
(d) Marines were encouraged to provide their own civilian apparel if necessary.[13]

As for clothes themselves, the Department of State specified those items that it would provide to each individual Marine on post.

Chart 3. Items to Be Furnished for Temperate Zone Assignments

Suit	4 — $40.00 each	$160.00
Overcoat*		40.00
Raincoat		15.00
Shirts	12 — 2.50 each	30.00
Ties	6 — 1.00 each	6.00
Handerkerchiefs	12 — .25 each	3.00
Sweaters	2 — 3.50 each	7.00
Belts	2 — 1.50 each	3.00
Garters	2 — 1.00 each	2.00
Gloves		5.00
Hat		8.00
Scarf*		3.00
Overshoes*		5.00
Mittens*		3.00
Headgear for Sweden, etc.*		10.00
	Total	$300.00[14]

*These items will not be necessary in a torrid zone, in which case the clothing allowance would be $239.

The clothing authorized for each Marine on embassy guard duty was to cover the two-year period that he was assigned to this duty and thus was to be a one-time issue. If there had to be a re-issue of clothing, replenishment took place "at a rate commensurate with the type of duty and type of clothing" required for that particular post.[15] For all other clothing allowances, "arrangements for the provision of civilian clothes" was parallel to the standards set for uniforms, in accordance with the above-mentioned table. In the event that a Marine's duty required him to wear civilian clothes, the State Department agreed to pay for eighty percent of the above-listed civilian clothes with the Navy Department picking up the balance.[16] As for the Marines' uniforms, the Marine Corps required each embassy guard to have 8 pairs of khaki trousers and 8 khaki shirts or "tropics" for warmer tropical climates, and for temperate zones 2 complete sets of "greens" that included 2 blouses and 4 trousers.

As for the selection, assignment and rotation of embassy guard personnel the process was very much the same as it is today with: (1) the Marine Corps in charge of selecting all Marine embassy guards in accordance with a standard set of criteria for determining a candidate's fitness for such duty; (2) specific post assignments will be determined jointly by officials of the Marine Corps and the State Department in accordance with a placement schedule drawn up pursuant to this agreement; and (3) the Marine Corps and the State Department will provide jointly and informally in the interest of flexibility, whatever training is considered appropriate. For its part, the Marine Corps remained responsible for the provision of the necessary inoculations, physical examinations, and dental care before the departure of the embassy guards from Washington, D.C., to their first assignments.

As for the actual instructions governing the employment of the Marines assigned to embassy guard duty, the State Department, under the terms of the Memorandum of Agreement, was charged with issuing the "necessary instructions to the appropriate Foreign Service establishment to govern the Marines as security guards." These instructions covered the specific duties of the Marines while on post in an embassy or consulate:

1. Marines are being assigned for the principal purpose of protecting Foreign Service establishments, under the direct control of the Chief of Mission or the principal officer, for security function exclusively, with emphasis on the primary activity of security Guard duty. The Marine Guards are responsible to the Chief of Mission or the principal officer, through the Senior Marine Commissioned officer and the Naval Attaché where one is assigned.
2. Special instructions, assignment of guard posts, reporting violations, and other operational details will be under the direction of the Chief of Mission or his designated representative.
3. Marine Guards will be required to wear while on duty, either Marine uniforms or civilian clothes only. In no case will improvised uniforms be prescribed. Locations where civilian clothes will be worn on duty or will be required for liberty will be prescribed by the State Department....
4. The State Department and Marine Corps will jointly develop and issue to the field instructions as required to implement this agreement.[17]

Finally, the last points of the Memorandum of Agreement concerned provisions regarding health care and reimbursements. By the terms of the agreement the State Department provided each Marine on embassy guard duty with full and complete medical care, insofar as was permitted within the existing facilities of both the Navy and State Departments.[18] As for reimbursement procedures, the MOA stipulated that the regular pay of Marines assigned to the Security Guard Program were to be paid by the naval attaché or State Department's disbursing officer and charged to the general account of advances inside the Navy Department. If per diem were deemed necessary, the State Department officers posted throughout the world were charged with its disbursement according to the rates established by the Navy

Department. Thus, the Memorandum of Agreement, signed on 15 December 1948, was both comprehensive and attempted to cover any problem that might arise as the Embassy Guard Program commenced.

Before the ink was dry on the MOA, Headquarters Marine Corps had already assigned the first group of 83 Marines to the Foreign Service Institute. While December 15, 1948, is cited as the actual signing date of the formal agreement between the State and Navy Departments that assigned leathernecks to Marine Security Guard duty, the first group of Marines had already been selected and was in training at both Henderson Hall and Foreign Service Institute. Here, the Marines received a very brief course on State Department procedures and courtesies (such as table etiquette and manners), as well as a brief familiarization course of small arms and the handling and proper storage of classified material. The Marines assigned to embassy duty also received their clothing issue from the Robert Hall Department Store in downtown Washington, D.C. It might be added that the Foreign Service Institute served as a "school" for all diplomatic personnel assigned to the Foreign Service. According to Warrant Officer George V. Lampman, one of the first Marines assigned to Marine Security Guard (MSG) duty, "the Marine Corps began to recruit for MSG duty as early as the summer of 1948 with the issuance of an ALMAR (All Marines) bulletin seeking prospective candidates."[19] Gunner Lampman recalled that the ALMAR stipulated that volunteers for this new program "had to be clean shaven, have a clean serviceman's record book, agree not marry during the length of duty on MSG, and have at least three years of active service remaining on their contracts or agree to extend their enlistments."

While a formality, it was not until September 1949 that General Clifton B. Cates, Commandant of the Marine Corps, ratified the agreement. Meanwhile, negotiations between the State Department and Marine Corps further clarified the position of the Marine Guards within the ordinary chain-of-command at Foreign Service posts. To this end both the State Department and Marine Corps issued a joint declaration that it was the intent of the State Department and Marine Corps that Marine guards would serve directly under the security officer of the post for all duty and administration. Also, the role and authority of the naval attaché was clarified by this declaration. In order to place the Marines under direct jurisdiction of the Navy Department, the naval attaché was to serve as the senior naval officer present with no power to exercise over the Marines on post beyond that of senior counselor and reporting senior. All matters concerning breaches of naval laws and discipline were turned over to the Marine Corps' judge advocate general for action.

While it was difficult to identify all problems that might occur while the Marine served on post, the matter regarding marriage received prompt attention. As above-mentioned, Marines selected for this program agreed not to marry while on post. Those caught in violation of this provision were promptly returned to the Fleet Marine Forces. As for the presence of the wives of senior staff noncommissioned officers selected to oversee the proper administration of a Marine detachment, the State and Navy Departments thought it at first prohibitive in terms of cost as travel, allotments, housing, and security screening were all involved with dependents. This was later modified in 1951 when Headquarters Marine Corps determined that senior noncommissioned officers, who oftentimes were married, provided a more stable group of NCOs, were better disciplined, and served as examples to the younger Marines on post.[20] The assignment of veteran staff and non-commissioned officers likewise insured that camaraderie developed between the Marines assigned to post. It further maintained the link with the Marine Corps as a whole, which prior to this oftentimes became obscured as individual leathernecks came to identify with the diplomatic personnel on post.

Inevitably there were disciplinary problems. Marines who violated the laws governing diplomatic personnel, breaches of naval and military law, and unethical conduct were summarily removed from the program at the discretion of the ambassador and State Department and returned to the United Sates for disciplinary action. By far, however, the single greatest cause for relief in those early days involved violation of the standing order regarding marriage to native women.

Manpower and the Marine Security Guard Program, 1949–1952

One of the earliest and most pressing problems faced by the Marine Corps during the early days of the Marine Security Guard revolved around the drain of critical manpower. Even as the first Marines trained at Henderson Hall and the Foreign Service Institute, the winds of the Cold War between the United States and the Soviet Union began to affect the use of Marines as embassy and security guards. As early as 21 January 1951, the secretary of state requested from his counterpart in the Navy Department to provide an additional 40 Marines to carry on guard duties at the eight Mutual Defense Assistance program missions spread throughout war-ravaged Western Europe. In the same letter, the secretary hinted that "a further request might be made to increase the overall number of Marines serving at Foreign Service posts."[21] The personnel ceilings placed on the numbers of Marines permitted to serve on embassy guard duty, coupled with a provision of the Mutual Defense Act that prohibited payment of military salaries from funds allocated to this program, presented a major obstacle to the State Department's plans to increase the number of Marines on embassy duty. With the outbreak of war on the Korean peninsula on June 25, 1950, the rapid expansion of the Marine Corps brought with it additional funds and manpower. With this increase the Marine Corps agreed to cover the cost of basic salaries of Marines who had been ordered to Foreign Service guard duty in excess of the initial quota of 300 Marine Security Guards. Also, the rapid increase in manpower brought with it the assignment of a total of 64 Marines to serve as security guards with the Mutual Defense Assistance program.[22]

During the fall of 1950, the Department of State, the Marine Corps, and the Bureau of the Budget engaged in a series of talks to clarify the financial support of Marine Security Guards. At the conclusion of these discussions the Bureau of Budget ruled, "If the guarding of American missions abroad is essential to the security of the United States, then that guarding is a defense function and should be carried out by the Military Establishment without reimbursement of basic costs." The Bureau of the Budget then asked that the Defense Department assume direct responsibility for the guarding of Foreign Service posts abroad and to assign that duty to the Marine Corps. For its part, the State Department requested that the Marine Corps "be allowed to increase its personnel ceiling by 650 enlisted positions in order to provide for Marine Guards that were thought to be necessary for completing an effective security defense."[23] The Defense Department and the Marine Corps agreed to accept the full responsibility for the security of embassies and consulates. On February 15, 1951, General Cates ordered his director of personnel to "increase the number of Marines available for duty with the Foreign Service by 311."[24] This increase in Marines assigned to Embassy Security Guard duty brought the total number to 675 guards.

Two major administrative changes occurred that placed the Marine Security Guard Program on a firm basis with the State Department. The first occurred within the Office of Security of the Department of State, which had originally been designated as the main bureau directing the overall security program of embassies and consulates. In an attempt consolidate and simplify the chain of command between the State Department and Marine Corps, the Secretary of State ordered that the Office of Security of the Department be officially designated as "main contact point within the Department of State for all Marine Security Guard matters." The second administrative change occurred in June of 1952, with the appointment of junior Marine officers to each of the Regional Security Headquarters of the Department of State to work with the regional security supervisors on all matters pertaining to the Marines. Shortly after the approval of the appointment of Marine officers, now designated as regional Marine officers, the State Department assigned these new regional security offices to Paris, Cairo, Manila, and later Rio de Janeiro. These officers directed the morale, discipline, administration, and other affairs of the Marine guards, and were to make semi-annual inspections of the guard detachments within their areas of responsibility.

To pay for the assignment of regional Marine officers, the Foreign Service Act of 1946, which specified that only enlisted men could be used in such a program, the Marine Corps agreed to pay the costs of these Marine officers. The assignment of the regional Marine officers brought with it a marked improvement of the Marine Security Guard program as a whole. Eventually, the regional Marine officer system was able to provide coverage to detachments spread throughout the world.

By the end of 1952, the success of the Marine Security Guard program was very much in evidence: a worldwide poll of U.S. ambassadors and regional security officers voted for a further increase by 125 Marines to the existing program. The request for more Marines came not only from ambassadors and consular officials but other agencies and missions attached to the Foreign Service. By and large, Headquarters Marine Corps, despite the ongoing war in Korea, recognized the importance of the program to the State Department, and thus proved willing to assign experienced Marines to the program.

The importance of Marines on security guard duty was further enhanced with the revision of the original memorandum of agreement in 1952 and later in 1953. The need for a revised agreement between the State Department and Marine Corps became evident as the program continued to expand. In fact, a memorandum circulated at both the State Department and Marine Corps emphasized the need for a revision of the original memorandum of agreement due to the fact that "it was seen to have become too restrictive to provide effectively for the administration of the program."[25] After two years of intense negotiations between the Departments of State and Defense, a revised "draft" agreement was created. This new agreement, signed into law by Secretary of State John Foster Dulles and Secretary of Defense Charles E. Wilson, restated the provisions for the use of military personnel for custodial (i.e., security) duty at all Foreign Service establishments. This last revision, with some minor amendments, is still in effect today as the legal basis for the use of Marines as embassy guards.

Training and Curriculum for Marine Security Guards, 1949–1954

As the first Marine Security Guard students trained at the Foreign Service Institute, it became apparent that there was a need for a standardized training program and curriculum. Whereas the original program had a limited curriculum of customs, courtesies, manners, and weapons familiarization taught at Marine Corps Base, Quantico, Virginia, that lasted a couple of weeks, a revised and more complete training syllabus was introduced as the Marine Security Guard program expanded. As Master Sergeant George A. Bader recalled, the program was, in fact, very basic. Master Sergeant Bader, who was part of one of the original classes of Marine Security Guards and saw duty in La Paz, Bolivia, specifically remembered that there was very little "military training," or preparation for oversees duty while at Henderson Hall in those early days of the program: "Other than preparation such as receiving the required inoculations, passport Application, and shopping at Robert Hall men's clothing store in downtown D.C., for civilian clothes, the only military training was qualification with the .45 cal. Pistol."[26] There was little if any formal curriculum or detailed training program in place to train Marine Security Guards. Moreover, as Master Sergeant Bader recalled, there was absolutely no familiarization with the posts or the country where they were being sent. The lack of a formal training program and country briefs given Marines at Henderson Hall by both the State Department and Marine Corps changed as the program expanded in the early 1950s.

In early 1954, officials in both the State Department and Headquarters Marine Corps suggested that it might be "to the mutual advantage of the Department of State and the Marine Corps to inaugurate an enlarged and improved training program." The program suggested would last a total of thirty days and "would provide Marine Corps personnel assigned to Foreign Service duty with a general knowledge of their new assignment." As part of the revised Memorandum of Agreement, the State Department and Marine Corps agreed upon a formalized, four-week course that would train anywhere from forty to fifty Marines per class at Henderson Hall, which was designated as the official training site for Marine Security Guards. Furthermore, in pursuance of a more formalized, and one might add rigorous, training schedule, both the Marine Corps and the Department of State assembled a staff of highly qualified instructors and specialists. Here, Marines received classes on weapons familiarization, security briefings on levels of classification, internal security measures, screening of personnel, diplomatic terms and courtesies, etiquette, and physical training. The first class to undergo this new curriculum began on November 4, 1954.[27] Thereafter, a new class was to convene monthly, starting on the first Monday of each month.

As the Commandant of the Marine Corps General Lemuel C. Shepherd, Jr., outlined in a letter to the commanding officer, Headquarters Battalion, located at Henderson Hall, the new training syllabus was to provide a "thorough training of applicants" with the emphasis to be placed on "those aspects requisite to proper performance of duty in Foreign Service Missions."[28] General Shepherd emphasized that the course was not only designed to train new Marine Security Guards but to "screen those applicants who are morally, mentally, or physically unsuited" for such duty.

The most important aspect in the approved training syllabus was the fact that it provided an official mission statement for the Marine Corps to operate a formalized school in the training of new security guards. The syllabus approved by General Shepherd stated that the purpose of the Marine Security Guard School was to "train specially selected Marines to perform the duties of a member of Marine Detachment operating under control of State Department Foreign Service Mission." Types of instruction included lectures, demonstrations, practical application exercises, conferences, and examinations. Applicants were required to undergo two formal interviews during their training. If at any time the commanding officer or State Department officer felt that an applicant was unsuited for Marine Security Guard duty, he was dropped from the program without prejudice. As for the subjects studied, the training was hard and intensive, and was intended to provide the new Marine Security Guard with the basic requirements he would need while on post.

CHART 4. CMC APPROVED SYLLABUS FOR
MARINE SECURITY GUARD SCHOOL (1954)

Subject	Hours	Type of Instruction
Inspections and Drill	24	Practical Application
Foreign Service Establishment*	4	Lecture, Examination
Interior Guard Duty	4	Lecture, Demonstration, Practical Application, and Examination
Weapons Instruction	6	Lecture, Demonstration, Practical Application
Security Procedures and Classified Material*	36	Lecture, Demonstration, Examination
Administration	4	Lecture, Demonstration, Practical Application
Driver Training	2	Lecture, Demonstration, Practical Application
Education (Foreign Languages, MCI, Correspondence Courses)	3	Lecture[29]
Photography	2	Lecture, Demonstration, Practical Application
Fingerprinting	3	Lecture, Demonstration, Practical Application
Personal Conduct Overseas*	8	Lecture, Demonstration
Military Courtesy	4	Lecture, Demonstration, Practical Application, and Examination
Current Events*	8	Demonstration, Practical Application
Director, MSG Time	68	Clearances, administrative and command time. Interviews of prospective Marine applicants.
Leadership	4	Lecture, Conferences

*Courses administered by the State Department

While the original curriculum agreed upon by the Marine Corps and the Department of State included officials from both agencies, it was hoped that in time the instruction at the Marine Security Guard School be administered entirely by Marines.

As the Marine Corps Security Guard program expanded, so too did the curriculum at the Marine Security Guard School. As time went on, courses were added or dropped as suggested by both the State Department and Headquarters Marine Corps. The most important development, insofar as the training of a Marine for embassy duty was concerned, however, revolved around the fact that for the first time a formal school and curriculum existed for training new Marine embassy guards. The formalized nature of embassy guard training meant, among other things, that the Marine assigned to an embassy or consulate was well-trained and could perform his mission under any adverse circumstances.

Summary

By the end of 1952, there were a total of 800 Marines on embassy security duty. Besides the substantial increase in Marines on duty in embassies and consulates world-wide, the further clarification of the Memorandum of Agreement of 1948 brought with it a more effective level of cooperation and coordination between the various branches and departments of the government and the Marine Corps. From the outset of the program, the further clarification of the working relationship between the State Department and Marine Corps as outlined in the Memorandum of Agreement and subsequent amendments insured a smoother implementation in the use of Marines as security guards and regional officers. As the Marine Security Guard program expanded, so did the curriculum and infrastructure used to train Marines. One important administrative changed occurred in 1954 with the organization of the Marine Security Guard School within "Fox" Company located at Headquarters Battalion. Prior to this move, Marine Security Guard School had been administered by Casual Company at Henderson Hall. With the formation of "Fox" Company, the Marine Security Guard program could be better administered and could concentrate on its primary mission in training Marine embassy guards. Despite the fact that the Marine Corps was heavily involved in the fighting on the Korean peninsula, Marine leaders from General Cates on down deemed the Marine Security Guard program as one of the most important tasks assigned to the Marine Corps since its birth in 1775. As the following years (1953–1980) demonstrated, Marines stood ready to guard U.S. embassies and diplomats in an increasingly dangerous world.

CHAPTER 5

The Early Years: Revolutions, Coups, Civil Wars, 1949–1964

By early January 1949, eighty-three Marines had been assigned to the Foreign Service Institute for training as Marine Security Guards. By January 28, 1949, the first fifteen Marines had departed for their first assignments: six sent to Bangkok, Thailand, and nine to Tangier, Morocco.[1] Within two years of the program's inception there were approximately 675 Marines serving at various embassies and consulates throughout the world. For the next two decades, Marine security guards were in the forefront in the defense of U.S. embassies and consulates as invading armies in Korea (1950) and Hungary (1956) ravaged the respective capital cities where they stood guard. Other Marine security guards witnessed revolutions throughout the developing Third World (Latin America, Africa, and Asia). As a result of these early experiences, Marines assigned to "Post One" remained vigilant and ready to defend American lives and property in what had become an increasingly dangerous and challenging mission.

The Eve of War in Korea

For the Marine Security Guards attached to the U.S. Embassy in Seoul, Korea, the invasion of the Republic of Korea (ROK) on the morning of 25 June 1950 by elements of the North Korean People's Army (NKPA) became the first real test of the Marine embassy detachments under fire. Prior to the invasion, the first Marine embassy guards who reported to Seoul on January 9, 1949, had been informed by the State Department that the post was, according to Warrant Officer 1 George Lampman , "a civilian clothes assignment, under the control of the State Department."[2] Not identified as Marines, Lampman stated that he and his fellow security guards were addressed as 'Mister' and that their only identification was a special passport colored green. At that time, the U.S. Embassy in Seoul was located in the 5th floor of the Banto Hotel. Built by the Japanese during their occupation of Korea (1910–1945), it was a fortified structure with steel shuttered strong points guarding the first two floors and surrounded by a moat. The ambassador at the time was Mr. John J. Muccio, a career diplomat who had been in Korea since 1947.

This first Marine security guard detachment to Seoul consisted of a 20-man detail of specially handpicked seasoned Marine staff officers. The senior staff noncommissioned officer in charge, a master sergeant, was assisted by two gunnery sergeants as well as two platoon sergeants, all of whom were veterans who had served in China before and after World War II.[3] The same was true for the "buck" sergeants who had experienced combat in the South and

Central Pacific during World War II. The remaining noncommissioned officers were on their second enlistments. "Gunner" Lampman recalled that while at Henderson Hall the Marines selected to go to Korea received a brief course on the history of Korea and lectures on security and how to handle what State Department officials called "situations." This referred to the limits of what the Marines could and could not do while carrying out their duties. The Marines selected to guard the U.S. Embassy in Seoul likewise received weapons familiarization, an issue of civilian clothes, and identification cards from the State Department. This class of Marine Security Guards completed their training on December 20, 1944, and within several days after graduation, boarded a Military Air Service flight on December 27 to Seoul. The Marines were anxious to assume their duties, and Warrant Officer Lampman remembered that upon arrival in Seoul the security officer there "had no preconceived notion of what they were capable of doing." In fact, as Lampman noted, this was the period of "trial and error," as the Marine Security Guard program was in its infancy. Yet within two weeks, the first Marine embassy guards had "snapped in" and had established a "well-oiled system of posts and watches in the mission headquarters."[4]

Due to the high-threat environment, two Marines, Technical Sergeant Jack Edwards and Sergeant Lloyd Henderson, had been assigned as bodyguards for Ambassador Muccio. Both Marines lived in the ambassador's official residence in Chung Dong. In addition to providing security for the ambassador, the Marines established a three-man, 24-hour a day, seven day a week watch at the converted mission headquarters at the Peninsula Hotel. Additionally, five Marines were assigned daily to maintain security on the outside of the embassy. A Marine stood guard at the entrance and logged visitors in and out of the building. Another Marine guard positioned himself on outside the embassy's offices on the fifth floor of the Banto Hotel. At nighttime, and prior to the admittance of the Korean cleaning personnel, Marines conducted a "shakedown" of the offices to insure that no classified material was carelessly left out.

Warrant Officer Lampman recalled that with the exception of the ambassador's bodyguards, the workload was evenly distributed with everyone taking turns at each assignment. The veteran Marine remembered that this arrangement "worked very well," and that there were "few incidents or any major problems." The first and last goal of the Embassy Guards was to protect the staff and property of the embassy.

Sergeant Paul Dupras recalled, "Our obligation to protect the staff and property was always first in the mind of the members of the detail but we also tried to be friendly with those we met and worked for either American military (occupation forces) or civilian both American and Korean. It must have worked quite well as two of the Marines married Korean girls who worked for the Embassy (this was after they had finished their tour of duty) and three others married State Department gals. One, George Wickman didn't wait for his tour to end and when he married was relieved, as was his wife, and sent back to the States." Sergeant Dupras added that the embassy staff invited the Marines to parties and many dinners. The Marines in turn reciprocated and held many parties themselves. Dupras stated that the largest party he attended while in Seoul was the Marine Corps Birthday on November 10, 1949, when over 200 guests came to watch Ambassador Muccio cut the birthday cake.[5]

War Comes to Korea, June 25–27, 1950

This routine changed, however, in the early pre-dawn hours of June 25, 1950, when elements of the North Korean People's Army spearheaded by Soviet-supplied T-34 tanks streamed across the 38th Parallel that separated communist North Korea from its democratic neighbor. Warrant Officer Lampman recalled that he and his fellow Marine Security Guards all realized that they were witnessing "history in the making" as war broke out on the Korean Peninsula.

On the night prior to the North Korean invasion, Warrant Officer Lampman remembered that there were two other Marines on duty beside himself standing the 12:00 A.M.–8:00 A.M. watch. The entrance to the embassy, controlled by what the Marines called the "Blueboy Post," served as the home base and call sign for the limited radio net operated by the Marine Security Section. The second post protected by the embassy guards was located on the 1st floor of the Banto Hotel while the third post, code-named "Rover" consisted of a radio jeep that continually patrolled and visited all the embassy-occupied hotels, warehouses, open storage areas, and outlying residences. Lampman wrote, "During working hours, this third Marine would control entrance to the Embassy main lobby. Also on the net were the fire chief and the Embassy security officers."[6]

In the pre-dawn hours of June 25, 1950, Lampman stated that the security phone rang at 5:30 A.M., with callers asking him, "What's going on?" Lampman responded to the callers that there was nothing that he knew of. He then dutifully entered the calls into the logbook. When Jack James and Sarah Parker, reporters for the *New York Times* appeared at the lobby and asked the same question, Lampman responded that he knew of nothing. Unknown to him and his fellow Marines, the North Korean Army had crossed the 38th Parallel at 4 o'clock that morning.

Relieved by Sergeants Paul Dupras, Glenn "Tiny" Green, and Corporal William "Bill" Lyons at 0800, Lampman and the other two Marine Security Guards returned to their quarters in the Capitol apartments, two blocks away from the South Korean Capitol Building, for some much needed sleep. At about 8:45 A.M., correspondent Jack James re-appeared at the U.S. Embassy with the news that the NKPA had crossed the 38th Parallel in full force. As the excited reporter spoke to the Marines, Ambassador Muccio appeared at the embassy and immediately contacted Robert Heavey, the recently arrived security officer, who after a short consultation with the ambassador ordered a general recall of embassy guards.

Meanwhile, tired from their long day of duty, Lampman and the two other Marines fell asleep, only to be awakened by the clerk at the front desk saying that he, Lampman, had a phone call. On the phone was an excited Sergeant Dupras, who exclaimed, "Get back to the Embassy immediately with any of the guys you can find. And bring any weapons you have with you." About 10:00 A.M., Lampman and Sergeant Augustus "Gus" E. Siefken were on their way back to the embassy in an embassy jeep (painted orange) when suddenly overhead two Soviet-built Yak fighters flown by North Korean pilots turned and headed toward the leathernecks. After making two strafing runs aimed at the South Korean Army Headquarters, the Yaks peeled away. As Sergeant Glenn recalled, "the Yaks were not interested in us."[7]

After the attack by the North Korean fighters, Warrant Officer Lampman and Sergeant Siefken made their way to the U.S. Embassy, where they were met by the Noncommissioned Officer-in-Charge Sergeant John F. Runck, who was in the process of making assignments and checking on the security of the embassy. Told to go into the dining room to stand by, Lampman and Siefken began to eat breakfast. Shortly thereafter, Runck and the embassy security officer, John Heavey, began to issue assignments and collect arms in order to defend the embassy and its personnel. Lampman stated that quickly, "our arsenal had suddenly blossomed from our normally carried .38 caliber pistols, a Thompson submachine gun, a few M-1's (Garands), and shotguns."[8] Both Heavey and Runck dismissed the notion that this was a false alarm when they told the Marine security guards: "This is no drill ... the North Koreans were on the way in strength."

Several Marines acted as drivers to meet U.S. embassy personnel arriving at the train station from the port city of Pusan while others were sent to alert embassy families in the outlying and isolated residences to begin preparations to evacuate if so ordered by the ambassador. Meanwhile Ambassador Muccio cabled Washington, D.C., at 9:30 A.M. after meeting with South Korean President Syngman Rhee with descriptions of the fighting, based mostly on ROK Army accounts.[9] Later, Ambassador Muccio made the decision to evacuate all dependents and non-essential diplomatic personnel in the early morning hours (12:00 A.M.) of June 25, 1950. Mr. Everett Drumwright, Ambassador Muccio's deputy, reported that "by that time [12:00 A.M.], it was clear the North Korean forces headed for Seoul through the Uijongbu Corridor could not be stopped."[10]

After returning from the railroad station where he escorted a team of diplomats to the American embassy, Lampman ate dinner and went to sleep. Early the next morning, June 26, Lampman and Dewy Lowe were given the task of destroying all of the embassy's vehicles in the motor pool that were not running and were, in fact, "on dead line." Lampman and Lowe then set out to sabotage the vehicles so that the NKPA could not cannibalize them: "So, with a couple of M-1's and cases of AP [armor piercing ammunition], we went to the motor pool and we shot, and shot, and shot [each dead lined vehicle]! Lift each hood, aim exactly into the block just behind the flywheel, and put in a couple of rounds. This type of identical damage would prevent the North Koreans from cannibalizing some of the vehicles to make the others work.... It took us several hours to execute the task."[11]

Gunner Lampman wrote that by midnight of the June 25–26, 1950, the evacuation of dependents was underway. Comprised primarily of women and children, the evacuees were taken to the port at Inchon where they boarded a Norwegian fertilizer vessel. Several Marines acted as escorts for the bus convoy to Inchon. On the afternoon of June 26, another bus convoy comprised of single American Embassy personnel were taken to the Kimpo Airfield outside of Seoul, where they were flown out by C-54 transports belonging to the U.S. Air Force's Far East Air Force. While at the airfield a dogfight erupted between U.S. Air Force twin-engine P-51 Mustangs and two Yaks, which were shot down by the American airmen. During the evacuation of American citizens and dependents Lampman and his fellow Marine security guards were able to depend on the U.S. Air Force's ability to maintain an "air cap" over the Kimpo Airfield and land routes to the airfield. Lampman recalled that the evacuation and security of the Americans and their dependents became one of the primary functions of the Marine Embassy Guards.

Meanwhile, as reports of an imminent breakthrough filtered back to Ambassador Muccio, he and the embassy staff began to screen and burn classified material. Lampman recalled that despite the invasion by the NKPA, the scene inside the embassy was relatively calm. With the scene outside the embassy in chaos, Ambassador Muccio ordered the embassy staff to remain inside and away from the roof because of the North Korean aircraft overhead. Inside, the Marine Security Guards, the military attaché and diplomatic personnel began a systematic burning of classified documents and manuals. Not having pyrotechnics, the Marines used the embassy's furnace to burn the classified documents. In fact, this became the main concern of the majority of the Marines at the Embassy as they "manned dollies and collected the classified materials which the embassy staff stacked outside office doors. They trucked the material down to the basement and fed the furnace — all day Sunday and into the night. With short, infrequent breaks for food and rest — and sometimes serving as convoy escorts to Inchon and Kimpo Airfield—they hauled and burned and drove from Sunday morning straight through to Tuesday afternoon. They got the job done."[12]

The Marines and embassy personnel soon discovered, however, that the furnace in the basement of the Banto Hotel was incapable of handling such a voluminous load of classified material.[13] To expedite the burning of the classified material and prevent the furnace from blowing apart, Sergeant Dupras and several other Marines built a cage made up of chain link fencing and steel posts in which to burn the documents. Set up in the parking lot of the embassy, the fire soon attracted the attention of the Seoul Fire Department, which was brought to the scene several times.[14]

By the evening of the June 26, the ambassador had ordered a further evacuation of embassy personnel. Corporal Ervin Krouse oversaw a group of dozen Korean watch supervisors and about fifty Korean watchmen who were to safeguard the embassy. As panic-stricken South Korean soldiers and civilians ran through the streets of Seoul, Corporal Krouse kept a watchful eye in order to prevent looters and vandals from ransacking the embassy. As the NKPA approached the South Korean capital, the Korean watchstanders and supervisors began to disappear.

Meanwhile, Lampman had been given the assignment of destroying the embassy switchboard, which he and "Tiny" Green accomplished in two hours with the help of two sledgehammers. Lampman recalled that when the North Koreans occupied the city, the NKPA forced the former South Korean embassy employees "at gunpoint" to repair the switchboard. Later, North Korean leader Kim Il-Sung reportedly used the Banto Hotel (U.S. Embassy) as his headquarters and the switchboard during his brief stay there. With that mission complete, Lampman was sent to insure that the French Embassy had received word of the impending evacuation.

In addition to destroying the switchboard, Lampman and several other Marines took the embassy code machines to the sidewalk in front of the building and hooked them up to a jeep battery. The code machines were thermite-encased and upon starting the jeep, the machines began to melt. Several minutes later the code machines resembled two lumps of molten metal. Lampman and Dupras then emptied the U.S. currency found in the embassy safe into a large regular U.S. Mail bag. With no receipt and no lock on the bag, the money nonetheless found its way safely to the U.S. Embassy in Japan, where the Marines placed it in a safe.[15]

The Last Ones Out of Seoul, June 27, 1950

With the classified material nearly destroyed (it would all be by the afternoon of the 27th) the ambassador and his party left Seoul to go south to join President Syngman Rhee. Accompanying Mr. Muccio was only one of the two Marine bodyguards, Sergeant Jack Edwards. That same afternoon the rest of the embassy personnel and Marine Security Guards departed the embassy compound and headed for the Kimpo Airfield, where they awaited evacuation to Japan. As the Marines pulled out of Seoul, North Korean Yaks strafed the entrance near the U.S. Embassy.

Sergeant Lloyd Henderson recalled, "When the plane came in the late evening [of June 27] we could hear the explosions and machine gun fire very close. Ours was the last plane out and we boarded it with only our weapons and the clothes on our backs."[16] George Lampman remembered that as the Marines and American civilians made their way to the Kimpo Airfield, the roads were clogged with refugees heading south. The final evacuation of the embassy personnel that had remained in Seoul was overshadowed by the NKPA's rapid advance. There was also some concern that the airfield might be overrun, with the Marines becoming prisoners of war. Lampman recalled the actual flight to Japan, however, was non-eventful.

The Marines and rest of the American and Korean citizens evacuated arrived safely at Kimpo prior to the flight out to Japan. The Marine warrant officer wrote that the C-54 transport plane had been filled to capacity with both American and Korean citizens. Though the plane was seriously overloaded, Mr. John Stone, the American consul general in Seoul, nonetheless continued to shuffle people aboard as the engines roared. Lampman remembered that by the time he and the remaining Marine Security Guards prepared to board there was "standing room only" in the forward section of the airplane.[17] In spite of the now overloaded airplane of 110 passengers, the pilot yelled, "Oh, what the hell, come on board." With that, the doors were sealed and the plane, rocking and dipping, took off. In scenes reminiscent of the evacuation of Saigon, Republic of Vietnam, in April 1975, the pilot ordered the passengers to discard everything, including suitcases, weapons, bags, boxes, and even survival gear in order to gain altitude fast. As the plane lifted off the sounds of machine gun fire could be heard all along the airfield perimeter. As the overloaded C-54 gained altitude and made its way across the Strait of Tsushima, Lampman completed his final evacuation order: he received permission to open the little round navigator's Plexiglas porthole and dropped the "Great Seal of the United States" into the water below. Arriving in Inazuke, Japan, "Gunner" Lampman and his fellow Marine security guards made their way to the U.S. Consulate in Kyoto, Japan, where they deposited the money from the embassy safe and other materials that required storage.

While all twenty Marine Security Guards of the Seoul detachment made it safely out of Korea, the same was not true for the South Korean civilians (drivers, dining room staff, hotel employees, switchboard and communications personnel), who had worked for the Americans. Many of them had remained on the job until the NKPA entered the city several days later. Lampman stated that the majority of these brave South Koreans were probably executed along with their families as collaborators.[18]

When the U.S. and South Korean Marines entered Seoul after the Inchon landings on September 25, the Marines who had been assigned to the U.S. Embassy returned and immediately set about re-establishing the facility prior to its re-occupation by Ambassador Muccio and his staff. As Sergeant Charles Goff recalled, "Seoul was in ruins and had suffered a great deal of destruction since June 25th."[19] After the re-establishment of the U.S. Embassy in Seoul and return of the Marine Security Guard detachment, Technical Sergeant Jack Edwards, whose assignment had been to guard Ambassador Muccio, participated in the ceremonies, officiated by General Douglas MacArthur, that had marked the return of the capital to South Korean President Syngman Rhee. Technical Sergeant Edwards recalled that he attended the ceremony with both a .45 caliber pistol and an M-1 Carbine in order to guard both Ambassador Muccio and General MacArthur, and had the honor of his own place at one of the desks of the National Assembly. Edwards whimsically stated, "So there I sat with my pistol on my hip and my carbine on my desk as Dr. Africa of the United Nations, General MacArthur, Ambassador Muccio, and Syngman Rhee made speeches."[20]

When the North Koreans and Communist Chinese forces entered Seoul in January 1951, the Marine Embassy Guards once again assisted in the safe and orderly withdrawal of American diplomatic and civilian personnel.

War in Peace: Revolutions, Coups, and Protests, 1952–1965

As Marine Security Guards discovered in Korea, embassy duty could be very dangerous. While Marines drew such posts as Rome, Italy, Paris, France, or London, England, as their first assignments, most of the duty was in Third World areas considered by the State Department as "hazardous duty." Master Sergeant George Bader stated that such was the case with his first assignment as a security guard to La Paz, Bolivia. The retired Master Sergeant recalled "During the years I was at La Paz, the country was in great turmoil [with] many small and not so small revolutions. Although the embassy and ambassador's residence were hit by small arms fire it is my belief most hits were from stray shots. Perhaps the most violent revolution was the so-called 'Holy Week' battle in 1952. It was bloody and scary but no U.S. citizens were harmed."[21]

The "Holy Week" revolution Master Sergeant Bader referred to was the result of nearly a decade of political instability and peasant unrest in the Andean nation. The unrest began with the installation of a series of military governments commencing with the government of Bolivian Army General Enrique Penaranda, who came to power in 1940. General Penaranda's government had been responsible for the brutal massacre of peasant tin miners who had organized themselves into a labor union to protest the low wages, health risks, and long hours under dangerous conditions found in the tin mines. Fearing a "communist" insurrection, the Penaranda government's crackdown only inspired more violence. Well armed with rifles, pistols, captured machine guns, shotguns, and dynamite (which they used with great effectiveness), the Bolivian miners, primarily Indians, waged a relentless guerrilla war against the military government.[22]

In 1943, the miners and a group of middle-class intellectuals and socialists formed the National Revolutionary Movement (MNR) that eventually forced a change in government. Unfortunately, the government of Major Gualberto Villarol proved just as brutal as its predecessor and forced the MNR underground. From 1946 to 1952, political instability gripped

The Marine Security Guard detachment in La Paz, Bolivia, poses for a photograph with the U.S. Navy's chief of naval operations. Left to right are MSgt. Robert Amacher, an unidentified Marine Security guard, Sergeant George Bader, Sergeant Robert Brown, and the chief of naval operations, Admiral William M. Fechteler (George A. Bader collection).

In a staged photograph, revolutionaries are poised to shoot it out with the Bolivian Army. MSgt. Bader noted that by the time this photograph was taken, "some of the Bolivian soldiers had already sided with the rebels" (George A. Bader collection).

Bolivia. The armed insurrection resulted in a decade of military rule in this land-locked Andean nation. Led by Victor Paz Estenssoro, a university professor at San Andres in La Paz, the MNR waged a relentless guerrilla war that culminated in the violence Master Sergeant Bader and his fellow security guards experienced during Holy Week of 1952.[23]

As the next decade and a half demonstrated, the revolt in La Paz, Bolivia, was but one of the many troubled spots in light of the post–World War II de-colonization period (1945–1974). The revolution in Bolivia and elsewhere, in fact, ushered in one of the most turbulent periods in American foreign policy in not only South America and Central America, but in Eastern Europe, the Middle East, Asia, and Africa.

Coups in Egypt, Jordan, Iran, Saudi Arabia, and Palestine

In defiance of Egyptian nationalists who had launched a wave of demonstrations, riots, and limited military engagements against British targets throughout the country, Great Britain announced in early January 1952 that until further notice, she would maintain its troops and colonial officials in both Egypt and the Sudan, "regardless of Egypt's unilateral denunciation of her international commitments." This announcement by the British government resulted in the outbreak of a serious riot between 1,500 British troops and Egyptians at Ismailia that resulted in the death of forty Egyptians.[24] The very next day, known as "Black Saturday," the

Egyptian capital, Cairo, "exploded" with riots and demonstrations against the British, foreigners, and authority in general (i.e., King Farouk I). The wave of damage ran into the millions of dollars as elements from the outlawed Muslim Brotherhood, fascists, socialists, and communists, as well as a little know group of Egyptian Army officers called the Revolutionary Command Council (RCC), led by Lieutenant Colonel Gamal Abd-al Nasser (and his assistant–Anwar Sadat), vied for power amidst the chaos that engulfed Egypt. In desperation, King Farouk appointed Ali Maher Pasha as his minister of the interior in order to restore security in the capital. Among other measures Mahar had the leader of the Young Egypt Movement (*Misr-al-Fatah*) and the Muslim Brotherhood arrested. This arrest made a tense situation even worse in a country on the verge of revolution.[25]

Eventually, on July 23, 1952, the civilian-led government in Egypt was overthrown in a *coup d'état* by Major General Muhammad Nagib. In a radio broadcast upon his assumption of power, General Nagib told the Egyptian people that "his group of officers sincerely believed that steps were necessary to inspire Egyptians with a new spirit and determination to go ahead and work toward fulfilling Egypt's national aspirations." Three days later after Nagib went before the Egyptian nation, King Farouk I abdicated the throne in favor of his infant son. After the appointment of a civilian-led cabinet under the former minister, Ali Maher, attempts were made to restore order and eliminate corruption. The Egyptian military, impatient with Maher, overthrew the civilian government and assumed control of the country in a military *coup d'état*.

While rioters aimed the bulk of their hostility toward the British and the Egyptian monarchy, some of the violence spread to the other embassies in Cairo. One such embassy was that of the United States. Sergeant Ronell Harwood recalled that he and his fellow Marine Security Guards had been warned of the distinct possibility of anti-foreign sentiment and potential violence. Sergeant Harwood stated that upon arriving at the airport in Cairo in October 1951: Sergeants McQueen, Greer and Harwood "were met at the airport by one of the Marines we were replacing. He immediately informed us that we would have to travel through Cairo to the Embassy by a round-about route as there was the distinct possibility we would meet the rioters. We did wonder what kind of a greeting this was, but climbed in the jeep and headed out. Needless to say, we made it really without incident."[26]

Sergeant Harwood stated that the Egyptians "really liked Americans," and could tell the difference between them and the other Westerners by the wide, rather "loud" neckties the Marine Security Guards wore off duty.

Despite the fact that the Egyptians held no animosity toward the Americans, the violence that swept Cairo nonetheless affected the U.S. Embassy in January 1952. Sergeant Harwood recalled that when "Black Saturday" occurred, Marine Security Guards could see the fires burning from the top of the U.S. Embassy and the USIA Building. The rioters, noted Harwood, burned every place (including American-owned) that had signs in English. The Marine sergeant noted that the Egyptian police and firemen, probably in sympathy with the rioters, refused to arrest them and just stood by and watched as the fires burned.[27]

Fearing that the rioters might turn their attention to the United States' and other embassies, Sergeant Harwood's staff noncommissioned officer in charge, Staff Sergeant Albers, "who was rather an imposing figure armed with a tommy gun,"[28] turned some rioters away when they reached the front gate of the embassy. Staff Sergeant Albers, who feared an assault on the U.S. Embassy, ordered the Marines to their assigned posts with their Marine Corps–issued shotguns and carbines. Harwood stated that shortly thereafter, the Egyptian Army moved in and things calmed down rather quickly.[29]

Marine Security Guards in the Middle East, 1956–1958

Egypt was not the only Middle East country to experience revolutionary turmoil during the 1950s. As the various Middle Eastern countries discarded the shackles of colonialism, socialists, communists, monarchists and soldiers all vied for power amidst the power vacuum created by Great Britain's withdrawal "east of Suez." Three such countries were Palestine, Iraq and Jordan. On October 7, 1956, two Marine Security Guards at the U.S. Consulate in Jerusalem held off an angry mob that attempted to force its way into the consulate. Amidst the shouts and shoving by the crowd into the consulate, Master Sergeant Bertrum Strickling and Corporal Thomas E. Rhodes were able to hold the angry crowd at bay until the Arab Legion arrived and dispersed it.[30]

Sergeant William D. Steeves, Jr., who served on Marine Security Guard Duty from May 1957 to December 1959, remembered a similar incident while on duty at the U.S. Embassy in Amman, Jordan. Sergeant Steeves' tour would be memorable due to the political instability that shook the region in light of the Suez Crisis and Second Arab-Israeli War in October 1956. Present at the annual Arab Army Day celebration held in Amman in early 1958 were King Hussein of Jordan and his cousin King Faisal of Iraq. Both monarchs were signatories to the recently formed Arab Federation, which was a direct response to the formation of the United Arab Republic (Egypt, Saudi Arabia, and Syria). The event was memorable, as it was the last meeting between the two monarchs in public; King Faisal was later overthrown and assassinated in a military coup led by General Abd-al-Karim Kassim in Baghdad on July 14, 1958.[31] Sergeant Steeves wrote that the "old tanks and armored vehicles" that rumbled past the reviewing stand where the two monarchs stood presented themselves as an excellent opportunity to stage a *coup d'état* when they turned the turrets toward the two monarchs to salute them.[32]

Not all the duty on post centered on the security of the embassy. Many assigned to Marine Security Guard duty took time to get to know the people and enjoy the many interesting facets of everyday life of their host country, which in Sergeant Steeves' case was in "the land of Aladdin." Sergeant Steeves recalled a humorous incident where he and another Marine Security Guard, Sergeant Donald C. Cook, were out in the desert and spotted some Bedouins with their "beautiful Arabian steeds." Steeves recalled that Sergeant Cook, a Texan, said to him, "Let's go horseback riding." Managing to convey to the Bedouins that they would like to ride their horses, the two Marines mounted the horses and shortly after that Steeves was "hanging on for dear life," as he recalled. With both Arabs and Sergeant Cook in hysterics laughing, they assisted Steeves in sitting upright in the saddle. With that the two Marines "kicked" the horse and both steeds took off at a manageable gallop. Recognizing that Sergeant Cook could ride, one of the Bedouins challenged him to a race. Eventually, the Bedouin, who now rode the horse Steeves had been riding, managed to beat Sergeant Cook in what his partner described as a "photo finish."[33]

Sergeant Steeves likewise recalled one day when he was on liberty in Amman in the Hotel Philadelphia that he met up with an Iraqi citizen named Kakhi who in "perfect harmony" sang the "Marines Hymn." Astonished that such a hymn would be popular in the Arab world, Steeves asked "Kakhi" where he had learned it. Kakhi replied that he was an Iraqi Air Force lieutenant and he had to "learn this song in flight school." Sergeant Steeves wrote that he was amazed in that "it struck me just how well known the USMC was around the world, especially out in the middle of nowhere, or so it seemed at the time."[34]

The Suez Crisis of 1956

The Middle East continued to be the scene of political unrest throughout the 1950s. Internal reaction to the immediate post-decolonization period was a series of coups, revolutions, and fears of imminent invasion either by the United States or, as in the case of Lebanon and Iraq, the Soviet Union. In October–November 1956, as Soviet tanks crushed the Hungarian freedom fighters in the streets of Budapest, both Great Britain and France sought to wrest control of the vital Suez Canal from Gamal Abdul Nassar, who had nationalized that strategically important waterway on 26 July 1956. In a three-pronged assault, led by Israel, which had invaded Egypt on October 29, British and French jets attacked Egyptian oilfields while British and French Marines and paratroopers landed to re-open the blocked Suez Canal (4 November 1956). The world seemed on the brink of a nuclear war as Soviet Premier Nikita Khrushchev threatened to launch atomic rockets against London and Paris. In order to defuse the situation, the secretary general of the United Nations called not only for the withdrawal of the British, French and Israeli troops but for an international police force to be sent to re-open the Suez Canal and restore order in Egypt. President Dwight D. Eisenhower, already faced with a tense situation in Hungary, ordered the evacuation of all Americans from Egypt.

On duty at the U.S. Embassy in Cairo was Sergeant Ed Vasgerdsian and seven other Marine Security Guards who were armed with a "single Smith & Wesson .38 caliber revolver with four rounds of ammo." Sergeant Vasgerdsian added that this was "our regulation issue back then [and] that was our official armament.... More weapons found in the vaults of the Army, Navy, and Air Force Attachés included a Thompson submachine gun, one carbine, and a couple of Springfield '03 rifle, all remnants of World War II. Judging by the condition of the ammunition, our personal shotguns would be more reliable." As the situation in Cairo continued to deteriorate, Sergeant Vasgerdsian recalled "plans were finalized to evacuate 1,300 Americans to Alexandria where the Navy's Sixth Fleet awaited. Evacuation also meant the relocation of the Marine Security Guard's Regional Office to Beirut, Lebanon."[35] Finally, Sergeant Vasgerdsian concluded that the evacuation had its interesting moments:

> The American Embassy became the living quarters for us and a skeleton force of Foreign Service men and women. Tension grew as British Canberra jets appeared over Egypt. The remaining embassy personnel, who may have been indifferent to us before, now suddenly treasured our presence, and Marines found eager Foreign Service Officers listening to weapons instructions from a kid who up until then was considered just a guard. Marines worked around-the-clock emptying mail pouches containing sensitive information and feeding them piecemeal into a fire.[36]

As the standoff between the British and French on one hand and Egyptians on the other deepened, President Nasser's regime severed all relations with the two former European colonial powers and demanded an immediate and unconditional withdrawal from Egyptian soil. Nasser likewise ordered an around-the-clock guard to ring the two European countries' embassies as well as to shut off all electrical power and deliveries of food. While water was still available, food supplies in the British embassy grew dangerously low. Sergeant Vasgerdsian recalled, "The Marines devised a plan to help ease their food shortage by heaving cans of food — including fruit and sardines — over the embassy wall," even as Egyptian soldiers and police guarded the exterior walls. Eventually, the Marines along with the rest of the embassy staff were evacuated to the Marine Security Guard's Regional Office located then in Beirut, Lebanon.[37]

By November 11, 1956, the situation had calmed so much that the Marines were able to return to the embassy in Cairo just in time to celebrate the Marine Corps Birthday. Despite the rather subdued atmosphere inside the U.S. Embassy, Sergeant Vasgerdsian stated that "the festivities were enjoyed by all ... people regardless of grade came ... and really let their hair down." Later, Ambassador Raymond E. Hare commended the Marines for their "outstanding loyalty and devotion to duty during the Suez Crisis"

Sergeant Vasgerdsian stated that as a result of the actions by the Marine Security Guards during the Suez Crisis, "We ... found among the Foreign Service Officers and staff a renewed appreciation for our presence." After the crisis atmosphere began to subside, duty inside the embassy returned to normal as Marine Security Guards conducted inspections of all staff offices and buildings for security violations, received and greeted visitors, dispatched government vehicles, handled diplomatic and military telegrams, controlled keys to all offices, burned classified information and accepted mail pouches from diplomatic couriers.

Marines in Beirut, Lebanon, 1958

The political instability that rocked the Middle East in the mid to late 1950s brought increased attention to the role of Marine Embassy Guards as an American Embassy's first line of defense. As Sergeant Steeves recalled, "At the height of the 1958 Middle East Crisis, the United States Marine Corps became more prominent and well known due to the news coverage (radio, we did not have television) of the landings (by Marines) in Lebanon."[38] Marines had been landed in Lebanon at the request of President Camille Chamoun, who had feared communist subversion from both Egyptian and Syrian agents who had been flown into his country in order to foment a revolution among the three political factions that existed in Lebanon.[39] With the brutal murder of King Faisal in Iraq by Brigadier General Abdel Karem Kassim in a *coup d'état*, President Dwight D. Eisenhower, at the advice of his military advisors, ordered the Marines of the 2d Provisional Force (Battalion Landing Teams [BLT] 1st Battalion, 8th Marines and the 2nd Battalion, 2d Marines) ashore, "in order to prevent Syrian or Egyptian forces from intervening in Lebanon." When the Marines landed in Beirut on July 15, 1958, their first task was to establish a defensive perimeter around Beirut International Airport. The next day, the 16th, the leathernecks attached to BLT 2/2 proceeded into the city itself, where they took up positions around the dock area and bridges, and furnished guards for the American Embassy and the Ambassador Robert McClintock's residence. As Steeves recalled, when news had reached the U.S. Embassy in Amman, Jordan, that the Marines had landed in Beirut and British paratroopers in Jordan, some anti–American demonstrations took place. In one instance, a bomb exploded near the U.S. Embassy in Amman, then located on Jebel Luebdih, directly across from Ambassador Mallory's residence on Jebel Amman. Steeves, who was on the night watch, recalled that shortly after the bomb had gone off the telephone rang, and the voice at the other end of the receiver said, "This is the Ambassador Mallory speaking, is my embassy still there?" Sergeant Steeves replied in the affirmative, "Yes Sir," and with that the ambassador said, "Thank you sergeant, good night."[40]

Expansion in the 1950s

During the 1950s the Marine Security Guard program expanded rapidly. Master Sergeant Rolland L. May recalled that many of the Marine Security Guard posts were three-man detachments. Assigned to the U.S. Consulate General in Madras, India, Master Sergeant May's duty was interesting and uneventful in a country made famous by British author Rudyard Kipling and others. Master Sergeant May wrote that after a long, tortuous journey, the Marines had been informed that they were to ship all of their uniforms home, as the Indian government forbade the Marines to wear their uniforms on duty. Also, the government of India would not allow the Marines to have firearms. May discovered upon arrival in Madras that the Indian government had provided the consulate with external security in the form of a detachment of Ghurkas, the legendary fighters from Nepal.

May remembered that his two years of duty in Madras were "extremely interesting," though proved to be "very routine." Master Sergeant May recalled that the only incident of note occurred when Ethel and Julius Rosenberg were executed for treason in the United States. The master sergeant remembered that in protest of the executions, "The Communist Party of India organized a demonstration against the U.S. Information Library, which was located on the ground level of the building in which the Consulate occupied the second floor. The demonstrators were able to break the glass windows before the employees were able to lower

The Marine Security Guard Detachment in Tegucigalpa, Honduras, poses with the Chargé d'Affaires, at the American Embassy in 1957. (Left to Right: Sgt. Lloyd Shank, Sgt. William McCain, Chargé d'Affaires Mr. John C. Pool, GySgt. Anton Hagan, SSgt. Harold Johnson, and Sgt. David Mall) (Sergeant Lloyd Shank collection).

The Marine Security Guard Detachment at the first Marine Corps Birthday Party held in Madras, India, November 1953. Left to right are TSgt. E.K. Minnick, SSgt. R.L. May, Cpl. B.W. Hackett and Cpl. T.C. Bunker (Sgt. Maj. R.L. May collection).

the protective steel shutters. Other than that, the rest of the action was outside and was handled by the local police."[41]

Apart from the riot staged by the Indian Communist Party, May stated that duty in Madras was routine with the annual event for Marine Embassy Guards being the Marine Corps Ball of 1953. Watches in the consulate were "long, eight hours on week-days and twelve hours on weekends." Duty consisted of standing watches at Post One and conducting security sweeps once the staff departed for the day. The Marines, in fact, were not officially known or listed as "Marines," but were, instead, referred to as "special assistants." May stated, "Apparently the Indians, having been dominated by the British for so long, apparently did not wish to acknowledge the presence of foreign military in their country."[42] In any event, May enjoyed his stay in Madras even though it was pretty routine. While in India, May developed a taste for the local dish of curry, a spicy meat that became the favorite of the entire Marine Security Guard detachment. They even hired a special cook to make this local delicacy at the Marine House.

Tom Stevens recalled that his duty as regional Marine security officer for Region 3 was just as interesting. Back then, Region 3 consisted of all U.S. embassies in Manila, Republic of the Philippines; Seoul, South Korea; Taipei, Taiwan; Rangoon, Burma (now known as Myanmar); Bangkok, Thailand; Djakarta, Indonesia; Saigon, Vietnam; and consulates in Hong Kong and Singapore. Headquartered in the U.S. Embassy in Manila, Stevens served under retired Fleet Admiral now Ambassador Raymond A. Spruance, the "fighting admiral" and commander of the U.S. 5th Fleet during World War II. Stevens remembered that dur-

Kilton, the Marine House in Madras, India, in 1953. The ground level was occupied by an officer from the U.S. Information Agency with his family. Marines occupied the apartment on the second level (Sergeant Major R.L. May collection).

ing the Marine Corps Birthday Ball of 1953, Ambassador Spruance gave an emotional speech as he recalled "his Marines" during the march across the Central Pacific during the war.[43]

Stevens' duties included fixed posts such as the front desk at Post One and roving patrols, and security checks and sweeps of the embassy and of the adjacent grounds. Stevens wrote that there "would occasionally be special assignments," such as providing security for the first Southeast Asia Treaty Organization Meeting in 1954, and the second one that was held in Bangkok, Thailand, in 1956. In particular, Stevens recalled the visit by then–Vice President Richard M. Nixon as he toured the Far East.[44]

On the island of Taiwan, where Chiang Kai-shek had established his Nationalist regime after being forced off the Chinese mainland by Mao Zedong's Communist armies, anti–American violence often placed Marine Security Guards in harm's way. As was often the case, both protestors and hopeful immigrants stormed the U.S. Consulate periodically in order to either protest U.S. policy toward Taiwan or in search of passports or visas to the United States. One such incident occurred when members of the Marine Security Guard Detachment at the U.S. Consulate in Taipei were faced with "a screaming mob of several thousand Chinese." The small Marine Security Guard, fearful that any show of force might result in either the death or wounding of the embassy staff, ordered the evacuation of the embassy. Unfortunately, rioters wounded a Marine Security Guard during the evacuation.[45]

Coups and Revolutions

Not all of Marine security guard duty was routine. As Staff Sergeant Lloyd E. Shank, who served on the Marine Security Guard program from January 1, 1956 to December 31, 1957, in Tegucigalpa, Honduras, noted, standing post in many developing countries could be extremely dangerous. Sergeant Shank recalled one such incident while on post in Tegucigalpa when on the night of July 31–August 1, 1956, rioters fired rounds from rifles and pistols in front of the U.S. Embassy located then on Quartel de San Francisco Street. Hearing gunshots, Sergeant Shank, alone in the embassy, as the ambassador was on vacation, looked about outside the front gate of the embassy. Much to his amazement there was not a soul to be found. Nonetheless, gunfire continued to fly through the front of the U.S. Embassy until finally Honduran police began patrolling the street outside the embassy grounds and airplanes could be heard buzzing overhead. Sergeant Shank later wrote that the disturbances had been part of what later turned out to the revolt of an infantry battalion stationed in the capital in an apparent *coup d'état*.

Not taking any chances, Sergeant Shank thought, "Something is definitely out of whack," and then drew an extra twelve rounds of .38 caliber ammunition and an M1 Carbine and twenty-round magazine from the embassy's armory. Gunfire that now included machine gun and sub-machine gun fire continued to rake the embassy. Looking over the balcony, Sergeant Shank recalled that he still could not see any targets,"[46] though he could hear the moans and mutterings of what turned out to be a man wounded. After the wounded man had been picked up by Honduran troops and placed in an ambulance, Sergeant Shank returned to his post and made a complete sweep of the embassy, where he found nothing disturbed. Sergeant Shank recalled that he then saw a Red Cross ambulance pick up two dead bodies that had been placed on the street in front of the embassy. At about 0340 that same morning Sergeant Shank then saw a six-man patrol heading down Quartel Street armed with five M-1 Garand and M1903 Springfield rifles. After phoning Master Sergeant Earl J. Payne, the detachment commander, and advising against a reinforcement of the embassy due to what Shank recalled was the "trigger-happy nature" of everyone shooting at everything that moves, Shank reported that "there is no way possible to get the other Guards into the Embassy without some or possibly all being casualties."[47] Shank likewise wrote that he continued to wear his flak jacket due to the gunfire that continued to hit the U.S. Embassy.

It was at about 4:30 A.M. that the Honduran minister of defense called the duty desk and inquired if there were any other Americans besides Shank inside the embassy, to which the Marine replied that he was the only one. The minister informed Shank that there had been some infiltration by the opposition into the Quartel and that the Honduran police and military were retaking the street by force. He also informed Shank that the Honduran military intended to flush the rebels out with mortars, tear gas, and possibly low-level air strikes. Shank wrote that at about 0630 a 1.5-inch shell landed in the patio of the embassy emitting tear gas. Shank recalled, "These shells were certainly made to do their job. Being no air circulation in the building it is raising heck with me. The front of the flak jacket is wet from my tears. Personally, I prefer the gas chamber in Boot Camp."

Sergeant Shank remembered that by 8:15 A.M. Honduran troops and police had retaken the Quartel. The Honduran police had rounded up many of the rebels and brought them handcuffed and in leg irons into the Park Valle in front of the Quartel. Shank recalled that many of the prisoners begged their captors to shoot them, as many of them did not wish to be confined to the prison located in the capital a few blocks away as it had enjoyed a notorious reputation for its cruelty.

In a letter of appreciation to the Commandant of the Marine Corps General Randolph McC. Pate, the U.S. Chargé d'Affaires Mr. John C. Pool commended Sergeant Shank for his "coolness, calmness, composure and good humor" during the night of July 31–August 1, 1956. In his letter to General Pate, Mr. Pool commended

> his coolness, calmness, composure and good humor which he consistently maintained even though he had some bad moments, as when the mortar fire came dangerously close, and when a tear gas grenade exploded in the Embassy patio. Not only did he carry out admirably his primary duty of screening the Embassy, but also he observed and reported usefully on events outside the premises. He took it all in his stride, showed great self-reliance, and conducted himself in the highest tradition of the Marine Corps.[48]

Mr. Pool likewise noted in his commendation of Sergeant Shank that the British minister to Honduras, Mr. Geoffrey Jackson, who talked to Sergeant Shank twice on the night of the revolt, had included his praise of the Marine's performance in an attached letter. Mr. Jackson was very much "impressed" by Sergeant Shank's keeping him "up-to-date" of the ongoing revolt and did so with "a clarity, calmness and good humor that in the circumstances I found quite admirable." The British minister stated that Sergeant Shank clearly deserved the warm commendation from his superiors for his actions during the revolt in Tegucigalpa on 31 July–1 August 1956, as he could not reach anyone inside the U.S. Embassy except for the lone Marine on duty.[49] In his commendation General Pate praised the newly promoted Staff Sergeant Shank for the "calm efficient manner in which you performed your duties this tense situation."[50]

The End of an Era: The Coup d'État Against Syngman Rhee

In another *coup*, Master Sergeant W.V. "Bill" East, who served in the Marine Security Guard program from 1959 to 1962, had been assigned to his first posting at the U.S. Embassy in Seoul, Korea, in 1959. For Master Sergeant East and his fellow Marine Security Guards, the highlight of their duty in Korea came when President Dwight D. Eisenhower, as part of his Far East tour in 1960, visited the U.S. Embassy and chatted with the Marines. Master Sergeant East was on duty in Seoul when President Syngman Rhee was overthrown in a military *coup d'état*. Master Sergeant East recalled that shortly after the coup all Marines serving at the U.S. Embassy were asked to leave the country.

Part of a twelve-man Marine Security Guard Detachment assigned to the U.S. Embassy in Seoul, Master Sergeant East recalled that duty there went well until students began protesting against the authoritarian rule of President Syngman Rhee and the other right-wing politicians. Master Sergeant East remembered that one of the first duties the Marine Embassy Guards were given was to protect the Korean vice president, Chung He Pak from the students.[51] As for the riots that followed, Master Sergeant East recalled that the Marines and embassy personnel oftentimes were caught in the crossfire as police and students fought it out on the streets surrounding the U.S. Embassy in Seoul. As Master Sergeant East stated, knowledge of escape routes and avenues in which to safely evacuate the embassy would have proved extremely useful, had the U.S. ambassador ordered an evacuation. Recounting the protests and overthrow of President Rhee, "Top" East wrote that:

> The compound in which the Embassy personnel lived, including the Marines was approximately 10–12 blocks from the embassy. Normally, we were shuttled back and forth between the compound and the embassy by a Korean national. When the rioting began, it was impossible to move

in a vehicle anywhere. All civilian employees were restricted to the living compound, which was protected by Korean police. The only persons allowed/required to leave the compound were the Marines, and some select embassy officers ... Fortunately, we had been in Seoul long enough to know some back routes to and from the embassy and the compound. Most of the time during the riot, it was very violent, warfare between the police and students. Often we were caught in crossfire, and had to jump over the walls for our own safety. These riots lasted about a week, until Sygmun Rhee left the presidential palace in utter disgrace.[52]

According to Master Sergeant East, the rioting continued even after Rhee stepped down. As Vice President Pak left the U.S. Embassy compound in an official limousine, students surrounded his car and dragged both the vice president and his driver out of the vehicle and beat both of them to death. The students, still not satisfied, jumped on top of the car until it was "no more than three feet high." Two days after the death of Vice President Pak and his driver, the Security Officer and the Marine detachment commander informed the Marine Security Guards that due to their involvement in protecting the Vice President they "had only 24 hours" to pack their belongings and leave the country." Doing as they were ordered, the Marines hastily packed, leaving behind clothes still at the laundry and tailor shops.

Retired Central Intelligence Agent Peer de Silva, who had been assigned to the U.S. Embassy in Seoul, recalled that during the coup against President Rhee, the Marine Security Guards played an extremely important role in maintaining order in the embassy amidst the violence and uncertainty spawned by the coup. De Silva recalled that the military officers and South Korean officials maintained a steady flow into the U.S. Embassy, a factor that kept the Marine Security Guards who were on duty at Post One "very busy." The former CIA agent recalled one incident when Captain Pak Chung Gyu, a spokesman for the coup leaders (which came from the South Korean Army) appeared at the entrance of the embassy to discuss the reaction of the U.S. government to the coup against the aging president. De Silva wrote that the Marine Security Guard on duty phoned him to report that, "a ROK[53] Army captain with my name and card was there and wanted to see me right away. I told the Marine to send him up but was told the man was armed. I said to tell him to leave his gun and come on up. Two or three minutes later there was a knock on my door. There stood a marine escort and Captain Pak Chung Gyu."[54] De Silva noted that caution and wariness with which the Marine Security Guard used when he turned over the captain's pistol to him before he departed the embassy.[55]

After a brief period of duty at the U.S. Embassy in Tokyo and Manila in the Philippines, Headquarters Marine Corps reassigned Master Sergeant East and three other Marine Security Guards from the Seoul detachment to the U.S. Embassy in Saigon, Republic of Vietnam. Master Sergeant East recalled that while in Saigon during the days before the large-scale U.S. commitment to defend that country against Communist aggression, "We endured several anti–American demonstrations, with one bombing in the Consular Section." Fourteen years later, Master Sergeant East was present in Saigon as a member of an EOD (Explosives, Ordnance and Demolition) team assigned to the U.S. Embassy in Saigon prior to the evacuation in April 1975.[56]

A Revolution in Budapest, Hungary, October 1956

By late 1953, the death of Soviet leader Josef Stalin (March 5, 1953) and the end of the Korean War brought about a slight relaxation or "thaw" in the tensions aroused by the onset of the Cold War between the United States and the Union of Soviet Socialist Republics. In the power struggle that followed in the Kremlin among Stalin's heirs was the foment of nationalism in the Soviet Empire in Eastern Europe. "While none of these events [revolutions] led to disintegration" of the rigid Stalinist system emplaced in Eastern Europe at the end of World War II, they nonetheless led to three separate uprisings, in East Germany (1953), Poland (1956), and by far the most serious one, in Hungary in 1956.[57] It was in Hungary that the rebels actually succeeded for several days in shaking off Soviet rule. Also, it was in Hungary that Marine Security Guards played a vital role in the defense of the U.S. Embassy as the Hungarian patriots and Soviet soldiers and their Communist allies fought each other in the streets of Budapest in mid–October 1956.

The Hungarian Revolution started, ironically, as a peaceful demonstration by Hungarians protesting the pro–Stalinist government of Stalin-Rakosi and Erno Gero on October 23, 1956, inspired in large part by the recently concluded Polish uprising (October 1956) that forced the Kremlin to liberalize its strict controls over Poland. When pro-government troops and the demonstrators began battling each other in the streets of Budapest, Soviet tanks and armored cars "joined the battle and restored order." As the envoys of Soviet leader Nikita Khrushchev, Anastas Mikoyan and Mikhail Suslov rushed to the Hungarian capital to restore not only order but also to prevent further bloodshed, the Hungarian Communist Party elevated two of its members — Imre Nagy and Janos Kadar — to initiate a series of reforms that liberalized the press, disbanded the hated secret police, and created a coalition government that included non–Communists. Repudiating the terms of the recently signed collective defense pact known as the "Warsaw Pact" and membership in the Soviet bloc, the Hungarians held out hope that the United Nations would prevent the Soviet Union from intervening to restore its tight control of their country.[58]

Both Mikoyan and Suslov arrived amidst what was the brief taste of freedom Hungarians would not know again until the collapse of the Soviet Union in 1991. Determined not to allow Hungary to be the first "socialist" country to defect to the West, even if they had declared themselves to be neutral in the ongoing East-West ideological struggle, the Soviet leaders deemed it necessary for Soviet troops to intervene in order to restore socialism in Hungary. First of all, the Soviets recognized Janos Kadar as Hungary's new leader and then responded favorably to his request for Soviet troops to smash the "sinister forces of reaction" and to "restore order and calm."[59] Acting upon Kadar's request to restore order, Soviet tanks, infantrymen, and armored cars rolled across the borders of Hungary from all points north and east in order to snuff out this rebellion. Anticipating only strong-worded rebukes and condemnations from the West, Soviet soldiers and pro-Communist forces battled the Hungarian freedom fighters as the rest of the world, distracted by events in Egypt,[60] watched helplessly and anxiously. Despite being out-numbered and ill-equipped to stand up to tanks and armored personnel carriers, the Hungarian freedom fighters fought the Soviets and their allies for several days starting on November 3, in a fight that became not only very bloody but a house-to-house, street-to-street duel. As the fighting raged outside the American Embassy, the Marine Security Guards, led by Master Sergeant Wade H. "Lucky" Ducksworth, had a first hand view of the brutality employed by units of the Soviet Army in suppressing the rebellion. As the fighting grew more intense, the leathernecks continued to maintain a close watch over the embassy and its grounds.

Two of the Marine Embassy Security Guards, retired Marine Chief Warrant Officer 4 G.J. Bolick and Sergeant E. Parauka, who had a ringside seat, recalled with much clarity and detail the events prior to, during and after the Hungarian Revolution (November 3–8, 1956).

Their reflections illustrate the duties and responsibilities as well as the dangers Marine faced on embassy duty during the Cold War.

Chief Warrant Officer G.J. Bolick recalled that the demonstrators began their protest "arm-in-arm" with members of the Hungarian Army who had been posted throughout the city to maintain order. On their way to Parliament Square, the demonstrators chanted slogans, sang the Hungarian national anthem, and waved banners and Hungarian flags (minus the hated Communist emblem). The crowds, Bolick observed, ended up in Parliament Square, where they remained and continued to protest until about 6:00 P.M., when they began to disperse for the evening. Sergeant Bolick recalled that events now began to happen very fast as the protestors once again returned to Parliament Square. After being directed by Master Sergeant Ducksworth to meet with him at the American Legation, about seven blocks from where the Marine security guards were quartered, about 8 P.M. that evening, Sergeant Bolick had to pass through Parliament Square. Here, the Marine sergeant he saw Imre Nagy standing on a balcony overlooking the square, which by this time had once again filled with literally thousands of people, and asking that "they disperse, be calm, and to restrain themselves."[61] Attempting to gain the attention of his countrymen, Imre Nagy yelled out "Comrades," to which someone in the crowd shouted back, "no more comrades, no more communism!"

Bolick remembered that about 9:45 P.M. someone called the legation desk and stated that a crowd of about 10,000 Hungarians had once again gathered in Stalin Square and pulled down the icon of icons — Stalin's statue — from its pedestal. Events now turned ugly as "we heard weapons being fired about 10:00 P.M., we were to learn later these shots originated from Magyar Radio, supposedly, these were the first shots fired in the Hungarian Revolution of 1956." Gunner Bolick wrote that "the remainder of the night was filled with sounds of firefights" between the insurgents and pro-government forces in most sections of the city.[62] Turning on the radio to monitor the events in the streets, Bolick wrote that a situation report being read indicated that heavy fighting had broken out between the dissidents and the AVH (Hungarian Secret Police). By this time members of the AVH became targets of the protestors; the American Legation officer noticed that several police vehicles, old second-hand Buicks and Pontiacs used by the AVH to follow foreign diplomats about the city, had been overturned on their sides. Policemen likewise tore off their red stars and emblems identifying themselves as members of this despised police force. As the early morning hours progressed the fighting in Budapest became more intense as a full-scale war broke out between the insurgents and the pro-government forces.

By the dawn of the 24th, Soviet tanks, infantry carriers, and troops had rolled into the city and were engaging the dissidents in pitched fire fights, block to block, building to building. Soviet gunners fired indiscriminately into the crowds and at the surrounding buildings, including the U.S. Legation. The firing was so severe that Anton Nyerges, one of the legation staff officers, found several of the shirts hanging in his closet riddled with Soviet 12.7 mm bullet holes.

As for the protestors in Parliament Square, Sergeant Bolick recalled that the scene was "catastrophic" as the Soviet soldiers then turned their attention and weapons on the Hungarians chanting against the Russian invasion. On March 25, there was a loud explosion in the square that at the time was filled with Hungarians. Sergeant Bolick stated, "It was reported that an estimated 1,000 people were in Parliament Square when the ordnance charge detonated and the Soviets started firing their weapons. No official statistics were published regarding the number of people killed or wounded, but survivors stated that the majority [in the square] did not survive the attack."[63]

Bolick and his fellow Marine Security Guards recalled that during the "Five Days of Freedom" that began on March 29, most of the public utilities (gas, electric, telephone, and water) continued to work despite the devastation that had occurred (which according to Bolick was near total). While the Marines were permitted to go about the city, they were required to travel in pairs and then for no more than two hours at a time. There was very little looting despite the fact that store windows had been broken and buildings gutted. Perhaps the most telling sounds came not from machine guns or explosions but from the church bells that continued to ring throughout those five days. As Bolick wrote, "The church bells had a wonderful sound, the sound of Hope for Hungary."[64]

During the first few days of the revolution, in order to prevent being hit by a stray round or mistaken for Hungarian Freedom Fighters, several of the Marines were moved from their apartment complex into the legation until March 29. Another Marine Security Guard, Sergeant Edward R. Parauka, recalled that for those who remained in the apartment complex, the situation was very dangerous. Ordered to remain inside the apartment until further notice by Master Sergeant Ducksworth, the Marine guards settled in as Russian tanks and armored vehicles parked right in front of the apartment building (that had an American flag flying outside) apparently searching for snipers atop the surrounding buildings. Sergeant Parauka remembered on the morning of the 26th, after the Marines made their morning coffee, they then went out onto the balcony to observe the night's activities and had noticed that the Soviet tanks had positioned themselves between the buildings with their crews looking curiously up at the Marines. By this time, the Marines put on a Glenn Miller album on the phonograph and sat, with their coffee, on the balcony looking down at the Russians who were looking up at them. This situation remained until snipers began shooting at the Russians. Sergeant Parauka recalled:

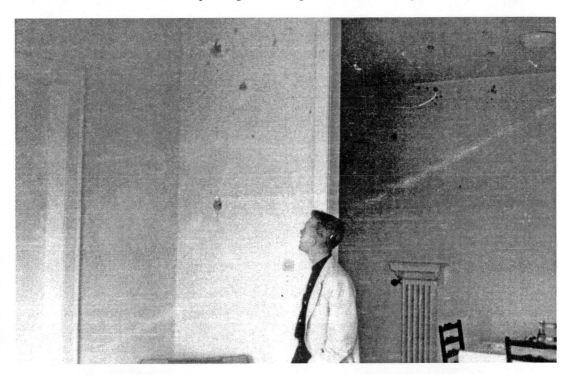

Sergeant Gene Comer assesses the damage to the second floor of the Marine Security Guard apartment caused by the Soviet attack on October 25, 1956 (U.S. Marine Security Guard photograph).

Just as we were getting comfortable with each other, over our heads, on top of our apartment building, some Hungarian Freedom Fighters started shooting down on the troops below us. All hell broke loose! The young Soviet soldiers, kids just like us, having their coffee and chow around their vehicles, jumped quickly back in, and manned their positions. The armored personnel carrier just below us, about 25 feet or so, maybe more, was getting ready to fire. One of them climbed into the forward turret with the machine gun, and before he could traverse the damn thing upwards toward the roof, started firing right away. Which meant, when we saw what was likely to happen, that we had better get inside right away and hit the deck.... [W]e got inside just in the nick of time. The bullets came flying in just above our butts as we lay on the floor. Looking up we could see the rounds going into the walls and ceiling. Jesus, that was scary![65]

Sergeant Parauka recalled that the firing didn't last very long, possibly about five minutes or less. Nonetheless, some of the rounds, incendiary mostly, caused the sofa inside the legation to catch on fire, which the Marines quickly put out with fire extinguishers. The Marines then gathered what civilians there were in the legation and ordered them into the cellar until the firing stopped. In fact, the Marines remained inside the legation for about four to five days until given permission to return to their apartments. Sergeant Parauka whimsically recalled that during those five days he ate quite a few "peanut butter and jelly sandwiches" as he and his fellow security guards burned classified material and stood regular guard duty.[66]

Walking among the Hungarians after the Russians briefly pulled out of Budapest, Sergeant Parauku recalled that Hungarians, with the help of many Hungarian soldiers who defected to the Freedom Fighters, were "proud they kicked the Russians out." Hungarians would stop and ask the Marines, "When are the American soldiers coming to help them win the whole

During the uprising in Budapest, Hungary, in October-November 1956, Freedom Fighters pose with Sergeants G.J. Bolick, Gene Comer and Edward Parauka. The man on the front row to the far left is holding a bottle of gasoline, which the Freedom Fighters used to destroy Soviet tanks (U.S. Marine Security Guard photograph).

country, not just Budapest?" Parauka and Bolick acknowledged that the freedom fighters held onto the belief throughout the ordeal that the United States' military would come to their assistance. Parauka sadly said, "I had no answer for them." President Eisenhower refused to send in American or NATO troops to assist the Hungarians in their attempt to free their country from the Soviet Union.

In the early morning hours of November 4, 1956, the Marines inside their apartment could hear the loud rumble of tanks, trucks, and armored personnel carriers in the streets below. The Soviets had come back, as Sergeant Parauka said, "with a vengeance."[67] Within a few days, the Hungarian Revolution had been brutally suppressed as Soviet troops and Freedom Fighters fought it out in the streets and alleys, with the end result being the restoration of Communist rule in Hungary.

The last act of the Hungarian Revolution, however, was not over. Sergeant Bolick remembered that while making his initial checks of the security points at the U.S. legation, as he arrived at the last point, he noticed from outside the main door a lone Hungarian armored car approaching and then stopping. Leaving the vehicle were two Hungarian Army officers escorting two men, both in clerical robes, toward the entrance to the U.S. Legation. The order came down to Sergeant Bolick, "Let them in." After reaching the door the two Hungarian Army officers waited as the two clerics stepped inside the Legation — sovereign U.S. territory — and then departed. One was a priest, and the other one was Cardinal Mindszenty. As Sergeant Bolick approached the two men, Master Sergeant Ducksworth yelled down to the Marine, "Do your duty." He greeted the Cardinal and the priest. Sergeant Bolick saluted the two Hungarian officers, who returned the salute, then did an about face and departed, leaving the two clerics standing at the door of the U.S. Legation.

After the two men entered the legation, the staff of the legation knelt down to kiss the cardinal's ring and greeted Monsignor Turcsanyi, the other cleric. Mr. Wailes, the U.S. minister, then read from a telegram handed to him moments before from the State Department in Washington, D.C., to the cardinal and legation staff that, "the United States had granted asylum to Cardinal Mindszenty."[68] Escorting the cardinal to the legation's third floor, Minister Wailes informed him that the office and its two adjoining rooms were now his home. Shortly after the cardinal had settled in, a Soviet T-55 tank appeared on the sidewalk in front of the legation's main entrance door with Soviet troops now walking guard duty on the legation front and side street sidewalks. At 1100, Radio Budapest announced that the Soviet Army intended to storm the legation and take the Cardinal into custody and intern the staff.

There arose the question that if captured, would the Marine Security Guards, who were in civilian attire, be afforded protection under the Geneva Convention or rules governing diplomatic personnel? Sergeant Bolick stated that the Marines realized there would not be enough time to retrieve their uniforms in the apartment building several blocks away, "even if we could have gotten past the Soviet guards at our front door." Fearing capture and possible execution as spies, the Marines "prepared for a last ditch stand." Sergeant Bolick recalled that the Marines gathered up all the arms they could muster. This included "six .38 caliber revolvers, two AK-47 (post–World War II vintage) assault weapons with four clips of ammunition (someone had traded a policeman a carton of Winston cigarettes for the AK's and ammunition), one meat cleaver and two knives."[69] Sergeant Bolick stated that the Marines had developed "a grand plan" in dealing with a possible Russian intrusion into the legation. Bolick said, "When a Soviet soldier presented himself at our front door, a Marine guard would open an inner glass window panel flanking the door, so a Russian speaking Legation official could tell the soldier we were on United States soil and they could not enter."[70]

Monsignor Turcsanyi, who spoke fluent English, met with the Marine Security Guards and thanked them for their protection and said that both he and the cardinal were more concerned about the safety of the Marines and other Americans than their own well-being. After insuring for the safety and comforts of Cardinal Mindszenty, Monsignor Turcsanyi made three unsuccessful attempts to leave the U.S. Legation for Vienna. On the fourth try and escorted by a Hungarian-speaking American, the monsignor was eventually captured by Soviet and Hungarian border guards and later executed by the government of Janos Kadar.[71]

Embassy Duty in Germany in the 1950s

The "Cold War" affected Marine Embassy Guards throughout Western Europe and Asia during the 1950s. As tensions between the United States and the USSR increased, security at U.S. embassies and other diplomatic posts became even more important. Even in posts far removed from the two armies facing each other across "Checkpoint Charlie" in Berlin and along the West German–Czechoslovakian border, Marine Security Guards maintained their readiness to respond to any emergency.

Sergeant William "Bill" Owens and his fellow Marine Security Guards were among the first Marines to stand duty first in Brussels, Belgium (February 1949 to April 1950), and later at the U.S. Embassy, Stockholm, Sweden (April 1950 to April 1952). Sergeant Owens, who entered the MSG program during its inception, trained at Fox Company, then under the command of Captain Sartor, and his staff of a lieutenant, a first sergeant, and three Marine clerks. After receiving instruction in diplomatic security, customs and courtesies, and weapons familiarization at the Marine Base at Quantico, headquarters posted Sergeant Owens to the U.S. Embassy in Bogota, Colombia. Switching posts with another Marine due to the latter's inability to pass a physical for the Belgian Embassy assignment, Sergeant Owens reported to the U.S. Embassy in Brussels and took up his duties as a Marine Security Guard. Sergeant Owens and the other leathernecks assigned to the embassy[72] reported directly to the embassy's security officer, Mr. Anderson, who gave Owens an extensive briefing as to the duties and responsibilities of the Marine detachment.

Sergeant Owens recalled that upon arriving in Belgium he discovered that the physical security there was the responsibility of civilian guards made up of ex–World War II U.S. Army soldiers who had married Belgium women during the war and remained in Europe at the conclusion of the war. Shortly thereafter, Marine Security Guards set up a watch schedule "to begin standing guard duty in tandem with our civilian counterparts. After each Marine had stood indoctrination watches, approximately two each, the Embassy Guard took over the responsibilities for the physical security of the Embassy."[73]

Sergeant Owens noted that the main task of the Marines every day was to insure that no classified material remained out on the desks of the embassy staff. The U.S. Embassy in Brussels, located on the second and third floors of the Shell Building, presented a challenge to the Marines who stood at Post One. After the embassy staff left for the day, the Marines on duty had the oftentimes routine task of observing everything on or near their post through a locked and barred gate. Owens stated, "To guard against any surreptitious entry," the Marines on duty constantly patrolled the two floors of the U.S. Embassy in order to prevent any unlawful intrusion. "It wasn't long after the arrival that the Marine Guard was functioning effectively in achieving our mission in Belgium."[74]

Sergeant Owens recalled that a frequent visitor to the U.S. Embassy was Ambassador-at-Large Robert Murphy. With the onset of the Cold War and the formation of the North Atlantic Treaty Organization (NATO) in 1949, Sergeant Owens stated, "Ambassador Murphy, at the time, was probably the highest level trouble-shooter in the Department of State." Owens attributed the bulk of Ambassador Murphy's visits to the formation of the NATO headquarters in Brussels.[75]

While the duties in Belgium were primarily of a routine nature, Owens recalled that the Marines kept daily records of all the nightly patrols during non-working hours. Each morning the embassy security officer met with the Marines on duty for the past twenty-four hours in order to discuss new orders and problems that may have arisen during that period of duty. Owens remembered that there were incidents and disturbances, usually carried out by individuals "trying to call attention to themselves, create an incident in the Embassy, or seeking to promote a political cause."[76]

Sergeant Owens remembered that the first serious incident occurred six to eight months after the Marine Embassy Guards had arrived in Brussels when tensions flared between the two principal Belgian political factions, the Wallons and the Flemish peoples. Owens recalled that both groups blustered and made inflammatory speeches that amounted to very little in terms of open violence. Despite the absence of violence, Sergeant Owens recalled that the U.S. Army's attaché to the Belgian Embassy contacted him and offered to issue the Marine guards Thompson submachine guns. The embassy staff likewise briefed the Marine Guards that there was a possibility of riots or demonstrations.

At the height of this internal political crisis, Owens remembered, the local Communist Party organized a series of demonstrations and protests in front of the U.S. Embassy. This prompted the ambassador to recall all of the Marine Embassy Guards. Sergeant Owens wrote, "Posts were manned throughout the Embassy to provide a 100% security alert." After a second day of demonstrations, the protestors demanded a meeting with the U.S. ambassador. Sergeant Owens recalled that a compromise between the ambassador and the demonstrators was agreed upon, whereby "Arrangements were made for only one of the demonstrators to visit the Embassy proper. This person was allowed entry and visited with an Embassy representative. The next day, the communist newspaper carried a report of this visit."[77] Sergeant Owens recalled that besides describing the contents of the meeting with the embassy representative, the newspaper also carried "the description of a big, tough, security type individual present when the Communist representative entered the Embassy lobby." Owens said that the "big, tough, security type individual" was Marine Security Guard George Netio, who was on duty at the time of the meeting. After several more incidences of anti–American violence (mostly intimidation and harassment) calm prevailed among the two factions, and the country returned to normal.

Being a young Marine security guard duty in a Communist-bloc nation brought with it not only the excitement of duty in a foreign country but certain risks. Among these risks was the fact that their very symbolic presence as representatives of the United States made them vulnerable to exploitation by the host government. As the Cold War grew more intense toward the late 1950s, the KGB, the Soviet secret police, targeted the Marine Security Guards as a means of not only penetrating U.S. embassies in order to gain access to U.S. intelligence information, but also to bring discredit on the leathernecks standing watch over these installations. Just how vulnerable the Marines were came to light in 1959 when ten Marine security guards "were sent home after a Polish defector charged they had had been compromised by women controlled by the Polish intelligence service." While it was never established that the embassy's security was damaged by these alleged compromises, it was clear that the Soviet-controlled foreign intelligence services located throughout Eastern Europe had specifically targeted the Marines in their main intelligence-gathering efforts.[78]

Duty in Europe and Asia in the 1950s

Marine Security Guard duty in Europe during the 1950s had its lighter moments too. Many young Marines were able to see a part of the world that their fathers and grandfathers had seen in a much different role. In November 1955, Marine Security Guards attached to the U.S. Embassy in Paris, France, participated in a ceremony at the U.S. Military Cemetery located at Camp des Loges, Chateau Thierry, where 2,280 American Marines and soldiers lay buried. In a solemn ceremony commemorating the heroics of both U.S. Marines and soldiers in the fighting in the Aisne-Marne sector during the First World War, Marines attached to the U.S. Embassy in Paris honored their fallen comrades with a wreath-laying ceremony. As a lone bugler played taps with the entire Marine Security Guard detachment, commanded by First Lieutenant James Tomlin, at "present arms," two Marines brought forth an enormous wreath and solemnly placed it in front of the American Memorial.

Oftentimes, Marine Security Guards, such as Sergeant (later Lieutenant Colonel) William

During a wreath laying ceremony, an honor guard of U.S. Marines stationed at the U.S. Embassy in Paris and European Command presents arms at Camp des Loges at the American Military Cemetery in the late 1950s (courtesy U.S. Marine Corps).

C. Curtis, had the opportunity to meet with and assist American tourists that either wandered into a U.S. embassy or consulate or greeted them in their native language. One such encounter occurred with Sergeant Curtis while he was taking a break at the U.S. Embassy in Rome on a Sunday in 1962.

> On that particular day, as I was standing outside briefly enjoying the sun and watching the hustle and bustle of the Via Veneto, I noticed a man and a woman — obviously American tourists. They hesitantly walked past the CPS guards and slowly approached me. I, of course, was wearing Marine modified blues ... white barracks cover with glittering Brasso'ed gold Marine insignia. The equally brilliant tie clasp, and waist plate reflected the sunlight. Khaki colored long sleeved shirt and royal blue trousers with scarlet stripe. Attached to the snow white 4" wide belt was a highly shined black holster with .38 caliber Smith & Wesson pistol inside.
>
> It was pretty evident that these two senior citizens from my native land had no idea who, or even what, I was. I politely waited for them to get close enough for me to ask if I might be of some assistance. As they neared me, I could see the lady was about to speak, so I remained silent. The couple stopped, quickly, looked around ... taking in the imposing Embassy, the American Flag, the Great Seal of the United States with the words around the eagle, "Embassy of the United States of America," and back to me ... and then she asked those words which are still crystal clear to me even after all these years ... Excuse me, do you speak English?[79]

Not all of Marine Security Guard duty was spent around the embassy or in conducting official ceremonies. Marines were encouraged, whenever and wherever possible, to visit the sites and talk with the peoples many of them had only read or heard about as teenagers or from veterans who had served in Europe during the Second World War. Staff Sergeant Vernon A. Ogletree of Union Point, Georgia, was able to chat with a French gendarme in front of the Eiffel Tower in Paris, France. Other Marine embassy guards, such as Private First Class James W. Duvall, who served in Port Lyautey, had the opportunity during a visit to Rabat, Morocco, to watch the elaborate changing of the guard at the royal palace.

Besides the numerous sightseeing opportunities, Marines likewise had the chance to taste the culinary delights of their host countries. As was the case with Master Sergeant Rolland L. May, Marines found the food not too different or exotic than American cuisine. Sergeant Bill Owens recalled that during off duty hours, the Marine Security Guards frequented "Moms," a local restaurant that served "entrecôte and pomme frites" or "steak and fries" to the hungry leathernecks. Sergeant Owens wrote that "Moms" was a popular gathering place for the large American community in Brussels. Besides serving the best food in Brussels, it "served some of the best beer in the world."[80]

Sports also dominated the off-duty time. Master Sergeant East recalled that while assigned to the U.S. Embassy in Saigon, the Republic of Vietnam, the Marines' fast-pitch softball team won the Far East Championship for 1961. Also, Master Sergeant East, himself an avid rugby fan, played on the French rugby team.

Protestors in Rangoon, Burma, February 1961

In Burma, U.S. policy focused on support of the remnants of the Koumingtang (KMT — Nationalist Chinese) Army where it battled the Chinese Communist forces near the borders of the Shan state of Kentung along the Laos-Thailand border. Burmese students waged sit-down strikes and protests in front of the U.S. Embassy. United States–Burmese relations were further strained when Burmese troops shot down a Chinese-manned American airplane over Burmese territory ferrying arms and men to the KMT troops. Already walking a political tightrope between Beijing and Washington, the opposition party in Burma, the AFPFL,[81] forced the government of U Nu to issue formal protests to both Washington and the United Nations. In anticipation of trouble, the U.S. Embassy in Rangoon dismissed its staff at noon on 21 February 1961, leaving only a skeletal staff of mostly Americans behind.[82] The demonstration, led by the Rangoon University Students Union and sanctioned by the local police, was one of Burma's worst riots since the end of colonization in 1948. The focus of the rioters centered on U.S. assistance to the renegade KMT troops where the political opposition and U Nu government's policies remained steadfastly opposed to U.S. assistance to Chiang Kai-shek's ousted Nationalist troops.[83]

As police surrounded the demonstrators, the students managed to force their way to the American Embassy on Merchant Street, near Sule Pagoda Road and Barr Street in Rangoon. Here, a wall of baton-waving and fire hose-wielding policemen greeted the demonstrators and tossed tear gas bombs to break up the protestors. By 3:15 P.M., the demonstrators broke through the police barricades and attacked the embassy. Once inside the compound, the students smashed every window facing Merchant Street. Meanwhile, the staff who had remained inside made their way to the second floor of the building as the Marine guards inside took precautions to destroy the important documents should the rioters enter the building itself. At the time, a Marine sergeant, corporal, and lance corporal as well as a half-dozen Marines stood ready to repel the invaders.[84] After a tense stand-off, the police in Rangoon regained control of the situation outside the U.S. Embassy, though not before two people were killed and 53 wounded, mainly protestors, in the melee with the police. The Marine Embassy Guard stood by its posts, watched and waited anxiously as the Burmese army and local police eventually restored order, and enforced a dusk to dawn curfew in the city.

The Lighter Side of Marine Security Guard Duty

There were, of course, humorous moments on embassy duty. A lonely embassy or consulate at night oftentimes produced imaginary as well as real enemies. Sergeant George H. Morrow recalled one such incident while standing watch at the American Consulate in Stuttgart, Germany, in the summer of 1957. Sergeant Morrow remembered that even during the summer the American Consulate, situated in the Bavarian Alps, could be a cold, uninviting place, a glass and steel structure that made all kinds of noises as the temperatures changed from night to day. Sergeant Morrow compared the American Consulate to living in the desert and recalled that "the changes in temperature resulted in a rather noisy place in late night and early morning hours."[85]

Since Sergeant Morrow was the "new guy" on the Marine Security Guard detail, the detachment commander, Master Sergeant Joseph Mariotti, assigned him to the "graveyard shift," from 1:00 to 4:00 A.M. As Sergeant Morrow recounted, the events of his third night proved to be quite an introduction to the duties (and pitfalls) of Marine Security Guard duty:

> The guard office was located on the 3rd floor next to the open staircase well. The U.S.I.S. offices were located on the 2nd floor, next to the finance office's secure vault. On my 3rd mid-watch, with the building making its usual scary noises, I was sitting in the guard office having just completing my rounds and checks. While shining my shoes, I thought I heard voices. Good God, I just completed my rounds and being fresh out of school, I knew every nook and cranny of that place had been checked by me, from the sub-basement to the roof. But again, I heard voices. Should I call my NCOIC, The Marine House, the Army M.P.s or go it alone and check it out.

Hell, I thought, I'm a MARINE [emphasis Sgt. Morrow's], get on with it. I crept down the stairs in my stocking feet. My leather soled shoes with cleats (this was 1957!) Don't allow for "sneak and peak." Proceeding to the 2nd deck the voices were clearer. Next to the vault I saw a light flicker. Drawing my weapon and clicking through the empty chamber (next chamber held a round) I began crawling toward the voices and the light. Arriving at the doorway, I proned and slithered to the opening. Light switches are lower there than in the U.S.A. so I reached up to its level on the outside. Quick as a bunny I reached in the room, clicked on the light and cocked the pistol on a live round. In my best German I yelled, "Your DEAD!!" As my eyes focused on a bust of George Washington, sitting on top of the radio, all body systems locked. Fortunately, I got the cylinder of my weapon open, re-positioned, un-cocked and holstered without shooting myself or equipment. After my heart and lungs began working again, I returned to the Guard's Office. Subsequent to the spilled coffee, and lots of cigarettes, I made a log entry — "0137 — Noise on 2nd deck. Investigated and found U.S.I.S. equipment running. No unusual events or actions noted." ...

After relating my eventful night to TOP, all he could do was giggle. Ever see a MSGT giggle? "Quick Draw McGraw" had no other noteworthy mid-watches for the remainder of my tour."[86]

In short, Marine Security Guard duty could be dangerous, at times humorous, and very often routine. Throughout the 1950s and early 1960s, Marine Security Guards discovered that at a moment's notice, they could be thrust into the middle of a war or *coup d'état*. Duty oftentimes brought these young Marines in harm's way between two warring combatants. What made the difference was their training as Marines first and second as security guards.

Ambassadors in Blue in the 1950s

Marine enlisted men were not the only leathernecks representing the United States abroad. Following in the tradition of Brigadier General John H. Russell, Jr., in Haiti, General Thomas Holcomb in South Africa, and Colonel William Eddy in Saudi Arabia, other notable Marine officers served in quasi-diplomatic posts throughout the world during the 1950s. President Dwight D. Eisenhower appointed General Lemuel C. Shepherd, Jr.— following his retirement on 31 December 1955 as the twentieth commandant of the Marine Corps — chairman of the Inter-American Defense Board. Sergeant Lloyd E. Shank, who served at the U.S. Embassy in Tegucigalpa, Honduras, recalled that the Marine Security Guards, in direct contradiction to standing orders from the Honduran government that forbade foreign militaries to wear their uniforms, organized a special honor guard when General Shepherd's plane landed.

After General Shepherd's plane touched down at the international airport and the passengers began to disembark, the former commandant spotted the five-man Marine detachment standing perfectly erect in full dress blue uniforms. General Shepherd immediately headed toward the Marines, whereupon Master Sergeant Earle J. Payne, the NCOIC of the Marine Security Guard detachment, whipped off a smart salute. General Shepherd then proceeded to inspect the Marines prior to inspecting the Honduran Honor Guard. As Sergeant Shank recalled, "This really made our day!" Later, Shank remembered that General Shepherd spent about an hour talking with the Marines at the U.S. Embassy in Tegucigalpa. Sergeant Shank wrote that their security guard detachment in Honduras was the only one to render such honors to General Shepherd during his tour of duty on the Inter-American Defense Board.[87]

After the acceptance of an armistice between the Israelis and Arabs in 1948, a number of Marine officers served on the staff of the United Nations Truce Commission. Lieutenant General William E. Riley served successfully from 1948 to 1953 in what was described as an "extremely difficult post" as chief of staff of the United Nations Truce Supervision Organization in Palestine. After retirement from the Marine Corps, Lieutenant General Riley later served with Foreign Operations Administration as director of the U.S. Operations Mission in Turkey.[88]

Marines also served as a security force at the newly established United Nations office in New York City. Secretary General Trygve Lie requested and eventually was provided a force of 75 Marines for a few months until a permanent United Nations guard force could be organized.[89] Some environments were less benign. In February 1961, two hundred protestors in the African country of the Congo (formerly Belgian Congo) injured a Marine Security Guard while protesting the death of Congolese leader Patrice Lumumba. The next year (1962), a bomb blast at the U.S. Embassy in Cairo, Egypt, injured a Marine Security Guard as it destroyed several rooms and blew out fifty windows near where the Marine had been standing post.

Changes in the Memorandum of Agreement, 1955

By 1955, the size and mission of the Marine Security Guard had expanded ten-fold since the original Memorandum of Agreement signed in 1948. Signed by Secretary of Defense Charles E. Wilson and Secretary of State John Foster Dulles, the new Memorandum of Agreement, signed September 22, 1955, further clarified the roles and assignments of enlisted Marines assigned to Marine Security Guard Duty. This new Memorandum of Agreement (MOA) further specified in greater detail the "relationships and terms of agreement between the Department of State and the Department of Defense with regard to the utilization of Marine Corps officers and enlisted personnel at Foreign Service establishments."

The updated memorandum re-emphasized the roles of both officers and enlisted Marines and their relationship with the embassy staff (most important the chief of mission or ambassador). It outlined the increase in funds for the purchase of civilian clothing for Marines going out on post for the first time. It also detailed the instructions governing utilization of both Marine Corps officers and enlisted personnel as a diplomatic security force.

The new memorandum for the first time specified the type of firearms to be used by Marines in the embassy. Whereas Marines had a variety of World War II–era weapons (such as M-1 Carbines, 45 caliber pistols) and shotguns to defend the embassy staff, there had been no provision in the 1948 Memorandum of Agreement specifying the types of arms and conditions in which they could be used. The amended MOA specified that Marines would be trained and have available .38 caliber pistols and ammunition, as well as .12-gauge riot guns, tear gas and incendiary grenades to defend the immediate area of the embassy or consulate and the compound.[90]

The amended Memorandum likewise specified that "Marine Security Guards should not be assigned as receptionists, couriers, or to other duties which do not pertain to security functions." It stipulated that the Department of State would provide Marine Corps personnel with transportation to and from their living quarters or other places of duty as specified by the chief of mission when either he or the Department of State determines that "local transportation facilities are unsafe or unavailable." Finally, the amended Memorandum of Agreement of 1955 increased slightly the amount of money given to each newly assigned Marine

Security Guard. From the original average of $300 given to each Marine, the amended MOA added fifty dollars (less ten dollars for those going to a warmer climate).[91]

Fox Company and the Marine Security Guard Mission, 1955–1964

As the Embassy Guard program expanded during the 1950s, so too did the requirements in the preparation of a Marine for this arduous duty. Many of these changes were eventually introduced into the curriculum of the Marine Security Guard School at Henderson Hall in Arlington, Virginia.

By 1962, the training of a Marine Security Guard took on added importance as the Cold War grew much colder and the Soviet Union re-focused its efforts, at more clandestine efforts particularly in regards to espionage at U.S. facilities abroad. The increased efforts at training Marines for this duty at F Company can be seen in the seven Marine Security Guard classes held each year. Each class, six weeks in length, spent the first week in formation and the other five toward training. With a three-week interval between each class, Marines entering MSG School were now given a very thorough period of training that included special night sessions in the handling of classified material given by instructors from the State Department. Gone were the two-and four-week classes of the early 1950s.

The emphasis the State Department placed on the handling of classified material at an embassy or consulate can be seen in a letter to Lieutenant Colonel Eugene H. Haffey, the commanding officer of Company F, from Mr. William O. Boswell, director of Office Security for the U.S. State Department, who emphasized the need for Marines to have more on-the-job training in the handling of classified material and general embassy security systems. Mr. Boswell wrote: "The sole duty of the guards receiving this training will be to examine offices to insure that classified material is not exposed. This requires the examination of safes, file cabinets, tops of desks, desk drawers, shelves, bookcases, wastepaper baskets, and the preparation of notices of violations when violations are discovered."[92]

Mr. Boswell emphasized to Lieutenant Colonel Haffey that Marines would also learn the differences in classifications "Top Secret," "Secret," and "Confidential," and other administratively controlled material labeled "Limited Official Use" and "Official Use Only." The leathernecks also received classes in the proper storage of classified material. Boswell noted that under no circumstances were Marines undergoing training to interfere with regular State Department officials and employees on duty.

By November 1963, Fox Company had nearly completed implementation of the changes promulgated by the revised Memorandum of Agreement of 1955 with the writing of the first Standard Operation Procedures or SOP. By 1963, the Marine Security Guard School had completely reorganized its administrative procedures with the establishment of a company administrative section handling the service records of Marines in the field. Also created was a school administrative section, charged with the task of administering students "from the time of their arrival at School until they depart CONUS (Continental United States)." Colonel M.J. Dunbar, the commanding officer of Fox Company, emphasized in a memorandum to the commanding officer of Headquarters Battalion, Headquarters Marine Corps, that the split in the administrative functions, "has proven quite satisfactory," in that it reduced the operational workload of Fox Company personnel. Colonel Dunbar also noted that it reduced the backlog in paperwork that accumulated with every class.[93]

Colonel Dunbar likewise noted that a staff study on foreign language training was nearly complete and that preliminary results indicated the need for "the testing of Marines on Post to measure language proficiency, the teaching of languages [foreign] at English-speaking posts, and the opportunity for gifted Marines to continue their language study beyond the present 100 hours minimum." Finally, Colonel Dunbar informed the commanding officer of Headquarters Battalion that the commandant of the Marine Corps had approved the assignment of married staff non-commissioned officers to unaccompanied tours at single Marine Security Guard posts. The colonel believed that this last would create a much larger pool of qualified SNCOs for the program and it would provide for more manpower at undermanned posts.[94]

Summary

During its first full decade of existence, the Marine Security Guard expanded tenfold as a major war in Korea, hostilities between the United States and USSR, revolutions in Honduras, Lebanon, and Hungary as well as peasant uprisings in Bolivia and South Vietnam created environments of instability. As always, the fine, smart detachments of U.S. Marines stood watch and oftentimes reacted as the violence from these events spilled over onto the grounds of the various U.S. embassies and consulates in Europe, the Middle East, South and Central America, and throughout all of Asia. Marine Security guards stood watch over an ever-increasingly violent and complex world as the 1950s ended and a torch was passed to a new generation of Americans. As were their contemporaries in the line companies deployed to South Vietnam in March 1965, Marine Security Guards were about to undergo their most severe test as an embassy security force as the United States deepened its commitment to the Republic of Vietnam during the 1960s to the mid–1970s.

Throughout the first decade and a half of the Marine Embassy Guard program, Marine Security Guards spread out throughout the world to guard U.S. embassies and consulates, and their training likewise expanded. This training, which took into consideration the changing nature of embassy security, the handling and destruction of classified material and the increasingly sophisticated and complicated nature of security in the Cold War era, adhered to the time-tested principles of Marine Corps interior guard and security. Also, the demand for more Marine Security Guards and an ever-increasing tense international situation placed an additional requirement for a well-trained force schooled in the use of firearms. As Marine Security Guards demonstrated throughout the 1960s and 1970s, this training paid large dividends, as they were repeatedly called to defend their embassies and other U.S. government–owned buildings, oftentimes in the face of an overwhelmingly superior enemy force.

CHAPTER 6

Embassy Guards at War: Vietnam, Cambodia, and Laos, 1962–1975

For the U.S. Marine Corps, the war in Vietnam was fought on many fronts, from the jungles and coastal enclaves in and around I Corps to the villages and hamlets around Da Nang, as well in the skies above South Vietnam to the grounds of the U.S. Embassy in Saigon. The first known U.S. contacts with Cochin China, as South Vietnam was then known, occurred in May of 1845 when Captain John Percival, USN, commanding officer of "Old Ironside," the USS *Constitution*, dropped anchor off Touron (Da Nang). Captain Percival's mission was to make a friendly port call and establish relations with the local Vietnamese officials. While meeting with the mandarins Captain Percival received a message from Monsignor Dominique Lefebreve, a French missionary who had been imprisoned and placed under a sentence of death by the Vietnamese for "spreading Christianity," that informed Percival of his plight and impending death sentence. Placing diplomacy aside, Percival demanded the immediate release of Father Lefebreve and, as a show of force, landed on May 15, 1845, a combined force of 80 bluejackets and Marines to back up his demand. He also briefly held the four mandarins hostage before releasing them to French officials. Upon hearing of Lefebreve's release, Percival released the mandarins, re-embarked his bluejackets and Marines and sailed away. Disavowing Captain Percival's actions, the State Department apologized to the Vietnamese ruler, Thieu Tra, who had already accepted an apology from the French for Lefebreve's actions after local French officials paid a small indemnity and apologized.[1] One hundred twenty years later almost to the day (May 8, 1965), elements of the 9th Marine Expeditionary Brigade landed on those same beaches where Captain Percival's Marines and sailors came ashore in 1845.[2]

Early U.S. Relations with Vietnam, 1920s to the 1950s

U.S. relations with French Indochina remained relatively unimportant throughout the early half of the 20th century. In fact, U.S. diplomatic affairs were normally handled through the U.S. Consulate in Shanghai or Beijing. In 1923, journalist Gertrude Emerson observed that in Haiphong, the port city nearest Hanoi, "An American Consul was non-existent, there was not even a tourist bureau to offer expensive tours...." The American consul general in Saigon, Harris M. Cookingham, wrote to Secretary of State Charles Evans Hughes that Indochina was "almost cut off, commercially from the United States."[3]

Prior to 1940, the American consulate in Saigon handled United States' affairs in

Indochina. Before the fall of France to the *Wehrmacht* in June 1940, the United States opened up a consular office in Hanoi, though shortly thereafter closed it when Japanese forces invaded French Indochina in August of 1940. At the end of World War II, the United States, in order to counter the Soviet Union and People's Republic of China's recognition of Ho Chi Minh's Communist-dominated Democratic Republic of Vietnam (DRV), recognized the French-installed government of Emperor Bao Dai in Cochin China (South Vietnam).[4] In mid–March of 1946, the State Department established the first U.S. Consulate in Hanoi.[5] After the defeat and withdrawal of the French from Indochina in 1956, the United States assumed the primary responsibility for the training and equipping of the newly created Army of the Republic of Vietnam (ARVN). As the U.S. commitment grew over time to the government of Ngo Dinh Diem, the U.S. Embassy in Saigon became the most important symbol in the South Vietnamese struggle against subversion and intimidation by communist North Vietnam.

Protests and Coups: Marines in Saigon, 1960–1965

For the next nineteen years, the U.S. Embassy in Saigon was the symbol of the U.S. support for a series of successive South Vietnamese governments that began in 1956 with Ngo Dinh Diem and lasted until the final evacuation of the Marine Embassy Guard detachment and members of the 9th Marine Expeditionary Brigade from the South Vietnamese capitol in April 1975. Charged to guard this vital installation was a detachment of U.S. Marine Security Guards.

Master Sergeant William V. "Bill" East who as a sergeant had been assigned to Marine Security Guard duty at the U.S. Embassy in Saigon in 1963, recalled that duty there at times could be "pretty tense." He noted that demonstrations became more frequent and vocal in their opposition to not only toward President Ngo Dinh Diem but also toward the United States. Master Sergeant East remembered upon his arrival, after a brief tour of duty at the U.S. Embassy in Manila, "we encountered several anti–American demonstrations during the next year and a half (1963–1965). The embassy was bombed, as well as USOM." Master Sergeant East recalled that during one of these riots in Saigon: "I took a position on a balcony each night. All communications were disrupted, so I couldn't call or make contact with anyone else. I stayed on the balcony each night, as that was when the crowds were the heaviest and the rowdiest. During the day I would get some sleep, or rummage the annex rooms for something to eat.... There were several incidents of this sort during the rest of my tour."[6]

Not all the duty in Saigon was onerous. According to Master Sergeant East, "During this tour, it was not all bad, we had some very good times. The Marines fast pitch softball team won the Far East championship, playing against some very good military and civilian teams." Besides baseball, Marine Security Guards spent their off-duty hours playing rugby at the Circle Sport Athletic Club in Saigon or, took in the sights in Saigon. Master Sergeant East recalled that "until the buildup of military forces, and particularly the Tet offensive of 1968, Saigon was a beautiful city, with a great French influence. Many sidewalk cafes, flowers galore.... Even though we had a few rough times, all the guys seemed to enjoy this tour."[7]

Prior to the build-up of American combat troops in the Republic of Vietnam in the mid–1960s, the Marine guard at the U.S. Embassy in Saigon numbered only six men.[8] By early 1965, however, the Marine Security Guard in Saigon numbered thirty Marines.[9] By 1966, it had grown to sixty-two Marines and was the largest Marine Security Guard detachment in the world.[10] As Gunnery Sergeant Jerry N. Lorrelli, the staff non-commissioned officer in

As a Marine Security Guard (in white shirt and tie) casts a watchful eye, U.S. Ambassador Henry Cabot Lodge (in suit) leaves the U.S. Embassy in Saigon in 1963 for an appointment with South Vietnamese officials (courtesy U.S. Marine Corps).

charge of the Security Guard, said, "Our situation here is unique." This was due, of course to the commitment of U.S ground combat troops in spring of 1965. While the duty of the Marines remained the protection of American diplomats and citizens working in the embassy and its adjoining buildings, the primary role performed by the leathernecks was to be "constantly on the alert for security violations." As Gunnery Sergeant Lorrelli added, "Security is our business." Marines kept close tabs on persons entering and departing the embassy as well as remaining alert for suspicious packages. In a city where terrorist bombs went off almost daily, this became major concern for all Marine embassy guards.

This concern for potential terrorist bombs became reality on March 30, 1965 when, at 10:50 A.M. (Saigon time), a powerful car bomb went off in front of the U.S. Embassy. The explosion killed twenty-two and wounded over two hundred Americans and Vietnamese citizens who were in the embassy and in proximity of the explosion. The deputy U.S. ambassador to South Vietnam, U. Alexis Johnson, recalled that there were two terrorist attacks aimed at the U.S. Embassy in Saigon, both of which were unsuccessful prior to the more damaging attack on March 30. The third attack, however, turned out to be very bloody as the off-duty Marine Security Guards reacted to the powerful bomb blast in front of the U.S. Embassy.

As the deputy ambassador prepared his morning brief with General William C. Westmoreland, the commanding general, United States Military Assistance Command, Vietnam, Sergeant Donald J. Borbas, who had been relaxing in the Marine House after completing his shift, heard the powerful car bomb go off. In a vain attempt to call the embassy to find out what had happened (all of the telephone lines had been severed by the blast), he and several other Marines rushed to the embassy about two miles away on foot, bicycles, and in taxis. Upon arriving the leatherneck guards found the grounds of the embassy smothered with bodies, twisted metal, rubble and shattered glass.

Inside the embassy, Lance Corporal Theodore Little, who had been at Post One and had been knocked off his feet by the concussion of the blast, was already performing his duties when Sergeant Borbas and the other off-duty Marines arrived.[11] As Ambassador Johnson recalled, the scene was horrific as embassy personnel and Vietnamese civilians, many of whom had been on the ground floor applying for travel visas and passports, struggled to make their way out of the shattered building. Deputy Ambassador Johnson recalled the attack and its aftermath in painstaking detail:

> At 10:46, a man on a Lambretta motor scooter drove by the six Saigon police guards stationed outside the embassy and parked across the street. Then a Renault sedan slammed into the curb alongside the embassy (where parking or stopping was strictly prohibited) and the driver jumped out. When the guards (who I am ashamed to say we nicknamed "white mice") ordered him to move the car, he pulled out a gun and began shooting. So did the motorcyclist. The guards returned the fire. One guard was wounded, the Renault driver was killed, and the other gunmen fled.
>
> Our Consular Section, which handled passports, visas, and so on, was on the ground floor with a large window facing the street. When the car screeched to a halt just a few feet from the window and the shooting started, everyone dropped to the floor. Upstairs, most people, myself included, went out the nearest window to see what the commotion was all about. At that moment the 250 pounds of plastic explosive filling the back seat of the car exploded, hurling a storm of glass shards and metal window frames into the faces of those who had gone to see. Shielded by a concrete ledge just below the window, only three of the many visitors and employees of the Consular Section were killed, but many were wounded. A packed Chinese restaurant across the street collapsed and caught fire, and the bodies of many killed and wounded passers-by littered the street. The last thing that Peer deSilva,[12] the CIA station Chief, saw from his third floor window was the driver of the car lighting the fuse stuck in the explosive. Professional that he was, Peer recognized the fuse for what it was but did not react in time to shield himself and was blinded in both eyes. Happily, unlike some others, he recovered partial sight in one eye after some months of intensive treatment in the United States.[13]

Ambassador Johnson was extremely critical of the structural aspects of the U.S. Embassy in Saigon. He said the building's defects contributed to its being targeted by the terrorists:

> I had never liked our Saigon embassy building, an aging French structure located on a busy intersection near the port. It was a rabbit warren, poorly designed for office work and impossible to protect against attack. It had only one narrow staircase that spiraled around its one creaky elevator. There were no fire escapes or emergency exit routes to other buildings, and I had often worried about what we would do in case of fire. Getting money out of Washington to build a new embassy had been one of my pet projects since I arrived, but to no avail.[14]

One of the foremost thoughts on the deputy ambassador's mind was that the explosion was but a precursor to a full-fledged assault on the embassy by the Viet Cong:

> My first thought after the blast was that the supporting pillars had been blown away, as they had at a troop billet in Qui Nhon and the whole embassy would collapse. Betty and I quickly got in a doorway for protection. When the building appeared to be standing intact, we quickly locked away our loose papers and waited to see if Vietcong would come charging up the stairs brandishing Kalashnikov submachine guns or if fire would cut us off from escape. Soon we smelled smoke and heard the flames crackle, but the fire appeared to come from the Chinese restaurant opposite

us. I went down the stairway, checking each office to see that there were enough able-bodied to aid injured. Then I went out to the street, down stairs already slippery with blood. Fire trucks, ambulances, and military police were beginning to arrive, summoned by General Westmoreland, who had seen the blast on his way to an 11:00 appointment with me. I directed the rescue workers to the worst-hit areas and returned inside to the communications section, where the operator was standing by his post. I got off a quick message to Washington on the one working military circuit saying we had been heavily hit but I was unhurt and would report further as soon as I could size up the situation.[15]

General William C. Westmoreland recalled that his first concern upon seeing the destruction caused by the explosion was the safety of Ambassador Johnson. The MACV commander "made sure that Army medics and military police were on the scene." The general likewise contacted the deputy ambassador by phone to see if he was all right. Assured that Johnson was okay, General Westmoreland then sent a cable to his superiors in Washington reporting the bombing. The MACV commander later recalled, "To have lost such a stalwart member of the U.S. Mission would have been a serious blow."[16]

Peer de Silva, who was seriously wounded in the attack, recalled that prior to the car bomb going off, was able to clearly see the device used by the Viet Cong terrorist to detonate the C-4 plastic explosives. The CIA station chief remembered that the explosives had been packed into the frame of the old gray sedan used in the attack. De Silva wrote that just moments before the detonation of the explosives, he looked out the window of his office and saw the driver of the vehicle arguing with one of the South Vietnamese policemen, who was armed with a M-1 carbine. De Silva wrote, "I remember an enormous thud, which since reminded me of being inside a base drum when beaten heavily. My next conscious thought, apparently a few seconds later, was being on my hands and knees next to my desk, facing away from the window. My hands, buried in rubble and glass, were bleeding."[17]

As for the Marine Security Guards, the situation inside the embassy remained chaotic as they conducted sweeps throughout the embassy to check for wounded and to secure classified material in the vault in case of further attacks. Led by Staff Sergeant William D. Kerakos, the Marine Security Guard Detachment conducted a massive security sweep throughout the embassy, which by mid-afternoon was back to its normal routine.[18]

Ambassador Johnson recalled that there was one "amusing footnote to this tragedy," which involved the Marine Security Guard who manned the front desk that morning. Apparently the British ambassador, whom Mr. Johnson described as "an old school type" had arrived punctually for his noon appointment with him. Knowing of the attack an hour before his arrival, however, he became "very upset when he learned I was visiting the hospital." The British ambassador repeatedly "kept insisting to the guard that, I would return to keep my appointment after all." Ambassador Johnson recalled that he had not phoned to cancel, a fact that the Marine Security Guard attempted to pass on to the British ambassador. Only with the greatest difficulty and patience was Lance Corporal Theodore Little able to persuade the British diplomat that "waiting would be futile." Ambassador Johnson stated, "The next time I saw him [the British ambassador] his arched eyebrows implicitly condemned me for my dreadful breach of proper manners."[19]

Ambassador Maxwell Taylor, who was absent from Saigon on the morning of the attack, was pointedly upset with the delays that occurred in the U.S. Congress and its failure to appropriate funds for a new embassy. In a telegram to Secretary of State Dean Rusk a month after the attack, Ambassador Taylor asked for help in securing passage, as quickly as possible, of the spending bill authorizing the construction of a new embassy which would be, in the words of the ambassador, "permanent and dignified."[20]

In spite of the fact that President Lyndon B. Johnson requested over $1 million from the Congress in the immediate aftermath of the bombing, several months passed after Taylor's telegram to Secretary of State Rusk before construction actually began.

Duty in Saigon, 1965–1967

There was no other incident until the Tet offensive of January 1968 that "demonstrated to the Marine Security Guard detachment that it too was in the frontlines."[21] Due to the fact that the Marines lived under the constant threat of terrorist bombs and attacks, just like their comrades in the line companies, Marine embassy guards in Saigon received combat pay. Staff Sergeant Carl D. Sanders, who survived an attempted *coup d'état* in neighboring Vientiane, Laos, only a month before (February 1965), commented that "I witnessed more fighting there than I have had here." The veteran staff sergeant recalled that while in Vientiane, the U.S. Embassy came under intense rocket attack that in turn prompted Headquarters Marine Corps to authorize combat pay for that month.[22]

While on duty in Saigon, Marine embassy guards worked forty to seventy hours a week, depending on the events in the embassy or its adjoining buildings. While on duty, Marine guards screened visitors to the embassy and the consular section, conducted daily security patrols of the embassy and its environs, and conducted after-hours inspections of the embassy's

Gunnery Sergeant Jerry Lorrelli (left) and First Lieutenant Philip Tucker (right) make their inspection rounds of all the Marine Security Guard posts inside the U.S. compound in Saigon (courtesy U.S. Marine Corps).

As a true "Ambassador in Blue," Sergeant J.C. Dunn is like a father to these blind Vietnamese girls in Saigon as they play on a swing set (courtesy U.S. Marine Corps).

offices in search of security violations of classified material that might have been left on an official's desk inadvertently. Above all else, however, because Saigon itself was considered a combat zone, vigilance was the main job of all the leathernecks at the Saigon embassy. Gunnery Sergeant Lorrelli recalled that only two days after his arrival he was reminded that Saigon was, indeed, on the "front lines." On "his second day on the job he thought he heard someone knocking on his door. That knock had been the muted explosion of two Claymore mines, aimed at a floating restaurant less than a block away from the embassy. The gunny had received a warm welcome to Saigon."[23] Corporal James Plank, who had only just arrived in Saigon in early 1966 from Fox Company in Washington, D.C., after graduation from Marine Security Guard School, recalled that he also received a "welcome" from the Viet Cong. While manning Post One, a Vietnamese woman "nonchalantly dropped a cluster of three grenades" in front of the same floating restaurant at My Cahn.

Due to the ever-present threat of terrorism, Marine embassy guards were instructed never to take the same route twice and never to frequent the same establishment more than once, and were required to observe the strict Saigon curfew which ran from midnight to four in the morning. One Marine guard compared duty in Saigon to being on a "reconnaissance patrol.... You go one way and come back another."[24] Despite the ever present reminder that a war was being fought in the countryside and the threat of Viet Cong terrorists, Marine Security Guards selected from a variety of recreational activities to break the boredom and arduous duty of standing endless hours of watch. Besides the numerous clubs, bowling alleys and golf courses in and around Saigon, Marines from the embassy oftentimes took "R&R" in Bangkok, Hong Kong, Taipei, Tokyo, Manila, and Singapore.[25] As for pay, because Saigon was in an area designated to receive combat pay, a sergeant with over seven years made (in 1966) $477 a month. This included his normal pay, State Department pay, combat pay, and overseas pay.

Even at the Marine House, which was located on Con Truong Street in Saigon and had been a former French dispensary, the ever-present danger of Viet Cong terrorists attack kept Marines on alert. One Marine Security Guard remarked, "We were always on the alert. In fact, even on liberty, the men are prepared to return at a moment's notice. Their whereabouts are constantly plotted back at the house, just in case they're needed in a hurry." As for the Marine House, Master Sergeant William East remembered that it "was a huge villa, in a very nice neighborhood. The grounds were very well cared for by gardeners."[26]

In spite of the war and their mission, the Marines at the U.S. Embassy in Saigon acted as true "Ambassadors in Green," when they donated 2,000 Vietnamese piastres to a school for blind girls in Cholon, Saigon's sister city. Administered by three Catholic nuns, the school had been primarily subsidized by the South Vietnamese government. The donations and other assistance provided by the Marines nevertheless heartened the operators of the school. In fact, by the time Marine First Lieutenant Philip E. Tucker assumed command of the Marine Security Guard Detachment in April 1966, the Marines assigned to the Saigon Embassy had become surrogate fathers to the handicapped children, many of whom had been blind since birth.[27] By the end of 1966, the Marines had built the girls a chicken coop, a project that Lieutenant Tucker had not only praised Sergeant Dunn and the other Marine Security Guards for undertaking, but also one that he himself "wholeheartedly endorsed."

By the time Lieutenant Tucker succeeded Gunnery Sergeant Lorrelli as the commander of the Marine Security Guard in Saigon, the detachment had reached strength of sixty-eight Marines.[28] In time, it became the largest Marine Security Guard detachment guarding an embassy or other U.S. government building worldwide.

A Year of Preparation, 1967

By 1967, the Marine Embassy Guard in Saigon numbered one officer and sixty-seven enlisted Marines. Administered by Company C, Marine Security Guard Battalion (State Department) and headquartered in Manila, the Saigon detachment's "chain of command" consisted of "one of the longest small unit command links in the world. " In fact, the links ran 650 miles from Saigon to Manila and over 9,000 miles to the battalion's headquarters at Henderson Hall in Washington, D.C. In overall command of the Saigon Detachment was First Lieutenant Tucker and newly arrived Staff Sergeant Gary G. Stoces.[29]

As the Marine detachment grew in Saigon so too did the mission. The Marines assigned to the embassy "protected American lives and property within the Embassy and its associated U.S. Agency in International Development (USAID) and U.S. Information Service Buildings (U.S.I.S.)." The Marine guard was broken down into administrative and watch sections. The watch section was further divided into three separate units: the Guard Section, charged with protection of the embassy and the USAID and USIS compounds; an Ambassador's Residency Guard; and the Ambassador's Personal Security Unit (PSU), which protected Ambassador Henry Cabot Lodge and his wife. A State Department official, Mr. Robert A. England, who was the embassy's civilian security officer, exercised operational control of the detachment through First Lieutenant Tucker. Due to their mission, the Marines assigned to the embassy "had no connection with the Marines elsewhere in Vietnam."[30]

The equipment used by the Marine Security Guard differed very little from that found at the other U.S. embassies worldwide. In Saigon, however, the Marine Security Guard's equipment (including armament) reflected the higher state of readiness and need to communicate at a moment's notice. As was the case elsewhere throughout the world, the U.S. State Department provided the weapons and radio equipment for the Marine detachment in Saigon. In fact, "the detachment's highly sophisticated radio net consisted of extremely reliable fixed and the portable units which linked guard posts, vehicles, the detachment office, and the security offices." Weapons included the standard issue Smith and Wesson .38-caliber, 4-inch barrel revolver. Because of the highly sensitive nature of their mission, Marines assigned to the Residency Guard carried the 2-inch barrel Smith and Wesson .38, while the leathernecks assigned to protect the ambassador and his wife with the Personal Security Units carried the Colt .357 Magnum "Python." Both the Residency and Personal Security Units had the 9mm Beretta sub-machine guns that they carried in an unobtrusive attaché case.[31] Other weapons used by the Marine Security Guards at the various internal posts included Remington 12-gauge shotguns loaded with "00" buckshot shells.

One last piece of equipment available though never used by Marine Security Guards was non-lethal riot control gases. Throughout early 1965, memorandums among President Lyndon B. Johnson's special assistant for national security, McGeorge Bundy, and the Department of State, most notably William S. Bundy, dealt with the issuance of such non-lethal gases to U.S. forces in South Vietnam. Given specific mention in this debate was the use of such non-lethal gases in the defense of the U.S. Embassy and consulates. Despite the international outcry that surrounded the apparent use of such "non-lethal gas" by South Vietnamese troops (Army of the Republic of Vietnam), McGeorge Bundy, in a memorandum to the president, outlined the reasoning behind and countering the argument against their use. The assistant to national security attempted to deflect the criticisms expressed by the British government, among others, over the use of such gases. In a memorandum dated March 23, 1965, McGeorge Bundy informed President Johnson that:

1. The riot-control gases used in Vietnam are standard issue for all U.S. troops with riot control missions, and authority to use them has been delegated to subordinate commanders for many years.
2. These gases are also standard issue under Military Assistance Programs to friendly troops with riot-control missions.
3. These gases are non-lethal, and their effects are temporary. They are totally different from the poison gases against which international conventions and humanitarian feelings are directed.
4. There are three known uses of these riot-control gases in Vietnam (two cases were in efforts by Vietnamese troops to rescue U.S. advisors — this is a good point at home but not abroad).
5. There has been absolutely no NSC discussion of this problem precisely because riot-control gases are standard equipment. There has been no proposal at any time for the use of poison gas in this theater or elsewhere.
6. Finally, these gases are precisely analogous to those used by police forces all over the world.[32]

President Johnson informed both British Foreign Secretary Sir Michael Stewart and Ambassador Sir Michael Stewart that the gases in current use in South Vietnam by U.S. forces and ARVN were those used "by our own police forces."[33] The president added that the gases in question were "frequently employed for quelling riots, and were stocked by many countries."[34] Despite the widespread criticism aimed at the United States over the use of such gases, U.S. and South Vietnamese forces continued to use them in quelling riots or when dislodging Viet Cong terrorists from buildings. In fact, U.S. Marines used such non-lethal tear gas during the Tet offensive during the battle for Hue City.

One of the most difficult problems faced by Lieutenant Tucker and his Marine Security Guards was the fact that "his command expanded so fast that only he and his one staff NCO were hard put to exercise control. As a result, sergeants supervised watch sections of as many as 30 Marines, located at different posts in a potentially insecure city." After the appointment and arrival of Captain Robert J. O'Brien as the officer-in-charge in April 1967, and the assignment of Gunnery Sergeant Alexander Morrison earlier in February 1967 as the staff noncommissioned officer-in-charge (SNCOIC), the command and watch arrangements improved dramatically in Saigon.[35]

After the terrorist bombing of March 1965, the U.S. Congress authorized the construction of a new U.S. Embassy, which ironically heightened security concerns, as Marine Embassy Guards were now required to stand a 24-hour watch during the construction. In fact, "During the construction period, the Marines guarded the site on a 24-hour basis, and because of security considerations, monitored the workers on the job. The Marine Guard requirements constantly changed at the new building site and the contractors did not finish the new complex until the fall." This close monitoring was undertaken in order to prevent Viet Cong terrorists from either planting bombs or becoming familiar with the building's overall layout.[36]

For the Marine Security Guards 1967 remained an uneventful year as the Viet Cong failed to launch any similar attacks on the U.S. Embassy. Despite the lack of threats to the U.S. Embassy, its personnel and missions the Marines continued to "conduct routine training drills, alerts, passive defense measures, and tests of the security system."[37]

The Tet Offensive: The First Test, 1968

As Marine Security Guards in Saigon continued to train into the new year, the North Vietnamese and their Viet Cong allies prepared to launch what became the turning point of the Vietnam War. At center of this NVA/VC offensive was the Marine Security Guard guarding the U.S. Embassy in Saigon. Alerted by the Regional Security Office (RSO) of the possibility of a Viet Cong attack during the Vietnamese New Year, known as "Tet," on the afternoon of January 30, 1968, Captain Robert J. O'Brien, the detachment commander, "immediately increased the alert status and put a second man on all one-man posts" at the U.S. Embassy and the other buildings guarded by the Marines.[38] Contrary to the post–Tet offensive criticisms that the embassy was caught off-guard on the night of January 30–31, 1968, by the Viet Cong, Captain O'Brien had, in anticipation of an attack, had placed a two-man team on the roof of the Norodom compound adjacent to the U.S. Embassy compound. At approximately 1:30 A.M., on January 31, 1968, Captain O'Brien and a Marine sergeant checked each post prior to returning to the Marine House, where he left strict instructions to be awakened if anything unusual occurred prior to his next round of checks at 0300 (3.00 A.M.).

At 0245 A.M., a reinforced squad of Viet Cong sappers, later identified as coming from the Viet Cong's *C-10 Battalion*, "armed with satchel charges, automatic weapons, and grenades" blew a hole in the wall surrounding the embassy compound near the northeast gate. Two members of the U.S. Army's 716th Military Police Battalion attempted to raise the alarm but were shot by the intruders, as were two more military policemen from the same battalion who attempted to assist their fallen comrades and died in a burst of Viet Cong machine gun fire.[39]

Sergeant Ronald W. Harper, one of the Marine Embassy Guards posted in the Embassy Chancery, and who had been drinking coffee with one of the Marines on duty in the guardhouse near the Norodom complex, suddenly looked up and saw an unidentified Vietnamese standing near the two Marines. Shortly thereafter Sergeant Harper heard an explosion and a burst of machine gun fire that caused him to rush back to the entrance of the embassy, where he found Corporal George B. Zahuranic on the telephone at the receptionist's desk calling for assistance.

Sergeant Harper recalled that as soon as he recognized the shadowy figures as being enemy soldiers, he immediately

> dashed out of the guard shack and hollered to the guards that I had to get back to the Chancery to help Zach (Cpl. Zahuranic). I did not see the Vietnamese that I had seen a couple of seconds earlier as I ran past the Consular Building. I didn't slow down until I reached the entrance by the generator building and when I got there I only hesitated long enough to make sure that I wasn't running into any V.C. Then I dashed for the corner of the Embassy near the Norodom Compound. As I was running, I saw one driver running toward the generator building and I also saw one driver in the Embassy vehicle nearest the entrance of the Embassy stretching from his front seat into the back seat trying to get something. I also glanced toward the MPs and I couldn't see them. All I could see was dust flying from the MP's post where rounds from the V.C. were hitting the cement located there. There could have been V.C. at the gate too but I didn't notice them as all I was concerned with was getting back into the Chancery....
>
> At this time I ran for the armory and the rocket hit the wall at Post #1. I was located about one step from the armory and Cpl. Zahuranic was still at the telephone.
>
> The blast knocked me to the floor but I only received small shrapnel. Cpl. Zahuranic was also knocked down but he was injured. He said he thought his leg was broken and he was bleeding severely on the right side of the head and ear. He managed to get himself in the armory while I loaded my beretta. I fired three rounds at the receptionist's desk to make sure that my beretta was functioning properly. Cpl. Zahuranic was trying to load a beretta but he wasn't able to while he was on the floor. Then I rushed into the bathroom in the armory and grabbed a bunch of paper towels which I had Cpl. Zahuranic put on his head and apply pressure while he laid in pain on the floor.

Then I went back to the armory where Cpl. Zahuranic lay unconscious and I applied a first aid bandage to his head. At this time a grenade was thrown in the Embassy through the window at Post #1 which didn't touch either of us. I finally got into contact with the duty officer and told him to get help to evacuate Cpl. Zahuranic. I also told this to my other posts which were calling in.

Then a soldier (PFC Fisher) came downstairs and I gave him a beretta. Cpl. Zahuranic then started to shake and move his head around on the floor, so I had the soldier try to hold him still while I opened the elevator doors and locked them. The soldier then covered for me as I pulled Cpl. Zahuranic into the elevator. I gave the soldier a shotgun, a pistol and an ammo box of shotgun shells and gave him orders to take Cpl. Zahuranic to the Duty Officer on the fourth floor and to take the shells to Sgt. Soto on the roof.

A few minutes later, the duty officer contacted me as the soldier couldn't get on the roof as it was locked and Sgt. Soto thought the V.C. were trying to get in. He was out of ammo so he had to stay hid in case they succeeded in breaking in. I tried to call Sgt Soto but he wouldn't answer the telephone as he thought the V.C. were at his door. I then had Mr. Griffith from communications come down in the elevator and I threw him the master key and a pistol with ammo so he could get to the roof. By this time MACV (Major Hudson) had a helicopter on the way to get Corporal Zahuranic so Mr. Griffin and the Duty Officer took the injured Marine to the roof from the fourth floor and at this time I told Mr. Griffith to lock the elevator upstairs in case the V.C. did penetrate the building.[40]

Corporal Zahuranic and Sergeant Harper had been assured by both Captain O'Brien and Gunnery Sergeant Allen Morrison that "there would be no trouble" that night. Corporal Zahuranic recalled that this was not to be the case as he and Sergeant Harper began their shift at midnight on January 31:

Going on midnight duty at the front desk on January 31, 1968 at the U.S. Embassy was no different from any other time. Little did I suspect any of what was to follow. Two Marines were at the front desk and there was one extra guard stationed on the roof. There were some reports of V.C. activity in the area, but nobody was really concerned. At about 2:00 A.M. Sgt. Harper and I were visited by Capt. O'Brien, Gny [Gunnery Sergeant] Morrison, and Mr. Leo Crampsey. Leo was a big shot security officer for the State Department. They stayed for about 15 minutes and assured us there would be no trouble. After they left, Sgt. Harper and I went about our regular duties. A short time later Harper said he was going to check with the MSG's next door to see if they wanted anything. I was sitting at the front desk with my feet propped up on the counter when I heard an explosion outside. I didn't know what it was, but I thought we were taking mortars. I jumped up and started around the counter to close the huge wooden doors. Sgt. Harper came running in the back door, and when he was almost at the front desk I grabbed the phone to call for help. That's when the rocket hit the window knocking us both to the ground. I got the worst of it and don't remember much from then on. I do remember a lot of automatic fire coming in the windows and couple of more rockets hitting the embassy. I also remember more explosions that I later learned was one of the V.C. throwing grenades in the window. The V.C. also had satchel charges and to this day I don't know why the V.C. never got into the embassy. The other MSG's arrived shortly and engaged the 20 or so V.C. outside. One of these Marines was Corporal [James C.] Marshall.

Later I was taken to the [helicopter landing] pad on the roof and waited for a chopper. Several attempts were made to land, but the helicopters were turned back by enemy fire. I finally got aboard and thought I was now safe. Boy was I wrong! As we lifted off from the Embassy roof, I could hear the rounds hitting the bottom of the chopper. Some of the bullets came through the floor, and since I was laying on the floor, I'm sure you can understand my concern. Just when you think things can't get any worse, they do. I heard the pilot say "We're going down." We made a forced landing in a rice paddy and I was transferred to another chopper. That was the last time I saw the U.S. Embassy.

I feel I owe my life to all of the Marine Security Guards stationed at the Saigon Embassy. To

Ronnie Harper for his quick thinking. To Jimmy Marshall who gave his life so that we all could live....[41]

After Corporal Zahuranic had been evacuated by helicopter, the battle for the U.S. Embassy continued. On the roof of the chancery was Sergeant Rudy A. Soto, Jr., who had been assigned there by Captain O'Brien, armed with a 12-gauge shotgun. Here, Sergeant Soto witnessed a similar scene as experienced by Zahuranic and Harper overlooking the embassy compound. As the Viet Cong — armed with AK-47 assault rifles, rocket-propelled grenades, and satchel charges — blasted their way into the embassy courtyard, Sergeant Soto's weapon jammed. Despite having a radio with him the Marine sergeant was unable to contact Harper or the wounded Zahuranic. Acting on the presumption that the Viet Cong had penetrated into the embassy, Sergeant Soto radioed the Marine House and "informed them of the situation as he knew it."[42] In fact, from the roof of the embassy, Sergeant Soto had an excellent vantage point in guiding the relief efforts of the beleaguered embassy compound and relaying information as to the whereabouts of the enemy intruders:

> Looking down, I could see men coming from across the vacant lot and on the street in front of the Embassy wall. A few seconds later a hole was blasted through the wall (corner Mac Dinh Chi and Thong Nhut). At this time the Dragon distress signal was used (10–13 Emergency). As soon as the hole was blown in the wall, the MPs started firing in that direction. When the firing stopped, two Vietnamese got through the hole and took a position to the left front of the Embassy lobby doors with a rocket launcher.
>
> From the roof I could see the tracers from the MP's M-16's. Also at this time I tried loading the shotgun twice and both times it jammed. I put the shotgun down and commenced firing my .38 caliber pistol which only had five (5) rounds, at the two Vietnamese located in front of the Embassy hiding behind a planter. The Vietnamese with the rocket launcher shot several rockets into the area where Post # 1 was located. I then transmitted again on the Dragon Net that Post #1 had been hit at least 2 or 3 times.
>
> After this I ran to the door leading to the roof and secured it. I then took a position at the rear of the Embassy where I could hear small arms firing coming from the Mission Coordinator's House....
>
> There was also some small arms firing at the MP entrance and the front of the Embassy and Norodom Compound. Throughout the whole morning it was much until 0400 0555, when I heard a sound like someone trying to open the door to the roof. This was when I alled Dragon #20, #27, and Sgt Keady about the voices and someone at the door. GySgt Morrison then called me on the Dragon Net and told me to secure the doors. I told him that they had already been locked. The voices were heard again about 0610 so I called again and told Dragon #20, 27, and Sgt Keady that I was going to try to get to the helipad....
>
> Just before I started crawling toward the helipad door, I started receiving machine gun fire. It sounded like it was coming from the hotel across the street or the vacant lot in front of the Embassy. When I reached the door to the helipad, 0625 or 0630 I saw light shining down on the steps from the helipad. I yelled and said that I was a Marine Guard. The person with the light was Mr. Wendt, the Duty Officer.
>
> I went up to the helipad and saw three (3) other persons. Two man [*sic*] from Page Communications and Corporal Zahuranic. I asked Corporal Zahuranic if he was alright and he said that he was. About 3 to 5 minutes later, the helicopter that was to evacuate us attempted to land. When the helicopter landed, he unloaded about 6 cases of M-16 ammunition. After the ammunition was unloaded, one of the crew members motioned us to get into the helicopter. I pulled Cpl Zahuranic up the stairs, until he was able to crawl into the helicopter.
>
> The Duty Officer started going down the stairs toward the 6th Floor. As soon as Cpl Zahuranic, one man from Page Communications (Army) and myself were in the helicopter, one of the crew members asked me if that was all. I told him that there were still more (3) people, one on the steps of the helipad and two on the six[th] floor. As we were taking off, small arms fire started

Two Marine Security Guards examine the damage to the entrace of the U.S. Embassy in Saigon. One rocket-propelled grenade round hit the Great Seal of the United States, and knocked it off the embassy's front doors. Today, the emblem is on permanent display at the Marine Security Guard Battalion at Quantico, Virginia (courtesy U.S. Marine Corps).

again. Then a round whizzed through the bottom of the helicopter missing Cpl Zahuranic's head by 7 inches. Called GySgt Morrison informing him that Cpl Zahuranic was being evacuated and that he was okay.

Flying about 2 or 3 minutes, the helicopter landed somewhere in the rice paddies, Gia Dinh about 3 to 5 miles south of Saigon. Cpl Zahuranic was then transferred by a crew member and myself through high grass and water waist high. As soon as we were aboard the second helicopter, I noticed that the shotgun was left in the first helicopter or else fell into the tall grass. The second helicopter then took off, heading to the hospital at Long Binh.

At Long Binh, I waited until they told me that Cpl Zauranic was okay. I waited at Long Binh as they had a flight to Tan San Nhut heliport. There I spent the night....[43]

As Sergeant Soto fired on and reported the enemy positions to Captain O'Brien and the other Marine Security Guards, Viet Cong sappers, armed with rocket propelled grenades, moved to the center of the embassy grounds and fired several rounds at the doors. The blast knocked out the windows behind the steel bars and penetrated, but did not knock down the doors secured by Corporal Zahuranic and Sergeant Harper. The blast did, however, damage the Great Seal of the United States, and knocked it off the wall near the entrance of the embassy.[44]

Awakened by Corporal Dennis J. Ryan, the duty non-commissioned officer at the Marine House, after initial rounds of explosions, Captain O'Brien made his way toward the embassy along with Sergeant Richard G. Frattarelli, his driver. The U.S. Embassy, located four blocks from the Marine House, was now a battleground. Captain O'Brien, Sergeants Frattarelli, Patullo and Reed, and Corporal Timothy P. Inemer headed toward the embassy where Sergeants Harper and Soto as well as the U.S. Army military policemen had been engaged in a furious firefight with the Viet Cong sappers. As Captain O'Brien's team approached the embassy in a jeep, South Vietnamese military policemen stopped the would-be rescuers at a hastily erected checkpoint about a block away from the grounds. Leaving their vehicle at the police checkpoint the Marines continued toward the embassy on foot.

The Battle Joined: The Fight for the Embassy

As Captain O'Brien reached the embassy he called out to the military policemen who were supposed to be there but instead saw six of the Viet Cong still inside the grounds. Meanwhile, Gunnery Sergeant Morrison took charge of the situation at the Marine House and remained in frequent contact with the U.S. ambassador and a reaction team, led by Staff Sergeant Leroy J. Banks and five other Marines. In fact, Gunnery Sergeant Morrison and his reaction team proceeded to the embassy to restore order and kill the remaining Viet Cong guerrillas still inside the compound. As Staff Sergeant Banks' team made its way, two U.S. Army military policemen stopped the Marines about 300 yards from the compound and told the Marines to leave the area, as "the VC were attacking." Banks' reaction team dismounted from their vehicle and proceeded on foot, reaching the Norodom building that housed "the Consulate and other U.S. government offices, on the southwest side of the Embassy." Here, Staff Sergeant Banks attempted to find a way into the embassy. As the Marines probed the entrance, they came under fire "from edgy [South] Vietnamese police-men." Unable to reach the embassy compound, Staff Sergeant Banks' reaction team "returned to the Norodom building and joined the Marine security guards already there."[45]

Captain O'Brien and his team of Marine Security Guards, as well as the two State Department security officers, meanwhile prepared to launch a furious counterattack against the Viet Cong. Upon reaching the embassy's Mac Dinh Chi entrance, O'Brien's team encountered intense automatic weapons fire from the Viet Cong hunkered down inside the diplomatic compound. As Captain O'Brien later recounted, the fighting was as intense as that ongoing in the countryside surrounding Saigon:

> Sergeant Reed killed one (1) perhaps two (2) Viet Cong at this time. We now took up firing positions behind trees on the opposite side of the street and exchanged fire with the Viet Cong. About 0300, Mr. Crampsey and Mr. Furey, Embassy Security Officers, arrived and joined in the firefight. The Viet Cong were kept under fire all this time. During the course of the early morning, repeated attempts were made by Mr. Furey and Marine Security Guards to shoot off and break the locks of the gates and enter the Embassy Compound; all of these attempts were unsuccessful. During the hours of darkness, several attempts were made by Marine Security Guards to get where we had to leave our vehicles with communications at the Cahn Sat Station about 200 yards from the Embassy. The Cahn Sats (Vietnamese Police), apparently thinking us Viet Cong fired on each attempt by Marine Security Guards to reach the vehicles/radio. A number of other times during the early morning hours the Cahn Sats fired in our direction. This firing on the Marine Security Guards by the Cahn Sats put the OIC [Captain O'Brien] out of communication with Marine House for about three and one half (3 1/2) hours until about 0630. About 0330, six (6)

Two U.S. Army military policemen advance toward the U.S. Embassy in the early morning hours of January 31, 1968, during the Tet offensive (courtesy U.S. Marine Corps).

Military Police arrived and joined in the fight with the Viet Cong, a couple of them were sent up on the roof of a building under construction adjacent to the Embassy, and they were able to fire down on the Viet Cong in the front yard of the Embassy. About 0400, the OIC and Mr. Crampsey climbed onto the roof tops of the buildings along the rear wall of the Embassy Compound facing the Mission Coordinator's House. From here we saw two (2) or three (3) Viet Cong at the rear of the house, and brought them under fire from that direction. About 0630, the OIC directed the MPs to hold in place along Mac Dinh Chi while preparations were made to re-deploy the Marine Security Guards along the rear wall for the assault on the Embassy Compound with the coming of day light. Sgt Reed was now able to get to the radio vehicle and call Marine House for more Marines and Ammunition. The OIC and Sgt Patullo had climbed up on the rear wall and were ready to jump over when Sgt Patullo was hit in the thigh by fire from the vicinity of the Mission Coordinators House, knocking him to the ground.

Shortly after this, Sgts Bothwell, R.L. Johnson and [Joseph S.] Wolff arrived with weapons and ammo. They were directed along with Sgt Reed, to take up positions on the Generator Roof, while, the OIC, Sgt Bothwell and Mr. Crampsey layed down a base of fire from our original roof top position. Once in position all along the rear wall we were able to direct a heavy, accurate volume of fire on the Viet Cong in the parking lot, along the chancery wall and in the Mission Coordinators house. During this time Sgt Bothwell killed two Viet Cong, Sgt Reed and Johnson each killed one Viet Cong.

About 0730, from our position on the roofs along the rear wall we could see SSgt Banks' Marine Security Guards and MPs moving into the Embassy Compound from the vicinity of Norodom Compound. At this point the OIC's forces moved over the wall and down from the generator roof linked up with SSgt Banks force of Marine Security Guards and MPs, swept across the back yard of the Embassy toward the Mission Coordinator's House where the last of the Viet Cong had holed up.[46]

Fighting at the Norodom Building and the End of the Siege

While Staff Sergeant Banks attempted to maneuver his reaction team into the beleaguered embassy, Captain O'Brien and his team of Marines and six U.S. Army military policemen continued to "lay down a base of fire" until reinforcements could arrive to retake the embassy in the morning. At the Norodom building, Staff Sergeant Banks placed his men into defensive positions with several of them on the roof, "where they could fire down on the VC in the compound." Meanwhile, Staff Sergeant Banks and a small group of leathernecks attempted unsuccessfully to enter the embassy compound through the Norodom gate as the Viet Cong let loose a volley of automatic weapons fire. Despite having been reinforced by a U.S. Army Military police lieutenant and seven military policemen, the Americans still found themselves severely out-gunned by the Viet Cong, as they had but a handful of M16s, three Beretta submachine guns and .38 caliber pistols at their disposal.[47] Captain O'Brien recalled that the fighting in and around Staff Sergeant Banks' position grew more intense as the reaction team inched its way into the compound:

> About 0300 SSgt Banks reaction team, after being stopped by MPs at the corner of Hai Ba Trung and Thong Nhut arrived at the Norodom Compound gate, he split his force into two groups, leaving one group at Norodom, he led the other group along the Embassy wall toward the main front entrance. Heavy automatic weapons fire and grenades drove them back toward Norodom Compound. SSgt Banks moved all of his men into Norodom and had them take up firing positions with the men already there. SSgt Banks placed some of his men on the Consular Section roof from where they could bring fire to bear on the Viet Cong inside the Embassy grounds. About 0330, a group of about six or seven MPs arrived at the Norodom and joined in the fire fight with the Marine Security Guards. About this time some of the Marine Security Guards had worked their way behind the Consular Buildings and found the rear gate by the maintenance shacks open. Both Marine Security Guards and MPs tried to get into the Embassy grounds through this gate but were prevented from doing so by heavy automatic weapons fire and rocket fire from the Viet Cong inside the Embassy Grounds....
>
> About 0600, Cpl Marshall[48] was killed by Sniper fire from the apartment building at #1Mac Dinh Chi across from the Embassy. Cpl Marshall had remained on the Norodom Roof all through the fighting and had been accounted for several of the Viet Cong dead and wounded.[49]

With the scarred walls of the U.S. Embassy hit by enemy rocket-propelled grenades as a backdrop, two Viet Cong sappers lie where they were killed by Marine crossfire on the night of January 30–31, 1968 (courtesy U.S. Marine Corps).

Captain O'Brien noted that as the battle for the embassy compound ended, helicopters carrying Company C of the 502d Infantry, 101st Airborne Division landed on top of the embassy's chancery and mopped up the last pockets of enemy resistance. At 0900, Captain O'Brien and a group of Marine Security Guards conducted a room-by-room search to insure that "none of the attackers somehow taken refuge there." Sergeant Harper recalled that in those last moments prior to the order to cease fire, he "called Post #12 again, and they informed me that the Marines were coming over for tear gas so I opened the lobby entrance near the parking lot and the MSGs came and got tear gas, masks and flak jackets to finish off the V.C., in Colonel [George] Jacobsen's House. The 101st came down from the roof a few minutes later."[50] Both Captain O'Brien and Sergeant Harper asserted in their after-action reports that throughout the siege at the U.S. Embassy Compound "at no time during the fight did a V.C. enter the Embassy building."

The fighting, however, did have a toll on the embassy itself. As Captain O'Brien noted, "the lobby of the Embassy was in shambles from rocket fire and grenades and it was virtually impossible for the Marine Guards to effect any kind of adequate control because people were everywhere interfering with any attempts to maintain order." Also, once the Marines and soldiers cleared the embassy it soon became the focus of reporters, television cameramen, and U.S. and South Vietnamese government officials who "milled about" and continually stopped

Marine Security Guards to gain information on the attack. As Captain O'Brien noted in his report, "It was late morning before the crowd began to thin out and some semblance of order was effected."[51]

Steady Nerves and Valor

Far from the property damage, however, was the toll it took on the Marines and enemy alike. From the time of the first rocket propelled grenades hitting the embassy to the final assault on the Chancery and Norodom Buildings, the Marines suffered one killed in action (Corporal Marshall) and nine wounded in action. The U.S. Army's 716th Military Police Battalion suffered four killed in action and a like number wounded. The Viet Cong paid an even stiffer price for their failure. Of the twenty attackers from the elite Viet Cong *C-10* Battalion, the Marines and military policemen killed eighteen while two were taken prisoner.[52]

In honoring the men who defended the U.S. Embassy in Saigon, including Corporal James C. Marshall and the five Marines wounded during the siege, Secretary of State Dean Rusk praised the bravery and professionalism they demonstrated during the enemy assault in Saigon. On February 16, 1968, two weeks after the enemy assault on the U.S. Embassy in Saigon, in a ceremony held at Henderson Hall, Secretary of State Rusk told a graduating class from the Marine Security Guard School and their families that another "luminous" chapter had been added to the history of the Marine Corps in defense of a U.S. Embassy:

> Less than three weeks ago "our" Marines added another luminous chapter to the great history of the Corps. They suddenly were confronted with a situation which called for instant decision, fast action, and steady courage ... a situation in which they had to fight to carry out their two-fold mission: the protection of classified material, and the protection of lives and property. In the early morning hours of January 31 our Embassy in Saigon was subjected to a vicious surprise attack with rocket launchers, automatic weapons, grenades, and small arms. In that critical moment our Marines once again demonstrated their resourcefulness, their steady nerves and their valor....
>
> I cannot help but feel overwhelming gratitude and pride in the conduct of our Marine Security Guard in Saigon — and of our Marine detachments throughout the world — and in all of you sitting here before me....
>
> My colleagues an I know that — given the same circumstances, which we hope will never recur — our Marine Security Guards all over the world would react as effectively and courageously as did the detachment in Saigon.[53]

After delivering this address, Secretary Rusk presented General Leonard F. Chapman, the commandant of the Marine Corps, with a unit citation for the Marine Security Guard Detachment in Saigon. The citation was given in recognition of the "effective defense" of the U.S. Embassy during the Viet Cong attack in the early morning hours of January 31, 1968.[54]

The Attack on the Embassy and the Lessons Learned

Despite the psychological "victory" achieved by the Viet Cong in their attack on the U.S. Embassy in Saigon, the assault was a mere sideshow in the larger scheme of events of the Tet Offensive. From an operational standpoint, the attack failed to achieve any of its objectives and instead floundered as the Marine Security Guards, U.S. Army and South Vietnamese military policemen quickly gained control of the situation and launched a series of counterattacks against the enemy sappers. The Marine Security Guard program benefited from the lessons learned in the attack, the first of which was the need to expand the detachment at Saigon with a further 39 Marines. Also, as a result of the assault on the embassy during the Tet Offensive, Headquarters Marine Corps and the State Department reorganized the Saigon-based Marine Security Guard Detachment as a separate company, Company E. In time, this expansion of a detachment into a full company served as the basis for the expansion of the Marine Security Guard program as whole during the 1970s and 1980s. Prior to the Tet Offensive, there were four separate Marine Security Guard Companies (A, B, C, and D) that operated overseas in support of the Department of State's mission. A direct result of the Tet Offensive was the recognition on the part of both State Department and Marine Corps officials of the volatile nature of world events and the need for an expansion of the Marine Security Guard program. After the Tet Offensive in January 1968, the MSG program underwent its first major expansion since its organization in 1948. On "...29 April 1968, a *Memorandum of Understanding (MOU) between the Department of State and the Marine Corps* (based on the authority contained in a DOS [Department of State]/DOD [Department of Defense] Memorandum of Agreement of 1 August 1967) was signed to modernize and streamline the administrative and control aspects of the MSG program as well as reinforce Company Headquarters procedures abroad. During the same year, the MSG detachment at the American Embassy, Saigon, Republic of Vietnam, was reinforced and re-designated Company E."[55]

Also, many of the lessons learned, such as protection of the ambassador, his staff, and the embassy itself were incorporated in a Personal Security Unit Manual. Originally, a manual of this type was specifically written in response to a request from Ambassador Henry Cabot Lodge, Jr., in 1965 for a set of standard operating procedures for Marines handling diplomatic security. The updated manual, published and approved by Mr. Marvin L. Garrett, the regional security officer in Saigon in early 1971, incorporated many of the lessons learned during the 1968 siege of the U.S. Embassy. Specific topics covered by the Personal Security Unit Manual included: (1) the creation and training of an eight-man Personal Security Unit that consisted of Marine non-commissioned officers; (2) motorcade security for the ambassador; (3) security for in-country trips; (4) protection for the ambassador; (5) emergency equipment, and; (6) PSU credentials. While the manual was intended for use in the Republic of Vietnam, this document served as a guidebook later incorporated into Marine Security Guard training.[56]

While the Viet Cong achieved an initial surprise in their assault on the U.S. Embassy, the results for the enemy were, in fact, suicidal. As was the case throughout the Tet Offensive, the steadfastness of the Marines, soldiers and the South Vietnamese during the battle at the U.S. Embassy turned back this all-out assault. Despite the loss of life suffered by the United States and South Vietnam, the fact remained that the training, discipline, and professionalism of the Marine Security Guard detachment in Saigon paid huge dividends in the defeat of a very determined and well-trained enemy. This came, however, with a heavy price, as Corporal James C. Marshall became the first, but not the last, to die in the defense of the U.S. Embassy in the Republic of Vietnam and in neighboring Cambodia.

A Quiet Interlude: Marine Security Guards in the Republic of Vietnam, 1969–1973

In comparison to the tumultuous year of 1968 and the surprise attack on the U.S. Embassy, Marine Security Guard duty in Saigon from the end of the Tet Offensive through the end of

1971 remained relatively routine interspersed with high level visits and special duties. In 1969, Captain Roger M. Jaroch replaced Captain O'Brien in command of Company E. Later, Captain Jaroch was succeeded by Captain Robert P. Lacousiere and later Major Harry J. Shane. In turn, these officers led the five officers and 155 enlisted Marines assigned to the Saigon embassy throughout the next year. In contrast to the enemy's January 31, 1968, attack on the embassy during the Tet offensive, the year 1969 proved to be a very quiet one. During the course of the year, President and Mrs. Richard M. Nixon, as well as Secretary of State William P. Rogers, paid a visit to the U.S. Embassy in Saigon. In addition to the visit by their commander-in-chief, the Marine Security Guards received an inspection visit by the commandant of the Marine Corps, General Leonard F. Chapman, and the sergeant major of the Marine Corps, Sergeant Major Joseph E. Daily. While the year was relatively free of terrorist threats and activity aimed at the U.S. Embassy, the only serious incident that occurred was the attempted assassination of Tran Van Huong, premier of South Vietnam. The assassination attempt, which occurred only fifty yards from the embassy grounds, failed, however, as South Vietnamese police managed to capture and later charge four suspects in the incident. No U.S. Embassy personnel were injured in the attack.[57]

As the U.S. began to "stand down" and re-deploy its forces throughout 1969 and into 1970 in the Republic of Vietnam, Marine Embassy Guards assigned to Company E continued in its mission to guard classified material and protect U.S. personnel and property. Even as the redeployment of U.S. forces continued under President Richard M. Nixon's policy of Vietnamization, Company C, headquartered in Manila, Republic of the Philippines, created a new five-man Marine Security Guard located in Phnom Penh, Cambodia. Meanwhile, Captain Herbert M. Steigelman, Jr., assumed command of Company E from January to November 1970.

During this same period, Company E was re-organized into three elements (a headquarters section of two officers and 10 enlisted Marines; an interior guard force of one officer and 90 enlisted Marines; and an exterior guard force of one officer and 46 enlisted Marines). The exterior guard, essentially a reinforced rifle platoon, now assumed the task of responding to any further enemy assault on the embassy. In fact, the organization and mission of this Marine exterior guard, once the mission of the host country, became the first of its kind throughout the Marine Security Guard program. More important, however, was the addition of an exterior Marine guard designed to prevent a re-occurrence of the disruption and tactical delay experienced by the Marine Security Guards in Saigon during the 1968 Tet Offensive. In addition, "a reinforced rifle platoon was formed to control access into the compound and provide a reaction force in the event of another attack."[58]

With the organization and deployment of an exterior guard, a detachment of seven Marines "was selected as the Ambassador's Personal Security Unit (PSU). The PSU provided compound security and conducted route reconnaissance when the Ambassador left the compound."[59] Also, "all posts, vehicles, and buildings in the compound were connected by a sophisticated communications system, known as the 'Dragon Net,' which was manned by a five-man [Marine] detachment." The average monthly strength of Company E throughout 1971 was five officers and 150 enlisted Marines. This was, in fact, an increase of 10 men over that of the previous year (1970). This addition of manpower came about as Company E received added security responsibilities. In May 1971, the Saigon-based Marine detachment received the additional mission of providing a temporary five-man detachment for the American consulate located in Da Nang, Republic of Vietnam. This assignment became permanent in June 1971 as the Da Nang detachment, which consisted of one non-commissioned officer (a sergeant) and nine watchstanders. While the Marine Security Guards of the Da Nang detachment remained under the administrative control of Company E, this detachment fell under the operational control of the consulate general.

One last administrative change occurred on March 1, 1970, when operational control of the defense of the U.S. Consulate, Da Nang, Republic of Vietnam, transferred from the Marine Security Guard Detachment's tactical area of responsibility to the U.S. Army's XXIV Corps. As III Marine Amphibious continued to re-deploy from Vietnam back to Okinawa and Camp Pendleton, XXIV Corps assumed full operational control of the 3d Military Police Battalion by March 9, 1970. In turn, the XXIV Corps' officials assigned the 3d Military Police Battalion, Fleet Logistics Command, Fleet Marine Force Pacific, commanded by Lieutenant Colonel C. Fimian, with the defense of the American consulate and its personnel. Along with its other duties of law enforcement and the guarding of enemy prisoners of war, the 3d Military Police Battalion maintained a round-the-clock defense of the American Consulate as a reaction force. On May 31, 1970, the military policemen provided security for Ambassador Ellsworth Bunker as he toured the large Marine base at Da Nang. The military policemen assigned to Company D, 3d Military Police Battalion, continued in this role as a consulate defense force until the battalion re-deployed back to its base in the United States in late September 1970. In May 1971, five Marines "were sent to Da Nang on temporary additional duty to establish external security functions for the American consulate there." The State Department later increased the size of the detachment at Da Nang with five more Marines later that June when the ten Marines formally became a fully fledged Marine Security Guard detachment of one non-commissioned officer and nine watchstanders (lance corporal and below). The detachment was placed under the operational control of the consulate general and the administrative control of Company E.[60] As Company E resumed its role in the protection of the U.S. Consulate in Da Nang, the Marines stationed at the U.S. Embassy in Saigon, commensurate with the U.S. Marine Corps' redeployment to bases in Japan and the United States, likewise began to reduce the size of the embassy guard.[61]

Civic Action

In spite of their main assignment of embassy defense and protection of classified material, the Marines assigned to Company E were also "Ambassadors in Green," as they conducted their own version of civic action while in the Republic of Vietnam. In keeping with their time- honored tradition of "Toys for Tots," the Marines of Company E held, on December 24, 1970, a Christmas Party for the Vietnamese children of the Go Van Number II Orphanage. While the children enjoyed their Marine-cooked meal at the Marshall Hall enlisted quarters and later at Marine House Number Two, "Santa Claus" passed out presents, donated by the embassy staff, United States Agency for International Development, and the Joint United States Public Affairs Office. The following spring, Company E assumed responsibility of the My Hoa Orphanage. On Easter Sunday, 1971, embassy Marines visited the children of the orphanage, where the leathernecks brought the children gifts of toys, food, and clothing donated by the American Legion of Punta Gorda and Naples, Florida, and by the citizens and merchants of Immokalee, Florida, through the efforts of the mother of Company E's staff non-commissioned officer, Gunnery Sergeant Robert M. Jenkins.[62]

Like other commands throughout Vietnam, Company E was not immune to the disciplinary problems that wracked the U.S. Armed Forces in the wake of the redeployment of

U.S. forces from Vietnam. Company E, in fact, "like all other sizable Marine commands in Vietnam, had its share of discipline and drug problems." From the period of January to June 1971, Captain William E. Keller, Jr., who had assumed command of the Saigon-based company in November 1970, conducted company-level non-judicial punishment on 27 Marines, while two more were sent to battalion at Henderson Hall in Virginia. Five of the twenty-nine Marines disciplined "were ultimately removed from duty when found unsuitable for retention in the Marine Security Guard program. An additional five Marines during the same period were recommended for discharge by "reasons of unfitness for possession of dangerous drugs."[63]

As was the case in 1969, the Marine Security Guards of Company E played host to a number of dignitaries and U.S. civilian and military officials. Included in this group was Vice President Spiro T. Agnew, who met with Ambassador Ellsworth Bunker during a brief stay in Vietnam on January 1–2, 1970. A few days later, General Leonard F. Chapman, Jr., and Sergeant Major of the Marine Corps Joseph W. Daily followed Vice President Agnew's visit, and inspected the Marines of Company E on January 9, 1970. In July of that same year, Secretary of State William P. Rogers stayed at the embassy for a series of intense meetings that took place over a three-day period. The secretary of state was followed once again by Vice President Agnew, who returned to confer for two days with Ambassador Bunker in August of 1970.[64]

On October 28, 1971, Company E received a new commanding officer, Major Edward J. Land, who replaced Captain William E. Keller. Major Land, a veteran of both the Korean and Vietnam Wars, had previously served as the commanding officer of Scout-Sniper Company at Da Nang with the 1st Marine Division, and was about to face some of "the biggest challenges of his Marine Corps career" as he took charge.[65]

De-Activation and Withdrawal, 1971–1974

Amidst the background of a war that seemed endless, the Marines assigned to Company E maintained a steady and constant vigil over the ambassador, his staff, and the embassy itself. As the active U.S. involvement in the Vietnam War ended, the U.S. Embassy remained the object of terrorist violence and enemy rocket attacks. During the last half of 1971, the city of Saigon prepared for elections throughout the country. During this same period Company E's main concern revolved around security in and around the embassy compound. In order to prepare for any possible contingency, particularly an enemy sapper attack on U.S. and South Vietnamese installations located throughout city, routine training was briefly cancelled to meet any emergency. The Marine Security Guard's "Scramble Reaction Team," designed to repel terrorist and enemy attacks, responded that fall to over 140 bomb threats and detonated over 29 bombs sent to the embassy. Also, the Viet Cong maintained their pressure on U.S. personnel as they launched a total of 122 rockets on the city. On December 25, 1971, Christmas Day, a Communist terrorist threw an M26 fragmentation grenade into the Exterior Guard's Marine House.[66] The blast injured Sergeant Michael L. Linnan and a local security guard, Salay Mag.[67]

By June 1971, as U.S. forces in Vietnam continued to re-deploy back to the United States and Japan, Company E, along with Sub-Unit 1, ANGLICO, and the Marine Advisory Unit became the "only U.S. Marine Commands remaining in Vietnam." By mid–1971, the remaining elements of the 1st Marine Air Wing and 1st Marine Division re-deployed from Vietnam after having carried out six years of sustained combat operations. Eventually, administrative control of Company E was transferred back to Company C, headquartered in Hong Kong, on June 30, 1974. Prior to this transfer, Headquarters Marine Corps, on May 20, 1974, de-activated the Exterior Guard Platoon of Company E, which it had created in response to the Viet Cong's attack on the U.S. Embassy in January 1968 during the Tet Offensive.

With the de-activation of the Exterior Guard Platoon, the Marine Security Guards who remained in Saigon and the other consulates throughout Vietnam continued their vigilant watch as their comrades in the field units and forward squadrons began to leave Vietnam for bases in the United States and Japan. In recognition of their outstanding performance and steadfastness, Ambassador Bunker, on April 29, 1971, presented the Marines of Company E with the Meritorious Unit Commendation. The citation read, in part, "for meritorious service as the immediate defense and security force for the U.S. Mission, Saigon, Republic of Vietnam, from February 1, 1969 to December 31, 1970."[68]

Once again, the most visible presence of the United States in South Vietnam became the Marine Security Guards of Company E. Ultimately, the Marines of Company E became the last American unit evacuated from South Vietnam, nearly four years after the Marine Corps' tactical role ended on April 30, 1975.[69] It would be this distinguished unit of Marine Security Guards that would write the last valorous chapter of the U.S. involvement in the Vietnam War.

The Attack on the U.S. Embassy in Phnom Penh, Cambodia

While Company E maintained a vigilant watch over the U.S. Embassy in Saigon, the war in Southeast Asia spread into neighboring Cambodia. On March 18, 1970, the neutralist god-king Prince Norodom Sihanouk, whose neutralist position during the Vietnam War turned Cambodia into a North Vietnamese-Viet Cong base of operations, fled first to France for medical treatment and later into exile in Beijing, China, leaving General Lon Nol and Sisowatch Sirik Matak (Sihanouk's cousin) in charge. Shortly thereafter, the North Vietnamese, who had been training and arming the Cambodian communists or Khmer Rouge, infiltrated approximately 12,000 Cambodian guerrillas who at once launched an insurgency against General Nol's government.[70] Cambodia erupted into anarchy by late March 1970. As was the case in neighboring South Vietnam, the trouble soon spilled from the countryside into the cities, particularly the capital, Phnom Penh. This would shortly involve the five-man Marine Security Guard Detachment.

The Marine Security Guard Detachment in Phnom Penh came under heavy rocket and mortar attack on the afternoon of September 26, 1971. In the terrorist attack on the U.S. Embassy compound, Sergeant Charles W. Turberville was killed and four other Marines wounded while playing softball. This necessitated the dispatch of reinforcements taken from Company E in neighboring South Vietnam. This five-man Marine Security Guard team, under the command of Master Sergeant Clenton L. Jones, reinforced the Marine Embassy Guard in the Cambodian capital.

An Uneasy Peace, 1973–1974

Despite the lull in the fighting that took place after the Paris Peace Accords were signed on January 27, 1973, the war in Southeast Asia was far from over. As the last U.S. combat forces withdrew from South Vietnam, the North Vietnamese leadership planned for the next phase of their campaign to unite the two countries under Hanoi. With an estimated 140,000 to 300,000 North Vietnamese troops still inside South Vietnam, it became apparent to U.S. military and political leaders that the Paris Peace Accords were but an interval before the next round of fighting took place.[71]

As for the Marines of Company E, the short interval before war once again called upon their services was a time of reduction and re-organization. Major Gerald E. Diffee, who commanded Company E, oversaw one of the largest contingents of Marines in Southeast Asia following the signing of the Paris Peace Accords. Prior to his handing over the company to Major Daniel Bergen on September 15, 1973, the duties and responsibilities of Company E had grown considerably in wake of the American withdrawal from the actual fighting. Besides the U.S. Embassy Compound, the USDAO Compound at Thon Son Nhut Airbase, and the Personal Security Unit protecting Ambassador Graham Martin, the Marine Security Guards assigned to Company E likewise staffed the consulates located at Da Nang, Nha Trang, and Bien Hoa. Organized into a headquarters and three platoons, with two platoons assigned to the interior and exterior guard detachments at the embassy and consulates, the third platoon protected the ambassador, his family, and his residence.

Beginning in mid–1973, the average strength of the company stood at five officers and 143 enlisted Marines.[72] As the situation in Saigon and South Vietnamese countryside stabilized, Headquarters Marine Corps reduced Company E's strength. By 1974, in fact, the Exterior Guard had "absorbed the Ambassador's Residence Platoon" with the Interior Guard Platoon "re-designated the Marine Detachment, Saigon, and placed under control of the Hong Kong–based regional company, Company C, Marine Security Guard Battalion (State Department)."[73] On the same day, the Exterior Guard Platoon, organized in 1968 in response to the Viet Cong attack on the U.S. Embassy, was also de-activated.[74] In a letter to Major Bergen, Commanding Officer of Company "E" announcing the de-activation of the Exterior Guard Platoon, Ambassador Graham Martin praised the efficiency and steadfastness of the Marines assigned to this platoon over the past six years of its existence:

> On this date, the last day of duty for the Exterior Guard Platoon of Company "E," I would like to express my appreciation to all the Marines of the Exterior Guard Platoon who have served the Embassy so well over the past six years.
>
> As you know, prior to the communist Tet offensive of January 1968, the Marine Security Guard at the Embassy here in Saigon was not unlike that of other embassies throughout the world. Since then, approximately three-hundred and fifty Marines have served with the Exterior Guard Platoon. These Marines, unlike those of all other embassies, were assigned to duty without benefit of any formal guard training whatsoever. Most of them came to Company "E" directly from Individual Training School or "boot camp"; it is to their great credit that they learned and performed their assignment in typical Marine Corps fashion. They have served at the Consulates General in Da Nang, Nha Trang and Bien Hoa and at a variety of posts of the American Mission here in Saigon. Their overall performance has been nothing short of outstanding and I congratulate them all.
>
> There is no question that with the passage of time, the Marines of the Exterior Guard Platoon will join their legendary fellow Marines of the Peking Legation Guards in the annals of Marine Corps history and tradition.
>
> Please convey to the members of the Exterior Guard Platoon my thanks and appreciation for a job well done. I wish them well in all future assignments and endeavors.[75]

Meanwhile, Captain (Major-Select) James H. Kean, Company C's executive officer, arrived in Saigon to re-organize the Saigon Detachment. Captain Kean not only re-assigned the Interior Guard Platoon but also coordinated the transfer of the consulate detachments. The Marine captain likewise traveled to the American Consulate at Can Tho, where he began to plan for the establishment of a Marine Security Guard detachment. Other administrative moves saw the deactivation of Company E and its re-assignment to Addis Abada, Ethiopia, in February 1974. It was left to Major Daniel F. Bergen, the commanding officer of Company E, to officially de-activate the company on June 30, 1974. The remaining 90 enlisted watchstanders who comprised the Exterior Guard Platoon and the detachments located at Da Nang, Nha Trang, and Bien Hoa administratively became a part of Company C.[76]

Once again under the administrative responsibility of Company C, Master Sergeant Juan J. Valdez assumed command of the Marine Security Guard detachment, U.S. Embassy, Saigon, Republic of Vietnam. Staff Sergeant Roger F. Painter became the staff non-commissioned officer in charge of the Marine Security Guard detachment located at the U.S. Consulate, Nha Trang. Staff Sergeant Walter W. Sparks assumed temporary command of the Security Guard detachment at Bien Hoa prior to the arrival of Gunnery Sergeant Robert W. Schlager. Prior to their assumption of command over the respective Marine Security Guard detachments, State Department officials emphasized to these Marine staff non-commissioned officers that "their primary mission was to protect the American consulates and their classified material." To this end, all of the Marine Security Guard throughout South Vietnam "trained regularly to improve its readiness and enhance security of its consulate."[77]

Upon Captain Kean's assumption of command of Company C from Major Donald L. Evans on June 16, 1974,[78] his first task was to activate the Marine Security Guard detachment at the U.S. Consulate located in Can Tho, "the first ever in that city," in the province of Phong Dinh. Placed in charge of the Marine detachment was Staff Sergeant Boyette S. Hasty, who later played a leading role during the final evacuation from Saigon a year later in April 1975.[79]

Meanwhile, next door in war-torn Cambodia, Gunnery Sergeant Clarence D. McClenahan's 11-man Marine Security Guard detachment at the U.S. Embassy in Phnom Penh, continued to carry out a series of alerts and quick responses as the situation in that country worsened on a day-to-day basis. In fact, as the situation in Cambodia deteriorated, "there was talk of an evacuation," which in turn prompted Gunnery Sergeant McClenahan and his Marines to prepare, if so ordered by the ambassador, for a possible evacuation of American dependents and destruction of classified material.

Planning for a possible evacuation did not just occur in Cambodia. Colonel Nicholas M. Trappnell, Jr., who headed a special planning group attached to the Saigon-based U.S. Defense Attaché Office, began to examine the possibility of an evacuation of U.S. and foreign nationals from Saigon if necessary as early as March 1973. After the North Vietnamese launched its war-ending January 1975 offensive, the Special Planning Group, headed by Colonel Pat Howard, USMC, began to plan for the evacuation of Saigon over the objections of Ambassador Graham Martin, "who had refused to entertain any discussion of such an eventuality."[80]

Operation Eagle Pull: The Planning Stages, 1973–1974

On April 13, 1973, U.S. military planners attached to the United States Support Activities Group (USSAG), headquartered at the Royal Thai Air Force Base at Nakhon Phanom, began planning for a possible non-combatant emergency evacuation operation of all American citizens and designated aliens from Cambodia. "Marines were involved in the operation from the very beginning of the planning phase. Marine officers in key planning billets on the

USSAG staff early recognized the absolute necessity for rapid reaction to evacuation requirements and relied heavily on the responsiveness of the forward deployed Marine forces to meet these requirements."[81] Among those who played a major role in the planning for an evacuation from Cambodia were the Marines assigned to the U.S. Embassy in Phnom Penh.

The original plan, as worked out by USSAG, called for the evacuation of all designated persons from the Pochentong Airfield, outside the city of Phnom Penh by commercial aircraft with the ambassador maintaining "complete control of the entire operation."[82] A second plan called for the non-combatant evacuation of all citizens and designated personnel via U.S. Air Force fixed-wing aircraft flying out of Pochentong Airfield. The latter operation would be controlled entirely by USSAG in Thailand.

A third plan evolved that assumed that due the psychological effect on the morale and resolve of Lon Nol's government, the U.S. ambassador and his staff would be the last to leave. Hence, USSAG planners focused on the selection of several egress sites to facilitate evacuation by helicopter. This worst case option was "recognized from the outset as being the most likely option."[83] A reinforced Marine rifle company, approximately 360 Marines, would be used to secure the airfield and egress sites.[84] Other plans envisaged the use of a reinforced company of about 150 Marines coming from an offshore Marine Amphibious Unit (MAU). This force would use only Marine CH-53 helicopters in the extraction of the American and other foreign nationals from Phnom Penh. Meanwhile U.S. Air Force helicopters would arrive from bases in neighboring Thailand in order to extract the landing force. The last plan USSAG planners suggested was the use of both Marine and Air Force helicopters flying multiple sorties while a 240-man Marine landing force secured the landing zones. The security force would be extracted as helicopter space became available.[85] Eventually, Marine planners assigned to USSAG selected the third option: the use of a reinforced Marine rifle company that would secure an airfield and other egress sites near the embassy while helicopters did "one complete turn-around (i.e., in and out twice)."[86]

As for the Marine Security Guard detachment, they were to protect the ambassador and his staff, and insure that no classified material was left inside the embassy in case an evacuation took place. John Gunther Dean, Jr., the U.S. ambassador to Cambodia, passed instructions that the Marine Security Guards were to notify and organize the evacuees into marshalling areas. The Marines inside the embassy were to erect barriers at the south entrance of the U.S. Embassy in Phnom Penh. As events turned out, Marine security guards played a more pivotal role when the evacuation took place on April 11, 1975.

Evacuation from Phnom Penh, 3–12 April 1975

Throughout the remainder of 1974, the situation in Cambodia stabilized as the government of Lon Nol consolidated its gains against the Communist-backed Khmer Rouge. This did not end planning by USSAG, however, as it was felt that the situation in Cambodia was far from stable. Events soon proved USSAG planners correct, as renewed offensive operations in the Cambodian countryside by the Khmer Rouge began to press in on the capital as Lon Nol's beleaguered forces fell back. More important for USSAG and III MAF planners, however, was the fact that the Khmer offensive occurred almost simultaneously with that by North Vietnamese forces along the Demilitarized Zone in Military Region 1. This renewed communist military activity signaled the commencement of the last phase of planning for the evacuation of both Phnom Penh and Saigon by USSAG planners.

By the last week in March 1975, it had become apparent to all inside the administration of President Gerald R. Ford[87] that it was only a matter of a few weeks that Phnom Penh would fall to the Communists. Meeting with members of the Senate Foreign Relations Committee as the Marines and U.S. Air Force personnel began the evacuation of Phnom Penh, President Ford told the reluctant senators that the United States "couldn't just cut and run. We had to consider the people of Vietnam and what might happen to them, especially those who had supported us." The same applied for Cambodians who had supported the U.S. war effort.

The Evacuation of Phnom Penh Commences

Standing off the coast of Cambodia in the Gulf of Thailand were elements of the 31st Marine Amphibious Unit/Amphibious Ready Group (ARG) aboard the attack carrier USS *Hancock* (CVA), and USS *Okinawa* (LPH), ready to carry out an evacuation of U.S. and other foreign nationals from Phnom Penh. Marines from 2nd Battalion, 4th Marines, and helicopters from HMH-463, commanded by Lieutenant Colonel H.M. Fix, positioned themselves aboard the *Okinawa* and *Hancock* and awaited the final word before they commenced evacuation operation ashore.

One of the most important lessons learned during the evacuation of both Phnom Penh and later Saigon was the close integration and working relationship of U.S. Embassy personnel and the Marine Air Contingency Battalion Landing Team. In fact, one of the legacies of the Vietnam War was the inter-relationship between Marine Security Guards and other Marine forces ashore and afloat. These are lessons Marine Embassy Guard detachments routinely plan and prepare for today.[88] Staff Sergeant Thomas J. Sabanski, USMC, who participated in both Operation Eagle Pull and later Frequent Wind, the evacuation of Saigon, recalled the events leading up and during the evacuation from Phnom Penh:

> My duties as the Battalion Comm[unications] Center Chief necessitated a daily read board of all messages sent and received by the Battalion Staff officers to be readied by before 0700. It was my task to peruse this board prior to it being delivered to the Battalion Adjutant section and assure its completeness and readability. After several days ... I noticed that we were getting a disproportionate volume of messages for a unit our size. Upon closer examination of the file copies, the read board was already in the staff sections, I noticed that most of the messages carried a high precedence and security classifications were higher too. I decided to start reading the messages rather than just skipping over them. Before I had a chance to go over the back files, I and everyone else found out what was in the wind, the hard way....
>
> Everything aboard our ship and the other four ships carrying the rest of the Battalion and our support units, took on an importance unlike our previous training. Maps and aerial photographs of the city, possible landing sites and the surrounding countryside came out of the S-2 (Intelligence) office at an outstanding rate. Briefings were held on every facet of the operation. Landing plans, evacuation procedures and communications plans were formulated and discussed. Every man, officer, and enlisted, that would go ashore as the landing party was given specific instructions and then quizzed on their assignments. Those of us that remained aboard ship were given tasks to perform once the flow of refugees started coming aboard....
>
> No one aboard our tiny fleet was left out of the planning or assignments. At last, the word came down to "Land the landing force" and as the rotor blades of the helicopters began moving, Marines in battle dress poured out of the openings in the ships to board them.[89]

In the early morning hours of April 11, 1975, President Ford issued the orders that began Operation Eagle Pull with Marines boarding helicopters in order to carry out the evacuation.[90]

Staff Sergeant Sabanski recounted, "The word came down from LtCol. Slade [that] we were going to evacuate the Americans and high ranking officials from Phnom Penh, Cambodia ... things fell into place ... Operation Eagle Pull was now in effect and 2/4 had the task of carrying it out."[91] Staff Sergeant Sabanski recalled that the main objective of the Marines aboard the *Hancock* and *Okinawa* was to evacuate the American and foreign nationals from Phnom Penh:

> The "whump, whump, whump" of the rotor blades could be heard throughout the day as one after another helicopter would take off or land. The round trip or shuttle of Marines and equipment into the embattled capitol of an almost conquered nation and the refugees from there had started. The day passed quickly for us on ship because we were busy processing the staggering flow of wretched humanity forced to leave their homes. Everyone was subjected to a body search of themselves and all the pitifully small [amount] of belongings they were allowed to carry out with them. Allied military personnel were required to turn in all weapons, for which they got a receipt, and all ammunition. The latter was handled by the Explosive Ordnance Disposal (EOD) teams attached to the unit, and most of it was thrown over the side of the ships. The civilians had to turn in weapons of any kind, which included guns, knives, scissors, nailfiles, etc., and also got a receipt. Then everyone had to suffer the indignity of having one of two Staff NCOs. (Me and another man who was assistant Mess Chief) search their body and belongings. Once past us, other Marines and sailors guided them to the messdecks to eat and later to a compartment where they had to stay until we reached Subic (Bay in the Philippines) again. Some of the Americans balked at this, but it had to be so that we could get everyone on board the ship....
>
> The operation proceeded smoothly aboard our ship and from reports we got much later from the members of the returning landing force, everything ashore moved along according to plan. Finally, as the sky darkened, the helicopters would shut down instead of lifting off again and a long day was over. Also over was Operation Eagle Pull and our ships, now packed with humanity, turned their bows to the East and Subic Bay once more.[92]

As Marines from 2nd Battalion, 4th Marines, HMH-463 and HMH-462 evacuated the American citizens the Marine Security Guards, under the leadership of Gunnery Sergeant Clarence D. McClenahan, they assisted embassy officials in disabling the embassy's remaining vehicles and placing them at the southern accesses to the landing zones.

Marine Embassy guards likewise assisted in the processing of foreign nationals for evacuation, as well as searching the embassy for infiltrators and stragglers, burning and shredding classified material, and destroying sensitive communications equipment. Like clockwork, helicopters from aboard the *Hancock* and *Okinawa* swooped in and out with evacuees. As the last helicopter prepared to take off, Ambassador Dean and his Marine guard folded the colors that flew atop the U.S. Embassy in Phnom Penh and removed the Great Seal of the United States of America. As the helicopter prepared to lift off, Captain William R. Melton, the commanding officer of Company G, 2nd Battalion, 4th Marines, discovered that two of his Marines were missing. After a frantic search, Captain Melton's men found the two leathernecks still manning their post, totally unaware that the order had been given to leave. Boarding the last helicopter from HMH-462, the ambassador, his guards, and the remaining Marines from 2/4 flew out to the USS *Okinawa*, having successfully evacuated all of the American citizens, foreign nationals, and Marine Security Guards as well as safely extracting the entire landing force without a single casualty.

A Successful Evacuation

Operation Eagle Pull was by far one of the most successful evacuations ever to take place at a U.S. Embassy. Not only did Marines and Air Force personnel successfully extract 84

American citizens but they also evacuated over 204 foreign citizens. More important was the fact that not one Marine or airman became casualties or was left behind.[93] Although the same could not be said for events in neighboring Saigon, tragically, the extraction of Americans and foreign nationals from Phnom Penh became the model of "how to perform a successful evacuation." The evacuation from the Cambodian capital likewise demonstrated the close working relationship between the Marine Air Contingency Battalion and Marine Security Guards. Finally, *Eagle Pull* demonstrated the utmost necessity of close cooperation and coordination of the units involved.

Operation Frequent Wind, March 25–April 30, 1975

As the planning for *Eagle Pull* was underway, a similar group of Marine and Air Force officers began to develop plans for an evacuation of U.S. and South Vietnamese officials from South Vietnam. Complicating any potential evacuation operation was the lack of a strong U.S. military presence in Southeast Asia.[94] Falling under the command of either the U.S. Seventh Fleet or USSAG/Seventh Air Force, an already confused situation was compounded by the several layers of command and control that would oversee any evacuation operation. With the fall of Military Region 1 to North Vietnamese forces in late January 1975, General Homer D. Smith, Jr., U.S. Army, the defense attaché, directed Colonel Eugene R. "Pat" Howard, the senior Marine officer in South Vietnam and a member of the Defense Attaché Office staff, to begin planning for the evacuation of Saigon. As in neighboring Cambodia, the Marines assigned to the U.S. Embassy and consulates played a decisive role in this planning.

The final phase of the Vietnam War began in late December 1974 when the North Vietnamese Army launched its war-winning offensive in Phuoc Long Province in Military Region 3. Meeting minimal resistance from the South Vietnamese Army (ARVN) as well as no response from the United States, the North Vietnamese sent more forces south in what became a major invasion of South Vietnam and, more importantly, a violation of the Paris Peace Accords. After the capture of Phuoc Long Province, the North Vietnamese Army (NVA) consolidated its gains and prepared for the drive on its next targets, the strategically important Military Regions 1 and 2. On March 4, 1975, the NVA resumed the attack on Military Region 1 and by the end of the month had taken all of the major cities once fought over by U.S. forces in I Corps.[95]

In response to the North Vietnamese Army's violations of the Paris cease-fire accords, President Nguyen Van Thieu ordered the ARVN to withdraw from the Central Highlands. After the fall of Da Nang, this withdrawal turned into a full-fledged retreat as civilians and soldiers fled from the advancing NVA. As the ARVN retreated southward toward Saigon it became apparent to the U.S. Marine and U.S. Army planners that an evacuation of U.S. citizens would be necessary from Saigon and the other South Vietnamese cities.

For the Marine Security Guards, the evacuation from the U.S. Consulate in Da Nang foreshadowed the events to come as they now dealt with not only the evacuation of American diplomats and citizens but a flood of refugees seeking evacuation from the coastal enclave. During the "confusion and chaos caused by the collapse of the defensive perimeter surrounding Da Nang," the six Marine Security Guards "played a major part in the successful removal of Americans from the besieged area." Led by Staff Sergeant Walter W. Sparks, the detachment commander, the unit included Sergeants Venoy L. Rogers, Lazaro Arriola, and William S. Spruce III, and Corporals Leonard A. Forseth and Ronald W. Anderson.[96] The six Marines shortly put to use everything they learned while on MSG duty, as the orderly evacuation that began on 25 March turned into bedlam. Panic took hold among the South Vietnamese civilians as they rushed past the leathernecks hoping to board one of the "freedom flights" by World Airways at Da Nang's airstrip. In one instance, a crowd of South Vietnamese soldiers and civilians surrounded one of the Boeing 727s hoping to force their way onto the airplane, while others drove vehicles right onto the runway in a desperate attempt to flee from the advancing North Vietnamese Army. Marine Security Guards had a difficult time as "all sorts of illegal persons crowded on board, making it impossible to stay within either the legal limits for emigration or those for aircraft loading."

The most dangerous situations encountered by the Marine Security Guards in Da Nang as well in Saigon later on were the "thousands of armed South Vietnamese troops who were out of control roaming through the city."[97] "One of the detachment's gravest concerns was the ever-present threat of uncontrolled crowds, mobs of deserters, and criminals prowling the streets." As a result of the violence and the dangers it posed to the consul general and consulate, the Marine Security Guards "spent their final days in Da Nang in the consulate rather than the Marine House."[98] Staff Sergeant Sparks correctly assessed that protection of the consul general and consulate was more important than protecting the entire diplomatic compound. Staff Sergeant Sparks recalled that the potential for violence directed against the consul general and consulate was in place, as the threat of uncontrolled crowds, many of whom were mobs of armed South Vietnamese Army deserters who prowled the streets in search of airplane tickets that would take them away from Da Nang, blanketed the city. In response to what Staff Sergeant Sparks called "cowboy riding," or the robbing, looting, and killing of innocent civilians for plane tickets by renegade ARVN troops, the Marine staff non-commissioned officer moved the Marines to the safety of the U.S. Consulate on March 22, 1975. Despite the fact that "the consulate was not getting attacked ... there were crowds of people, trying to come in and get tickets" for evacuation by sea or air,[99] as tickets were handed out only to past and present South Vietnamese employees of the consulate and the U.S. government.

Staff Sergeant Sparks based his precautionary move on the violence and anticipation of violence in what had become an extremely volatile situation. In fact, Staff Sergeant Sparks fears materialized several days later when, at the Da Nang Airfield, a force of heavily armed South Vietnamese soldiers who, in their desperation to leave Military Regions 1 and 2, pushed their way through the crowds and at one point, opened fire with their weapons, killing members of their own families in order to take what became the last flight out of Da Nang on March 29, 1975.

Moved to the safety of the U.S. Consulate on March 22, 1975, Staff Sergeant Sparks and the other Marine Security Guards "immediately began destroying all classified records." Four days later, on Wednesday, March 26, Consul General Albert A. Francis asked Ambassador Graham Martin in Saigon for permission to evacuate via helicopter the 50 American employees and Marine Security Guards from Da Nang, as a land evacuation was now all but impossible.[100]

As the violence continued outside the walls of the U.S. Consulate, "the Marine detachment continued to do what Staff Sergeant Sparks saw as its primary duty: destruction of classified material and protection of classified material and protection of the consulate and its staff." As one Marine shredded classified documents, a second one placed them in "burn bags" and incinerated them. Two Marines were posted as guards at the vehicle gate and secured the pedestrian gate to prevent any unlawful entry of the consulate. The sixth Marine guard assisted Consul General Francis and his staff with security and administrative duties.[101]

One of the major problems that contributed to the chaos and turmoil at the U.S. Consulate was the American citizens who refused to leave Da Nang, even as the situation there grew more dangerous as each day passed. Staff Sergeant Sparks stated that in spite of all of the warnings of urgency from the consul general, there were many Americans who simply refused to leave Da Nang "until the last possible moment." Sparks recalled that these Americans "kept thinking maybe the tide would turn and everything would turn up rosy." While Consul General could "advise them to leave," he could not, according to Sparks, "compel them to leave." Many American citizens had hoped to catch the last flight out, or at best, the last helicopter lift out. Staff Sergeant Sparks recalled that he said to many Americans, "What are you still doing here?" to which they replied, "You're here." Sparks reminded them, "Yes, partner, but maybe there ain't going to be room on the helicopter that I'm leaving on."[102]

As the Air America planes continued their frantic pace in ferrying out American citizens and their dependents, Secretary of State Henry Kissinger sought assistance from the Military Sealift Command to aid with the remaining evacuees and other designated South Vietnamese civilians. By this time, panic had gripped the crowds still hoping to board what few flights landed at Da Nang's airport. When it appeared that the crowds would overwhelm the planes as they landed, Consul General Francis ordered that the smaller aircraft such as the venerable C-47's be diverted to the nearby helicopter pad at Marble Mountain to maintain security and ensure safety. The move came just in time, as the Saigon government ordered the suspension of further flights into Da Nang. Staff Sergeant Sparks recalled that by now there was a "creeping sense of finality to it all." As the end appeared, Sparks remembered talking to an Air America employee who, the Marine Security Guard stated, "wasn't panicked. At least on the radio he was calm. He said, It's all over. We can't get them out anymore; the planes won't land."[103]

The Last to Leave

Even as Air America suspended its flights into Da Nang, Consul General Francis and the remaining Americans, including the Marine Security Guard detachment, returned to the U.S. Consulate in Da Nang to insure the destruction of all classified material and await evacuation by helicopter. Meanwhile, Francis, his small staff, and Marines were now faced with the daunting prospect of leaving Da Nang amidst the continuing violence. Shortly thereafter, the consul general ordered the remaining Americans to proceed to the airfield for evacuation. Staff Sergeant Sparks remembered, "We drove down there, this was about 1830, we got to the LZ [landing zone] and it was very calm and quiet there." Assembling in the area located at the Da Nang airfield known as the International Commission of Control and Supervision's landing zone, the Americans discovered that there would be no more helicopter flights due to the fact, Staff Sergeant Sparks recalled, that "the pilots had used up all their fuel and the Vietnamese would not give them any more."[104]

Faced with the prospect of abandonment, Consul General Francis and his staff decided that evacuation would have to be by sea. From his residence on the consulate grounds, Francis requested, in the early morning hours of 29 March, that the Alaska Barge and Transport Company send in one of its tugs to push a barge in front of the consulate so it could be used to evacuate the remaining American personnel from Da Nang. After the tug had completed this task, Consul General Francis ordered his staff, the Marines, and the Vietnamese employees to board an awaiting Vietnamese truck to take them to the pier. As they rode toward the pier, Staff Sergeant Sparks and the other Marine Embassy Guards were horrified at what they now saw as they dismounted from the truck and proceeded across the dock. Staff Sergeant Sparks described what occurred next:

We got off the truck and helped the people on this barge. That ... was one of the most tragic things I have ever seen in my life, and I have been in combat a few times.... Women and old people were throwing their babies to that barge for people to catch, and they were missing and falling into the water. Old people crawling up this rope, trying to get to the barge and falling off, and the barge would come back and crush them.[105]

Offshore awaiting the American and Vietnamese evacuees was the MSC ship *Pioneer Contender*. In order to assure the safety of the crew and passengers, and prevent the ship from being hijacked, the captain of the *Pioneer Contender* asked that the Marine Security Guards disarm and maintain control over what had now become a mass of humanity. This task lasted until the vessel docked at Cam Rahn Bay near Saigon. Meanwhile, as the ship plodded southward, the crew of the *Pioneer Contender* lashed the barge carrying Vietnamese refugees to the side of the ship as the refugees were taken aboard the MSC ship. Staff Sergeant Sparks recalled that as the *Pioneer Contender* headed out to sea, refugees still came alongside to escape the advancing North Vietnamese Army. Sparks said: "We started loading these people on.... They would not behave themselves, they would not sit down, they would not relax. They would not help themselves. I saw a Vietnamese major stomping on babies to get up the ladder instead of trying to help his people. Fathers pushing their own wives and children out of the way. The old people being crushed and small babies being crushed." Sparks added that "for the individual Marine ... it became a question of risking your life."[106] Indeed, the mission had become one of risking lives as a detachment of Marine Security Guards was given the assignment of handing babies up the ladder and assisting the elderly South Vietnamese to board the ship even as the barges and reeking fishing boats bobbled in the rough surf. Added to this was the gunfire from angry South Vietnamese soldiers who demanded that they be taken aboard the *Pioneer Contender*. Amidst the rough surf, rickety vessels and intermittent gunfire Staff Sergeant Sparks, Sergeants Arriola and Rogers, and Corporal Anderson were given the grisly task of searching for survivors in the now emptied barge that contained two dozen corpses. As the Marines searched the barge, they discovered an elderly Vietnamese man who had suffered a broken leg and his wife, who had been buried among a pile of dead Vietnamese. After recovering the two survivors and returning aboard *Pioneer Contender*, the Marines cut loose the barge that soon drifted out to sea. By the afternoon of 30 March 1975, the *Pioneer Contender* arrived at Cam Rahn Bay, just in time to play a part in the final episode of the second Vietnam War. As the ship pulled into Cam Rahn Bay, reports circulated that renegade Vietnamese soldiers were shooting anyone who appeared to threaten their safety. Despite reports that some Americans remained aboard the MSC ship and despite pleas from the captain of the *Pioneer Contender* and Staff Sergeant Sparks to assist in restoring order, the Marine Security Guards were ordered to remain in Saigon as the ship headed back to Da Nang. As the *Pioneer Contender* headed back toward Da Nang, "the history of the Marine Security Guard Detachment, Da Nang officially ended at 0330, March 28, 1975." Events and attention now focused on the main Marine Security Embassy Guard detachment located in and around the city of Saigon as the South Vietnamese Army collapsed in the face of North Vietnam's massive onslaught directed toward the South Vietnamese capital.

The Curtain Falls: The NVA Advance to Saigon, March–April 1975

The final phase of the Second Vietnam War for both the Marine Security Guard detachment in Saigon and of America's involvement in the war began on March 25, 1975, as Major

General Carl W. Hoffman readied the III Marine Amphibious Force for the evacuation of American personnel, their dependents, and South Vietnamese citizens from Da Nang and Saigon. Planners of the evacuation dubbed the operation *Frequent Wind*. Even before the fall of Da Nang on 28 March 1975, the 1st Battalion, 4th Marines, received its warning order from III MAF to support possible evacuation operations from Da Nang. According to Lieutenant Colonel Walter J. Wood, commanding officer of the 1st Battalion, 4th Marines, recalled, "We were to embark aboard the [USS] *Blue Ridge* (the amphibious transport) for immediate departure to Da Nang where we would reinforce U.S. facilities." Lieutenant Colonel Wood's primary assignment was to prevent their capture by the NVA. Meanwhile, the 2d Battalion, 4th Marines, commanded by Colonel John Roche III, had positioned itself off the western coast of Cambodia in the Gulf of Thailand on February 28, 1975, and readied itself for the evacuation of the U.S. Embassy and other foreign nationals in Phnom Penh, Cambodia's capital.

Placed under the overall command of Colonel Alfred M. Gray, the commanding officer of 33rd Marine Amphibious Unit (33rd MAU), the 4th Marines received the mission of supporting the evacuation of American citizens. The order also extended to assist in the evacuation of designated evacuees (primarily ARVN officers and enlisted men, as well as other South Vietnamese who had worked for the U.S. government) located in Da Nang. Along with Company D, 1st Bn, 4th Marines, the *Blue Ridge* (LCC 19), now part of Task Force 76 led by Rear Admiral Donald E. Whitmire, departed for South Vietnam from bases in Japan and the Philippines. The remainder of 1st Bn, 4th Marines, eventually joined Task Force 76 on board the amphibious transports USS *Dubuque*, USS *Durham*, and USS *Frederick*. Augmented by the helicopters of Marine Medium Squadron (HMM) 165, commanded by Lieutenant Colonel James P. Kizer, the Marines assigned to Task Force 76 were to establish and secure possible evacuation sites at Da Nang.

When Da Nang fell to the Communists on March 28, Marines assigned to the 33d MAU received a new mission, one that harkened back to the 19th century: Marine security details aboard ships. As the amphibious task force headed toward South Vietnam's coastline, the deteriorating battlefield situation of ARVN had caused many South Vietnamese civilians to take to the open seas where they had hoped to be rescued by American ships and taken to some safe haven, preferably the United States. At sea, the ships of the Military Sealift Command (MSC) that had positioned themselves off the coast for a large-scale evacuation operation. Meanwhile, the Joint Chiefs of Staff had authorized the embarkation of Marine Security Forces for the purpose of security and assistance in refugee processing. The 1st Battalion, 4th Marines, quickly responded to this new mission by organizing and distributing its rifle companies according to their Marine Corps' letter designations.[107]

CHART 5. MARINE SECURITY FORCES' ASSIGNMENTS FOR OPERATION FREQUENT WIND, MARCH–APRIL 1975

Rifle Company	Commanding Officer	Ship
Security Force "A"	(Captain Harry Jensen, Jr.)	USS *Durham*
Security Force "B"	(Captain Robert T. Hickinbotham)	USS *Frederick*
Security Force "C"	(Captain Maurice O.V. Green)	USS *Dubuque*
Security Force "D"	(Captain Walter J. Wood)	USS *Blue Ridge*

Augmenting the Marine rifle companies assigned to the security force detachments were special evacuation teams that included detachments of military police, engineers, communicators, counterintelligence and interrogator-translators. As could be expected, each attachment had a specific mission. Military policemen provided expertise in crowd control, searching procedures, and the movement of refugees once on board ship. The engineers aided in the location and detonation of explosives, mines, and booby traps. Counterintelligence personnel provided expertise on how to counter any sabotage and single out individuals suspected of being terrorists. The communicators assisted in the establishment of command and control nets, and links with air and ground forces on board ship and in the air space above the task force. The Vietnamese-speaking interrogator-translators provided on-the-spot translation services to task force personnel and as a link between the ship's personnel and Vietnamese refugees. One final mission of the special evacuation teams was that they could assist U.S. Embassy personnel ashore, most notably the Marine Security Guards who by now began preparations for an evacuation of all U.S. and designated South Vietnamese personnel when the time came.

Once aboard their designated ships, company commanders from the Marine Security Forces met with their respective ships' captains and formulated a plan for the embarkation, searching, and moving refugees, and for the overall security of ship. Each plan was, in fact, tailored to conform to the overall dimensions of the ship in question. With the threat of enemy sappers mingling in with the refugees, or disgruntled and armed South Vietnamese soldiers seeking passage to the United States, Marines and sailors quickly established designated areas where the refugees would be either denied or permitted access.

On April 4, 1975, as NVA forces continued their offensive toward Saigon, Marines aboard the USS *Durham* picked up the first group of 4,000 cold, hungry, and above all else, frightened Vietnamese refugees, and began the process of screening and feeding them.[108] Meanwhile, with the decision by the Joint Chiefs of Staff to use the ships from the Military Sealift Command and to place additional Marines aboard them as a security force, III MAF now faced the prospect of finding additional manpower to carry out this more extensive mission. In the face of the deteriorating situation in both South Vietnam and neighboring Cambodia, and the strain this had already placed on Marine and Navy forces in the Pacific, General Hoffman nevertheless alerted all of his commanding officers to form additional security detachments to man these vessels.

A New Old Tactic

On the evening of April 4, 1975, the Marine Security Force aboard the USS *Frederick* received its first call to restore order aboard a Military Sealift Command ship, the SS *Pioneer Contender*. A platoon of Marines, reinforced by a M-60 machine gun squad and two Navy corpsmen, led by Second Lieutenant Robert E. Lee, Jr., boarded the *Pioneer Contender* with a minimum of notice at the request of its captain in order to quell a series of disturbances by the refugees who threatened to take over the ship. With no accessible ladder to board the ship from their landing craft (LCMs), Lieutenant Lee's Marines had been forced to board the *Pioneer Contender* by way of a "Jacob's ladder," suspended from the leeward side of the ship. Upon boarding the ship, Lieutenant Lee reported to his commanding officer that the ship possessed neither food nor drinking water, and that many of the passengers were armed and in an "ugly mood." Despite this situation, and as the vessel set sail, Lieutenant Lee and the Marines quickly restored order. In only one instance were Lieutenant Lee's Marines forced to fire a "warning burst" from the attached M-60 machine gun squad as they sought to restore order when distributing food. This tradition-based tactic was a marked departure in the use of Marines in the modern era but was anticipated by both General Hoffman and Admiral Whitmire as the only means of providing security to the ships and men aboard as the task force carried out its mission.

In fact, the tactics employed by Lieutenant Lee's platoon of Marines illustrated the flexibility displayed by the Marines of the 33d MAU:

> This new use of Marines specially tailored, reinforced, platoon-sized security forces for Military Sealift Command's ships — required new planning. Each of the four rifle companies was broken down into three "security" forces, task organized with support from the weapons platoon, medical section, engineers, military police, and interpreters. Two additional security detachments were formed out of the various headquarters elements, as backups should they be needed. Various attached personnel — doctors, counter-intelligence specialists and some interpreters — were kept in a central pool to be used in general support. This security force structure was supported by ships of the Task Group 76.8 and the helicopters of HMM-165. Each force was prepared to mount out with enough supplies to last a week.[109]

During the final evacuation of the U.S. Embassy from Saigon, a similarly configured Marine security team was helo-lifted into the compound in order to augment the Marine Security Guards, who were then in the process of destroying classified material and safeguarding the ambassador and his remaining staff. Both the Marine Security Guards and the security rifle platoon accomplished their missions even as the U.S. Embassy in Saigon became deluged with asylum-seekers as the North Vietnamese Army entered Saigon in the final days of April 1975.

As Task Force 76.8 with its attached force of Marines contended with the Vietnamese refugees now plying the waters off South Vietnam's northern coastal area, the military situation in Military Region 3 continued to deteriorate. The South Vietnamese Army sought to regain the initiative against the enemy, while the North Vietnamese Army, emboldened by its swift victories in the northern section of the country, prepared for its final offensive aimed at Saigon.

The Final NVA Offensive, April 1975

As Marine Security Guards and special evacuation teams prepared for an evacuation of American, foreign, and Vietnamese nationals, the NVA planned its long-awaited war-ending drive toward Saigon. On April 1, 1975, the Marine Security Guard Detachment positioned at the U.S. Consulate at Nha Trang, headed by Staff Sergeant R.F. Painter, assisted in the successful evacuation of all American and Vietnamese citizens as the North Vietnamese Army continued its advance toward Saigon.[110] The North Vietnamese Army now held most of Military Region 2 as the major cities of Qui Nohn, Nha Trang, and Dalat had been abandoned. Meanwhile, the NVA launched a heavy combined arms attack against ARVN positions along Routes 1 and 22 located in the eastern portions of South Vietnam's long coastline. The fighting soon shifted to Xuan Loc, the capital of Long Kahn Province. Here, four NVA divisions commenced attacks on 9 April in order to surround and cut off the 18th ARVN Division defending Xuan Loc, and thereby gain control of Highway 1, the main access route into the Bien Hoa/Saigon area. Badly demoralized from their earlier defeats in Military Regions 1 and 2, without much of their heavy weaponry, ARVN forces quickly moved to reinforce Xuan Loc in order to thwart this latest and most crucial Communist offensive. Organized from the survivors of the various ARVN military units, South Vietnamese soldiers who fought at Xuan Loc proved surprisingly very effective. The 18th ARVN Division, commanded by Brigadier

General Le Minh Dao, launched a series of counterattacks on 10 April and retook a considerable amount of the city they had lost the day before. The next day, ARVN repulsed an attack by the NVA's *165th Regiment* of the *75th NVA Division* and supporting regiments from the 341st and 6th NVA Divisions.

The South Vietnamese Army's victory at Xuan Loc, temporary in nature, nonetheless renewed hopes in some South Vietnamese and U.S. government and military circles that the NVA's spring offensive could be halted and Saigon itself saved. If the Communist onslaught could be stopped then the Marine Amphibious Brigade (MAB) and its units could refocus efforts toward a canceled Marine amphibious exercise.

Despite this heroic though futile stand by ARVN, the NVA retook Xuan Loc on April 20, 1975, and resumed its attack westward toward Bien Hoa. Meanwhile other NVA units advanced southward from Xuan Loc in order to interdict the main Bien Hoa–Vung Tau highway (Route 15). The battle of Xuan Loc not only signaled the end of major organized resistance by ARVN in the eastern portions of Military Region 3, it also opened the way for attacks against Bien Hoa and Saigon.

On April 21, 1975, President Nguyen Van Thieu resigned and fled the country. Vice President Tran Van Huong, who initially assumed a militant policy of continued resistance against the NVA, likewise resigned several days later. Before his departure, Huong turned over the presidency to former ARVN General Duong Van "Big" Minh. General Minh immediately set out to negotiate a cease-fire with the North Vietnamese, who by this time had approached the outskirts of the city. After General Minh rejected several of the NVA's preconditions for a cease-fire, the North Vietnamese launched their final assault on the South Vietnamese capital on April 26, 1975.

As truce talks broke down the NVA resumed its offensive, striking out at ARVN units in the Long Thanh and Long Binh areas. Puoc Long, near Vung Tau, likewise came under attack and was quickly taken, thereby isolating the Vung Tau Peninsula. North Vietnamese forces then overran the Bear Cat Armor School and Long Thanh District, which prevented South Vietnamese forces (and potentially any U.S.-led evacuation) from entering or leaving Saigon to the sea over Route 15. When Route 15 fell to the Communists so to went the escape routes then situated on the Vung Tau Peninsula. On April 28, the NVA renewed the offensive with a direct attack on Long Binh. Defended by the scattered remnants of ARVN units, the NVA quickly maneuvered through them as the defenses at Long Binh collapsed under the weight of the NVA advance. The quick advance of the NVA forced the South Vietnamese Air Force units that had operated out of Bein Hoa Air Base to fly to Can Tho. Also, on the 28th, Saigon and the vital Tan Son Nhut Air Base came under heavy rocket and mortar attacks. The NVA likewise brought up Soviet-supplied Zu-23mm antiaircraft guns and artillery to further neutralize the South Vietnamese Air Force. At the same time, ARVN units in Cu Chi, Lai Khe, and virtually all positions around the city of Saigon came under intense artillery and mortar fire. In keeping with its strategy of destroying all pockets of resistance in and around Saigon, the NVA slowly tightened the noose around ARVN. At the same time the NVA's rapid southward advance made it increasingly likely that any U.S. evacuation from Saigon and other South Vietnamese cities would be by air.

As ARVN's defensive perimeter continued to shrink, a combined Navy-Marine Corps task force positioned itself off the southeastern coast of Vietnam as elements of the 9th Marine Amphibious Brigade prepared to evacuate Americans and thousands of Vietnamese citizens seeking political asylum. Inside the American embassy in Saigon, at the remaining consulates, and Defense Attaché Office, Marine Security Guards hurriedly prepared to carry out their mission by destroying classified material and screening the thousands of asylum seekers as Operation Frequent Wind began in the early morning hours of 29 April 1975.

Their Finest Hour

The South Vietnamese Army's victory at Xuan Loc temporarily halted the NVA's drive into Saigon. As ARVN troops and South Vietnamese Marines fought in what was by now a lost cause, U.S. military and civilian planners hastily put the finishing touches on evacuation plans from the remaining consulates and U.S. embassy in Saigon. Overall responsibility for the evacuation fell to the 9th Marine Amphibious Brigade, under the command of Brigadier General Richard E. Carey. The actual operation was carried out, however, by Regimental Landing Team 4, commanded by Colonel Alfred M. Gray, with air support from Colonel Frank G. McLenon's Marine Air Group 39. The ground composition of RLT-4 consisted of the 1st Battalion, 9th Marine Regiment (BLT 1/9), 2nd Battalion, 4th Marines, and 3rd Battalion, 9th Marines. Combat Service Support came from the Brigade's Logistic Support Group. Other aviation units came from HMH-462, HMH-463, HMM-165, and HML-367. By April 19, the 9th Marine Amphibious Brigade had arrived off of the South Vietnamese coast and, in order to better execute any withdrawal from Saigon, integrated its operational plans with that of the fleet and planners ashore.[111]

The staff of the 9th MAB and USSAG planners had concentrated its withdrawal from Saigon upon five possible evacuation sites where American citizens and their dependents, as well as the South Vietnamese that had assisted the U.S. war effort, could be safely evacuated. Among the five were the DAO/Air America Complex, the U.S. Consulate at Can Tho, rooftops in Saigon, the U.S. Embassy and the adjacent compound, and Vung Tau — considered the "largest of all possible evacuation sites."[112] Of the sites most affecting the Marine Security Guard detachments the DAO/Air America complex, the U.S. Consulate at Can Tho and U.S. Embassy in Saigon proved the most challenging for planners as the situation in and around Saigon changed from hour to hour.

Based on operational realities both USSAG and 9th MAB planners centered their evacuation plans upon the DAO/Air America complex at Tan Son Nhut Air Base, Can Tho, and the U.S. Embassy in Saigon. Adjacent to the Tan Son Nhut Air Base was the Defense Attaché Office and Air America airlines' offices. Planners concluded that the DAO, separated by planners into two separate components known as the "Alamo," which housed the main headquarters buildings and Emergency Command Center, and the "Annex," housing a gymnasium and post exchange, required no less than three battalion landing teams "if the scope of the operation were broadened to provide security for fixed-wing evacuation flights out of Tan Son Nhut."[113] A Marine ground force would also be required for the U.S. consulate at Can Tho, located fifty miles southwest of Saigon, which was supposed to be able to evacuate about 2,000 evacuees. The U.S. Embassy in Saigon proved to be the most difficult insofar as its limited rooftop space necessary for any large-scale evacuation. In fact, planners at USSAG and 9th MAB believed that, at best, only one hundred refugees could be flown out by helicopter. Additional space could be made available in the courtyard of the embassy only if a large tree and other obstacles could be cut down. As it turned out, this is precisely what occurred when the final evacuation took place. Major Kean ordered a detail of Marine Security Guards to chop the tree down when it became apparent that Saigon would play the pre-eminent role during the evacuation.

The Bien Hoa Consulate

The stand at Xuan Loc, heroic though futile, merely delayed the NVA's advance southward by days. In fact, "the loss of Xuan Loc ... catapulted both the consulates at Bien Hoa and that at Can Tho into hectic preparations for what now appeared to be the inevitable."[114] Standing in the path of the NVA was the U.S. Consulate located at Bien Hoa, which made it particularly vulnerable to enemy rocket and artillery fire. With this in mind, Consul General Richard Peters directed his staff and the Marine Security Guard Detachment Commander, Sergeant Ronald E. Duffy, to prepare for an evacuation. Sergeant Duffy and the other Marine Security Guards (Sergeant James M. Felber, Corporals Carlos R. Arraigna and Gary

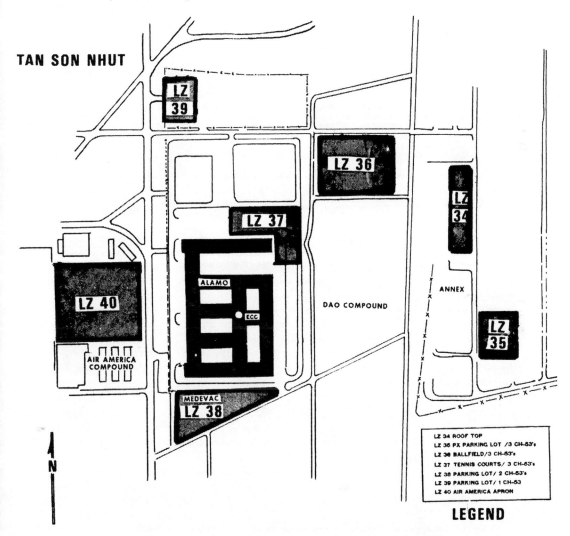

DAO /AIR AMERICA COMPLEX

Diagram 1. The Evacuations at Bien Hoa and Can Tho. The Defense Attaché Office/Air America Complex at Tan Son Nhut Airfield outside of Saigon (Dunham and Quinlan, *U.S. Marines in Vietnam: The Bitter End, 1973–1975*, page 191).

L. Lindholm, and Lance Corporal Dean M. Kinzie) began to either transfer to Washington, D.C., or destroy the highly classified material and other sensitive gear located there. The Marines were determined that neither would fall into the hands of enemy forces. When it became clear that ARVN could not hold Xuan Loc, Consul General Peters, on 24 April 1975, ordered the consulate staff and Marine Security Guards to Saigon, where they were incorporated into the embassy's staff, took down the U.S. flag and Great Seal of the United States, and closed the consulate. When it became obvious that no negotiations would be held with the NVA, Deputy Consul General Charles Lahiguera and two of the Marine Security Guards returned to the facility a few days later to officially close its doors. This left only the consulate at Can Tho and U.S. Embassy in Saigon as the last two diplomatic facilities remaining.

Can Tho

As the situation in and around Saigon became more desperate the third non-combatant evacuation operation took place at the U.S. Consulate General at Can Tho. Prior to its attack on Can Tho, the NVA launched a powerful artillery and rocket bombardment against the city on April 12, 1975. This signaled the commencement of withdrawal operations from the consulate and nearby city of all remaining American and South Vietnamese civilians. Staff Sergeant S.B. Hasty, the Marine Security Guard's staff non-commissioned officer in charge, and his staff of five Marine non-commissioned officers[115] ordered all personnel to remain calm and seek cover so as not to cause a general panic. Meanwhile, Marine Security Guards organized the defenses inside the compound and pre-positioned all fire-fighting equipment to better respond to fires that would be spreading. Sergeant John S. Moore, one of the Marine Security Guards at Can Tho, recalled that Staff Sergeant Hasty's instructions were clear and very concise:

> Upon instructions of the NCOIC I assumed control of the emergency radio net command and control center, and relayed radio messages, while Sergeant [Terry D.] Pate on Post Number One, handled the telephones. Enemy rounds were landing nearby, and started a roaring fire in the area behind the Consulate. At about 2200 I was informed that the Consul General had arrived and had gone up to the roof to meet the NCOIC and assess the situation. At this time I received a report that two (2) tanker trucks were parked in the compound, so I turned over control of the Radio Control center to the incoming Communications Officer, and went outside to ascertain the contents of the trucks. I discovered that one contained water and the other contained POL. I informed the Consul General and the NCOIC of the situation and was instructed to remove the fuel truck at all costs, as high winds had spread the fire to within less than 200 meters of the Consulate, and showed no signs of stopping. I assigned Sergeant [John W.] Kirchner, Corporal [Lee J.] Johnson, and Corporal [Lawrence B.] Killens to the task of removing the vehicle. Corporal Johnson and other Consulate personnel went to the nearby GSO motor pool compound to attempt to locate keys to the vehicles, while the rest of the Marines broke into the vehicles to push them out of the way of the fuel truck. Shortly afterwards Corporal Johnson and the other personnel returned without having located any keys, but with a tow truck they had found with which to remove the disabled tanker. By this time the major portion of the fire had started about 20 meters away. The Marines quickly attached the fuel truck to the tow, and with Sergeant Kirchner, who volunteered to steer it, it was removed to a safer area, with Corporal Johnson driving in a vehicle behind it in case the tow should break. Meanwhile Corporal Killens and I and other personnel maneuvered the water truck to the rear of the compound in order that a hose could be brought into operation on the rear of the building and the houses behind it. The Consul General and the NCOIC then dispatched me to organize emergency fire hoses and fire fighting equipment at nearby American compounds. I returned with the equipment and assisted Staff Sergeant Hasty in positioning the hoses where he felt that they would do the most good. At 2300

the last enemy round fell, and the fire was brought under control a short while later. At approximately 0030 the Consul General passed the word to stand down. At this time I again mustered the Marines in the lobby and had them return to the Marine House to stand by in case of other action.[116]

The quick response by Staff Sergeant Boyette S. Hasty and the other Marine Security Guards insured the safety of all U.S. personnel inside and near the U.S. Consulate. Staff Sergeant Hasty recalled in his after-action report that while the shelling was intense, it appeared that the NVA intended it for ARVN's IV Headquarters that was nearby and not the U.S. Consulate. He added that:

On or about 2130, 12 April 1975, VC/NVA forces commenced an artillery attack upon the city of Can Tho. The enemy rounds and resulting fires were close enough to directly endanger the Consulate General. Marines of the Marine Security Guard Detachment reacted to the Consulate General Headquarters area immediately. During the hours that followed the Marines ordered nearby civilian personnel to seek cover, kept a count of the incoming rounds, spotted the impact areas, stood by to pick up casualties and form damage control parties, and monitored the emergency radio net.

Colonel Boyette S. Hasty, USMC, who served as both a watchstander and later detachment commander at Can Tho, is shown here as commanding officer, Marine Security Guard Battalion at Quantico, Virginia Col. Hasty was in charge of one of the last consulates evacuated prior to the fall of Saigon in April 1975 (courtesy U.S. Marine Corps).

Members of the Detachment calmed down civilian personnel and attempted to keep a casualty and damage report. When the fire started by the artillery flamed out of control and threatened the Consulate, the MSG's removed a potentially dangerous fuel truck from the area and organized and emplaced emergency fire-fighting equipment to defend the compound from the spreading fire. At approximately 2300, the enemy shelling ceased, and the fire soon was brought under control after having advanced at one point to within 20 meters of the compound. At 0300 the order to stand down was received, and the Marines returned to their quarters to stand down for further action. Casualties and damage during the attack were 16 killed, 42 wounded, with 112 buildings destroyed. No MSG's or other American personnel were injured during the attack, and damage to U.S. Government property was minimal. Intelligence analysis leads us to believe that the attack was directed against the nearby ARVN IV Corps Headquarters rather than against the American Consulate.[117]

The quick thinking by all the Marines Security Guards at Can Tho in the removal of the POL tanker averted what could have been a very tragic incident. Also, unknown to Staff Sergeant Hasty and his Marines, they had, in fact, laid the groundwork for the final evacuation of the Can Tho consulate that began shortly after dawn on Tuesday, April 29, 1975. As events turned out, the Marines assigned to the Amphibious Evacuation Security Force (AESF) were among the first to realize that an evacuation had been organized as two helicopters appeared on the horizon near Can Tho on the morning of April 29, 1975.

Within minutes of the helicopters' landing, Central Intelligence operatives loaded Vietnamese civilians into the two Air America helicopters that quickly took off and headed toward the amphibious transport dock ship USS *Vancouver* (LPD 2).[118] Among the evacuees were Vietnamese members of the consulate staff, the resident CIA staff members and other Americans and foreign nationals.

By 1100 that morning, the evacuation of Can Tho was well underway. Sergeant John Moore, one of the Marine Security Guards at Can Tho, on duty in the communications center at the consulate, recalled that Consul General Francis T. McNamara had been informed by Mr. Jacobson of the Saigon Embassy that Ambassador Martin had "given the order to evacuate Can Tho immediately."[119] With that, Sergeant Moore informed Staff Sergeant Hasty of the conversation between Consul General McNamara and Mr. Jacobson. Staff Sergeant Hasty instructed Sergeant Moore to assemble all of the Marine Security Guards, who were to pack only a small bag with their weapons and muster in the adjoining parking lot, where they would be transported to the Delta Compound portion of the consulate. Sergeant Moore then transported the Marines, some leftover munitions and ordnance and boarded a LCM that was procured for the evacuation. By 1200, the Marines, the remaining consulate staff, and other Vietnamese refugees, including SSgt. Hasty's mother and father in-law, boarded another LCM procured by the Marine staff sergeant prior to the commencement of the evacuation and headed down the river.[120] After being stuck in the mud due to the outgoing tide, the LCMs were briefly stopped by a South Vietnamese Navy patrol boat that demanded the Marines hand over all draft-age males. Assured that there were no such males aboard the boats the South Vietnamese sailors allowed the convoy to continue unhindered.

At one point barges carrying the refugees and Marines came under intense NVA and Viet Cong rocket fire. According to Lance Corporal Lawrence B. Killens, prior to their departure from Can Tho, the Marine Security Guards were given explicit instructions concerning the rules of engagement and ordered to return fire if fired upon.[121] Thus, in response to the enemy's fire "all Marines and some civilian personnel returned the fire with an assortment of weapons." Assisted by one of the consular officials, Mr. David Sciacchitano, Sgt. Moore recalled, " I myself manned and fired a BAR...."[122] Moore stated that this return fire "discouraged the enemy from further hostile fire and we continued throughout the remainder of the trip without further assaults." Sergeant John W. Kirchner recalled that the fighting was both sharp and intense as the LCMs proceeded down river:

> I saw what I believed to be a rocket and turned out to be a B-40 rocket (RPG-7). I put my M-16 on automatic and opened up on a smoky area on the shoreline; pulling out the clip, I locked and loaded to use up the second clip. I then picked up my M-79 (grenade launcher) and squeezed off a round but found it to be short. I raised it a little further and fired another round. In all, I fired two full magazines and five HE (M-79) rounds. I'm not sure if we hit anything, but one thing for sure is that either we hit him or scared the living daylights out of him/them.[123]

Traveling in almost complete darkness with no means to contact Saigon or any other friendly units in the vicinity, the convoy continued on as an American RF-4 Phantom jet roared overhead. Staff Sergeant Hasty's most vivid recollection of the journey was that it was done in a driving, cold rain that "obscured us from sight by the VC/NVA along the banks of the river." Shivering from cold rain, SSgt. Hasty nonetheless maintained his watch as he manned an M-60 machinegun. Hasty recalled that Mr. Sciacchitano was kind enough to throw a field jacket over him to protect him from the elements, "which helped a great deal."[124]

Finally, the convoy reached the mouth of the Bassac River where no ship could be seen (it was nighttime) except for a few Vietnamese fishing boats. Shortly after midnight of 30

April, the *Pioneer Contender* came into view. Unable to communicate with American officials aboard that ship, the consulate's administrative officer, Mr. Christian, came aboard one of the LCMs with a walkie-talkie in order to communicate with the leathernecks. Within minutes of pulling alongside the *Pioneer Contender*, the task now focused on loading the refugees aboard the ship. This in itself would prove to be even more difficult as the Marines assisted the Marine security force detachment aboard ship, commanded by Captain David A. Garcia, the assistant S-3, communications detachment officer, 9th Marines, in loading the refugees aboard the *Pioneer Contender*. Hasty recalled, "the Marines worked quickly and accurately and by 0200 the offloading was complete."[125]

After loading the Vietnamese refugees aboard the *Pioneer Contender*, the Marines remained aboard the vessel after which, Hasty recalled, "we sailed north to Vung Tan. At that time we were attached to Captain Garcia's Marine Security Forces' detachment. We assisted in the loading and transfer of refugees off of Vung Tan, until that afternoon, when we boarded a Japanese tug boat for transfer to a Korean LST. The next day we were picked up by helicopters and flown t o the USS *Blue Ridge*."[126] As Hasty later noted, the Marines and other American citizens were transferred to the USS *Blue Ridge* (LCC 19) via Huey helicopters from Marine Helicopter Squadron HMM-165. To prevent the Vietnamese refugees from storming onto the flight deck in order to seize the helicopters, SSgt. Hasty ordered the Marines to surround the helicopters until all Americans were aboard. Evacuated to the *Blue Ridge*, the Marines and other American citizens were frisked for weapons and other items, and then escorted to more suitable quarters. Before they could clean up, A Marine colonel informed Hasty and the Marines that they did not have to "in process," but were instead taken to a wardroom. Here, Brigadier General Richard E. Carey, Commanding General of the 9th Marine Amphibious Brigade, asked SSgt. Hasty and his men several questions before offering them some cold iced tea.[127] Dismissed by General Carey shortly thereafter, Hasty and his men were taken below deck and given quarters. With the closure of the Can Tho consulate on 1 May 1975, the last detachment of Marine Security Guards assigned to a consulate had been evacuated safely and without loss of life. Such was not to be the case at the DAO/Air America complex, where two more Marine Security Guards made the ultimate sacrifice.

As for the work of the Marines at Can Tho, Ambassador McNamara had nothing but praise for "his Marines." The ambassador, in particular, had special praise for Staff Sergeant Hasty, who he called "bright and willing [and] could produce the most incredible flashes of youthful courage bordering on the vainglorious. At times I found the young sergeant's enthusiasm terrifying, but his youthful weaknesses were far outweighed by his many virtues."[128] Major Kean likewise praised the efforts of the Marine Security Guard detachment at Can Tho. After meeting with Brigadier General Carey ended, Major Kean walked up to Staff Sergeant Hasty and the exhausted Marine security guards and congratulated them on a job well done. Then, in a thunderous vote of confidence, Major Kean turned to Hasty and the leathernecks and said, "You did the good job we expected."[129]

Operation Frequent Wind Commences: Action at the DAO/Air America Complex

Against the backdrop of a heavy NVA artillery and rocket attacks, aimed at the Tan Son Nhut airfield, General Carey and the MAU commander, Colonel Alfred M. Gray, landed at 1350 at the DAO Compound. Here, they established an austere command post prior to the arrival of the main ground security force, 2nd Battalion, 4th Marines. Staff Sergeant Thomas J. Sabanski recalled that the call for 2/4 came suddenly as Ambassador Martin himself realized that "the ARVN's could not hold back the tide of Communist aggressors and the time-honored call went out ... Send in the Marines."[130] This signaled the commencement of Operation Frequent Wind, the evacuation from Saigon. At about 1506 that afternoon the main wave of Marines from BLT 2/4, a reinforced rifle battalion, aboard CH-53's began to land at the DAO Compound. Quickly taking defensive positions, the leathernecks began to load the first of 6,968 evacuees (American, Vietnamese, and other foreign nationals) aboard the awaiting helicopters.[131]

As the first increment of refugees took off from the DAO Compound, Lieutenant Colonel George P. Slade, BLT 2/4's commanding officer, reinforced his existing positions with Marines from the second increment. With the Alpha increment — which consisted of a command element, two rifle companies, and an 81mm mortar platoon — around the DAO Compound's headquarters building, known as the "Alamo," the call went out for reinforcements.[132] Shortly thereafter the Bravo command group — commanded by Major Thornton L. "Luke" Youngman and having two rifle companies and a 106mm recoilless rifle platoon — came ashore and assumed responsibility for security of the DAO Annex and its adjoining landing zones. Also assigned to the DAO Compound was a eighteen-man Marine Security Guard detail attached to the Marine Security Guard Detachment located at the U.S. Embassy in Saigon, commanded by Gunnery Sergeant Vasco D. Martin. Among the Marines assigned to this detail were two Marine Security Guards, Corporal Charles J. McMahon of Woburn, Massachusetts, and Lance Corporal Darwin D. Judge of Marshalltown, Iowa, who would be the last Americans to die in the Vietnam War.

As Lieutenant Colonel Slade's Marines took up positions around the DAO/Air America Compound, Gunnery Sergeant Martin assigned Corporal McMahon and Lance Corporal Judge to a two-man outpost situated at the northwest corner of the compound. As the rifle companies assumed their positions around the compound, the NVA launched a furious rocket and mortar attack. In the pre-dawn hours of 29 April 1975, at approximately 0400, a "number of rounds of heavy artillery and rockets impacted in the DAO Compound, and around Tan Son Nhut Airfield. One round scored a direct hit on the road-block post, killing the two Marines instantly and destroying or setting afire a number of motorcycles in the area, upon which they were apparently seated." Despite the continued heavy bombardment, Sergeant Doug Potratz was able to have McMahon's and Judge's bodies placed in body bags and transferred to the mortuary of the Seventh Day Adventist Hospital located near the grounds of the DAO Compound. Unfortunately, amidst the pandemonium surrounding the final evacuation from Saigon, the bodies of the two young Marines were inexplicably left behind.[133]

As the rifle companies from BLT 2/4 assumed their defensive positions around the DAO perimeter, other Marines burned classified material and loaded the frightened refugees aboard the awaiting Marine and U.S. Air Force CH-53's. One of the pilots, Major John F. Guilmartin, USAF, the senior Air Force pilot aboard the USS *Midway*, complimented the team of Marine air controllers guiding the helicopters into and out of the DAO Compound. Working amidst the shelling and heavy gunfire from the NVA, Major Guilmartin stated that these Marine air controllers, headed by Major David A. Cox and positioned atop one of the buildings in the DAO Compound, were "very cool and professional." Major Guilmartin added, "Their landing procedures worked like a champ."[134] The airlift, which had begun at 0830, ended at approximately 1100 that same morning.

By daylight of the 29th, the DAO was in chaos, with enemy fire threatening the air evacuation and refugees running about the compound in search of space on one of the many Air America or Marine helicopter flights taking off. Gunnery Sergeant Vasco D. Martin, Jr., recalled that one overcrowded helicopter never made it off the ground. "It made two or three attempts ... and the last attempt he swung around in a cloud of dirt and dust, and he couldn't see where he was going, and his tail blade ended up hitting [a] mound of dirt, and when he did that, part of the blade flew across the road and hit the building where we had been billeted." Gunnery Sergeant Martin remembered that the pilot and co-pilot, as well as the crew and passengers simply exited the crippled helicopter as its main rotor blade kept spinning.[135] Despite the intensity of the enemy's fire, the Marines and Air Force helicopters were able to evacuate over 395 U.S. citizens and 4,475 other refugees from the DAO Compound.[136]

Operation Frequent Wind: The Last Phase, April 29–30, 1975

As the evacuation continued at the DAO Compound, Major Kean, the commanding officer of the Marine Security Guard Detachment in Saigon, awaited the word to begin the evacuation from the U.S. Embassy. Having been reinforced by a 40-man Marine security force from the *Blue Ridge,* the Marine embassy guards began to shred the mounds of classified material and burn them in the embassy's incinerator, as well as establish perimeter defenses. In spite of the confused signals coming from President Gerald R. Ford and National Security Advisor Kissinger, who believed that the North Vietnamese might still negotiate, and Ambassador Martin's hesitation to order an evacuation, Marines nonetheless continued to prepare for just such an operation. In order to prepare a suitable landing pad for helicopters, Marine Security Guards, acting on orders from Major Kean, chopped down a large tamarind tree that stood in the courtyard of the embassy. The Marines acted fast, as Ambassador Martin had refused Major Kean's earlier request to cut the tree down, fearing that it might send the wrong signal to the South Vietnamese and cause an even faster collapse than what actually occurred.

Events proceeded quickly, however, as President Ford, now fully briefed as to the gravity of the situation that had been unfolding in and around Saigon, ordered Ambassador Martin, his staff, and all Americans out of South Vietnam. At 2:30 P.M., twelve Marine CH-53 "Sea Stallion" helicopters lifted off the decks of the USS *Blue Ridge,* USS *Peoria,* and USS *Vancouver,* while Navy and Marine fighter jets streaked off the flight deck of the aircraft carrier USS *Coral Sea,* headed once more over the familiar skies of South Vietnam, in order to protect not only against the NVA, but from a vengeful South Vietnamese military and populace angry with the United States for having abandoned it to the enemy. Inside the beleaguered embassy, Marine Security Guards frantically burned and shredded what seemed be a ton of classified messages as the Armed Forces Radio Network and other South Vietnamese radio stations played the song "White Christmas" over and over again. The song was, in fact, a code that signaled the commencement of the evacuation.

Inside the embassy, as the Marine Security Guards shredded classified material, other leathernecks conducted a room-by-room search for anything that might be of use to the enemy and destroyed it. Reinforced by three platoons (130 men) of BLT 2/4 that came directly from the DAO Compound, Marine Security Guards also had the task of holding back a growing, frantic crowd of South Vietnamese refugees seeking asylum. By late afternoon, the Marine strength in the embassy compound stood at 171 officers and men.[137] As afternoon receded into

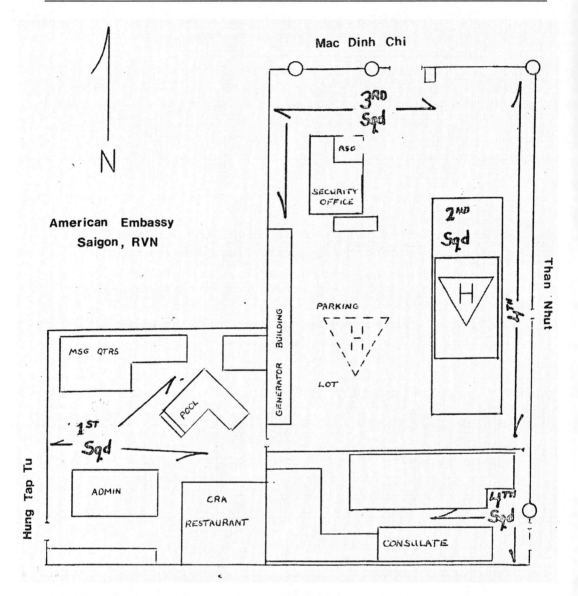

Diagram 2. The American Embassy in Saigon, Republic of Vietnam (U.S. Marine Corps Security Guard Bn., After Action Report on Evacuation from Saigon, July 1, 1975).

early dusk, the crowds grew in size and became more aggressive as it now appeared that the evacuation itself was starting to wind down.

As was the case at the DAO Compound, the situation at the nearby Tan Son Nhut Airfield had likewise greatly deteriorated as the NVA pounded the compound with rocket and artillery fire. Despite the intense enemy fire, the Marine Security Guard detachment and a reinforced rifle platoon, the 3rd Platoon, Company C, 1st Battalion, 9th Marines, commanded by First Lieutenant Bruce P. Thompson-Bowers, successfully defended the compound and suffered no casualties.

As Frequent Wind continued into the evening hours, Ambassador Martin still refused to leave. In fact, to Colonel John H. Madison, Jr., head of the U.S. Delegation to the Four

Party Joint Military Team, who had up until now monitored the Paris Peace Accords, it appeared that Mr. Wolfgang J. Lehman, the deputy chief of mission, was in effective charge of activities going on at the American Embassy as Ambassador Martin seemed unable to grasp the fact that the war was, indeed, over. When it became clear that Ambassador Martin would remain to the very end, General Carey ordered Major Kean to inform the ambassador that he had been ordered out of Vietnam. Shortly thereafter, Major Kean and two Marine Security Guards who belonged to the ambassador's Personal Security Unit (PSU) went to the ambassador's office where Kean instructed the two Marines to escort the ambassador to the rooftop of the embassy and insure that he was placed aboard an awaiting helicopter.[138]

One of the Marines who belonged to the Ambassador's Personal Security unit, Staff Sergeant Broussard, recounted that as Ambassador Martin was placed aboard the helicopter, he turned and "bid us all a farewell and stated ... "I owe you boys a 5th of Scotch!'"[139]

As the airlift entered its final phase, Major Kean became concerned over the safety and evacuation of the remaining Marines, including those who belonged to the rifle platoons sent from the *Blue Ridge* and *Duluth* to secure the compound and its environs.[140] After Ambassador Martin had departed for the USS *Blue Ridge*, the Marine major moved his force of 11 Marines into the embassy, where he barricaded its doors and moved to the roof. Prior to the evacuation of the ambassador, it was announced that there would be six more flights that would take the remaining South Vietnamese refugees seeking evacuation. Unknown to Major Kean, President Ford and Dr. Kissinger had abruptly ordered an end to all helicopter flights. The evacuation was over.[141] Still on the ground in the embassy, however, were Major Kean and his Marines, who by this time had positioned themselves on the top of the embassy in order to await evacuation. Informed that there would be no more evacuation flights, Major Kean ordered his men to the rooftop and used CS (tear) gas.

Sergeant Richard G. Paddock, one of the Marine Security Guards, recalled that despite the confusion that existed inside and outside the embassy, the Marines that remained in Saigon carried out their assigned tasks in an orderly fashion. In an after-action report filed three months after the fall of Saigon, Sergeant Paddock provided a detailed insight into the squad assignments of the Marine Security Guards starting on April 28 and ending two days later on April 30, and how each of these insured a successful operation.

The Last Out: The Embassy Is Evacuated

As the last refugees were loaded onto the awaiting helicopters, Major Kean's attention focused on the withdrawal of his Marines. Master Sergeant Juan J. Valdez, acting on Major Kean's orders, "assembled the Marines and started drawing infantry from the perimeter and gates, and with the MSGs, we set three perimeters outside the lobby entrance to the embassy."[142] As the Marines withdrew inside to the rooftop of the embassy, many of the Vietnamese who had hoped to be evacuated realized now that they were not going to be airlifted out. Sergeant Paddock recalled that a group of ARVN soldiers and civilians clambered aboard the embassy's fire truck and rammed the door to the embassy open. The crowd spilled into the embassy's lobby and climbed the stairwell that led to the roof. Master Sergeant Valdez wrote that the Marines were ready for this:

> At this time also, people who were at the gates began coming over the top. Also, the masses who were in the CRA compound started coming in. Before the last group of Marines could get in, they were overrun by the people, and they had to shove them out. Finally, we were able to get

the double doors buttoned up. The Marines who were inside the lobby started going up to the embassy roof.... We secured the final door on the roof and people began coming toward the roof. They had forced open the main door of the embassy and were appearing on the [roof's] helo pad. About 40 or 50 people. They never actually got on the main roof.[143]

There is some confusion as to whether the remaining Marines used CS agents to keep the South Vietnamese at bay. Master Sergeant Valdez discounted Sergeant Paddock's assertion that the onrush of the crowds necessitated the use of CS or tear gas, as the many of the Marines had "already discarded their masks," and it "would've been foolish for us to use gas and not have the means of protecting ourselves." Major Kean, however, confirmed the use of CS gas employed by the Marines, who he said used the chemical agent in order "to clear the ladder wells of the Embassy as we made our way to the rooftop. CS was used to clear these ladder wells on an intermittent basis until the final eleven [Marines] cleared the Embassy."[144]

Finally, it was time for the Marines to close the chapter on the U.S. involvement in Vietnam. At approximately 0753, "Dodging small arms fire and using riot control agents against people attempting to force their way to the rooftop, " Major Kean and the 10 Marines boarded "Swift 2–2," a CH-46 from HMM-164 and flew off the top of the now abandoned embassy. The Second Vietnam War was over. Even as the Marines boarded the last helicopter, random shots rang out at the rooftop, fired by disgruntled South Vietnamese soldiers angry toward the Americans for abandoning them. Major Kean recalled that as the Marines climbed aboard the CH-46, a motorcade appeared below. He believed that inside the limousine was President Minh, who apparently ordered his guards to fire upon the crowd so as to allow the Marines a safe evacuation.[145]

The last man to board the final helicopter was Master Sergeant Valdez. As the veteran Marine boarded the helicopter he perhaps looked back and wondered about those many young Americans who gave their all for their country in this faraway land. More important, however, was the satisfaction he must have felt that in those final days, the Marines, Navy, and Air Force evacuated over 6,968 persons of whom 1,373 were American citizens.[146]

Anti-American Rioting in Vientiane, Laos, May 9, 1975

As the last Marines left atop the rooftop of the U.S. Embassy on April 30, 1975, anti–American sentiment spread throughout Southeast Asia, most noticeably in neighboring Vientiane, Laos. Staff Sergeant E.L. Wagner, the staff non-commissioned officer in charge of the Marine Security Guard, recalled that on May 9, 1975, at approximately 10 o'clock in the morning, he received a call from the NCOIC at Post One. The Marine on duty told Staff Sergeant Wagner that there "would be an anti–American demonstration by the students" supported by the Communist Pathet Lao. Eventually, the demonstration turned into a seven-day siege of the U.S. Consulate. Staff Sergeant Wagner later recounted that it was as intense in Vientiane as it had been in Saigon during the final days prior to the execution of Operation Frequent Wind. His after-action report illustrated the confusion and pressures Marine Security Guards faced in Southeast Asia during this period:

> During the siege of the USAID Compound Sgt. Murphy and Sgt. Wilburn kept reports coming day and night as to what was happening inside of the compound. The two Marines had to put up with constant movement from the students who now occupied the compound. Almost all of the buildings were looted except for the two occupied by the Marines. The Chargé [d'affaires] was already having daily talks with the Prime Minister and student leaders but it was quite clear he

wasn't getting anywhere. Sgt. Wilburn's building contained all of the weapons but very little food. Sgt. Murphy's building had lots of "C" rations but no weapons. So after careful consideration and a lot of planning with the NCOIC a roof top exchange was made by the two Marines, Sgt. Wilburn receiving two boxes of "C" rations and Sgt. Murphy a .38 Caliber revolver and 15 rounds. From time to time after checking each other's roofs, one would go up on the roof and check the entire compound radioing back what he saw. On the fourth it was clear the compound was to be turned over to the students so the destruction of classified material began.[147]

Staff Sergeant Wagner stated that even though a truce of sorts had been worked out between the chargé and the students, the Pathet Lao was clearly behind the incident. For this reason, the chargé and RSO deemed it necessary to order the evacuation of all non-essential Americans. In the period that followed, the Marines processed between 800 and 850 Americans, whose homes were looted by the students shortly after they abandoned them. No building was safe, as looters broke into the Marine House and walked away with clothes, furniture, and other personal items that belonged to the Marines. The Laotian prime minister likewise ordered that the Americans reduce the size of their consulate staff including the Marine Security Guard detachment down to 40 State Department officials and 10 Marine security guards. From the fifteen Marine Security Guards five were ordered home.[148]

The MSG's Ultimate Test

Up to this point, the Vietnam War was the ultimate test of the Marine Security Guard program. More significant is the fact that as the end came closer and it became apparent an evacuation would take place, the Marine Security Guards asked permission to be the "last out of Vietnam." They were granted this request as the leathernecks insured that no American citizen was abandoned or classified material fell into enemy hands. According to Master Sergeant Valdez, amidst the chaos that wracked Saigon in those last days, not one piece of classified material was left in the embassy's vault. Master Sergeant Valdez added, "The primary mission of the MSG is the protection of classified material. Our secondary mission is the protection of American lives. I believe we did it all." As the last helicopter flew off the U.S. Embassy, the Marines were, as history has dutifully recorded, the first in and the "last out."

Tragically, however, this honor came with a terrible cost, as four Marine Security Guards paid the ultimate price in carrying out their missions. The deaths of Sergeant Charles Turberville, Corporals James C. Marshall and Charles McMahon, and Lance Corporal Darwin D. Judge once again demonstrated the dangers associated with the Marine Security Guard mission. More importantly is the fact that the war in Vietnam proved to be the ultimate test of the Marine Security Guard program and its training and mission.

CHAPTER 7

_____

Standing Watch Over a
Troubled World, 1961–1979

As Marine Security Guards in Southeast Asia watched over U.S. diplomatic interests throughout Southeast Asia during the mid to late 1960s, other leathernecks stood guard at Post One over a troubled and unsettled world. The steadfastness and professionalism of the Marines standing guard at Post One was repeatedly tested during the 1960s through the mid–1970s from Burma to Africa, and in the Western Hemisphere in El Salvador, Bolivia, Panama and Nicaragua. From political coups in the Republic of the Congo (September 1960–December 1965), the Dominican Republic (April 1965), as well as ethnic and religious violence on the island of Cyprus, in the Middle East, and Central America, Marine Security Guards faced numerous challenges in these highly volatile parts of the world.

Crisis in the Congo, September 1960–December 1961

The first of these tests came in September 1960 during trouble in the Republic of the Congo when President Joseph Kasavubu dismissed his premier, Patrice Lumumba on September 5, 1960. Lumumba in turn fired President Kasavubu. This move by Lumumba prompted the Congolese Army's chief of staff, Colonel Joseph Mobuto, to seize control of the Congolese government. Premier Lumumba was seen by President Dwight D. Eisenhower as a "genuine threat" to U.S. security. Whether or not Lumumba was a Marxist made little difference to President Eisenhower, who was determined not to have another "communist" such as Fidel Castro coming to power, as occurred in Cuba in 1959. The Eisenhower administration instead sought to control the situation in the former Belgian Congo through a variety of assassination plots aimed at the elimination of Lumumba. President Eisenhower made no secret of his concern over the situation in the Congo and of President Kasavubu's precarious position. The Eisenhower administration's concern was genuine, as it appeared by mid–June 1960 he was losing his power struggle with Lumumba as each day passed. Sharing President Eisenhower's view was U.S. Ambassador to the Congo, Clare Timberlake, who said Kasavubu acted more and more like a "vegetable ... while Lumumba continues to display brilliant broken field running."[1] On July 6, 1960, in response to a possible Soviet move in the former Belgian colony (and a victory by Lumumba), President Eisenhower ordered a Marine landing force to reinforce the carrier task force then sailing off the coast of the Congo. The Marines and sailors were ordered to prepare for a possible landing in order to evacuate American and foreign citizens. The violence in the Congo came to a head on January 17, 1961, when Colonel Mobuto's troops allegedly killed Lumumba while he was under house arrest in the city of Eliza-bethsville, located in the heart of the Congolese province of Katanga. The murder of Lumumba set off a wave of civil unrest and political violence that shook the capital, Leopoldsville,[2] and elsewhere throughout the Congo.[3]

In fact, in Leopoldsville, the violence was especially heavy as rioters and disaffected sol-diers targeted western embassies and consulates that now became the scene of shootings, bomb blasts, and protests. These attacks prompted ambassadors and consular officials to undertake severe security measures to protect them and other foreign nationals. The violence continued on into the New Year, as the administration of John F. Kennedy (1961–1963), which had promised during the election to "put African affairs on the front burner," dealt with its sec-ond, and perhaps most volatile, foreign crisis inherited from the previous administration.[4]

Throughout the summer and fall of 1961, Katangan guerrillas, led by Moise Tshombe, fought government and other tribal forces in a bid to control Katanga and secede from the Republic of the Congo. Eventually, after much bloodshed, Tshombe notified the United Nations that he was ready to end his rebellion. In order to guarantee his safety, however, Mr. Tshombe sent a personal request to the White House and asked that the United States bro-ker a ceasefire with his opponents. Mr. Tshombe sent a personal telegram to President Kennedy and informed him that he was prepared to talk with Congonese Prime Minister Cyrille Adoula at a neutral site. Through Secretary of State Dean Rusk, President Kennedy informed Mr. Tshombe that he would appoint Mr. Edmund A. Gullion, U.S. ambassador to the Congo, as his special representative in order to facilitate the meeting.[5] Acting United Nations Secretary General U Thant likewise appointed noted American Civil Rights champion Ralph Bunche as his special special representative. Through the efforts of Ambassador Bunche, and with assis-tance from the United States, France, Great Britain, and a host of African and European countries, the warring factions were brought to the negotiating table. Meeting at the air base in Kitona, the city in the Congo where the negotiations took place, Tshmobe sat down with Mr. Adoula and hammered out an agreement that briefly unified the Congo for the first time since July 1960.

Prior to the start of the Kitona Conference, Secretary of State Rusk, as well as U.S. Ambassador Gullion, in a move to guarantee the success of the negotiations, offered the use of Marine security guards to protect the conferees against any random violence. Ambassador Gullion, in fact, pointed out in a telegram to Secretary Rusk that the "U.S. handled all details ... but promised U.S. Marines." As expected, the Marine Security Guards met the airplane at Kitona Airfield carrying what one observer noted was "a very agitated and nervous Mr. Tshombe," and remained within the Katangan leader's sight most of the time of the confer-ence. In order to deflect criticism that the African leaders were being coerced into meeting against their will, Ambassador Gullion reported later to Secretary Rusk, "Tomorrow when international press arrives [the Marines] will, at [Ralph] Bunche's request, merely guard the bedroom serving as small U.S. office."[6]

The Marine Security Guards assigned to protect President Tshombe were Staff Sergeant Harold W. Leach, the staff noncommissioned officer-in-charge of the Marine Security Guard Detachment, and Corporal Arthur F. Williams, both of whom had been assigned to the U.S. Embassy in Leopoldsville. Both Staff Sergeant Leach and Corporal Williams flew from Leopoldsville with Ambassador Gullion on December 19, 1961. Tshombe felt he was being set up for assassination and Ambassador Gullion assured him of U.S. protection by bringing Staff Sgt. Leach and Cpl. Williams as bodyguards. Meeting at the Kitona airbase, Adoula and Tshombe signed an agreement and agreed to lay down their arms and resolve the matter of

Katangan independence peacefully. Unfortunately, the Kitona peace conference resulted merely in a ceasefire between the warring parties that did not last; violence broke out even before the ink was dry on the treaty. At the conclusion of the Kitona Conference, Staff Sergeant Leach and Corporal Williams flew back to Leopoldsville via Ndola, Rhodesia,[7] two days later on December 21, 1961.[8]

MSGs and Political Turmoil in the Congo, 1964–1967

As the ink dried on the agreement between Adoula and Tshombe, the seeds of the 1964 *coup d'état* against the government in Leopoldsville were sown, as the Republic of the Congo wavered between an uneasy truce and violent uprisings along the Katangan border. For the next two years, the United States attempted to prevent mineral-rich Katanga from seceding from the rest of the Congo. By early 1964, however, disaffected political groups took to the street as rioting and looting, aimed primarily at Westerners, broke out in Leopoldsville and throughout the Congo.

One of the disaffected political groups, the Simbas, reportedly supported by both the Soviet Union and Cuba, and led by General Nicholas Olenga, led a rampage through Stanleyville on August 5, 1964, where for the next two weeks, they and their supporters killed some 2,000 to 4,000 Congolese. In the wake of the political anarchy that now swept all of the eastern Congo, the Simbas killed several Belgians and an American doctor. One of the targets of the Simbas was the American Consulate in Stanleyville. Here, Consul General Michael Hoyt and his five-man staff bolted themselves inside the communications vault and awaited rescue either from the Congolese, the Belgians or the American forces that were on alert at Fort Bragg, North Carolina. As the American diplomats awaited rescue, the U.S. ambassador in Leopoldsville, G. McMurtrie Godley, prepared a rescue operation that involved military personnel from the U.S. Military Mission in the Congo (COMISH), embassy staff, the Marine Security Guard Detachment, and two C-47 transports, two T-28 fighter-bombers, and an H-21 helicopter.[9] The rescue, known as Operation Flagpole, was abruptly canceled on orders from Secretary of State Dean Rusk, who prohibited Ambassador Godley from the use of overt force. After several months of captivity, which at times at the hands of the Simbas bordered on fear and terror, Belgian paratroopers eventually freed Consul General Hoyt and his staff. Despite the successes (and failures) of Operations Dragon Rouge and Dragon Noir, the sub-continent of Africa and Middle East broke out in a wave of anti–American, anti– British, and anti–Belgian protests and demonstrations. In Cairo, Egypt, demonstrators burned and ransacked the USIA Library, while Kenyans in Nairobi burned cars outside the American, British, and Belgian embassies. For his part, President Lyndon B. Johnson, pre-occupied with the situation in South Vietnam, did not "desire to get tied in on the Congo and have another Korea or Vietnam" in the middle of Africa.[10]

The revolt by the Simbas did not, however, end the political turmoil in the Congo. One Marine Security Guard, Lance Corporal Larry Bell, recalled that when he arrived in Leopoldsville, Africa had become "the mercenary center of the world," as African rulers, businessmen and western intelligence agencies competed for the services of these free-lance soldiers-of-fortune. As for the Congo, after the defeat of the Simbas, Moise Tshombe assumed a tenuous hold on the Congo for the next several months until he was overthrown in a *coup d'état* by General Sese Seko Mobutu. Eventually, the United States recognized Mobutu as the legitimate ruler of the Congolese Republic. As Lance Corporal Bell discovered, Marine Security Guard duty in Africa was "anything but dull," and was, in fact, a lesson in survival amidst Africa's frequent political and social chaos.

Marine Security Guard Duty in Leopoldsville, 1966–1967

Upon his arrival in Leopoldsville after a fourteen-hour flight from New York, Lance Corporal Bell settled into a regular routine of standing watch, conducting after-hour searches of the diplomatic offices, daily physical training, and dealing with the local population. Bell recalled that upon his arrival at the airport in Leopoldsville, he was met by Staff Sergeant James Kenney, NCOIC of the MSG Detachment, and the off-duty guard he was to relieve. After what he described as a "bewildering ride" through miles of a "grubby shantytown," the Marines arrived at the Marine House, situated cattycorner to the U.S. Embassy and located less than fifty yards from it. The lance corporal recalled that the Marine House was

> a large villa situated on a large fenced yard.... The house consisted of four bedrooms, a billiard room, formal dining room connected to a large living room with a wet bar. The kitchen included a servant's laundry room to do ironing, a pantry room, and a large informal dining room, where we normally ate our meals. Out back, we had a shed we dubbed the 'atomic room' since the US Army attaché's had a gizmo inside that reportedly sniffed for French and South African testing of atomic weapons. The sole security of this equipment was a key lock.[11]

Lance Corporal Bell wrote that before leaving him, Staff Sergeant Kenney went over the routine of the Marine Security Guard that included PT every morning at 0700. Exhausted after a long journey, Bell "slid into bed about 11:00 P.M.," only to be awakened two hours later by "two grinning drunks," who happened to be his fellow Marine Security Guards, determined to show the new Marine Security Guard "the town." Failing to persuade them that he was tired, Bell reluctantly dragged himself out of bed, dressed, and accompanied his fellow leathernecks into a strip of a bars located near the embassy, punctuated by loud music, and patronized by Congolese women and "very drunk" mercenaries. After one of the Marines barely avoided an altercation with one of the mercenaries, the other two decided it was time to go back to the Marine House. Bell recalled later that "This was only the beginning of two years of drunken bar fighting, embassy parties, hunting trips, rescue operations, and general mayhem that would have normally caused an embassy Marine to get a free trip home."[12] A typical day for a Marine Security Guard began at 0700 when Staff Sergeant Kenney arrived in PT gear to take his Marines on a five mile run (past a leather factory toward the airport) and conduct sit ups, pull ups, broad jumps, and push ups. Bell, who usually worked 2nd shift, ate dinner at 4:00 P.M., prior to staring his shift that began at 5:00 P.M.

Oftentimes, MSG duty could be boring and monotonous, but as Bell recalled, the Marines found ways to break the monotony of a backwater post. After returning from a typical night of partying, Bell was walking alone in the streets of Leopoldsville and saw flapping in the wind in front of a Catholic cathedral two Congolese flags he believed would make great souvenirs. After successfully pulling the flagpole halfway out of the ground, the top of the pole hit the concrete and scraped against the face of the cathedral. Finally, the pole broke apart. As the pole bounced onto the pavement below it made a loud noise, resembling a Chinese gong that alerted four Congolese policemen who were standing nearby. The policemen, upon hearing the pole hit the concrete, rushed to the site of the suspicious noise. To their amazement upon their arrival at the cathedral, the policemen found Lance Corporal Bell holding onto the pole, which he had attempted to place back into its original upright position. The frightened Marine Security Guard told the policemen that the pole had inexplicably come down and that he had attempted to put it back up. Bewildered, the Congolese allowed Bell to leave, but only for a moment, as they soon gave chase to the Marine, who by this time had made it back to the Marine House. After a narrow escape from police, who had a reputation for cruelty, Bell decided that he had had enough adventure for one night and it "was time to go to bed!"

Lance Corporal Bell recalled another incident that involved a pellet gun brought out by one Marine to shoot at the lizards that abounded in the embassy compound. As Bell wrote, "that kept us busy for two days," before someone decided lizards were no fun to shoot at and instead began to target unsuspecting Congolese. After hitting their first victim, the Marines, who were "giggling like a bunch of little kids," searched for other victims. Deciding to try his luck, Bell took the pellet gun and climbed atop the Marine House via a microwave antenna used by the embassy. Ducking behind a small ventilation hood, Bell waited in "ambush" and fired at a Congolese man in front of the house. The victim, however, spotted his attacker and threw a large rock back at Bell and proceeded to chase after him. Incensed at this attack on the property of the United States, Bell, shouting in French "go away," fired again as his attacker drew near, and hit him in the back of the neck, and the retreated into the sanctuary of the Marine House. Later, as the Marines prepared to go out on the town, two Congolese policemen and the victim stood on the porch of the Marine House looking for his attacker. Thinking quickly, Corporal Bell informed them in French, "This is U.S. Embassy diplomatic ground," and that they had to leave.

Shortly after awaking the next morning, Corporal Bell received a phone call from Lance Corporal Langley, the duty Marine, who informed him the assistant detachment commander, Staff Sergeant Giles, wanted to see him "now" concerning the shooting incident. Informed that the security officer, Mr. Philips, wished to see him, Staff Sergeant Giles looked up at Bell and tersely told him, "You have some explaining to do." The consular officer explained that the Marines had been watching a western movie that had been the source of the gunfire that the victim had heard. In a further move to resolve the issue, Corporal Bell, Staff Sergeant Giles, and Mr. John Mowinkel, the director of the USIS Library, met with the victim, who once again recounted that Bell had shot him in the back of the neck. Mr. Mowinkel, who appeared sympathetic to the victim though not desiring to see the incident ruin Bell's career, asked the Congolese man to show him the "bullet wound." Asking him if he bled very much or had a bullet hole, the victim gyrated and shook his head in the negative. Mr. Mowinkel then turned to the victim, and in perfect French told him "If this young man had shot you in the back and neck you would've bled, correct? And of course you would have bullet holes in your body. Since you didn't bleed and there are no holes, obviously he didn't shoot you." Thanking the Congolese for coming in, he took their notes and wished them a good afternoon. Driving back to the Marine House, Staff Sergeant Giles, who had been silent on his way to the USIS Library, turned to Bell and said, "Don't get on the roof again!"[13]

Amidst the routine duty and monotony of the post, duty in the Congo could be quite dangerous. By September 1966, border clashes between the Portuguese, who still maintained control over neighboring Angola and the Congo, broke out over an assassination attempt on guerrilla leader Holden Roberto, who was fighting for Angolan independence. Radio Kinshasa began broadcasting inflammatory rhetoric over the airwaves blaming Portugal for this and other crimes along their mutual border. While the tension was not readily apparent in Kinshasa itself, this all changed on the morning of 24 September 1966, when Kinshasans gathered outside the Portuguese embassy, only a few yards away from the U.S. Embassy, and began to shout insults and hurl stones at Portugal's building. Shortly thereafter, the violence spread to the neighboring U.S. Embassy. The Marine Security Guards, many of whom had just stumbled out of bed, quickly got dressed and rushed to the U.S. Embassy. Staff Sergeant Kenney, referred by the Marines as "Gunny," who had been at the embassy that morning doing paperwork, ordered the Marine Security Guards to prepare for possible trouble. Corporal Bell recalled:

When we arrived approximately four hundred demonstrators consisting of thugs belonging to the "Volunteers for the Congo" were standing in the road chanting something, but maintaining a distance from the front of the Portuguese embassy. As we prepared for trouble by distributing baseball bats and moving oil and concertina wire into stairwells, organized groups of more demonstrators approached marching in military formation. It became apparent that the entire demonstration was a government sponsored event. All the demonstrators were wearing a bandana of General [Sese Seko] Mobutu's political party. With the arrival of the additional groups the entire crowd had swelled to over 700 semi-organized ranting hoodlums. Demonstrators attempted to stay directly in front of the Portuguese embassy, but with the additional numbers, small groups or individuals started getting aggressive. We had remained in the lobby, but several of our embassy personnel who had arrived there were standing in our driveway watching it like it was a sporting event. Suddenly, three babbling drunk demonstrators decided to haul down our flag which was in the middle of the small island in front of our doors. "Gunny! a couple of them are trying to haul down the flag!" SSgt Kenney had been talking to an embassy officer and turned to see the Congolese unraveling the flag pole landyard. "Stop the mother...!

Looking like black water going down an open drain, hundreds of Congolese rushed for the open doors shoving and hitting trying to get inside the embassy. "Gunny! Gunny! They're inside the embassy! The roar of the crowd drowned out Jone's screams back towards the mall crowd on our front foyer watching in horror. Not seen by any of us was the immediate abduction of the Charge d'Affaires, Ressano Garcia, who was dragged forcibly to a waiting vehicle and whisked away to the headquarters of General Mobutu's political party sponsoring this demonstration. A few crazed demonstrators lunged at me trying to grab my shirt. I swung the baseball bat at head level and made contact repeatedly. Suddenly Congolese appeared on the embassy's second floor balcony holding loot they had gathered up in their rampaging through the embassy. Telephones, lamps, papers, everything seemed to be carried out and flung over the balcony banister into the crowd below. With each arm load the crowd would roar approval.

Screaming and twisting in their hands a female stenographer, Maria Helena Silve, was carried out with the crowd screaming to the looters to throw her. Jones and I looked on in horror as it became apparent she would be tossed. I yelled, "Gunny, They're going to throw her out!" Just then they did. With a loud roar of approval the gang on the balcony heaved her out into space. Luckily for her the crowd below her didn't react quick enough and she landed on several of them breaking her fall. Jones and I instinctively had leaped over the separating wall charging into the crazed crowd. Bats swinging we ran towards her with the crowd scattering in front of us. Just then the looters on the second floor brought an embassy male out on the balcony, Third Secretary, Carlos Milheirao, and threw him over. Unfortunately, no one was below him when he hit the ground. The Portuguese embassy's third secretary sustained severe contusions and a broken arm from his fall. In a drunken frenzy a rioter had doused Mr. Milheirao with gasoline as he lay in agony. The rioter was only stopped from lighting Mr. Milheirao up by another demonstrator with a little sanity. Jones and I grabbed Ms. Silve up from the ground dragging her up and over the wall towards our front door.

SSgt Kenney had belatedly run towards us the moment Jones and I had leaped the wall yelling for us to stop. He assisted getting the lady into the embassy front doors where the nurse had come out to provide aid. During this bedlam police sirens could be heard coming closer. In a few moments several police jeeps and trucks with Congolese Army troops had pulled up and began dispersing the crowd. Jones and I were standing in our embassy's front driveway watching the dispersing mob, our bats hanging down in exhaustion.[14]

The next day, Sunday, 25 September 1966, the demonstrators, about 2,000 of them, marched through the streets of Leopoldsville and stopped once again in front of the Portuguese Embassy. This time, however, the Marines, Congolese policemen, and soldiers were able to prevent a repeat of what occurred the day before, and quickly dispersed the crowd.

After a brief period of hospitalization, Ms. Silve and Mr. Milheirao, both of whom had suffered severe trauma as a result of their ordeal, were sent home to Belgium. Mr. Garcia, who had suffered multiple bruises as well as severe head injury, was eventually released through the personal intervention of President Mobutu, though not before his kidnappers had attempted to strangle and torture him as they took him to Mobutu's political headquarters.[15]

During his tour of duty in the Republic of the Congo, Corporal Bell likewise served as a courier for the CIA Station chief. Along with another Marine Security Guard, Corporal White, the Marines had been ordered to rescue two cryptographers from the U.S. Consulate located in Elizabethsville, located near the Angolan and Zambian borders. While the mission was clearly a violation of the duties performed by the Marine Security Guard, it did have the approval of Ambassador Godley, who along with the CIA Station chief, Mr. Lawrence Devlin,[16] assured the Marines that the secretary of state and director of the CIA in Langley, Virginia, had been informed of the mission.

Armed with Belgian FN 7.62mm FAL rifles, magazines and accoutrements, the Marines, along with a U.S. Army major who had been the embassy's military attaché headed to the besieged consulate. Upon their arrival at the consulate in Elizabethsville, the Americans, dressed and equipped as Belgian soldiers, became involved in an intense though brief firefight with Simba guerrillas, all whom the Marines quickly disposed of as they freed the two trapped cryptographers. Gathering a small amount of gear, the cryptographers, Marines and Army major boarded an awaiting Belgian helicopter that whisked them to an awaiting airplane where, after a short flight, they arrived back to Leopoldsville. In praising the efficiency of their work, Ambassador Godley and Station Chief Devlin sent congratulatory telegrams via the secretary of state and director, CIA, addressed to General Wallace M. Greene, the commandant of the Marine Corps, who likewise praised the efficiency and steadfastness of the Marine Security Guards involved in the mission.

Despite the fact that this was a CIA-sponsored mission, U.S. State Department officials were visibly upset over the use of Marine Security Guards in such a dangerous mission. Upon receipt of Staff Sergeant Kenney's report of the mission, the regional security officer in charge, headquartered in Beirut, Lebanon, immediately preferred courts-martial proceedings against the Marine staff sergeant for his violation. General Greene, who retained administrative control over the Marines on embassy duty, dismissed these charges, as both Ambassador Godley's and Mr. Devlin's congratulatory messages made it clear that SSgt. Kenney had been acting on orders.[17]

Corporal Bell and his fellow Marines endured one last state-sponsored demonstration against Portugal and United States while in Leopoldsville, on August 15, 1967, as President Mobutu attempted to deflect criticism from his ever-increasingly heavy hand as ruler of the Congo. In a replay of the September 24, 1966, demonstration that injured several Portuguese and American embassy officials, the Congolese were stopped at the last minute from ransacking the U.S. Embassy when President Mobutu himself rode through the crowd in a jeep and ordered his people to disperse and go home. After dispersing the crowds, President Mobutu, escorted by Bell and another Marine Security Guard, met with the new U.S. ambassador, Mr. McBride, who was visibly upset over this latest outrage against the United States. Despite the fact that President Mobutu continued to express his sorrow over the attacks and that it was all a "terrible mistake," Ambassador McBride told the president to leave his office immediately. Even before Mobutu could utter another sentence on how sorry he was, Ambassador McBride looked straight at the African president and told him, "Get the hell out of my embassy!" whereupon the "General," Bell wrote, "got the hint and left." The damage done to the U.S. Embassy was considerable, as it was later estimated that the rioters caused over $120,000 worth of damage in broken windows, destroyed offices, broken doors, and office equipment. Paraphrasing President Mobutu, Corporal Bell recounted that the riot really was just "a big mistake."[18]

Later on, Vice President Hubert H. Humphrey, on a tour of Africa, visited the Congo and met with President Mobutu. In his report to President Lyndon B. Johnson, Vice President Humphrey praised Mobutu's sincerity and that of his people. Mr. Humphrey reported later to the President that while on a tour of the Agency for Internal Development at an assisted housing project in Kinshasa, "the crowds gave us an enthusiastic welcome as we drove in Mobutu's open car." The vice president added that this "greatly overshadowed an earlier minor incident in which a small number of Communist-organized students sought to embarrass the West."[19] Mr. Humphrey likewise praised Mobutu's apparent strong nationalism and sense of pride in the direction that he was taking Congo (soon to be Zaire). The vice president re-affirmed Mobutu's strong desire for a "strong friendship" with the United States, and his hope that Congo can steer clear of the internal chaos that plagued the country for nearly eight years.[20]

As events three decades later demonstrated, this would not be the last time the Marine Security Guard detachment in the Congo would be on the front lines of anti–Western, anti-government protests. In the mid–1990s, Marine Security Guards were once again thrust into the vortex of Congolese politics and, like their predecessors, met the challenge with the same cool professionalism displayed by Staff Sergeant Giles, Sergeant Jones, Corporals Bell and White, and the other Marine Security Guards assigned to the Congo in the mid–1960s.

Crisis in the Dominican Republic, April–June 1965

As Marine Embassy Guards stood guard in revolution-torn Africa and Asia, events closer to the United States involved the Marine Corps, and more specifically the Marine Security Guard Detachment assigned to the U.S. Embassy in Santo Domingo City, in the Dominican Republic in the spring of 1965.

For nearly thirty years, the Dominican Republic remained under the authoritarian, often-times described as more totalitarian, rule of Rafael Leonidas Trujillo Molinas, a former member of the U.S. Marine–organized and trained *Guardia Dominicana*, and who assumed power in 1930 through a rigged election. Through intimidation, murder, and a carefully orchestrated public relations campaign with supporters in the United States Congress, Trujillo and his cronies retained their grip on the Dominican Republic. On May 30, 1961, however, Trujillo was assassinated by a group of conspirators who had hoped to return the country to democratic rule. Unfortunately, the late dictator's son, Air Force General Rafael Trujillo Martinez, took savage reprisals against those who he thought responsible for his father's death. The senior Trujillo's death, however, sent a signal to those opposed to the Trujillo clan's hold on the country, as they now openly opposed any return to the authoritarian rule by members of Trujillo's family.

In November of 1961, after sacking the country's treasury, General Trujillo fled the country for a self-imposed exile in Europe. After the failure of an abortive coup by two members of Trujillo's immediate family, President John F. Kennedy, in an overt display of force and support for the forces opposed to the Trujillos, dispatched an amphibious task force spearheaded by a Navy-Marine Expeditionary Task Force to waters off the Dominican Republic.[21] Shortly after the departure of General Trujillo, a caretaker government, comprised of a seven-man interim council known as the Council of State, assumed office on January 1, 1962. The seven-man council began to prepare the country for elections scheduled for December of that same year. Despite the threat that existed from the supporters of the ousted Trujillos and their supporters, the country elected its first president, Juan Bosch, the leader of the liberal Dominican Revolutionary Party (PRD). Bosch remained president of the Dominican Republic for only seven months, when he was ousted in a military *coup d'état* by Air Force Brigadier General Elias Wessin y Wessin. In an attempt to mollify the United States, which had refused to recognize the military junta that had overthrown the popular Bosch government, General Wessin eventually appointed a seven-man civilian junta led by Donald J. Reid Cabarl. Reid's government shortly thereafter dismantled the 1963 Constitution that had established the first republican government in the Dominican Republic since Trujillo's rise to power in 1930.

In a government controlled by the more conservative elements of Dominican society, the political forces opposed to this curtailment of its hard-earned political and personal freedom refused to recognize Reid's government. Over the next fourteen months, political opposition to Reid continued to gain momentum. Most active in their opposition to the civilian junta was a coalition of communist and communist-front organizations (the APCJ, MPD, and PSPD), many of whom had been trained in Cuba under Fidel Castro.[22]

Also opposed to Reid were a growing number of "influential conservative" officers of the armed forces, member of the country's upper classes, and the hierarchy of the Catholic Church, who feared a disruption of their traditional positions of power within the country.[23] In effect, the Dominican Republic became a battleground of two competing political philosophies, both groups which sought the removal of the unpopular Reid government. Against the backdrop of this political instability was the release of a U.S. Army intelligence study that concluded, "It is extremely doubtful that the Dominican Republic, still in a state of political immaturity, will achieve any semblance of political stability in the foreseeable future."[24] As the political situation remained unsettled, rumors of an impending coup against the Reid government scheduled for the weekend of April 24–25, 1965, began to filter into the U.S. Embassy during the last week of April 1965.

Despite knowledge of an impending *coup d'état*, U.S. Ambassador to the Dominican Republic William Tapley Bennett, Jr., left the country on April 23, 1965, in order to visit his ailing mother in Georgia, and follow through with a scheduled trip to Washington, D.C., to brief the secretary of state on the situation in the Dominican Republic, while other members of the embassy were either off on assignment or vacation. Meanwhile, the anti–Reid forces prepared to launch what they thought would be a popular uprising throughout the Dominican Republic, and would restore the popular leader Juan Bosch to power.

At noon, on Saturday, April 24, 1965, a small group of pro–Bosch army officers and enlisted men, "acting in the name of Juan Bosch," arrested the army chief of staff at his headquarters outside Santo Domingo. Meanwhile, pro-Bosch supporters seized control of a local radio station and began to broadcast reports that the Reid government had been overthrown. Shortly thereafter, Dominicans in Ciudad Nueva appeared in the streets and began shouting "Bosch, Bosch," in an apparent show of support for the rebels. Even as the government-controlled Radio Santo Domingo denied reports of a coup against Reid, rebels stormed into the station and began to broadcast reports that the Reid government had indeed fallen. This was short-lived, as loyal police forces forced their way into the radio station and arrested the rebels. The die was cast, however, as supporters of Bosch, many of whom comprised the lower classes living in the major cities, filled the streets and voiced support for the ousted president and the rebels.

Support for the coup leaders did not come exclusively from the poor. Members of the armed forces, primarily the Army, began to defect over to the side of the rebels. In a major blow to the Reid government, General Wessin y Wessin refused to intervene on behalf of the government. With this refusal, President Reid Cabral and his fellow junta member, Ramon Caceres, resigned and fled the capital. Word of Reid's resignation soon reached the crowds, who now filed into the streets in a defiant show of support for the coup against the ousted president. While the majority of the Dominicans voiced support for Rafael Molina Urena, the leader of the PRD, in lieu of President Bosch's re-assumption of power, General Wessin y Wessin and other members of the armed forces had hoped to forestall the latter's return to power through the installation of a military junta. The country was now in turmoil as both factions girded for a showdown.

Eventually, when Air Force chief of staff General Juan de los Santos Cespedes threw his support to General Wessin y Wessin, the supporters of President Molina were given an ultimatum: either disarm and abandon their plans or face the consequences of an all-out military assault. As the country now tottered on civil war, President Molina and twenty of his top military and political advisors met with Ambassador Bennett, who had returned to Santo Domingo City. In his meeting with Ambassador Bennett on April 27 in the U.S. Embassy, President Molina implored the U.S. diplomatic representative to intercede with the military junta and arrange a cease-fire. The rebels' hopes for a cease-fire and recognition were soon dashed, however, as Ambassador Bennett reportedly insulted and admonished them for starting the coup in the first place. The rebel leaders reportedly emerged from the meeting more determined than ever to carry through with the overthrow of Reid Cabral — even if it meant civil war.

Having dismissed the rebels and their *coup d'état* as a reckless adventure doomed to fail, Ambassador Bennett feared that the violence would now be turned against U.S. citizens and interests. That evening, Ambassador Bennett requested that a force of Marines be dispatched to Santo Domingo to assist not only in the evacuation of U.S. and foreign nationals, but also to defend the U.S. Embassy, which was already on a heightened state of alert. Ambassador Bennett felt that the rebels would target American interests in the aftermath of the meeting with President Molina.

As the situation in Santo Domingo City and its environs deteriorated into a state of anarchy, President Lyndon B. Johnson and his staff became increasingly concerned as to the long-range implications of any coup in the Dominican Republic. Having already dealt with the Cuban Missile Crisis of 1962, many advisors in the Johnson administration and in Congress feared the installation of a government in the Dominican Republic with ties directly or indirectly to Castro's Cuba. They believed that the presence of another leftist-oriented government, no matter how popular to the average Dominican, threatened hemispheric stability. It also raised the possibility of the creation of another Communist-dominated Caribbean nation — not unlike the one in neighboring Cuba.

For President Lyndon B. Johnson, the Dominican Crisis could not have occurred at a worse time. He was already pre-occupied with the ongoing troop build-up in South Vietnam, and a regime dominated by Marxists and supported by Fidel Castro was both an unthinkable and unacceptable prospect. Also, due to the country's strategic position at the entrance of the Caribbean and approach to the Panama Canal, President Johnson "could not ignore U.S. interests in and around the Dominican Republic and the deteriorating situation in that country." With reports that approximately fifty or so of the guerrillas had been trained in Cuba, the Soviet Union, and in the People's Republic of China, President Johnson realized that a failure to act might bring about another communist regime in the hemisphere. President Johnson likewise made it clear that he would act quickly and decisively to resolve the crisis in the Dominican Republic.[25] With U.S. troops committed to the defense of South Vietnam, the president told his advisers early on in the crisis, "What can we do in Vietnam if we can't clean up the Dominican Republic?"

Send in the Marines

Events in Santo Domingo City and elsewhere throughout the Dominican Republic began to worsen even before President Johnson received word at Camp David, Maryland, of the

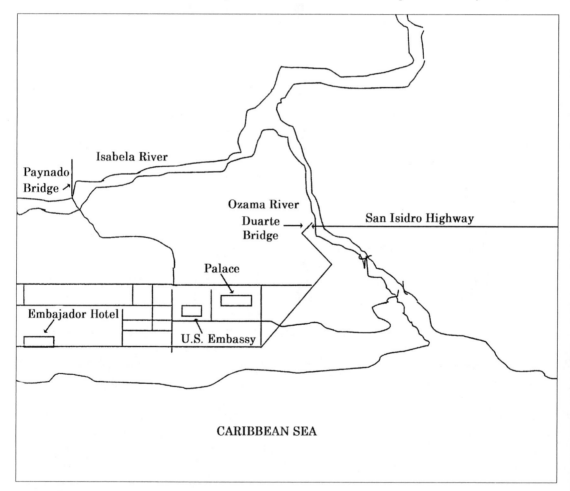

Map 3. Santo Domingo, Dominican Republic, in 1965 (Yates, *Power Pack: U.S. Intervention in Dominican Republic*).

coup d'état. Deputy Chief of Mission William Connett, Jr., who was in charge of the U.S. Embassy in the Dominican Republic during the first few days of the revolt,[26] reported to his superiors in Washington, D.C., that the coup threatened the lives of the 1,200 Americans living there, and that troops were needed to assist in their safety and probable evacuation.[27] At the time of the crisis, the Marine Security Guard at the U.S. Embassy in the Dominican Republic consisted of one NCOIC and six watchstanders.[28] One of Ambassador Bennett's first moves upon his arrival back in Santo Domingo City was to request reinforcements in order to safeguard the embassy, its classified material, and above all else, all personnel assigned to the embassy's staff.

Already alerted and steaming toward the Dominican coast were Marines and Sailors of Ready Amphibious Task Group (TG 45.9), comprised of the 6th Marine Expeditionary Unit. The infantry element assigned to the 6th MEU was the 3d Battalion, 6th Marines (Reinforced), commanded by Lieutenant Colonel Paul F. Pedersen. Conveniently, 3/6 was close by when the crisis began, having just completed an amphibious landing on the island of Viques, Puerto Rico. After embarking aboard the USS *Boxer*, all of the battalion's line companies — minus Company M, which had been left behind on Guantanamo Bay, Cuba, as part of the base defense force — received word that their next destination would be Santo Domingo City. Unknown at the time to the Marines of 3/6, however, Colonel George W. Daughtry, the commanding officer of the 6th MEU, had ordered the battalion, along with its supporting helicopter squadron, Marine Medium Helicopter Squadron 264 (HMM-264), to proceed in haste to the waters off the Dominican Republic. Here, the leathernecks and sailors were to assist in the evacuation of an estimated 1,200 American and foreign nationals, as well as reinforce the Marine Embassy Guard in defense of the embassy and its staff.[29]

Upon their arrival off Dominican waters, helicopters of HMM-264 airlifted Company K, 3/6, ashore in order to direct the evacuation of Americans and foreigners from the beleaguered capital. At approximately 2 P.M. on April 28, the U.S. Embassy received a call from Junta President Colonel Paul Benoit, who informed the ambassador that it might be prudent to land 1,200 Marines to assist in the restoration of peace and stability in the country.[30] At first, Ambassador Bennett believed it unnecessary to land such a large force. His attitude quickly changed, however, when rebel sniper and small arms fire began to target the embassy. Late on the afternoon of the 28, Ambassador Bennett requested that the Marines from the *Boxer* be sent ashore "to insure the safety of the evacuees and to reinforce the Marine guard at the Embassy."[31]

Within minutes of Bennett's call to Washington, D.C., scout snipers and the lead platoon of Kilo Company, 3/6, took off from the deck of the *Boxer* in order to secure a landing zone necessary for the evacuation of the estimated 1,200 Americans and foreign nationals from Santo Domingo City. Once on shore, the leathernecks of Kilo Company discovered that the number of Americans and foreigners to be evacuated had risen to 3,000.[32] Undaunted, the Marines established a defensive perimeter around the polo fields located on the grounds of the Embajador Hotel, where helicopters from HMM-264 began a rotation of airlifts to and from the USS *Boxer*. Only days before, on April 27, prior to the full-scale evacuation from Santo Domingo City, helicopters belonging to HMM-264 had logged 59 hours and approximately 102 sorties in the evacuation of approximately 558 Americans and other nationals from the Port of Haina. As events later turned out, this was but a prelude to the evacuation from Santo Domingo City.[33]

As the evacuation from Santo Domingo City commenced, Marines from Kilo Company established a patrol along the perimeter adjacent to the landing zone. Meanwhile, on the afternoon of April 29, 1965, rebels fired on the U.S. Embassy. The next day, April 30, Colonel Daughtry ordered the rest of 3/6 ashore. As dusk started to cast its shadow over the task force off shore, the remainder of the Battalion Landing Team began to assemble for the brief flight ashore. By midnight of May 1, the remainder of 3/6 was ashore in what was surely a tremendous accomplishment, given the short notice Lieutenant Colonel Pedersen had received from the MEU staff. In fact, within hours of the order to land the entire battalion, HMM-264 shuttled 536 Marines and 18 tons of equipment ashore. With each returning flight civilians were placed aboard the helicopters. By the time the shuttle ended, 684 civilians had been brought aboard the *Boxer*.[34]

By the early morning hours of 1 May, the Marines of BLT 3/6 had expanded the original defensive perimeter to include the road leading into the hotel from the northern part of the city to prevent rebels from entering the landing zone. Hiding behind trees and buildings along Calle Leopoldo Navarro on the east side of the city, rebels re-directed their fire toward the U.S. Embassy. The local security policemen, assigned to augment the Marine Security Guard, did what they could to help the Marines inside the embassy. As Major General R. McC. Tompkins later recounted, "this was little enough and it was clear from the rebels' actions that they had it in mind to try something more adventurous than simple sniping. At the ambassador's request, a platoon from the 3d Battalion, 6th Marines came in by helicopter and sought out thoughtful firing points in the embassy grounds.[35] Augmenting the Marine Security Guard inside the U.S. Embassy was a rifle platoon that had been organized by Lieutenant Colonel Pedersen, who quickly took charge of the situation prior to the battalion coming ashore. Colonel Pedersen was ready to land this security platoon once Ambassador Bennett sent word that additional Marines were required to defend the embassy. The 27-man "clutch" platoon, composed of personnel organized from H&S Company under the command of Second Lieutenant Phil Tucker and Master Sergeant Harold E. Lanter, was quickly brought ashore by helicopters from HMM-264. As soon as they touched down at the Embajador Hotel, the platoon departed for the embassy in a variety of civilian vehicles provided by the embassy. In charge of the convoy carrying the Marines was Commander Richard Holmes, USN, of the Military Advisory and Assistance Group (Dominican Republic), who led the convoy directly into the embassy's courtyard. Along with their small arms, the leathernecks brought with them food and much-needed medical supplies.[36] Disembarking from the vehicles, the Marines quickly took up tactical positions alongside the wall that surrounded the embassy compound to prevent the rebels from entering the embassy grounds. As Major General Tompkins wrote, "Ashore the Marines at the Embassy traded shot for shot with enthusiastic rebels, to the detriment of the latter."[37]

Aboard the *Boxer*, Lieutenant Colonel Pedersen began to organize another force to augment the Marines already ashore. This force, headed by Second Lieutenant Phil Tucker, was instructed by the commander of BLT 3/6 to defend the embassy and its staff. Lieutenant Tucker recalled later that he and his Marines were "ready for anything," though he emphasized that he had carefully instructed his men as they rode through the tense city not to be too "trigger happy."[38]

Second Lieutenant Tucker's platoon, which had already been ashore guarding the Embajador Hotel polo field, recalled that Lieutenant Colonel Pedersen specifically selected his platoon for the mission ashore, as it was the most readily available:

> I was in the wardroom on Wednesday, April 28, about to eat chow when the colonel gave me the word that my platoon was to land. We had been ashore before, around the Embajador Hotel and the polo grounds in Santo Domingo. We went in to evacuate Americans and other people fleeing

the turmoil in the city. We had gone in strictly as an MP group and we had left our combat gear on deck. I think that is the reason we were picked. At about 1715, we drew ammo, put on flak jackets, and boarded HMM-264's choppers to fly to the polo grounds. We were to be met by transportation from the U.S. Embassy. Marines had been requested to secure the Embassy area.

We landed after only a few minutes in the air. Five choppers were used. One received ground fire. The platoon set up a perimeter defense around the area. I made contact with the Embassy people who were to take us into town. They had panel trucks, Volkswagens and sedans. We loaded and headed out in what must have been a pretty spotty convoy if anyone was paying attention. There were no incidents on the way into the city....

We all got to the Embassy, and my platoon sergeant and I set up a perimeter defense. I located Gunnery Sergeant Jack Moorman, the NCOIC-in-Charge of the Embassy Guard, and he advised me on what should be guarded, and the layout of the Embassy grounds....

I incorporated 38 Dominican policemen into the platoon. They had had a pretty rough time, and seemed tired, making sure there were Marines around them, because it appeared they were jumpy and suspected they would be a bit trigger happy. Fire discipline was crucial at this time....

The Embassy told me there's been tanks in the area. I knew we couldn't handle tanks with our small arms, so I called Company for 3.5 rockets and machine guns. At about 2300, two trucks pulled up with two of each. Everyone at the Embassy was glad to see us. They were armed with nothing but .38 caliber revolvers, and had been subject to two days' sniper fire.[39]

Sniper fire continued to harass the Marines and civilian personnel inside the embassy compound as Lieutenant Tucker's 27-man platoon established defensive positions in and around the walls of the compound. Despite the rebels' sporadic fire, Tucker's Marines maintained their fire discipline and refrained from firing back. Lieutenant Tucker recalled, "Our orders were not to return fire." This changed, however, as the rebels continued to fire on the leathernecks who had positioned themselves along a wall inside the embassy. Lieutenant Tucker said that as the embassy staff and Marine Security Guards burned classified documents in the courtyard, the flames from the fire illuminated the positions of Marines silhouetted against the wall. The Marine lieutenant added that bullets whizzed about from all directions, "but nobody got hit," as the Dominicans were poor shots and were shooting at the leathernecks without aiming. This sniper fire continued well into the night.

Despite this incessant fire, the Marines held on to their positions, firing back whenever they could make out a target. Lieutenant Tucker, not wishing to injure or kill innocent civilians, and acting on orders from the ambassador, passed the word to his Marines that they were not to fire indiscriminately into the row of houses adjacent to the embassy. As a light rain fell over Santo Domingo City, the Marines, who were covered with only their ponchos, settled into their positions and waited for morning. Despite the fact that they were tired and thirsty, and it was raining and very humid, the Marines remained awake throughout the entire night.

About 0400, the rebels opened up with a heavy volume of fire. Lieutenant Tucker recalled that one bullet nearly hit in the head a Marine who "peeked over the low wall." As the bullet impacted the cement near the startled Marine, Tucker could hear him cuss and say to his fellow Marines, "I want to go get that guy." Another bullet whizzed by Lieutenant Tucker, who barely escaped being grazed in the shoulder by an errant round. Having never been in combat, Lieutenant Tucker recalled that he was "damned mad" at the rebels, though, as he later recalled, "the troops maintained their sense of humor and displayed excellent fire discipline."[40] When morning light peeked over the horizon, Lieutenant Tucker passed the word that the Marines were to return fire on the snipers. As Tucker later recounted, "The snipers gave us hell and we gave it back to them. We didn't use automatic weapons, since it didn't seem necessary."

The next day, Thursday, brought more enemy activity as rebel fire continued to pepper the Marines' positions. Also, the snipers began to target the visitors who were brave enough to drive into the embassy's courtyard unescorted by policemen or the Marines. Angered over the continued rebel fire, Lieutenant Tucker decided to act. Informing the ambassador that he could not "control the situation" inside the embassy without removing the snipers, Tucker received permission to clear the snipers off the roofs of the adjoining buildings with fire teams organized from his "clutch platoon." Lieutenant Tucker recalled:

> One fire team cleared a building and went to the top. Five snipers were spotted, and we killed one. I think two others were hit, but we found only one body. They knew we were after them in earnest now, and the situation changed for the better. Still, after we had cleared the building, we had to return to the Embassy grounds. Each time we returned, the snipers would go back and re-occupy the building. We cleared it six times. A group of rebels fled down the street, and the Dominican policemen chopped them up. Another fire team went out again to clear another building. They killed one sniper, wounded one. The same thing happened. The snipers couldn't be discouraged. They moved back in. We killed another one. If we could have moved in and occupied the buildings, we could have held their fire down. Moving back to the Embassy grounds put us at a disadvantage. One of my Marines looked over the wall, and the cement splattered next to his head. He was mad, and jumped up and caught the sniper dead center. On one of our trips to clear a house, we found four big Dominican boys, all looking suspicious and guilty, but they weren't armed, and we had no evidence. We let them go. We received fire from the other side of the Embassy — from Trujillo's old palace — and a Dominican policeman opened up with an automatic carbine and killed the sniper. We never went out more than 150 to 200 yards from the Embassy wall, and then only when we had someone definite to chase. The situation remained much the same through Friday.[41]

Pinned down for three days by intense rebel fire, the embassy staff, Marine Security Guards, and Lieutenant Tucker's platoon were, the young lieutenant added, "sure glad to see the rest of the company, and eventually the rest of the battalion, come up and give us a break."[42]

As Lieutenant Tucker stated, the remainder of BLT 3/6 linked up with the Marines inside the embassy. As the Marines continued to battle the rebels near the U.S. Embassy, two U.S. Army airborne battalion combat teams (BCTs) from Ft. Bragg, North Carolina, were flown into nearby San Isidro Airfield, where they secured the airfield and screened the east and north perimeters from rebel fire.[43]

Meanwhile, the leathernecks from 3/6 continued to root out the rebels, who continued a desultory fire against the embassy and the Marines. Moving from building to building in squad rushes, and covered by grenadiers carrying M-79 "Bloopers," the Marines eventually established a method of rooting out the snipers. Marines quickly figured out the pattern of fire the snipers used:

> Usually the hostile fire came from the windows of nearby buildings. These windows had built in louvered blinds with slats about three inches wide, which could be opened just enough for a sniper to poke the muzzle of his rifle through. After a couple of hostile rounds the sniper usually would be located. The first round from an M-79 grenade launcher would blow the entire set of blinds into the room. The second M-79 round quieted things down nicely. The rebels soon got the message — you shoot at the Marines and they will kill you.[44]

From the grounds of the embassy, the Marines, along with their supporting weapons (Ontos anti-tank vehicles, M-48 tanks, and LVTs) moved into the barrios where much of the resistance had been concentrated. Advancing in squad and fire team rushes, supported by machine guns, Company I under the command of Captain William G. Davis eventually cleared the area of the rebels after a day of hard fighting. As the Marines entered the neighborhood, only a block north of the embassy, the rebels withdrew carrying with them their wounded. The Marines entering the neighborhood discovered two rebel bodies. As for the Marine casualties, the 1st Platoon of Company I suffered four wounded. Enemy fire wounded four more leathernecks as the company moved to its next objective, about five blocks north of the embassy. The battalion suffered its first death due to hostile fire when a sniper killed one Marine as the members of his platoon maneuvered a 3.5 rocket launcher into action against the well-entrenched rebels. Company K, commanded by Captain Robert C. Cockell, joined in the fight, and established a roadblock three blocks south of the U.S. Embassy. While the Marines from Company K received no incoming fire that first day, nighttime brought out the snipers, who harassed the Marine positions throughout the night into the next morning. Meanwhile, Company L, commanded by Captain Horace W. Baker, set up another roadblock four blocks south of I Company. In a series of raids, the Marines cleared one building near the company's command post that had been a "hornet's nest" of resistance. In the ensuing firefight, the Company K Marines killed one rebel and scattered the rest. On May 1, 1965, the Marines of 3/6 and the two BCTs from the Army's 82nd Airborne Division linked up and proceeded to clear out the remaining enemy resistance. While the Marines suffered no casualties, snipers killed two paratroopers from the 82nd Airborne and wounded two more.[45]

By May 1, the Marines from 3/6 were joined by Marines from the 1st Bn, 6th Marines, 1st Battalion, 2nd Marines, artillery support from the 2nd Battalion , 10th Marines, and finally, leathernecks from the 1st Battalion, 8th Marines, all based at Camp Lejeune, N.C. Upon landing at San Isidro Airfield, Marines from 1/8, commanded by Lieutenant Colonel Edward F. Danowitz, a veteran officer, took up positions around the Embajador Hotel and adjacent Bella Vista Golf Course. Here, they initiated a series of motorized patrols in the immediate vicinity. On May 4, 1965, the Marines from 1/8 came under sporadic sniper fire. On May 9, leathernecks from the 1st Battalion, 8th Marines, relieved the 3d Battalion, 6th Marines, in and around the U.S. Embassy. Here, they set up checkpoints, established defensive positions and searched all vehicles entering the area for bombs and other explosive devices. Marines also maintained a sharp lookout for suspected rebels known to be operating in the vicinity of the embassy.

Alerted to the possibility of major rebel counterattack against the embassy, Lieutenant Colonel Danowitz's Marines kept the diplomatic compound under constant surveillance. A tense moment occurred when a loyalist plane made a strafing run over the Marines' positions. The Marines from the 1st Battalion, 8th Marines, maintained their positions in and around the embassy despite continued sniper activity. By the time the battalion withdrew to an awaiting transport offshore in early June, the Marines from the 1st Battalion, 8th Marines, killed 13 snipers and wounded 10 others, while it suffered four wounded.[46]

By June 1, 1965, tensions in Santo Domingo City had eased sufficiently to warrant a withdrawal of the Marines from the Dominican Republic. On this date, in fact, Marines from the 1st Battalion, 8th Marines, turned over their peace enforcing duties to the soldiers from the U.S Army's 1st Battalion, 325th Infantry, and withdrew to an awaiting transport, the USS *Monrovia* (APA-311). All Marines, in fact, departed the Dominican Republic by 5 June 1965, and returned to their base at Camp Lejeune.

In response to the professionalism and steadfastness displayed by all of the Marine forces ashore in the Dominican Republic, including those assigned to the Marine Security Guard Detachment, American Embassy, Santo Domingo, Secretary of the Navy Paul H. Nitze awarded them a Navy Unit Commendation citation with an accompanying ribbon. The cita-

Sergeant Major A.T. Oates (left) and the Marine Security Guard Detachment, U.S. Embassy, Tripoli, Libya, pose for a photograph with Ambassador David Newsom, center (Sgt. Maj. A.T. Oates collection).

tion, presented to the commandant of the Marine Corps, read, "The fact that the entire evacuation and troop landing operations were successfully conducted in the face of unusual conditions and obstacles, is a tribute to the dedication of all personnel involved and was in keeping with the highest traditions of the United States Naval Service."[47]

During the crisis in the Dominican Republic, Gunnery Sergeant Moorman's Marine Security Guards carried out their traditional functions of burning classified documents, processing American citizens for evacuation, and maintaining order and security inside the embassy compound. They rose to every challenge and skillfully carried out their assignments despite the fact that they remained under constant rebel sniper fire during the crisis.

The Six-Day War, 7 June 1967

The outbreak of the Six-Day War among the Arab countries of Egypt, Syria, Jordan, and Israel in June 1967 once again tested the steadfastness of the leathernecks guarding U.S. embassies and consulates in what was fast becoming an increasingly volatile part of the world. In Jordan, Beirut, and Cairo, Marine embassy guards stood ready to assist in the evacuation of American and foreign nationals as Arabs protested the United States' support for Israel. After the Egyptian government ordered all U.S. diplomatic personnel out of Cairo, the U.S.

chargé d'affaires, Mr. David Gulick Nes, ordered the Marine Security Guard non-commissioned officer in charge to begin the destruction of all classified files and code machines on the roof the U.S. Embassy. As Chargé Nes recalled, the Marine sergeant "apparently misread the directions, and a considerable fire ensued on the chancery roof where the machines and files had been taken. This resulted in consternation among the Egyptian troops 'protecting us,' who assumed it was a bomb, and the equivalent of five to six alarms were sent into the neighborhood fire houses. The resulting confusion and noise was awesome! The fire was quickly put out without Egyptian assistance."[48]

Informed that same evening by the interior minister that the Egyptian government could not guarantee the safety of the diplomatic personnel inside the embassy, Chargé Nes ordered the immediate evacuation of all personnel. Over four hundred Americans were rounded up in Cairo and placed aboard trains destined for the port of Alexandria. Meanwhile, Nes and two Marine Security Guards, who were armed with hand grenades, returned to the official residence in order that the chargé could collect his personal belongings packed into two bags. He then sent two Marines in an embassy vehicle to pick up Ambassador-designate Richard Nolte at his official residence, and drive him to the train station where he and the remaining Americans boarded a train and proceeded to Alexandria. Upon their arrival in Alexandria, the Americans boarded the passenger ship *Carina* with their final destination being Greece. Two U.S. Navy warships assigned to the U.S. Sixth Fleet escorted the *Carina* with her American passengers on board all the way to Greece.

In neighboring Libya, the war likewise affected the Marine Security Guards, who soon found themselves in the midst of a wave of anti–Americanism. Sergeant Major A.T. Oates, Jr.—who, as a gunnery sergeant, was NCOIC of the Marine Security Guard detachment in Tripoli throughout this crisis—recalled that the start of the war caught everyone off guard. He first heard about the war between the Israelis and Arabs while taking his wife and daughter to the doctor. Realizing that he would be needed at the embassy, Gunnery Sergeant Oates shortly thereafter left the doctor's office and gathered up his other children and dropped his entire family off at the Family Center. Returning quickly to the embassy compound, Gunnery Sergeant Oates recalled that the number of protestors located in front of the building forced him "to hop a fence and enter through the back door." There, Oates was greeted by a Marine Security Guard and an Army sergeant, who was part of the Military Advisory and Assistance Group stationed in Tripoli. Gunnery Sergeant Oates recalled:

> The ambassador, David Newsom, gave the order to evacuate and left me in charge of securing the building. Windows were shuttered shut, doors locked and the front stairwell blocked. We left the beach stairwell open as an escape route to the roof where helicopters would pick us up. The back stairwell was secured with a steel gate. Intelligence informed us of a Friday attack which is an Arab holy day. The remaining met on Thursday and it was decided that everyone would leave the building save for me and my four Marines. And it came to pass that I was left in charge of the Embassy (Pretty good for a Gysgt!) In the meantime, American dependents had been evacuated and my family went to California and waited till it was safe to return to Tripoli (This occurred 4 months later).
>
> Securing the Embassy meant destroying all classified documents. I posted one Marine at the front door and the other three Marines and myself set about the task. With only one burn machine these proceedings took 48 hours. The last to be destroyed was the Crypto gear. The war was over Saturday. The attack never came. We were at the Embassy for five days before the staff returned. It took about a week for things to return to normal.[49]

Sergeant Major Oates recalled one incident in particular during the war that left a deep impression on him. A Jewish family that lived directly across the street from the embassy had been surrounded by Libyan troops. Unable to leave their house, the family faced starvation. Fortunately, one of their friends, a brave Libyan, put food in a bucket the family dropped from a front window. After the war, the Libyan government ordered the evacuation of all Jews from the country. Allowed only one suitcase, and crowded onto dusty, dirty buses, these unfortunate deportees were then taken to an airfield outside the city and flown out of the country to Rome.

Marine Security Guards and the Special Security Detail

In response to the violence aimed against U.S. diplomatic personnel and U.S. allies at home and abroad during the tumultuous 1960s, the State Department's Protective Security Division, charged with the protection of foreign heads of state and dignitaries when they visited the United States, began a unique domestic protective service program to prevent their assassination or being kidnapped by terrorist groups hoping to either embarrass or disrupt relations between America and its allies. With an overstretched, under-manned and aging diplomatic protective force, and due to the fact that Marine Security Guards already guarded U.S. embassies and consulates worldwide and were thus familiar with State Department security procedures, as well as possessing security clearances, officials from the U.S. Department of State Office of Security, in June of 1966, decided that they would seek approval to use a

Marine Security Guards assigned to the Special Security Detail Number 1 protected foreign heads of state when they visited the United States. Pictured here are the first six Marines assigned to this detail. Left to right are Sergeants R. Verell, Thomas Okeson, J. Garner, SSgt. M. Keller, Sergeants F. Wilkins and D. Kottlowsk (courtesy U.S. Marine Corps).

select group of Marines from each MSG class as temporary special agents in guarding foreign heads of state. As a result, State Department officials approached the secretary of the Navy and commandant of the Marine Corps, General Wallace M. Greene, and requested that three Marines from each graduating Marine Security Guard class at Fox Company be assigned to the State Department's Office of Security, Division of Protective Security, then headed by Special Agent Keith Lynch. Sworn in as federal agents, the Marines were then issued federal agent credentials and provided with a federal badge along with a set of handcuffs and a Smith and Wesson .357 magnum. Unlike their MSG counterparts, the Marines assigned to this detail wore civilian clothes and were under strict instructions not to identify themselves as Marines. They were likewise forbidden to wear either a "high and tight" or a crew cut. In short, they were to look like State Department security agents. The first Marines assigned to SSD-1 included SSgt. Michael Keller, Sgt. Thomas Okeson, and Sgt. David Kottowski, all of whom

were Vietnam veterans and graduates of Marine Security Guard School.

Even though the Marines were assigned to SSD, the Marine Corps still had administrative oversight of them, insofar as promotion, pay, and other typical military matters were concerned. At the time of the program's inception, oversight of the SSD 1 Marines by MSG officials came in the person of Colonel Forest J. Hunt, a veteran infantry and intelligence officer, his executive officer, and the company gunnery sergeant.

Staff Sergeant Thomas Okeson, who had been selected as one of the first three Marine security guards assigned to SSD, entered the Marine Corps in June 1964, and after recruit training at Marine Corps Recruit Department, San Diego, California, was sent to 2nd Infantry Training Regiment, located at Camp Pendleton, California, before being re-assigned to MCRD San Diego as an administrative clerk. Meritoriously promoted to lance

Among the foreign dignitaries protected by Marines assigned to Special Security Detail 1 were President Ferdinand Marcos and his wife Imelda. Here they are shown aboard Air Force One on a visit to the United States in September 1966. Standing behind the Marcoses is Special Agent (Sgt.) Thomas Okeson (courtesy U.S. Marine Corps).

corporal and later corporal, SSgt. Okeson, who joined the Marines at the time of the Gulf of Tonkin Resolution prior to the U.S. involvement in the Republic of Vietnam, and wanted to "see the world" began to apply for "just about every school I could to get out from behind a typewriter ... even Demo[lition] School...." "I didn't join the Marines to become a Remington Raider," SSgt. Okeson said. One day he saw his chance after reading a message asking for volunteers to Marine Security Guard School in Washington, D.C., at Henderson Hall. SSgt. Okeson applied for and was accepted by the MSG program and attended in the spring of 1966. Several weeks before graduation, officials at the school called the students to be interviewed; Marine officers and staff noncommissioned officers as well as civilians asked them a series of questions. "Of course, no one had known about this beforehand," SSgt. Okeson added. He said that of all the questions asked by this committee, the one that mystified him the most was the one asked by a civilian member of the board: "What would happen of the Marine Corps detailed you to guard a person and that if you knew there could be bodily harm against the person with a pistol or rifle or something, and your mission was to get that person into a car and out of the area, and if you had a weapon with you and shots were fired, what would you do?" Staff Sergeant Okeson recalled that he told him, "Of course, I would push him into the car and tell the driver to escape and throw my body over the top of him [the principal being guarded] because that was my mission."[50] Later the former Marine SSD 1 member said, "What they were looking for was essentially someone willing to put their body in front of a bullet and the person they were guarding."[51]

Master Sergeant Michael Keller was also one of the first Marines selected for SSD. He also became the detail's first NCOIC. A combat veteran of Korea and Vietnam, Master Sergeant Keller recalled that MSG School was "more intense than anything he had ever known." Selected to become the first NCOIC of SSD, Master Sergeant Keller said that the Marines assigned to the Special Security Detail received about six months of training even as they protected the various heads of state.[52] The Marines, who were constantly reminded of the assassinations of presidents John F. Kennedy and Abraham Lincoln, underwent intensive training that included firearms training, defensive driving courses, how to handle a riot control stick, and hand-to-hand combat. For firearms training, the Marines utilized the firing ranges of the Fairfax County Sheriff's Department. Originally billeted at Henderson Hall, Keller said the Marines assigned to SSD soon moved out and were housed in a special house on Van Dorn Street in Alexandria, Virginia. Here, they lived alongside the other Marines on the program in a central location near Henderson Hall with accessibility to the State Department. This was done primarily to prevent the Marines from being given extra duties at Henderson Hall and to allow them to carry their firearms and handcuffs with them instead of worrying about securing them in a wall or footlocker. The goal of SSD, MSGT Keller said, "was to get the Principal they were assigned to guard on the plane ALIVE!" He said that during his two years on duty, he became familiar with how to handle the press corps, crowds, and uncooperative heads of state.

Staff Sergeant Virgil Melton and SSgt. Ed Robbs, who were members of SSD in late 1969–70, said that by far the hardest and perhaps most difficult "principal" to guard was Abba Eban, Israel's foreign minister. Both Marines acknowledged that Mr. Eban oftentimes took nighttime strolls from his lodgings at the Hilton Hotel in downtown Washington, D.C., bolting past his own security as well as that of the Marine guards to purchase a pack of cigarettes, a newspaper, or have a cup of coffee from one of the many small restaurants located near the hotel. The Marines and Israeli security agents would have to accompany the foreign minister until he turned in for the evening.

There were the interesting moments too. Staff Sergeant Ron Trottier and SSgt. Virgil Melton recalled an assassination attempt against Premier Chiang Ching-kuo (son of Chiang Kai-Shek) of Taiwan in 1971 in New York City. Fortunately, one of the State Department security agents was able to block the rounds fired from the assailant's pistol while a New York City policeman wrestled the would-be assassin to the ground. The only damage that occurred was to the watch of the State Department agent who accompanied the premier. In gratitude for saving his life, the premier replaced the agent's damaged watch with his own — a solid gold Rolex. Other frequent visitors to the United States during the late 1960s and early 1970s were President Ferdinand and Imelda Marcos. According to SSgt. Edward E. Robbs, the Marines accompanied Mrs. Marcos on many of her infamous shopping sprees, and oftentimes held the brief case full of money she used to purchase clothes and other items. All of the Marines who guarded Mrs. Marcos candidly admitted, however, that she was very kind to the Marines, as she would always converse with them and acknowledge their presence — something the other heads of state rarely or never, did. Gunnery Sergeant Jeptha E. Turner recalled the visit to the U.S. made by President Mobuto Seso Seko of Zaire, who spent two weeks at Disneyland in Florida. "Imagine spending two weeks at Disneyland," GySgt. Turner said laughingly.[53]

In the mid to late 1960s and into the 1970s, demonstrators against the Vietnam War posed a serious threat to officials in both the Lyndon B. Johnson and Richard M. Nixon administrations. This prompted the State Department to post Marines of SSD at the homes of Secretaries of State Dean Rusk and later William P. Rogers (1971–1974). Special State Department Agent Richard Heckman said, "The Marines grew fond of both men, as both senior diplomats treated their 'leathernecks' like family."[54] Finally, after Marines guarded various heads of state for eight years, Secretary of State Henry Kissinger, in 1974, disbanded the Special Security Detail, with their duties taken over the Secret Service. Despite cancellation of the program, the Marines of SSD agreed with MSGT Keller, who said, "we never expected this. We didn't realize what we had gotten ourselves into, but we did know that this detail was a once in a lifetime thing."[55]

Anti-Americanism in the Middle East and Athens, Greece, 1970

As Marines battled Dominican rebels in the streets of Santo Domingo, and other Marine Security Guards fought Viet Cong terrorists inside the very compound of the U.S. Embassy in Saigon, the leathernecks standing watch at Post One throughout the world now found themselves on the front lines of a new war — against terrorism. Indeed, Marine Security Guards became the most visible reminders to those opposed to U.S. policies in Southeast Asia, the Middle East, and in Europe. In fact, many of the protestors directed a large part of their violence abroad at the very symbol of the United States' presence in their countries — the U.S. embassies and consulates. This in turn placed additional burdens upon Marine Security Guards as local authorities, in order to protect their own policemen, periodically withdrew police protection and oftentimes informed the U.S. ambassador or his assistants that they could not guarantee the security and safety of Americans in their respective countries. While this was often the case in those countries hostile to U.S. foreign policies, it sometimes occurred in friendly host countries such as in Istanbul, Turkey, Amman, Jordan, and Athens, Greece.

While most anti–American sentiment remained confined to protests and demonstrations, it sometimes would take the form of more violent actions, such as the planting of bombs inside the U.S. Embassy or, as occurred in Latin America, attacks on Marine Security Guards at the Marine House. In all cases, the violence was due to some U.S. foreign policy decision that would incite crowds to undertake attacks on U.S. interests and personnel.

While not confined to one specific area, by 1970, much of the violence directed against the United States originated from radical Arab countries in the Middle East, the Horn of Africa, and along the shores of the Eastern Mediterranean, most notably in Greece and on the island of Cyprus. Indeed, the roots of the current war on terror had its origins in the violence spawned in the Palestinian refugee camps in Lebanon and Jordan, and in the terrorist training camps in Libya, Somalia, the Sudan, and Syria during the mid to late 1960s. Furthermore, the war against terrorism waged by the Marine Security Guards in the late 1960s was but the forerunner to the post–9-11 war against these same faceless extremists.

The violence was not, however, confined to these rogue Middle Eastern and African nations. Indeed, Marine Security Guards became subject to attack in such European cities as Athens, Greece, where protestors planted bombs inside the U.S. Embassy on two separate occasions in 1970.

The Middle East

On September 1, 1969, Colonel Mu'ammar al-Qaddafi led a group of military officers in a *coup d'état* against King Idris of Libya. After forcing King Idris into exile, Colonel Qaddafi proclaimed the "Popular Socialist Libyan Arab Jamahiriyah." Colonel Qaddafi's overthrow of the pro–Western King Idris brought to power one of the first of several radical Muslim regimes that openly proclaimed its hostility to the State of Israel and to U.S. policies in the Middle East and North Africa. Upon his assumption of power, Qaddafi ordered the closure of the U.S. Air Force's Wheelus Air Force Base and the British Royal Air Force's El-Adam military base, as well as nationalizing all western oil interests in this oil-rich North African country. Almost from the day he seized power, the Libyan leader vociferously incited the Libyan peoples against the United States, Israel, and moderate Arab regimes. Indeed, from the start of his rule of Libya, Colonel Qaddafi, calling to mind British and Italian colonization, adopted a confrontational policy and incited his people toward what he believed was an "imperialistic-Zionist" plot aimed at Libya's vast oil resources.[56] In time, Qaddafi used Libya's oil profits to sponsor various radical terrorist groups, including Yassir Arafat's Fatah and other radical Palestinian Liberation Organization terrorist groups, and the Irish Republican Army. The Libyan leader likewise requested Soviet military assistance for his anti–Western activities, to which the Soviet leadership enthusiastically responded with massive shipments of arms.

For the Marine Security Guards and their veteran detachment commander, Staff Sergeant Marvin Z. Gray, stationed inside the U.S. Embassy in Tripoli, tensions remained very high as Qaddafi repeatedly called for the expulsion of all foreigners from "the People's Jamahiriyah." Throughout the 1970s, particularly during the Yom Kippur War of October 1973, "Marines in Tripoli [operated] in an increasingly hostile environment."[57]

In neighboring Sudan, the government likewise sponsored a virulent anti–American and anti–British campaign as state-sponsored demonstrations marched against U.S. and British support of Israel in Khartoum. The Sudanese government likewise proved very obstructive when it refused to issue visas to the new incoming Marine Security Guards and the Regional Security Officer in Beirut, Lebanon, and denied them permission to enter the country.

Also in Africa, in Aden, South Yemen, Marine Security Guards protected the embassy, its contents, and the ambassador against the local populace, who had been incited by anti–American propaganda for its support for Israel. From July 1967 to January 1968, the Marine Security Guard Detachment, under the greatest hardships, and amidst two wars that were ongoing at the time — the war on terror as well as the counter-insurgency between the British Army and insurgents in the Dhofar — "provided security to the compound and additionally assisted in maintaining a vital communications link between Embassy officers and the Department of State."[58]

Not far from Tripoli, in Amman, Jordan, the radical Palestinian groups Black September, Fatah, and the Popular Front for the Liberation of Palestine, stepped up its campaign of violence and terrorism against the peoples of Israel, Jordan and Lebanon, in order to drive Israel out of Palestinian lands. Radical Palestinian groups, such as Dr. George Habash's Popular Front for the Liberation of Palestine (PFLP) and Yassir Arafat's Fatah, inaugurated a campaign of intimidation and terror aimed at Western governments and their support for Israel. In September 1969, in a coordinated terrorist attack, the PFLP hijacked three airliners and flew two of them to Jordan and one to Egypt. They subsequently blew up the plane in Egypt in a media-staged event designed to highlight their grievances. Terrorists aimed much of this violence toward the United States, mainly against its embassies and consulates throughout the Middle East and its diplomatic personnel overseas. These tactics directly targeted the most visible presence of the United States — the Marine Security Guards.

Living in the hundreds of refugee camps established after the 1948 Arab-Israeli Wars, Palestinians clung to the hope of returning to their homes now occupied by the Israelis. Frustrated and with little hope, many of these young Palestinians took up arms and inaugurated a wave of terrorist attacks under the direction of the radical PLO leaders such as George Habash, Wadi Haddad, Abu Iyad, Ahmad Jibril, and Yassir Arafat, aimed primarily against Israel and Jordan. To highlight their cause, Palestinian terrorists hijacked Western airliners and diverted them to such countries as Jordan in order to bring attention to their cause.

In one of the most spectacular and bloodiest of these hijackings, members of the Black September terrorist group hijacked two international airliners — TWA and KLM, in July 1970, and flew them to an abandoned airstrip inside Jordan. In a calculated attempt to attract the Western media and force King Hussein's government to grant the Palestinians the right to operate more freely from Jordanian soil against Israel, the Palestinian fedayeen and Jordanian troops clashed in what soon became an open war. Fearing an Israeli backlash and survival of his own throne, the Jordanian monarch moved against the Palestinians forcefully and eventually evicted the fedayeen and Palestinians to refugee camps located in Lebanon.[59]

Some of the violence in Jordan spilled over into the chancery of the U.S. Embassy. In fact, up until the situation in Beirut, Lebanon, in 1976, the situation in Amman, Jordan, in early 1970 placed an enormous strain on the abilities of the Marine Security Guards to protect American lives and to safeguard classified material. When the Jordanian government proved itself unable or unwilling to control the thousands of anti–American demonstrators, who attacked the chancery on several occasions and inflicted severe property damage on the facility, Marine Security Guards provided invaluable service in guarding the embassy. During the periodic exchanges of gunfire between Jordanian army units and the Palestinian fedayeen, Marine Security Guards shredded non-essential classified material and guarded the ambassador and his staff. Marine Security Guards likewise assisted in the evacuation of non-essential personnel, including the wife of Gunnery Sergeant Joseph A. Smith, the detachment's SNCOIC, to various "safe havens" located throughout the capital.[60]

Back at the embassy, the Marine Security Guards, who were protected on the outside by a small contingent of Bedouin guards, became the target of intense mortar, machine gun, and sniper attacks September 17–30, 1970. Cut off from the outside for period of about a week, the Marine Security Guards were forced to venture out into the hostile atmosphere in search of food, water, and fuel. Armed only with M1 Carbines and .45 caliber pistols, and "facing an enemy which was armed with automatic weapons, including Kalashnikov rifles," the leathernecks nevertheless succeeded in their foraging missions. While the Bedouin guards were able to repel the Palestinian fedayeen's final assault on the U.S. Embassy, the Marines were nonetheless prepared to "fight to the end" in order to protect the ambassador and the civilian staff inside.[61]

Indeed, U.S. embassies and consulates throughout the Middle East became targets of these terrorists. One such consulate was located in Jerusalem, where the State Department, fearing possible retribution for U.S. support for Israel, assigned a six-man Marine Security Guard detachment to stand guard inside the consulate, ringed by a wrought iron fence that stood 9 feet high. The horizontal support was topped off with pointed pikes to impale anyone attempting to scale the fence. Local Israeli militia guarded the outer perimeter against potential terrorist attacks.[62]

Similar anti–American demonstrations threatened American lives and property in Beirut, Lebanon, during the same period. In fact after one such attack, Gunnery Sergeant Gerald E. Vanhoose placed his entire Marine Security Guard detachment on full alert in order to repel any intrusion of the embassy or attempts to seize its classified material. From the period of April 1, 1975, to January 31, 1976, Marines assigned to the U.S. Embassy in Beirut endured shelling, sniper attacks, bombing, and mortar attacks as the country headed toward civil war. Adding to the problem were the various Palestinian groups that had arrived in Beirut after their expulsion from Jordan by King Hussein in 1970. Beirut, in fact, became one large gladiatorial combat ring as the various Lebanese communal factions (Maronites, Sunni Muslims, and Druze) jockeyed for power amidst the deteriorating political situation in Lebanon. When full-scale civil war broke out in 1976, the Marines assigned to the U.S. Embassy in Beirut experienced terrorism like no other Marine embassy would in the years to come.

Indeed, two Marines, Corporal William H. Phister and Sergeant Chamberlain, became the first casualties in this "new war" when they were injured during two separate mortar attacks on the embassy compound on August 7 and October 13, 1978. During the first attack, a mortar round injured Corporal Phister when it slammed into the ambassador's residence at Yarze on 7 August 1978. The attack resulted in the Marine Security Guard's hospitalization. In the other attack, another mortar round on the embassy two months later, slightly injured Sergeant Chamberlain and forced his medical evacuation. The injuries to Sgt. Chamberlin were not severe, however, as the Marine sergeant returned to duty later that same day.[63]

On March 1, 1973, a group of armed terrorists belonging to the Black September Organization conducted an armed attack on the Saudi Arabian Embassy and abducted the U.S. ambassador and the former U.S. chargé d'affaires. Upon hearing the news of the attack and abductions, the Marines assigned to the U.S. Embassy in Khartoum immediately went on full alert and increased the physical security of the American Embassy. Marines manned switchboards and restricted the flow of visitors. Also, the "Marines at the observation post identified, described, and reported all activities which could be observed or heard in or near the Saudi Arabian Embassy."[64] During this crisis, the entire Marine Security Guard detachment worked around the clock, putting in a total of 60 hours, and "operated at maximum efficiency and performed extraordinary unusual tasks at the highest level of effectiveness in spite of near exhaustion." When the terrorists killed the ambassador and chargé, the Marines established an honor guard over each of the flag-draped coffins, and conducted a brief, moving, and dignified departure ceremony for the two slain diplomats. In recognition of their performance under the greatest difficulties, the secretary of the Navy, with the concurrence of the commandant of the Marine Corps, General Robert E. Cushman, awarded the Marines assigned to the Khartoum-based Marine Security Guard detachment a Meritorious Unit Commendation for "their superior professional competence ... and their dedication and courage" during the hostage crisis.[65]

Anti-American Violence in the Cradle of Democracy, 1970–1974

Peaceful opposition to U.S. war in South Vietnam as well as its support of conservative governments in Western Europe turned into bloody confrontations as pro–Communist and other leftist-oriented factions marched throughout the streets of European cities in order to force their respective governments to pressure changes in Washington's policies. Ambassador Jack Bloom Kubisch wrote that during the negotiations over the Paris Peace Accords between the United States and North Vietnam, anywhere from 10,000 to 30,000 demonstrators marched past the U.S. Embassy in Paris.[66] The ambassador stated that this was nothing compared to what took place upon his arrival in Athens, Greece, in late summer 1974, when Greeks protested U.S. support of the military junta as well as Washington's alleged complicity in sanctioning the Turkish invasion of Cyprus in July 1974.

In Athens, Greece, anti–American feelings coalesced with dissatisfaction with the right-wing military junta that came to power in April 1967, in a *coup d'état* that quickly suppressed civil liberties and removed many centrist and leftist politicians. In a move that further alienated the Greek populace, the military banned all political activity, including that of the Popular Progressive Centre Union (EPEK), led by George Papandreou.[67]

Coupled with the continued stalemate over the status of the island of Cyprus and U.S. support for Turkey, the junta's seizure of power led to increasing attacks on U.S. personnel and facilities throughout Greece. One of these groups, the Revolutionary Popular Struggle (ELA), whose goal was to drive Greece out of the North Atlantic Treaty Organization and eliminate the U.S. military presence in the country, inaugurated a campaign of intimidation and bombings against high-profile targets such as embassies and U.S. military bases and facilities.[68]

The attacks, uncoordinated and unsophisticated as they were, nevertheless called upon the vigilance of all U.S. personnel to be on guard at all times. Amidst the wave of anti–Americanism that existed in Greece (and elsewhere in Europe), terrorist groups such as the ELA began a campaign of bombings and shootings, with some of them aimed at the U.S. Embassy in Athens. Prior to the arrival of the new U.S. ambassador to Greece, Mr. Henry J. Tasca,[69] the terrorist groups demonstrated their ability to strike whenever and wherever they desired in early January 1970.

On the afternoon of January 5, 1970, a cleaning lady discovered a bomb taped to the underside of the toilet in the men's room in the Consular Section of the embassy. The explosive, connected to an ordinary alarm clock, was set to detonate, according to a de-classified State Department telegram, at approximately 10 o'clock that evening, when the building would be vacant. The terrorists apparently sought to minimize the chances of killing or wounding anyone who happened to be in the building when the bomb went off. According to witnesses at the scene, the embassy's regional security officer, Mr. Frank Durfey, a former Marine, immediately ordered the Marine Security Guards to seal the area off and vacate the embassy. Mr. Durfey then called in Greek military demolitions experts, who defused the explosive device. A phone call later received at the U.S. Embassy told the operator that a "Militant Strike Group of Athens had placed the bomb in the embassy."[70]

This was not an end to the violence aimed at the United States in Greece. On September 2, 1970, terrorists planted a car bomb that detonated in the parking lot adjacent to the north side of the U.S. Embassy. According to the non-commissioned officer-in-charge of the Marine Security Guard Detachment, Staff Sergeant Johnnie P. Hirst, "No alert had been issued and no preparations made" prior to the bomb's detonation.[71]

Staff Sergeant Hirst recounted that the bomb killed the occupants of the car, a man and a woman, whose bodies were found amidst the debris and fragments of the destroyed vehicle. In his special incidence report addressed to the commanding officer, Marine Security Guard Battalion, Staff Sergeant Hirst not only described the sequence of events after the blast occurred but detailed the Marine Security Guard detachment's immediate response to guard against an attack on the embassy itself:

At approximately 1600 on 2 September 1970, a bomb exploded in the parking area on the North side of the Embassy. No alert had been issued and no preparations made. NCOIC [Hirst] and Sgt. McDaniels, who was on duty at Sentry Post #1, were in Guard Office, Room 101, AmEmb. NCOIC ordered Sgt. McDaniels to contact RSO [Mr. Durfey] and call in all MSG's, and proceeded immediately to blast area to investigate.

NCOIC noted, on arrival at parking area, one car almost totally destroyed and two adjacent cars burning. In grassy area between parking lot and the Embassy, a distance of approx. 25 yards, was a man's body. Close inspection revealed that the head, hands and clothing (except for shorts, socks and shoes) had been blown off by the explosion. As the flames subsided, NCOIC checked the cars for possible injured persons and discovered a woman's body, whose hands and clothing were blown off, in the front seat of the car in which the blast occurred. At this time, RSO and Admin Officer, arrived at the scene.

NCOIC informed RSO that MSG had been ordered to report for duty. RSO then ordered the Embassy be closed for Security Reasons and that a systematic check for additional explosive devices inside the building be conducted as son as the Guard arrived. On arrival at Guard Office, NCOIC relayed orders from RSO to Sgt. McDaniels. At this time, approximately 1625, seven MSG's, who were at the Marine House at the time of the explosion, reported for duty. NCOIC instructed them to form three groups of two and conduct a thorough search of the building for explosive devices. Sgt. Benson remained to assist at Sentry Post #1. At approx. 1645, Sgt. Wilburn, who was on liberty, reported for duty and joined the search.

NCOIC then joined RSO and Admin. Officer on the Embassy grounds. At approx. 1730, at the request of RSO, NCOIC escorted three (3) members of the Athens Bomb Squad to the roof of the Embassy to search for bomb fragments. Fragments of bomb and car were found scattered over rooftop, even to far side of building, nearly a block from site of explosion. Also, NCOIC discovered a small portion of the man's head, which was later identified as part of the jawbone. At conclusion of search, NCOIC escorted the Bomb Squad back to the parking area where blast occurred and returned to Guard Office....

At approx. 1830, RSO ordered an extra guard be posted, because almost all the ground floor windows and most of the second and third floor windows on the North side of the Embassy had been shattered by the blast. NCOIC then set up a Special Guard Roster to maintain two men at Sentry Post #1 during non-working hours; one man to act as continuous roving patrol of ground floor offices. All personnel were informed of duties of Special Guard and assignment of watches. Extra guard was posted and remaining MSG's relieved and returned to the Marine House at approx. 1900. This Special Guard was maintained until the morning of 5 Sep 1970, when all openings on the ground floor of the Embassy were close. No MSG's were injured in this incident.[72]

For Marine Security Guards, vigilance against car bombs and other explosive devices in Athens and throughout U.S. embassies and consulates in Europe during the 1970s became routine as terrorist groups, such as the ELA, the West German Red Army or "Baader Meinhof Gang" targeted American interests and military personnel. This terrorist campaign was relentless in its avowed goal of driving the United States military presence from Europe. As events on the island of Cyprus demonstrated in April 1974, however, the violence directed at American embassies and interests came not just from the left but from being caught up in the domestic politics of the host country.

The Turkish Invasion of Cyprus, 1974

Since its conquest by the Ottoman Turks in 1571, the island of Cyprus, located in the Eastern Mediterranean, and the gateway to the Middle East, had been the scene of continuous religious and ethnic struggle between the Greek Cypriots and its Turkish masters. This situation continued on into the modern era as both the Greeks and Turks who lived on the island were convinced "that in the end the other was out to rob it of its birthright; each seeing itself the victim," and were, according to former Secretary of State Henry Kissinger, "prepared to preempt fate by wreaking vengeance on its neighbor."[73] As Secretary of State Kissinger asserted, "the Greek-Turkish" conflict on Cyprus, indeed, belonged "to the blood feuds of history."

Despite the fact that after World War II both Greece and Turkey became members of the North Atlantic Treaty Organization, the situation on Cyprus only grew worse, as it became the eye of the storm between these two supposed allies. In 1960, the British mandate ended with Cyprus gaining her independence. Archbishop Makarios III, who represented the

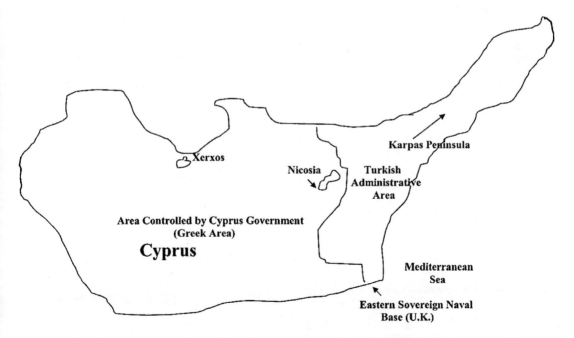

Map 4. The Island of Cyprus (Central Intelligence Agency: *Atlas of the Middle East,* January 1993, page 22).

Orthodox Greek Community on the island prior to independence, and later chosen president of the new republic, had initially agreed to a limited degree of self-rule for the Turkish minority on the island. After independence, however, Archbishop Makarios reneged on this agreement, and within months of coming to power he instituted a series of laws and restrictions against the Turkish community. This merely inflamed the situation insofar as Ankara, the capital of Turkey, was concerned, as it now appeared that the Turkish minority on the island would lose whatever rights it had in regards to the Greek Cypriot majority. When Turkish leaders threatened to invade the island, President Lyndon B. Johnson, already consumed with troubles in the Middle East and Southeast Asia, sent a stern warning to the general staff in Turkey against any preemptive move against Nicosia (The Cypriot capital). In deference to the United States, the Turks backed down, though as Secretary Kissinger wrote, Turkish leaders vowed that there would be no *next time*, and that they would not hesitate to take action even if it meant an all-out invasion of the island[74] (author's emphasis).

A U.S. Army field artillery officer, Lieutenant Colonel Joseph L. Allred, who had been assigned to a U.S combat detachment stationed at Erzurum, Turkey, as a linguist, recalled that tensions remained high during his tour of duty in Turkey. Lieutenant Colonel Allred recalled that "Cyprus was recognized as an independent state and had been admitted into the United Nations, although it had a majority of ethnic Greek Cypriots and a minority of ethnic Turkish Cypriots, each desiring a closer union with their motherland. The only group on the island who wished to have both Greek and Turkish influence eliminated were those who called themselves Cypriots."[75]

The situation on Cyprus remained extremely tense throughout the late 1960s and early 1970s. The *coup d'état* in Athens that brought to power a violently anti–Communist military junta did little to help the situation on Cyprus, as the generals became alarmed over Makarios' "flirting" with leftist-oriented Third World countries, and began to plan for a possible takeover of the island. The Turks likewise became alarmed over Makarios' stockpiling of arms, as they believed that it would only lead to an all-out invasion by Athens. With memories still fresh of Makarios' campaign of intimidation aimed at the Turkish minority living on the island, any change of the status quo or alteration of the provisions that gave some protection to their ethnic kin on the island was unacceptable to Turkish leaders.

Events on Cyprus drifted toward open conflict, as Archbishop Makarios was overthrown in a *coup d'état* on July 15, 1974. Replaced by Nikos Sampson, who had reportedly been put into power by the EOKA-B and the Cypriot National Guard, and had favored a union with Greece, it now seemed to all that war could not be avoided. For their part, the Turks demanded that Makarios be restored as the legitimate ruler of Cyprus, this despite the fact that the archbishop had been, as Dr. Kissinger wrote, responsible for some of the worst violations of human rights on the island aimed against the Turkish minority.[76] By insisting on Makarios' return, it became obvious to President Richard M. Nixon and Secretary Kissinger that Ankara's insistence on Makarios' being restored to power was merely the pretext for an invasion of the island.[77] Lieutenant Colonel Allred remembered that

> the colonels [in charge in Athens] sent a special operations team onto Cyprus to convince Makarios to peacefully relinquish his authority to Greece; however, when he did not do this he was ousted as the president and fled the country. As he headed for the United Nations to make his appeal for his state, the Turkish government reacted swiftly to the overthrow of the legitimate government of Cyprus and demanded the withdrawal of the Greek military presence from the island and return Makarios to power. If they did not do it within a period of days, Turkey, under the authority of the agreement would invade the island to protect Turkish-Cypriots and restore legitimate government to the island.[78]

When the Greek government refused to do so, the Turks began to assemble an invasion force and made preparations to invade the island.

Throughout the month of July, as Secretary of State Kissinger and his assistants tried fervently to avert war in an already volatile part of the world, Ankara prepared for an invasion of the island, which came in the pre-dawn hours of July 19, 1974. As Turkish marines and soldiers came ashore in LCMs and LCUs on Cyprus that summer morning, the Marine Security Guards on duty in the U.S. Embassy prepared for a situation that would place a supreme test on their training and readiness.

Assigned to Company B, headquartered in Beirut, Lebanon, the Marine Security Guard Detachment located at Karavas, Cyprus, consisted of its NCOIC, Staff Sergeant Guitierrez, and six watchstanders. One of the watchstanders, Lance Corporal Robert A. Lynn, provided an excellent account of the Turkish invasion that he and his fellow Marines now found themselves right in the middle of. Assigned to guard the United States' Foreign Broadcast Information Services (FBIS) building in Karavas, an annex of the U.S. Embassy located in Nicosia, Lance Corporal Lynn had been previously assigned to the Marine Security Guard Detachment, Amman, Jordan.

After a short stopover in Beirut, Lebanon, Lynn reported to the MSG detachment at Karavas. At no time did the Marine corporal realize that he was about to become an eyewitness to the Turkish invasion of Cyprus:

> One cannot believe that it's been thirty years since that hot day in July 1974 on Cyprus when the Turks invaded that beautiful and enchanting island. I had been ordered to the U.S. Marine Security Guard Detachment at Karavas, Cyprus in from the U.S. Marine Security Guard Detachment, Amman, Jordan via Company B Headquarters in Beirut, Lebanon.
>
> Located at Karavas on the north coast of Cyprus, the FBIS or Foreign Broadcast Information Service Mediterranean Bureau, an annex of the American Embassy, Nicosia, is situated on six acres of U.S. Government-owned land which accommodates the operations and supports buildings as well as two official residences. An additional 167 acres are leased to provide an antenna field.
>
> The Bureau was established here, 7 miles west of Kyrenia and 25 miles from Nicosia, the island's capital, in 1949. Its full staffing complement at the time of the Turkish invasion was 85 employees, including 13 Americans.
>
> When hostilities erupted at daybreak on Saturday, 20 July 1974, the Bureau was manned by one U.S. staff employee, seven U.S. Marines, and 18 local employees.... The U.S. Marine Security Guard Detachment Karavas consisted of the following: Guitierrez, Benda, Bibeau, Lynn, Sampson, Veasey, and Wilson. To the best of my knowledge, the detachment was organized in early 1974 in response to a request by FBIS personnel because of the uneasy political climate on Cyprus. But there were some who saw us as an extension of the U.S. Marine Security Guard Detachment Nicosia, Cyprus....
>
> Days prior to the Saturday, 20 July 1974 invasion by the Turks, myself and other Marines in the detachment were discussing that coup that had been engineered by EOKA-B and the Cypriot National Guard on the morning of 15 July 1974. Nikos Sampson, editor and publisher of the widely circulated Enosist[79] paper *Makhi* (Struggle) was appointed as president. He was a fanatical enosist (union with Greece) and was one of two dozen powerful right-wing warlords who maintained small private armies for attacks on the Turkish enclaves. With the coup, Sampson also established a curfew.
>
> This curfew resulted in all available cots and mattresses being placed inside the station before the invasion as the swingshift personnel began sleeping overnight. As the days passed and more personnel came to the station; we would find that we needed more but individuals utilized chairs and even floors to sleep on.
>
> The Turkish government made it clear that Sampson had been chosen as a "willing mouth-

piece" for the Greek junta in Athens and that the goal of the military government would be unification with Greece. But immediately, Sampson proclaimed the continued independence of Cyprus and he further promised to restore unity and peace to Cyprus through inter-communal talks with the Turkish minority on the island. They continued to be suspicious though and the stage was set for the invasion.

At 0700, on 20 July 1974, I relieved Bibeau and assumed the duties of that post. The invading Turks had already been on the island for almost three hours and SSGT Guitierrez, our NCOIC, quickly gave orders to all Marines to physically secure the building and protect all FBIS employees and dependents. The total number of personnel in the building came to 34 and thus the storing of food and water became our first priority. The other Marines went back to the Marine House, located about 2 or three miles from the station, to gather all food from our residence and get a change of clothes. Within the hour, they had all returned safely to the station.

We were then ordered to place flattened cardboard cartons over the windows in all rooms to prevent shattered glass and other objects from becoming flying shrapnel and to enforce the blackout. Our commercial power was lost early on 20 July, but the station's three generators were sufficient to meet essential power requirements (one generator was lost the second day with a hole in the radiator, a second one was having voltage regulator problems, but was still functioning at the time of the evacuation of 23 July 1974). We couldn't operate the air conditioning units and thus the temperature inside the station remained high. On the outside, it was about 98 degrees.

After ensuring that all personnel were taken care of in the station, the Marine Detachment immediately set up a watch on the roof looking for troop movements, where shelling was directed, rocketing by aircraft, choppers and troop plane targets were to the station. With naval bombardment and air attacks against the mountain emplacements, many fires were set. In spite of this, we continued to feed the vital information to the American Ambassador, Rodger Davies, and the American Embassy in Nicosia, Cyprus on our emergency net.

As night fell, the mountains were ablaze from west to east. A strong wind from the west, combined with heat-induced drafts, made an inferno of the once beautiful mountains.

Secretary of State Kissinger commented that the Turkish invasion "met unexpectedly strong resistance" from the Greek Cypriots,[80] an observation also made by Lynn. Lance Corporal Lynn noted that as the day wore on into evening, the fighting drew more intense as it came closer and closer to the FBIS building:

About 2100, on July 20, 1974, we noticed a tremendous small arms and machine gun firefight erupting to the east. We could see arching tracers from the opposing forces, and flashes of artillery fire provided a timing reference which indicated the battle was only 2 miles east of the station. It was late in the night that the station was caught in artillery crossfire that was probably the most intense in our area between the warring parties. It was this artillery exchange that was responsible for all employees being bedded down in the central corridor of the station. Food was provided by our own "house mothers," Marge Weiss, Imogene Clegg, Pat Werrell, and Beth Seely. A 81mm mortar round landed just outside the kitchen door at about 0435 Sunday and was potentially the most dangerous of all which landed in the vicinity of the station. Certain death would have resulted had anyone been in the kitchen or first aid room. Only personal observation or photographic evidence can show the force of the impact and the fortune of our staff. The shrapnel-riddled flag which was attached to the side of the building, bears brutal evidence of this attack....

There was a skirmish by what we considered squad-sized units just outside the station compound between 1200 and 1400 Monday, 22 July 1974. None of the fire was directed toward the station, but it was so close that everyone kept down during most of the exchange. Also about this time, a decision was made by J. Thomas Weiss, Dennis P. Sheehan, Alvis B. Clegg, Jr., SSgt Guitierrez, and Sgt. Veasey on how best to evacuate. Both Guitierrez and Veasey said they wanted to rig up the buses with U.S. flags so that we would be prepared to evacuate by land or by sea. This was done.

On Tuesday morning, 23 July 1974, we were notified that the evacuation — described by the

American Embassy as a mini–Dunkirk — would take place either by landing craft or helicopter. Prior to waiting for the appropriate signal, Guitierrez ordered all detachment members to the roof and we began to destroy all classified material in brown barrels. This assignment was completed within 30 minutes.[81]

Lance Corporal Lynn recalled that the confusion that resulted in the decision to evacuate was because the evacuation plan had not been updated since 1970. Indeed, as Major W. Hay Parks, USMC, wrote in a post-evacuation analysis of the Cyprus evacuation, "The embassy's evacuation committee was defunct, even though the committee was required to meet and update the evacuation plan every six months. The plan was 75 percent dependent on an airlift by a military unit no longer on Cyprus."[82] This in turn placed an even greater demand upon the resourcefulness of the ambassador, the RSO, and the detachment commander of the Marine Security Guard to formulate an effective and expedient evacuation plan.

With the U.S. Sixth Fleet already pre-committed elsewhere, the Americans on Cyprus came to depend on the British Royal Navy, who sent the aircraft carrier *HMS Hermes* to assist in the evacuation of all foreigners from war-torn Cyprus, including the Americans and foreign nationals at the FBIS Station in Karavas. Lance Corporal Lynn noted that once an evacuation plan had been established, the Marine Security Guards quickly put it to work as the fighting grew more intense around the FBIS building.[83]

For their outstanding performance "above and beyond" the call of duty, Secretary of the Navy J. William Middendorf, Jr., awarded Lance Corporal Lynn and his fellow Marine Security Guards a Meritorious Unit Citation for "their extraordinary performance and selfless devotion to duty during this most chaotic time…. The Marine Security Guard Detachment … ensured the safe evacuation of the personnel when the Station came under fire. Through their professionalism and untiring efforts, they successfully formed two convoys when the American Embassy was evacuated, thus ensuring the safe transport of American citizens and third country nationals to Dhekelia. After the evacuation, they were responsible for monitoring security outside the building as well as maintaining a strict security posture inside the Embassy. When the Embassy was demonstrated against and attacked, the Marines remained calm and stood ready to resist any intrusion into the Embassy proper."[84]

Tragically, however, the chaos that lingered behind in Nicosia took the life of Ambassador Rodger Davies, when on 19 August 1974, rioting Greek Cypriots unleashed a hail of gunfire into the U.S. Embassy. Also killed in the melee was Miss Antonette Varnava, who met her death while trying to assist the fatally wounded ambassador. Miss Varnava, called "Toni" by her friends and all who knew her, was known as a warm, caring person, whom colleagues eulogized "as a joy to work with … and we will long feel her loss. She stuck with the Embassy through its most difficult days when her warmth and friendship were a source of strength for everybody." Both President Gerald R. Ford and Secretary of State Kissinger extended their deep, personal condolences to Miss Varnava's family and praised her bravery in assisting the mortally wounded ambassador.

At a memorial service for the slain envoy, President Ford and Secretary of State Kissinger praised the dedication and sacrifice Ambassador Davies displayed during the Turkish invasion of Cyprus and throughout his career with the Foreign Service. He was, as President Ford told the ambassador's grieving family, "a professional in the fullest sense. His services to our country embodied the best time, of effort and competence. He loved and worked for peace and he lost his life in the search for all America and all the world."[85] Dr. Kissinger likewise praised Davies' dedication and professionalism. He added that in the diplomatic entrance to the Department of State, the American Foreign Service Association maintains plaques that list the names of those members of the Foreign Service who gave their lives under heroic or tragic circumstances in the service of their country. Dr. Kissinger solemnly added that, tragically, "another name will be added to the list."[86]

"Those Marines ... did a wonderful job"

Ambassador Davies' death and the sacking of the U.S. Embassy in Nicosia was not, however, an end to the violence in the Eastern Mediterranean Sea. The Turkish invasion of Cyprus and the alleged U.S. support for the junta sparked yet another round of anti–American violence in Athens, once again aimed primarily at the U.S. Embassy and its personnel. Ambassador Jack Bloom Kubisch, who had only recently arrived in country, recalled that never before had he seen anything like the violence displayed in Athens in the aftermath of the Turkish invasion.

Ambassador Kubisch recalled that demonstrations in Athens often occurred with crowds that ranged anywhere from 200,000 to 400,000 people "that gathered in the center of town all day long," and ended the day with a march past the U.S. Embassy. Here, the demonstrators, marching 200 to 300 people abreast, shouted "the worst, most obscene epithets in language," and often tried breaking into the embassy compound. The American envoy specifically remembered one such demonstration where the protestors succeeded in breaking into the embassy and tried to set the place on fire. In the end, they caused over $100,000 in damage."[87]

Ambassador Kubisch remembered that there was a pattern to these demonstrations, almost as if the leftist and other anti–American elements in Greece choreographed them prior to their execution. While Greek authorities attempted to protect the embassy against the demonstrators, these efforts oftentimes failed, as the crowds proved too large to control. It was, as Ambassador Kubisch acknowledged, often left to the Marine Security Guards in such situations to protect the embassy, its contents, and personnel against the outrages of the demonstrators.

Ambassador Kubisch stated that these protests were easy to detect as they always started with huge crowds gathering downtown, about midday, to witness the burning of the American flag and inflammatory anti–American speeches. The embassy, defended by a couple hundred Greek police, remained open until about 4 P.M., when the ambassador sent the embassy staff and employees home. Before departing, Kubisch placed the regional security officer, the Marine guards, and several other unnamed individuals in charge of the Embassy's defense. Ambassador Kubisch then specifically instructed the Marine Security Guards "not to draw a pistol and shoot anyone because they were looking for a martyr, the demonstrators, the leaders of the demonstration, to try and bring on even more anti–American sentiment in the country." During one such "break in," Ambassador Kubisch

> told the Marines not to draw their pistols or shoot anyone unless, as we used to say in the navy in World War II, you were in the last extremity where they had you down, they were about to do you terrible damage, then you could draw your pistol and shoot. And those Marines, we had twelve at the time in the Marine Security Guard, did a wonderful job. They fought off the people breaking into the embassy with brooms and fire extinguishers and chairs and so on. A lot of people were hurt. There were a lot of broken bones, broken arms, broken clavicles and so on. A lot of police were badly injured, but no one was killed.[88]

The following spring, 100,000 demonstrators once again marched on the U.S. Embassy in Athens. Surging past the local guards, the students and rioters managed to force their way into the compound of the embassy before being repelled by the Marine Security Guards and local police. Mr. Verne F. St. Mars, chief of the Division of Foreign Operations, wrote in his after-action report that the presence of the Marine Security Guards "precluded extensive damage.... All persons on duty inside the Embassy performed with great credit. As to be expected, the Marines on duty carried out [their] duties in an exemplary fashion."[89] Mr. St. Mars concluded that during this latest outrage against the U.S. Embassy, "the Athens Marines should be commended for a job well done." He added "This only tends to emphasize the value of the selection, training, and discipline of the Marine Security Guards. They were prepared."[90]

One final incident in Nicosia, Cyprus, occurred on October 4, 1975, when Greek Cypriots discovered the fact that U.S. State Department had brought in more Marines to defend the U.S. Embassy. This was shortly followed after the news reached them that the U.S. Congress had lifted the ban on sending arms to Turkey it imposed after the latter's invasion of the island in July of 1974. The Greek Cypriots reacted angrily to this latest provocation when it was rumored that the Marines had been ordered "to kill if necessary citizens of the Cyprus Republic." Indeed, the Greek Cypriot press reported that these Marine Security Guards came "armed to the teeth [in] field uniforms, in cars loaded down with weapons, walkie-talkies, machine guns, pistols, and radios ... and black briefcases." Greek Cypriots likewise protested the installation of security cameras and monitors, which they said were "provocative and unnecessary measures."[91]

During this period of intense anti–American feelings in the Greece, the Turkish invasion of Cyprus in July 1974, and the killing of Ambassador Davies that same August, Marine Security Guards found themselves involved in the some of the most intense and professionally demanding situations since their organization in 1948. As Ambassador Kubisch, Lieutenant Colonel Allred and Lance Corporal Lynn noted, the situations Marine Security Guards and U.S. soldiers oftentimes found themselves in during the Turkish invasion of Cyprus called upon their professionalism as representatives of the United States.[92] One misstep, one accidental shooting, could've had terrible consequences with world-wide ramifications. The Marines who stood guard at Post One during this intense period of American foreign relations walked a "fine line" that called upon their excellent training and professional bearing.

Anti-American Protests in India, 1971

Protests against U.S. policies were not confined to Europe. One of the largest anti–American demonstrations to call upon the capabilities of Marine Security Guards occurred prior to the visit of Dr. Henry Kissinger, President Richard M. Nixon's national security advisor, to New Delhi, India, in June and July of 1971. The demonstrations occurred as a result of Washington's shipping arms to India's arch rival on the sub-continent — Pakistan.

In a situation Marine Security Guards would face in Athens, Greece, three years later, the leathernecks assigned to the U.S. Embassy "were alerted for demonstrations at USIS" that never materialized. During the period of 5–13 July 1971, protestors, primarily from the Delhi Youth Federation, a leftist-oriented student organization, as well as the Communist Party of India (CPI), conducted large-scale demonstrations past the U.S. Embassy Compound.[93] Staff Sergeant Robert A. Creedon recalled, "With the exception of the incident of 6 July the Embassy had been warned of demonstrations in advance. The off duty watch had been mustered and posted. On each occasion local police were in force at the main gate. Their presence precluded penetration of the Embassy compound." Staff Sergeant Creedon noted that at any given

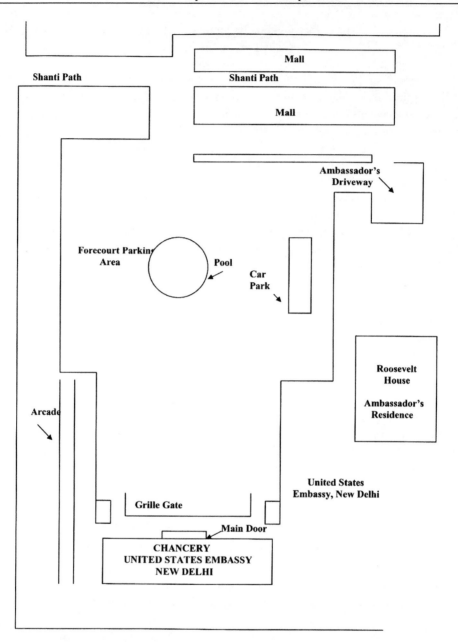

Diagram 3. The U.S. Embassy in New Dehli, India, in 1973 (U.S. Marine Security Guard Battalion).

time protestors numbered at most 75 individuals, and the demonstrations themselves were peaceful in nature.

All of this began to change, however, a week prior to Dr. Kissinger's arrival. The number of demonstrators averaged between 300 on 24 June and 450 on 28 June, respectively, and their actions escalated as well. According to Staff Sergeant Creedon, the protests originally were rarely violent, as the main goal of the demonstrators was to be arrested. On both July 6 and 13, 1971, this changed when two demonstrations, led by the leftist-oriented Delhi Youth Federation and the CPI, became violent.

Upon his arrival in New Delhi, members of the CPI awaited Dr. Kissinger's aircraft in what turned out to be a downpour. As the American envoy emerged from the aircraft, members of the CPI, flanked by "more policemen than there were demonstrators," began to wave their black flags and shouted, "Kissinger go back" and "Murderer go back." They also waved large banners that said "Kissinger of Death Go Back."[94] Dr. Kissinger and his entourage were then hustled into the awaiting cars that then sped off before the demonstrators realized, much to their dismay, that the Americans had already departed the airport. Frustrated that they had missed their intended victim, the protestors pelted all of the vehicles leaving the airport with rotten eggs and tomatoes.[95] At the U.S. Embassy Compound, even before Secretary Kissinger arrived, approximately forty demonstrators penetrated the grounds and made their way to the entrance guarded only by a few local policemen. Before the Marine Security Guards were able to act, several jeeps of local policemen, coming mainly from the grounds of the Soviet Embassy, were rushed to defend the American compound. Before the doors of the U.S. Embassy were broken open the policemen swooped in and conducted a massive arrest of all the protestors, who offered no resistance. Before they were arrested, however, the protestors were able to plant a red flag into the lawn of the U.S. Embassy and shouted anti–American and anti–Kissinger slogans.[96]

Staff Sergeant Creedon recalled that prior to the arrival of the local police, the penetration of the embassy's grounds was "a cause of momentary consternation" among the Marine Security Guards inside the embassy. "Frustrated in their efforts to stage a successful show of force due to the large local security force and deluge of rain," the demonstrators turned their attention to the U.S. Embassy where they believed Dr. Kissinger was possibly staying prior to his meeting with Indian officials.[97] Approaching the embassy, the demonstrators, who

numbered approximately one hundred and fifty moved up to the Embassy's main gate. Realizing there were no local police thirty to forty charged past the main gate watchman and attempted to breach the Chancery main door. They were immediately followed by a second group of forty to sixty persons. Fortunately at that moment, Sergeant Dennis F. Beska who was in the process of relieving Lance Corporal Steven A. Lonas as Sentry Post #1, observed the mob push past the watchman. Sergeant Beska and Lance Corporal Lonas implemented the Immediate Action Plan, securing the main and stairwell doors and the elevator and alerted the off duty watch. At the same time, Sergeants Garnett A. Slade and Ernest W. Judge and Corporal Diehl were returning from the Ashoka Hotel (special Sentry and Escorts for classified material). Upon seeing the mob they entered the Chancery through the basement garage, securing the garage gates, and continuing with the Immediate Action Plan.

A detachment of local security police, stationed at the Russian Embassy, observed the mob forming. This detachment was approximately 500 meters from the American Embassy. Upon realizing the potential danger, part of the detachment was dispatched. Upon arrival they contained the demonstrators and ushered them from the compound. However, during this time the mob shook and climbed upon the grill gate, pushing sticks through the grill attempting to break the glass doors. This was accompanied by a great deal of shouting and flag waving. No damage was incurred. Marines were not required to become further involved.[98]

The main reason that the demonstrators failed to enter the embassy was due, as Staff Sergeant Creedon wrote, to "the rapid reaction of the Marine Security Guard." The Marine staff sergeant admitted, however, that "the mob moved at such a rapid rate, rushing cross the Embassy forecourt (pool and driveway area), that they were within twenty meters of the front door, before the sentry was able to secure the front grille gate."[99]

Staff Sergeant Creedon wrote that this was the most serious of all of the demonstrations that took place during this period, though it was not the only one of any consequence. Prior to the demonstration on July 13, in fact, local police officials notified the regional security officer at the embassy that "there was a good possibility the demonstrators would be violent." This forced the Marine Security Guards to implement an Immediate Action Plan. The RSO mustered the entire MSG Detachment while 300 local police gathered to form a barricade in front of the embassy. As the sun began to set, at approximately 6:25 p.m, "125–150 demonstrators approached the police lines. The demonstrators immediately charged the police who took 60–70 into custody. By 1835, all the demonstrators were disbursed." Staff Sergeant Creedon remembered that "this was the first time during my tour that I have witnessed mass arrests of demonstrators at the Embassy. It appeared the motive of the demonstrators was to be arrested. No Embassy personnel [were] involved."[100]

The People's Republic of China and Taiwan

On February 18, 1972, Air Force One touched down on the tarmac at the airport in Beijing, the People's Republic of China (PRC). On board was President Richard M. Nixon, who was greeted by Chinese Premier Chou En-Lai. As a cold wind blew across the tarmac and the two enemies shook hands, so ended twenty-three years of official hostility between the United States and the People's Republic of China. While President Nixon met with Chinese officials, including Chairman Mao Zedong, United States and Chinese diplomats, including Secretary

A lone Chinese security guard stands outside the U.S. Embassy in Beijing. The first Marine Security Guard detachment to the People's Republic of China was established immediately after relations were restored between the two countries in 1972 (U.S. Marine Security Guard Battalion).

of State Henry Kissinger, discussed a wide range of geo-strategic issues including an agreement that re-established low-level diplomatic contacts between the two countries. Part of the normalization process involved in diplomatic relations between two countries included the exchange of envoys and the establishment of interest sections in each other's country. The agreement between the U.S. and PRC stopped short, however, of formal diplomatic recognition between the two Asian powers.

Even before the ink was dry on the agreement that re-established low level contacts with the PRC, State Department officials assigned the first Marine Security Guard Detachment to the new United States Liaison Office (USLO). The detachment, consisting of Staff Sergeant Royal G. Osborne, Sergeant Robert E. Jones, and Corporals Roy E. Macdonald and Mark A. Worrell, crossed over into the PRC from nearby Hong Kong on May 2, 1973. A brief journey first took them to Canton and then on to Shanghai, where, during the first three decades of the twentieth century, leathernecks guarded U.S. interests in the International Settlement area. After dinner, the Marine Security Guards boarded an airplane that took them to Beijing, where they took up residence at the Peking Hotel, the first office of the USLO. The Marines were joined by two additional leathernecks, Sergeants Clarence N. France and Geary E. MacMurray, who flew into Peking directly aboard a U.S. Air Force C-130 transport based on the island of Guam. On May 3–5, 1973, the Marines assisted in moving equipment into the temporary office. On May 5, the Marine Security Guards began to stand post in this temporary embassy.[101]

On May 14, 1973, Mr. David K.E. Bruce, the first U.S. ambassador to the PRC, arrived. There at the airport to greet the ambassador was Chinese Vice Foreign Minister Chiao Guan Hua and the entire staff of the USLO, including all of the Marines (with the exception being the guard on Post One). As the diplomats exchanged pleasantries, the USLO was officially opened for business. On May 16, 1973, the Marines attended a reception and dinner given for the USLO staff by Vice Foreign Minister Chiao Guan Hua. In an atmosphere of friendship and cooperation, the Marines settled into their new post, mindful of their predecessors who once stood guard over the U.S. Embassy prior to World War II in the ancient Chinese capital and rode the sturdy little Mongolian ponies in endless parades and polo matches. In fact, in keeping with this tradition, the leathernecks participated with the other foreigners living in the city in a boat race at the Summer Palace on May 17, 1973, where they placed second to the Canadian team.[102]

On June 26, 1973, Marine Embassy Guards raised the "Stars and Stripes" for the first time in over two decades over the ancient city of Beijing. On hand for the flag-raising ceremony was Major Donald L. Evans, Company C's commanding officer, who had arrived in Beijing in order to inspect the Marines assigned to the USLO.

Initially, PRC officials permitted the Marines to wear their uniforms while on duty. This situation changed shortly after the Marines settled into their usual routine, when the deputy director of protocol, Chu Ch'uan-Lsien, summoned U.S. Deputy Chief of Mission Mr. Alfred M. Jenkins to the Foreign Ministry in order to discuss a variety of topics, including the issue of Marine Security Guards wearing their uniforms and carrying sidearms while on duty. Chu told the deputy chief of mission that the practice of wearing uniforms and carrying firearms went against the uniform practice of the other foreign missions in China. Chu also informed Mr. Jenkins that Chinese military personnel were not permitted to wear their uniforms while in foreign countries. Chu reminded Mr. Jenkins that Dr. Kissinger, President Nixon's secretary of state, had initially agreed that U.S. personnel would wear civilian clothes and would not carry arms openly.

The American envoy explained to Mr. Chu that the issue of wearing uniforms instead of civilian clothes had already been discussed in Washington, D.C., with the decision taken that due to morale and discipline problems, the Marines would be required to wear their uniforms on duty. As for the carrying of arms in the open, Mr. Jenkins reminded the deputy director of protocol that the United States attempted to use civilians to guard its embassies and consulates abroad after World War II but that in the long run, it proved unworkable and ultimately failed. Mr. Chu reminded Jenkins, however, that at least on one occasion, a uniformed Marine had searched a Chinese consular official. Chu likewise told Jenkins that "this was both unnecessary and an inappropriate departure from local custom."[103]

In order to maintain friendly relations with the Chinese, Ambassador Bruce summoned Staff Sergeant Osborne to his office on July 4, 1973, and informed him that the Marines were henceforth not to wear their uniforms while on duty. Marines nevertheless took this in stride and became true "Ambassadors in Blue," as they organized numerous softball games, soccer matches, and even good old American football games within the diplomatic community.

Chinese officials, however, persisted in their campaign to rid the country of the Marine Security Guards. On November 5, 1973, Chinese officials summoned Mr. Bruce to the Foreign Ministry and informed the American envoy that "the Marine Corps Birthday will not be celebrated in Peking." Bowing to Chinese pressure, Mr. Bruce informed the Marine Detachment commander that "he was ordering the ball to be cancelled." In the same meeting with Chinese Foreign Ministry officials, the host country renewed its demand that the Marines be withdrawn from the PRC. Ambassador Bruce once again informed them that he did not have the authority to order the Marines out of Peking. He told the Chinese that he would have to inform Washington of the Chinese request to remove the Marine Security Guard detachment.[104]

When Secretary of State Henry Kissinger arrived in Beijing for consultations with Chinese officials, the question over the status of the Marine Security Guards was again brought up. After discussions were held with PRC officials over the matter, the latter agreed to allow the Marines to remain and that the matter would be dropped, at least for the time being.

On December 22, 1973, Marine Security Guards played Santa Claus and hosted a Christmas party for all of the children in the diplomatic community. To Marines, Christmas would not be Christmas without the time-honored tradition of "Toys for Tots." At the party, Marines presented each child in attendance with a toy or gift.

Despite the goodwill and camaraderie engendered by the leathernecks in Beijing, Chinese officials renewed their efforts to remove the Marine Security Guards. On April 16, 1974, Ambassador Bruce was once again called to the Foreign Ministry, where he met with Lin Ping. The Chinese Foreign Ministry official demanded that "the Marine Security Guard Detachment get out of China 'speedily.'" Once again, Ambassador Bruce reminded his hosts that he alone did not possess the authority to order the Marines home, and that "this could only be done by the Secretary of State and other officials in Washington, D.C." The American official agreed, however, to bring the matter up with his superiors once again back at the State Department. Finally, after much wrangling and heated discussion, U.S. State Department officials decided to gradually withdraw the Marine Security Guard Detachment and replace it with civilian guards at the USLO. Prior to its de-activation, the Marine Security Guard detachment in Beijing was awarded the Meritorious Unit Commendation for its services in the PRC.[105] When the United States formalized relations with the PRC on January 1, 1980, Marine Security Guards returned to take up positions in Beijing and at the other U.S. consulates throughout China.

Marine Security Guards in Taiwan, 1975–1978

Meanwhile, one hundred miles across the Taiwan Strait on the island of Taiwan, Marine Embassy Guards witnessed the end of another era—the death of Generalissimo Chiang Kai-Shek and the cessation of formal U.S.-Taiwan relations. Relations between the United States and Chiang dated back to 1927, when the United States recognized the Nationalist leader as the legitimate ruler of China. When Chiang fled to Taiwan at the end of the Chinese Civil War (1946–1949), the United States transferred its support to his regime on this disputed island for the next twenty-four years. As the news spread of the rapprochement between the United States and their sworn enemy, the People's Republic of China, many on Taiwan, particularly the Nationalists (or those who had fled the mainland) felt betrayed. This frustration turned to anger as demonstrators ransacked the outer walls and compound of the U.S. Embassy in Taipei and hurled heavy objects at its infrastructure in protest of the United States' recognition of the People's Republic of China.

Marines had long been familiar with the island of Taiwan. In fact, leathernecks assigned to the Pacific Squadron participated in several landings against the inhabitants of the island in 1867 and 1894.[106] As a result of China's defeat at the hands of Japan in the brief though decisive Sino-Japanese War of 1894, and the subsequent Treaty of Shimonseki that ended the war in 1895, China ceded sovereignty of Taiwan to Japan. From 1895 until the end of World War II in 1945, Taiwan became an integral part of the Japanese Empire. At the conclusion of World War II, U.S. forces briefly occupied the island before the arrival of Nationalist Chinese troops who were sent in February 1946. For nearly three years, with Chiang's attention diverted toward the civil war with the communists on the mainland, Taiwanese enjoyed a slight degree of independence. During this tumultuous period of Chinese history, Chiang's Nationalist government claimed Taiwan as a province of China. Chiang Kai-Shek who had hoped to re-establish himself and his regime back on the mainland, used this historic claim to seize the island and use it as a base of operations for the Nationalists' eventual return to the Chinese mainland.[107] As it became more and more apparent that the Nationalists would never return to Mainland China, Chiang accomplished on Taiwan what he never could achieve on the mainland—political stability and economic security. Over time, Taiwan became one of the leading economic powers in Asia, rivaled only by Japan and the United States.

Also, because of his anti–Communist credentials, Chiang became the recipient of a massive amount of U.S. foreign and military assistance. Indeed, until his death in April 1975, Chiang Kai-Shek became one of the pillars of U.S. security interests in Asia. Nevertheless, the formal relationship between Washington and Taipei changed with the U.S.-PRC rapprochement that began under President Nixon in February 1972, and ended with the formal recognition of the PRC on January 1, 1979.

As the relationship between Beijing and Washington, D.C., grew in importance, the relationship between the two old friends diminished, as the historic bonds of friendship between the Taipei and Washington gave way to the strategic priorities of the mid to late 1970s. This change in relationship between Taipei and Washington was highlighted upon the death of Generalissimo Chiang Kai-Shek, who died shortly after suffering a massive heart attack on April 5, 1975. Despite the decision to down-grade its contacts with the Nationalist regime on Taiwan, and in recognition of the long friendship between the United States and Nationalist China, President Gerald R. Ford sent Vice President Nelson Rockefeller to Taipei to represent the United States at the generalissimo's state funeral. Fearing anti–U.S. riots and possible attempts on the vice president's life, the Marine Security Guards stationed at the U.S.

Embassy in Taipei provided a security detachment for Mr. Rockefeller as he moved about the Taiwanese capital as a part of the funeral procession.[108]

The downgrading of relations with Taiwan continued into the presidency of Jimmy Carter. As the Carter Administration continued to downplay its relationship with Taipei in preparation for its eventual recognition of Beijing as the "true representatives of the Chinese people," both Nationalist Chinese and native Taiwanese became increasingly concerned as to their future in this arrangement. Many Taiwanese directed some of this frustration against the very symbol of their anger: the U.S. Embassy in Taipei. When President Carter announced that the United States would normalize relations with Beijing and discontinue official relations with Taipei as of January 1, 1979, angry Taiwanese, on 16 December 1978, stormed the U.S. Embassy, broke windows, and heaved bricks, ink wells, and other heavy objects at the embassy's outer walls. They also attempted to penetrate the besieged compound. In a demonstration of forceful resolve, Marine Security Guards immediately implemented riot control procedures and eventually were able to repel the demonstrators with tear gas.[109]

In an attempt to re-assure the Taiwanese that Washington was not totally abandoning them, President Carter sent a special representative to Taipei to discuss the future of U.S.-Taiwanese relations in wake of normalized relations with Beijing. On December 29, 1978, as the motorcade of Assistant Secretary of State Warren Christopher made its way to the U.S. Embassy in Taipei, angry demonstrators attacked the envoy's party. In response to this and the other violence directed toward the United States and its property, State Department officials made the decision to augment the strength of the Marine Security Guard detachment on the island. By December 30, 1978, two days before official relations between Taipei and Washington came to an end, six additional Marine security guards joined their comrades in Taipei in order to repel any attack that might occur against the embassy and its personnel. At sunset on December 31, 1978, as "Evening Colors" was played, Sergeant D.J. Buchanan and Corporals R.A. Stowell and W.E. Kuskowski lowered the colors for the last time from the American Embassy in Taipei.[110]

As Marines in Taipei lowered the flag over the U.S. Embassy, another Marine Security Guard detachment lowered the United States flag over the U.S. Consulate in the British Crown colony of Hong Kong. As in Taipei, the State Department placed the Marine Security Guard Detachment on alert in wake of the normalization of relations between the United States and Beijing.

Despite the damage inflicted on the U.S. Embassy in Taipei, there were no casualties among the Marines or protestors. This was due to the riot control procedures Marine Security Guards were taught at the MSG School that stressed non-lethal defensive measures. In recognition of their steadfastness in the face of the angry mobs in Taipei, Secretary of the Navy W. Graham Claytor, Jr., awarded the Marine Security Guard Detachment there the Meritorious Unit Commendation for

> Meritorious achievement in support of the United States Embassy, Taipei, Taiwan, from 16 to 21 December 1978. During this period of severe diplomatic tension, the Embassy was surrounded by a hostile mob numbering in the thousands. The Chancery was bombarded with rocks, bricks, pieces of metal fencing, paint, dye, and bottles of ink. All windows on the right side of the Chancery were broken, all outside equipment was heavily damaged, and large objects were thrown with such force that some of them penetrated the walls themselves. When the embassy gates were opened to admit vehicles, the mob constantly attempted to gain entrance, forcing the Marine Security Guards to use nightsticks to control the mob and close the gate. At about 2330 on 16 December, the mob broke into the Embassy grounds and under direct attack, the Marines executed riot control procedures with chemical agents to drive the mob back into the street. The Marines of the Taipei Detachment remained on full alert for 96 hours and lived in the Embassy during that period. Their presence was a source of reassurance to the ambassador and the entire Embassy Staff.[111]

An Admirable Response in Tokyo, October–November 1974

Anti-American sentiment affected American embassies and consulates in other parts of Asia. Prior to a state visit by President Gerald R. Ford, the regional security officer placed the entire Marine Security Guard detachment at the U.S. Embassy in Tokyo, Japan, on full alert as it enacted a range of security measures and prepared for the expected anti–American protests by various Japanese groups. Of particular concern was the Japanese Red Army (JRA), an extremely violent anti–American terrorist group that had, in August 1975, temporarily seized the U.S. Consulate in Kuala Lumpur, Malaysia, and seized 52 hostages, including the consul and the Swedish chargé d'affaires. After the terrorist group threatened to blow up the embassy, the Japanese government agreed to the demands of the JRA, which was the release of seven of its members from various jails in Japan.[112]

Linked to the JRA was the Marxist Youth League, which was comprised of student groups opposed to the U.S. military presence in Japan and supported the overthrow of the Japanese government. On November 14, 1974, shortly before the arrival of President Ford, the Marxist Youth League attacked the U.S. Embassy. The Marine Security Guard detachment "responded admirably," as they quickly contained the riot and prevented "the unpleasant incident from becoming a tragedy," and ensured the protection of the president, his party, and the embassy itself. Later, the commandant of the Marine Corps awarded the Marines stationed in Tokyo a Certificate of Commendation for its admirable job in protecting the president and the embassy against the terrorists.[113]

Trouble in Latin and South America, 1971–1979

Not all of the violence directed toward the United States and its diplomatic missions during the late 1960s and 1970s occurred in Asia and the Middle East. Some of that violence was closer to home, in Central and South America. At the root of this violence was the political and economic instability characteristic of this region in the 1960s and 1970s. Many of the governments in the region were either run by military juntas or by authoritarian figures. Many of the leftist groups, some of whom were openly Marxist and sympathetic to Fidel Castro's and revolutionary leader Che Guevara's calls for revolution throughout Latin America, found support from the peasantry and the growing urban masses that swelled cities. American embassies and consulates, located in cities such as La Paz, Bolivia; Tegucigalpa, Honduras; Managua, Nicaragua; San Salvador, El Salvador; Guatemala City, Guatemala; and Montevideo, Uruguay, became primary targets for these leftist guerrilla groups, openly supported by Fidel Castro's Cuba with arms, money, and training. The ultimate goal of these groups was to bring attention to their cause of revolution. Often taking the brunt of the assault on the American diplomatic compounds were the Marine Security Guards assigned to Company D.

Violence in La Paz, Bolivia, October 1970

In the evening hours of 6 October 1970, a *coup d'état* occurred which brought out scores of demonstrators and protestors who stormed the U.S. Embassy in La Paz, Bolivia, bombed the American-sponsored Bi-National Center, and drove away with American-owned automobiles, parked in the embassy's parking lot. The next day, October 7, 1970, an estimated

125 Bolivian nationals gathered outside the Marine House and forced their way inside as they smashed the front door and entered the building. Some of the protestors carried loaded pistols while others carried sticks, knives, and in one case a hatchet. Two Marines were seized by the mob security guard and questioned about "their status with the CIA as to where the weapons were stored." One protestor questioned a Marine with a loaded pistol pointed against the Marine's head. Before they left the Marine House, the mobs ransacked the place, broke up furniture, and went through each room and stole both military and civilian clothing, as well as the personal effects of the Marines. After about a half an hour, the crowds departed but not before they released unharmed the two Marine Security Guards held captive.[114]

Also in La Paz, on August 20–22, 1971, Marine Security Guards came under intense machine gun and rifle fire as the country exploded in revolution. On August 20, as the revolution got underway, small arms fire impacted against the U.S. Embassy. At approximately 10:30 P.M., on August 21, an explosion caused by a blast from a charge made from dynamite damaged the front wall of the Marine House. This attack was followed by intense rifle fire aimed at the occupants inside. Fifteen minutes after the initial blast, another blast occurred and more rifle fire poured into the Marine House. This latest attack as well as the earlier one trapped five Marines inside. As the attackers surged into the first and second floors of the Marine House, the five Marine defenders made their way to the third floor and set up a defensive barrier. The mob, however, continued to fire at the Marines using rifles, automatic weapons, and tear gas at sporadic intervals until about 12:30 A.M. on August 22. Despite the fact that the Marines possessed the means to fire back, they nevertheless held their fire, and instead rolled tear gas grenades down the stairs to turn away the attackers.[115]

As was the case in Africa, the Middle East, and even in Europe, American diplomats in South America faced the day-to-day threat of terrorist attacks, inspired by such notorious terrorists as Manuel Ruben Guzman's *Sendero Luminoso* or Shining Path of Peru, Rodrigo Asturias' Guatemalan National Revolutionary Unity, and Joaquin Villalobos' Farabundo Marti National Liberation Front of El Salvador, which was responsible for the deaths of four Marine Security Guards in 1985. All of these groups had one major goal: to drive the United States from their respective countries, and to end its support of the repressive governments they were fighting.

In Montevideo, Uruguay, American and other foreign diplomats endured bombings, bomb threats, sniper fire, kidnapping, and constant street demonstrations on a day-to-day basis. One attack, on April 6, 1971, targeted the American Embassy with a burst of small caliber automatic fire and a bazooka-type round that hit the Marine House. While no one was injured, the attacks served as a constant reminder of the day-to-day dangers endured by American diplomats and the Marine Security Guard Detachments throughout Central and South America.[116]

As demonstrated in Guatemala City, Guatemala, these attacks could be deadly. In January 1968, the Marxist-oriented Guatemalan National Revolutionary Unity Group (URNG) machine-gunned and strafed the U.S. Military Mission and U.S. Naval Attaché's office in Guatemala City. In the attack, the URNG wounded two U.S. service members. The deadliest attack launched by the URNG occurred in August 1968, when they killed U.S. Ambassador John Gordon Mein, after he openly resisted an attempt to kidnap him on a busy Guatemala City street.[117]

In Tegucigalpa, Honduras, Marxist rebels placed a bomb on a wall surrounding the courtyard of the U.S. Embassy. The explosion was so powerful that it threw several Marines to the ground. Also, throughout the early 1970s, Marine Embassy Guards protected the embassy against the many violent, anti–American demonstrations that crowded the streets of Teguci-galpa.[118]

Throughout 1972, as violent anti–American demonstrations occurred in Quito, Ecuador; Rio de Janerio, Brazil; and even peaceful San Jose, Costa Rica, Marine Security Guards stood ready to repel any attempt to violate the embassy or its surrounding buildings. In Santo Domingo, Dominican Republic, the Marines faced bomb attacks and sniper fire aimed at the U.S. Embassy despite the imposition of a dusk to dawn curfew in the city.

While Marines continued to man Post One, others guarded the ambassador and his fam-ily on numerous occasions against any harm from these same demonstrators. In Rio de Jane-rio, Marine Security Guards established a round-the-clock guard for the ambassador and his family as "positive" threats were made. In Santiago, Chile, supporters of the leftist President Salvador Allende carried out violent anti–American demonstrations and threw stones at the U.S. Embassy and the personnel inside. As in Rio de Janerio, Marine Security Guards estab-lished a round-the-clock guard of the ambassador and his family in response to several threat-ening phone calls to the embassy's switchboard.[119]

The most serious attacks against the U.S. Embassy and its personnel occurred, however, in San Salvador, El Salvador. Starting in the early 1970s, the country of El Salvador was chal-lenged by threats from a Marxist-oriented group known as the Farabundo Marti National Lib-eration Front or FMLN.

Almost immediately, this violence spilled into the diplomatic compound of the U.S. Embassy in San Salvador. While the majority of attacks consisted of random shots fired at the outer embassy wall, stone-throwing, demonstrations, and bomb threats, the violence remained sporadic. As 1979 dawned, however, this changed, and the security situation through-out El Salvador deteriorated as government troops, supported and advised by U.S. military advisors, fought off a major Marxist-led insurgency aimed at toppling the country's legiti-mate government.

On the afternoon of October 30, 1979, approximately 100 to 150 demonstrators, armed with rifles, automatic weapons, and hand-held explosive devices, and shouting "We will take the embassy" and "Down with imperialism," attacked the U.S. Embassy in San Salvador. In their attempt to minimize casualties and not let the situation get out of hand, Marine Secu-rity Guards lobbed about sixteen tear gas canisters from the roof at the protestors, who fired their weapons into the air while other demonstrators lobbed Molotov cocktails at the embassy.

During the attack on the embassy, two Marine Security Guards were wounded as they resisted the protestors that stormed into the compound. One of them, Gunnery Sergeant Csabon, the NCOIC of the Marine Detachment, was wounded when a bullet took a piece of his ear off as it whizzed by. Thankfully, he was wearing his helmet. Another Marine, Cor-poral Fowler, was likewise slightly wounded when a bullet ricocheted and shattered his teeth. Both Gunnery Sergeant Csabon and Corporal Fowler were later awarded Purple Hearts for wounds received during the attack in San Salvador.[120]

To disperse the crowds, the Marine Security Guards fired two blasts from their shotguns into the air. While the exact number of casualties among the protestors was not known, two of them were apparently wounded in the attack. The Marines saw them being carried off the street into awaiting vehicles that quickly left the scene. After about thirty minutes, units of the Salvador National Guard arrived to break up the demonstration and restore order.[121] For its cool professionalism displayed in the attack on October 30, 1979, Acting Secretary of the Navy J. James Woolsey awarded the Marine Security Guard Detachment in San Salvador the Meritorious Unit Commendation.

Several months later, on May 12, 1980, demonstrators once again stormed the U.S. Embassy in San Salvador in protest to U.S. policies in El Salvador. The protestors met with the same determined resistance by the Marine Security Guards, who once again lobbed tear gas grenades at the protestors and worked their way to rescue U.S. Ambassador Robert E. White from his official residence. Marine Security Guards "rode shotgun" as they escorted the ambassador to the U.S. Embassy guarded in two bullet-proof four-wheeled vehicles and the ambassador's limousine.[122]

In neighboring Nicaragua, a violent revolution led by the Cuban and Soviet sponsored Farabundo Liberation Sandinista Nicaragua (FSLN) against the U.S.-supported government of Anastasio Somoza Deboyle resulted in the evacuation of 1,435 American citizens and other non–United States nationals. The Marine Security Guard Detachment located at the U.S. Embassy in Managua, Nicaragua, worked around the clock to process and assist these individuals to safely evacuate this war-torn country. Marines also drove the embassy-owned vehicles, and served as escorts and cargo handlers. As part of their duty to protect the classified material inside the embassy, Marine Security Guards loaded boxes and shredded classified documents into boxes and burn bags. They likewise stood guard at Managua International Airport as American citizens boarded jets to take them back to the United States. Secretary of the Navy E. Hidalgo later awarded the Marine Security Guard Detachment in Managua, Nicaragua, a Meritorious Unit Commendation for their "sterling display of professionalism, selfless initiative, and steadfast dedication to duty."[123]

Marine Security Guards likewise became the target of anti–American harassment in Managua as the Sandinistas consolidated their hold on Nicaragua. Typical of this harassment campaign was the arrest of Sergeant Steven T. Hughes, USMC, by two policemen outside the Tropicana Club in Manuagua in the early morning hours of October 29, 1979. Taken to a local jail, Sergeant Hughes was briefly interrogated by Sandinista police officials. Allegedly, the Sandinistas had detained the Marine sergeant for no other "crime" than the possession of a walkie-talkie that he carried in his hip pocket in order to communicate with the embassy in the event of an emergency. During his interrogation, the Sandinistas attempted to force him to sign a statement, which he refused. After several hours of interrogation, the Sandinistas released him and transported him back to the embassy. The policemen, after being questioned by the Regional Security Officer and the embassy's administrative officer, informed the two American officials that Sergeant Hughes had been picked up near the sports stadium, "inebriated" the night before and that they were to take him to the American Embassy." After being further debriefed by American officials, Sergeant Hughes was found to be completely innocent of any wrongdoing and was, in fact, commended by the RSO for his "cool and level headedness during an extremely tense and volatile situation."[124]

From Diplomatic Security to Disaster Relief in El Salvador and Nicaragua, 1971–192

Not all of the work involving the Marine Security Guards centered upon the defense of the embassy or other traditional duties. In 1971, Marine Security Guard Detachments throughout Europe provided security for the Strategic Arms and Limitations Talks (SALT) held between the United States and the USSR. Marines guarded the SALT III talks that were held in Helsinki, Finland (August 1–October 30, 1970); the Salt IV Talks in Vienna, Austria, (March 3–May 12, 1971); and Salt V Talks (July 3–August 31, 1971), once again in Helsinki,

Finland. Marine Security Guards likewise provided security for Secretary of State William P. Rogers when he visited Lisbon, Portugal, on May 30, 1971, and later for President Richard M. Nixon when he visited Madrid, Spain, from September 30 to October 7, 1971. Later, the Marine Security Guard Detachment in Moscow, Russia, provided security for President Nixon when he met with Soviet General Secretary Leonid I. Brezhnev, on May 15–30, 1972.[125] In December 1972, Company A, from where the Marine Security Guards were detailed, received a Meritorious Unit Commendation for their services and professionalism displayed during these conferences: "Disregarding their own safety and concerned primarily with the safety of other persons and U.S. property, the Marines of Company 'A' ... repeatedly placed themselves in a position of forming the only line of defense before the diplomatic mission whose security they are charged with."[126]

As for disaster relief, the Marine Security Guard Detachment in San Jose, Costa Rica, assisted local officials with the distribution of food and other necessary supplies to the flood-ravaged countryside. When two hurricanes struck the Nicaraguan countryside in September 1972, Marines collected food, medicines, and other necessary supplies, and aided local officials for nearly five days (September 12–17, 1972) in their distribution.

Assassination of Ambassador Adolph "Spike" Dubbs in Afghanistan, February 1979

As Afghanistan slowly slipped into civil war during the mid to late 1970s, the Marine Security Guard Detachment maintained a close, watchful eye as they guarded the U.S. Embassy in Kabul. When the fighting between the different political and tribal factions as well as growing Soviet involvement intensified, the United States attempted to maintain strict neutrality amidst this chaos. Unfortunately, the U.S. ambassador to Afghanistan, Adolph "Spike" Dubbs, a seasoned Foreign Service officer, became one of the victims of Afghanistan's tumultuous civil war that began with the bloody *coup d'état* against the government of Mohammad Daoud in April 1978.[127]

On February 14, 1979, terrorists abducted Ambassador Dubbs, whom they intended to use as a bargaining chip in the release of political prisoners. While Afghan police and army units negotiated with the kidnappers, the commander on the scene gave the order to storm the building in order to free the American diplomat. In the ensuing gun battle, Ambassador Dubbs died in a hail of bullets during the botched rescue attempt. Shocked and outraged at this senseless act of violence against an American diplomat, President Jimmy Carter and Secretary of State Cyrus R. Vance not only denounced this blatant act of terrorism, but also questioned the tactics used by the Afghan police to rescue the envoy.

As word reached the U.S. Embassy of the kidnapping and murder of Ambassador Dubbs, Marine Security Guards were placed on full alert. Later, as their Meritorious Unit Commendation stated, the Marine Security Guard Detachment

> responded cooly and efficiently to provide increased security for the embassy under the direction of the Regional Security Officer. Working many hours with little sleep, the Detachment constantly maintained their image of calm confidence and were able to advise mission personnel regarding various safety procedures and courses of action to take in emergencies. Following the kidnapping and murder of Ambassador Adolph Dubbs on 14 February 1979, the Detachment was placed on total alert and provided additional security for the Charge d'Affairs until the arrival additional Department of State security support. By their continuous display of professionalism,

sterling teamwork, and unswerving devotion to duty, the officers and enlisted personnel of the Marine Security Guard Detachment, Kabul, Afghanistan, upheld the highest traditions of the Marine Corps and the United States Naval Service.[128]

The Marine Security Guard Detachment participated in a memorial to Ambassador Dubbs. Later, a Marine honor guard escorted the body of the slain ambassador to an awaiting airplane at Kabul International Airport, where his flag-draped coffin was then flown home to the United States. In a ceremony at Andrews Air Force Base, President Jimmy Carter praised the late ambassador, who he said was "a good ... courageous man, who served his country well and who gave his life for it." Secretary of State Cyrus R. Vance told Dubbs' widow, Mary Ann, and daughter, Lindsey, "It is tragic that a man whose life and career were dedicated to the cause of peace, was killed as a result of terrorism and violence." In recognition of Ambassador Dubbs' service to his country, Secretary Vance awarded him the Secretary's Award for his dedication and devotion to duty.[129]

The End of the Beginning

The 1960s and 1970s witnessed the maturation of the Marine Embassy Guard as it was put to the ultimate test in such places as Amman, San Salvador, Kabul, Managua, and Leopoldsville. Indeed, as the Marine Security Guard program grew, so too did its missions abroad. Even as the Marine Embassy Guard program adjusted to more challenging roles and responsibilities, leathernecks found themselves face-to-face with an implacable foe — the terrorist. As the 1970s ended and gave way to the 1980s, Marine Security Guards found themselves meeting new challenges in an ever-increasingly dangerous world that would call upon their professionalism and steadfastness as the United States' front-line troops in the war on terror. Secretary of State Vance stated at Ambassador Dubbs' memorial service, the United States "will spare no effort to protect our diplomats overseas, and we will fight terrorism with all of our resolve and resourcefulness."[130] The Marines who manned Post One assumed their positions along the front lines on this new war on terrorism with renewed confidence and more determination than ever to carry forward in this fight against those who, to paraphrase President Carter, participated in such despicable acts of violence.[131]

CHAPTER **8**

Embassies at War
and in Peace, 1979–1991

The death of Ambassador Adolph "Spike" Dubbs signaled the beginning of a wave of violent anti–American demonstrations that spread from Tehran, Iran (1979–1980), Islamabad, Pakistan (November 1979), and Beirut, Lebanon (April 1983), and from San Salvador, El Salvador (1985), to the U.S. Embassy in Kuwait during Desert Shield/Desert Storm (1990–91). For Marine Security Guards, the violence directed against Americans was not new. Indeed, from the period radical students seized the U.S. Embassy in Tehran in 1979 to Iraq's invasion of Kuwait in 1990, Marine Security Guards bore the brunt of this violent anti–Americanism. From 1979 to 1991, the violence aimed at U.S. embassies claimed the lives of six Marine Security Guards.

The Hostage Ordeal in Iran, January–November 1979

The origins of the hostage ordeal that resulted in the detention of fifty-two American diplomats, staff, and Marine Security Guards dated back to the political and socio-economic dislocation caused by Shah Mohammed Reza Pahlavi's White Revolution.[1] Linked to this socio-economic dislocation was the corruption and political unrest associated with Iran's relations with the West — particularly the United States. Aside from the socio-economic dislocations caused by the influx of both semi-skilled and skilled foreigners — notably from Korea, Pakistan, and the Philippines — landless peasants and unemployed industrial workers crowded into the shantytowns of Tehran and other Iranian cities looking for what little work existed. Besides the landless peasants and unemployed industrial workers were the hundreds of thousands of Western and Iranian educated college graduates who had very few employment prospects in a country dominated by the Shah's handpicked elite. Discontent ran deep among all classes in Iran.

In time, these shantytowns along with their disaffected populations became fertile recruiting ground for opponents of the Shah, most notably from the Shi'ite clerics, led by a longtime opponent of the monarchy, the Ayatollah Ruhollah Khomeini, and the Marxist-oriented Mujahedin Khalq, led by Masoud Rajavi. For his part, Rajavi's Mujahedin Khalq had advocated the creation of a classless Iranian society built on the principles of Marxism and Islam. Meanwhile, the Ayatollah Khomeini, who spent the majority of the 1970s in exile in either Najaf, Iraq, or on the outskirts of Paris, France, along with the other Shi'ite clerics, mostly located in the holy city of Qom, called for the creation of an Islamic state, free of western (most notably U.S.) influence.

Part of Khomeini's appeal was his repudiation of Western culture and values, which the cleric denounced as "satanic" and contrary to the teachings of Islam. In time, Iranians of all classes began to identify all of Iran's ills with the more than 50,000 American military and civilian personnel living in Iran, largely at the invitation of the Shah.[2] Most Americans living in Iran, in fact, saw no harm in their behavior, which they considered normal. The disregard shown for Iranian culture and the growing discontent for the Shah's heavy-handedness in dealing with political opponents, largely through his secret police known as the SAVAK, led many Iranians to openly resent the presence of so many foreigners in their country.[3]

Sergeant Joseph R. Svinth, whose first tour of duty as a Marine Security Guard took him to the U.S. Embassy in Tehran, recalled that he and his fellow Marines felt the growing tide of anti–American resentment when he first arrived there in October 1977. In order to avoid any problems with the local population, the American diplomatic community and Americans confined their activities to dealing with either the Shah's officials or the other embassies.

The American Embassy, located on twenty-three acres in the heart of downtown Tehran, on property purchased from a wealthy Iranian family deep in debt in 1928, had become the symbol of everything wrong with the Shah's rule. By the time Sergeant Svinth arrived to take up his duties in Tehran, the embassy had become a virtual town in and of itself, surrounded by concrete walls bordered on Roosevelt and Tahkte-e Jamshid avenues. The Marine Security Guard detachment in Tehran consisted of one NCOIC and thirteen watchstanders. While Marines stood guard inside the walled compound, local police complemented the security arrangement on the outer perimeters of the U.S. Embassy. Svinth remembered that Tehran was, by all accounts, a hardship post, with certain segments of the city either off limits or, to paraphrase the Marine sergeant, "not a place you really wanted to be as an American with a flat tire!" Svinth, in fact, compared Tehran to the Watts section of Los Angeles.[4]

Sergeant Svinth recalled that the Marine Security Guards in Tehran were, for the most part, constantly on call, as the political situation there had already began to deteriorate by the time of his arrival:

> The posts at Tehran were post one (inside the lobby), a roving patrol (post two), the front gate, the consulate, and the information agency. The last three posts were manned only during working hours. The consulate was where most of the problems occurred. From the Marine standpoint, there were several problems. One was that consular officers were slow as molasses. Another was that they were rude. And then, when they'd outraged somebody, they'd call the Marines to throw the guy out.... The CIA folks evidently resented wasting their valuable time giving out visas, no matter what their technical job description. The Commerce people never had such problems of, course.[5]

As for interaction with the local Iranian police, Svinth wrote that:

> The waiting room at the consulate was a big open room. Usually the Iranian security guards took care of most problems, but when they had problems they'd call for Marines, too. Now that always made no sense to me — the Marine usually spoke no Farsi, the Iranian spoke just as little English, and the Marine was supposed to defuse the situation. But usually, it worked, Lord knows why. Sergeant Mike Mayhem had the best solution for problems I'd heard, though. He'd walk out there and start looking around. Then he'd hold up a gas grenade and say, "Excuse me. Excuse me. I lost the pin to my grenade around here someplace. It's this round thing, you know? If you see it, could you let me know? The place would clear out like magic. Then he'd go back to drinking tea from glasses with the Iranian guards.[6]

Sergeant Svinth recalled that the Iranian guards oftentimes "got a little hostile" in their dealings with the Marines. While these tense situations with the Iranian guards (and civil-

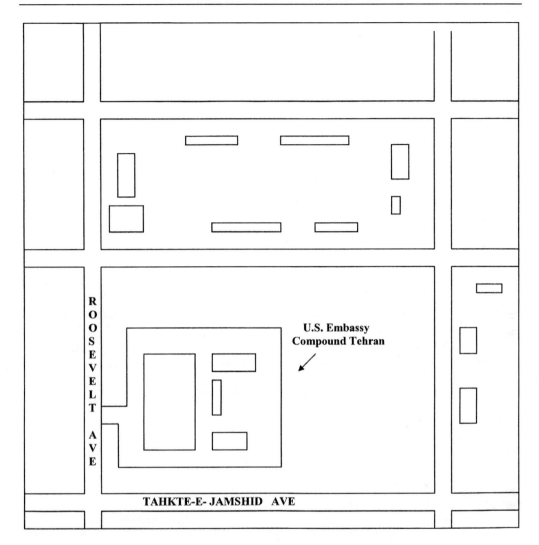

**U.S. Embassy
Compound Tehran**

Map 5. Location of the U.S. Embassy in Tehran, Iran (S-3 Archives, Marine Security Guard Battalion).

ians) were oftentimes resolved without incident, this clash of cultures served as one of the causes of the Iranian Revolution — the perceived arrogance of the Americans and their insensitivity to Iranian culture. Svinth later recalled that he and the other Marine Security Guards were "tolerated," and not too well liked. Indeed, Svinth remembered that when his tour of duty ended in Iran (four months prior to the overthrow of the Shah), he was all but glad to be leaving. Svinth stated, "The whole time I was in Iran the embassy folks kept telling us that the Iranians loved us. 'Hmm'— every time I rode from the consulate to the embassy in uniform I felt like George Armstrong Custer attending a convention of Lakota hairdressers. Walking around town out of uniform wasn't a whole lot better. I figured if hassled I'd say I was from Penticton Landing, BC, which is about three hours east of Vancouver."[7]

Sergeant Svinth admitted that part of the problem Marine Security Guards in Tehran had was that "there was little attempt to get us involved with the local community." This was due to fears on the part of the embassy officials that the Marines might become either a target for terrorists or singled out because of their association with the Shah's regime. In fact, Svinth recalled that this was one of the few criticisms he had of State Department officials in Tehran. The former Marine Security Guard claimed that this non-fraternization policy further exacerbated a tense situation at Tehran that was already a hardship post. "Instead," Sergeant Svinth remembered, "everybody, from the ambassador on down, dealt almost solely with the Iranian officials and the U.S., Canadian, and British communities. Worse, only rarely did anyone leave downtown Tehran. A very depressing way to exist, I assure you."[8]

By the time of the Shah's exile on January 16, 1979, the anti–Americanism that Svinth and his fellow Marines felt in Tehran in the late 1970s began to spill over onto the world stage by the seizure of the U.S. Embassy in Tehran by supporters of the Ayatollah Ruhollah Khomeini.

The First Hostage Crisis of 14 February 1979

From January through December 1978, the Shah attempted with little success to silence or suppress the street demonstrations that demanded his abdication. From Paris, Khomeini continued his daily barrage of anti–Shah broadcasts that had found a receptive audience among the Shah's loyal army. One serious incident occurred on September 7, 1978, in Tehran in a bloody confrontation between the Shah's police and the demonstrators who shouted "Death to the Shah." On that day alone, hundreds of demonstrators were reportedly killed by bursts of machine gun and automatic rifle fire. As the demonstrations grew more and more violent, the Shah's response bordered on a series of weak compromises to the revolutionaries and religious authorities, and the appointment of Dr. Shahpour Bakhtiar, a Western-educated moderate who had supported the first revolution against the Shah in 1951.[9] Dr. Bakhtiar, who was the last prime minister appointed by the Shah, immediately called for the Shah to leave Iran, the secret police to be disbanded, and the punishment of those who had killed demonstrators. The Shah, not wishing to drown the streets of Tehran with the blood of his citizens, and under increasing pressure from the United States to abdicate, left Iran on January 16, 1979. What was left of the Shah's army soon defected and joined the ranks of demonstrators, who now clamored for the establishment of an Islamic republic.[10]

As Iranians battled each other in the streets of Tehran and elsewhere in Iran, Ambassador William Sullivan asked for and received permission to augment the Marine Security Guard detachment in Tehran by six guards. These additional Marine Security Guards came directly from posts throughout Company B. As early as December 24, 1978, the violence that had engulfed Tehran for nearly eleven months touched the United States when Iranian revolutionaries conducted a terrorist-type attack against the main gate of the U.S. Embassy in Tehran. As a result, Ambassador Sullivan decided to replace the local guards on the outside wall with Marines. In spite of the fact that this went against normal operating procedures, Ambassador Sullivan's decision was meant to prevent the embassy from being penetrated by terrorists.[11]

Throughout the month of January, as the political situation in Iran continued to deteriorate, the Marines were subject to harassment by local Iranians as well as intermittent sniper fire. Occasionally, a stray round would find its way into the embassy compound. When the Iranian military proclaimed its neutrality in the struggle between the various political factions, the Iranian troops that had previously guarded the outer perimeter of the embassy were withdrawn. Ambassador Sullivan, who realized that this move further endangered the remaining personnel inside the embassy, placed the Marines and other U.S. military personnel on 24-hour alert, and armed them with a variety of weapons that included Uzi submachine guns, M-16s, shotguns (with # 9 skeet shot shells), and .38 and .357 Magnum pistols. Svinth added that most of the Marines also had the means to employ the shotgun with tear gas, as they were familiar with the employment of tear gas grenades and knew when to use them.[12] Despite the departure of the Shah and appointment of Shahpour Bakhtiar as prime minister, the violence continued, as pro-shah, Marxist, Kurd, and pro–Khomeini supporters battled each other in the streets of Tehran.

The government of Shahpour Baktiar lasted only a month as the forces loyal to Ayatollah Khomeini turned their venom toward the Shah's appointee. On February 1, 1979, a huge *Air France* jetliner landed at Tehran's Mehrabad Airport carrying the man who from a half a continent away laid the foundation for the ouster of his arch enemy, Shah Mohammed Reza Pahlavi. As the Ayatollah Khomeini emerged from the aircraft and entered an awaiting vehicle that shortly thereafter whisked him through the streets of the capital, the crowds jammed the streets and greeted their new supreme ruler, shouting pro–Khomeini, anti–Shah slogans.

Shortly after establishing himself at the Alawi Girls school in Tehran, Khomeini began to lay the groundwork for what he had clamored for in France: an Islamic republic. Shahpour Baktiar, who had already fled Iran, had been replaced in the interim by Dr. Mehdi Bazargan, an Iranian nationalist and Islamic scholar, who became the Western façade of a revolution that was now experiencing dissension from within its own ranks. Much of this opposition came from the Iranian Communists (Tudeh), Mujahadin Khalq, and several moderate religious clerics, including the Ayatollahs Ali Shariati and Teleghani.[13]

Meanwhile, the deposed Shah, now a man in essence without a home, began his long odyssey that would eventually take him to the United States and trigger one of the most humiliating affairs in U.S. history. After spending several days in Egypt as the guest of President Anwar el-Sadat, the Shah flew on to Morocco, where he remained as the guest of King Hassan before flying to the Bahamas on March 30, 1979. The Shah had hoped that the United States would grant him permission to live in exile there. Events in Tehran, however, soon forced the Carter administration to refrain from any invitation to the deposed monarch that might possibly trigger a violent response against the Americans living there. One of these events occurred on February 14, 1979, when Iranian militants launched the first of two attacks on the U.S. Embassy in Tehran.

Somewhat oblivious of the internal opposition to his rule, Khomeini continued to implement his vision of an Islamic republic. While Bazargan formed his cabinet, Iranian Marxists saw a window of opportunity in the confusion and mayhem that existed in Tehran after Khomeini's seizure of power. In fact, the Mujahedin Khalq and other pro–Marxist groups who allied with the anti–Shah forces to overthrow the monarchy now turned their attention to overthrowing Khomeini, who they feared would begin purging them along with members of the former regime. In a centuries' old Iranian practice of using foreigners to influence elections, the Mujahedin Khalq and other dissident Iranian political groups sought to use this method as a political leverage against their opponents — the mullahs and other Islamists in Khomeini's government. Part of this strategy was to seize foreigners as hostages.[14]

Throughout the confusion and bloodletting of the Iranian Revolution, the U.S. Embassy in Tehran remained untouched by the sea of violence swirling about the city. Nonetheless, the State Department soon ordered non-essential personnel home. In fact, since the beginning of the events that led to the Shah's exile and Khomeini's return, over 25,000 of the estimated 40,000 American citizens had already left Iran. By February 1979, there were still an

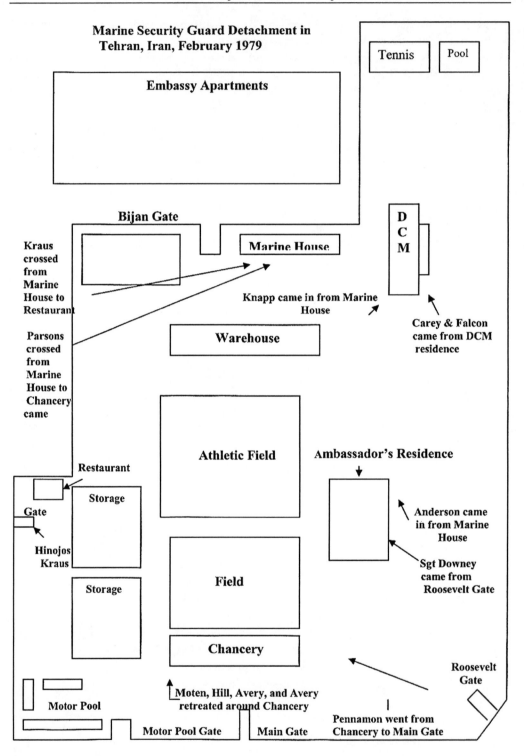

Diagram 4. Marine Security Guard positions inside U.S. diplomatic compound during the first hostage crisis in Iran, in February 1979 (U.S. Marine Security Guard Battalion).

estimated 10,000 Americans in Tehran and throughout the country. The U.S. ambassador to Iran, William Sullivan, acting on orders from Washington, D.C., warned the remaining Americans that "all American citizens except diplomatic personnel could no longer be protected and should leave the country."[15] Quietly, Americans began to leave Iran on chartered and individual flights. Despite the constant anti–American rhetoric that streamed from the daily protests and officials in Khomeini's entourage, "no American had been attacked." This changed, however, as the Iranian revolutionaries sought to resolve their internal political differences through the use of the most convenient target inside Iran: the U.S. diplomatic community in Tehran.

Prior to the seizure of the American hostages, Marine Security Guards had been operating under some confusion as to the rules of engagement if, indeed, the embassy were to be seized by the militants. As the Iranian Army withdrew from the embassy's outer perimeter, Ambassador Sullivan instructed Gunnery Sergeant Willie Sutton to position his Marine Security Guards in a manner in which they could defend the perimeter of the embassy. Besides the tactical positions they assumed inside the compound, the Marines were unsure as to the rules of engagement, particularly when and whom they could fire upon. Indeed, throughout the entire ordeal, starting on 10 February 1979, Marine Security Guards assumed that they were under strict orders not to use their weapons except as a last resort. Likewise, "all were sure that the Ambassador did not want them to defend to the death, but none were sure of their authority to engage." While all of the leathernecks inside the embassy compound realized that there would be "some type of terrorist attack" made against the embassy, none of the Marines thought that the attackers would seize the entire compound.[16]

At approximately 10:00 A.M., local time, Sergeant Gary N. Downey observed two Iranians in uniform on the top of the embassy's gatehouse roof. While Sergeant Downey immediately reported the presence of the intruders, one of the Iranians began looking around the compound. The intruders were shortly joined by four more uniformed and jean-clad Iranians, who sprayed the compound with automatic rifle fire. Even as Sergeant Downey reported the initial sighting, two of the Iranians jumped into the compound, shot the lock away to the main gate, known as the Roosevelt Gate, and swung it open. Sergeant Downey, who was watching all of this unfold while he was on the radio, asked for and received permission to fire tear gas grenades at what now appeared to be a flood of people pouring through the gate. The Iranians, who numbered about fifty, and had successfully penetrated the U.S. Embassy's compound, took aim at Sergeant Downey with automatic weapons and opened fire. The Marine sergeant, who had let loose a bombardment of five tear gas grenades via a launcher, began to lob the grenades himself as it was faster and allowed him to cover a wider area. As the Marine sergeant prepared to lob the last grenade, a bullet whacked the grenade from his hand. Unhurt though startled, Sergeant Downey radioed Post One for permission to fall back toward the ambassador's residence. Along with a soldier from the U.S. Army, the Marine Security Guard fell back to the patio of Ambassador Sullivan's residence. Here, another Marine Security Guard, Corporal Roarke L. Anderson, joined the two Americans who had heard Sergeant Downey's transmission and request to open fire with tear gas grenades while still in the Marine House several hundred yards away from the ambassador's residence.

As it became apparent that the embassy was under attack, the other Marine Security Guards, who had just finished their shifts, quickly dressed and rushed to their assigned positions. By now, there was firing everywhere as sniper fire pinned down two Marines, Sergeant Kenneth L. Kraus, who eventually made his way to the restaurant despite the murderous fire, and Sergeant Glenn R. Parsons, who had to cross an open field. As expected, Iranian snipers made the crossing difficult.[17]

Throughout the first hours of the siege, the action focused on the deputy chief of missions' (DCM) quarters. Lance Corporal William M. Carey, Jr., whose assignment was the DCM's residence, radioed for assistance. Within minutes, Sergeant Donald R. Knapp and Corporal Anderson joined him on the patio of the diplomat's residence. Sergeant Downey, meanwhile, continued to radio for assistance. Borrowing Sergeant Carey's walkie-talkie, Corporal Anderson informed Downey that he was on his way. Meanwhile, enemy rounds began to hit all around Carey and Anderson. By now, enemy fire engulfed the compound as the Marine Security Guards re-grouped. As he prepared to move out toward a warehouse located on the embassy grounds, Sergeant Carey noticed seven men on top of a building north of the compound. Pinned down by enemy fire, and armed only with No. 9 skeet shot, the Marine corporal nevertheless emptied his shotgun toward the intruders and re-loaded with No. 4 shot and continued to fire as he maneuvered toward the warehouse. When he was in position to make one last dash, he radioed Knapp to open the door to the warehouse. As the door opened to the warehouse, Corporal Carey rushed inside.[18]

The firing inside the embassy compound continued. Armed with only .38 pistols and shotguns, Sergeant Miller and Corporal Rayfield scanned the walls of the main gate in search of the sniper fire that seemed to have come out of nowhere. As the two Marines fell back from the main gate in order to obtain a better field of fire, Iranian snipers opened up all around the now exposed Marines. Joined by another Marine Security Guard, Sergeant Ronald Miller, the three Marines built a makeshift barricade from empty packing crates. This proved to be only a temporary measure, however, as bullets tore away at the flimsy defenses. Nevertheless, all three Marines were able to make it into the warehouse where the other MSG's were hunkered down. Gunnery Sergeant Sutton approached "cowboy," Ambassador William Sullivan's code-name for inter-embassy communications, and asked permission to return fire. Ambassador Sullivan told Sutton, "If you need to protect yourselves, you may fire. If you can arrange to surrender, do so."[19]

At the motor pool, Sergeant Steward D. Hill and Corporals Theodore Avery, Jr., likewise received a heavy volume of sniper fire. Despite the fact the Marines had Ambassador Sullivan's permission to return fire, they had failed to sight any visible target to shoot at. Not wishing to hit innocent bystanders, the Marines continued to hold their fire.[20] As they made their way across the embassy's parking lot, Sergeant Hill and Corporals Avery and Leonard Moten came across two unarmed civilians who they left hiding underneath a parked car.

Later, it was discovered that the attackers, both men and women, belonged to the *Cherikhaya Fedaye Khalq*, a Marxist guerrilla group that had hoped to embarrass the government of Ayatollah Khomeini into granting it political concessions. Meanwhile, fighting broke out in other parts of Tehran, where the guerrillas and their supporters fought Khomeini's loyalists and Iranian soldiers. At one point, fighting raged at the National Radio Station between the two sides. In an appeal to his followers, Khomeini urged his followers to put down the rebellion that he said had been caused by members of the former Iranian secret police, SAVAK, and other pro–Shah elements seeking to embarrass the Islamic Republic. In fact, in a scenario that would not be repeated nine months later, Tehran Radio broadcast appeals from Khomeini and the ruling Revolutionary Council to their followers to rescue the trapped Americans at the embassy.

Eventually, both Sergeant Downey and Corporal Anderson were the first to heed the ambassador's advice and surrender, and this only after a heroic stance inside the Ambassador's residence forced the two Marines to lay down their arms. Sergeant Larry A. Pennamon as well as a member of the U.S. Navy fought attackers that attempted to storm the main gate in front of the chancery. Both Americans stubbornly fought off the attackers with shotguns and pistols. Running out of ammunition, both sought cover inside the gatehouse, locked the door and hid their weapons. Eventually, both Pennamon and the Navy man were forced to surrender to the guerrillas.

William Branigin, a reporter with the *Washington Post*, recorded that upon receipt of the Ambassador's order to lay down their arms, one of the Marines "dejectedly replied, *aye aye sir*" and surrendered to the Iranians. At 11:37 A.M., the fighting inside the compound went on. In one instance, a Marine was overheard on a walkie-talkie telling another Marine still resisting, "How can I surrender? There's too many people around me shooting. How can I surrender?"[21] Corporals Fred J. Schmidt, B.D. Garcia, Michael Rayfield, and Michael Laurent, as well as Sergeant Donald Knapp, battled the guerrillas at the Bijan Gate where, prior to the attack, Corporal Rayfield had been talking with an American woman who was trying to get a passport for her Iranian husband. After the attack began, Corporal Rayfield escorted the woman and her husband into the safety of the Marine House.

Meanwhile, the fighting shifted from the ambassador's residence to the adjacent restaurant where Sergeants Kenneth L. Kraus and Jack M. Hinojos and Corporal Henry C. Lojkuc had assumed their defensive positions as the siege began. Armed with pistols and shotguns, the Marines quickly began gathering up about 30 civilians who had sought refuge in the abandoned restaurant, in order to protect them from the mob. With the compound and ambassador's residence seized, the last two buildings yet to be penetrated by the guerrillas were the restaurant and Main Chancery.

Still refusing to surrender, the Marines prepared to defend the restaurant with what few weapons they had in their possession. Also, the Marines broke broom handles and stuffed them inside the door to prevent them from being forced open. All of these measures were temporary, however, as the demonstrators were able to force their way through the doors and into the restaurant. All the while this was occurring, a local Iranian girl attempted to talk to the guerrillas into letting them all leave. Then,

> As the attackers broke into the restaurant, a local employee stepped into their [the guerrillas] view and was shot. He fell between [Sergeants] Kraus and Hinojos. All the people in the restaurant were ordered outside. Their captors were dressed in civilian clothes, and several had on business suits. Three Marines were made to kneel in a row, and each one thought they were going to be shot. One of the captors approached Kraus and implied that he did not know how long he could hold the others back unless the weapons were turned over to them. Lojkuc was struck several times by some of the other captors, and several of the civilians were being pushed around and struck. Kraus agreed to show them where the weapons were. He returned to the restaurant with three of the captors and showed them where he had hid his shotgun. The man in the suit asked where the rest of the weapons were. Kraus said there were no more, that they were only security troops and all they had were light weapons. A second man struck Kraus in the ribs with his rifle butt, knocking Kraus to the ground. The man who had retrieved the shotgun then aimed it at Kraus and suddenly it went off. Kraus heard, rather than felt the explosion, and wasn't sure if he had been hit or not. He lapsed into semiconsciousness. He does remember that he was bleeding from the head. [Sergeant] Hinojos and [Corporal] Lojkuc heard the shot but did not know what had happened until Kraus was brought out on a stretcher. Hinojos believed that Kraus was alive because he saw him move and could see him breathing. He was not sure how badly Kraus had been injured, but he did not see much blood. Kraus was then removed on the stretcher, and Hinojos and Lojkuc were taken to the Ambassador's residence by the guerrillas.[22]

As the guerrillas assaulted the embassy, and it became apparent that the entire compound would be overrun, Ambassador Sullivan ordered the Marines and remaining diplomatic staff inside the Main Chancery and communications room to begin shredding classified material and destroying communications equipment. In fact, when the siege began, Sergeant Glenn C. Parsons, Lance Corporal Edwin C. Falcon, and Gunnery Sergeant Sutton were on duty in the Main Chancery. As the other Marines took up their respective positions inside and around the embassy compound, Gunnery Sergeant Sutton, Sergeant Parsons, and Lance Corporal Falcon were able to monitor the battle as it proceeded toward the Main Chancery, by way of the many cameras positioned all around the embassy. In fact, as the attackers steadily overwhelmed the other Marines, it became apparent to the three Marines inside the chancery that it wouldn't be too long before the attackers turned their attention toward the Main Chancery itself. As Lance Corporal Falcon gave Sergeant Downey permission to open fire, a bullet penetrated the main door of the chancery. Both Gunnery Sergeant Sutton and Lance Corporal Falcon quickly hit the floor as more rounds followed. As Lance Corporal Falcon looked at the monitors for any activity while Gunnery Sergeant Sutton, who by now had heard over the radio that a group of Marines were heading toward the chancery, got up and headed for the basement to open the door for them. As the cameras outside the chancery were now destroyed, Lance Corporal Falcon observed a large crowd heading toward the main entrance of the chancery and main gate. The main action then turned to the mob that had entered the chancery. The main concern of the Marines turned toward the destruction of classified material and any sensitive equipment. As the Marines secured the door, the other leathernecks fired their weapons into the air to provide cover.

By this time, the chancery had become a bullet "magnet," as a large volume of fire ricocheted off the building and more specifically, the front door. Sergeants Thomas and Parsons, as well as Corporals Avery and Moten, continued to lob gas grenade after gas grenade at the demonstrators, who by now were trying to get inside the chancery. Gunnery Sergeant Sutton later wrote that during the attack, the Marines valiantly fought to prevent just such a penetration:

> Several of the Marines grabbed nearby objects and attempted to blockade the door, Parsons noticed bullets digging into the floor as if fired from a high angle. As firing increased against the doors and windows, the Marines retreated down the hallway. As they cleared the hallway, Thomas began to throw tear gas grenades down the hall. Parsons joined him, and the two of them threw several dozen grenades. The persons handing the grenades to them were pulling the pins, and one of the grenades went off in Thomas' hand, burning him on the arm and shoulder. Falcon, had heard the transmission that Downey and Anderson had surrendered, and also the transmission that the Marines at the Bijan Gate had retreated into the warehouse. Shortly after these transmissions, the word was passed for everyone to get upstairs. The Ambassador announced for everyone to lay down their weapons and surrender if possible.[23]

One of the Marine Security Guards, Corporal Wade S. Jeffries, who had been sleeping in the Marine House after having stood his watch, awoke to the sound of intense gunfire. While gunfire in Tehran was not unusual, the Marine corporal thought nothing of it until three Iranians showed up at the Marine House. Corporal Jeffries remembered that he then turned his radio on and heard something to the effect that the ambassador had just ordered the Marines to surrender. Realizing that the embassy probably had been under siege, Jeffries locked the door and waited for about thirty minutes in his room before the three Iranians forced the door to his room and captured him.

At the chancery the Marines continued to assist State Department officials and staff with the destruction of the communications equipment and shredding of classified documents. This continued until the attackers managed to break down the door leading to the second floor, where the remainder of the embassy staff had assembled, and entered the room where the destruction of equipment and documents had been taking place. All of the personnel were ordered into the ambassador's suite. As the Marines were the only ones in uniform, the attackers repeatedly searched and treated them rather roughly. Several times during this process, the attackers screamed at the Marines and pointed their loaded weapons at them. Several of the Marines likewise observed the attackers pushing Ambassador Sullivan around as well as putting a knife to his throat.[24]

By this time, all of the Marines, with the exception of the ones in the warehouse, had been captured and repeatedly searched. The RSO then got on the radio and ordered all the remaining Marines (Laurent, Rayfield) to lay down their weapons and surrender. Once Corporals Laurent and Rayfield emerged for the warehouse, the other Americans followed shortly thereafter. The attackers then gathered them up, searched them, and took them to the ambassador's residence, where the other Americans were being held.

At 11:49 A.M., a cheer went up among the American captives as it had been reported that followers of the Ayatollah Khomeini had arrived, and had been fighting the Marxist guerrillas in and around the embassy compound. For the next several hours, the fighting continued with Khomeini's followers (identified by an armband with the words 'Islamic Army' on them) eventually gaining the upper hand. In fact, one representative of a *komiteh* (a revolutionary committee) armed only with a bayonet managed to reach Ambassador Sullivan amidst all of the confusion. Hugging the ambassador, the *komiteh* official assured the American diplomat that they had come to liberate them. Many of Khomeini's supporters, in fact, repeatedly assured the Americans, "You are our brothers. Don't worry." Sergeant Glenn C. Parsons, however, thought that Iranians had assembled the Marines together in order to execute them. The Marine sergeant believed that a BBC camera crew filming the embassy takeover was an execution squad until he saw the ambassador talking to an Iranian in a robe.[25]

After several hours, the attackers were eventually driven off or had simply melted away from the American Embassy into the streets of Tehran. During the attack on the embassy, the Marine Security Guards managed to kill three of the attackers while one local Iranian civilian had been accidentally killed in the restaurant. Two Marine Security Guards were wounded in the attack.[26]

"One of our Marines is missing"

Once order had been restored, the Iranians restricted the movement of the Marines inside the embassy and placed three Iranian guards at each entrance. Meanwhile, Gunnery Sergeant Sutton re-assigned his Marines to their respective posts. Still unresolved, however, was the whereabouts of Sergeant Kenneth L. Kraus, who had been wounded during the siege. Apparently, the Iranians had taken him first to a local hospital where doctors treated his wounds before revolutionary guards kidnapped him from his hospital bed and took him to a nearby prison. While the Carter administration secretly negotiated for his safe return, the ambassador downplayed the Marine's disappearance from the Tehran hospital by telling newsmen that Sergeant Kraus had been transferred to another hospital. At the prison, Kraus was still wearing pajamas issued by the hospital. The Iranians interrogated him and attempted (with no success) to have him make anti–American and anti–Shah statements as well as sign false confessions. At one point during the interrogations, Iranian Assistant Prime Minister Amir Entezam hinted at the possibility that Kraus would be "tried for crimes" committed at the

General Louis H. Wilson, commandant of the Marine Corps (1976–1980), accompanies Marine Sergeant Kraus (front) as he makes his way off the airplane that brought him home from captivity in the immediate aftermath of the first hostage crisis in Tehran, Iran, February 1979 (courtesy U.S. Marine Corps).

time of the attack on the U.S. Embassy. Mr. Entezam made specific reference to the deaths of the three Marxist guerrillas supposedly killed by the Marines as they attempted to storm the embassy. Ambassador Sullivan dismissed the charges, however, by stating that the guerrillas died as a result of the cross fire that erupted in the courtyard of the compound.[27] After a week-long captivity, the Iranians released the Marine sergeant, who was eventually flown home to Lancaster, Pennsylvania, to a hero's welcome, for which Governor Richard Thornburg proclaimed "Sergeant Kenneth L. Kraus Day" in honor of the freed Marine Security Guard.[28]

For their bravery while under fire during the siege at the U.S. Embassy in Tehran, five of the Marines were recognized for heroism and awarded Navy Commendation Medals. Corporal Roark L. Anderson's citation noted that he "held off his attackers until his tear gas grenades were expended." Sergeant Gary N. Downey was cited for "staying at his post until a gas grenade was shot from his hand and he was forced to surrender." Sergeant Jack M. Hinojos was likewise cited for having "moved civilians to the kitchen [of the restaurant]" to safety before helping to secure an outside gate and returning to the restaurant. Lance Corporal Edwin C. Falcon, who was at Post One when it came under fire, was specifically cited for his bravery under fire and having remained at his post in order to monitor the embassy's television cameras "that allowed him to open the doors letting in Americans trapped outside." Lance Corporal Falcon's citation noted the fact that upon being ordered to leave the desk, he helped in the destruction of classified material until captured by the guerrillas. Sergeant Kraus, who had been awarded a Purple Heart for wounds he received during the attack, was also awarded a Navy Commendation Medal for bravery while under fire and later his refusal to give into the demands of his Iranian captors.[29] Embarrassed by the hostage takeover, the first of two at the U.S. Embassy in Tehran, the government of Medhi Bazargan apologized to President Carter for the incident and pledged good relations with the United States.[30] This first takeover of the U.S. Embassy gave notice that the U.S. Embassy and its personnel were now pawns in the power struggle waged among the Marxists, the clergy, and other dissident groups over who would control Iran.[31]

Before the Deluge: An Uneasy Peace in Tehran, March–October 1979

As the Marine Security Guards in Tehran resumed their routine assignments, the situation in Iran temporarily stabilized. Ambassador Sullivan, who had hoped to establish a dialogue with the revolutionary government, passed instructions to his staff, including the Marine Security Guards, that they were to avoid at all times any incident that might provoke a repeat of the February 14 takeover. Indeed, during the siege the Iranians singled out the Marines for "special treatment." Sergeant Glenn Parsons, who had moved rather slow when one of his captors ordered him to move along, was spat upon and subjected to some verbal abuse about the United States in Vietnam. During his brief captivity, Sergeant Parsons "went out of his way to antagonize his captors," particularly over the way in which the demonstrators ransacked the Marine House. Ambassador Sullivan ordered Sergeant Parsons out of Tehran as a precautionary move to avoid another attack on the embassy.[32] Also, by November of 1979, the State Department had replaced all of the Marine Security Guards present during this first siege with new arrivals to prevent bad feelings from spilling into the streets of Tehran.

President Carter ordered a reduction in the diplomatic staff to less than 75 people, down from the 1,100 or so who resided there before the overthrow of the Shah.[33] Also, as President Carter wrote, those involved "revamped the embassy's security features," placing a greater reliance on the host government's ability to prevent a hostile takeover.

Besides the increased security measures, the State Department replaced Ambassador Sullivan with Chargé d'Affaires Bruce Laingen as the head of the U.S. Embassy in Tehran. The change in personnel (including the normal rotation of the Marine Security Guards) and improved security measures were undertaken by the Carter Administration to prevent a repeat of the embassy takeover and lessen tensions with the government of Ayatollah Khomeini. Iranian Foreign Minister Ibrahim Yazdi had indicated as much in a speech on May 5, 1979, where he called for, among other things, an improvement in relations with the United States.[34] Tragically, events in Mexico and Tehran during the spring and summer of 1979 would lead to a second, longer-lasting takeover of the U.S. Embassy.

In Mexico, Shah Mohammed Reza Pahlavi had been diagnosed with lymphoma, a cancer that demanded hospitalization and treatment. At the urgings of both former Secretary of State Kissinger and banker David Rockefeller, President Carter permitted the exiled Shah to enter the United States for treatment in a New York City hospital. The Iranians, who had long memories of the overthrow of Prime Minister Mossadeq by the Central Intelligence Agency and SAVAK, saw this move on the part of the Carter Administration as a veil to re-install the Shah back on the throne in Iran and overthrow their revolution.

As the Shah flew to New York, the various Iranian political factions jockeyed for power as Khomeini's followers continued to lay the foundation for the creation of an Islamic state that by the end of the summer of 1979 began to take shape. With Medhi Bazargan's moderate government now dominated by four clerics close to the Ayatollah Khomeini (including Ali Akbar Hahemi Rafsanjani and Ali Khameni), the Assembly of Experts unveiled a draft constitution that was far from what Khomeini and his Revolutionary Council had envisioned. The document, moderate even by strict Islamic standards, was ultimately rejected and replaced by one that recognized Khomeini as the *Faqih* or *Supreme Jurisprudent*— the supreme religious and political figure. By terms of the constitution, Iran became an Islamic state in theory and practice, run by the mullahs.[35]

A week before Iranians were to vote on the new constitution with Khomeini becoming *Faqih*, the ayatollah warned his followers that "dissenters" conspired to defeat the referendum and plotted the destruction of the Islamic republic through the election. This was the signal that triggered the second and longer-lasting hostage crisis at the U.S. Embassy.

The Second Embassy Takeover, 4 November 1979

About 9:00 A.M. on November 4, 1979, a group of about 100 protestors, who called themselves The Students Following the Imam's Line,[36] sent a group of chador-covered[37] women, who shouted over and over "Death to America" and waved pro–Khomeni, anti–American banners as a much larger group of students, numbering about 1,000, marched passed the U.S. Embassy shaking their fists and shouting the same slogans as the Iranian women. While the Marine stationed at Post One observed the group in front of the embassy via the gate-mounted camera, a group of students were observed climbing over the gate that led to the motor pool. Many of the local guards on duty shortly thereafter abandoned their posts, virtually leaving the outer embassy compound defenseless against what was now a large number of protestors. The Marine Security Guard, realizing that another siege was in progress, alerted his comrades living in the Marine House, located behind the main chancery outside the compound. Before these leathernecks could react, however, protestors broke into the Marine House, forcing the Americans to go to the 7th floor, where they watched with amazement the events now unfolding.[38]

Meanwhile, Marine Security Guards on duty in the chancery detected that intruders were now in the basement. With loaded shotguns and tear gas grenades, two Marines went downstairs to investigate. Reaching the stairwell to the basement, the Marines discovered that a crowd of Iranians had entered the building. The Marines pointed their shotguns toward the demonstrators and ordered them to halt. Still awaiting permission to open fire from Mr. Laingen, who was at the Iranian Foreign Ministry, the Marines pulled the pins of the tear gas grenades though did not let go of the spoon. In the excitement, however, two or three of the grenades dropped out of their carriers' hands or exploded, sending a cloud of tear gas onto the crowds that momentarily halted their ascent up the stairs of the main floor of the chancery. Meanwhile, the regional security officer (RSO) emerged to talk with the crowd outside the embassy to try to defuse the situation. This was to no avail, as the demonstrators threw a rope around his neck and tied his hands behind his back. The RSO then ordered the Marines to open the door of the chancery so the students could enter the building and perform a "sit in." The Marine NCOIC refused until ordered a second time by the RSO, who by now ordered that all of the Marines thrown down their weapons and surrender. As all of this was going down, Marines inside the vault room were busily shredding classified material until the bound and blindfolded RSO appeared outside the room with his captors and demanded that they stop what they were doing.[39] Inside the chancery, the Iranians who had managed to enter through the unlocked window in the basement proceeded to round up every American in the building, including the Marine Security Guards. The Iranians then marched the Americans, blindfolded and with pistols to their heads, out of the Main Chancery to an army of protestors and world journalists. All of the Marines, including the diplomatic personnel inside the embassy, were paraded outside to the crowds and scores of reporters who had gathered to watch the event. Eventually, all of the Americans inside the compound were taken hostage and herded together with the other American captives. Day One of what would be a siege of 444 days had begun.

While the Carter Administration wrestled with the Iranian government and a chorus of domestic critics who demanded a tough response to this outrage, President Carter cautioned his countrymen that for the time-being, diplomacy, not military force, was the best option to insure the safety and release of the hostages. Meanwhile, the Iranian government sought to divide the American nation in its order to the students that all women and African Americans be released. This action by the Iranian government set off a wave of protests among former Marines and concerned Americans, who seemed confused over what appeared to be an act of treason on the part of the three Marines released.

As stated by Islamic revolutionaries, the Iranians released the Marines and Air Force members, all of African-American descent, and several women, out of humanitarian concerns, because the former were part of an "oppressed minority." The Marine Security Guards included Sergeants David Walker and Ladell Maples, and Corporal Westley Williams. They were joined shortly thereafter by fellow Marine Security Guard Sergeant William E. Quarles.[40]

What had touched off the controversy surrounding their release were statements made by those released, either out of coercion or naiveté over the presence of the Shah then in the United States, on the activities of the CIA in Iran, and the general anti–Americanism, fed largely by Iranian domestic politics.

Several critical letters that followed noted what the authors considered inappropriate behavior — abandonment of their fellow Marines and violation of the Code of Conduct that governs U.S. service members while in captivity. All of the letters, coming mainly from former Marines, and addressed to the commandant of the Marine Corps General Robert H. Barrow, cited a "breakdown in tradition," that Marines do not leave fellow Marines behind. One letter, written by a former Marine from Rochester, New York, to General Barrow stated:

> It has been my greatest displeasure to learn of the gross breakdown in tradition in the Marine Corps. According to a Canadian correspondent, he says that one of the two first Marine guards released from the American Embassy in Iran revealed openly to his captors where the Secrets were kept because he thought they would kill him. This is wonderful? ... Moreover, the women secretarial staff except for one were tied day and night to their chairs, yet these black guards were totally unharmed. They are not to be treated as heroes but should be tried for a general court martial![41]

Another former Marine was even more blunt in his assertion that the statements made by Sergeants William E. Quarles and Ladell Maples bordered on cowardice. To prove his point, the author of this letter, a Marine that had served throughout the Pacific campaign during World War II, returned his "honorable" discharge to the commandant's office. The Marine added in his letter to General Barrow that: "Their actions [Quarles and Maples] ... and the mouthings attributed to them, since their desertion of duty, is inexcusable to say the

Bottom to top: Sergeants Ledell Maples, William E. Quarles, David Walker, and Corporal Westley Williams, all members of the Marine Security Guard Detachment in Tehran, Iran, as well as several female members of the U.S. Embassy, exit an airplane after being released by their captors several weeks after the seizure of the embassy. The release of these Marines ignited much controversy as to the training and the adherence to the Code of Conduct governing captivity (U.S. Marine Security Guard Bn. photograph).

least. They have soiled the names of the Corps and the memory and spirit of all those who embraced them as comrades and shipmates. Even now as I write my mind races with the memory of the names and faces of wounded and dead comrades whose sacrifices and pain have been made a mockery of by these two unworthies."[42]

Another citizen, who went so far as to send his letter of displeasure to his Congressional representatives, claimed that the Marine Security Guards who left Iran "had a sworn duty and are honor bound to protect the citizens of the United States and to uphold the honor and integrity of our country."[43] The individual likewise claimed that the Marines who left Iran brought "disgrace and dishonor to those valiant men who have upheld this tradition in the past and who will do so in the future." One individual insisted that either the Marines who left Tehran and deserted their comrades be court-martialed or that the Marine Corps be disbanded. This same person added, "such cowardly behavior in World War II would have guaranteed a Japanese victory," and asked the question, "Where are our patriotic politicians?"[44] Finally, a former Marine officer, Homer B. Pettit, who had served in World War II and Korea, asserted in his letter to General Barrow that it was "inexcusable to me that these two would voluntarily leave their comrades behind after publicly espousing the 'revolutionary theme.' You and I know that no matter how frightened we might be it would have been unthinkable to leave before the others." Mr. Pettit pointedly asked the Commandant "how the Marine Corps could possibly recruit such people in the first place and then compound the mistake by sending them to a known trouble-spot like Iran — if we are to have guards at embassies they should be some of our very best. It was obvious to me that and others that these men were ill-equipped to handle this assignment and were fair game for the 'rebels.'"[45]

While Headquarter Marine Corps insisted that the Marines who left Tehran had not violated the Code of Conduct and that the Marines did nothing improper, it did little to stifle the wave of criticism aimed at the freed Marine Security Guards.[46]

As for the freed Marines, all insisted that they did nothing improper and, in fact, had participated in the defense of the Main Chancery on November 4, 1979. Corporal Westley Williams told reporters that he and another Marine "sweated heavily as they labored to pry open a case of rifles and .38-caliber revolvers kept on hand for emergencies. As they looked over their shoulders ... shouting militants mounted the stairs" as the Marines succeeded in breaking open the case. They stuffed pistols and tear gas grenades in their pockets, rushed to the second floor and took refuge behind a heavy security door. Corporal Westley Williams recalled that as he made his last entry in his log at 10:40 A.M., he noticed demonstrators were attempting to climb over the wall of the front gate of the embassy.[47]

Captivity at the Hands of the Iranian Militants, November 1979–January 1980

Eventually, the storm over the returned Marine Security Guards subsided as attention focused on the remaining Marines and diplomatic hostages, all of whom began one of the longest periods of captivity for U.S. service personnel since the return of the U.S. prisoners of war from North Vietnam in 1973. As the hostage crisis stretched into December 1979, the Carter Administration focused on the safe return of the captives. Meanwhile, the Marine Security Guards and other U.S. service members held prisoner continued to maintain their professionalism and dignity despite the efforts on part of the captors to force them to sign "confessions," and the repeated threats to place them on trial for espionage. Not all of the captured military personnel were Marine Security Guards. Other hostages taken included an Air Force officer and a army staff sergeant assigned as a military attaché. In fact, Staff Sergeant Donald Hohman, assigned to the U.S. Embassy in Tehran as an assistant military attaché, like his fellow Marines and airman, upheld the fine traditions of the U.S. Army while held captive by his refusal to collaborate with the Iranian militants.

During the initial period of captivity, which lasted from November 4, 1979, through January 1980, the hostages were moved from the U.S. Embassy to undisclosed locations throughout Tehran, partly to prevent any U.S. rescue attempt. "They (the Americans) were told from the very first that they would not be harmed, and they would be held as hostages until the Shah was released by the President." After the first two days of the crisis, the militants set about to organize the prisoners and move them from room to room or building to building. No one was together with another for more than two days. By the second day, most of the blindfolds had been removed, except for period when the militants transferred them. By the fourth day of the crisis, only two to four hostages were kept at the same location, as they were moved about Teheran approximately every four days.

They were fed regularly and ate the same food as the guards, who remained outside the room where the prisoners were being held. If a hostage required medical care, the captors provided a doctor or medical care. Captain Neal "Terry" Robinson, an administrator in the embassy's budget section recalled that the captors "were our fathers and mothers. We had to ask for everything."[48] While the prisoners were instructed to maintain their silence, there was little or no punishment if they spoke, as they were simply moved to a room by themselves. Many of the captors were students who were from 18 to 25 years old, and were eager to talk to the hostages about the crimes of the Shah. They told the American captives that "they would follow the wishes of Khomeini." They indicated that if the Ayatollah Khomeini instructed them to release the hostages, they would do so.[49]

As for the Marine Security Guards, they continued to resist the demands of their captors and were singled out by the Iranians. During their initial capture

the Marines were hostile, and were treated more roughly than the other prisoners. They were identified for the most part by their uniforms, and to some degree by their haircuts. There is some indications that members of the mob also knew the Marines. When the Marines were initially herded into the buildings, they were escorted by two Iranians, one on each side, while nearly all of the others were escorted only by one person. They [the Marines] were slow to carry out orders, very observant as they were taken to their rooms, and in general tried to find out what was going on. In three cases, they were kept blindfolded well after the blindfolds of the others had been taken off. Three of the Marines were taken to the Chancery building and ordered to open the safes. All three refused. All the Marines were aware of their obligations under the code of conduct. All of them believed that they have not collaborated with anyone in any way. None of them viewed the students as enemy. When the petitions were passed around for the prisoners to sign, the Marines first refused to sign anything. There was no threat from the guards, and no coercion to sign any document. When they were presented with later opportunities to sign documents, three of the four did sign, but signed with a view that nothing they did was degrading to themselves or to the U.S. They reviewed the wording of the statements, and they reviewed the names of those persons who had signed the statements. Among the names, was that of the Embassy Political Officer. Most of the Marines believed that because of that signature, it was all right to sign. The Marines were told they would be released shortly before the actual release. They were not told if anyone else was dead or alive, or if anyone else had been released. The first two who were released were told that they would be given a press conference prior to their release. At that press conference they answered nearly one hundred questions, and it was obvious that some of the answers were not satisfactory to their captors. But they were never pressured to change answers or say anything. The second two who were released were subjected to the same tactic, but were also told that two other black Marines had been released. When they were informed of this, both refused to leave, but were informed by the head of the press conference that they had no choice, since Khomeini had ordered it. They then went to the man and informed him that they did not want to leave unless all of the Marines were expelled, since none of the Marines were spies. The man they talked to said he would take that into consideration, but they would still leave. Both of these Marines were extremely bitter. (Both also were extremely sensitive to say anything because of the fact it may affect the other Marines.)[50]

From Desert One to Freedom, April 1979–January 1981

For the first few months of the hostage crisis, President Carter wisely chose to avoid threatening the Iranians, as he feared that the Iranians might retaliate and harm the American captives. In fact, as time went by, the Iranians set out to use the hostages as bargaining chips with the United States, which had frozen all Iranian assets and still refused to hand over the Shah, who by this time was dying of cancer.[51] The hostages had taken on a domestic political significance in the struggle for control of Iran between the hard liners in Khomeini's government and the moderate political leaders. The political hard liners, led by Khomeini, saw the hostages as a means of diversion while they strengthened their hold on the country while the moderates, led by Abolhassan Bani-Sadr and Sadegh Ghotbsadeh, favored their release. In the end, the hard liners won out, as both Sadegh Ghotbsadeh was later executed on the charge of treason and Bani-Sadr forced into exile.

Exasperated as to the endless rounds of negotiations that seemed to be going nowhere, President Carter was finally convinced to attempt a rescue mission. After a month of meticulous planning, and using a specially organized task force, U.S. Special Forces attempted to land on an abandoned landing strip 275 miles from Tehran, code-named Desert One. Once on the ground, the Special Forces, led by Colonel Charles Beckwith, were to head to Tehran in vehicles brought in by six C-30 Hercules and eight RH-53D Sea Stallions flown off the deck of the USS *Nimitz*. Once in Tehran, the force, known as Delta, was to storm the U.S. Embassy, kill or immobilize the Iranian guards and rescue the hostages. From the start of the operation, however, things went wrong. A sandstorm immobilized two of the helicopters and sent a third crashing into a parked C-130, killing eight servicemen. With news of the disaster at Desert One, President Carter immediately ordered an end to the rescue attempt.[52] Immediately, the Iranians saw this as another attempt by the United States to overthrow the legitimate government of Iran. The failure of Desert One not only sealed the fate of the hostages for another seven months but also gave Khomeini the excuse he and the other hardliners in his government had been looking for in order to "launch their final drive for absolute power."

The failure of the Iranian Rescue Mission went unnoticed by the hostages, as their Iranian captors imposed a complete news blackout. According to Corporal Steve Kirtley, after the failed rescue attempt the Iranians dispersed the hostages throughout Iran in case the United States should try another such mission. Corporal Kirtley, who completed Marine Security Guard School in July 1979 and whose first assignment brought him to Tehran, recalled that immediately after the failed rescue mission, conditions for the hostages once again worsened, as the Iranians feared an American attack. Corporal Kirtley recalled:

We were tied up for the next two months. Our shoes were taken away and we were forbidden to speak to one another. After a time, I and two others were taken on a bus to Isfahan where we were held for months. The two others got sick and were moved. I got sick, too, but I recovered and was kept there. Other hostages were then brought to where I was in Isfahan, and there were four of us when a van came to pick us up in July 1980. On the way back to Teheran [*sic*], the van had an accident and I was taken to the "holy city" of Qom, where we were held for about five days.[53]

Kirtley recalled that he and several of his fellow hostages eventually learned of the failed rescue mission when one of the Iranian captors let one of the hostages who, as it turned out, spoke fluent German, have a German magazine that had an article detailing the mission.[54]

In a large sense, the 444 days of captivity in Iran were interspersed with random acts of kindness and periods of extreme terror by the militants holding the Americans. According to Marine Lieutenant Colonel W.B. Clark, coordinator, Marine Corps Iranian Hostage Task Force, the hostages were eventually able to communicate with family members. At one point in March 1980, the Iranians permitted Corporal James Gallegos to call his father to let him know that "all of the hostages were basically ok." Corporal Gallegos likewise informed his father that "the students treat them well [and] say that they will not be harmed, but remain insistent that the hostages will not be released until the Shah is returned to Iran."[55]

Sometimes this benevolence did not always exist, as was evident in the accusations brought by one Iranian man, who claimed that he strangled his sister to death in order to "save my family's honor," because she had been allegedly made pregnant by one of the 50 American hostages. The hostage, later identified as Staff Sergeant Michael Moeller, apparently had intercourse with the woman, a student at Tehran's Teacher's College prior to the commencement of the hostage crisis. After discovering she was pregnant, she told her brother that she had been "raped by a taxi driver." Seeking to avenge the family's honor, the brother beat up the cab driver. Later, the woman confessed that "she had sexual relations with one of the spies now in the Embassy." The brother, enraged by the accusation, killed his sister in an abandoned alley in downtown Tehran, trying to make it appear as if she had committed suicide. The brother then turned himself in and told the Iranian magistrate, "This American spy must be executed ... I killed my sister only to save my family's honor and to erase from my family the disgraceful male seed left by this American spy."[56] After blood tests and several interviews, Iranian officials determined that Staff Sergeant Moeller was not, in fact, the father of the child, and that the charges had been false from the very start.

The captors would likewise distress the American victims by using their mail from home as psychological weapons. Here, the hostages would be subjected to the captors holding up the mail from home, and then to their horror, the letters would be set on fire. The Iranian militants would conduct mock executions with the hostages, play Russian roulette with the female hostages, and rouse their captives in the middle of the night on so-called "Gestapo Raids." There was physical abuse as well. Marine Sergeant Johnny Mckeel, Jr., remembered that one of these instances occurred when the Iranians, in order to extract military information, told him that his mother in Balch Springs, Texas, had died. When he still refused to talk, the Iranian guards knocked out a tooth. Other hostages were beaten repeatedly and placed in solitary confinement as punishment for trying to escape.[57]

In spite of the physical and psychological torture the Iranians subjected the American hostages to, the discipline exhibited by the Marine Security Guards served as an example for all who had come into contact with them. In fact, as Major Jeffrey T. Roland discovered in his interviews of the Marine captives in Tehran, each of the Marines, at one time or another, thought about escape, though decided at the last minute that it was unwise, as the embassy had been surrounded by chanting students. The Marine captives were more inclined to follow orders, which in the long run saved lives and prevented them and the civilian hostages from doing something that could have resulted in exacerbating the situation.

Major Roland pointed out that the Marines felt that the Department of State, and more specifically, the regional security officer, had betrayed them by not permitting them to defend the embassy in order to give the persons inside the vault more time to destroy classified information. "the Marines personally believed that they had not been kept informed of the developing situation, and were therefore not trusted, and not ready to do the best job." In short, the Marine Security Guards held hostage firmly believed that the situation in Tehran, while not avoidable, could have been better managed had a better working relationship with the Department of State and RSO existed. Also, as the hostage crisis unfolded, the curriculum and training at Marine Security Guard School quickly absorbed many of the lessons learned in Tehran. The visible lessons of the hostage crisis were soon applied to the training of future Marine Security Guards in order to prepare them for similar situations.[58]

The Crisis Ends

As the hostage crisis lingered, the American captives became part of the political tug-of-war between the moderate politicians and the hard-line supporters of the Ayatollah Khomeini. In March of 1980, the Iranian government took control of the hostages from the militants. At first, this seemed to send a glimmer of hope that the crisis could be resolved. Impasses over return of the Shah, who died in July 1980, the release of Iranian financial assets held in the United States and elsewhere, and the continued internal struggle for control of Iran, however, sabotaged any chance of resolution throughout the spring and summer of 1980.

With the Shah dead, it seemed that the last major obstacle had been removed in settling

The Marine Security Guards from the U.S. Embassy, Tehran, Iran, after their release from 444 days of captivity. They are shown here with Commandant of the Marine Corps Robert H. Barrow (center) on January 27, 1981 (courtesy U.S. Marine Corps).

the differences between the United States and Iran. As President Carter engaged in a bitter re-election campaign and an insurgency from within his own party, led by Senator Edward Kennedy, and later with his Republican rival, former California Governor Ronald Reagan, the crisis lingered into the early and late fall. Finally, what may have convinced the Ayatollah Khomeini that the hostages no longer served a domestic political purpose was Iraq's invasion of Iran on September 22, 1980. Already isolated in the world's diplomatic community for its seizure of the American hostages, as well as its vociferous support for the overthrow of the more moderate Gulf States in the Persian Gulf, the Ayatollah Khomeini ordered the Americans released. In its last snub of the Carter administration, the Iranian government, after settling the issues over Iran's frozen assets and other issues, thanks largely to the efforts of the Algerian government, held the American hostages to the very hour of President-elect Ronald Reagan's inauguration on 21 January 1981.

On the morning of January 21, 1981, all of the 52 American hostages boarded an Algerian airliner at Tehran Airport, and as President-elect Reagan raised his right hand to take the oath of office, the jet took off, ending one of the most humiliating incidents of modern American diplomatic history. In the 444 days the Americans remained captive in Iran, it was a credit to the training and professionalism of the Marine Security Guards who set the example during the entire crisis that maintained the spirits of all 52 hostages.

In a letter to Mrs. Lisa Moeller, the wife of Staff Sergeant Mike Moeller, Chargé d'Affaires Bruce Laingen praised the Marine Security Guard's professionalism and told her "of the fine job" he did in Tehran. Mr. Laingen likewise praised the entire Marine detachment as "being the finest he had ever known." Laingen wrote: "I have said frequently that the Marine Detachment here was the finest I have ever known. Mike [SSgt. Moeller] helped ensure that the regulations remained that way. ... The Marines here were, and are, an outstanding group of young Americans. I am proud of them, and I am confident that all Americans are."[59]

Embassy in Flames: Trouble in Islamabad, Pakistan, November 1979

As the hostage crisis in Tehran lingered into its third week, the American Embassy in Islamabad, Pakistan, became the scene of protest by a crowd of Muslim fundamentalists. These Muslims initially believed that the United States, in response to the Iranian seizure of the hostages, was behind the seizure of the Grand Mosque in Mecca, Saudi Arabia.

With tensions already high as a result of the takeover of the American Embassy in Tehran, Marine Security Guards throughout the Middle East were on high alert. In neighboring Islamabad, Master Sergeant Lloyd G. Miller and his seven Marines stood guard over a very tense situation that erupted into violence shortly after noon on November 21, 1979.

The violence had been sparked by radio reports, attributed to the inflammatory remarks by Ayatollah Ruhollah Khomeini in Iran that the United States "and its cronies" had instigated the attack and seizure of the Grand Mosque in Mecca." While untrue, the rhetoric fueled an already growing anti–Americanism in Pakistan, due in part to the military takeover by President Zia ul-Haq and his crackdown on opposition to his rule. In the middle of this were the Americans assigned to the U.S. Embassy.

The demonstrations that resulted in the ransacking of the U.S. Embassy began about 12:20 P.M. by about 50 to 75 Pakistanis throwing rocks at the embassy's metal gate. Master Sergeant Miller, who had already been alerted by the Marine at Post One of the presence of the protestors who had been throwing rocks, realized that this was no ordinary anti–American demonstration. MSGT Miller, who had just returned from the dentist, went immediately to Post One, where he saw two busloads of demonstrators from Islamabad's Quaid-I-Azam University pull up in front of the embassy. He immediately posted his Marine Security Guards, all of whom had been recalled, except for one who had been hospitalized and one on liberty, to their assigned positions. On the top of the embassy, Corporal Steven Crowley and Sergeant S.A. Segobiano looked down at the gathering crowd while Sergeant Ralph Purry and Lance Corporal Robert G. Bledsoe took up positions at Post Two.[60]

By 1:00 P.M., over 2,000 students were in front of the U.S. Embassy, where Pakistani police made a half-hearted attempt to disperse the crowd. Despite the deaths of two Pakistani students, the Pakistani police were able to temporarily disperse the crowd. By 1:45 P.M. the crowds swelled to over 20,000 demonstrators who were chanting "kill the American dogs" and other anti–American and anti–Carter slogans. When the Pakistani police opened fire on the crowds, the demonstrators surged forward, forcing the police to flee the scene as the students lunged toward the largely undefended American Embassy. Of those policemen who remained on the scene, the mob quickly stripped them of their weapons and then turned their fury to the Main Chancery. Meanwhile, gunshots rang out toward the Marines from the students below, who had managed to grab the weapons from the Pakistani police. One of the shots hit Corporal Steven Crowley on the left side of his head and exited through his left ear. The Marine corporal slumped to the floor of the roof into a pool of his own blood. Sergeant Segobiano recalled that even as the crowds below let loose a heavy fusillade, his main attention was on the fate of Corporal Crowley:

> At this time, the demonstrators were still outside the main gate, but other rioters were coming over the compound wall in the vicinity of the car port. At this time I saw or heard shots. They were coming from the police on the compound firing over the heads of the rioters near the main gate. The police had retreated to the vicinity of the flag pole, which is right in front of the lobby door. I saw firing and heard shots. I looked over at Cpl Crowley who was kneeling on the edge of the roof behind the wall. He was peering over the edge observing the rioters. I then saw the NCOIC come onto the roof from the door leading to the 3rd floor. Shots were still being fired. He came over to me and told me to pack up my gear and report to Post #1. He then started walking over to Corporal Crowley. At this time I noticed that Cpl Crowley was laying down on the roof. It looked as if he was hurt. The NCOIC arrived at Corporal Crowley's position and I started over also. MSgt Miller motioned for me to stop and to go below and get a stretcher. I couldn't find any but eventually someone found a piece of board. I picked up Cpl Crowley and his gear and with the help of Alvin Morrell, MSgt Miller and two other people. Other people inside took over and carried him down into the vault. I then went to Post #1 where the rest of the Marines were.[61]

Master Sergeant Miller recalled that upon seeing Corporal Crowley lying on the roof, "I immediately knew something was wrong when I noticed the way he was laying on the roof. Blood was all over. I laid him down and took off his helmet. I tried to stop the bleeding but that was impossible. He had been shot in the head over the left eye.... I called for help on my radio and Bob Lassard, Gary Schoen, and Sgt. Sebobiano arrived. We put Cpl Crowley on a board and carried him down to Sam Carden's office. Nurse Fran Fields was there and I turned him over to her care due to continued troubles in the lobby."[62]

When Master Sergeant Miller returned to the lobby to check on the other Marines, he discovered that the demonstrators had continued to pelt the embassy with rocks. Reaching Sergeant Purry at Post Two, MSgt. Miller instructed him to gather all up all his gear and report to Post One. Master Sergeant Miller, in fact, had arrived just in time, as the demonstrators had taken a metal cart from the cafeteria and had forced the door behind Post Two open by ramming it with the cart. When they saw Sergeant Purry with his shotgun, however, they immediately backed off.

At this point in the siege, the rioters were now on the first and second floors, as well as on the rooftop. MSgt. Miller replied that "as far as I knew," by 1400, all of the employees of the U.S. Embassy were in the vault. Miss Marcia Gauger, a *Time* magazine correspondent who was among those evacuated into the vault, recalled that the scene was chaotic, as "some 90 of us were herded into the vault," and many individuals were forced to stand on chairs and desks in order to make room. As the Americans headed into the vault, they began to smell smoke and feel the effects of the tear gas, as many began crying and belching. As Miss Gauger later recounted, "We were pretty packed in."[63]

With the Americans now safe at least for the time being inside the vault, the students smashed their way into the embassy itself and onto the first two floors while the Marines continued to lob tear gas grenades at them from the third floor. As the Marines continued to hold off the demonstrators, Sergeant Purry saw several students carrying buckets of gasoline and starting fires. Despite the frantic calls to Pakistani Foreign Ministry officials as well as officials back at the State Department in Washington to do something to get the Pakistani Army to move in and quell the riot, there was no reply. Ambassador Arthur Hummel, who was at his residence and was in touch with the embassy staff in the vault via a radio, assured the Americans that help was on its way, as "the Pakistani Army was just a few minutes away."[64]

As the Americans awaited help and evacuation from the Pakistani Army, James Thurber, the Embassy's public affairs officer, handed Miss Gauger a message written on notepaper that at 3:35 P.M., Corporal Crowley had died of his wound. Upon hearing the bad news, Gauger wrote, "Tears started to my eyes." With the Americans safely in the vault, the Marines valiantly tried to hold the demonstrators from coming onto the third floor. Sergeant Michael J. Sirois recalled that along with Master Miller, Sergeant Purry, Sergeant Sagobiano, and Lance Corporal Robert Bledsoe, the Marines continued to lob tear gas grenades toward the oncoming demonstrators. In what seemed like an eternity, Lance Corporal Bledsoe recalled that the Marines held this position for almost two hours before, as Sergeant Sirois stated, "the smoke was so thick that we couldn't see so we headed toward the third floor." By this time, the Marines had "emptied all the gas and smoke grenades from the cabinet by the vault door into the vault before entering the vault. All the employees were in the C&R Vault. TCU people, the nurse, Corporal Crowley, Mr. Shroan and Mr. Lassard were in the TCU vault. The Marines, DEAs, Mr. Powers and Mr. Sayles and the RSO Mr. Koritko were in the outer vault. We entered the vault at approximately 1500 hours."[65]

Despite frantic calls to the ambassador and to the Pakistani Foreign Ministry, the Pakistani Army's arrival was mysteriously delayed by three crucial hours, a fact that wasn't lost on anybody inside the vault. President Carter, who had been notified of the situation by Secretary of State Cyrus R. Vance, called President Nigannad Zia ul-Haq, and demanded that the Pakistani Army rescue the trapped Americans.

By this time, all the Americans, including the Marines, were inside the vault. At 4:11 P.M., someone inside the vault yelled, "The embassy is on fire — the theater building and the entrance, and there is smoke pouring out of the motor pool. The Pakistani military are not doing anything at all. The front of the second and third floors is on fire."[66] It was at this point that Sergeant Sirois remembered that "smoke was seeping in from the vault door and live small arm fire was being fired from the roof into the disentegrated tube and ventilation vents. The smoke was getting bad so we decided to make a move out of the vault and down the third floor to the exit of the ambassador's office."[67]

Corporal Paul M. Sima, who was not on duty that day, called Sergeant Sirois at 12 P.M. and informed him that he was going to the Holiday Inn for a brief period. When he arrived back at the Embassy, much to his amazement and horror, he saw smoke billowing out of the embassy. A local Pakistani policeman, sensing the danger posed to all Americans, screamed at Corporal Sima, "Get the Hell out," and led him back to his car. Corporal Sima remained determined, however, in his desire to somehow get into the U.S. Embassy. The Marine corporal, frustrated in his attempt to enter the embassy from the front, recalled that he

> attempted to reach [the] Embassy from the other side via road by old Brit Club, people seen all over that area. Not many people were outside compound. My visitors left and people called me into Canadian Housing Compound #1. Went to top of Mr. Ferguson's house on corner. He said to change my shirt. From balcony I observed smoke from direction of Club area. Carryall in front of house was in flames. Theatre was, also, Motor Pool and parking area. More students were coming (walking) up side of road. One section of steel grille on left side of MSG Post #1 was out, main gate intact. Mob was attempting to break this, and mob was getting larger. Canadian Ambassador was also with us.[68]

At 2:15 P.M., Corporal Sima reported that the mob was

> attempting to break windows using bricks from construction site. Flag was gone. NCOIC office window was smashed and what appeared to be a molotov cocktail was thrown in. ODRP window smashed and same happened. First floor appeared to be smoking. Second floor was starting. People were using rope on flag pole to get on roof. No weapons were seen from balcony, but heard from small arms from Club area. Saw buckets being carried from center of mob to Embassy. Did not see source of supply. 30–40 people now on roof tearing down antennas. I attempted to call Embassy/NCOIC residence, no reply. Called Handley from AID [Agency for International Development] and told him what was happening so he could relay to vault by radio. We then heard local military was supposed to arrive in 5 minutes. The German Ambassador drove up in his car; one Army helicopter was now circling Embassy, later joined by a smaller second one. Half of the mob surrounded the German Ambassador's car. Small arms fire continued, smoke got thicker. Helicopter was just circling.[69]

By 2:45 P.M., Corporal Sima informed Mr. Handley via radio that something had to be done as the people inside the vault were suffocating from the fumes that began to seep into the crowded space. As for the Pakistani Army, the Marine corporal reported that upon their arrival, they just "stood around."[70]

With smoke now filling the room, and the searing heat melting the floor tiles inside the vault, MSgt. Miller and State Department officials decided that it was time to evacuate everyone before it was too late. Miss Gauger recalled that everyone inside the vault was drenched in sweat, and with the smoke getting thicker, people were now "finding it hard to breathe." At this point, the administrative officer, Mr. Fields, the RSO and MSgt. Miller

> finally decided to go out the vault door and to try to go down the hall to the Ambassador's office and then down the stairs and get out. I went out with Randy Sayles, Sgt. Sirois and Bill Powers. The smoke was too thick and rioters were on the stairs. We went back to the vault. The only way out was up to the roof. When we no longer heard the rioters beating on the trap door, we tried to open it and get out. The door was too badly damaged to get out. I took Sergeant Purry, Sgt. Segobiano, and Randy Sayles and found our way to the roof. I set up a perimeter and began briefing people from the vault. As they came up we took them to the auditorium roof and then down to the ground. Sayles had found a ladder. I went back and got Cpl. Crowley's body and carried him up out of the vault and to the ground. On the ground the Pakistani military tried to take our weapons but we refused to let them.[71]

It was at this point Randy K. Sayles, special agent for the Drug Enforcement Agency, recalled that the RSO passed the word that the vault was to be evacuated, and that the Marines were to make their way to the rooftop and secure the area. Mr. Andrew Koritko, the regional security officer, then gave Master Sergeant Miller and the Marines permission to use deadly force in order defend the remaining Americans and friendly Pakistanis from the mob. Mr. Sayles added that prior to the decision to evacuate via the roof, Master Sergeant Miller led an assault team made up of Sergeant Sirois, himself, and Mr. C. Williams Powers, the other DEA agent, through the hallway of the third floor in order to check out any alternate escape route. After leaving the vault, the team made its way to the stairwell of the 3rd floor near the ambassador's office and attempted to go down the stairs but were met a crowd of angry demonstrators. The team then retreated back up the stairs without firing any weapons. It was at this point that the team decided to evacuate through the roof.[72] Mr. Powers, the other DEA agent, recalled that Koritko decided that the roof would be the best escape route due to the "fire, smoke and some of the mob at the ground floor entrance."[73]

The RSO gave the word that everybody was to proceed to the rooftop. Mr. Koritko recalled that by this time "the conditions became so unbearable, that an escape from the vault had to be attempted no matter how dangerous." Also, an attempt to force open the trap door inside failed, as the rioters on the roof had made it impossible to open from inside the vault. Also, it was still not known if rioters were still on the roof. Regardless, MSgt. Miller, Sgt. Purry, Sgt. Segobiano and DEA Agent Sayles volunteered to find a way to the roof so that those trapped in the vault could escape. They managed to get to the roof through the fire, smoke, and tear gas. Finding the roof empty of the rioters because of the heat, they quickly secured it and managed to open the trap door. All Marines then assisted those in the vault to gain the safety of the roof and from there they led them to a lower level and ultimately to safety.[74]

"It was our Marine Guards who saved us. Nobody else"

Marcia Gauger shared the view of all when she stated that had it not been for the Marines, all would've either died of asphyxiation or have been burned alive inside the smoldering vault. Miss Gauger recalled:

> It was the Marines who led the way up the stairs to the hatch. The first Marine opened the hatch and stuck his head out into the darkness. He had no way of knowing what might be waiting for him out there on the roof. It had gotten quiet; the shooting had stopped, the hammering and pounding had stopped. But it could well have been a trap. We didn't know. The only thing we had going for us was the darkness itself, and I guess the fires too. That must have been what drove the rioters away.
>
> With the Marines standing guard over the hatch, two groups of women went out on the roof, then some men, then some more women. A burst of fresh air suddenly hit me; very cold, very fresh. There was a strange glow around the edges of the roof from the fire that was consuming the building beneath us. The Marines warned us in whispers. "Stay down! Stay down!" They could not be sure there were not still rioters somewhere on the roof.... We came out all by ourselves. It was our Marine guards who saved us. Nobody else.[75]

Lance Corporal Bledsoe stated that Master Sergeant Miller and Sergeant Purry led the assault team out of the vault onto the roof, where they opened the hatch and began to assist the people up onto the roof. From there, Lance Corporal Bledsoe and the rest of the Marine Security Guards "assisted everyone else in getting up the ladder onto the roof, across the roof to the auditorium, and finally down to the ground where the Pakistani military assisted us in getting to the British High Commission."[76]

Nobody, however, was as praising of the Marines as was the RSO — Mr. Koritko. The RSO especially commended Master Sergeant Loyd G. Miller, who, "throughout the entire incident ... maintained complete control of his detachment. His outstanding leadership, steadiness, dependability and control of his detachment enabled them to provide the maximum protection for the American and Pakistani personnel whose lives were in danger. His efforts and those of the entire Marine detachment were responsible for minimizing the loss of life during this attack."[77]

Despite the apologies from President Zia for the damage done to the U.S. Embassy, the Pakistani government remained silent on the death of Corporal Crowley, U.S. Army Warrant Officer Bryan Lee Ellis, and the two Pakistani civilians killed during the initial period of the demonstration. It is a fact that the Pakistani Army took five hours to arrive on the scene, and when they did arrive, they stood helpless and watched the embassy burn. As one survivor claimed, "The Pakistanis didn't do s---." This view was further reflected in the after-action report written several days after the embassy fire in Islamabad. Major Jeffrey T. Ronald wrote, "The Pakistani Army's contributions to the protection and rescue of American lives were negligible." Major Ronald added that the last-minute rescue of the American personnel was in no way "attributable to the host government's actions." Instead, the rescue came as a result of both divine intervention and "a few good Marines."[78]

Both Major Ronald and Master Sergeant Miller likewise asserted that had the Marine Security Guards been given permission to defend themselves and personnel in the embassy, the outcome of the siege might have been different. In his after-action report, Major Ronald wrote, "The situation in Islamabad might have been resolved sooner and the lives of Corporal Crowley, W.O. Ellis and two Pakistani employees saved if the on rushing, determined mob was presented with an equally determined defense."[79] Master Sergeant Miller added, "If we had been allowed to fire on the rioters while they were trying to start fires at the front and back gates, I think that we could have kept them out of the Chancery. Nothing could have been done to save Corporal Crowley, who was shot very early in the riot, but it would have saved the Pakistani employees who died on the first floor."[80]

Apologetic of the events that had transpired on 21 November, General Zia ul-Haq extended his "personal apologies to President Carter and to the American people," and "insisted that his government would pay for all the damages."[81] No apology, however, could bring back the lives of Corporal Crowley, Warrant Officer Ellis, or the two innocent Pakistanis killed during the attack. In recognition of the young Marine's bravery while on the rooftop of the embassy, the secretary of the Navy awarded Corporal Crowley a posthumous Purple Heart and Bronze Star. Both Warrant Officer Ellis and Corporal Crowley were likewise eulogized for their bravery under fire and buried with full military honors. In the case of Corporal Crowley, both President Carter and General Robert Barrow, the commandant of the Marine Corps, attended the young Marine's funeral. Tragically, Corporal Crowley became the fifth Marine Security Guard killed in the line of duty. While his death may not have been preventable, as Master Sergeant Miller asserted, it nonetheless was a tragedy all the same, as the young Marine "gave his all" in defense of the U.S. Embassy in Islamabad.

For their defense of the U.S. Embassy in Islamabad and the safe evacuation of 137 American and foreign service nationals, the secretary of the Navy awarded Master Sergeant Miller and the Marine Security Guard detachment a Meritorious Unit Citation for meritorious service in defense of the Embassy of the United States of America in Islamabad, Pakistan on 21 November 1979. When the American Embassy was surrounded and subsequently attacked and burned by hostile demonstrators, members of the Marine Security Guard Detachment held their post and, when directed, crawled through smoke-filled corridors in order to throw tear gas canisters at pre-selected positions to block the advance of the mob which resulted in one Marine being fatally wounded. When the situation became critical, they assisted in directing the Embassy employees to safety of the third floor vault.... The Marines then assisted those in the vault to gain the safety of the roof and led them to the security of the ground level. By their outstanding resolve, unparalleled dedication to duty, the enlisted personnel of the Marine Security Guard Detachment, Islamabad reflected great credit upon themselves and upheld the highest traditions of the Marine Corps and the United States Naval Service.[82]

Corporal Steven J. Crowley, who had been promoted only weeks before, was posthumously awarded a Bronze Star and Purple Heart with a Combat "V" for his bravery and dedication duty during the first hours of the siege in Islamabad. In presenting the two medals to Mrs. Georgene B. Crowley, Cpl Crowley's widowed mother, Major General Robert E. Haebel, who represented the commandant of the Marine Corps, praised the young Marine's selfless dedication to duty and his steadfastness during the siege. The accompanying citation with Cpl. Crowley's Bronze Star reflected Major General Haebel's comments:

> When the hostile attack began ... he took his assigned position on the roof of the Embassy Compound. Cpl Crowley was immediately subject to a barrage of rocks and various other objects hurled onto the roof, and very shortly, to small arms fire from the hostile force. Despite the fact that he was in an exposed position, he remained at his assigned post and continued to provide surveillance of the situation and information for the Embassy officials.... Corporal Crowley's aggressiveness, initiative, and coolness under fire contributed to the delay of the attacking force, which saved the lives of U.S. personnel, and enabled the destruction of sensitive material. His courageous actions were in keeping with the highest traditions of the U.S. naval service.[83]

Brief Siege in Tripoli

Besides the takeover of the American Embassy in Tehran and the sacking of the U.S. Embassy in Islamabad, 2,000 Libyan protestors demonstrated in front of the U.S. Embassy in Tripoli on December 2, 1979. As was the case in Islamabad, the protestors were able to break through to door of the main entrance into the Main Chancery where they then set fire to furniture as the 14 American occupants escaped unharmed through a side door. U.S. State Department spokesman Hodding Carter later told reporters that the demonstrators destroyed the first floor and damaged portions of the second in the four-storied building. Carter added that the Libyan government of Mohammar Qadaffi "made no attempt to disperse the demonstrators or protect the mission despite repeated appeals by embassy officials during the hourlong attack."[84] Eventually, an automatic tear gas system forced the demonstrators to leave the embassy. Libyan officials later lodged an official protest to the U.S. State Department over the use of tear gas, as many of the protestors had been hospitalized due to the tear gas inhaled during the brief embassy siege.[85]

The MSG Detachment in Beirut, 1982

Political and religious strife throughout the Middle East remained strong throughout the 1970s and early 1980s. No more was this in evidence than in war-torn Lebanon. In addition

Sergeant Luis G. Lopez, Jr. (with shotgun), on duty immediately after the bombing of the American Embassy in Beirut, Lebanon, on April 18, 1983 (courtesy U.S. Marine Corps).

to the civil war that had began in 1976 among the different religious-ethnic groups was the ongoing war between Israel and the Palestinian Organization (PLO), led by Yasir Arafat. The PLO, after having been expelled from Jordan in the 1970s, shortly thereafter took up residence in neighboring Lebanon, a country that was already divided along confessional lines of Maronite Christians and Sunni and Shia Muslims. By mid–1976, the power-sharing arrangement that had been held in place since 1943 by the French began to fall apart, as each party began to jockey for more political power amidst the already deteriorating situation close to Lebanon's border due to the ongoing Arab-Israeli struggle. By the spring of 1976, various Lebanese militias began to openly fight each other in the streets of Beirut, the capital that had been once hailed as "the Paris of the Middle East." Also, the arrival of thousands of Palestinian refugees and the resultant rise in terrorist activity in Southern Lebanon brought the Israeli Army into the picture as it soon created its own militia — the Army of Southern Lebanon (ASL) to act as its surrogate in the region.

For the Marines who stood guard at the U.S. Embassy in Beirut, dodging stray bullets and mortar rounds became a daily occurrence as the country slipped further into civil war during the late 1970s. With his seizure of power and creation of the Islamic Republic of Iran, the Ayatollah Khomeini and his surrogates likewise set out to export the Islamic Revolution to other countries in order to battle whom they labeled the so-called "Great Satan," or the United States and the state of Israel. Added to Lebanon's political woes was the unholy alliance between Iran and Syrian leader Hafez Al-Assad, both of whom saw that country's state of anarchy as an opportunity to further their own religious and political objectives.

As Lebanon tore itself apart in factional fighting, the Marine Security Guard detachment inside the U.S. Embassy in Beirut hunkered down for any situation that might arise. While Lebanese security forces and leftist militia fought each other in an area adjacent to the U.S. Embassy for three straight days (January 7–10, 1982), Marine Security Guards "manned their defensive positions" until the fighting subsided.[86] On 31 March 1982, Marine Security Guards provided cover for several embassy staff members and rescued them after they were pinned down by hostile fire. On April 11, 1982, when an Israeli citizen opened fire and killed several innocent Palestinian worshippers in front of the Dome of the Rock, one of the holiest sites in all of Islam, the U S. Embassy in Beirut came under intense small arms and rocket propelled grenade fire.

The increased violence in Beirut forced the U.S. ambassador to order the creation of several new defensive posts inside the embassy. For the next six weeks, from April 11 through May 17, Marine Security Guards stood an average of 70 hours per week on duty due to the heightened security. When Israeli jets bombed West Beirut in retaliation for mortar attacks along the Lebanese-Israeli border, the Marines evacuated all non-essential personnel and prepared to destroy all classified material if the embassy should be stormed, as occurred in Tehran and Islamabad in 1979. Likewise, terrorists let off car bombs, attacked the French Embassy, and posed threats to all Western diplomats, as Marine Security Guards remained on duty virtually 24 hours a day.[87]

Tensions in Lebanon exploded into violence when terrorists critically wounded Mr. Shlomo Argov, the Israeli ambassador to Great Britain. The attack had been carried out by the splinter Palestinian terror group with ties to both Syria and Iraq and led by the late terrorist Abu Nidal. It forced the hand of Prime Minister Menachem Begin, who ordered an all-out offensive aimed at the annihilation of the Palestinian Liberation Organization, who, it might be added, denied any complicity in the attack, once and for all.[88] In an action dubbed Operation Peace for Galilee (1982), the Israeli Army drove Yasir Arafat's Palestinian fighters all the way to the outskirts of Beirut. Here, other terrorist groups, notably Hezbollah ("Party of God") and Hamas, both supported by Syria and Iran, as well as the other leftist militias, declared a "holy war" or "jihad" against the Israelis, their Lebanese Christian allies, and the Americans.[89] Inevitably, however, the focus of the terrorists' hatred turned toward Israel's main supporter — the United States.

On June 4, 1982, Israeli jets pounded Palestinian positions inside West Beirut, the site of the Palestinian refugee camps. This bombing triggered a whole new round of intense fighting between the militias and the advancing Israeli troops. Gunnery Sergeant James G. Watson, the NCOIC of the detachment, placed all the Marines on 100 percent alert as terrorists called in bomb threats to the embassy. Also, as a precaution, the Marines also wore their

Amid the rubble and debris, General Robert H. Barrow (center, with hands clasped) and his staff are briefed by U.S. State Department officials on the damage done to the U.S. Embassy in Beirut in the aftermath of a suicide bomber that killed one Marine Security Guard (U.S. Marine Security Guard Battalion).

REACT Gear at all times, even when they slept, as the embassy was subjected to daily mortar, small arms, and rocket propelled grenade fire.[90] On June 7, 1982, a fragment from an errant round wounded a Marine Security Guard as he stood his post during an intense shelling. Meanwhile, the Marines maintained the embassy's emergency generator and began to destroy all classified material. A week prior to the evacuation of the Marines from the embassy, the State Department informed the Marines that "in case of a forced evacuation 3 Marines were expendable," in order to safeguard whatever presence remained behind in Beirut.[91] On that afternoon, four leathernecks were evacuated to the Ambassador Morris Draper's residence in the hills overlooking the embattled city. On the 24th, the four Marine Security Guards who remained behind made a final sweep of the entire embassy. The determination displayed by the Marines may have discouraged an assault on the embassy by the various militias that surrounded the embassy compound. As the situation in Beirut stabilized, the Marines who were left behind served as a "an island of stability" to the few Americans who remained in Beirut. When the rest of the Marines rejoined their colleagues in Beirut, the Marine Security Guard Detachment rigorously applied itself to its regular duties and earned an "Outstanding Rating" on its semi-annual inspection for that year.[92]

Prelude to Tragedy: Beirut, September 1982 to April 17, 1983

As part of the Multi-National Force agreement, agreed upon by all of the warring parties in order to bring order out of chaos in Lebanon, the 32nd Marine Amphibious Unit (MAU) began the evacuation of the Palestinian Liberation Organization. The MAU remained in Beirut for several days as it loaded Palestinian guerrillas to transport them to locations

The Marine Security Guard Detachment, Beirut, Lebanon, stands "at parade rest" in the aftermath of the terrorist bombing that killed Lance Corporal Robert V. McMaugh (U.S. Marine Security Guard Battalion).

throughout the rim of North Africa. On September 10, 1982, the 32nd MAU left Beirut. While heading toward its home port of Naples, Italy, the Marines heard the shocking news that President-elect Bashir Gemayel, a Maronite Christian, had been killed by a powerful bomb. On the heels of this tragedy was the massacre of innocent Palestinians by pro-Israeli Lebanese Christian militiamen at the Sabra and Shatila Refugee Camps. Beirut stood on the verge of another round of open warfare as the new president of Lebanon, Amin Gemayel, requested the return of the 32nd MAU to help stabilize the situation until the newly constituted, American-trained Lebanese Army could assert its authority.[93]

Throughout the late fall of 1982 and into the winter and early spring of 1983, the Marine Security Guard detachment worked closely with the Marine units that comprised the American portion of the Multi-National Force. In fact, during the first week of April 1983, Colonel James M. Mead, commander of the 22nd MAU, wrote in his weekly report that "the situation in Beirut had become unusually quiet."[94] All of this began to change, however, when French and Italian soldiers of the Multi-National Force came under attack, with the result of one Italian peacekeeper being killed. On the evening of April 17, 1983, Private First Class Kenneth E. Simpson, a member of Company F, 2nd Battalion, 6th Marines, was shot at by an unknown assailant as he stood sentry duty outside the MEU headquarters. Fortunately, the Marine was unharmed, though the round did tear away his cargo pocket on his utility trousers. This attack was the prelude for one of the most devastating attacks aimed at an American Embassy since the Vietnam War.

"How dare anyone strike at the U.S. Embassy"

On April 18, 1983, at approximately 1 P.M., a white van, later found to be stolen from the grounds of the U.S. Embassy, drove right past a lone Lebanese sentry who had been asleep and came to a halt directly in the lobby of the U.S. Embassy. The suicide bomber then set off a 2,000 pound load of explosives, with the blast ripping through the front portion of the seven-story structure, killing instantly Lance Corporal Robert V. McMaugh, who had been on duty at Post One along with 52 embassy employees and innocent Lebanese.[95] The blast also severely wounded 7 other Marines who were on duty in the embassy. Despite having suffered injuries in the blast, the Marines nevertheless put into operation an emergency action plan and began to assist the wounded. The Marine Security Guards, fearing a further assault on the embassy, quickly established an external security force until the arrival of French Marines, who were members of the Multi-National Force, and in whose sector the U.S. Embassy had been located.[96]

Upon hearing of the blast from a staff sergeant in the S-3 Section of 22nd MAU headquarters, Colonel Mead, who had arrived on the scene just 20 minutes after the blast, ordered the area off limits. He then organized a reaction company from Battalion Landing Team 2/6, which relieved the French Marines on the scene. Here, the Marine Reaction Company took up security with elements of the Lebanese Armed Forces.[97]

While Colonel Mead's Marines and the Lebanese Army set up a 24-hour security detail, the Marine Security Guards began the laborious, painful process of picking through the rubble of the shattered embassy. Marine Security Guards, in particular, were to "recover valuable U.S. government property," classified material and, most importantly, the body of their slain comrade — Lance Corporal McMaugh. The Marines placed his flag-draped body on a litter, and then carefully removed him from the debris and placed him in an ambulance that

A Marine from 22 Marine Amphibious Unit stands guard duty on a road leading to the U.S. Embassy in Beirut after the terrorist attack on April 18, 1983 (U.S. Marine Security Guard Battalion).

took him away for proper identification and notification of the next of kin. Lance Corporal McMaugh became the sixth Marine Security Guard to die in the line of duty.

For the next two weeks, all of the Marines of the MAU, regardless of his assigned duty, stood guard at the U.S. Embassy. In fact, "some of the MAU Marines did not get more than four hours of sleep a night during the two-week period immediately following the blast. They would get up to go on patrol, return to their positions ... and might get two hours to take care of personal matters, and so on, have chow, and go back out on line, standing post around the security effort at the embassy site."[98]

The reaction of the Marines who arrived on the scene shortly after the blast was one of "absolute anger." Colonel Mead remarked later, "How dare anyone strike at the U.S. Embassy." Others asked each other candidly, "Who was next?" Despite the shock and anger over the destruction of the U.S. Embassy, the Marines of 22nd MAU assisted the Marine Security Guards in the search through the rubble for classified material and anything else of value. Battered though determined, Colonel Mead praised the professionalism and efficiency of the Marine Security Guards, who he said "performed magnificently" during the immediate aftermath of the bombing.[99] In a show of defiance to the terrorists, the Marine Security Guards raised the American flag over the Embassy's ruins at the request of Ambassador Robert S. Dillon.

When it was concluded that the U.S. Embassy was uninhabitable, the British Ambassador, Sir David Roberts, in a gesture of solidarity with his American cousins, offered Ambas-

Lance Corporal Anthony Viscarando, USMC, sits in the turret of his Assault Amphibian Vehicle with his M203 grenade launcher at the ready in downtown Beirut, Lebanon, looking for snipers in the area surrounding Beirut International Airport in the spring of 1983. (Leo J. Daugherty III collection).

sador Dillon space for the political, military, and consular sections. The British Embassy, located along the Mediterranean Sea, was soon home to a platoon of U.S. Marines, as Sir David Roberts had personally requested the leathernecks in order to prevent a similar strike from occurring at the British Embassy. Colonel Mead quickly assigned a platoon of Marines, commanded by Lieutenant William G. Leftwich III, to the British Embassy, which marked "the first time in history that you have U.S. Marines guarding a British Embassy." Marines also stood guard in front of the Durrafourd Building, located near the British Embassy, which became the temporary headquarters for U.S. diplomats and their staffs. Another platoon of Marines stood guard over the residence of Ambassador Dillon in Yarze, in the hills just east of Beirut. Finally, a platoon of Marines from 22nd MAU stood guard over a delegation of State Department and Central Intelligence Agency personnel sent to Beirut to accompany the bodies of their slain colleagues as well as that of Corporal McMaugh.[100]

Secretary of the Navy John Lehman, in response to the professionalism and dedication to duty displayed by the Marines assigned to the U.S. Embassy in Beirut from the period of 1 January 1982 to 30 April 1983, awarded the Marine Security Guard Detachment, Beirut, Lebanon, a Navy Unit Citation for "their cool reaction to crisis, determination in the face of adversity, and selfless dedication to duty. He said the "enlisted personnel of the Marine Security Guard Detachment, Beirut, Lebanon, reflected great credit upon themselves and upheld the highest traditions of the Marine Corps and the United States Naval Service."[101]

Even more tragic than the destruction of the U.S. Embassy in Beirut was the suicide bombing of the Marine Barracks located at Beirut, Lebanon, on the morning of October 23, 1983. The bombing killed over 243 Marines, sailors, and several soldiers who were asleep in the BLT's headquarters when a suicide bomber with a van packed with explosives drove past a lone Marine sentry and headed straight for the barracks. Mourned by their countrymen in the days and weeks to follow, the Marines who perished in the bombing of the barracks, as well as Lance Corporal McMaugh, were "Ambassadors in Blue."

This was not an end to the violence aimed against the United States in Beirut. On September 20, 1984, a suicide bomber once again targeted the U.S. Embassy, killing U.S. Navy Petty Officer Michael R. Wagner and U.S. Army Chief Warrant Officer 2 Kenneth V. Welch, both assigned to the Defense Attaché's Office. Wounded in the same attack were four Marine Security Guards. The wounded included Staff Sergeant Jimmie Brown, Sergeant Richard P. Leydet, and Lance Corporals Kenneth W. Gasmire, Jr., and Larry W. Gill. Staff Sergeant Brown, who had been in Beirut only eleven months before this latest bombing, said that he volunteered to return to Beirut because "I was upset, to say the least," about the previous bombing here on 18 April 1983. The Marine staff sergeant added that the Marines in Beirut knew the risks associated with such a high-profile post, and as such, "we consider the threat here extreme because we know we're on a list somewhere."[102] Despite the dangers, all of the 14 Marine Security Guards in Beirut were volunteers and had specifically asked to be transferred from various posts throughout Europe, North Africa, and Southwest Asia. While there were daily reminders of the dangers present in Beirut, Staff Sergeant Brown indicated the Marines were there by choice and as such were fully prepared for any crisis that might arise at the makeshift embassy.

Sergeant Major (then Staff Sergeant) Jimmie Brown, USMC, receives the Silver Star from Major General Dennis Murphy, commanding general, 2d Marine Division, Camp Lejeune, North Carolina, for actions while under fire in Beirut (U.S. Marine Security Guard Battalion photograph courtesy Sgt. Maj. Jimmie Brown).

Death in San Salvador: The Murder of Four Marine Security Guards in June 1985

During the 1980s, both Nicaragua and El Salvador became the focal point of the Cold War between the United States and proxies of both Cuba and the Soviet Union. In Nicaragua, the leftist government of Daniel Ortega fought the U.S.-supported anti–Communist guerrillas or "Contras." In neighboring El Salvador, the U.S.-supported government battled an insurgency waged by leftist guerrillas, primarily directed by the Farabundo Marti National Liberation Front (FMLN), supported by Nicaragua, Vietnam, Cuba, and the Soviet Union. While the government of El Salvador fought off the attacks of the FMLN, terrorists once again sought to weaken the resolve of the United States when they struck at the very heart of the U.S. presence in the country — the U.S. Embassy in San Salvador.

In the early evening hours of June 19, 1985, four off-duty U.S. Marine Security Guards assigned to the U.S. Embassy in San Salvador were enjoying the music and a few drinks in a sidewalk café when a pickup truck stopped in front of their table. Without warning, several men, dressed in military uniforms, "leaped from the truck and opened fire with submachine guns and automatic rifles."[103] According to an eyewitness, the gunmen specifically singled out the Marines as they methodically went from table to table and checked out the other patrons who were on the floor underneath the tables, looking for individual targets. When it was over, the gunmen, later identified as leftist guerrillas, had killed four Marines, two American civilian contractors (George Viney and Robert Alvidrez) and seven Salvadorans. Salvadoran Deputy Defense Minister Reynaldo Lopez Nuilia told reporters later he believed the Marines were the target of the gunmen.[104] Two of the eyewitnesses, Manual Argueta and Mario Orellana, both of whom were wounded in the attack, said that the "gunmen fired their submachine guns and automatic rifles first at the tables where the Marines were seated and afterward sprayed the bullets indiscriminately."

The Marines, all members of the Marine Security Guard Detachment, U.S. Embassy, El Salvador, were identified as Sergeant Bobby Joe Dickson, of Tuscaloosa, Alabama, Sergeant Thomas T. Handwork, of Boardman, Ohio; Corporal R. Kwiatkowski, of Wausau, Wisconsin; and Corporal Gregory H. Weber, of Cincinnati, Ohio. Politicians in the United States and El Salvador denounced the killings and vowed that the murders would not shake the resolve of the United States and El Salvador in defeating the leftist insurgency.

President Ronald Reagan, in a speech to the American nation, eulogized the four Marines as "the victims of vicious evil," and that as a nation, "we grieve for their loss and for the other innocent victims of that vicious attack." The President added, "No one can treat such men and women as they deserve, because what they give us is beyond our power to repay. So when they're taken away from us, when they're taken because they wore our uniform with love and pride, when they're killed because they put themselves in harm's way for our sake, then we feel an anguish that cuts at the heart. We cannot forget."[105] The president spoke of the selfless dedication that all four young Marines gave to their country, and how all of them dreamed when they were young of joining the Marines. In his speech, President Reagan specifically cited the father of Corporal Gregory H. Weber, who said that his son told him before he left for embassy guard duty in San Salvador, "They need a few good men down there." President Reagan concluded his tribute to the four Marine Security Guards with a verse out of the Marines' Hymn: "And now today we grieve for four young men taken from us too soon. And we receive them in death, as they were on the last night of their lives — together, and following the radiant light, following it toward heaven, toward home. And if we reach, or when we reach, heaven's scenes, we will truly find it guarded by United States Marines."[106]

The deaths of Sergeants Bobby Joe Dickson and Thomas T. Handwork, and Corporals Kwiatkowski and Weber were mourned by the entire nation. More tragic, however, was the fact that four more Marine Security Guards paid the ultimate price while serving their country in a war-scarred nation wracked by civil war. Of the Marines killed in El Salvador, President Reagan said in remarks to the nation that "they were all volunteers," and accepted the inherent dangers that went along with being Marine Security Guards. Still, like the deaths of the six Marine Security Guards before them, the deaths of these four leathernecks were tragic all the same.

Upheaval in Kampala, Uganda, August 30, 1985, to March 31, 1986

When civil war erupted in Uganda during the summer of 1985, the fighting eventually spread to the capital, Kampala. As the situation became more violent from day to day, the chargé d'affaires of the American Embassy there requested additional security in the form of an emergency Temporary Additional Duty (TAD) Marine Security Guard detachment. By the time the crisis subsided, four additional MSG detachments were assigned to the Kampala embassy from October 1985 through March 1986. These Marines provided the necessary security that enabled the diplomatic staff to continue its mission throughout the bloody and merciless civil war that plagued Uganda.[107]

In praising the performance of the Marine Security Guards assigned to the U.S. Embassy in Kampala, Lieutenant Colonel Rollin G. Napier, who commanded Company F later wrote:

"Operation Kampala" was a highly successful small unit operation. The Marines went into Kampala to protect the American Embassy, a forward and sovereign portion of the United States. During "Operation Kampala" Marines were engaged in actual combat operations. Their obvious, vigilant presence, twenty-four hours a day protected American lives and property. When the battle between the UNLA [Uganda National Liberation Army] and NRA [National Resistance Army] raged around them, the Marines ... successfully deterred the enemy forces from carrying out any attack against the Embassy, the Ambassador's residence or any American official. As a result, no American lives were lost, no American property was destroyed and American honor in that portion of the world remained intact. In summary, "Operation Kampala" was a successful Marine Corps operation.[108]

In addition to being awarded a Navy Unit Citation their bravery and coolness under fire, the assistant detachment commander, Staff Sergeant Casimir Puchalski, was awarded the Bronze Star for his actions while defending the ambassador's residence during a period of intense fighting in Kampala.

Betrayal in Moscow

Throughout the six weeks of intensive training prior to their first assignment, Marine Security Guards receive many hours of instruction in the care, storage, and destruction of classified material. The safeguarding and proper storage of classified material is the primary mission of a Marine Security Guard when posted to a U.S. embassy or consulate. This fact alone made Marine Security Guards primary targets for foreign espionage services during the

Cold War (1947–1989). In fact, an aggressive, hostile intelligence service (HOIS) or more specifically in this case, the Soviet Union's Committee for State Security or KGB, considered Marine Security Guards, like embassies and consulates in their own backyard, "high priority targets." Hence, the Soviet state security services thus sought to exploit what Kremlin leaders may have thought was "the key to the classified vaults" in U.S. embassies abroad.[109] This exploitation by the KGB-led Eastern European security services of Marine Security Guards was not new. In Warsaw, Poland, in 1959, Headquarters Marine Corps relieved ten Marine Security Guards over allegations that they solicited Polish prostitutes who turned out later to be Soviet agents. While no compromise of the embassy or its classified material took place, the Marine Corps and State Department re-doubled its efforts to prevent just such an incident from occurring. This changed, however, in the summer and fall of 1986, when a Marine Security Guard, Sergeant Clayton J. Lonetree, admitted to a series of charges that he aided and abetted several known KGB agents in the compromise and penetration of the U.S. Embassy in Moscow. With the assistance of a Russian woman — Violetta Sanni, with whom he had become romantically involved, Sergeant Lonetree betrayed not only his country and Corps, but his fellow Marine Security Guards.

The Making of a Traitor: Sergeant Lonetree and the MSG Program

Sergeant Clayton J. Lonetree graduated from Marine Security Guard Battalion School in the early fall of 1984 and was assigned to the U.S. Embassy in Moscow, Russia. For Sergeant Lonetree, this was an assignment come true, having read about Nazi Germany, World War II, and on the Soviet Union and Communism while in high school. A Native American, and member of a tribe that prided itself on military service, it was therefore not out of the ordinary that he enlisted in the Marine Corps in late 1979 on the delayed entry program. Lonetree entered boot camp at MCRD, San Diego, in July 1980 and, after advanced infantry training at Camp Pendleton, was assigned to Marine Forces, Guantanamo Bay, Cuba, as a 0311-Marine rifleman. After taking a few correspondence courses on history and international affairs, Lonetree soon applied for and was at first turned down for an appointment to the Marine Security Guard program due to his General Classification Test (GCT) score. Re-assigned to Camp Pendleton, Lonetree, now a corporal, re-applied for the MSG program, and with assistance from Senator Rudy Boschwitz from Minnesota, barely passed the entrance test. Eventually, the Marine Corps conditionally accepted him into the program on the provision that he re-enlist, and informed him that there was no guarantee that he would graduate.[110]

While a student at MSG School, Sergeant Lonetree was repeatedly counseled for below-average scores on clothing and uniform inspections. Lonetree received average or above-average scores, however, in such tasks as physical fitness tests and rifle and pistol marksmanship. He graduated from Marine Security Guard School with the class of 5–84 in September 1984. Though he requested a preference for East Germany, he nonetheless received as his first assignment the U.S. Embassy in Moscow.[111]

Assignment to Moscow

During the first months in Moscow, Sergeant Lonetree carried out his regular duties as a Marine Security Guard. An introvert, Lonetree continued to read about the Soviet Union, rode the Moscow Metro system by night, and continued to fantasize amidst his new surroundings. While on duty one day in the embassy, Lonetree became fixated on a beautiful young Russian woman, Violetta Sanni, who worked as a translator at the U.S. Embassy.[112]

Officially forbidden by the rules that governed Marine Security Guards to befriend or date a member of the opposite sex in a Communist country, Lonetree and Violetta nevertheless met several times at her apartment and in specially arranged places in Moscow away from the embassy. Unknown to Lonetree was the fact that the KGB had targeted him for blackmail in order to gain access to classified sources inside the U.S. Embassy through his lover Violetta Sanni. As it turned out, Ms. Sanni was what the intelligence community called "a honey pot," designed to trap unsuspecting or naïve young Americans in romantically compromising situations. These "situations" are in turn used by the KGB to first blackmail and later use as a means of gaining intelligence data or, as occurred in the case of Lonetree, access to areas inside the embassy off-limits to foreign nationals.

After several of these 'liaisons' with Ms. Sanni, who kept her KGB handler — Aleski Yefimov, who went by the name "Uncle Sasha"— informed of the meetings, Lonetree began to pass classified material to this Soviet agent. This material included photographs, floor plans of the U.S. Embassy in Moscow, and the names of Soviet citizens in service of the United States. Over time, Lonetree became a "willing go-between" for the Soviets, all for the price of sex and affection. This relationship culminated when Violetta asked Lonetree to allow "Uncle Sasha" into several rooms, including the secure communications room off-limits to citizens of the host nation.

In mid–1986, Sergeant Lonetree transferred to his next assignment, the U.S. Embassy in Vienna, Austria. Here, the Marine Security Guard continued to write Violetta, with whom by this time he had fallen in love, and provided "Uncle Sasha" with information and other intelligence data as it became available. In December 1986, several days before the embassy's annual Christmas Party, the reality of what he had been doing began to catch up with Sergeant Clayton J. Lonetree. At first, he thought of committing suicide with his .38 caliber pistol, though when the time came to pull the trigger he hesitated and, instead, decided to turn himself over to the embassy's resident political officer.

On December 14, 1986, the day of the party, and after pouring himself a drink, Sergeant Lonetree approached the embassy official and told him, in a private conversation, that he had turned over material of a non-classified nature over to Soviet intelligence agents for about seven hundred U.S. dollars.[113] When asked by the officer if either a woman or blackmail had been involved, Lonetree hesitated at first, and then categorically denied any sexual impropriety or substance abuses were involved. He was eventually arrested on a charge of espionage, and a deeper investigation revealed that Clayton J. Lonetree had, in fact, been a willing accomplice of the KGB. Further charges followed, which included disobedience to standing orders for all Marines in sensitive posts, unauthorized contacts, and a sexual liaison. Placed under arrest, and interviewed by both the Naval Investigative Service and Central Intelligence Agency, Clayton J. Lonetree was transferred to the Marine Corps Base at Quantico, Virginia, where the Marine Corps formally charged him with no less than five counts of espionage, treason, and disobedience of lawful orders. The Marine Corps placed Lonetree in solitary confinement in the Quantico brig, where he awaited trial.

Even before Lonetree admitted that he had violated the State Department's policies concerning fraternization with unauthorized females, Sergeant Arnold Bracy, another watchstander in Moscow, admitted to the RSO in Moscow, in June 1986, that he had contact with a Soviet female who had formerly worked in the Marine House. After assurances that he would discontinue further contacts with the woman, later identified as the Marine House's cook, Ms. Galya Gallotina, Sergeant Bracy was seen once again in her company. State Department officials promptly requested Bracy's removal from the program and the Marine Corps complied. While awaiting orders back at Marine Security Guard Battalion at Quantico, Sergeant Bracy was demoted to corporal for disobedience of a lawful order. As he awaited orders to return to the Marine Corps, he was indicted for espionage. After a lengthy investigation by the Counterintelligence Branch at the Department of State, it had been concluded that there had been no security leaks and all charges against Corporal Bracy were eventually dropped. Corporal Bracy was then re-assigned to Marine Corps Base, Twenty-nine Palms, California, where he finished his tour of duty and left the Marine Corps.[114] Subsequent investigations during and after the Bracy trial concluded, however, that there had been a severe breakdown in the discipline and morale of the Marine Security Guard Detachment in Moscow. This last fact was revealed in later investigations when it was determined that all of the Marine watchstanders, including the detachment's assistant NCOIC, Staff Sergeant Stufflebeam, had been guilty of "unreported sexual encounters with Soviet females, currency violations, black marketeering, and unauthorized travels." The majority of the Marines assigned to Moscow were tried and, in most cases, either given summary court-martials, or had other non-judicial disciplinary actions taken.[115] All of the Marine Security Guards in Moscow were eventually relieved and replaced by newly assigned graduates of MSG School.

Lonetree's Trial and Conviction, July–December 1987

At Sergeant Lonetree's general court-martial, Lieutenant General Frank E. Petersen, the convening officer of the trial, ordered the Marine Security Guard to stand trial on charges of espionage. Lonetree was to be tried on five specific counts stemming from his activities in Moscow: espionage; unlawful and unauthorized contacts with Soviet citizens; the passing of classified information to a hostile foreign intelligence service; and the identification of Soviet citizens in the service of the United States to a hostile foreign intelligence (i.e., the KGB).[116] For his defense, Sergeant Lonetree's father hired the activist lawyer William Kunstler, who questioned whether Lonetree "gave the Soviets anything of value" and whether he was aware of his actions. Finally, Mr. Kunstler questioned the Marine Corps' contention that Lonetree's offenses equated to acts of espionage.[117]

The trial of Clayton J. Lonetree commenced on July 22, 1987, and after several months of hearing testimony, the jury of eight Marines found him guilty on all five counts. The jury recommended and the judge concurred that the Marine was to be reduced to the rank of private, forfeit all pay and allowances, fined $5,000, given a dishonorable discharge, and serve no less than thirty years in prison. Shortly after his conviction, Lonetree was transferred to the Federal Disciplinary Barracks located at Fort Leavenworth, Kansas, where he served his sentence. In 1993, a Military Court of Appeals rejected the contention by Lonetree's lawyers that their client had committed a "mistake" in turning classified material over to the KGB, and that the original sentence of thirty years was too harsh. Instead, Lieutenant Colonel David Anderson, the presiding judge, accepted the prosecution's contention that Lonetree's actions warranted the maximum sentence, and thus reduced the ex–Marine's sentence a mere five years, from thirty to twenty-five years.[118]

Changes in the Marine Security Guard Program

The Lonetree and Bracy affairs sparked significant changes in the training and adminis-tration of Marine Security Guards throughout the program. These changes occurred at all levels of the program: from the Department of State, the relationship with the other inves-tigative branches of the U.S. government (Naval Investigative Services, Defense Investigative services, and Central Intelligence Agency); and the relationship between the Department of State and Marine Corps. One of the most significant changes to take place at Marine Secu-rity Guard School was the screening of all applicants prior to and during training at Quan-tico. Prior to the Lonetree investigation, only detachment commanders and "marginal" candidates received psychological evaluations for fitness in order to determine whether they were retained in the program. The "lessons learned" in the aftermath of the Lonetree trial concluded that all future watchstanders were to be constantly evaluated during training in order to prevent a re-occurrence of the events in Moscow.[119] Finally, the profiles of each new MSG candidate is retained in order to detect any change in behavior on both liberty and duty once on post.

Second, a Navy chaplain was added to the staff of Marine Security Guard Battalion. During the course of Lonetree's trial, it had been revealed that his tumultuous family back-ground had much to do with his behavior in Moscow and his decision to "turn coat" and assist the KGB. The chaplain would perform so-called "crisis intervention" that would help counsel or resolve problems of the individual Marine prior to his or her assignment to post. This in turn would prevent a Marine from being assigned to such a high profile post or being accepted into the program in the first place.

Third, a Designated Country Board was established prior to a Marine Security Guard's assignment to an embassy or consulate. This would insure that only those best suited would be assigned to a high threat post or where the intelligence threat to the United States was at its highest. Board members would now consider the Marine's psychological profile and test-ing, his or her grades, and "any other information that could be considered detrimental to a Marine's character" for suitability in the MSG program.

The amount of operational training increased twofold at MSG School. Increased empha-sis was now placed on integrity, performance of assigned duties with little or no supervision, and critical independent thinking, and finally, a more intensive, stressful environment that would "weed out" those unsuited for the rigors of embassy duty. Also, as a part of the school curriculum, counter intelligence training was increased. This included providing specific briefs to all Marines going to designated countries. Finally, as a means of improving the lives of Marines once on post, the living standards at the Marine House were vastly improved. Added to this was the implementation of much tighter controls over social functions (i.e. the serv-ing and availability of alcohol). This last reform was undertaken largely to prevent the excesses that reportedly took place in the Marine House and the subsequent breakdown in discipline and morale of the Marines assigned to the MSG Detachment in Moscow.

The Marine Corps likewise instituted greater oversight of the 134 Marine Detachments throughout the world with the institution of inspections twice a year by company headquar-ters with visits by their company commanders and first sergeants twice a year. Also, the com-manding officer, Marine Security Guard Battalion, and sergeant major now made official visits to each and every detachment once every two years. This last measure insured greater over-sight and administration of the program.[120]

In order to improve the working relationship between the Marine Corps and the Department of State, a separate Marine Security Guard Section was created within the Security Branch at Headquarters Marine Corps. The goal here was "to insure increased oversight of the MSG program, and provide a higher level of liaison with the Department of State. Finally, the creation of the MSG Section at HQMC vastly improved the sharing of information between the State Department and Headquarters Marine Corps."[121]

As for the Department of State, an internal investigation in wake of the Lonetree incident revealed that deficiencies existed in its Diplomatic Security Service relating to counterintelligence issues. Efforts were made toward "improving records-management systems, training programs, interagency communication and coordination, and program management."[122]

Furthermore, a greater working relationship developed between the Federal Bureau of Investigation (FBI) and the Bureau of Diplomatic Security. The FBI would now provide an individual for a two-year assignment to the Bureau of Diplomatic Security, in order to advise and train members in counterintelligence techniques and procedures. Likewise, all Foreign Service officers assigned to Eastern Europe or other highly sensitive posts were to receive training in counterintelligence.

Finally, in order to prevent a reoccurrence of the misunderstandings that occurred during both the Bracy and Lonetree investigations, the Bureau of Diplomatic Security signed a Memorandum of Understanding with the Naval Investigative Service. This memorandum between the State Department and NIS clearly defined and established common practices and investigative procedures between the two agencies in order to avoid the confusion and "turf wars" that occurred during Corporal Bracy's and Sergeant Lonetree's investigations.

In sum, there were some positive lessons learned from the Lonetree and Bracy espionage affairs. Internally, the Marine Corps was able to correct and adjust its Marine Security Guard Program while at the same time continue to train and prepare Marines for embassy duty. Secondly, a better working relationship developed among the agencies responsible for investigating internal and external security of a U.S. Embassy. Lastly, the Marine Corps and the State Department made it be known that treason will not be tolerated, in any form, a fact illustrated in the stiff penalty issued to Clayton J. Lonetree. As Major Ronald Rogers told Lieutenant Colonel Anderson before the Military Court of Appeals, what made Lonetree's acts all the more unforgivable was the fact that "he's wearing a Marine Corps uniform. And to those of us who believe in the Corps and believe in our country ... he used his office as a Marine to come into contact and gain information which he passed to the Soviet Union," information that was in turn used against the United States and its allies during the Cold War.[123]

Operation Just Cause, Panama, December 1989

From the mid–1800s through December 1989, Marines had on numerous occasions landed in Panama to quell insurrections, protect American civilians and diplomats, and later, after 1903, defend the Panama Canal. In 1904, Marines under the command of Major John A. Lejeune began construction of the first semi-permanent barracks near Panama City. In 1923, a permanent Marine presence was established with the construction of the Marine Barracks located at the U.S. Naval Submarine Base, Coco Solo. During World War II, Marine strength in Panama reached its peak of 36 officers, 3 warrant officers, and 1,571 enlisted men, as they guarded the Canal Zone against enemy saboteurs.[124] By 1987, Headquarters Marine Corps re-designated the force of five officers and 125 enlisted Marines stationed in Panama as Marine Corps Security Force (MCSF) Company Panama. This force of leathernecks remained at the U.S. Naval Station, Panama Canal, known as the Rodman Naval Station, located on the western shore of the Canal near the Pacific Ocean exit of this vital waterway.[125]

During this same period, American relations with Panama fluctuated between one of benevolence to periods of strained relations as Panamanians struggled to regain control of the Panama Canal from the United States. In 1977, after years of negotiations and bitter debate inside the U.S. Senate, President Jimmy Carter and Panamanian strongman General Omar Torrijos signed the Panama Canal Treaty that provided for complete Panamanian control of the canal by the year 2000.[126] Assured by General Torrijos that the United States would have full and complete passage through the canal, relations between the United States and Panama remained amicable until General Torrijos' death in a plane crash in 1981. Unfortunately, General Torrijos' successors, appointed largely by General Manuel Antonio Noriega, proved unable to maintain favorable relations with the United States. By 1988, in fact, the military strongman began to consolidate power through control of the Panamanian National Guard, which he later combined with the Air Force and Navy in order to create the Panamanian Defense Forces (PDF). By 1988, through his position as commander-in-chief of the PDF, General Noriega virtually controlled Panama. Through the use of the so-called "Dignity Battalions," who were little more than unemployed laborers trained by PDF officers and non-commissioned officers, Noriega harassed Panamanian politicians as well as U.S. interests in the Canal Zone, including Marines and Navy personnel assigned to the Rodman Naval Station.

Despite General Noriega's history of cooperation with American intelligence agencies, his involvement in drug smuggling and racketeering eventually made him a liability. When Noriega was indicted by two Florida-based federal grand juries, Panamanian President Eric Arturo Delvalle sought his removal as head of the PDF. Instead, Noriega struck first and engineered President Delvalle's dismissal Along with Delvalle's dismissal, came a wave of anti–American sentiment and activity, led primarily by the Dignity Battalions and other hired thugs.

President George H.W. Bush responded to this harassment by Noriega's forces when he assigned a platoon from the Norfolk, Virginia–based Fleet Anti-terrorist Security Team (FAST), Marine Corps Security Force Battalion (MCSF), to Panama, in order to protect the Naval Station's Arraijan Tank Farm, and later to augment the Marine Security Forces (including the Marine Security Guard detachment located at the U.S. Embassy) in Panama.[127]

For the Marine Security Guards assigned to the U.S. Embassy in Panama, the period from July 1, 1987 through June 8, 1989, witnessed an increase in anti–American activity, as American diplomatic personnel and their families became the target of much of this anti–American sentiment by the PDF. At one point during the period prior to Operation Just Cause, Noriega instructed the PDF to "shut off all electrical power to the Embassy building and residences" inside the U.S. diplomatic compound. This in turn forced all of the embassy's families to move into one hotel, then into a second one until power was eventually restored. In response to the escalating violence in Panama, the State Department, in May 1989, ordered all the families of the Company Headquarters personnel out of Panama. Later that month, the State Department ordered Company D, then headquartered in Panama City, to re-locate its base of operations back to Miami, Florida. This move became permanent in December 1989.[128]

In the year prior to Company D's re-location to Miami, the Marine Security Guards serving inside the U.S. Embassy became the targets of Noriega's "Dignity" Battalions and thugs from the PDF dressed in civilian clothes. On February 2, 1988, a protestor threw a rock through the windshield of an empty Marine vehicle. A month later, on 4 March 1988, a demonstration by a handful of Panamanians at the U.S. Embassy, who demanded that the

U.S. leave Panama immediately, forced a recall of the Marine Security Guards in order to prepare for a possible seizure of the embassy. Five days later, another demonstration at embassy forced the detachment commander to request reinforcement from the nearby Marine Barracks.[129] This harassment continued throughout 1988 as Noriega and his supporters sought to exploit the United States' fast-approaching withdrawal date from Panama.

Prior to the arrival of the FAST Marines, and in the waning days of his presidency, President Ronald Reagan had ordered the Marine Barracks Panama reinforced, in order to meet any contingency should Noriega become more aggressive with his rabid anti–American campaign. Additional Marine units assigned to Panama during the spring and summer of 1988 included India Company, 3rd Battalion, 4th Marines, led by Captain Joseph P. Valore, who arrived in April 1988; a platoon from the Fleet Anti-Terrorist Security Team (FAST), based at the Marine Barracks, Norfolk, Virginia, and a company from the Camp Lejeune–based 2d Light Armored Infantry Battalion. Supporting this force were command and combat service support elements from Brigade Service Support Group 6. Headquarters Marine Corps designated this force MARFOR, Panama. The mission of MARFOR Panama was to protect American lives and property, including the reinforcement of the Marine Security Guards inside the U.S. Embassy.[130]

President Bush's tough stance against General Noriega prompted the Panamanian strongman to increase the tempo of his harassment and intimidation of Americans. General Noriega and his supporters directed the bulk of this anti–Americanism toward the Marine presence in Panama. Likewise, the general's nullification of the results of a popular election on 7 May 1989 that witnessed the defeat of his chosen candidates, and subsequent beating of President-elect Guillermo Ford by his supporters, prompted the Bush administration to initiate plans for the invasion of Panama.[131]

In order to meet any emergency, FAST Marines, supported by U.S. Army helicopters, conducted, on August 15, 1989, a "fast-roped" reinforcement exercise that involved all of the Marines inside the U.S. Embassy and at the ambassador's residence. The exercise was dubbed a "complete success" for the Marine Security Guards who had been recalled to full alert status five days prior to the start of the exercise.[132]

Demonstrations against President Bush and the United States, in general, continued on into the fall of 1989. On October 3, 1989, the ambassador placed the entire Marine Detachment on full alert as reports reached the U.S. Embassy of an attempted coup against Noriega. By late November 1989, Noriega's defiant behavior, coupled with his refusal to recognize the results of the May 7, 1989, elections, forced President Bush and his advisors to consider invading Panama in order to restore democratic rule and apprehend the Panamanian leader on drug charges.

The final act that drew a swift response from President Bush was the murder of Marine First Lieutenant Robert Paz and detention of Navy Lieutenant Adam J. Curtis and his wife by members of the PDF on the evening of December 16, 1989. Already incensed over Noriega's "declaration of war" against the United States, President Bush put into motion the executive order that called for swift, retaliatory strikes against the Panamanian Defense Forces and the capture of the Panamanian dictator in an operation later known as Operation Just Cause.

The Attack on the U.S. Embassy, December 19–20, 1989

As U.S. forces assembled at bases throughout the United States, the PDF launched a well-coordinated attack against the U.S. Embassy. At approximately 10:32 P.M. on December 19, 1989, the U.S. Embassy came under heavy attack from rocket-propelled grenades fired at it by members of the PDF. In fact, "a total of 6 rocket propelled grenades impacted into the front and rear of the Embassy causing extensive damage. Throughout the attack the Marines maintained the integrity of the Embassy as well as making damage assessments and checking for fires."[133]

When the attack on the U.S. Embassy began, the eight-man Marine Security Guard, led by Staff Sergeant Michael S. Pellow, awaited reinforcement from the FAST detachment that had been assigned to reinforce the Marines inside the U.S. Embassy. Unfortunately, the FAST team became involved elsewhere. As the Marines hunkered down to defend the embassy, two light armored vehicles from the 2nd Light Armored Infantry Company, known as Task Force Gator, arrived and positioned themselves on the streets near the embassy. While they welcomed the arrival of more Marines and these armored vehicles, Staff Sergeant Pellow and his Marine Security Guards realized that "for the most part, they were on their own throughout the night" until reinforcements could arrive. Lieutenant Colonel G.G. Robinson, the commanding officer of D Company, informed Staff Sergeant Pellow that pending the arrival of reinforcements from MARFOR Panama, the Marines inside the embassy "were to take as many of them as you can with you," if the PDF had decided to storm the compound.[134] Staff Sergeant Pellow then ordered the Marines to load their shotguns with solid shot and await orders to open fire.[135]

At approximately 1:20 A.M., the embassy came under attack, primarily from members of Noriega's Dignity Battalion. At 1:45 A.M., a Marine Security Guard spotted a suspicious person with a radio positioned in front of the embassy. Staff Sergeant Pellow ordered the Marine to fire a gas grenade in the direction of the intruder. When the gas grenade impacted, the Panamanian fled the area. To prevent either the PDF or "Dignity Battalion" members from infiltrating the embassy compound, Staff Sergeant Pellow ordered the Marine Security Guards, who were armed with only shotguns and .357 revolvers, to saturate the area with gas grenades.[136]

Staff Sergeant Eric T. Howe, a watchstander during this attack, recalled that as "Just Cause" got underway, the U.S. Embassy received many rocket-propelled grenade (RPG) impacts into the chancery. Nevertheless, the Marines held their positions, despite being covered from head to toe (in SSgt. Pellow's case) with masonry and dust from the impact of the rocket propelled grenades on the walls of the chancery. As the fighting intensified all around the embassy, the Marine on duty recorded the following in the log book: "0246, via Argentinia y Espana possibly Dignity Bn. Forming up ... 10–12 blocks from Emb." At 0337, the log noted "steady mortar fire ... 0341, 4 Mortar rounds reported getting closer ... 0442, Mortar close trying to hit column, landed in back street ... 0516 ... Marine BEQ O.K., Ground Radios Dead; ... 0600 Updated Intel: Noriega Alive & puts serious threat on Emb."[137] Staff Sergeant Howe asserted later that he became deaf from all of the explosions going off around him. He recalled that when the attack began:

> The first explosion hit a palm tree next to the flagpole in front of the Embassy. My position was in the Ambassador's conference room which over looked the front of the deck, and started to low crawl out of this small place, and get to somewhere where I could return fire. Just as I dropped down, two RPGs slammed into the conference room, the room was in shambles. I was deaf from the explosions. The fire alarms were going off, and we could still hear heavy explosions coming from the city. It seemed to me like mass confusion. My primary position was destroyed, so I deployed to my secondary, which was the DCM's office. I got there and moved the couch away from the window, and removed the metal grating that protected the windows. I had to smash the glass out so I could try and acquire a target. Just at that time a RPG came in from behind me and

exploded about four feet from me. It slammed me into a wall and knocked me unconscious. SSgt Raymond Boretti was there in a few seconds after the blast, he dove on me, and started checking for wounds. Somehow I didn't even get a scratch. While Boretti and I were contemplating the situation, another RPG slammed into the Ambassador's suite. The tail fin from the rocket motor rolled up next to us.... We turned to one another and laughed. To this day I have never been that afraid.

Meanwhile at Post One, SSgt Michael Pellow [the detachment commander] had been one the phone with the Company Commander (LtCol Robinson) when the first blast occurred. Sgt. Staples tried to call in FAST to help us.[138]

Then, Staff Sergeant Howe stated that all of the civilians in the embassy

were still locked in the CPU vault. AK-47 fire swept the compound. We were unable to acquire any enemy to fire at. Later we spotted a Panamanian carrying what appeared to be a PRC-77 radio. At that time Cpl Richard Krout maneuvered to a position, and launched several CS canisters in the area surrounding Dubbs the Embassy. That seemed to stop the enemy from firing into the compound. These four hours went by quickly, but we didn't know if they were going to launch another attack.

Now we were subject to sniper fire. Still we had no support, the FAST Marines from Rodman had been given another such mission. We felt like we were hung out to dry. During this intense time we had destroyed much classified material. The State Department personnel in the vault had began destroying classified [material] when the first rounds began hitting the embassy. The Admin officer who was the senior American at the Embassy, made the decision to call the Pentagon situation in DC. He told them to send someone quickly, because the embassy was possibly going to be overrun!

The next morning the Army Rangers arrived. We were happy to see them. The next two weeks we lived in the Embassy, and in a hotel behind the Embassy.

There were several firefights in the direct vicinity of the embassy. Later in the afternoon of the 20th the FAST Marines arrived. They stayed for two weeks on the Embassy compound, and at the ambassador's residence.[139]

As Staff Sergeant Howe noted, the Army Rangers eventually came to the assistance of the Marine Security Guards after a harrowing night under fire by the Dignity Battalions and the PDF. After battling the PDF and remnants of the Dignity Battalions for nearly seven weeks, American forces (U.S. Army Rangers, Delta, and paratroops, Marines, Navy SEALS, and aircraft from the Air Force) gradually scattered the few pockets of resistance that remained after the initial assault. In the end, the American forces cornered Noriega inside the Papal Nuncio, where he eventually surrendered on January 3, 1990, and was taken into captivity by Drug Enforcement Agents, who served him with the warrants for his arrest. Transported to the United States for trial, the U.S. Federal Court in Miami convicted General Noriega of drug smuggling and racketeering and sentenced him to forty years in the federal prison in Atlanta, Georgia.

Commenting on the performance of the Marine Security Guards who withstood nearly twenty-four hours of fire, General Maxwell R. Thurman, Commanding General, Southern Command, summed it up best when he stated, "an infantry company of lesser men could not have done well as the eight embassy Marines."[140]

Closure of the U.S. Embassy in Kabul, Afghanistan, January 1989

Surrounded by the fighting that engulfed Afghanistan shortly after the murder of Ambassador Adolph "Spike" Dubbs on February 14, 1979, the U.S. Embassy, situated in the heart

The Marine Security Guard Detachment, Kabul, Afghanistan, poses for a last photograph prior to its deactivation in 1989 (U.S. Marine Security Guard Battalion).

of Kabul, the capital, and located near the Presidential Palace, was a "sea of stability" in an otherwise dangerous part of the world. For the next ten years, the U.S. maintained a reduced staff of diplomats and Marine embassy guards as the Soviet Army, its puppet Afghan Army, and Mujahadeen or "Warriors of God" fought each other in and around Kabul. Eventually, and with increased U.S. and other foreign aid, much of it clandestine, the Mujahadeen fought the Soviet Army to the bargaining table, where it finally agreed to leave the country by February 15, 1989. Secretary of State James A. Baker III feared that the American envoy, Mr. Jon D. Glassman, and his staff (including several Marine embassy guards) could become either hostages or casualties to any of the dozen or so factions fighting the Soviets, the government of Najibullah, or themselves. Secretary Baker thus ordered the embassy in Kabul closed as a precautionary measure so as to protect the Americans living there.[141]

On January 30, 1989, in a solemn ceremony marked by sounds of distant gunfire and explosions, Chargé d'Affaires Jon Glassman "watched a small Marine detachment lower the American flag." As the "Stars and Stripes" slowly made its way down the flagpole, the Marines "gently folded the flag and handed it to Mr. Glassman, who walked to a small slab of marble on the other side of the compound that honors Adolph Dubbs, the former U.S. Ambassador."[142] Chargé Glassman later told reporters, "The people of Afghanistan will enjoy peace and freedom once again. That is our wish.... We say goodbye, and God Bless the United States of America. We are going home."[143] The next day, the American party boarded an Indian transport aircraft that transported them to New Delhi, where they boarded planes bound for the United States or assignments elsewhere.

Marine Security Guards in Kuwait, August 1990

In the early evening hours of 1 August 1990, while Marine Embassy Guards hosted a social function at the Marine House in Kuwait City, Kuwait, approximately 120,000 Iraqi troops, tanks, armored personnel carriers, and troop-carrying helicopters, which had been poised at the border between Iraq and Kuwait, poured across the border into western Kuwait. The Iraqi invasion of Kuwait had begun.[144] As Iraqi troops stormed into Kuwait City, the Marine Embassy Guards inside the U.S. Embassy quickly went on full alert, as it became obvious that it was not be "business as usual" inside the diplomatic compound.[145]

In fact, in the pre-dawn hours of August 2, 1990, as he stood duty at Post One, Sergeant Paul G. Rodriguez overheard a conversation between the duty officer, Mr. Kevin Briscoe and the ambassador that Iraqi forces had "penetrated into the Western Border of Kuwait and did a sweep up along the northern border taking out all police posts and [had] taken over the oil rigs."[146] At approximately 5:20 A.M. the ambassador gave the order to recall the Marine Embassy Security Guards. Sergeant Rodriguez then

took a deep breath and counted to 10 rather quickly and called the Marine House. Cpl Royer answered the phone and I said, "We're going hot this is not a drill. The British EMB is taking rounds." I then called the DET CMDR and RSO and both were already in route. By this time a lot of small arms fire could be heard north of the compound. At approx. 0525 the RSO and DETCMDR came aboard. By this time the DET was still not aboard. Post #1 waited for what seemed an eternity. At Approx. 0527 the DET came aboard, locked and loaded with the weapons we had in the safe at the Marine House. The situation was apparent. The mission was understood. The execution was well rehearsed and the following internal defense positions were assigned.... Not long after the Marines were in position, the destruction of classified material was ordered by the Ambassador. The night before the invasion we knew that the destruction was not part of our duties.

I was also monitoring and reporting all activity by the Iraqi forces outside the compound with help from our local guard force positioned at our front gate and back gate and I also had a good view with our cameras all around the compound. I also was still taking phone calls from a lot of scared people in Kuwait. I was told to tell them to just stay inside where it was safe. My biggest concern was to report as much of the Iraqi forces going by the compound to Major Freeley who was then in turn reporting it by radio to CENTCOM. A lot of tanks and troops drove by so what we did was to have our local investigator, who was also in charge of the guard force, stay at the back gate and write down everything that went by to include any and all flags and uniforms that the troops were wearing. He then just reported approximately every hour to Post #1 and I then passed it to Major Freeley, vice calling every minute when a tank or troop carrier went by. Still, on the first day of the invasion the destruction of classified took approximately 6–8 hours....

By this time we had a minimal staff from various sections to include approximately 6 other military, 4 secretaries, Ambassador, DCM, and approximately 8–10 other key personnel. Day 1 was extremely long. I had phone and radio contact with several people who gave me eyewitness accounts of assaults on the palaces and build ups in the city. Kuwait National Guard forces still stood their ground outside the compound. Some fire fights broke out the back gate with the Kuwaiti forces taking cover behind their vehicle barriers. Iraqi forces were stopping cars and taking them for "joy" rides. Once the Kuwaitis found out at the back gate they began to check all the cars going by. The back gate local guards reported that the Kuwaitis found two Iraqi troops in a car and pulled them out and reported that they were going to kill them.[147]

Sgt. Rodriguez stated that on August 3, Day 2 of the invasion, the Marines remained at their assigned positions. They likewise established radio contact with the other Allied embassies. When the Marines received a report that the Kuwait International Hotel across the street from the U.S. Embassy had moved all of its guests and staffs away from the compound, the Marines assumed that "they would be the Iraq's next on call target for a mortar attack."[148]

When Sergeant Rodriguez returned to his post on the night of August 4, the Marines received their second red alert in the form of threatening phone calls that were "claiming that there would be some men dressed as Arabs that would attack the compound." Sergeant Rodriguez claimed that the callers identified themselves as angry "Palestinians." One of these alerts consisted of Iraqis dressed as Kuwaitis in traditional dish-dashas, so as to blame it on the local government. As Staff Sergeant Smith later wrote, "None of these alerts ever materialized."[149] Later that evening, while he waited for "any attack," Sgt. Rodriguez noticed on his cameras five 1-ton trucks dropping off approximately 50 Iraqi troops outside the back gate of the embassy. Once the troops disembarked from the trucks, they made camp and there they stayed until the U.S. ambassador ordered the embassy evacuated. During this same time, the Marine sergeant reported that the Kuwaiti troops guarding the American compound removed their uniforms and fled their posts outside the compound walls.

When the Iraqi ambassador requested a meeting with all foreign diplomats in Kuwait City, the American ambassador refused and, instead, asked the Canadian ambassador to represent the United States. Sergeant Rodriguez later remembered that while he could not recall the nature of the meeting, he did note that the Canadian diplomat was visibly shaken when he returned from this meeting with Iraqi officials. In any event, on the night of August 7, the ambassador ordered the Marines to remove their uniforms and put on civilian clothes. At approximately 6:00 A.M. on August 8, the ambassador ordered all of the weapons in the React Room destroyed. After several Marines questioned the order, Staff Sergeant Smith snapped to the Marines, "Just do it." Sergeant Rodriguez and the other Marine Security Guards then began to systematically "smash all 870P Shotguns, all .357 pistols, all .38 pistols, 1 Uzi 9mm, also destroyed 2 Gerber knives belonging to the USLOK as gifts, and also destroyed the Ambassador's personal Colt .44 Magnum Python."[150]

Staff Sergeant Smith emphasized that during the first three days of the Iraqi invasion, the ambassador had authorized the use of deadly force. At the end of the third day, however, permission to use deadly force was withdrawn without the verbal consent of the ambassador. Sergeant Rodriguez recalled that this and the destruction of the firearms resulted in a severe blow to the morale of the Marines, who remained determined to carry out their mission and protect the Americans and other foreigners who now resided in the U.S. Embassy compound. Sergeant Rodriguez wrote that as it turned out, the RSO misread the ambassador's order that read "to render all weapons inoperable," and not destroy them, as Staff Sergeant Smith ordered the Marines to do on the morning of the 8th.

At no time during the Iraqi invasion did the Iraqis attempt to breach the walls of the embassy. Staff Sergeant Smith noted that the embassy did "take on fire from small arms into the buildings of the compound including the Chancery and Marine House," and that "tank and artillery rounds were fired over the Embassy Compound," hitting a building adjacent to the compound. The Marine SNCOIC noted that none of the staff, civilians or Marines inside the compound were injured by Iraqi or Kuwaiti fire. Staff Sergeant Smith did note, however, that throughout the exchange of gunfire between the invading Iraqis and Kuwaitis, the Marines remained in their defensive positions throughout the embassy. The only time the Marines left these positions were to look and, if necessary, rescue civilians seeking refuge from the fighting.[151] On August 10, Staff Sergeant Smith requested from the ambassador that the Marines be permitted to wear their camouflage utilities. As SSgt. Smith noted, the ambassador complied with the request. Despite being allowed to wear their camouflage utilities, both Smith and Sergeant Rodriguez noted that the morale of the Marines "dropped to its lowest level of the entire time in Kuwait." Corporal Mark E. Royer said the Marine Security Guards maintained a constant state of readiness, as they slept on the floor of their positions and remained with the ambassador at all times.[152]

The Marine Security Guards and the defense attaché officer performed an important intelligence function by relaying information on the movement of the Iraqi forces to American military officials at Central Command Headquarters. Staff Sergeant Smith noted, "The information passed to the officer did not interfere in any way with the operation of Post #1, nor the Detachment's responsibility to the defense of the Embassy. This was vital information that Central Command relied upon for its intelligence on Iraqi forces that were heading south to the Kuwait/Saudi Arabian border along Arabian Gulf Road which passes between the Embassy and the Persian Gulf."[153] On August 23, 1990, the ambassador, acting on an earlier decision to evacuate the Marine Security Guards from the area, ordered the detachment and all non-essential personnel to convoy north to Baghdad. Here, they were to board airplanes for the United States. The next morning, at 7:00 A.M., upon receiving the word to evacuate the embassy, Marine Security Guards "rode shotgun" as they guarded the convoy of over thirty vehicles carrying embassy staff, their dependents and other evacuees. As the convoy headed out of Kuwait, Iraq's invasion turned into a full-scale occupation of that country until coalition forces forced the Iraqis out of Kuwait in February 1991.

Baghdad, August 1990–January 1991

While Iraq's invasion came as surprise to most of the world, a Department of State (DOS) Task Force had sensed that an evacuation of the region might be necessary as early as 20 August 1990. It was on this date that State Department officials informed the Marine Security Guard section at Headquarters Marine Corps that it had ordered the Marine Security Guard, along with other non-essential employees and dependents from Baghdad, Kuwait, and Sanaa, to leave for Amman, Jordan. On August 21, 1990, Lieutenant Colonel Lonnie Messick, Company B's commanding officer, informed officials at the DOS that the Marine Security Guards from Baghdad were safely in Amman, awaiting transportation back to the United States. Two days later, on 23 August 1990, officials at HQMC informed officials at the State Department that the Marine Security Guard Detachment in Kuwait had been stranded in Baghdad, where it was "manning the posts at the embassy."[154]

Staff Sergeant J.B. Smith recalled that originally, the Marine Security Guards had been detailed to provide command and control of the convoy of American and other foreign dependents in order to "lessen the likelihood of being a group target." While the dependents were being moved, an elderly woman broke her hip and received other wounds in an auto accident that required hospitalization. Sergeant David K. Hudson volunteered to take the woman back to a hospital in Kuwait City where, after assurances that the woman would be taken care of, the Marine Security Guard returned to the convoy now inside of Iraq headed toward Baghdad.

After the Marines arrived in Baghdad, Iraqi officials informed the Marine Security Guards that they were to be kept as hostages. Staff Sergeant Smith later recalled that the Marines shortly thereafter "assumed responsibilities of Post 1 at 1200, on August 24, 1990."[155] Upon arriving in Baghdad, SSgt. Smith immediately conversed with the chargé d'affaires "on what he desired of the Detachment." The chargé informed both SSgt. Smith and the RSO "that the Detachment was to assume all responsibilities as an MSG Detachment." Unlike in Kuwait immediately after the Iraqi invasion, the chargé authorized the Marine Security Guards to use deadly force if necessary to protect the embassy and all personnel inside the compound.[156] In fact, as Smith recalled, the chargé emphasized that "deadly force and all duties inherent to the position were to be enforced." After the chargé issued these instructions to the Detachment Commander, he immediately rescinded the order and instructed that the Marines were to have only "exit and entrance duties," with no deadly force or security sweeps authorized. Furthermore, the Marines were not permitted to use mace, handcuffs, all ammunition, and PR-24s, all of which were to be secured in a safe near Post One. This policy remained in effect until October 1, 1990, when Mr. Jim Blystone, an administrative officer from the State Department, arrived in Baghdad to inspect the facilities and security at the near-deserted embassy. Much to his surprise, Mr. Blystone discovered that "the MSG's were not being utilized properly." The diplomatic envoy concluded "that they should be afforded the ability to accomplish their mission as MSGs."[157] Three days later, on October 4, 1990, after both the chargé and RSO met with Mr. Blystone, the former authorized the use of deadly force and permission to conduct security sweeps. As SSgt. Smith noted, "These security sweeps consisted of the Administration building, the USIS building, and the Chancery."

Now "guests" of Saddam Hussein's government, the Marines settled into a daily routine inside the U.S. Embassy. Staff Sergeant Smith wrote, "The initial billeting of the Detachment was in the Chancery. After approximately four days we were billeted in the Commercial building and the Chancery, with the breakdown being four Marines in the Commercial building and two Marines in the Chancery. The Detachment Commander and Assistant Detachment Commander were billeted separately. On approximately October 25, 1990, the Detachment was then billeted in the Consular officer's residence, one block from Chancery. The Detachment Commander was billeted four blocks from the Chancery. This at any one time would leave one Marine on duty, and three Marines at the residence and myself at my residence. This would keep us separated and not bunched up at any one place."[158] The accommodations were Spartan. Sergeant Hudson recalled, "During the first two months in Iraq we slept on floors in the Commercial Building."[159]

Despite the ongoing military buildup by the United States and its Coalition partners in Saudi Arabia, relations with the Iraqis in Baghdad and the embassy remained tense, though without incident. The Iraqi government permitted one Marine Security Guard, Sergeant Ward, to leave the embassy for home, as his father had passed away in November 1990. To keep the focus of the Marines on their job, Staff Sergeant Smith noted that a regular routine of physical training, guard school, and React Drills were adhered to. While the Iraqi government permitted the Marine Security Guards to take liberty, they were restricted to an area within a twenty-five mile radius of Baghdad. Staff Sergeant Smith noted, however, that the Marines were required to obtain his permission, and that no liberty was granted on an ad hoc, spontaneous basis.

Surprisingly, the Iraqi people "showed no animosity toward the Americans other than the government sponsored demonstrations at the Embassy." The detachment commander did note, however, that the number of Iraqi soldiers guarding intersections, armed with rifles and pistols were numerous, but they never did approach or make provocative gestures toward the Marines or other Americans in Baghdad.[160] Staff Sergeant Smith did note, however, that the Iraqi secret police followed the Marines wherever they went.

On December 7, 1990, the chargé informed the Marine Security Guards that Saddam Hussein would release all foreign hostages, including the Americans. Two days later, on December 9, 1990, the American envoy relieved the MSG Detachment of its duties and responsibilities as the "MSG's for the American Embassy Baghdad, Iraq." At 8 P.M., the Marine Security Guard Detachment departed Baghdad and landed in Frankfurt, Germany. They arrived at Andrews Air Force Base, Maryland, the next day, on December 10, 1990. On December 11, 1990, all of the Marine Security Guards reported to Marine Security Guard Battalion at Quantico.

The Liberation of Kuwait, February 24–28, 1991

On February 24, 1991, the United States and its Coalition partners launched Operation Desert Storm, with the objective of driving the Iraqi army from Kuwait. Within two days, elements of the 1st Marine Expeditionary Force, along with Saudi and Kuwait forces, arrived on the outskirts of Kuwait City. As Marine reconnaissance and pathfinder teams fanned out throughout the abandoned city, one of those teams, under the command of 1st Lieutenant Brian G. Knowles, headed for the U.S. Embassy. Upon entering the U.S. compound, First Lieutenant Knowles found a tattered American flag still flying proudly above the embassy's courtyard. Lieutenant Knowles' Marines then conducted an extensive clearing operation, checking for booby traps and assessing the damage to the diplomatic compound. At 10:10 P.M. that same evening, Lieutenant Knowles declared the embassy secure.[161]

Into the Future

The liberation of Kuwait took only four days. After nearly a month and a half of aerial bombardment by U.S. and Allied aircraft prior to the commencement of the ground war, the Iraqi army had been whittled down to where it was no match for American and coalition forces. On February 24, 1991, President George H.W. Bush ordered American and Coalition forces to launch Operation Desert Storm. In one of the most lopsided victories in American military history, U.S. Marines, soldiers, airmen, coast guardsmen, and sailors along with NATO and Arab allies defeated the Iraqi Army, once heralded as the world's "4th largest army." While they were not present in Iraq during the victory, the Marine Security Guards who stood guard of the U.S. Embassy in Kuwait City played a vital role during those early, critical days of Iraq's invasion of Kuwait. Undaunted by the threat posed by this hostile force inside Kuwait and later Baghdad, the Marine Security Guards maintained their professionalism and carried out their duties until ordered out of Iraq in December 1990.

CHAPTER 9

Coups, Non–Combatant Evacuations, and the War on Terror, 1991–2007

While the Marine Embassy Guard in Baghdad maintained a vigilant watch over the now practically abandoned U.S. Embassy in the Iraqi capital, Marines from both I and II Marine Expeditionary Forces (MEF) continued to make preparations for a ground war that was now all but inevitable. As the Marines in Saudi Arabia busily prepared for combat, clashes between the forces of Siade Barre and anti-government forces in Mogadishu, the capital of Somalia, threatened the lives of both U.S. and other foreign nationals residing in the city. Violence and political chaos in Liberia likewise threatened the security and lives of the U.S. diplomatic community in Monrovia. Both crises eventually necessitated the execution of Non-Combatant Evacuation Operations (NEOs) by Marines from I MEF in early January 1991. At the forefront of these operations, respectively dubbed *Sharp Edge* and *Eastern Exit*, Marine Security Guard detachments stood ready to defend yet another U.S. Embassy against the outrages of the numerous local gangs and private armies in these two war-torn African countries. During the decade of the 1990s, Africa and Southwest Asia became the focus of these "Ambassadors in Blue," as they dealt with several *coups d'état* and the numerous Non-Combatant Operations.

Commencing with the defense of the U.S. Embassy in Monrovia, Liberia, in 1990, Marine Security Guards remained vigilant at embassies throughout the continent of Africa throughout the 1990s. This vigilance included the humanitarian interventions in Rwanda and Burundi (1994 and 1996), in Brazzaville, Congo, in 1997, and in the Republic of the Congo in 1998, and finally, the destruction of the U.S. embassies in Kenya and Dar Es Salaam in 1998.[1]

The Non-Combatant Evacuation Operation in Liberia, May 1990–January 1991

Prior to and during Operation Desert Shield, Marines found themselves carrying out nearly simultaneous non-combatant evacuation operations in both Liberia and Somalia. At the forefront of these operations were the Marine Security Guard detachments located in Monrovia, Liberia, and Mogadishu, Somalia. As political unrest and *coups d'état* unseated President Samuel K. Doe of Liberia (September 1990), and Siad Barre in Somalia (1991), Marine Security Guards once again found themselves in defense of American and foreign nationals as the security situation around them deteriorated. Once again, the Marines inside the embassies and members of the Camp Lejeune–based 22nd Marine Expeditionary Unit (Special Operations Capable) (MEU[SOC])), demonstrated the close working partnership between the State Department and the Marine Corps in the defense of U.S. embassies and personnel.

The insurgency against President Samuel K. Doe, a former master sergeant in the Liberian army, began in December 1989 and was led by Charles Taylor, leader of the National Patriotic Front of Liberia (NPFL), and Prince Johnson's Independent National Patriotic Front of Liberia (INPFL). Both the NPFL and INPFL were implacable foes of Doe and sought his removal from power. By late May 1990, both rebel armies had overtaken key installations, including the coastal town of Buchanan, and threatened to march on Monrovia, the capital, unless President Doe capitulated and fled the country.[2]

As the warring armies jockeyed for power in Liberia throughout late spring 1990, the 22nd MEU(SOC) continued to train for any contingency. As the leathernecks and sailors of 22nd MEU(SOC) trained in Toulon, France, the MEU's forward command element (FCE) drew up a series of contingencies that involved the execution of an NEO from Monrovia.[3] On May 27, 1990, the National Command Authority ordered the 22nd MEU to stand by and make the necessary preparations in order to conduct "a NEO, the reinforcement of the U.S. Embassy in Monrovia, security for the communication sites,[4] humanitarian assistance, and the possible extraction of key personnel."[5]

Pre-deployment training paid off during Operation Sharp Edge, as the plans developed in early May 1990 were exactly the same ones executed later that August. Detailed planning and continued rehearsals prior to and during the prolonged periods of MODLOC (Miscellaneous Operational Details, Local Operations) factored into 22nd MEU's state of readiness, resulting in the execution of a simple, unchanged plan. The 22nd MEU(SOC)'s "laborious pre-deployment planning paid big dividends in a crisply executed actual contingency mission, months after the Marine Amphibious Readiness Group 2–90's (of which 22nd MEU had been attached) deployment from CONUS." As occurred during Operation Eagle Pull, the evacuation from Phnom Penh in March 1975, the Marines of 22nd MEU(SOC) were ready when the order was given to execute the mission.[6] Starting on May 20, 1990, the BLT staff and tactical commanders received daily intelligence briefs on the situation in Monrovia. Also, in a move to provide more riflemen, the MEU commander ordered the formation of provisional rifle platoons from Battery I, Headquarters and Service Company, Light Armored Infantry, and the transformation of Weapons Company into a provisional rifle company. All Marines received briefs on the rules of engagement once ashore in Monrovia, and conducted extensive live fire weapons practice to enhance combat readiness.[7]

All MEU(SOC) exercises held prior to the MEU's deployment, known as SOCEXs (Special Operations Capable Exercises), involved scenarios focused on the defense and evacuation of a "notional" U.S. Embassy, where Marine Embassy guards participated on a regular basis. During Sharp Edge, both the Marine Embassy Guard detachment and local guards had been integrated into 22nd MEU's evacuation plan. When the time came to execute the NEO from Monrovia, these plans and practices produced "a force ready to execute the assigned contingency."[8]

Prior to the execution of Sharp Edge, Marine and Navy officers of the forward command element (FCE) coordinated both the reinforcement of the embassy, and its defense with the RSO. By using a map that illustrated the layout of the embassy and the surrounding buildings, the FCE was better able to plan for its defense. For Sharp Edge, "the plan encompassed securing the surrounding multi-storied building threat, outside, perimeter patrols along the U.N. Drive side of the Embassy wall, inner patrols along the Embassy walls, locating automatic weapons and key observation posts within the compound, and finally, the staging of a reaction force within the compound itself."[9] This plan included both the Marine Security Guard Detachment and State Department's own Special Security Forces (SSFs), both of which were under the direct supervision of the RSO. The FCE discounted the use of the local guard force, however, as it lacked the proper weapons to repel any penetration of the Embassy compound.

Besides the defense of the embassy, the FCE plan called for securing a key complex known as the Greystone Compound, where non-evacuees would be diverted to during the evacuation of most Americans and foreign nationals. Prior to the arrival of Ambassador James Bishop, the deputy chief of mission (DCM) outlined a plan for the defense of the compound by the insertion of a force of Marines to patrol both the inner and outer walls. The DCM authorized the positioning of machine guns at key observation posts within the compound, as well as the establishment of a reaction force placed on standby in the compound itself.

The DCM believed that in any event, a sizable force of Marines would be required to defend the Greystone Compound, as it lacked adequate physical barriers to prevent rioters from entering the complex. Upon assuming his post, Ambassador Bishop scrapped this plan and instead instructed all Americans living there to move into apartments inside the embassy compound.

By early July 1990, the situation on the ground in Liberia had worsened, as Johnson's NPFL had gained control over most of central and portions of eastern Liberia. Meanwhile, thousands of refugees began pouring into the capital, fleeing the advancing rebels. As Johnson and Prince's forces turned their attention toward Monrovia, and with it an upsurge in anti–American activities, Ambassador Bishop feared that the fighting in the countryside as it neared the urban areas could endanger American lives caught between the warring parties.[10]

On August 4, 1990, the situation took a turn for the worse when Prince Johnson's INPFL openly threatened to seize Americans and foreign nationals as hostages. This in turn prompted Ambassador Bishop to request an evacuation of U.S. citizens, foreign nationals, and other designated non-essential personnel. Accordingly, the commander-in-chief, Europe, issued the order for the evacuation to take place the next day on August 5, 1990. The executive order instructed 22nd MEU(SOC) to: (1) Evacuate American citizens from the two communication sites; (2) Reinforce the American Embassy in Monrovia with a reinforced rifle company; (3) Evacuate American citizens and other designated foreign nationals from the American Embassy; and (4) Provide logistical support, as required, to the American Embassy.[11]

"Send in the Marines": The Evacuation, 5 August 1990

At 9:00 P.M. on August 4, 1990, the FCE and MEU staff reviewed and refined final preparations for the insertion and evacuation. At 5:00 A.M. on August 5, the USS *Saipan* pulled to within six nautical miles of the coast of Liberia. A final brief was held prior to the launch of the first helicopters at 9:00 A.M. As the helicopters of HMM-261 lifted off through clouds, a thick mist and thunderstorms set in over Monrovia while refugees began to gather inside the U.S. Embassy into heli-teams. At 9:06 A.M., the first CH-53 helicopter from HMM-261 inserted a platoon of 45 Marines from Company E, 2/4 into the communications site. The men quickly fanned out and secured the landing zone. The first to be evacuated were 18 people assigned to the communications facility. By 013 all evacuees had boarded helicopters and were on their way to the *Saipan*. Minutes later, a CH-53 safely extracted all 45 Marines of Company E. At 9:26 A.M., helicopters airlifted another platoon from Company E into the transmitter site to pick up the three evacuees located there. In a show of force, the Marines discouraged about 20 of Prince's INPFL rebels from approaching the site. The guerrillas quickly backed off as CH-53's flew directly over their heads.

Meanwhile, back at the U.S. Embassy, Marines from Company H, BLT 2/4, by 9:10 A.M., had reinforced the Marine Security Guard detachment inside the U.S. Embassy compound. Once inside the embassy, the company commander established a series of small security forces at each gate. Once the Marines accomplished the tasks, forces were moved outside the embassy in order to prevent the rebels — the Armed Forces of Liberia or "AFL"— from entering the compound.

The MEU's pre-planning, as well as the cooperation with the RSO and Marine Security Guard detachment, paid off, as Company H quickly established defensive positions within the embassy itself. In fact, the leathernecks from Company H augmented the MSG's React capability as they set up their positions within and outside the embassy compound. Shortly thereafter, the Marines countered their first resistance, in the way of sniper and small arms fire. When a patrol of about 20 INPFL rebels approached the embassy near the intersection of U.N. Drive and Benson Street, a squad from Company H, in a show of force, convinced the rebels to withdraw through skillful negotiations with use of a bullhorn. Once the rebels cleared the area, the leathernecks then conducted a sweep to insure that there were no more insurgents in the area. They then established blocking positions at the same intersection to discourage further guerrilla movements toward the embassy.

By the evening of August 5, the reinforcement of the embassy had been completed. Rifle

Two U.S. Marines remain alert as they scan the approaches to the U.S. Embassy in Monrovia looking for rebels attempting to break into the diplomatic compound in 1996 (courtesy U.S. Marine Corps).

squads from Company H, supported by heavy machine guns mounted on two fast attack vehicles, manned blocking positions outside the embassy. Other Marines manned observation positions inside and outside the embassy in order to prevent the rebels from entering the compound. Meanwhile, due to both legal and political considerations, however, the commander-in-chief, Europe, ordered the Marines to abandon their positions outside the embassy and withdraw to inside the diplomatic compound.[12]

Company H remained ashore for eight days until relieved by Company E on August 13. When 18 soldiers from the Liberian Army attempted to pass by the embassy along U.N. Drive from the south, the Marines quickly turned them away by threatening to use riot control agents. As the Liberian soldiers cleared the area, a force of INPFL rebels approached the Marines, who likewise discouraged them from going any further.

Eventually, as the evacuation portion of the operation ended, the decision was made to reduce the size of force down to a reinforced rifle platoon. By 13 August, there were 65 Marines (including the MSG detachment) defending the embassy compound. Company E continued to be responsible for the defense of the compound as well as the evacuation of the remaining foreign nationals. By the time elements of 22nd MEU withdrew from Liberian waters, the Marines and helicopters of HMM-261 had removed 1,648 evacuees from the U.S. Embassy Compound in Monrovia.[13] In time, Marines and sailors from 26th MEU(SOC) replaced the 22nd, which pulled away and headed for home. Prior to 22nd MEU's departure, elements of BLT 3/8 relieved the leathernecks of Company H, BLT 2/4. The Marines from BLT 3/8 remained on station and were the last to leave when the commander-in-chief, Europe, declared Operation Sharp Edge at an end.

The Lessons of Operation Sharp Edge

The successful execution of Operation Sharp Edge validated the MEU(SOC) training syllabus followed by all Marine infantry battalions prior to their departure from Camp Lejeune, North Carolina, and Camp Pendleton, California. Furthermore, the success of Sharp Edge demonstrated the close relationship between Marine Security Guards and Fleet Marine Force units, and the importance of including Marine Security Guards in any pre-deployment training and planning. More important was the close integration of the FCE's plan for the defense of the U.S. Embassy in Monrovia. In fact, the coordination between the FCE and RSO, as well as with the Marine Security Guard detachment, insured that the operation ended in success. Furthermore, the cooperation of all three components insured that upon the order to execute the mission, all of the vital elements in the defensive and evacuation phases of the operation came together at the right time to insure its success. Like Operation Eagle Pull, planning beforehand by all key Marine and Navy components, as well with State Department officials, insured a smooth operation once the order was given to carry out the evacuation.

The most important lesson learned from Operation Sharp Edge, however, centered upon the fact that prior planning and coordination insured that there was not one single loss of life during the operation. Though Marine commanders did not give much thought to it in the aftermath of Sharp Edge, the final evacuation from Monrovia served as the model for the next successful non-combatant evacuation operation in neighboring Somalia.

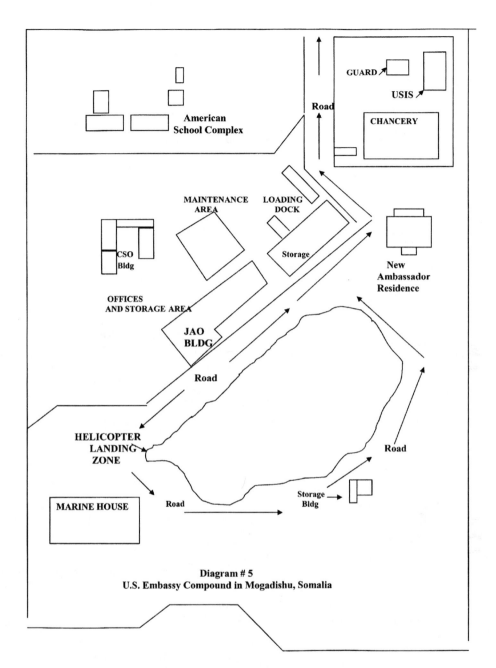

Labels within the diagram:

GUARD
USIS
CHANCERY
American
School Complex
Road
MAINTENANCE
AREA
LOADING
DOCK
Storage
New
Ambassador
Residence
CSO
Bldg
OFFICES
AND STORAGE AREA
JAO
BLDG
Road
HELICOPTER
LANDING
ZONE
Road
MARINE HOUSE
Road
Storage
Bldg
Diagram # 5
U.S. Embassy Compound in Mogadishu, Somalia

Diagram # 5. U.S. Embassy Compound in Mogadishu, Somalia (Siegel, *Eastern Exit*, Center for Naval Analysis, page 6).

Evacuation from Somalia in January 1991

As the U.S.-led coalition continued preparations for a possible confrontation with Iraqi forces in Kuwait, continued factional fighting in the strife-torn African nation of Somalia prompted U.S. Ambassador James K. Bishop to request the immediate evacuation of all non-essential American personnel from that country. As the forces of Somali warlord Mohammed Farah Aideed pushed the forces of President Mohammed Siad Barre into the capital city of Mogadishu, Ambassador Bishop cabled Washington, D.C., and asked that the embassy be evacuated. As the fighting between the two rival clans intensified, the State Department ordered elements from the 4th Marine Expeditionary Unit on standby notice in order to execute a non-combatant evacuation operation in the African nation.[14]

Due to Somalia's proximity to the Persian Gulf, authority to prepare and launch the rescue attempt was given to General Norman Schwarzkopf, who at the time was Commanding General, Central Command, and responsible for Desert Shield. On January 2, 1991, General Schwarzkopf ordered Vice Admiral Stanley R. Arthur's[15] naval forces "to launch Operation Eastern Exit to rescue those trapped in the diplomatic compound at Mogadishu."

Vice Admiral Arthur had decided to send a two-ship force from Amphibious Group Two along with a 60-man Marine and Navy SEAL force to assist in the defense and later evacuation of U.S. and foreign nationals from the Mogadishu embassy. Meanwhile, Major General H.W. Jenkins, commanding general of the 4th Marine Expeditionary Brigade (MEB), designated Colonel J.J. Doyle as the commander, landing force. The ground forces assigned to Eastern Exit included a reinforced rifle company, C Company, Battalion Landing Team 1/2, led by Lieutenant Colonel R.P. McAleer, and combat support and combat service elements from Brigade Service Support Group 4.[16] The force from 4th MEB augmented the five-man Marine Security Guard detachment assigned to the U.S. Embassy in Mogadishu to protect classified material and provide close-in protection for embassy personnel.[17]

Planners from Central Command settled on a two-phased plan of operation, which demanded perfect timing and precise execution. Reports of heavy fighting were coming from the U.S. Embassy and gangs armed with assault rifles and rocket-propelled grenades were trying to storm the compound's walls. The first phase called for a night reinforcement mission by CH-53s to the U.S. Embassy, to be immediately followed by the main evacuation operation that involved a ferry operation by CH-46s as Amphibious Group Two positioned itself off the coast of Somalia.[18]

In the late evening hours of January 2, 1991, the USS *Guam* (LPH) and USS *Trenton* (LPD) steamed toward their launch point off Somalia. Aboard were Marines and sailors from BLT 2/1, its Brigade Service Support Group 4 elements, 12 CH-46 helicopters from HMM-365 and an additional 12 from HMM-263, as well as two UH-1 Huey gunships, and two CH-53Es "Super Stallions" from HMH-461's.

As the force positioned itself off the coast of Somalia, the situation in Mogadishu grew more intense. At first, planners in both Washington, D.C., and at Central Command thought that an air evacuation might be the best option, and to that end, General Schwarzkopf dispatched a force of U.S. Army Reserve policemen to the Mogadishu airport. As the situation on the ground further deteriorated, Ambassador Bishop thought that the remaining embassy staff could not be assured safe passage from the embassy to the airport. While the distance was less than 1.5 miles, conditions were such in Mogadishu that Bishop thought an air evacuation "too dangerous," to undertake. Hence, officials decided that the best option was to use a force of Marines to conduct the evacuation by use of helicopters.[19]

By January 2, 1991, Ambassador Bishop's calls for help became "more strident." This in turn prompted General Schwarzkopf to order the insertion of a 60-man Marine force and a nine-man Navy SEAL team as a security force at the now surrounded U.S. Embassy. While the task force was still 1,500 nautical miles from its launch point, Navy and Marine officers decided to wait until its force was within 466 nautical miles. In the early morning hours of January 5, 1991, the giant CH-53 "Super Stallions" lifted from the flight deck of the *Guam* at approximately 1:45 A.M. On board the helicopters were a 46-man Marine security force and nine U.S. Navy SEALS. While the 46 Marines were to secure the landing zones for the follow-on rescue force, the SEALS were to augment the Marine Security Guards in the chancery.[20]

The Marines, part of BLT 1/ 2, were heavily armed, with most of leathernecks equipped with automatic and antitank weapons (this included Dragons, light anti-armor weapons and AT-4s. There was a concern among Marine commanders that the rescue operation might deplete existing ammunition stores being held in reserve for the upcoming operations against Iraqi force. Also, the grenades carried by the Marines could not be returned to their protective wrappings if left unused. As the rescue operation unfolded, concerns over ammunition expenditure was put aside as armed gangs targeted the U.S. Embassy with bursts of automatic gunfire.

Inside the embassy, Marine Security Guards shredded classified material and began preparations for an evacuation. Ambassador Bishop, who had been in a similar situation in Monrovia, Liberia, only months before during Operation Sharp Edge, issued strict orders concerning the rules of engagement that stated, "Marines could fire only if armed people displaying hostile intent breached the perimeter, and then only with his permission."[21] The ambassador likewise sought to tactically deploy his Marines (both Marine Security Guards and the leathernecks from BLT 1/2) in a defensive position, in order that they could better defend the embassy and its access to the helicopter landing zone.

Marine sniper teams positioned themselves on both the water tower and roof of the chancery, primarily to observe anything on or near the five-story apartment building known as the K-7 that could possibly harbor enemy gunmen. Before it could carry out its mission, the Marine sniper team (a sniper and spotter) placed on the water tower immediately drew fire from enemy gunmen. This prompted Lieutenant Colonel McAleer to immediately remove the team from the tower.[22] The ambassador assigned three Marines and six SEALS to augment the five-man Marine Security Guard to "ride shotgun" in the embassy's three hardened vehicles.[23] Lieutenant Colonel W.D. Oates, the Marine commander of all forces on the ground, placed one platoon of leathernecks to cover the northern and western walls of the embassy, as well as a platoon on the southern end of the compound. Colonel Oates deployed the Dragon antitank teams across from both gates (northern and southern walls), while the SEAL team took up positions on the roof of the chancery building.[24]

Unlike in Islamabad, Pakistan, or Tripoli, Libya, in November and December of 1979, the fear was not so much on the embassy being stormed by hostile crowds, but more so on stray rounds wounding or killing embassy officials. Most of the shooting was done by teenage "hooligans," riding about the streets of Mogadishu in armed pickup trucks, known as "technicals," and armed with AK-47's.[25] Due to the volatile situation in Mogadishu, American forces remained inside the compound while the crowds outside looted the city.

The only foray by the Marines and Navy SEALS was to accompany a four-vehicle convoy assembled to make a 20-minute run to the U.S. Office of Military Cooperation located about a quarter of a mile from the embassy along the Via Mekka Highway. This particular evacuation brought out four Americans and 18 foreign nationals, while another convoy brought out 38 Russians, including the Soviet ambassador and his wife. When night fell the Marines inside the embassy continued to prepare for an evacuation by organizing the 200 evacuees into helicopter teams. Marines likewise screened all evacuees for life-threatening medical conditions and conducted last-minute weapons searches. Leathernecks placed Chemlites on the children so that they could easily be found if they happened to wander away. The only problem faced by the Marines came from the order that allowed evacuees only one bag per person. Enforcing this rule shortly became a problem as Marines became caught up in escorting and assisting the evacuees to the awaiting helicopters.[26] Also, many of the evacuees came with their family pets that, due to space constraints, were forced to stay behind, as they could not be brought aboard the helicopters. Unfortunately, this forced many evacuees to kill their pets or, as in one case, forced the Marine security guard to kill the animal out of necessity.

By 11:00 P.M. on January 5, 1991, with the embassy now operating under blackout conditions (the electrical cables to the Marine House had to be cut), the Marine security force and embassy guards donned night vision goggles as the CH-46 helicopters made their way inland to begin rescue operations. The first CH-46 "Sea Knight" sat down inside the U.S. Embassy compound at 11:43 P.M., at which time the first group of evacuees boarded the helicopters as the Marine guards looked on. This scene repeated itself for nearly four hours as a stream of evacuees lifted off in helicopters from the darkened compound of the U.S. Embassy with little or no incident.

An Important Component of the Embassy's Defense

There was a tense moment, however, when a local militia commander, Major Sayeed, walked through the main gate with a hand-held radio and hand grenade and threatened to have his men "shoot helicopters out of the sky" if the 'unauthorized' violation of Somali airspace did not end. After hurried negotiations with the disgruntled Somali warlord, Ambassador Bishop was able to purchase Major Sayeed's "goodwill" with both cash and his choice of the embassy vehicles. With this threat removed, the evacuation continued. Throughout the evacuation, the five Marine Security Guards, a number of embassy security personnel, and the 30 Somali contract guards proved to be an important component of the embassy's defense as they assisted evacuees and the Marine Security Force from BLT 1/2.

One last incident nearly derailed a near-perfect evacuation as the last wave of helicopters prepared to take off with the ambassador, his staff, and the Marine Security Guards, when a two-man Marine communications team failed to rendezvous with the helicopters. Apparently, the Marines had failed to realize that this was the last flight out. Fortunately, an alert crew chief aboard one of the CH-46's spotted the two leathernecks still in the compound. As these two grateful Marines were hustled aboard the awaiting helicopter, the last wave lifted off from the makeshift landing zone. About 3:00 A.M., the two helicopters spotted the USS *Guam*, and by 3:43 A.M., both were safely aboard that ship. At 0343, in the pre-dawn hours of 6 January, the "evacuation was declared complete."[27] Even as the last helicopter lifted off from the landing zone at the U.S. Embassy in Mogadishu, looters forced their way into the compound and smashed what they could not carry off.

When it was over, the Marines and sailors of Amphibious Group Two had evacuated 281 individuals from 31 countries. Included in this group were diplomats from Germany, Great Britain, Kenya, Soviet Union, Kuwait, Nigeria, Oman, Sudan, Turkey, and the United Arab Emirates. In keeping with their roles as "Ambassadors in Blue," Marines and sailors from the amphibious ready group mustered spare clothes and hot meals, as well as providing medical attention to several wounded evacuees. Doctors aboard the *Guam* assisted in the delivery of the Sudanese ambassador's pregnant wife's baby. The birth of the child brought the total number of evacuees to 282 before the ship dropped anchor in Oman several days later.

After the amphibious task force reached Muscat, Oman, Ambassador Bishop addressed the sailors and Marines aboard the two ships and thanked them for their invaluable assistance and professionalism during the evacuation operation. In his speech, the ambassador acknowledged that "few of us would have been alive [without] your extraordinary efforts ... we will take a part of each of you with us for the rest of our lives."[28]

After the Marines had evacuated U.S. personnel from Mogadishu, rebels shortly thereafter forced President Siad Barre into exile. This in turn led to the nearly decade long civil war that caused widespread starvation and civil strife in this African nation a year later. In order to assist United Nations (UN) relief operations, President George H.W. Bush, in December 1992, ordered a force of Marines to Somalia as a vanguard in Operation Restore Hope, the UN-sponsored humanitarian and stability operation in that country.[29]

FAST to the Rescue in Somalia, April 1993

With the withdrawal of the Marine Security Guard detachment from Somalia during Operation Eastern Exit, the Commander, Joint Task Force Somalia, in order to provide security for the United States Liaison Office (USLO) in Mogadishu, requested a Fleet Anti-Terrorism Security Team (FAST). He requested the team in order to provide security prior to the arrival of a newly trained Marine Security Guard detachment. While in Mogadishu, the FAST unit patrolled the liaison office, controlled the access control points through it, and provided external and internal security for the office, now located in the United Nations compound, once the main body of Marines departed Somalia.[30]

The original FAST platoon consisted of 2 officers, 49 enlisted Marines, and 3 Navy corpsmen. Two additional Marines, a two-man communications team from I Marine Expeditionary Force, augmented the FAST platoon. One of these officers was Major Edwards, a liaison officer who had been sent over from Marine Corps Security Forces Battalion and who coordinated the activities of FAST with Central Command, Navy Central Command, and the Marine Expeditionary Unit. Upon FAST's arrival, State Department officials assigned it to the USLO and on a limited basis, and to the United Nations Operations in Somalia.

The duties assigned to FAST upon their arrival in Somalia included the defense of the inner perimeter of the U.S. Liaison Office in Mogadishu, and providing a reaction force and backup forces for both defensive operations and counterattacks. FAST members likewise "rode shotgun" alongside the U.S. Air Force's 436th APS for armed State Department and United Nations food convoys in order to protect them from ambushes set by the various warlords. Unlike Marine Security Guards, however, they came armed with a variety of weapons, and were under a different set of rules of engagement. Finally, the FAST platoon rotated with another team every four months, unlike Marine Security Guards, who were assigned to an embassy on a semi-permanent basis.

Also, according to Corporal C.J. Noble, who served as a member of 1st FAST at the U.S. Naval Base, Little Creek, Virginia, during the late 1990s, unlike MSG detachments, which are normally five to six Marines (a detachment commander and four to five watchstanders) at most posts, FAST units deploy as a platoon.[31] Each team has a platoon commander and a platoon sergeant, and its team members are infantrymen. Corporal Noble stated that FAST platoons are made up like any other platoon in the Marine Corps, three squads with four fire teams. They train extensively on a variety of weapons, including M16A2's, .590 shotgun, MP 5, M 4's, M-240 Gs, 60mm mortars, light anti-armor weapons, M-19's and 9mm pistols. Throughout their two-year assignments, FAST Marines are constantly honing their infantry skills. As occurred in Mogadishu, and later in various actions in Central Africa and Liberia, FAST Marines are trained, as Corporal Noble stated, to "take a hostile area then secure it as

During the 1990s, Africa became the focal point of MSG activities as civil warfare, famine, and political upheaval threatened the U.S. diplomatic community. Here, Ugandan soldiers guard the outer perimeter of the U.S. Embassy compound in Kampala (U.S. Marine Security Guard Battalion).

long as it takes." They are also trained to communicate with the PR-24, route control, martial arts, and reconnaissance tactics. Since the teams must sometimes deal with embassy takeovers, FAST members must have the ability to "fast rope or repel from helicopters in order to take an objective from the air." Like Force Reconnaissance, FAST adheres to a rigid deployment schedule to places such as the Middle East, Japan, and Italy, as its "mission is always changing." This change in mission is evident of the fact that since 1993, FAST and Marine Security Guard battalions have formed a vital partnership in the defense of U.S. embassies and consulates worldwide.[32]

Originally, Headquarters Marine Corps planned to replace the FAST platoon with either contract security guards or a reactivated Marine Security Guard detachment. As the security situation in Mogadishu remained fluid, the State Department requested that the FAST platoon remain in Somalia until "certain security measures are addressed and improvements are implemented." In fact, in a letter to Lieutenant General Norman E. Ehlert, USMC, Deputy Chief of Staff for Plans, Policies and Operations, Mr. Mark E. Mulvey, the State Department's director for diplomatic security, outlined these "measures and improvements," which included the relocation of the United States Liaison Office and the reactivation of a MSG detachment and motorcade safety.[33]

Mr. Mulvey requested the extension of the FAST platoon's stay in Somalia beyond its original departure date of August 26, 1993. In his reply, Lieutenant General Ehlert emphasized that while he sympathized with the Department of State's requirements for improved security, the Marine Corps could not support further extension of FAST platoon's stay in Somalia. General Ehlert stressed that such a request "goes beyond the basic mission for Marine Corps Security Forces (MCSF) as established by the Secretary of the Navy." The general wrote that while the situation in Mogadishu "is highly volatile and continues to support the deployment of FAST personnel to provide USLO site and convoy security until more permanent security arrangements can be made," he nevertheless "could not support expansion of the current MCSF mission to include convoy security."[34] The deputy chief of staff for plans, policies and operations likewise informed the director of diplomatic security "neither can I support expansion of the MSG mission to include convoy security, except as currently provided in the DOS-USMC Memorandum of Agreement on MSG Operations." The general recommended that Mr. Mulvey formally submit a request to the Department of Defense asking for a convoy security force. General Ehlert concluded that while the Marine Corps "would have to decline to provide such support," he emphasized that another military department would be willing to assume the mission.[35]

Prior to the reactivation of the Marine Security Guard Detachment in Mogadishu, Chief Warrant Officer 2 Felix M. Arnold, supply officer from Marine Security Guard Battalion, was sent by the battalion commander to oversee the safe transportation and weapons for use by the Marines at the USLO. In an after-action report submitted after his return to the battalion, the chief warrant officer outlined the main differences between the FAST platoon and Marine Security Guards, and their respective roles in defense of an embassy. CWO2 Arnold was complimentary of FAST's training but repeated throughout the report that the defensive nature of the Marine Security Guard's mission complements that of the anti-terrorist teams:

> Somalia is a very dangerous and intense situation. The situation is constantly changing and has the capability of exacerbating to an uncontrollable incident. Any unit in a defensive posture must be able to react and realign to prevent an uncontrollable incident.
>
> There are two distinct defensive missions; Exterior and Interior. My impression is that the FAST Plt should continue the exterior defense until the situation subsides and an MSG Detachment should conduct the interior defense mission. I think that it would be a mistake to relieve the FAST Plt once the MSG Detachment arrives.
>
> The FAST Plt has been trained to operate on the Forward Edge of the Battle Area (FEBA). The exterior of the compound is a FEBA. The Plt currently operates with defined sectors of fire for all posts established. Primary and supplementary positions are established. Channelizing entanglements have been established. The Plt believes that this situation is real and has prepared themselves accordingly.
>
> While I was in the compound I was adopted by the FAST Plt. It was a good thing. I spoke with the Plt Comdr CAPT Scott Campbell about the situation and his impressions. He feels very strongly that the FAST CO has a legitimate mission in Somalia. He also believes that an MSG Det should complement (but operate separately) the FAST CO Plt.
>
> The Plt is trained and has operated extensively in the mission they are tasked with. Escort vehicle driving, protective measures for vehicles, maintenance of the HUMMV, crew-served weapons operation and maintenance, the collection and interpretation of intelligence information, the planning and conduct of the tactical escort movements. In short, they are an infantry unit.
>
> In the time I that was exposed to this unit I was shown how flexible and adept they are to this mission. The T/O and training of the Plt fits. It was obvious that the Plt had cohesion and that this cohesion was a result of the confidence instilled through training and operation as a unit.[36]

CWO2 Arnold added that the capabilities and training of the FAST Platoon, as well as the fact that they are equipped for such missions, made them an ideal force for "exterior defense." In his report, the supply officer stressed the fact that if necessary, the Marines assigned to Embassy Security Guard duty could learn how to handle both the perimeter defense and "exterior defense" missions. CWO2 Arnold admitted, however, that FAST's unit cohesion, based on "confidence instilled through training and operation as a unit," made it better equipped to handle the stress of a "combat environment."[37]

Planners at Headquarters Marine Corps had been thinking along similar lines as had CWO2 Arnold, insofar as the employment of Marine Security Guards had been concerned. A memorandum from Marine Security Guard Battalion to Plans, Policies and Operations stressed the fact that prior to the activation of a Marine Security Guard Detachment in Mogadishu, it is required to perform the same missions as that of a FAST Platoon. These missions included convoy protection, personal protective details, and external defense. By mid-spring 1994, the Department of State re-established diplomatic relations with Somalia, and after a brief organizational period, set up the U.S. Embassy at the United States Liaison Office. Despite the continued after-effects of the battles between U.S. Army Rangers and 10th Mountain Division troops in October 1993, and only after careful preparation and a Post Validation Study, the State Department authorized the organization of a Marine Security Guard Detachment for the U.S. Embassy in Mogadishu in late 1994.

The use of a FAST platoon in Somalia demonstrated not only the flexibility of this highly motivated mobile tactical force, but also its interoperability with MSG detachments. Indeed, from their first introduction in defense of the U.S. Embassy in Mogadishu and "riding shotgun," FAST and MSG formed a viable partnership in defending embassies throughout Africa and the Middle East. In fact, as FAST's subsequent operations in Sierra Leone; Nairobi, Kenya; Dar es Salaam, Tanzania; and Monrovia demonstrated, FAST and MSG became partners and formed one of the most important teams in the day-to-day defense of U.S. embassies in an increasingly unstable portion of the globe.

A Terrorist Attack in Santiago, Chile, February 1991

Half a world away from the violence in Somalia and the preparations for war in Kuwait, Marine Security Guards in Santiago, Chile, were dealing with similar threats from terrorists, in this instance, working to end U.S. support for Chilean strongman General Augusto Pinochet. In Santiago the main focus of these terrorists[38] was the most visible sign of that support to the Pinochet regime: the U.S. Embassy.

On February 16, 1991, as Sergeants Gerald R. Konz and David K. Knutson, the assistant detachment commander, drove away from the Marine House on liberty, a "flash" was seen from behind a light pole. Later, investigators discovered that the "flash" was a U.S.-made light anti-armor weapon (LAAW) rocket. As the rocket impacted against the vehicle (which did not explode due to the distance traveled to impact not being sufficient to arm the rocket), another vehicle drove up to the Marine House and sprayed the vehicle occupied by the two Marines with M-16 and Uzi 9 mm machine gun fire. In what seemed like an eternity, the melee lasted for nearly 45 seconds, with two rounds from the M-16 penetrating the windshield of the Marines' vehicle. Despite the fact the windshield was made of bullet-proof glass, one of the rounds struck Sergeant Konz, who was sitting in the front seat. As Sergeant Knutson recalled later, Sergeant Konz was soon "bleeding heavily and in extreme pain." Fortunately, "no vital organs were hit."[39]

After opening fire on the Marines, the assailants sped away. Meanwhile, inside the car, Sergeant Knutson quickly administered first aid to his wounded comrade and immediately drove the injured leatherneck to the hospital. Sergeant Konz remained in a Santiago hospital for three days. Despite the severity of the wounds, Sergeant Konz "felt all the more wiser" for having survived an attack from one of Chile's most notorious terrorist groups. Later, on July 4, 1991, in a ceremony at the U.S. Embassy in Santiago, Ambassador Charles R. Gillespie awarded Sergeant Konz the Purple Heart for injuries he received during the February terrorist attack. While his left armed remained a bit stiff, and fragments from the LAAW remained in his arm, Sergeant Konz gave a "thumbs up" indicating that he was "still hard-core functional" to resume his duties at Post One.[40]

Terrorism in Lima, Peru

At approximately 5:30 A.M., on the morning of July 27, 1993, terrorists from the leftist guerrilla group *Sendero Luminoso* or Shining Path bombed the U.S. Embassy in Lima, Peru. As was the case in Santiago, Chile, the terrorists used two cars to carry out their attack. The first vehicle drove by the embassy with the occupants firing small arms and light machine guns at the entrance of the compound. The second vehicle, laden with explosives and unmanned, was then steered into the perimeter wall as a detonator set off the explosives packed inside this vehicle. The blast tore a huge gap in the outer wall of the diplomatic compound and shattered all of the windows along the northern side of the building. The explosion also set off numerous fires in the various office spaces of the embassy. The Marine Security Guards responded immediately and quickly secured the building in order to prevent the terrorists from entering amidst the confusion. The leathernecks, led by Staff Sergeant Richard Ontivero, quickly restored order and ensured the safety of all the embassy personnel until permanent repairs could be made on the structure. The ambassador recognized the entire Marine Security Guard Detachment for their bravery and outstanding efforts during this crisis.[41]

Violence in Congo-Brazzaville, September 1991

On September 30, 1991, attention once again focused on Africa, as Congolese soldiers rioted against President Mobuto Sese Seko, and in the process killed scores of their own countrymen in Congo-Brazzaville and neighboring Kinshasa, located across the Congo River. For the first time in the history of the Marine Security Guard program, Marines left the confines of the embassy in order to carry out an evacuation of 1,000 American and foreign nationals once they reached the west bank of the Congo River. Perhaps recalling the slaughter of foreign nationals by rampaging Simba troops during the early 1960s, the Marine Security Guards assigned to the Brazzaville embassy were ready to proactively help fellow Americans and foreigners escape the violence that had spread throughout Kinshasa and had claimed many lives.[42]

Throughout the evacuation the six Marines who were sent to protect the foreigners maintained contact with the main body of the Security Guard Detachment via hand-held radios as they gathered the evacuees on a ferry situated on the Congo River. Once safely on the west bank, the Marines conducted a mini–NEO, searching the baggage, screening for weapons, and placing the evacuees in teams (much like the helicopter teams used during Operation Eagle Pull in Phnom Penh, Cambodia in 1974), in order to facilitate their evacuation from the country. The Marines provided practically everything during the evacuation. This included arranging plane tickets, acting as translators (some of the leathernecks spoke French) for the

French-speaking Congolese, and caring for children. The Marine Security Guards also comforted those refugees who had been traumatized by the sudden violence that forced many to leave husbands and pets behind in the confusion.[43] Perhaps the most important task performed by the Marine Security Guards was the rescue of the detachment commander's family that had been caught up in the violence.

Mrs. Lucie Phillips, wife of the American ambassador to the Congo, who assisted the Marines during the evacuation, recalled that the "Marines were great volunteers for the humanitarian evacuation," as many of the refugees "went out of here in shock," and, one might add, with few possessions or money.[44] To this end, the leathernecks, out of their own pockets and embassy funds, purchased food and held a barbecue in order to feed the hungry refugees, many of whom had no money and had not eaten since being forced to evacuate from Kinshasa. The goodwill of the Marine guards paid off, as fear quickly turned to confidence and the refugees realized that these young Americans would safely see them out of the country. A doctor who had been sent to check the health of the refugees, and who quite naturally expected to be greeted by uncertainty and fear, instead found the refugees singing and glad to be have been rescued by the Marines.

Operation Distant Runner, April 12, 1994

Throughout the 1990s, the continent of Africa experienced nearly a decade of ethnic genocide and epidemics. This violence inevitably led to the involvement of the international community in withdrawing its citizens from these war-ravaged countries. In the case of the United States, this resulted in the use of Navy and Marine expeditionary forces as well as the local Marine Security Guard Detachment in rescuing Americans as well as foreigners caught up in the middle of these tragedies. Indeed, the ethnic and tribal warfare endemic in Liberia, Somalia, and Congo-Brazzaville in 1991 was but a precursor of events to come throughout the 1990s.

In the country of Rwanda, ethnic warfare took on an extremely violent form when the majority Hutus began a systematic persecution of the minority Tutsi tribe. While the administration of President Bill Clinton sought "an African solution to an African problem," the slaughter went on unabated.[45] Nevertheless, the 11th Marine Expeditionary Unit (Special Operations Capable) arrived off the coast of Kenya aboard the USS *Pelileiu* (LHA-5), where it awaited orders to go ashore in order to evacuate hundreds of American and foreign nationals trapped between the warring Hutus and Tutsis in neighboring Rwanda.[46] On April 10, 1994, U.S. Ambassador to Rwanda Mr. David Dawson closed the U.S. Embassy, and with 142 American citizens, left for Kigali, the capital of neighboring Burundi, to await rescue by the leathernecks. A day earlier, on April 9, a force of Marines from BLT 2/5 arrived in Bujumbura, Burundi, in order to assist in the safe evacuation of the American citizens and foreign nationals who had joined their American counterparts in leaving Rwanda.

The arrival of the 330-man force of Marines in this land-locked country was extraordinary, as Marines had boarded the giant CH-53E "Super Sea Stallion" helicopters and conducted a 636-mile inland journey to Bujumbura, the capital of Burundi, where Ambassador Dawson and the Americans awaited rescue.[47] Taking off from Mombassa, Kenya, and being refueled in mid-air from Marine KC-130 refueler-cargo aircraft, the leathernecks and corpsmen arrived in Bujumbura, where they loaded the thankful Americans and foreigners onto the awaiting aircraft. Meanwhile, other Marines from BLT 2/5 landed 90 miles south of

Kigali, where they conducted civic operations, bringing medical care as well as other community-action projects to the thankful villagers of Kipini, Kenya.[48]

A Complete Success and Team Effort

On April 12, 1994, Ambassador Dawson declared Operation Distant Runner a complete success, as the Marines and sailors from BLT 2/5 safely evacuated over 230 American and foreign nationals. Ambassador Dawson, in fact, dubbed the operation "an extraordinary" event. The very fact that the Marines were able to launch a rescue operation from 636 miles out was, as Ambassador Dawson added, "immensely significant" in getting the Americans and foreigner nationals safely out of Rwanda.[49] The ambassador credited the success of the operation to the professionalism of the Marines and sailors of the 11th MEU(SOC). The ambassador later told these Marines and sailors, "The knowledge you were here made it possible for us to get the cooperation needed [to get Americans out]." U.S. Chargé d'Affaires to Burundi Leonard J. Lange, who was the acting U.S. ambassador to that country added, "I really mean it when I say this was a team effort." Mr. Leonard emphasized that the close cooperation of all the agencies involved — including his staff, the Marine Security Guard Detachment, other State Department officials, U.S. European Command, local Burundian officials, and the Marines and sailors of the 11th MEU(SOC) — contributed to a successful end to a terrible crisis.[50]

The safe evacuation of the American and foreign nationals from Rwanda illustrated the versatility of the Navy-Marine team in rescuing American citizens. The rescue further emphasized the ongoing relationship between the Navy-Marine team and Department of State in defense of American nationals living abroad. Before the end of the decade, this concept would again be tested in Monrovia, Rwanda, Brazzaville and tragically, in both Kenya and Tanzania, as Marine Security Guards once again came to the rescue of a beleaguered embassy under attack in an unstable environment on the African continent.

"A few close calls at this post": Monrovia, Liberia, May 1996

As Marine Embassy Guards stood watch amidst the political changes that swept throughout Eastern Europe and the former Soviet Union, political instability on the African continent continued to require a visible and active Marine presence. No more so was this true than in Monrovia, Liberia. Despite the victory of Charles Taylor's NPFL in January 1991, the overthrow of President Doe was but a pause in the ongoing civil war. In fact, even after Doe's ouster, Liberia continued to experience internal chaos and disorder as the armies of the other warlords that helped in bringing down the Doe regime now focused their energies on ending Taylor's rule.

As always, caught up in the middle of this violence was the most visible sign of the U.S. presence in Liberia: the U.S. Embassy in Monrovia. At about 0300, in the early morning hours of April 6, fighting broke out between rival political factions in Liberia's transitional government. As the fighting spread throughout the city, over 20,000 Liberians sought refuge in the U.S. Embassy compound. To prevent overcrowding and assist those seeking a way out of the embattled capital, the United States and other nations evacuated these refugees to Sierra Leone and neighboring Senegal.[51] At one point during the fighting, the regional security officer personally rescued over 200 refugees as they sought the protection of the Greystone complex in Monrovia. Assisting the RSO were the Marine Security Guards and local guards assigned to the exterior walls of the compound. Meanwhile, chaos reigned throughout the city as rival gangs fought each and roamed the streets of Monrovia brandishing AK-47s, while other Liberians smashed storefront windows and looted stores and businesses.[52]

Eventually, after a month of heavy fighting, the United States sent in elements of BLT 2/2 (2nd Battalion, 2d Marine Regiment), assigned to the 22nd MEU to Monrovia, in order to protect the U.S. Embassy and evacuate the Americans living there and other foreign nationals who desired to leave. Once ashore, the Marines of BLT 2/2 turned the U.S. Embassy into a virtual fortress as they set up defensive positions atop the various gates of the diplomatic compound. While rival gangs avoided openly challenging the heavily armed Marines, they nonetheless posed a serious threat to an orderly evacuation.[53]

Lance Corporal Gary Squires recalled that while at the U.S. Embassy, "We had a few close calls at this post. A few days ago, there was a person with an AK-47 rifle riding on the trunk of a red sedan with most of the windows broken out. The car was moving very slowly as the person pointed his weapon in different directions. When the vehicles came closer, he placed the weapon on his shoulder and pointed it at us. That's when we racked [chambered] rounds.... Once he saw that we were serious, his weapon went down, and the threat was over."[54]

Most of the Marines had difficulty in recognizing both friend and foe. While all combatants wore pieces of military gear or webbing, most wore civilian clothes and carried Soviet-style assault rifles or other firearms. Corporal James Welch commented, "At this point, we consider anyone with a gun the enemy ... we look out there and we know there is supposed to be a good side and a bad side, but its hard to tell, so we stand ready to protect the Embassy against anyone."[55] Another Marine, who manned a tripod-mounted .50 caliber machine gun, aimed at the Mamba Point Hotel positioned on the second floor of the ambassador's residence, confidently told journalist Howard W. French that he and his fellow Marines could handle any situation that might arise. The Marine told French he had "already received incoming fire several times during his shift [and that] it doesn't really worry me too much.... I have faith in my training, and in my equipment. People who shoot at me tend to regret it pretty quickly."[56]

Eventually, a nine-man Marine team from BLT 2/2 came ashore and set up an Evacuation Control Center (ECC) to process the hundreds of evacuees seeking an exit from Monrovia. The members of the ECC were the first members of the MEU to enter the U.S. Embassy compound. Once set up, the Marines began to screen the refugees seeking a safe passage out of Monrovia. Corporal Tony Fleming said, "We've heard all kinds of stories from the people we are processing."[57] Among the stories told by the refugees were tales of cannibalism and threats to their person by the troops from the various armies.

As always, the Marines proved themselves be an island of stability amidst the violence and chaos that wracked Monrovia. Gunnery Sergeant Danny Ray Lanier, SNCOIC of the ECC, said, "When they [the refugees] first see us, they don't know what to expect.... Then we give them food and water, a place to sleep, talk with them and help them relax. When we put them on the helicopters, they extend their thanks and are very grateful for what we've done for them."[58] Echoing GySgt. Lanier's comments was Staff Sergeant James Sanders, an explosive ordnance disposal technician and the ECC's search and screening team leader. Staff Sergeant Sanders said, "Since we've been here, we have had zero problems with anybody. Most of the people are glad to be here and off the streets and out of harm's way. Once they are behind the walls of the embassy, they know they are safe until it's time for them to leave on the evacuation helicopter."[59]

By the end of the evacuation, the Marines from BLT had safely evacuated over 300 foreign nations and American citizens. Through the efforts of the United States and other African nations, a brokered arrangement brought much of the fighting to an end. Tensions remained very high, as President Taylor was able to stabilize much of the country for the next seven years.[60] Marine Security Guards inside the U.S. Embassy continued to guard the diplomatic compound and the Greystone complex amidst an extremely volatile atmosphere in the Liberian capital until President Taylor's forced removal in 2003.

The Coup d'État in Sierra Leone, May 1997

Liberia and the Congo were not the only African nations beset by internal disorder. In the *coup* that occurred in Sierra Leone in May 1997, Marine Embassy Guards withstood a siege that lasted for two weeks. The coup began when the military revolted against the government of President Tejan Kabbah, who fled to Conakry, Guinea. For nearly two weeks, soldiers undertook an orgy of looting and destruction in Freetown, the capital of Sierra Leone, until the Army leaders restored some semblance of order. Meanwhile, Major Johnny Paul Koroma declared himself head of the Armed Forces Ruling Committee (AFRC) and linked up with rebels of the United Front that resided in the countryside. As the two armies joined forces, the mutinous troops closed off the airport, the borders, and all roads leading in and out of the country. As Sierra Leone slipped further into anarchy, the ambassador ordered an immediate withdrawal of all Americans residing in Freetown. The ambassador requested assistance from the 22nd Marine Expeditionary Unit that had been placed on alert off the coast of Sierra Leone.[61]

Upon hearing automatic gunfire near the U.S. Embassy at approximately 5:45 A.M., Gunnery Sergeant W.E. Walters, the detachment commander, and the Marine Security Guards assigned to the embassy immediately manned defensive positions. Ten minutes later, at 5:55 A.M., the local guards had informed the detachment commander that the Marine vehicle had been stolen and had driven by with troops hanging out the windows. Also missing was one of the Marine Security Guards, Sergeant Joseph A. Arnold, who had been "carjacked on his way to the embassy" and taken hostage by a group of rebels not more than twenty years old. Sergeant Arnold recalled that kidnappers "obviously didn't have any idea what they were doing." After a tense exchange of some words, the rebels released the Marine sergeant as he skillfully negotiated his release.[62] "By 0800," GySgt. Walters recalled, "the entire city was in complete chaos and the heavy looting had begun." Given the scale of the looting, Gunnery Sergeant Walters and the RSO quickly surmised that the coup had been successful.[63] While sporadic gunfire could be heard coming from the city, the Marines and the RSO began rounding up all Americans living in Freetown or had ordered them to take refuge in pre-arranged safehavens. By 10:00 A.M., the rebels turned their attention to the grounds of the U.S. Embassy where they eventually succeeded in penetrating. Once in, they managed to steal several embassy vehicles before leaving.

Inside the besieged embassy, the Marine Security Guards set up the best defense they could. Meanwhile, representatives from the international community met with AFRC leaders who promised the foreigners safe passage out of the country. As the looting and shootings slackened, some travel throughout the city was possible. This also allowed the MSGs assigned at the embassy to be relieved, and allowed other Marines to position themselves at the "Smart Farm" compound where the RSO had established the command center. Plans were also made to begin the evacuation of all non-essential personnel and equipment from the embassy. Meanwhile, while the RSO planned the evacuation, the Marine Security Guards manned Post One, which acted as a communications center in order to keep all Americans and foreigners informed of any change in the situation in Freetown. The leathernecks likewise maintained internal defensive positions, and were fully prepared to defend against any penetration at the embassy, particularly as rebel fire, coming mostly from AK-47s and rocket propelled grenades, hit the outer walls of the compound as the coup began. As Sergeant Arnold recalled, the damage to the compound was quite heavy, with the offices of the ambassador and Deputy Chief of Mission Ms. Ann Wright taking most of the heavy hits.[64]

In sharp contrast to other embassy crises that wracked Africa during the 1990s, GySgt. Walters praised the efficiency and loyalty of the local guards, who, he said, "could be counted on" and remained at their positions throughout the crisis.[65] By Thursday, May 28, 1997, the fighting and looting resumed, which in turn prompted the ambassador to order the evacuation of the embassy. An ECC team from 22nd MEU arrived by helicopter to set up a processing center. As the leathernecks from 22nd MEU began to evacuate the Americans and others from the embassy, the Marine Security Guards began to shred and burn all classified material.[66] Sergeant Arnold recalled that the Marines from the 22nd MEU had taken up positions around the perimeter of the hotel nearest the embassy. The Marine sergeant candidly admitted that it "was good to see some people of your own with some halfway decent weapons."[67]

By May 30, 1997, over 900 Americans and foreigners living in Freetown, as well as the embassy staff and Marine Security Guards, had been safely evacuated to the ships carrying the 22nd MEU.[68] In his after-action report of the *coup d'état* in Sierra Leone, GySgt. Walters was very critical of the embassy' evacuation plan which, he said, was nonexistent, as was the intelligence prior to the coup. The detachment commander wrote that there was no intelligence or prior warning of the coup. Thus, the embassy staff failed to detect that a coup was imminent. This resulted in some initial confusion as to the course of action to take. As Gunnery Sergeant Walters wrote, "There were things happening prior to this coup that should have alerted us."[69] The detachment commander likewise was critical of the staff at the embassy, who he said were "in the way" at times and cared little about the events going on around them.[70]

Gunnery Sergeant Walters, however, praised the establishment of an effective communications center and plan that kept everybody informed and constantly updated. Walters noted, "Everyone in the Embassy had a radio.... This allowed reports of action from all over the city." Also, the establishment of an effective communications center allowed the State Department back in Washington to keep abreast of events in Sierra Leone, and was thus enabled to act much quicker than in other crises on the continent.

Gunnery Sergeant Walters maintained that the *coup d'état* in Sierra Leone offered many lessons in the preparation of future Marine Security Guards. Perhaps the two most important included sufficient pre-planning of all possible danger areas and establishing many escape and evasion routes located throughout the city from the embassy. Also, the detachment commander recommended that Marine Security Guards be schooled via sand table exercises as well as briefings on embassy evacuation, safe havens, and rules of engagement. He added that given the volatility of some posts, Marine Embassy Guards should have an overnight or "ditty" bag packed with underwear, clothing and toiletry items "ready to go" if an evacuation is ordered.

Finally, GySgt. Walters noted that there is no "book" or schoolhouse solution to all problems found in such circumstances. Marines, he wrote, should be able to at all times to "think out of the box" in such instances. In any event, Gunnery Sergeant Walters maintained that throughout the crisis in Freetown, "the Marines' presence was a calming effect on all Americans."[71]

Fighting in Congo-Brazzaville, June 1997

As was the case with most African nations possessing mineral resources, Congo-Brazzaville suffered from constant political turmoil and greed as rival political parties fought each other at the polls and in streets and countryside, jockeying for power and fighting for control of the country's treasury and resources.[72] A country the size of the state of Montana, Congo-Brazzaville, a former colony of France, had been ruled by a succession of Marxist-oriented politicians, politically oriented to the Soviet Union though dependent on her former colonial master to run the oil industry and mines. Indeed, "as long as ever more oil kept flowing, the semblance of a functioning state could be maintained."[73] Prior to the pro-democratic coup that occurred in 1993, Congo-Brazzaville was ruled by Denis Sassou-Nguesso, a flamboyant Army officer "with a keen taste for the good life" and a clique of Army officers. Sassou was eventually ousted by Pascal Lissouba, a Marxist and a member of a southern tribe hostile to Sassou's northern-led, Army-dominated government. Fueled by the bitter ethnic and political rivalries that existed in Congo-Brazzaville between Sassou and his political ally, the mayor of Brazzaville, Bernard Kolelas, on one hand, and Lissouba on the other, the stage was set for the ethnic and political unrest that resulted in the evacuation of the U.S. embassy in June 1997. Sergeant Thomas A. Ring, who stood MSG duty in Congo-Brazzaville from November 1978 to November 1980, recalled that "Congo-Brazzaville was ... a hardship tour [and while there] I had my share of the usual experiences, such as bomb threats, and African-style political unrest."[74]

Indeed, throughout the 1990s, Congo-Brazzaville lived up to its reputation as being "a hardship tour." In the weeks prior to the evacuation of the U.S. Embassy in Brazzaville, the rival gangs and soldiers of these African warlords "pounded one another and residents of the city [Brazzaville] with anti-aircraft guns and heavy artillery aimed at one another's neighborhoods."[75] In one incident, Lissouba's militiamen charged into Bakongo, a suburb of Brazzaville, and practically leveled the city with anti-aircraft guns, and later bludgeoned to death many of the residents. As Bernard Kolelas recalled, "By the end of three months of this kind of killing, we had cases where people would capture their enemies' babies and beat them to a pulp with a wooden mortar for revenge."[76] Sassou's militiamen, known as the "Cobras," were just as brutal against Lissouba and Kolelas' followers.

Toward the beginning of June, the ire of the rival gangs turned against the French community in Congo-Brazzaville. As could be expected, much of the anger directed toward Sassou centered on his ties to the French technocrats living in the city. The French, held responsible by the rebels for the greed and corruption that turned a bustling and booming economy into an economic disaster, were specifically targeted by Lissouba's and Kolelas' forces. The militiamen stopped cars and asked the terrified passengers to "speak" their native tongues to assure they were not hiding their French identity. Gunnery Sergeant Frederick A. Upchurch, the detachment commander at the U.S. Embassy in Brazzaville, recalled that at one point, "the French Ambassador's bodyguard requested use of a small American flag. He planned to affix it to the vehicle carrying both the U.S. and French Ambassadors."[77]

In fact, by the morning of June 5, 1997, much of the violence aimed against the rival armies turned its attention toward the foreigners, notably the French living in Brazzaville. As he conducted morning PT with his Marines, Gunnery Sergeant Upchurch noticed truckloads of government troops heading toward the compound of Denis Sassou. Here, they disembarked and surrounded the ousted leader's compound. Shortly thereafter, a firefight broke out between government forces and Sassou's "Cobras."

Sensing trouble, GySgt. Upchurch placed the Marines on full alert. The situation became increasingly tense as the day went on. As the situation in Brazzaville became more chaotic the deputy chief of mission (DCM), acting on behalf of the RSO, who had been out of the country, instructed the Marines and all embassy personnel to remain at their posts. The DCM likewise ordered all Americans living in the city to remain indoors and not to venture out unless it was absolutely necessary. Early in the morning of 6 June, the DCM informed the detachment commander that the embassy "had lost all internal communications."[78]

The next day, June 7, the ambassador arrived at the embassy in his armored vehicle and met with his principal staff, including Gunnery Sergeant Upchurch. Given the chaotic conditions that existed in Brazzaville, the ambassador instructed the Marine detachment commander to organize a two-vehicle convoy in order to collect all of the American citizens (AMCITs) and bring them into the embassy compound prior to their evacuation. From intelligence reports, it seemed that the greatest danger came from looters and not the warring armies. This rescue team, known as the AMCIT Rescue Team, conducted several rescue missions and managed to rescue all Americans living in the city and several French families that requested evacuation.

Throughout the rescue attempts, the rescue convoy passed through numerous barricades manned by both government troops and the rival armies. According to Gunnery Sergeant Upchurch, "The government troops manned the barricades closer to the city while bandits controlled those at the key intersection of Avenue De Maya Maya and Des Trois Martrys, and approximately two to three kilometers on both sides of the airport road." The only trouble experienced by the Marines was when the bandits became agitated over the constant movement of the rescue convoy toward the airport control point. Contributing to the belligerence of the bandits was the consumption of alcohol. "Gunny" Upchurch wrote, "We noticed that these bandits were consuming alcohol from bottles, possibly palm wine. This greatly contributed to the deteriorating situation."[79] As for the government troops, the Marine gunnery sergeant wrote that when not engaging Sassou's or Kolelas' forces, they spent most of their time looting electronic stores and stealing cars, household goods and food.

After several days, the Marines and local guards succeeded in rescuing the majority of the Americans (including two U.S. government officials trapped in the fighting) and other foreign citizens, including many French families. On June 8, 1997, the situation in Brazzaville became increasingly violent. With the U.S. Embassy in the direct line of fire, the DCM ordered all Americans, including the Marine Security Guards, into the safe havens. After checking their ammunition, food, and other supplies, the Marines complied with the order. They all remained there overnight (June 8–9). The next day, when the "all clear" was given, the Marine Security Guards conducted a room-by-room search of the embassy in order to insure that no intruders had penetrated the chancery. They also checked for structural damage to the chancery itself. The Marine Security Guards likewise provided a security detail for a meeting between the ambassador and a representative from the government.

As the situation in Congo-Brazzaville continued to deteriorate, the French sent in troops, who seized the airfield and set up their headquarters. While some of the French forces processed the evacuees, others prepared to repel the advance of the Cobras, who now threatened the airfield and the evacuation. Throughout the crisis, the Marine Security Guards and their French comrades-in-arms worked together to prevent the loss of the airfield or harm to the evacuees. When a Marine Corps MC-130 landed at the international airport to assist in the evacuation, French soldiers formed a "human wall" to protect the American evacuees until the aircraft lifted off.[80] With the safe evacuation of the American citizens, Gunnery Sergeant Upchurch and several Marine Security Guards, including Lance Corporal Robert Reichner, returned to the U.S. Embassy to begin final evacuation procedures.

Back at the embassy, Sergeants Furne, Penman, and Gousie, along with Sergeant Harckom continued to shred and burn classified material as well as conduct sweeps of the U.S. Embassy prior to its evacuation. When another firefight broke out near the Embassy, Gunnery Sergeant Upchurch ordered a REACT[81] and instructed the Marines to proceed to a designated safe haven. On the evening of June 10, 1997, the Marines resumed operations at Post One. As Gunnery Sergeant Upchurch noted, "Throughout the night there were fierce fire fights nearby and distant with heavy artillery going outward away from the embassy area."[82]

After the evacuation of five more American Embassy officials, the Marines continued to destroy all classified material inside the vault and communications room, which in and of itself proved to be a considerable problem, due largely to the volume of classified material kept at the embassy. In his summary of the evacuation from Brazzaville, Gunnery Sergeant Upchurch recommended that in the future, the amount of classified material be limited by section. He added that each section limit its holdings of classified material to only the most current and vital messages.[83]

On Wednesday, June 18, 1997, the ambassador gave the order to close the American Embassy in Brazzaville. At 7:30 A.M., the ambassador, his staff, the remaining evacuees, the

The Marine Security Guard Detachment from the U.S. Embassy in Brazsaville, Congo, stands ready in REACT gear to protect American citizens as they prepare to evacuate the Embassy on June 18, 1997. Left to right are Sgt. Furne, Lcpl Riechner, Sgt. Harkcom, GySgt Upchurch, Sgt. Penman, and Sgt. Gousie (courtesy of Corporal Robert Reichner).

Marine Security Guards and French troops boarded airplanes and headed for neighboring Kinshasa, a thirty-minute flight. Within a year's time, however, the situation in Brazzaville would be repeated. The Republic of the Congo experienced a similar fate as inter-ethnic and tribal warfare once again called upon the Marine Security Guards to undertake a similar evacuation.

Trouble in Kinshasa, Republic of the Congo, July–August 1998

As the Marine Security Guards evacuated the U.S. Embassy in Brazzaville, rebels in the Republic of the Congo, led by Laurent Desire Kabila, ousted the long-time leader of the country and U.S. ally Mobutu Sese Seko. The overthrow of Mobutu, who ruled Zaire for nearly thirty-one years, however, did not bring peace to the country, as neighboring Rwandans now sought Kabila's ouster. As in Brazzaville, peace seemed elusive, as the warring parties continued to kill and loot amidst a populace battered by decades of tribal and inter-ethnic warfare.[84] Kabila's overthrow of Mobutu was due largely to support from the so-called Tutsi-dominated "boy-soldiers" from Rwanda.[85] In return for their support in Mobutu's overthrow, Kabila promised to "seal off" the borders between the Congo and neighboring Rwanda in order to prevent Hutu guerrillas from entering and leaving the country at will. Meanwhile, disaffected politicians from the Mobutu era and Kabila's own tribesmen — the Katangans — likewise fed the ever-increasing rumors in Kinshasa of an impending *coup d'état* against Kabila's government.[86]

With opposition growing from within the Congo (which Kabila had renamed upon coming to power in 1997) and from the outside in neighboring Rwanda and Uganda, Kabila, on July 27, 1998, ordered "all foreign forces to leave the country immediately." The Congolese president likewise began to round up all Tutsis in the capital. The Rwandans initially complied with Kabila's order. On August 3, however, Tutsi military units living in the capital revolted and began to seize various cities in the eastern half of the country. As the Tutsis staged their *coup d'état*, other Rwandan military units launched their own uprising in Kinshasa. Kabila's forces put this revolt down almost immediately.[87] According to Staff Sergeant T. Richardson, the detachment commander at the U.S. Embassy in Kinshasa, the Rwandans and Ugandans turned against Kabila due to the way he ran the Republic of the Congo. According to SSgt. Richardson, "He didn't listen to advice and had no government experience [in] running a country."[88]

On August 2, 1998, the fighting became more intense as Banyamulenge and Congolese troops fought each other at Camp Tshatshi, approximately eight miles from Kinshasa. It was during this time that the commander of the 10th Brigade of the Congolese Army announced that he could no longer support Kabila's government. The proximity of the fighting to the American School of Kinshasa, where the children of the American diplomats and Foreign Service workers attended, sent alarm bells through the embassy, and prompted the ambassador to order the people who remained there to seek shelter in the safe havens. In Kinshasa itself, loyal Congolese troops enforced a dusk to dawn curfew, with roadblocks and checkpoints, checking identification cards and passports. Two days later, on August 5, 1998, the RSO ordered all non-essential personnel to evacuate the post. Embassy personnel placed all dependents on a chartered flight out of Kinshasa. An Emergency Survey and Assessment Team arrived from Washington, D.C., and began planning for a possible evacuation by helicopter if necessary. Meanwhile, erroneous reports coming in from CNN on the rebels' advance toward

Kinshasa and supposed wide-scale looting (all of which proved to be false) caused some panic. By week's end, there was a calm that descended over the city, as Congolese checkpoints became less rigid (as Staff Sergeant Richardson reported, some Congolese soldiers, in fact, slept at their checkpoints). Marine Security Guards nevertheless continued to shred and burn most of the classified material in the embassy vault. The RSO instructed the Marines to keep some message traffic but told them to be able to 'take care of [the rest of the classified material] in 15 minutes or less if we had to get out quickly."[89]

Marine Security Guards continued to man Post One, though they did set up a command post just in case the ambassador ordered a full-scale evacuation. The RSO, Staff Sergeant Richardson, or an off duty Marine Security Guard normally monitored the command post when not on duty. Throughout this period the city remained relatively quiet as Congolese went about their day-to-day business. Staff Sergeant Richardson noted that despite the coup, President Kabila remained popular with the average citizen.[90]

While there was a minor government-sponsored anti–American demonstration in front of the U.S. Embassy on 6 August by about 600 to 700 Congolese, who shouted anti–Western and anti–American slogans, the situation remained calm. Despite the calm, however, he RSO and the ambassador both recommended that American citizens leave the Congo as soon as possible, warning them that "this was the calm before the storm."

On August 13, the situation deteriorated as rebels seized the Inga Dam and had cut the power to Kinshasa, leaving most of the city in the dark and without electricity. The biggest fear among the citizenry was the potential for wide-scale looting to take place in the capital though fortunately, by the afternoon of 14 August, power had been restored to Kinshasa. This event convinced the ambassador that the time had arrived to close the embassy and evacuate all personnel. By late afternoon five more members of embassy left for Yaounde, Cameroon, with only twelve members of the core staff left behind. Included in this latter group was the Marine Security Guard detachment.

At 6:30 A.M., Staff Sergeant Richardson received a call from the Marine on duty at Post One, who informed him that the RSO wanted to see him. Arriving at the embassy, the RSO informed SSgt. Richardson that the embassy would close. All remaining classified material was to be destroyed and the Marines were to disable all weapons prior to evacuation. At a subsequent meeting, the deputy chief of mission informed the detachment commander that all of this had to be completed within the next to 4 to 5 hours.[91] Staff Sergeant Richardson recalled, "During the next hours, the remaining weapons were moved to the safehaven vault and disabled. The last bit of classified material was destroyed. Marines went about the embassy checking each office to make sure all windows were locked and safes locked. With the embassy semi-secured the focus was shifted to the Marine BEQ [quarters], securing it and packing a suitcase to take along."[92]

At 4:30 P.M., the last of the luggage was pre-positioned in front of the embassy. With the Marine House all secure, the RSO and Staff Sergeant Richardson conducted a room-to-room check of the entire embassy to ensure that nothing was left on, all computers turned off, and everything in the offices had been secured. A 1730, the Marines lowered the U.S. flag and handed it to the chargé d'affaires. Luggage was then loaded onto trucks as the remaining staff boarded vans and headed for the airport. At the airport, they boarded a chartered flight headed for Yaounde, and arrived there at approximately 11:15 P.M.[93]

As occurred in neighboring Congo-Brazzaville, the alertness of the ambassador and his staff, as well as the professionalism and dedication of the Marine Security Guards, from the detachment commanders through the watchstanders, ensured that not a single American had been hurt or killed by rebels or government troops. Staff Sergeant Richardson's after-action comments, however, suggest that similar problems existed in both Kinshasa and Brazzaville insofar as classified material had been concerned. Staff Sergeant Richardson noted that during the crisis, the embassy staff spent a better part of the night before evacuation destroying classified material. The detachment commander, like his counterpart, Gunnery Sergeant Upchurch, in Brazzaville suggested that a semi-annual review should be held to ensure that dated classified material is destroyed.

Staff Sergeant Richardson wrote that the relationship between the Marines and RSO was very good, and that the latter kept the leathernecks well-informed of the ongoing situation in the Congo. Unlike in Brazzaville, the safe havens in Kinshasa had an adequate supply of Meals Ready to Eat (MREs), thanks largely to the foresight of the Marine Security Guards. Finally, the Marine staff sergeant was very critical of CNN's reporting, which he wrote "was false" in both content and conjecture. Staff Sergeant Richardson added that throughout the crisis, CNN could not be relied upon for accurate or truthful reporting.[94]

As with the Marine Security Guard Detachment in Brazzaville, the Marines assigned to the U.S. Embassy in Kinshasa were ready when the word came to evacuate. Their professional training and dedication to duty during times of trouble ensured that a panic would not ensue among the embassy staff or other American citizens. In fact, as in both countries, the Marine Security Guards were a reassurance as to the need for calm and order, and remained, as Staff Sergeant Richardson concluded, "flexible," and thus were able to meet all the challenges in both of these complex and highly volatile cauldrons.

Terror Strikes in Kenya and Dar Es Salaam, 7 August 1998

During the 1990s, Africa's political and socio-economic instability made it a breeding ground for terrorism. The followers of Osama Bin Laden,[95] founder and financier of the group known as Al-Qaida or "the Base," targeted those states that had a sizeable or oppressed Islamic population and thus could provide "foot soldiers" in his war against the West. Several African states, including Sudan, Chad, and most importantly Somalia, served Bin Laden's purposes well during this period. On February 23, 1998, at a meeting in Khost, Afghanistan (Bin Laden's adopted homeland), all of the groups associated with Al-Qaida issued a manifesto that was, in essence, a declaration of war against the United States and its allies. This declaration of war, coming in the form of a fatwa, or religious decree, ordered all Muslims to "kill the Americans and their allies — civilians and military," and that it was a "duty for every Muslim who can do it in any country in which it is possible to."[96] Thus, at a single stroke, Bin Laden was able to hijack a religion and turn it into a cause that justified the murder and maiming of thousands of innocent people. His first target were the streets of Mogadishu with the ultimate objective situated on the streets of New York City, Washington, D.C., and the fields of Pennsylvania.

Osama Bin Laden's call for a "jihad" or "holy war" against Americans and the West found adherents in Africa, where Islam had long been a strong, dominant force. Coupled with Africa's seemingly endless factional and tribal fighting, Bin Laden's fatwa proved a highly volatile "call to arms." This fatwa, first experienced by the United States Army Rangers in Mogadishu, Somalia, in October 1993, was the first in a series of incidents that pitted the radical Muslim's fanatical followers against the interests of the United States in Africa and the Middle East.

The bombed out shell of the U.S. Embassy in Dar es Salaam after a suicide bomber's attack on August 7, 1998 (U.S. Marine Security Guard Battalion).

Not About Religion ... Not About Politics ... Simply Murder

On the morning of Friday, August 7, 1998, as Corporal Samuel Gonite stood guard at Post One at the U.S. Embassy in Nairobi, Kenya, Gunnery Sergeant G.B. Cross, the detachment commander, made his rounds throughout the embassy. At approximately 10:35 A.M., Sergeant Jesse N. Aliganga walked past Corporal Gonite and boarded an elevator headed to the bank in the embassy to cash a check. Within minutes of Sergeant Aliganga's arrival, "all hell broke loose," as an unidentified man demanded from one of the local guards access to the U.S. Embassy. Rebuffed by the local guard, the man took out a grenade and tossed it toward the guard. As this took place, a truck laden with explosives suddenly appeared on the scene and crashed into the rear wall of the embassy adjacent to an underground garage and exploded. According to Lieutenant Colonel Dennis G. Sabal, commanding officer, Fox Company, the force of the blast blew out nearly every closed window and frame on the building. The concussion of the blast knocked both Gunnery Sergeant Cross and Corporal Gonite to the deck of the embassy that was now in "shambles."[97] By the stopped clock located in the chancery of the embassy, the blast came at approximately 10:39 A.M., with the force of the explosion causing the small bank building behind the embassy to collapse. The walls located on all floors of the embassy, made of concrete that was about 12 inches thick, crumpled like thin plates of glass — such was the force of the explosion. As for the Ufundi House bank building adjacent to the U.S. embassy (which shared the same parking lot), the impact of the blast

A Marine from 2d Fleet Anti-Terrorist Security Team Company stands guard in the aftermath of the terrorist blast that killed over 200 innocent people in Nairobi, Kenya. FAST Marines were immediately airlifted to Kenya to guard the embassy and its environs (U.S. Marine Security Guard Battalion).

was so great that it turned into a "giant pile of sand."[98] Meanwhile, in the embassy, Lt. Col. Sabal noted, "There was not an office space that survived inside the embassy. Bodies were spread all over, most of which were buried under up to eight feet of rubble."[99]

Even before the smoke had cleared, all of the Marine Security Guards, including two leathernecks temporarily visiting Nairobi from other MSG detachments, rushed into the smoldering building to begin the search for Sergeant Aliganga. As several Marines began to search the rubble for their comrade, other Marine Security Guards manned defensive positions around the perimeter of the embassy in case the terrorists should follow up with another attack.[100]

At the same time that the U.S. Embassy in Nairobi was struck by a suicide bomber, another suicide bomber simultaneously drove an explosive-laden truck into gate in front of the U.S. Embassy in Dar es Salaam, Tanzania. At the time of the blast, approximately 10:40 A.M., Post One had been occupied by the RSO, Mr. John DiCarlo, himself a former Marine Security Guard, while the duty Marine Security Guard, Corporal Brian P. Johnson, made a head call. The force of the blast knocked Corporal Johnson to the floor. Picking himself up, the Marine corporal quickly donned REACT gear and alerted the other Marine security guards then at the Marine House, after which he immediately took control of the command center.[101] The impact of the blast at Dar es Salaam was just as powerful as the one that shook the

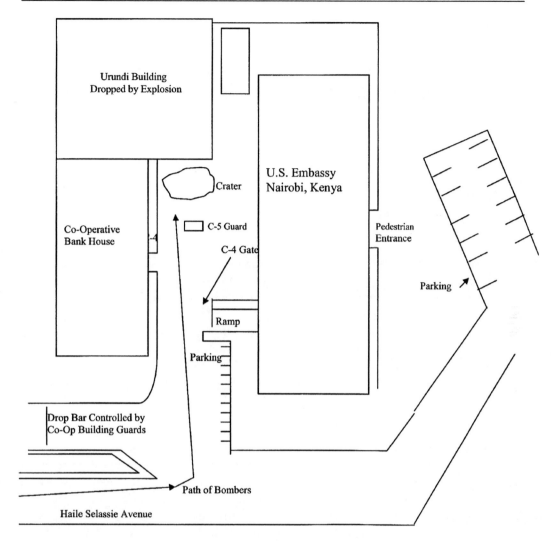

Diagram 6. Bombing of U.S. Embassy, Nairobi, Kenya, August 7, 1998 (U.S. Department of State).

U.S. Embassy in Nairobi, crumpling solid concrete walls into chest-high rubble, blowing computers off desks, and sending glass, aluminum, and steel into the air. In fact, the force of the blast was so great that it blew open the hardline doors located on the opposite sides of the embassy. The force likewise blew the emergency fire exit doors off their hinges.

Almost as soon as the blast impacted, Gunnery Sergeant Patrick Kimble began an immediate search for survivors. Among the injured Americans in Tanzania was GySgt. Kimble's wife, Cynthia, who had worked at the U.S. Embassy in Dar es Salaam, and suffered lacerations and bruises caused by flying glass. She and the other wounded were immediately evacuated and placed on emergency medical flights out of the country. Despite his concern for his wife's injuries, Gunnery Sergeant Kimble and Corporal Aaron Hatfield immediately set up an emergency command center, where they began to coordinate rescue efforts and assess the damage to the embassy.[102] Within five hours, the Marines assigned to the embassy in Tanzania were able to conduct a sweep of what was now a charred mass of twisted steel and concrete.

"Devil Dogs up! We got a job to do"

Corporal Johnson recalled that the scene at the embassy was one of "utter chaos." He remembered that after alerting the Marine House he grabbed his shotgun and waited for the other Marine Security Guards to arrive. Meanwhile, the Marine corporal assisted the civilians inside the destroyed embassy down the embassy's ladder well into the courtyard. Here, he saw one of his comrades, Sergeant Stivason, armed with a K-bar and a PR-24 radio. Even amidst the death and destruction, the Marines, Cpl. Johnson recalled, "knew what needed to be done, and we did it."[103]

As Corporal McCabe recalled, the Marines' working, training, and living together enabled the leathernecks to react quickly and efficiently. Corporal McCabe, who likened this attack to the one on the U.S. Embassy in Beirut in 1983, stated that he and the other Marines realized that it was time for "Devil Dogs up. We got a job to do." Donning their REACT gear, the Marines awaited for a follow-on attack that never came. After the smoke began to clear, the Marine corporal, Gunnery Sergeant Kimble, and another Marine made their way back into the embassy in order to get what ammunition and other supplies that they could. By 1800, everything began to settle down, and the Marine Security Guards in Tanzania had re-established Post One and re-instituted a watch schedule.[104]

Both Corporals Johnson and McCabe recalled that within forty-eight hours of the blast, a FAST team had been on the ground in Dar es Salaam, as well as a detachment of three Marine Security Guards from Echo Company. Corporal McCabe gave special praise to the efficiency of the Tanzanian Special Forces, who he said gave a good account of themselves in the aftermath of the explosion in setting up external security.

Meanwhile in Rome, Italy, on the morning of August 7, 1998, Secretary of State Madeline Albright received word of the twin tragedies and immediately issued statements condemning the attacks as both vicious and against all principals of civilized humanity. From the outset, the attacks had the imprint of Osama Bin Laden. The secretary of state, upon returning immediately to Washington, D.C., met with President Bill Clinton along with members of his National Security Team to discuss retaliatory strikes against Bin Laden, who had been hiding with his followers somewhere in Taliban-controlled Afghanistan. Ultimately, President Clinton "gave the green light for a retaliatory mission" in the form of cruise missile attacks aimed against Bin Laden and his followers.[105] With this decision made, Secretary of State Albright boarded a special Air Force plane and flew immediately to Nairobi, Kenya, where she was able to gain a first-hand assessment of the twin tragedies.

Bravery and Heroism

Even before Secretary Albright arrived in Nairobi, a FAST team from Norfolk, Va., immediately boarded a flight and flew directly into the Kenyan capital. Once on the ground, FAST relieved the Marine Security Guards who, despite having spent nearly 56 hours on duty, were still able to concentrate on securing the perimeter and locating their fallen comrade. In fact, after nearly 27 hours of continuous digging, the Marines came across the body of Sergeant Aliganga. Covering the body with an American flag, they reverently placed Sgt. Aliganga's body onto a stretcher. "Then," Lt. Col. Sabal wrote, "the Marines very purposefully marched him through the rubble and out of the embassy to the waiting vehicle. Although there were no cameras present, nor was there any music playing, the crowds seemed to stand still, and people stood erect, with tears running down their faces, as the body of another United States Marine, who gave his life in defense of his country, was ushered away."

Sergeant Aliganga was not the only American service person to die in the bombings. Also killed in the blast in Nairobi were Sergeant Kenneth R. Hobson III, U.S. Army, who was a veteran of Desert Storm, and Master Sergeant Sherry Lynn Olds, U.S. Air Force. Other victims included American Foreign Service personnel as well as the hundreds of Kenyans caught up in the impact of the blast on the embassy and Ufundi bank building. In fact, over fifty percent of the 200 occupants of the U.S. Embassy in Nairobi were casualties of the bombing. Twelve Americans and 34 local employees were killed. Another 50 required extensive medical care while over 200 Kenyans were killed and over 5,000 wounded.[106] Among the wounded was Sergeant Daniel Briehl, a Marine Security Guard who, along with the other wounded victims, was evacuated to a U.S. Military medical facility in Landstuhl, Germany.

As for the casualty figures in Dar es Salaam, the blast there killed 7 contractors and injured 7 others, including Mrs. Kimble and Elizabeth Slater, both employees at the U.S. Embassy.[107] The toll could have been much worse if had it not been for the fact that the embassy in Tanzania was built miles away from the populated sectors of town and was of much sturdier construction.[108] Nevertheless, both bombings were tragedies all the same.

During both crises, the Marine Security Guards worked tirelessly as they guarded the perimeters in Nairobi and Dar es Salaam until the arrival of the FAST teams. Assisting the Marine Security Guards in the immediate aftermath of the bombings was a group of U.S. Army Special Forces, who took over guard duty while the tired Marines slept in shifts. Once the FAST teams were in position around the embassies, the Marine Security Guards resumed their normal duties of searching the rubble for classified material and recovering vital equipment.

Lieutenant Colonel Sabal, in his letter to Colonel David S. Burgess, the commanding officer of the Marine Security Guard Battalion, had nothing but praise for the Marines assigned to both Nairobi, Kenya, and Dar es Salaam, Tanzania: "What must not be missed is the incredible bravery and heroism displayed by our Marine Security Guards. Without any regard for their own lives or safety, they maintained incredible presence of mind in the face of tremendous devastation. Each Marine continued to serve our country and our Department of State with distinction. Even through the chaos and the fog, our Marines never lost focus of their mission. They were models of strength to be emulated by all."[109] Lieutenant Colonel Sabal added that the bravery displayed by the Marines came as a result of the training each Marine received throughout his career before coming into the MSG program:

> Please keep in mind that we are talking initially about only six Marines. Four corporals with less than five months on the MSG program; one supply admin[istrative] clerk, one communicator, one tank crewman, and a canvass repair specialist, an 0311 Sergeant and a Gunnery Sergeant who is a legal chief. This situation brought true meaning to the fact that every Marine is a rifleman.... They have not missed a beat and will continue guarding Americans and America's interests abroad, as Marines have done for over 222 years.[110]

The chargé d'affaires in Dar es Salaam, Mr. John Lange, likewise praised the efficiency of the Marines in the immediate aftermath of the attack. In a statement issued after he met personally with the Marines, Mr. Lange praised the leathernecks for their heroism and outstanding conduct in the aftermath of the bombing. The statement specially commended the Marines for how "exceptionally well they performed their duties under extreme conditions of chaos and terror. Their bravery and heroism was displayed in such a confident and

The strain and tears of the Marine Security Guards can be seen as they carry the body of their comrade and friend, Sgt. Jesse N. Aliganga, wrapped in an American flag to an awaiting ambulance. Sgt. Aliganga was the eleventh Marine Security Guard to die in the line of duty (U.S. Marine Security Guard Bn. photograph).

purposeful manner that their very presence transferred to others, allowing them to get through the situation."[111]

Sergeant Jesse N. Aliganga Is Honored

Amidst the carnage of the twin bombings, the Marine Corps took time to honor yet another fallen hero who paid the ultimate price. In a memorial service at the Quantico Memorial Chapel, Sergeant Jesse N. Aliganga, the eleventh Marine Security Guard to die in the line of duty, Marines from MSG Battalion honored the young leatherneck for his bravery and his sacrifice as an "Ambassador in Blue." In attendance at the memorial service was Mrs. Clara Aliganga, Sergeant Aliganga's mother, his sister, Leah Colston, members

Sergeant Jesse N. Aliganga, USMC, killed in the terrorist attack of the U.S. Embassy in Nairobi, Kenya, on August 7, 1998 (U.S. Marine Security Guard Battalion).

of the Marine Security Guard Battalion staff, and the current students from MSG School. In a private ceremony at Marshall Hall prior to the memorial service, Colonel David S. Burgess presented Mrs. Aliganga with her son's Purple Heart, awarded posthumously for actions at the Kenya embassy. While presenting the medal to Mrs. Aliganga, Colonel Burgess praised the young Marine for his sacrifice and dedication to duty. Gunnery Sergeant Donald Cozine, Jr., an instructor with Schools Company, eulogized Sergeant Aliganga as one who "paid the ultimate price" as a Marine Security Guard. Gunnery Sergeant Cozine told the more than 250 people, which included Marine Security Guard students, battalion staff officials and relatives, that Sergeant Aliganga's spirit will never die, as it will always "linger here, at Nairobi, and at the recruit depot at Parris Island. He is our brother. He is our son." Gunnery Sergeant Cozine added, "The fact that he was chosen as an MSG shows he was of outstanding character ... very large in honor and in heart."[112] The finest, and perhaps most touching tribute paid to the memory of Sergeant Aliganga came from his mother who, in a tearful goodbye, quoted a line from a popular song of the day, "'Far longer than Forever, I'll hold you in my heart.' I love you Nathan ... Mom."

Sergeant Aliganga, like the soldier and Airwoman killed in the bombing in Nairobi, was eulogized as a casualty in the war the United States now found itself fighting on many fronts and on many battlefields. Like so many of the young men who went before him, Sergeant Aliganga represented the best our country had to offer and, and as GySgt. Cozine stated, "his spirit will live forever" in the Marine Security Guards who follow in his footsteps.

The Kenya and Tanzania Attacks: A Breakdown in Intelligence

In the aftermath of the twin terrorist attacks in Nairobi and Dar es Salaam, it became apparent that the bombings had all of the "calling cards" of Osama Bin Laden. More tragic, however, was the breakdown in intelligence that occurred prior to the two bombings. In his after-action report of the events of August 1998, Gunnery Sergeant G.B. Cross wrote that as detachment commander of the Marine Security Guards, he had not received any briefing on the threats posed by terrorists, most notably from Al-Qaida, whose supporters had been making numerous telephone bomb threats throughout the region prior to the attacks. Instead, Cross said, "the only information that the Detachment Commander [Cross] had received in the three weeks of his assignment were about crime threats, nothing at all about terrorist threats or activities in the local area." While Cross wrote in his report that corrective measures had been taken by the regional security officer insofar as intelligence briefings were concerned, it was too little too late to help the victims in Kenya and Tanzania.[113]

Operation Desert Fox and the MSG Detachment in Damascus, Syria

As the United States confronted this new enemy, American and British warplanes continued to enforce the "no-fly zone" over Iraq, as part of the cease fire that brought an end to the first Gulf War. The Iraqi leader, Saddam Hussein, however, continued to test the will of the coalition when he ordered his forces to fire on the American and British aircraft. Furthermore, in another direct violation of the cease fire agreement, the Iraqi leader expelled members of the United Nations Special Commission (UNSCOM), headed by Richard Butler, who had been sent to Iraq to catalog and begin the dismantling of Hussein's production of weapons of mass destruction. Mr. Butler's report, issued on December 15, 1998, outlined in precise detail that Iraq had failed to "turn over documents related to its chemical and biological weapons programs and had indeed obstructed another inspection."[114] As former Secretary of State Albright wrote, "This time there would be a price to pay." On the morning of December 16, 1998, President Bill Clinton met with his National Security Team and authorized a massive retaliatory strike aimed at forcing Hussein back into compliance. That afternoon and for the next two days, American and British planes flew over 650 sorties against selected military targets while sea-launched Cruise and Tomahawk missiles pounded a variety of security-related targets.[115]

The mixed response from neighboring Arab countries was both supportive and hostile. Most notable was the large anti–American and anti–British protests that took place in neighboring Syria, where hundreds of thousands of people took to the streets to protest this attack on a fellow Arab country. Already alerted to the possibility of trouble, the RSO and detachment commander, Gunnery Sergeant Donald Downey, Jr., "REACTED" the Marine Security Guards, who assumed defensive positions inside the chancery and throughout the compound.

CHART 6. MARINE SECURITY GUARD DETACHMENT, U.S. EMBASSY, DAMASCUS, SYRIA, DECEMBER 1998

Gunnery Sergeant Donald Downey	Detachment Commander
Sergeant Kevin G. Tinsley	Watchstander
Sergeant Louis O. Hernandez	Ass't. Detachment Commander
Sergeant Marc F. McDonald	Watchstander
Corporal Bryan Paxton	Watchstander
Master Sergeant Thomas C. Reed	Detachment Commander[116]

In order to deal with what had become a sizable crowd in front of the embassy, Sergeant Louis Hernandez, the assistant detachment commander, sent the Marine Security Guards to their assigned observation posts. As the crowds grew larger, they became more violent as they shouted anti–American slogans and demanded that the U.S. end its no-fly zone over Iraq.[117]

As the Marine Security Guards took up their positions, the crowds began to force their way into the embassy compound. At 9:40 A.M., the protestors, using portable No Parking Signs as steps, climbed over the exterior walls of the compound. Within ten minutes, the courtyard in the back of the chancery was filled with angry protestors. At 11:00 A.M., the RSO gave the order to the Marine Security Guards to use tear gas to repel the intruders. Sergeant Hernandez then activated the back entrance exterior T-Guard. Sergeant Marc McDonald let loose with three tear gas canisters filled with CS gas from the second floor of the chancery. The canisters fell onto the ground of the exterior wall and caused the crowd to immediately disperse. Before the crowds dispersed, four protestors managed to climb onto the roof of the chancery, where they tore the American flag off the flagpole. As the protestors slowly dispersed, Syrian police and fire trucks arrived and dispersed the crowds by spraying them with water from fire hoses.[118]

Meanwhile, another group of protestors stormed Ambassador Ryan Crocker's residence and trapped his wife inside the apartment. At 12:57 P.M., Mrs. Crocker informed the RSO that protestors had managed to enter the residence compound and were at her windows. The RSO asked Gunnery Sergeant Downey for volunteers to help rescue the ambassador's wife. Sergeants McDonald and Tinsley immediately volunteered to assist the RSO. Once chosen, Sergeant Tinsley accompanied the RSO to Mrs. Crocker's residence. Using a Syrian police car, the RSO and Marine sergeant successfully rescued Mrs. Crocker, her servants, and pets. Once inside the U.S. diplomatic compound, Sergeant Tinsley drove them to temporary quarters using the Marine vehicle and driver.[119]

Later that afternoon, at about 2:05 P.M., the protestors returned, this time targeting the entrance to the compound. At one point, the crowds managed to enter the chancery, though Syrian police immediately repulsed them and forced them out. By late afternoon, the protestors had dispersed thanks largely to the efforts of the Marine Security Guards and the local Syrian police and fire departments. In their wake, however, the protestors left a path of destruction, as the American Embassy, the ambassador's residence, the U.S. Information Services building, and the Damascus Community School all had been severely vandalized. Upon closer inspection of the embassy vehicles and Marine House, it was discovered the protestors had disabled the vehicles by pulling out the ignition wires and had smashed several windows at the Marine BEQ.

Corporal Bryan Paxton, who had been away on temporary additional duty in Cyprus conducting familiarization firing of all weapons found at a MSG detachment, returned on the morning of December 21, 1998, and immediately assumed his REACT position in the embassy.[120] As the after effects of Operation Desert Fox continued to be felt in Damascus, the RSO ordered the Marines to maintain their interior defensive posture until later that evening. At 5 P.M., the ambassador gave the "all clear" and the Marine Security Guards resumed their normal duties.

Other Incidents in 1998–1999

In November 1998, anti–American violence in Islamabad, Pakistan, affected the traditional Marine Corps ball. Gunnery Sergeant William B. Wheeler recalled that despite the ordered withdrawal of all non-essential personnel, the ball was held, albeit as a much subdued celebration at the American ambassador's residence.[121]

Other events in 1998 included the defense of the U.S. Embassy in Tirana, Albania, by the Marine Security Guard, when, in August, Albanians protested the assassination of Azem Hajdari, a political ally of their ousted president, Sali Berisha. When the violence spilled over into the U.S. Embassy, the Marine Security Guards were reinforced by a rifle company from the 22nd MEU(SOC), flown in from the USS *Austin* and USS *Saipan* in order to protect the embassy and the American citizens living there. Major Frank Carroll, commanding officer of the Marines from the MEU, said that while the additional Marines were there as more of an insurance policy, "he has enough troops to protect the Embassy and do the job."[122] Approximately 100 Marines from 22nd MEU(SOC) remained ashore in Tirana at the U.S. Embassy, hardening the embassy facilities to help ensure there was no repeat of the two terrorist attacks that devastated the American embassies in Nairobi and Dar es Salaam only weeks before.[123]

The following year, in neighboring Yugoslavia, when Serbian troops began a systematic massacre of ethnic Albanians in Kosovo, American and NATO warplanes pounded Belgrade, Yugoslavia's capital. Fearful of retribution by Serb strongman Slobodan Milosevic, President Bill Clinton ordered the closure of the U.S. Embassy in Belgrade. The Marine Security Guards assisted the ambassador in this operation by shredding classified material and insuring that all the American citizens had been evacuated.

They Attacked America "Because we are freedom's home and defender"

At approximately 9:00 A.M. on September 11, 2001, two jet airliners crashed into the Twin Towers of the World Trade Center in New York City. As the two buildings collapsed before a horrified nation, another jet shortly thereafter crashed into the Pentagon while yet another jet, reportedly headed for the White House, crashed into a field in southeastern Pennsylvania. Taking responsibility for these acts of war were the followers of Osama Bin Laden's terrorist group Al-Qaida. President George W. Bush, who had been visiting with school children in Florida, immediately boarded *Air Force One* and headed for Washington, D.C., where he could better assess the damage to the country and prepare America's response to the criminals who planned and carried out these outrages. That same evening, the president addressed a stunned nation and asserted that the individuals who have attacked America did so "because we are freedom's home and defender," and that he would pursue these "killers" wherever they hid in order to seek justice.

Activation of the 4th Marine Expeditionary Brigade (Anti-Terrorism)

For Marine Security Guards, this was not a new war. Indeed, long before September 11, 2001, terrorist attacks aimed against U.S. embassies and consulates worldwide throughout the 1970s 1980s, and 1990s had put Marine Security Guards on the front lines of this conflict. As a response to the new war on terror, Marine Security Guard battalion became part of the Marine Corps' "Anti-Terrorism Marine" or "ATM" concept. Henceforth, Marine Security Guard Battalion, along with Marine Corps Security Forces Battalion (i.e., FAST), the newly established Chemical and Biological Incidence Response Force or "CBIRF" and a rotating rifle battalion based at Camp Lejeune, N.C., became part of the 4th Marine Expeditionary Brigade (Anti-Terrorism). While MSG Battalion remained operationally under control of the State Department, the 4th Marine Expeditionary Brigade now controlled the day-to-day administrative and training functions. This modification to the original Memorandum of Agreement provided the Marine Corps with better coordination in its response to the war on terror.[124]

While the missions of MSG, CBIRF and MCSF battalions remained the same, the role of the infantry battalion assigned to the brigade is to "provide rapid deployment forces to detect, deter, defend, and conduct crisis response in order to combat the threat of terrorism world wide."[125] Brigadier General D.V. O'Dell, USMC, was subsequently appointed the first commanding general of this new unit, tailored to take the fight to the terrorists. The 4th MEB gave the Marine Corps–Navy team a capable, rapidly deployable force, well-trained in a variety of tasks, in order to meet any emergency world-wide in response to a terrorist act aimed against the United States or its allies. Upon the establishment of the 4thMEB(AT), Brigadier General O'Dell's mission was to "provide designated supported commanders with rapidly deployable, specially trained, and sustainable forces that are capable of detecting terrorism, conducting activities to deter terrorism, defending designated facilities against terrorism, and conducting initial incidence response in the event of chemical, biological, radiological, or nuclear terrorist attacks."[126]

For the Marines of Marine Security Guard Battalion, many of whom had already been "blooded" by acts of terrorism, there was very little change, as it remained under the operational control of the Department of State by terms of the Memorandum of Agreement. Under the new mission, MSG Battalion remained committed to provide trained Marine embassy guards for U.S. embassies and consulates worldwide.

Operation Enduring Freedom in Afghanistan

The first test for the 4th Marine Expeditionary Brigade (AT) came after Marines of the 26th Marine Expeditionary Unit (Special Operations Capable) (MEU[SOC]), entered the abandoned U.S. Embassy in

In wake of the attacks on September 11, 2001, Major General D.V. O'Dell was appointed the first commanding general of the newly-developed 4th Marine Expeditionary Brigade (Anti-Terrorism) headquartered at Camp Lejeune, North Carolina (courtesy U.S. Marine Corps).

Kabul, Afghanistan, shortly after U.S. and coalition forces occupied the city as both the Taliban and members of Al-Qaida fled. On 11 December 2001, a 'provisional detachment' of 80 Marines from the 26th MEU(SOC) entered the vacant compound of the U.S. Embassy after a twelve year absence without incident. Colonel Andrew P. Frick, the commanding officer of 26th MEU(SOC) later told reporters, "Unfortunately, when an embassy shuts down, the Marine security guards and the U.S. ambassador are always among the last to leave because they have the responsibility to lower the American flag from sovereign U.S. soil."[127] In surveying the abandoned embassy, Colonel Frick said, "I think it's only fitting that the Marines ... be the ones to stand with the new U.S. Ambassador as he raises the flag over sovereign American soil. It's a fitting and poignant moment, and we're happy to be part of it." The Marine colonel said that the reopening of the U.S. Embassy in Kabul held a special meaning, and that the Marines and sailors felt a certain satisfaction, particularly in light of the events of September 11. Colonel Frick added, "As I watched the events of 11 September, I knew that we [Marines] would more than likely play a significant role in our nation's war against terrorism." Colonel Frick emphasized, "To be here at this time and [know] that we not only answered our nation's call when she needed us, but that we had an integral role in the fall of the Taliban ... really brings it home."[128]

Sergeant Major Gerald N. Lane, the senior enlisted Marine of BLT 3d Battalion, 6th

Marine Regiment, who served on MSG duty as the detachment commander in Islamabad, Pakistan, from 1989 through 1991, knew exactly what needed to be done as the Marines entered the abandoned embassy. Sergeant Major Lane stated that the first order of business of the Marines was "to determine if the embassy itself and the other buildings in the compound are structurally sound." Sergeant Major Lane added, "Once they have that, then the establishment of Post 1, the main entrance to the embassy will be the first priority, and the recreation of the infrastructure will be the key. Cameras, structural reinforcements, housing for the Marines who will stand post [there], housing for the Ambassador and his family are all elements which need to be in place before a more permanent Marine presence can be introduced."[129]

The main task of the leathernecks from 26th MEU(SOC) was to provide security for a U.S. State Department assessment team as it measures the compound's suitability for a more permanent presence. In any event, the "the last out" became the "first in" as the leathernecks from 26th MEU(SOC), in a solemn ceremony shortly entering the compound, located a flagpole and affixed an American flag to it. As the first note of the national anthem blared out, Marines stood proudly at attention and, with a firm salute, raised the "Stars and Stripes." With the raising of the American flag at the U.S. Embassy in Kabul, the first and most important battle against the Taliban had been won.

An Embassy in Shambles

On January 1, 2002, a company of Marines from the 4th MEB (AT) replaced the Marines from 26th MEU(SOC) and took over the positions of the U.S. Embassy in Kabul. They shortly thereafter began the arduous job of cleaning the facility and restoring some basic services in the former U.S. diplomatic compound. Marines from both 26th MEU(SOC) and 4th MEB (AT) found the embassy in shambles after years of neglect.[130] Gunnery Sergeant William T. Sowers, Company L, Anti-Terrorism Battalion, commented that "handover of security at the embassy was fairly smooth," and that the Marines didn't really expect to find the embassy in good order. "Of course," Gunnery Sergeant Sowers asserted, "we're going to improve on things. They [elements of 26th MEU(SOC)] were only here for three weeks, and we're going to be here for a lot longer."[131]

Captain Farrell J. Sullivan, commanding officer, Lima Company, Anti-Terrorism Battalion, stated, "The main problems that the MEU faced were that they came in here on short notice and the place was in really bad shape. The situation around the embassy was a lot more uncertain than it is now.... Everything was trashed ... nothing was working. They didn't have a lot to work with when they got here, so they had to build from the ground up."[132]

While Marines from 26th MEU(SOC) constructed better security positions from which to defend the compound, as well as improving upon the living conditions inside the embassy, there remained quite a bit of work to do for the Marines from the 4th MEB(AT). Captain Sullivan stated that the Marines of 26th MEU(SOC) "managed to set up a very solid position here defensively for us to take over.... The problems that still exist are that we are in a tight cramped space ... and the power still comes on and off. As far as security goes it's not a problem; we have that. The living conditions for the Marines are the issues we have to tackle."

Gunnery Sergeant Sowers emphasized that when the Marines came off duty, they served as escorts for the foreign nationals who work in the embassy. GySgt. Sowers added that the Marines "went on working parties, filled sandbags, cleaned living spaces, and other things like that." Like a Marine Security Guard Detachment's mission, Captain Sullivan added, "Our immediate focus was the security of the embassy and improvement of our positions. A secondary mission was the improvement in the living conditions for our Marines." According to GySgt. Sowers, the Marines assigned to the 26th MEU lived in the Marine House portion of the embassy and left that place 100 times better than it was when they turned the compound over to the newly installed MSG Detachment in 2004.[133]

After years of intimidation and mismanagement by the Taliban, the stabilization of Afghanistan went forward. Throughout 2002 until the establishment of a Marine Security Guard detachment in June 2004, Marines from the 4th MEB (AT) rotated into Kabul on a company-sized basis in order to provide security at the U.S. Embassy.[134] From their first arrival in December 2001, the leathernecks from 4th MEB (AT) continue to uphold the dedication to duty that their fellow Marine Security Guards adhere to on a day-to-day basis, and serve as an inspiration to all that see them as America's "Ambassadors in Blue."

The Liberation of Iraq, March–April 2003

After nearly twelve years of United Nations–imposed sanctions and Iraq's flaunting of international law, the United States, along with Great Britain and other coalition partners, ended the brutal rule of Saddam Hussein with a massive invasion designed to liberate Iraq from his tyranny. Undaunted by skeptics at home and unwilling allies abroad, President George W. Bush, launched, with U.S. Marines as the spearhead, Operation Iraqi Freedom on March 20, 2003. After a war that lasted only three weeks, the Iraqi Army collapsed, with Hussein and his cronies fleeing for their lives in wake of the advancing coalition armies after the fall of Baghdad in early April of 2003. After his capture by U.S. soldiers on December 16, 2003, the former Iraqi dictator went on trial for crimes against humanity and against the Iraqi people and his neighbors.[135]

With Hussein in jail, his sons dead, and most of his associates either killed or captured, President Bush, on April 20, 2004, announced the appointment of Ambassador John Negreponte, a career diplomat and former U.S. representative to the United Nations, as the first U.S. ambassador to Baghdad. The move came nearly fourteen years after the president's father severed diplomatic relations with Iraq prior to the start of Operation Desert Storm in 1990. Guarding Ambassador Negreponte and the U.S. Embassy in Baghdad was a provisional detachment of Marine Security Guards, made up of a detachment commander and twelve watchstanders.[136] After Ambassador Negreponte's appointment and organization of interim Iraqi administration, the State Department requested the establishment of a formal Marine Security Guard detachment, which today stands duty at Post One in Baghdad. For the Marines assigned to Baghdad, they can say with some certainty that they represented "the last ones out [of Baghdad] and ... were the first to arrive" as goodwill ambassadors of the United States in a free Iraq.

Lessons from Operations Enduring Freedom and Iraqi Freedom, 2001–2004

According to Master Sergeant Richard K. Prather, operations chief for the Marine Security Battalion who served as a detachment commander, the Marine Security Guard Battalion,

Marines from the 4th Marine Expeditionary Brigade (Anti-Terrorism) patrol a section of Baghdad, Iraq, in the summer of 2004. The Marines are member of the Anti-Terrorism Battalion assigned to 4th MEB (AT) (courtesy U.S. Marine Corps).

in response to both Operations Enduring Freedom and Iraqi Freedom, implemented several lessons learned that have long-term implications for the program. In the months preceding the war, there was an increase in the number of demonstrations aimed at U.S. embassies and consulates. These demonstrations necessitated Marine Security Guards to respond with an increased number of REACT drills. During Operation Iraqi Freedom I (March–April 2003), Marine Security Guards worldwide stood ready to react to any threat aimed at an embassy or consulate. At the conclusion of the war, the demonstrations continued throughout the Persian Gulf and Middle East countries protesting the U.S. liberation of Iraq.[137] Before, during and after Operations Enduring Freedom and Iraqi Freedom, there were over 300 bomb threats, 250 demonstrations, and numerous incidents that included small arms fire, carjackings, and telephone threats aimed at U.S. embassies and consulates located in both the Middle East and throughout the world.

In the aftermath of both operations, Marine Security Guards also implemented a series of "lessons learned" and refined operational procedures in the two new detachments established in Kabul, Afghanistan, and Baghdad, Iraq. In direct reference to the environment in which they now operated, Headquarters Marine Corps labeled the MSG detachments as "provisional detachments," which referred to the special composition of the two MSG detachments, made up primarily of MSGs with an infantry-related military occupation specialty or "MOS."

As occurred in the MSG program at Company E in Saigon during the Vietnam War, special "combat ready" platoons were assigned to both Kabul and Baghdad due to the increased threat levels in both countries.[138] These "combat-ready" platoons were made up of Marine Security Guards with a 0300-series (infantry-related) MOS. Armed with standard TO/E weapons of an infantry platoon, Marine Security Guards in both Kabul and Baghdad are better able to "react" to threats from insurgents armed with a variety of weapons.

Sergeant Jose Martinez, one of the first Marines assigned to one of these combat-ready platoons in Baghdad, recalled that his infantry skills as a machine gunner came into good use during those early chaotic days in Baghdad. Sergeant Martinez stated that during this period the Marine Security Guards, known affectionately as the "Dirty Dozen," endured daily car bombs and indirect small arms fire, as well as direct fire by rocket propelled grenades and mortars in the so-called "Green Zone."[139] The Marine sergeant recalled that his introduction to life in post-war Baghdad were events "I could never forget." One particular incident occurred only two days after his arrival in the Iraqi capital when a car bomb went off, with the impact of the explosion knocking him off his rack. Sergeant Martinez and fellow Marine Security Guard, Sergeant J.D. Hutchinson, also rescued a State Department official struck in the head by indirect small arms fire.[140]

Outside of their job of protecting the U.S. Embassy and its personnel from insurgent attacks, the Marine Security Guards in Baghdad continued in their roles as "Ambassadors in Blue." Despite daily bombings, shootings, and mortar attacks, the Marines attempted to "win the hearts and minds" of the Iraqi people. Sergeant Martinez recalled that the Iraqi citizens he and his fellow Marine Security Guards came into contact with were "nicest people I ever met during my whole tour as a Marine Security Guard."[141]

A Coup in Monrovia, September–October 2003

In summer 2003, the United Nations Special Commission on War Crimes indicted President Charles Taylor on charges of sponsoring massacres in neighboring Sierra Leone. Using the indictment as their pretext to oust Taylor, rebels from the group known as Liberians United for Reconciliation and Democracy (LURD) began a multi-pronged assault on the forces loyal to President Charles Taylor in order to force the unpopular Liberian leader from office. As part of the unresolved civil war in Liberia, the fighting threatened to involve all of the countries of West Africa, as fighters, some as young as 12 and 13, roamed the streets of Monrovia and neighboring villages at will. The goal of the LURD and these "boy soldiers" was to force Taylor to resign and leave Liberia.

In response to the violence and potential danger to American citizens living in Monrovia, President George W. Bush ordered Marines from the 26th MEU(SOC) off the coast of Liberia, not only to protect American citizens and property, but to assist West Africans in separating the warring parties. President Bush took this action when mortar rounds slammed into the compound of the U.S. Embassy and the homes and schools where thousands of refugees had taken shelter to escape the fighting.[142] President Bush told reporters, "U.S. troops will be there to help [West African troops] go in and serve as peacekeepers necessary to create the conditions so that humanitarian aid can go in and help the peoples of Liberia."[143]

Despite ongoing operations in Iraq and Afghanistan, with the commitment of over 158,000 combat troops in both countries, the amphibious task force, comprised of the 26th MEU(SOC), along with the assault ships USS *Iwo Jima*, USS *Nashville*, and USS *Carter*, was fully prepared to go ashore and assist in securing a beachhead and protect the U.S. Embassy.[144]

In calling upon Mr. Taylor to resign, President Bush ordered the Marine Expeditionary Unit off of Liberia's coast in order to aid a larger peacekeeping mission that began to assemble in Nigeria. As the forces designated to assist Liberia began to gather, ordinary Liberians pleaded with President Bush to send U.S. troops ashore. One Liberian, Emmanuel Sieh, told an Associated Press reporter in Monrovia, "I want to tell George Bush to do something hurriedly, very fast and quickly.... People are dying every day."[145]

The Marines Land in Monrovia, July 20–21, 2003

A week prior to 26th MEU(SOC)'s arrival off the Liberian coast, Secretary of Defense Donald H. Rumsfeld ordered a Marine FAST team flown into Monrovia in order to protect the U.S. Embassy and adjacent Greystone complex. The 41-man FAST team, coming from the 3rd Platoon, 2nd FAST, based at Yorktown Naval Weapons Station, Virginia, landed on the morning of July 20 in HH-Pave Hawk helicopters inside the U.S. compound and set up defensive positions. Almost as soon as landing at the U.S. diplomatic compound, the FAST Marines assisted American as well as approximately 23 foreign humanitarian and United Nations workers to evacuate the country aboard the awaiting helicopters.[146] The FAST Marines likewise reinforced the five-man Marine Security Guard detachment in maintaining security at the U.S. Embassy

Attesting to the swiftness of the FAST team's arrival, Mr. Michael R. Wiest, chief of staff of Catholic Relief Services said, "We ... saw American Marines arrive in the embassy compound very quickly. From the point of view of humanitarian need, when we would have liked to have seen it? Several weeks ago."[147] Late or early, Randolph Eggley, a 51-year old Liberian who worked at Monrovia's International Airport, was overjoyed to see the leathernecks arrive. He exclaimed, "I am so happy. All these years we've been praying for America to come.... Today, maybe peace will begin."

By August 14, 2003, Marines from 26th MEU(SOC) came ashore as CH-46 Sea Knight and CH-53E "Super Sea Stallions" ferried about 200 Marines from the amphibious assault group and began peacekeeping operations. Once on shore, the Marines prepared the way for the West African peacekeeping force that arrived from Nigeria days later. Sergeant Michael Hobbs, an infantryman from 26th MEU(SOC), told reporters, "We are just here to help the people."[148] As Marines disembarked from their helicopters at the airport, U.S. Ambassador to Liberia John Blaney told reporters, "This operation today is going to be an important one.... You are going to see American boots on the ground, and a firm commitment to uphold humanitarian concerns in this country."[149]

As President Taylor fled the country in exile, the West African force, made up of troops from several West African nations and belonging to the Economic Community of West Africa States (ECOWAS), eventually assumed peacekeeping duties in Liberia. The FAST Marines, however, remained on duty at the U.S. Embassy for several months after the crisis. The arrival of the FAST Marines from 3rd Platoon, 2nd FAST, underscored the lessons learned in past crises on the African continent that these highly trained leathernecks complement the duties carried out by Marine Security Guards, who still remain as "America's front line soldiers on the war on terror."

Sergeant Jason R. Scamlin, USMC, the assistant detachment commander at the U.S. Embassy in Monrovia, recalled that the Marine Security Guard detachment there was very active in the defense of the U.S. Embassy despite the chaos and violence present on the streets of the Liberian capital. Along with the FAST Marines, the Marine Security Guards conducted exigent missions, in which they escorted water and fuel trucks in and out of the U.S. Diplomatic compound as well as the Greystone complex, as well as accompanying American and foreign personnel and evacuees throughout the city. They provided external security for likely avenues of approach, set up fields of fire, provided cover and concealment, and protected vital communication links and potential escape routes for the ambassador, his staff, and other American citizens.[150]

Sergeant Scamlin's report points to the fact that the Marines applied many of the "lessons learned" from their experiences in Somalia, Congo-Brazzaville, and Rwanda. These lessons learned included:

- A good working relationship with the local guard forces. This enabled the Marines (MSG, FAST, and 26th MEU) to build defensive positions on the roof of the chancery. It also gave the Marines better intelligence on the activities on the streets of Monrovia. It also kept open the "links" between all the warring factions.

- A clear evacuation order of the Marine House and other buildings ensured that no Marine or American citizen became tempting targets as hostages, as they were not permitted to return to their quarters once the fighting intensified.

- The Marine Security Guards learned that it is important to have loaded weapons in the safes. This cuts down the time it takes to load. They also learned the value of having nearby extra ammunition, MREs, water, and anything else readily available for "grab and go." The Marine Security Guards also found out that taking their REACT gear home with them (back to the Marine House) made them more "combat ready" when the time came to put it on.

- Once again, weapons maintenance was the key to readiness. This ensured that when the time came, no weapon malfunctioned.

- This time, the Marine Security Guards were prepared to leave the embassy at a moment's notice, as all the leathernecks had "bug out" bags packed and ready to go with essential items such as clothing, health and comfort items, important documents and money.[151]

What made the Monrovia operation an overriding success was the simple fact that the Marine Security Guards knew well in advance how to plan and prepare for most contingencies. Even though the Marine Security Guards could not anticipate everything that might happen once the fighting began, the success enjoyed by all U.S. forces in Liberia depended upon teamwork, flexibility, and professional training. These were all present in the Marines and sailors President Bush sent into Liberia in August 2003.

FAST Marines in Haiti, February–June 2004

On 5 February 2004, opponents of Haitian President Jean-Bertrand Aristide initiated a series of protests against the former Catholic priest's corrupt and authoritarian rule, and called for his immediate resignation. Aristide, who had been elected to office in Haiti's first truly democratic elections, had been in power off and on since 1991.[152] Re-elected to that office in 2000, President Aristide's rule had become more arbitrary as time went on. Eventually, after years of mismanagement, corruption, and inefficiency, Aristide's opponents mustered enough strength to launch what amounted to a *coup d'état*.

The Marine Security Guard Detachment in Port-au-Prince, Haiti, in April 2004 poses in full REACT gear. When Haiti exploded in political violence in February 2004, Marine Security Guards and a platoon from 2d FAST Company, based in Norfolk, Virginia, defended the U.S. Embassy against rioters and anti–U.S. protestors (U.S. Marine Security Guard Battalion).

As the rebels pushed Aristide's small police force back toward the capital, Port-au-Prince, the island exploded into violence; armed gangs took to the street when it became apparent that the president's days were numbered.[153] Shortly thereafter, representatives from France (Haiti's former colonial master), Canada, and the United States met to discuss the ongoing crisis in the impoverished Caribbean nation. In response to the pleas from ordinary Haitians, such as Yvon Neptune, who urged the international community to "save Haiti from terrorists who sow violence and death," President George W. Bush ordered a platoon from the Yorktown-based 2nd FAST Company to Haiti, primarily to protect American Embassy and prepare the way for a United Nations–led multi-national force, which eventually took control of Haiti on 3 June 2004. Colonel Michael Paulovich, commanding officer of the Marine Security Forces Battalion, said that the 2nd Company got the "green light," as it was "the FAST platoon at the highest state of readiness." This was the same company that provided security at the U.S. Embassy in Monrovia, Liberia, prior to the ouster of President Charles Taylor. Now, the FAST Marines were called upon once more to guarantee the safety of the Americans at the U.S. Embassy in Port-au-Prince and to assist the five-man Marine Security Guard detachment there.[154] Colonel Paulovich, a veteran of the intervention in Haiti in 1994, said that the FAST Marines from 2nd Company "are an experienced crew" and that "they'll know what to do once they get there."

Even as Secretary of State Colin S. Powell urged President Aristide to resign and leave

Haiti, the rebels gathered outside Port-au-Prince to launch what presumably was to be their final offensive. On February 24, 2004, 41 FAST Marines landed in the Haitian capital and immediately took up positions at the U.S. Embassy in order to reinforce the Marine Security Guards already on full alert. Meanwhile, a force of 200 Marines, primarily from the 3rd Battalion, 8th Marines, prepared to depart Camp Lejeune, North Carolina, for Port-au-Prince, where they reinforced the MSG detachment and FAST Marines already there.[155] Once on the ground in Haiti, the Marines from the 3rd Bn, 8th Marines, accompanied by light armored vehicles and approximately 130 French troops, established defensive perimeters throughout the city and patrolled Port-au-Prince's dirty alleys and market places. As a young leatherneck poured water over his head in order to cool off from the heat, Mr. Frantz Labissiere, a resident of Port-au-Prince, said, "I feel much safer now [that] the Marines are here.... I wouldn't be here if the Marines weren't here."[156]

Not all Haitians were happy to see the Marines (or the French). A few residents of Port-au-Prince recalled early 19th century history when Haitian guerrillas defeated a much larger French force sent by Napoleon I in 1804 to quell a slave insurrection. Others recalled the occupation of Haiti by U.S. Marines from 1915 to 1934. One Haitian, in fact, went so far as to accuse the United States of forcing President Aristide into exile. A crowd shouted out as a convoy of Marines passed by, "You took our president — now you're taking our country."[157]

Eventually about 1,500 Marines landed in Haiti, where they participated in a variety of humanitarian missions, including relief from devastating rains that flooded the de-forested countryside. As President Aristide fled the country into self-imposed exile on 29 February, an interim government was named to restore order and await the time when elections can be held under United Nations auspices. Meanwhile, as hundreds of U.S. Marines along with about 5,000 soldiers from France, Canada, Brazil, and several other South American nations patrolled the capital and countryside, Haitians set about the task of restoring their hard won freedom from decades of authoritarian and corrupt rule.[158]

In April 2004, Secretary of State Colin S. Powell visited the war-ravaged capital city of Port-au-Prince. One of the stops on his itinerary was the U.S. Embassy. Here, the secretary of state praised the ambassador, his staff, and most important, the Marine Security Guard detachment, for their steadfastness and professionalism during the *coup d'état* against Mr. Aristide. Secretary of State Powell posed for a photograph with "his Marines" and thanked them for a job well done. As the Marines of both MSG Battalion and FAST demonstrated during this and other political upheavals in Somalia, Congo-Brazzaville, Kinshasa, Monrovia, Burundi, and Rwanda, they both, as Colonel Paulovich said, "knew what do," as both organizations are "an experienced crew."

Car Bombing in Karachi, Pakistan, 26 May 2004

As Marine Security Guards worldwide stood guard over embassies now in the forefront of the war on terror, at approximately 1700 local time, on May 26, 2004, two car bombs exploded near the residence of the U.S. consul general in Karachi, Pakistan, as well as the U.S.-Pakistani Cultural Center. The first blast, which occurred just fifty meters from the U.S. Consulate, killed a Pakistani policeman. The second blast, which occurred only 25 minutes after the first one at the same location, wounded a passerby, eight journalists, several medical workers, and four policemen, who had responded to the emergency.[159] While no Americans were killed or wounded in either attack, the Marine Security Guard detachment, notified through the early warning Imminent Danger Notification System (IDNS), went on full alert. As a precaution to a possible full-scale assault on the consulate, Gunnery Sergeant Richard Eres, the detachment commander, ordered the Marine watchstanders to the consulate, where they donned REACT gear. Gunnery Sergeant Eres then ordered the leathernecks to stand by in the REACT room for further instructions.

After a meeting with the Consul General, GySgt. Eres informed Staff Sergeant Gary W. Shepherd, the assistant detachment commander, that the Marines were to remain on full alert until a full sweep of the area had been conducted.[160] After about thirty minutes, the consul general gave the "all clear" and sent everybody home from their safe havens. As a precaution against further potential violence, the consul general nonetheless ordered all the Americans and the foreign staff nationals to "avoid the blast areas" and go directly home.[161]

As a precaution against further attacks, the consul general advised all personnel "to adhere to the implemented security measures on a daily basis. The assistant regional security officer, Mr. Vincent Martinez, likewise instructed all of the Americans and FSN's "to remain vigilant, avoid setting routines, and to limit movement in and around Karachi."[162]

Terrorists Strike at U.S. Consulate in Jeddah, Saudi Arabia

In the late morning hours of December 6, 2004, terrorists, shouting "*Allah Akbar*," or "God is Great," attacked the U.S. Consulate in Jeddah, Saudi Arabia. The attack, which came at approximately 11:15 A.M. (local time) unfolded as the gunmen rammed their vehicle past the guards into a concrete barrier and set off small explosive devices or stun grenades. Exiting their vehicle, the terrorists then hurled hand grenades at the gates of the heavily guarded diplomatic compound and opened fire with assault rifles. They then stormed past the Saudi National Guardsmen who manned the outer perimeter and headed toward the Marine House and main chancery. They were able to force their way inside one of the buildings and temporarily seize several hostages as human shields.

As the attack unfolded, confusion reigned as to how the terrorists were able to enter the heavily guarded compound. Saudi officials initially reported that the attack started when "a car with three militants pulled up behind a consular car to the first checkpoint of the consulate. When stopped and told to turn around, terrorists jumped out and began firing [AK-47's] and throwing hand grenades. A second car with terrorists pulled up, two more terrorists ran out and started shooting as well."[163] According to Ms. Carol R. Kalin, a spokeswoman for the U.S. Embassy in Riyadh, the attackers attempted to drive into a side entrance of the compound, the one usually used by employees and visa applicants. Somehow, the vehicle they were driving managed to get past the first barrier into the closed lane used to channel traffic in the compound, but was stopped by another concrete barrier.[164]

The attackers then jumped out of their vehicle and opened up with a hail of automatic gunfire and set off small explosives. According to eyewitnesses, the first target of the terrorists was the Marine House, which shortly thereafter caught fire. The gunmen, who kept shouting, "Where are the Americans?" then tried, though with no success, to enter the main chancery as well as a bungalow adjacent to the consulate. Meanwhile, the Marine Security Guards, who by this time were already in REACT gear, had "gone to the main building and led most of the employees to a designated safe area." Even as the terrorists attempted to enter the diplomatic compound, the Saudi policemen and soldiers raked the ground with a heavy volume of fire.

According to Muhammad Mahmoud Fouad, an Egyptian who worked in the consulate and observed the fighting from its driveway, "There were so many people firing that it was impossible to tell how many were involved."[165] In fact, the front checkpoint, manned by Saudi National Guardsmen, as well as a guard tower that overlooked the compound, put up stubborn resistance. Despite the resistance by Saudi policemen, however, the terrorists managed to seize several hostages, all of whom were later released.

Despite the resistance by Saudi security forces, the terrorists managed to force their way past the main gate. Here, they encountered the Marine Security Guards who kept the terrorists at bay until Saudi Special Forces arrived and repelled the attack. U.S. Ambassador James Oberwetter said that the "Marines performed heroically protecting the chancery and the citizens who were inside [the chancery]."[166] The U.S. Marine Security Guards who manned the second checkpoint then proceeded to escort all Americans and their dependents to a designated safe area inside the compound. As reinforcements arrived to bolster the numbers of the Saudi National Guardsmen, a fierce gun battle raged inside the first checkpoint of the consulate. Eventually, Saudi troops managed to overwhelm the attackers, and in the process killed four and captured two of them, including one of Saudi Arabia's most wanted terrorists, Saleh Al Oufi. Once again, the Marine Security Guards prevented the main chancery from being breached. Before the terrorists were subdued, however, they managed to kill five non–American consular employees and wound four others, including two Americans. Prior to their neutralization, the terrorists, who were later linked to the Saudi faction of Al-Qaida and claimed to be members of the Fallujah Brigade,[167] managed to set a fire inside the compound. Residents of Jeddah later reported that they saw plumes of smoke rising from the general direction of the consulate. Despite the severity of the attack, eyewitnesses inside and outside the compound agreed that the Saudi policemen and soldiers acquitted themselves very well in beating back this vicious assault. Furthermore, the repelling of the attack by Saudi troops validated the concept that local guards should provide the main security at a consulate or embassy insofar as the outer perimeters are concerned. Also, it was obvious, as Ambassador Oberwetter noted, that the terrorists had "scoped the place out" before the attack and knew the traffic patterns entering and leaving the compound.

The world community was quick to condemn the attack by the Fallujah Brigade as a despicable act of terrorism. President George W. Bush, who at the time of the attack was meeting with Iraq's new interim president, Ghazi al-Yawer, in the White House, condemned the attack as another instance of terrorism aimed at intimidating the free world. In a direct comparison to the violence that existed in neighboring Iraq, President Bush told reporters, "These attacks in Saudi Arabia remind us that terrorists are still on the move — they're interested in affecting the will of free countries [and they] want us to leave Saudi Arabia.... They want us to leave Iraq, they want us to grow timid and weary in their attacks to kill."[168]

In the aftermath of the attack in Jeddah, President Bush vowed, "We will find out more about who caused these attacks." The president likewise praised the bravery of the Saudi National Guardsmen and police who repelled the attack, as well as the performance of the Marine Security Guards, who he said "did their jobs splendidly."[169] In a final tribute to the professionalism of the Marines on duty in Jeddah, Secretary of State Condoleeza Rice credited the "rapid reaction of the Jeddah MSG Detachment who were instrumental in protecting many of our [U.S.] personnel." Secretary Rice likewise cited the "alertness and dedication" of Marines worldwide, as they stood ready "in every clime and place."[170]

A Substantial Contribution

In response to the ongoing Global War on Terror, the Marine Corps faced new challenges as the demands of a three-front war affected the organizational and institutional structure of the Marine Corps. In fact, the wars in both Iraq and Afghanistan brought the Marine Corps into the realm of Special Operations with the establishment in 2001 of Marine Detachment One. The standing up of Marine Detachment One, in fact, was the "Marine Corps' first formal contribution to the Special Operations Command." Marines assigned to the 100-man strong Marine Detachment One, like U.S. Army Special Forces, shortly thereafter found themselves fighting alongside other Coalition troops in Iraq.[171]

With the establishment of the 4th MEB (AT) in the fall of 2001, and the emphasis on anti-terrorism as opposed to Marine Detachment One's counter-terrorism mission, Marine Security Guard Battalion soon found itself administratively under the command of the Commanding General, 4th MEB (AT). With increased demands for more Marines to decisively engage Al-Qaida and the jihadists in Iraq and Afghanistan, a shift soon took place in the defensive role of 4th MEB (AT) to that of a more offensive one. With this in mind, the Marine Corps, with pressure from the Office of the Secretary of Defense and the special forces community to become more of a team player in the realm of special operations, soon found itself setting up an entirely new command.[172] During the summer and late fall of 2005, intense negotiations between Secretary of Defense Donald H. Rumsfeld, the Commandant of the Marine Corps General Michael W. Hagee, and U.S. Army General Bryan Brown, commanding general of Special Operations Command, took place over the incorporation of elements of the 4th MEB (AT) into a more robust organization designed carry the fight to the terrorists worldwide. In late August 2006, the 4th MEB (AT) stood down in favor of the establishment of Marine Special Operations Component.[173] Absent in this new command arrangement was Marine Security Guard Battalion (MSG Bn.) and the Chemical Biological Incidence Response Force (CBIRF). After much internal debate as to where and whom MSG Bn. and CBIRF should fall under Headquarters Marine Corps, after discussions with the State Department, placed both Marine Security Guard Battalion and CBIRF under the administrative authority of the II Marine Expeditionary Force (II MEF) at Camp Lejeune, N.C.

President George W. Bush talks about the War on Terror at the National Defense University at Ft. Lesley J. McNair in Washington, D.C., on March 8, 2005 (photograph courtesy of White House, by Krisanne Johnson; reprinted with permission).

Marines, Soldiers and Expeditionary Strike Groups, 2004–2006

As the U.S. military responded institutionally to the challenges posed by terrorists world-wide, U.S. embassies throughout the Middle East and Southwest Asia grew in importance as central command and control facilities in the wake of natural and man-made disasters. One such disaster was the earthquake that struck Pakistan along its North-West Frontier on October 8, 2005. President Bush, in response to a request from the Pakistani government, ordered Expeditionary Strike Group 1 to the scene to provide immediate assistance in the wake of this tragedy and prevent terrorists from taking advantage of the chaos that ensued in the region. With the formation of the U.S. Navy's Expeditionary Strike Groups (ESGs), the "arm" of the United States grew even longer to respond almost immediately to these and other disasters. Lieutenant Colonel Terry L. Love, U.S. Army, who served with one such ESG, recalled the swiftness with which the strike group responded to the unfolding humanitarian disaster in Pakistan in the hours that followed the October 8, 2005 earthquake. Lieutenant Colonel Love, who had been assigned to the U.S. Military's International Humanitarian Assistance/Disaster Relief (HA/DR) effort following this devastating earthquake, and was in the lead element Joint Lessons Learned supporting Expeditionary Strike Group 1[174] in order to help stand up the U.S. military's footprint in the country, remembered that it was a team effort by soldiers, Marines, sailors, and non-governmental organizations that provided relief to the stricken Pakistani civilians within hours of the disaster. As an operations research systems analyst, it was LTC Love's responsibility to observe and report first-hand the disaster relief effort and

President George W. Bush, on a visit to the U.S. Embassy in Islamabad, Pakistan, thanks a group of U.S. military officers assigned to the U.S. Embassy there for their service in response to an earthquake that shook northern Pakistan in October 2005. Lieutenant Colonel Terry Love, U.S. Army, is standing to the far right, with hands clasped (courtesy of Lt. Col. Love).

document this relief for future reference. LTC Love added that it was also the team's responsibility to "provide joint operational expertise to the ESG-1 Commander, Rear Admiral LeFever, and his staff as they ramped up operational capabilities" of the relief effort.[175] With Marine riflemen from the strike group providing security to his team, LTC Love stated, "My activities during the Joint Lessons Learned Team (JLLT)'s initial 30-day stay involved making numerous observations from within the U.S. Military Command center as well as documenting the coordination and integration efforts with other countries, United Nations organizations, and a plethora of non-governmental organizations and international charities that were all converging on the area to help in the relief effort."[176] LTC Love, along with an U.S. Air Force major, conducted over 30 interviews with U.S. and Pakistani military and civilian officials as well as members of the United Nations and U.S. Embassy staff personnel based in Islamabad. LTC Love added he served with U.S. Marines who played "key and essential roles in what became formally named as Operation Lifeline–Disaster Assistance Center Pakistan."

During operations in Pakistan, LTC Love and his team oftentimes stayed within the walls of the U.S. diplomatic compound in Islamabad. Over time, LTC Love said, the U.S. Embassy, like the Chaklala Airbase, soon became the central command and control "hub" of the U.S. relief effort in Pakistan. During one such stay, President George W. Bush, LTC Love recalled, took the opportunity to "thank the members of the staff for what we had done and to assure us that our efforts during this operation made a huge positive impact in U.S. efforts" in fighting the global war on terrorism.[177] Like their predecessors before them, the Marines, Soldiers, Sailors, and Airmen served as "true ambassadors of goodwill" to the stricken people of Pakistan and gave each service member, as LTC Love concluded, "a chance to take part in sharing America's goodness to a part of the world that rarely saw that side of us."

A New Name: Marine Corp Embassy Security Command, June 2007

Along with the above-mentioned changes made in the institutional structure of the Marine Corps and MSG's ever-expanding mission as new detachments stood up, the title Marine Security Guard Battalion gave way to its new name: Marine Corps Embassy Security Command or MCESC in June 2007.[178] With its headquarters remaining at Marine Corps Base, Quantico, Virginia, MCESC's mission remained the same — the protection of classified material and diplomatic personnel.

Also changing are the names of the lettered companies. As the U.S. State Department increased the number of new embassies and consulates worldwide, the mission of the existing Marine Security Guard companies likewise increased. As a means of better administering these new detachments and aligning them with the State Department's regions, officials at Headquarters Marine Corps and in the State Department changed the names of the former lettered companies and renamed them by region.[179]

The rescue of American diplomats, American citizens, and foreign nationals in Mogadishu in January 1991 presaged the types of threats that Marine Security Guards faced throughout the 1990s and into the 21st century. Indeed, as events of the 1990s and early 21st century have demonstrated, there has been no let up in the war on terror, as Marine Security Guards have found themselves on the front lines. Despite the problems and scandals of the mid–1980s, the Marine Security Guard program demonstrated its resilience and adjusted very well to the changing nature of the threats to embassy security. Furthermore, with the advent of the FAST in 1987, embassy security became a joint effort as the world became a more dangerous place. This latter fact was highlighted throughout the 1990s and into the new millennium as events in Liberia, Somalia, Rwanda, Burundi, Kenya, and Tanzania called upon the professionalism of Marine Security Guards everywhere. Even in the midst of tragedy, including the bombings in Nairobi and Dar es Salaam in 1998, as well as above the skies of New York, Washington, D.C., and Pennsylvania in 2001, as well as in Baghdad, Karachi, and Jeddah, "these fine smart detachments" rose to meet these and other challenges.

CHAPTER 10

Not Just Fitting In ... But Standing Out: Marine Security Guard School, 1979–2004

In addressing the nation after the devastating attacks by Al-Qaida on the United States on September 11, 2001, President George W. Bush remarked that we were attacked "because we are freedom's home and defender." One of the key components of this defense are the young men and women who stand duty at a lonely post, surrounded by monitors and, as President Bush succinctly put it, the "enemies of freedom." Prior to the assumption of these posts, these Marines undergo a rigorous six-week course at Marshall Hall, the home of Marine Security Guard Battalion School. While many are selected, not all will finish the grueling curriculum designed to prepare these Marines for the difficult and oftentimes dangerous work they will face while defending an U.S. embassy or consulate.

Much goes into the training of a Marine Security Guard. The individual Marine is required to know how to defend themselves, the ambassador and the contents of that embassy against those individuals determined to destroy the very symbol of the United States in a foreign land. Since the assumption of the diplomatic security mission in 1948, the training of a Marine Security Guard has changed over the years, as new threats and new technology have emerged to make the job of defending an embassy or consulate all the more challenging. Also, the very composition of the Marine Security Guard program since 1948 has likewise changed, largely due to the evolving nature of the threats against the United States and, to the changes in American society, namely the inclusion of female Marines. This addition into the program, which commenced on an experimental basis in 1979, has been an important and lasting change that has reaped large rewards with the addition of these dedicated "Ambassadors in Blue."

Female Marines and the MSG Program, 1979–2004

In response to the increased number of women in the Marine Corps, General Louis H. Wilson, Commandant of the Marine Corps, initiated a novel program in 1978 at MSG School when HQMC ordered 19 female Marines to report to Marine Security Guard School, then located at Henderson Hall, Virginia. Fifteen of the original nineteen graduated from the school and were assigned to eight embassies considered to be "hardship" posts.[1] General Wilson's objective was to see if the female Marines "could keep up with men in training and how they were accepted in countries where women are not respected in the workplace."[2] After

Women Marines were assigned to MSG Battalion in 1979. Sergeant Deborah L. Caron (left) was assigned to the U.S. Embassy in Seoul, South Korea, while Corporal Jeanne Peterkin (right) was assigned to the U.S. Embassy in Kingston, Jamaica. Sergeant Neal Allen (center) reported to the U.S. Embassy in Belgrade, former Yugoslavia (courtesy U.S. Marine Corps).

graduation, the fifteen female Marines who completed the program reported to their first assignments as Marine Security Guards. Fourteen of the fifteen female Marine Security Guards completed their required 30-month tour of duty.[3]

An early indication of the successes from the employment of females as Marine Security Guards came from two of the "hardship" posts they served at during this early experiment. Major W.T. Tucker, commanding officer, Company C., headquartered in Hong Kong, reported that the first three female MSGs, Sergeants Caron and Bradford, members of the first class that had women in their ranks, reported aboard on August 4, 1979, and received a "warm reception" from the male MSG's, due in large part because the female Marines were, "out of necessity welcomed, and accepted as members of the group before anyone took notice of their sexual difference."[4] Major Tucker noted that because each male Marine MSG was standing in excess of 50 hours a week on post, "replacements that would decrease the work load were welcome regardless of sex." In fact, when the detachment received an additional female watchstander, Corporal E.J. Gorman, the male Marines "set about to train them" in order to reduce the heavy work-load.

As for their overall performance, Major Tucker wrote:

> Sgts Caron and Bradford daily performance has been rated excellent in all areas by the NCOIC and RSO. In my opinion both women eagerly accepted the responsibility of MSG duty and applied themselves in a determined and willing manner. Both have produced excellent results while requiring a minimum of supervision. They have fully participated in all areas of detachment affairs. Each woman is assigned additional duties which they accomplish with the same degree of professionalism exhibited in the performance of their regular duties.[5]

Major Tucker specifically noted Sgt. Caron's "resourcefulness" as custodian of the detachment's mess funds. The major likewise praised Sgt. Bradford's "enthusiasm" and skill for administration. While noting the fact that all three female watchstanders seemed to adapt very well to their new surroundings, Major Tucker noted that all three "expressed a strong desire to successfully complete this program regardless of obstacles encountered" and wanted only to become an integral part of the detachment."

Major Tucker specifically cited reports from the Seoul MSG Detachment where another female Marine watchstander had been assigned that indicated there were no cultural problems, even though Korea is a male-dominated society, where women take a subservient role to men. The Marine major noted that so far, the woman Marine assigned to the U.S. Embassy in Seoul had encountered no resentment toward her gender. The fact that she wore a uniform and that Koreans generally respect authority made her acceptance more palatable to a society that prided itself on its martial spirit and paternalistic nature.

Major Tucker did note two problems that surfaced almost immediately after the three female women watchstanders arrived, and that was in the isolation of the female Marines in a male-dominated detachment, and the use of the Marine Security Guard issued equipment, notably the baton and pistol. Major Tucker noted that because most female Marines tend to befriend Marines of their own gender more readily in units that traditionally have more women it its ranks, female Marines assigned to the embassy found it difficult to make friends with the other females among the State Department workers. This latter group tended to be much older than the female Marine Security Guards. They were also less inclined to include female Marines in their circle of friends or activities. Secondly, Tucker noted that the male Marines noticed that women tend to favor the use of stronger measures immediately, i.e., the use of the service pistol as opposed to situations that require the use of the baton, favored by most male MSGs. Major Tucker reported that while no such incidents had yet occurred, it remained a distinct possibility.

Major Tucker made special mention of the fact that the RSO at the embassy in Seoul noted an increased level of *esprit de corps* among the Marines since the women arrived. This enthusiasm was specifically noted "in the increased number of events staged by the detachment."[6] Finally, the "Charlie" Company commander noted that the only drawback in the use of women as Marine Security Guards was the fact that the male Marines were "overly protective" of the females during duty situations.

Major R.H. Kayser, the commanding officer for Company D, which covers all of Latin and South America, made similar observations on the use of the female Marines assigned to his detachments. Because Latin American society is more paternalistic with a heavy dose of what Major Kayser termed "machismo," female Marines encountered some initial problems in dealing with foreign nationals. In one instance, a belligerent male visa applicant threatened a female watchstander with physical harm as she escorted him from the building. From all accounts, the female leatherneck was praised for tactfully handling the situation even though the foreign national "threatened to knock her glasses off her head."[7] In Kingston, Jamaica, female Marine Security Guards were subjected to "lewd remarks and catcalls." Major Kayser noted that this situation made it undesirable for women to be assigned to this or any other detachment where there existed a high degree of sexually motivated crimes such as assault and rape.

Another problem encountered with the presence of women assigned to MSG duty was an incident when a female Marine security guard demonstrated "a tendency towards overt displays of affection for the male MSGs." While this individual was immediately counseled for her actions and that the incident was never again repeated, it nonetheless remained a source of major concern among most detachment commanders insofar as the assignment of women to a post.[8]

As for the physical limitations of the female Marine Security Guards, the Commanding Officer, Company F, based in Nairobi, Kenya, reported that for the most part, "Women Marines performed their normal Post #1 duties in a professional manner." Major R.G. Richard, Company F's commander, was more blunt than the other company commanders in his assessment of the use of women Marines as security guards:

> In several of our post, I don't feel the WM's could perform all of their duties in times of crisis. I am specifically referring to the physical attributes necessary in accomplishing duties during the emergency drills. I realize this notion is ridiculed and scoffed at by women supporters within the military; nevertheless, it is in fact the truth at a majority of the posts with Company "F." I feel an average woman would have a difficult time negotiating the obstacles involved in attempting to gain access to some chanceries by other than the main entrance. Many of these secondary access routes involve walls with glass on top, the use of rope ladders, the ability to swing oneself up on the ledges and the climbing on of adjacent buildings in order to gain secondary access to the chancery. Many of our posts use iron sliding doors for internal protection. Many male Marines have difficulty securing these doors, I feel most females would be unable to secure these protective barriers without outside assistance.[9]

Major Richards recommended against the use of women as watchstanders, particularly in such high-threat posts such as Company F or in the Middle East. The Marine major did recommend that if women were to be kept on the program, they should be assigned to posts "where the social restrictions and their physical handicap would not be as severe a problem."[10] The commanding officer of "Golf" Company voiced similar concerns and recommendations as those made by Major Richard in his evaluation of women security guards.[11]

The concerns expressed by Majors Kayser and Richard, as well as those from other company commanders, were taken into consideration when, after the death of Corporal Steven Crowley in Islamabad, Pakistan, in November 1979, General Robert H. Barrow canceled the pilot program for the use of women watchstanders. While the use of female Marines proved initially successful, it was felt that with an increase in anti–American sentiment, as well as the demonstrations and violence directed toward U.S. embassies, female Marines would be placed in potential combat-related situations.

In direct response to the hostage crisis in Iran and embassy takeover in Islamabad, a spokesman at Headquarters Marine Corps hinted that the commandant of the Marine Corps was, in fact, considering just such a move. He stated, "Consideration is being given to pulling out Women Marines in any of eight countries in which they are now assigned if ever they face situations similar to Tehran." When asked if the women would be removed if the situation warranted, a State Department spokesman reiterated, "There was not the remotest chance that the Women Marine Security Guards" assigned to Amman, Jordan, Karachi, Pakistan, and Bamako, Mali would be recalled. "They are Marines, and they're members of the detachments and they are essential personnel."[12] The State Department official indicated that ultimately, it was the Marine Corps that decided where embassy guards would be placed and routinely assigned them during the course of their tours of duty. Eventually, HQMC decided to re-institute the restrictions on the use of female Marines on MSG duty, and ended the experiment in training additional female Marine Security Guards.

The issue concerning the use of women as Marine Security Guards re-surfaced, however, after a commission reported to Secretary of Defense Caspar Weinberger that discrepancies existed among the four services (Army, Navy, Air Force, and Marine Corps) insofar as the Congressionally-mandated ban on women in combat had been concerned. Based on recommendations in the report, Secretary Weinberger, on 2 February 1988, "ordered an expansion of job opportunities for women in the Air Force and Marine Corps including the assignment of women Marines to Marine Security Guard duty."[13]

In line with Secretary Weinberger's directive, General Alfred M. Gray, the commandant of the Marine Corps, issued ALMAR 080–88 that outlined the fact that "Women Marines were eligible for Marine Security Guard Duty." Subsequently, five women reported to the Marine Security Guard School (Class 4–88), where three of them graduated and were assigned to a post.[14] While not opposed to the use of women as Marine Security Guards, General Gray was of the opinion that MSGs are expected "to protect lives and property by going on the offensive to quell or repulse any threat to our embassies and consulates. This duty should be performed by fully prepared, combat-ready Marines drawn principally from the combat arms occupational fields."[15]

As time went by, and more women entered the Marine Corps, they increasingly became an integral part of the day-to-day operations. Still restricted from combat due to congressional law, female Marines nonetheless continued to enter the Marine Security Guard program and, by 1991, were fully accepted by their male counterparts. By September 1991, in fact, female security guards once again stood duty as watchstanders though were not then, and still are not to this day, assigned to those countries where women were treated as "unequal to men," and living arrangements prohibit women from living in the local Marine House. These include most Muslim countries in the Middle East and several posts in Asia. Colonel Thomas Harkins, who commanded Marine Security Guard Battalion from June 1991 to June 1993, stated, "Cultural acceptance and living facilities are the primary factors considered when deciding whether to send women to a post."[16] Colonel Harkins added, "Where a women can be assigned is based on a thorough analysis of the post—whether culturally and socially a woman under arms providing security and access control to embassies and consulates can be respected in a local culture."

During the 1990s, female security guards served at 60 posts, including Company A, headquartered in Frankfurt, Germany, and at Company B, headquartered in Casablanca, Morocco.[17] Only one woman, however, during this early period, was assigned to a company headquarters: Lieutenant Colonel Mary V. Jacocks, USMC, who ultimately became the first woman officer to command a Marine Security Guard Company. Lieutenant Colonel Jacocks commanded Company A, with responsibility for the Marine Security Guards for all of Eastern Europe, Finland, Greece, Turkey, and Yugoslavia. Lieutenant Colonel Jacocks also became the first Marine Security Guard commander to establish a new MSG detachment, in Kiev, Ukraine, in the former Soviet Union. She recalled that this was quite an experience, and one that she would long remember. Lieutenant Colonel Jacocks noted that while she and First Sergeant (later Sergeant Major) Ronald Biggs made a survey to determine the location of the new Marine House there in 1993, she and the first sergeant had taken a drink of water directly from the tap in their hotel rooms, since bottled water was not available. Asked the next day by the embassy staff if they had drunk any of the water, they both admitted having done so the night before. To her amazement, the embassy staff informed her that the water in the Ukraine had been contaminated from the Chernobyl nuclear accident. As a precaution everyone was required to drink and use bottled water for everything, including brushing one's teeth, and to undergo a thyroid test to test for contamination.[18]

During the troubles in the Balkans between Serbia and Croatia in the mid–1990s, Colonel Jacocks noted that the conflict there oftentimes called for quick thinking and a "steady hand," as the violence affected the relations between the United States on the one hand, and Serbia and Croatia on the other. In one instance, the lieutenant colonel said that due to Ser-

Lieutenant Colonel Mary "Ginger" Jacocks was the first female Marine officer appointed to command a Marine Security Guard Company. Here she poses with other company commanders and General Carl M. Mundy, commandant of the Marine Corps, at Headquarters Marine Corps in August 1993 (courtesy of Lt. Col. Mary Jacocks).

At the annual Marine Corps Ball in Warsaw, Poland, in November 1993, Lieutenant Colonel Mary "Ginger" Jacocks, First Sergeant Brian Penzak and his wife Cathy enjoy a laugh together as they take a break from the festivities inside the ballroom (courtesy Lt. Col. Mary Jacocks).

bia's atrocities in the Balkans, the United States refused to recognize Yugoslav diplomats. She wrote that the Serbs responded in kind by denying visas to U.S. diplomatic personnel, to include Marine Security Guards. In one instance, a Marine detachment commander had to wait nine months before Belgrade granted him a visa. Another interesting situation took place in Zagreb, Croatia, when a Marine Security Guard reported that a pipe bomb had been found in a pothole after a vehicle had passed in front of the embassy.[19] While the bomb was later destroyed, it was surmised that the device was meant "to be affixed to a car until it detonated."[20] She commented, "There was one lucky person driving around Zagreb that day."[21]

Lieutenant Colonel Jacocks recalled that the most memorable event occurred in October 1993 in Moscow, Russia, when she and 1stSgt. Brian Penzak were scheduled to visit the MSG detachment. Due to political unrest aimed at Russian President Boris Yeltsin, the U.S. Embassy cancelled the trip at the last minute due to potential problems in the city. "A few days later," Jacocks noted, "I saw on CNN that there was a revolt in Moscow and that the Russian 'White House' was under attack by Russian tanks." Later that day, the lieutenant colonel remembered:

> I received a call from MSG Bn asking why I had not notified them that one of our Marines was wounded in Moscow; I had heard nothing of this but the Bn had gotten the information via State Department channels. Communications with the Embassy in Moscow was always unreliable and this time would be no different. When I finally got a call through to the embassy, the detachment

commander acknowledged that the information was correct, they had stopped the tanks on the street beside the embassy long enough to get the Marine to a hospital and his prognosis was good, even though his carotid artery had been cut by the bullet — he was alive only because of the clear thinking and quick action of a fellow Marine who was also manning that OP. I found myself for the first time being responsible for submitting recommendations for a Purple Heart, a Navy Marine Corps Medal, and a Marine Corps Unit Citation — all were approved as written and subsequently awarded.[22]

Lieutenant Colonel Jacocks was, in many respects, a pioneer, and acquitted herself extremely well as the first female Marine to assume command of a Marine Security Guard company. She was not, however, the last female Marine officer to be "a first" in the history of Marine Security Guard Battalion. Lieutenant Colonel Anna R. Smythe later became the first woman executive officer of Marine Security Guard Battalion in the late 1990s. Lieutenant Colonel Smythe later served as commanding officer of Company E, also based in Frankfurt, Germany, but was responsible for the Marine Security Guard detachments in Western Europe, Iceland, and Canada.[23] By the early 1990s, women Marines began to make great strides as Marine

Another pioneer at MSG Battalion was Lt. Col. Anna Smythe, who became the first female marine Battalion executive officer. Lieutenant Colonel Smythe later assumed command of Company A in Frankfurt, Germany (U.S. Marine Security Guard Battalion).

"Not just fitting in ... but standing out": a female Marine Security Guard corporal receives a hearty congratulations from the State Department's representative at her graduation ceremony in Little Hall, located at Quantico. At left is Colonel Boyette S. Hasty; second from right is Sergeant Major Jimmie Brown (U.S. Marine Security Guard Battalion).

Security Guards. In July 1992, a woman Marine staff sergeant reported to MSG Detachment, Brussels, Belgium, and became the first female assistant detachment commander. Within a month, in August 1992, the first woman SNCO to attend Detachment Commander School reported aboard Marshall Hall for training.

By the late 1990s, both Colonel Jacocks and Lieutenant Colonel Smythe represented what had by now become commonplace at Marine Security Guard Battalion. Women were not just "fitting in" but were "standing out" and making a real contribution to the program. While women still cannot serve at posts in the more conservative Muslim nations or those deemed extremely hazardous, they nonetheless serve everywhere else. More importantly, female Marine Security Guards stand guard today with both pride and vigilance, as did their predecessors when women first entered the Marine Corps in 1917.

The First and Only Soldier to Attend MSG School, 1983

While the Marine Corps has had primary responsibility in guarding U.S. embassies and consulates since 1949, the U.S. Army briefly had been charged with that responsibility in the immediate aftermath of World War II in West Berlin, Germany. After the senior Army leadership declined an invitation by the State Department to allow soldiers to guard U.S. embassies and other diplomatic facilities, officials there contacted the Navy Department, which agreed to the idea that Marines would comprise an embassy guard. In 1983, Staff Sergeant Lee Mahlstede became the first U.S. Army staff non-commissioned officer to attend Marine Security Guard School since 1954. Staff Sergeant Mahlstede, in fact, became the first Army SNCO to attend the detachment commander's portion of MSG School. Staff Sergeant Mahlstede was already familiar with diplomatic security, having been the non-commissioned officer in charge, United States Mission, Berlin, Security Detachment, a position that put him in charge of two assistant NCOICs and 12 military policemen. Upon reporting in to MSG School at Quantico, SSG Mahlstede said, "When I received the assignment, I knew I wanted our detachment to be as professional as the embassies' Marine Security Guards. So I asked the State Department for any kind of school that would help and I received orders to MSG School."[24]

Assigned to attend MSG School at Quantico, Staff Sergeant Mahlstede immediately got a high-and-tight haircut. "The Marines here," he stated, "stress appearance on and off duty. They're elite and I want to fit in." From the start of the class, where he "sat in" as opposed to being graded or evaluated, Staff Sergeant Mahlstede studied all of the subjects Marine SNCOs did to prepare them as detachment commanders. These courses included security inspection, emergency destruction, terrorist activities, foreign methods of espionage, as well as how to use a nightstick and handcuffs; he fired State Department issued weapons and did the Marine Corps' physical training.[25] The Army Staff Sergeant said, "I'm especially impressed with the counseling techniques we're learning here. It's definitely knowledge I'll take back to Berlin. I'm going to be just as demanding about appearance and conduct with my men as Marines are here."

As for the Marines with whom Staff Sergeant Mahlstede attended class, they were equally impressed with him. One Marine stated, "SSG Mahlstede is a very mature SNCO and does an excellent job, offering valuable advice because he was out there on post for 18 months before he arrived here. He possesses all the qualities of a good Marine SNCO."[26]

Marine Security Guard School in the 1960s and 1970s

The home of Marine Security Guard School in 1960s and 1970s was Henderson Hall, a complex of old, "H-shaped" barracks and buildings that served as Headquarters Marine Corps. Marine Security Guard School was located in the rear. The classroom and the battalion offices were mostly on the ground floor. Students slept in two squad bays on either end of the top floor. While Marine Security Guard School had been rumored to be "a second boot camp," the Marines who attended MSG School in the 1960s and 1970s found it to be far different than scuttlebutt had indicated. While most classes were held in Henderson Hall, Marines went over to the State Department building in Washington, D.C., a couple of times during the six-week course for classes on the Foreign Service and security matters. They spent two days during their stay at Henderson Hall at Quantico firing a variety of weapons and qualifying with the .38 revolver.

In addition to the rigorous academic subjects, emphasis then, as it is today, was on physical fitness training and appearance. Classes were divided into groups of eight to ten men, called detachments or "dets." The Marines lived in sections of the squad bays partitioned off by wall lockers for each detachment. In addition to the rigorous academic courses and numerous inspections, Marines did physical training, primarily running and weightlifting. One former Marine Security Guard during this period recalled that as the school progressed, inspections became more rigorous, as the Marines often spent hours preparing for these inspections.

As for the instructors, one Marine stated that they "varied in quality and reputation," and that the discipline was very strict. So strict, in fact, that "the slightest mistake could result in expulsion, especially as the end of the course neared." While normal attrition accounted for most of the "drops," medical, security, or discipline problems also reduced the size of the class. In some classes, as their course neared the end, Marines would find themselves out the door for seemingly minor errors. The strictness associated with MSG School can be seen in the comments made by Sergeant Carlos Simonetti, who attended Marine Security Guard School in 1967 after a tour of duty in Vietnam. Sergeant Simonetti recalled that members on the MSG Screening Board "had serious doubts" about him remaining in the program, due in large part "to my physical and mental immaturity." The Marine sergeant stated that officials at MSG kept him under close scrutiny before allowing him to complete the school.[27]

"We are not turning our embassies into fortresses": MSG School, 1979–1987

The seizure of the U.S. Embassy in Tehran in 1979 and burning and storming of the embassy in Islamabad initiated a comprehensive review of the training, assignment, and instruction of Marine Security Guards. Only days after the second embassy seizure in Tehran, Congressman Samuel S. Stratton, chairman of the House Armed Services Committee, requested from the Marine Corps "a detailed report on the employment of Marine Corps Guards at the U.S. Embassy in Teheran during the two seizures of that embassy in 1979."[28] The outcome of that review and subsequent congressional hearings brought about several immediate changes in the training of Marine Security Guards.

The review reinforced many of the lessons taught at MSG School and introduced new ones. Gunnery Sergeant D.W. Brennan stated that the most important lessons Marine Security Guard officials learned from the embassy seizure in Tehran and the brief takeover by Pakistani rioters in Islamabad in November 1979 was the absolute necessity in "maintaining composure in case of riots or mob action. [The Marine Security Guard] must know what to do if a bomb is found [and that] he will work closely ... in some cases with other members of the U.S. Army, Navy, and Air Force."[29]

The second lesson was the fact that despite the criticism that the Marine Guards did not resist the Iranians or Pakistani students, the "security guards" purpose is to protect classified information and to provide a limited defensive capability to counter small acts of violence directed against embassy personnel and facilities. They are not intended to be a fighting force capable of engaging a hostile population in a pitched battle."[30] Gunnery Sergeant Brennan said this point is emphasized throughout MSG School. Indeed, in a loud voice, he would ask his class, "Who can tell me what action you use before using deadly force? The Marines responded forcefully, "All other methods."[31] Equipped with only small arms, Marines are taught that it is the responsibility of the host government to protect the U.S. Embassy. Marine Security Guards are to delay as long as possible "the entry of a hostile group into the installation, long enough to destroy classified material, and aid in safeguarding the lives of embassy personnel."

Colonel James L. Cooper, who commanded the Marine Security Guard Battalion dur-

Students at the Marine Security Guard School practice defensive tactics in REACT gear with their protective shields and pistols (U.S. Marine Security Guard Battalion).

ing both Iranian hostage crises, said, "Our Marines are sent there to protect classified material, U.S. lives and U.S. property.... They are also capable of fighting a delaying action and holding a mob off long enough for diplomatic personnel to move in safely and destroy secret material."[32] Colonel Cooper added that the 13 Marine Security Guards "held off a crowd of hostile Iranians for three hours, allowing embassy workers to destroy secret communications equipment."

Colonel Cooper also stressed the fact that "we are not turning our embassies into fortresses." Marine Security Guards, armed with .38 caliber revolvers, riot sticks, 12-gauge shotguns and tear gas canisters, are likewise taught that the only time they can fire their weapons is in self defense, and even that has to be approved by the ambassador. In other words, if a Marine pulls his or her weapon, he or she has thought about it and has received permission from the Ambassador. Also, Marine Security Guards are not permitted to fire outside the grounds of embassies unless ordered to by the ambassador or RSO.

The Marine colonel emphasized that Marine guards do not have assault rifles or machine guns in the REACT rooms or armories. Marines have successfully repelled attacks without resorting to force. One such instance was in San Salvador in January 1979, where Marine Security Guards held off 300 intruders until government troops arrived. Unlike in Saigon in January 1968, when combat-equipped Marines guarded the embassy and took offensive action when attacked during the Tet offensive, Marine Security Guards are to remain "buttoned up" until host nation troops can arrive to stabilize or resolve the situation.[33] As Colonel Cooper said, defense of the embassy is the responsibility of the host government, "and if they don't live up to their international responsibilities, there's no way we can protect the embassy."

One major change in the curriculum as a result of the Iranian hostage crisis was a four-hour period of instruction on how to deal with hostage situations. The first class to receive such training at MSG School was the class that had been in session during the second seizure of the U.S. Embassy in Tehran in November 1979. Colonel Cooper told the leathernecks attending the class that if they are taken hostage, they are to "1. Survive. Stay alive. No. 2, do it with honor. If you have a choice just remain silent."[34] With the latter point, Colonel Cooper obviously had in mind the statements made by several former Iranian-held hostages while in captivity and upon their return to the United States.

As for the Marines attending MSG School during this period, Sergeant Richard LaBoyne stated, "If you think you're worth anything as a Marine, this is where you ought to be!" Sergeant LaBoyne said upon graduation, he was "prepared to give 100 percent while I am on post. I know it's not going to be a cocktail tour, and I know we'll not be playing games. Everything will be for real."[35]

The Aftermath of the Lonetree Espionage Affair, 1987–1988

In the aftermath of Sergeant Clayton Lonetree's admission that he willingly committed espionage against the United States in Moscow, the Marine Corps and State Department initiated a series of reforms aimed at preventing another such episode. Many of these reforms took place at Marine Security Guard School. The goal was not only to prevent a repeat of the Lonetree affair but also to better prepare young Marines for the new threats that emerged during the 1970s and 1980s.

In a memorandum to the secretary of the Navy and Secretary of Defense Caspar Weinberger, General P.X. Kelley, the commandant of the Marine Corps, said that the corps had undertaken a series of reforms aimed at the improvement of the Marine Security Guard Program. These reforms included: (1) Improved and tighter screening of applicants and their records; (2) The requirement that potential candidates and students, prior to attendance and during the length of the school, appear regularly before a screening board of highly qualified officers and staff noncommissioned officers to determine eligibility; (3) A critical examination of all applicants by several expert psychologists within and outside the government to identify those characteristics required for successful performance of MSG duties; and finally, (4) Establishment of an MSG Screening Team to visit major commands to identify, interview, and screen applicants in the field, thus extending the expert screening process from the training phase back to the applicant phase.[36]

As for training, General Kelley informed the secretary of the Navy that the staff at Marine Security Guard School was in the process of "a critical review of the training program that will be completed before the next MSG Watchstander and Detachment Commander classes commence in May (1988)." The commandant went to great lengths to stress that the MSG staff psychologist would explore additional techniques to augment courses such as stress management and substance abuse counseling for detachment commanders. In his memorandum, General Kelley indicated that the problems associated with the Marine Security Guard Detachment of which Sgt. Lonetree was a member were not confined to the Marines assigned to Moscow. The commandant indicated that there was also a problem in the relationship between the Marine Security Guard detachment commanders and the embassy staffs. Colonel C.J. Del Grosso, commanding officer of Marine Security Guard Battalion in the late 1980s, added that one of the major problems in the relationship between the State Department and the Marine Corps was a lack of coordination in the roles of detachment commanders and company commanders. Colonel Del Grosso indicated that there was a "tug of war" between HQMC and the Office of Diplomatic Security Services. While HQMC wanted more supervisory authority over the companies and detachments, the State Department apparently wanted to reduce the number of companies and their locations. General Kelley and his successor, General Alfred M. Gray, as well as Colonel Del Gross, pointed out that the Lonetree incident could have been avoided or the damage minimized had there been better supervision on the company and detachment levels. The lack of supervision inevitably led to the fiasco in Moscow.[37] General Kelley stressed the fact that the Department of State syllabus for regional security officers would be taught at the MSG Battalion at Quantico. Finally, General Kelley repeated that more emphasis would be placed on training the detachment commanders themselves. Marines and State Department officials who investigated how and why Sgt. Lonetree was able to successfully carry out his espionage virtually undetected concluded that there had been a serious breakdown in the chain of command in Moscow between the detachment commander and the watchstanders. General Kelley concluded that detachment commanders, who attend the 8-week course, would receive just as much screening and attention as the watchstanders who attend the 6-week course.[38] General Kelley wrote, "prospective detachment commanders will receive very careful scrutiny. The small-unit leadership skills these staff non-commissioned officers carry to their respective posts are critical to the success of the program." Both maturity and academic excellence are the keys to a successful tour as a Marine Security Guard or detachment commander.

Major General Carl E. Mundy, Jr., USMC, Deputy Chief of Staff for Operations at HQMC, emphasized this before the House Armed Services Committee. General Mundy told the lawmakers that "a lack of maturity and failure to maintain an acceptable grade point average were the frequent causes for failure at MSG School."[39] Major General Mundy added, "The curriculum for the Marine Security Guard School is determined jointly by the Diplomatic Security Service of the Department of State and the Marine Security Guard Battalion.... The curriculum is reviewed and updated annually."

Furthermore, General Mundy added that the Diplomatic Security Service provides professional and experienced security officers to MSG School in order to instruct the Marines in specific security subjects and the functioning of a diplomatic mission. General Mundy emphasized that the 6-week, 350-hour course is academically demanding and rigorous:

> The MSG students receive about 70 hours of instruction on performing security functions and coping with a foreign environment. Specific classes include: Conduct in a Foreign Environment, Reporting Contacts by Hostile Agents, Detecting Hostile Intelligence, Subversion, Classified Material Procedures, Conducting Security Inspections and Briefings on Soviet Bloc countries. 25 of these hours are taught by Department of State instructors. In all, over 50 hours of instruction are taught by the department of State personnel.[40]

Major General Mundy added, "The remaining instruction focuses on the physical security aspects of Marine Security Guard duty such as the employment of weapons, personal protective measures and operating security-related equipment." In short, Mundy concluded, "This training is extensive in order that Marines become familiar with the Department of

State security equipment and procedures and well versed and highly skilled in the application of deadly force."

Sergeant Laboyne acknowledged that his tour of duty as an embassy Marine "will be a true test of the confidence" others have placed in him. He also saw it as a self-test of his own integrity, and possibly, durability. Sergeant LaBoyne concluded, "I believe I can handle a situation where there are only 20 or 30 other Americans involved who are reliant on my judgement and ability."[41] Confidence and trust, as Sergeant Laboyne pointed out, are the two key words that define the objective of Marine Security Guard School. The Marines who graduate from MSG School are both the recipients and guardians of the trust and confidence of their superiors and fellow Marines in situations that are oftentimes life-threatening and hold international ramifications. Ramifications, one might add, that go far beyond the Marine's embassy detachment. Such has been the case since the inception of the Marine Security Guard program in 1948.

During an orientation at MSG School, located at Marine Corps Base, Quantico, Virginia, First Lieutenant (later Captain) J.P. Valencia briefs incoming students on what to expect for the next six intensive weeks (U.S. Marine Security Guard Battalion).

Marine Security Guard School and a War on Terror, 1991–2004

One of the greatest attributes of the Marine Security Guard program is its flexibility and ability to change with the times. Over time, as the MSG program evolved from a handful of Marines to a force of some 1400 men and women, so too has the curriculum and teaching methodology. During the 1960s and 1970s, instructors at MSG School varied in quality and reputation. Their sole purpose, it seemed at least to the students, was to instill fear into the minds of the Marines when they constantly shouted during instruction, "Attention to detail, men! Attention to detail."

While inspections still play an important role in the preparation of a Marine Security Guard, the emphasis today is on a host of subjects Marines must know before going out on post. In one of the large classrooms, Marines sit at long tables, each given a huge binder with course outlines and syllabuses on a variety of topics, and listen to lectures on "close-range weapons, police skills, state-of-the art security equipment, hostage survival, counter-intelligence and cultural do's and don't." The Marine security guards selected for the MSG program are, according to Major John D. Augsburger, who commanded Schools Company during the late 1990s, "mature, smart, and ambitious, and they all have a plan."[42]

Major Lewis D. Volger, the operations officer for MSG Battalion, said that Marine Security Guard School "is a total environment." It's a lot of responsibility for a profession where the average age is 21 years. Major Vogler added, "No where in the Corps — or even in life — will [a young person] get such feedback.... This not only serves them well throughout their Marine Corps career, but throughout life."[43]

One of the best examples of the discipline and dedication of Marine Security Guards can be seen in the career of 2nd Lieutenant Therrel Shane Childers. Lieutenant Childers, a veteran of Desert Shield and Desert Storm, who, as a young boy, aspired to become a Marine Security Guard, grew up in Tehran, Iran, where his father, a Navy Seabee, had been stationed as a security technician at the U.S. Embassy. Here, Lieutenant Childers saw a Marine Embassy Guard raise the American flag during morning colors. Later that night, Childers told his parents, "That's what I want to be." Entering the Marine Corps prior to Operation Desert Storm, Childers served as an assault amphibian driver with the 2nd AAV Battalion, 2nd Marine Division. After the war, Childers realized his dream when he graduated from MSG School. After completing his required two tours of duty, Sgt. Childers' next challenge was to become a Marine Corps officer. He entered the Citadel, where he majored in French and made the dean's list. Commissioned a second lieutenant after graduation, Childers' first assignment as an infantry officer was with "Alpha" Company, 1st Battalion, 5th Marines. At the commencement of Operation Iraqi Freedom in March 2003, Lieutenant Childers became the first Marine to die in combat as his company assaulted the Rumaila oilfields in southern Iraq. Throughout his career, Lieutenant Childers had, as Major Augsburger stated, a "plan," and in carrying it out, he never wavered nor looked back.[44]

Among some of the more important changes in the Marine Security Guard program since 11 September 2001 is the lengthening of the tour of duty. Formerly, Marine Security Guards were assigned to two 15-month tours of duty — one tour at what is considered a "hardship" post and the second one at a post of the Marine's choosing, if possible. In all cases, Marine Security Guards are assigned to posts according "to the needs of the Marine Corps" and State Department. As of May of 2004, Marines are now required to stand three 12-month tours of duty. According to Major Vogler, this new assignment policy is designed to offset a

Teamwork is an essential part of the defenses of an embassy. Here, MSG students practice tactical operations in the use of the pistol (U.S. Marine Security Guard Battalion).

shortage of Marines volunteering for MSG duty and the manpower demands of Operations Enduring Freedom and Iraqi Freedom II. Major Vogler added that this new policy "makes a good Marine even better," as it allows a Marine to "stay sharper during each tour, and be able to return to the fleet ... more well rounded."[45]

Future Marine Security Guards train on the latest state-of-the-art equipment such as the Indoor Simulator Marksmanship Trainer (ISMT). At Marshall Hall, two rooms are set aside for the ISMT that allows Marine Security Guards to practice on a "judgmental pistol-shooting range" that flashes incremental images of armed intruders and non-combatants. Here, Marines must make the determination when not to and when to fire. ISMT allows Marine Security Guards at MSG School and out on post, where many now have ISMT trainers, to constantly practice and refresh an important decision-making process of when and when not to use their issued side arms.[46]

The second important innovation is the Mobile Firearms Trainer, a movable, armor-plated truck trailer parked outside of Marshall Hall, installed in 1993. The instructor's monitoring gear and the shooter occupy one end of the trailer, from which the student "shoots at realistic life-sized computer images into a bullet trap at the other end. The trap is capable of stopping a standard NATO 5.56mm and lesser caliber rounds."[47] Inside the trailer, a student

Students at Marine Security Guard School located in Marshall Hall, Quantico, Virginia, practice how to use the riot baton in repelling intruders and demonstrators (U.S. Marine Security Guard Battalion).

walks toward a screen located at the front as a scenario is played out. "It could be an intruder, an employee brandishing a knife or simply someone refusing to stop for questioning. Each vignette responds to student commands. "As the danger in the video escalates, the student must decide what countermeasures to use — from verbal persuasion to deadly force."[48] According to Gunnery Sergeant Robert De Coito, an instructor at Marine Security Guard School, "This is a confidence tool.... There is nothing else like it in the Marine Corps."

Marine Security Guard students likewise train with the new Point Blank Ballistic Shield and body armor that is now standard equipment in all REACT rooms. The shield can stop a .44 magnum round and multiple hits from a 9mm sub-machine gun. The body armor Marine Security Guards train on and use on post "provides the same level of protection as the shield." Besides the .44 magnum and 9mm rounds, the body armor and Point Blank shield can protect against rounds from a .357 magnum, 12-gauge shotgun, .45 automatic, .38 Special, and .22 long rifle high velocity shell.

In the field of weaponry, Marine Security Guards now train on, in addition to the standard .357 magnum and 12-gauge shotguns, the 9mm pistol, which is now the standard firearm for Marine Security Guards on post. Marines at MSG School likewise are familiarized with the Ruger Mini-14 and Uzi 9mm sub-machine gun, as well as continued training and familiarization firing of the M16A2 rifle. In short, Marine Security Guards are trained on a variety of weapons in order to be prepared to defend an embassy until help arrives.

Marine Security Guards likewise receive extensive training on how to subdue an attacker without the use of firearms, as well as training with the PR-24 police baton, handcuffs, and other security equipment. In addition to the extensive classroom instruction, Marine Security Guard students conduct extensive hands-on training. This includes role-playing exer-

SSgt. Richard Roark explains the workings of the 870 (.12-gauge) shotgun to MSG students at the rifle range (courtesy U.S. Marine Corps).

cises, practice donning REACT equipment (Kevlar helmet, Point Blank body armor, the load bearing vest, chemical-biological protective masks, 12-gauge shotguns and Beretta 9mm pistols), and how to handle hostage situations.

Also, as a result of the events of September 11, 2001, there is an increased awareness made of nuclear, biological and chemical (NBC) training and evacuation operations during a catastrophic attack. According to CWO2 J.A. Pcola, MSG Battalion's NBC officer, all potential detachment commanders receive four days of training in mass casualty evacuation and operating in an NBC environment with the Marine Corps' Chemical and Biological Incidence Response Force or CBIRF, located at Indianhead, Maryland.[49] Here, the future detachment commanders are given familiarization classes in mass casualty evacuation during a terrorist attack, such as occurred in Nairobi and Dar es Salaam, as well as on 11 September 2001. These SNCOICs are taught how to evacuate individuals safely from a destroyed building surrounded by piles of rubble and debris. Their main task is to safely evacuate any casualties, represented in training by mannequins approximating the actual weight and height of human beings. They must be able to negotiate these "individuals" through narrow passages and amidst debris or in an NBC environment and pass them off to rescuers.[50] All MSG students are given classes on the various types of CS gasses, and are "pepper sprayed" in order to familiarize them with the effects of these chemical agents.

As with all Marine Corps Schools, Marine Security Guards conduct extensive physical training. This includes cardiovascular (running, sprints, basketball, etc.) as well as upper and lower body (pull ups, weightlifting, and leg lifting) exercises. Besides building teamwork, Marines are taught from day one at Marshall Hall that many times, an emergency such as

Like firearms, communications are vital to the success of a Marine Security Guard's mission. Mr. John Konicki lectures students at MSG School on the types of radios, frequencies, and systems found at all embassies or consulates worldwide (U.S. Marine Security Guard Battalion).

Islamabad, Pakistan, or a siege such as Tehran or San Salvador may call upon all of their energies and coordination. Hence, physical fitness constitutes an important part in a Marine Security Guard's overall training.

Students at Marine Security Guard School likewise receive extensive classes on administrative matters such as keeping accurate accounts of the MSG funds, maintaining a log book, and perhaps most important, procedures on issuing violations dealing with classified material. Also, as was the case in Santo Domingo in 1965 and Saigon in 1968, Marines are taught to use a variety of communications equipment and how to communicate on controlled security communications networks.

The most important function of a Marine Security Guard remains the destruction of classified material. As Gunnery Sergeant Frederick A. Upchurch, the detachment commander in Congo-Brazzaville, recalled, Marine Security Guards were called upon to destroy or burn large amounts of classified material. Gunnery Sergeant Upchurch stated that this proved to be, by far, the most taxing of all jobs undertaken by the Marines, even as they set out to evacuate the embassy. "Gunny" Upchurch added that when the Marines in Brazzaville began to destroy the classified material, they soon discovered that there was more classified material than was probably necessary in the embassy's vault. This, he said, required further scrutiny for future operations.[51] Indeed, in absorbing the lessons from Tehran, Somalia, Brazzaville, Monrovia, and Moscow, the destruction of classified material has evolved into one of the most important and perhaps one of the most demanding jobs of a Marine on embassy duty. Indeed, since the Lonetree affair, the protection and destruction of classified material has been the area of most concern to Marine Security Guard School officials, and has thus received more attention in recent years. Marines learn from the time they enter the school that it is the responsibility of a Marine Security Guard on post to insure that classified material, when no longer needed, is accounted for, stored properly or, destroyed.

The Recruiting and Advertising Teams

In wake of the war on terror and combat operations in Afghanistan and Iraq, attention shifted toward the retention and recruitment of qualified candidates for the Marine Security Guard program. Despite the shortage of Marines available for MSG duty, both the Marine Security Guard Battalion and State Department increased their efforts toward recruiting Marines for the program.[52]

To address the shortage of prospective candidates for the MSG program, Headquarters Marine Corps, in the summer of 2004, authorized the creation of a "Recruiting, Advertising, Screening Team or 'RAST.'" The "RAST," which is a permanent addition to the staff of Marine Security Guard Battalion, has the task of attracting prospective candidates to the MSG program. The first SNOIC of the team was Gunnery Sergeant Steve E. Rice, who served as a MSG detachment commander, and is now charged with the recruitment of new MSG candidates. According to Gunnery Sergeant Rice, "RAST" teams travel to the various Marine Corps bases throughout the United States, where they brief the local commands and Marines stationed there on the Marine Security Guard program.[53]

Summary

In sum, no effort is spared to properly prepare a Marine Security Guard for his or her assignment out on post. Marine Security Guards are today armed with five decades of some very hard "lessons learned." Since September 11, 2001, the tasks now faced by Marine Security Guards have become more demanding and more dangerous. With President George W. Bush's declaration of war on the killers who planned and carried out the coordinated attacks on the United States, Marine Security Guards stand confident and ready to meet any future challenges that they might confront while on duty.

CHAPTER 11

"Our Marines": A Retrospective

In the aftermath of the uprising in Kampala, Uganda, in 1986, Ambassador Robert G. Houdek said what most, if not all, ambassadors have thought over the years of the brave and dedicated Marine Security Guards, "They are my Marines."[1] From the time of the early Republic up to today, the Marine Corps and the State Department have forged one of the most important and most enduring relationships that exist between two government agencies. Former Secretary of State George P. Schultz stated on May 11, 1984, during a ceremony honoring Marine Security Guards, "The Marines and our diplomacy are tightly intertwined. Sometimes people have the mistaken idea that the strength represented by the Marines is an alternative to diplomacy. That's wrong. Strength and diplomacy go together. They need each other. And we in the State Department — people in the Foreign Service — are perhaps the most acutely aware of the importance of our Marines, because the Marines are with us in our embassies. Of course, that's what we're honoring here today. The Marines are usually the first people he sees when he comes to our embassy. And, of course, the Marines do far more than provide that immediate presence as their innumerable examples of exploits on the part of the

Marines with our embassies. To me, the Marines as we see them stand for the best."[2]

Former Secretary of State Madeline Albright echoed these sentiments when she spoke at a memorial service for the victims of the dual bombings in Nairobi, Kenya, and Dar es Salaam, Tanzania. In her moving eulogy, Secretary of State Albright praised the dedication and professionalism of the Americans killed in the blasts. The former secretary of state's comments were fitting commentary on the service of Marine Security

Secretary of State Madeline Albright speaks at the 50th anniversary of the signing of the Memorandum of Understanding between the State Department and the Department of the Navy in December 1948 (U.S. Marine Security Guard Battalion).

Guards worldwide, and in particular for the eleven Marines who died in the line of duty defending U.S. embassies:

> The most important thing we can do is to help the survivors to honor the friends we have lost; to add our prayers to those loved ones they leave behind; and most important, to keep alive the spirit of service and commitment that lent meaning to their lives. For these were honorable lives spent in service to our country and its ideals. These were good people who understood that life without purpose is merely existence and that the highest purpose resides not in what we can acquire for ourselves, but in what we can achieve through our kinship with each other. These were dedicated professionals who knew what we all know but seldom consciously feel or express — that this work we do is dangerous.[3]

Indeed, as Sergeant Derek Hawkins, a former Marine Security Guard stated, "A lot of Marines think [embassy guards] stand in front of a building with blues on." Sergeant Dawkins paraphrased Secretary of State Albright when he said that MSG duty "requires a high level of vigilance and self-motivation." Echoing this sentiment was an official at Headquarters Marine Corps, who said the impact a single Marine Security Guard "can be far greater than any one thing an infantryman assigned to Iraq could have."[4]

One of the most fitting tributes to the dedication and sacrifice by Marine Security Guards came, however, from the Foreign Service Officer in charge of the U.S. Consulate in Asmara, Ethiopia. In his last cable from the U.S. Consulate in Ethiopia, the foreign service officer-in-charge lauded the MSGs with his "unqualified respect for their dedication, discipline, and devotion. In a world of negotiable values, these men demonstrated a standard of performance which ranks among the most esteemed traditions of the Marine Corps."[5] The finest tribute to the men and women who stand at Post One came, however, came from former Sec-

"Not just about Dress Blues," Sergeant Paul M. Roberge USMC, stands "at ease" at Post One in Moscow, Russia. For most host-nation citizens, Marine Security Guards are the first Americans they will see when they enter an embassy or consulate (U.S. Marine Security Guard Battalion).

retary of State Henry Kissinger, who praised "the brave men of the Marine Corps with whom we have been through so much, side by side."[6]

Since the beginnings of the republic in 1776, the Marine Corps and the State Department have worked "side by side," as former Secretary of State Kissinger so eloquently stated, in an oftentimes hostile and dangerous world. Likewise, the bravery and dedication displayed by the Marines who stand duty at Post One has never flagged. Instead, the devotion to duty and high standards that have been the hallmark of the Marine Corps and its relations with the Department of State since 1798 remains strong and vibrant.

Chapter Notes

Chapter 1

1. First Lieutenant Anthony Gale served as lieutenant colonel commandant of the Marine Corps beginning on 3 March 1819 and was removed from office after being court-martialed and cashiered from the service on 8 October 1820. See Richard S. Collum, *History of the United States Marine Corps* (Philadelphia: L.R. Hamersly, 1890), p. 270.

2. Edwin H. McClellan, "French Naval War, 1798–1801," Chapter 12 in "History of the United States Marine Corps," Vol. 1, unpublished draft, Historical Section, HQMC, 8 July 1925, in possession of author, p. 23.

3. Edwin H. McClellan, "The Naval War with France," *Marine Corps Gazette*, December 1922, Vol. 7, No. 4, p. 348.

4. Captain Franklin Wharton served as lieutenant colonel commandant of the Marine Corps from 7 March 1804 to 1 September 1818. Collum, *History of the United States Marine Corps,* p. 270.

5. McClellan, "French Naval War," p. 18.

6. The most contemporary accounts of President Jefferson's campaign against the Barbary pirates is Joseph Wheelan's *Jefferson's War: America's First War on Terror, 1801–1805* (New York: Carroll and Graf, 2003).

7. According to Captain Harry A. Ellsworth, the United States offered to pay the bashaw an additional $100,000 as ransom money, which he promptly rejected. See Ellsworth, *One and Eighty Landings of United States Marines, 1800–1934* (Washington, D.C.: History and Museums Division, 1974), p. 157.

8. Collum, *History of the United States Marine Corps,* p. 48.

9. *Ibid.*; Ellsworth, *One Hundred and Eighty Landings,* p. 158.

10. Ellsworth, *One Hundred and Eighty Landings,* p. 159.

11. Charles N. Morris, "The Autobiography of Commodore Charles N. Morris, U.S.N.," *U.S. Naval Institute Proceedings,* 1880, Vol. 6, No. 12, pp. 184–5.

12. Clyde H. Metcalf, *The History of the United States Marine Corps* (New York: G. P. Putnam's Sons, 1939), p. 91.

13. McClellan, "History of the United States Marine Corps," 1st Edition, Vol. 2, Chapter 2, unpublished manuscript, p. 58. In possession of the author.

14. *Ibid.*

15. *Ibid.*, pp. 58–9.

16. McClellan, "Japan, 1846–1860," Chapter 28 in "History of the United States Marine Corps," Vol. 2, unpublished manuscript in possession of the author, p. 1.

17. Interestingly, Second Lieutenant Fowler's mission would not be the last force of Marines sent ashore in Cochin China. One hundred and thirty-one years almost to the day, the 9th Marine Expeditionary Brigade landed at Da Nang, precisely where the *Peacock* dropped anchor in the spring of 1834. *Ibid.*

18. McClellan, "Japan, 1846–1860," p. 3.

19. *Ibid.*, p. 4.

20. *Ibid.*, p. 5.

21. *Ibid.*, p. 6.

22. *Ibid.*, pp. 7–8.

23. Captain Glynn wrote this letter to President Fillmore on 10 June 1851. McClellan, "Japan, 1846–1860," p. 8.

24. Commodore Matthew Calbraith Perry was the son of the hero of the Battle of Lake Erie in 1813, Commodore Oliver Hazard Perry, USN, and had been given command of the expedition to Japan by President Millard Fillmore. See Mary H. Krout, "Perry's Expedition to Japan," *U.S. Naval Institute Proceedings,* February 1921, Vol. 47, No. 2, p. 215.

25. McClellan, "Japan, 1846–1860," p. 11.

26. *Ibid.*, p. 13; also see Commodore Matthew Perry, USN, *The Personal Journal of Commodore Matthew C. Perry.* Edited by Roger Pireau with an introduction by Samuel Eliot Morison (Washington, D.C.: Smithsonian Institution, 1968), p. 65.

27. Perry, *Personal Journal,* p. 165.

28. Perry used the term "poo-cchings." *Ibid.*

29. Ellsworth, *One Hundred and Eighty Landings,* pp. 100–1.

30. McClellan, "Japan, 1846–1860," p. 25.

31. McClellan, "Japan, 1846–1860," pp. 18–19.

32. *Ibid.*, pp. 28–9.

33. *Ibid.*, p. 30.

34. Perry, *Personal Journal,* p. 192.

35. Ellsworth, *One Hundred and Eighty Landings,* pp. 101–2; McClellan, "Japan, 1846–1860," pp. 30–1.

36. The Taiping Rebellion (1850–1864) was a peasant-based rebellion led by Hung Hsiu-ch'uan, who had characterized himself as the younger brother of Jesus Christ and had formulated a revolutionary ideology that one historian termed the "Chinese version of Protestant Christianity." The Taipings proposed not only to overthrow the Manchu dynasty but intended a sort of social revolution. Driven by Hung's messianic creed, the rebels aimed at improving the status of women, opposed the opium traffic, and introduced communal economic organization. They also embarked upon a reform of land tenure to achieve a better balance between the agricultural population and available arable lands and thus won support from the discontented Chinese peasantry. The Western powers (France, Britain and the United States) had an increasing interest in the survival of the Manchu dynasty due to trade and economic concessions as well as the United States being granted the right to establish a diplomatic presence in Peking, and in time came to support the Manchus against the rebels. Eventually, the rebellion was crushed after an estimated 20 million Chinese on both sides were killed. See O. Edmund Clubb, *20th Century China* (New York: Columbia University Press, 1966), pp. 12–13.

37. McClellan, "French Naval War," pp. 43–6.

38. Both the minister from Holland and Mr. Harris' secretary and interpreter were killed by the Japanese, who had hoped to return to their isolationist policies before Commodore Perry's visit. *Ibid.*, pp. 51–2.

39. Ellsworth, *One Hundred and Eighty Landings*, p. 102.

40. "Chronology of Marines and the State Department," in Marine Security Guard Battalion file marked "Chronologies" located at the History and Museums Division, U.S. Marine Corps, HQMC, Washington Navy Yard, Washington, D.C.

41. Caleb Cushing had been a member of the U.S. House of Representatives from the State of Massachusetts prior to his appointment as the first U.S. minister to China. He negotiated a treaty of extra-territoriality with the Chinese foreign minister, Ki Ying, at Wanghai on 3 July 1844. See Captain Evans Ford Carlson's "Marines as an Aid to Diplomacy in China," *Marine Corps Gazette*, February 1936, Vol. 20, No. 1, p. 30.

42. Metcalf, *The History of the United States Marine Corps*.

43. *Ibid.*

44. Ellsworth, *One Hundred and Eighty Landings*, pp. 25–6; Major Edwin H. McClellan, "The Capture of the Barrier Forts in the Canton River, China," *Marine Corps Gazette*, September 1920, Vol. 5, No. 3, p. 264.

45. Bernard C. Nalty, *The Barrier Forts: A Battle, A Monument, and A Mythical Marine* (Washington, D.C.: Historical Branch, G-3 Division, HQMC, 1962), p. 7.

46. *Ibid.*, pp. 7–8.

47. *Ibid.*, pp. 8–9.

48. Ellsworth, *One Hundred and Eighty Landings*, p. 27.

49. Nalty, *Barrier Forts*, p. 10.

50. *Ibid.*, pp. 28–9.

51. *Ibid.*, p. 29.

52. The shogun or "tycoon" was the head warlord who ruled nominally in the name of the emperor. This situation lasted until 1868, when full-scale civil war broke out in Japan in order to break the power of the shogun and the other warlords and restore the full authority of the Meiji ruler. Leo J. Daugherty, phone conversation with Dr. Doris T. Chang, 9 August 2001. Also see Mikiso Hane, *Modern Japan: A Historical Survey*. Second Edition (Boulder, Colo.: Westview Press, 1992), pp. 84–90.

53. Ellsworth, *One Hundred and Eighty Landings*, p. 104.

54. *Ibid.*

55. Ellsworth, *One Hundred and Eighty Landings*, p. 57.

56. *Ibid.*, p. 58.

57. *Ibid.*, p. 58. Collum, *History of the United States Marine Corps*, pp. 192–3.

58. *Ibid.*, p. 59.

59. Korea had been under the suzerainty of China during this period.

60. Captain George F. Elliott became the tenth brigadier general commandant of the Marine Corps in 1903. He served until 1910.

61. Ellsworth, *One Hundred and Eighty Landings*, pp. 59–60; Metcalf, *History of the United States Marine Corps*, pp. 243–4.

62. One of the best accounts of this landing comes from a member of the Japanese Diet in 1907 who transcribed it from official records. See Yosaburo Takekoshi, *Japanese Rule in Formosa*. Translated by George Braithwaite (London: Longmans, Green, and Co., 1907), pp. 75–6.

63. Ellsworth, *One Hundred and Eighty Landings*, pp. 83–4; Metcalf, *History of the United States Marine Corps*, pp. 237–8.

64. Takekoshi, *Japanese Rule in Formosa*, p. 76.

65. The U.S. Congress followed the lead of the British Parliament in passing a ban on the African slave trade in 1804. Unfortunately, this inhumane practice continued unabated until after the American Civil War in 1861. See Thomas A. Bailey, *A Diplomatic History of the American People*, Ninth Edition (Englewood Cliffs, N.J.: Prentice-Hall, 1974).

66. Mr. Joseph Jenkins Roberts was born a free Negro in Norfolk, Va., on 15 March 1809. After working on the docks in Norfolk and on barges on the James River, he immigrated to Monrovia, Liberia, where he became a leading soldier and statesmen of the emerging African state. He became Liberia's first president and remained active in political affairs until his death on 24 February 1879. *Makers of Modern Africa: Profiles in History* (London: African Journal, 1981), pp. 489–90; also see Russell Warren Howe, *Black Africa: Africa South of the Sahara From Pre-History to Independence, Vol. I: From Pre-History to the Eve of the Colonial Era* (New York: Walker and Co., 1966), pp. 136–7.

67. Peter Duignan and Lewis H. Gann, *The United States and Africa: A History* (New York: Cambridge University Press, 1987), p. 108.

68. Ellsworth, *One Hundred and Eighty Landings*, p. 75; Collum, *History of the United States Marine Corps*, pp. 218–19.

69. *Ibid.*, p. 219.

70. First Lieutenant John Harris would become the sixth brigadier general commandant of the Marine Corps (1859–1864).

71. McClellan, "History of the United States Marine Corps," 1st Edition, Part II, Chapter 2, p. 43.

72. *Ibid.*, p. 65.

73. *Ibid.*, p. 65; phone conversation between the author and Mr. Glenn Helm of the Naval Historical Center, Navy Department Library, Washington, D.C., 14 August 2001.

74. Metcalf, *History of the United States Marine Corps*, p. 139.

75. *Ibid.*, pp. 139–40.

76. *Ibid.*, p. 185.

77. Collum, *History of the United States Marine Corps*, p. 187.

78. Ellsworth, *One Hundred and Eighty Landings*, p. 121.

79. Ellsworth, *One Hundred and Eighty Landings*, p. 124; Bernard C. Nalty, *The United States Marines in Nicaragua*, 4th Edition (Washington, D.C.: Historical Branch, G-3 Division, HQMC, 1968), p. 4.

80. Major Charles Heywood, known as the "Boy Colonel" because of his youthful age, had won the Medal of Honor and was breveted for gallantry during the American Civil War while on blockade duty with the Union Fleet. He later became the 9th commandant of the Marine Corps and the first to hold that office as the brigadier general commandant (1892–1903).

81. For the best first-hand account of this landing see Collum, *History of the United States Marine Corps*, pp. 220–38.

82. *Ibid.*, p. 238.

83. Ellsworth, *One Hundred and Eighty Landings*, pp. 30–1.

84. *Ibid.*, p. 31; Metcalf, *History of the United States Marine Corps*, pp. 244.

85. Ellsworth, *One Hundred and Eighty Landings*, p. 32. For an excellent overview of the last years of the Manchu dynasty see Clubb, *20th Century China*, pp. 17–43; Frederic Wakeman, Jr., *The Fall of Imperial China* (New York: The Free Press, 1975), pp. 199–242. On the American experience and revolutionary China see James C. Thomson, Peter W. Staley, and John Curtis Perry, *Sentimental Imperialists: The American Experience in East Asia* (New York: Harper and Row, 1985), pp. 121–33.

86. Ellsworth, *One Hundred and Eighty Landings*, p. 33.

87. Captain Evans Ford Carlson, "Marines as an Aid to Diplomacy in China," *Marine Corps Gazette*, February 1936, Vol. 20, No. 1, p. 47.

88. *Ibid.*

89. R.R. Keene, "Samoa: Marines Intercede in Bloody Power Struggle," *Leatherneck*, 82 (April 1999), p. 16.

90. *Ibid.*, p. 18.

91. Private Hulbert would rise to the rank of sergeant major and retire in 1919. See Keene, "Samoa," pp. 20–1.

Chapter 2

1. Frederic Wakeman, Jr., *The Fall of Imperial China* (New York: The Free Press, 1977), pp. 215–16.

2. *Ibid.*, p. 217.

3. *Ibid.*

4. *Ibid.*, p. 218.

5. Metcalf, *History of the United States Marine Corps*, p. 280.

6. Born in Toledo, Ohio, on 14 January 1871, Private Oscar J. Upham entered the Marine Corps in 1898 and

served in the Spanish-American War. After the war he was ordered to sea duty aboard the USS *Oregon*. He was a member of a six-inch gun crew aboard that ship. During the Boxer Rebellion, Private Upham participated in the defense of the Legation Compound in China. He was awarded the Medal of Honor for this action. He died 19 February 1949. Mr. Fred Graboske and the heirs of Private Upham gave permission to quote from his diary. *Diary of Private Oscar J. Upham*, Washington, D.C., History and Museums Division, Archives Section, Marine Corps Historical Center.

7. Upham Diary, p. 2.
8. *Ibid.*, p. 7.
9. *Ibid.*, p. 8.
10. *Ibid.*, p. 156; *Upham Diary*, pp. 64–5.
11. Metcalf, *History of the United States Marine Corps*, p. 281.
12. Brigadier General A.S. Daggett, *America in the China Relief Expedition* (Nashville, Tenn.: Battery Press, 1903 Reprinted 1997), p. 16.
13. *Ibid.*, p. 18.
14. Upham Diary, pp. 8–9.
15. *Ibid.*, p. 9.
16. The best and most up-to-date text on the Boxer Rebellion is Diana Preston's *The Boxer Rebellion: The Dramatic Story of China's War on Foreigners that Shook the World in the Summer of 1900* (New York: Berkley Books, 2000), p. 57.
17. Upham Diary, p. 15.
18. *Ibid.*, pp. 16–17; Metcalf, *History of the United States Marine Corps*, p. 281.
19. Upham Diary, pp. 29–30.
20. Allan R. Millett, *Semper Fidelis: The History of the United States Marine Corps* (New York: Macmillan, 1980), p. 159.
21. Major (Major General) William P. Biddle eventually became the eleventh major general commandant of the Marine Corps (1910–1914). During his tenure as commandant, General Biddle instituted a mandatory three month period of recruit training at Marine Corps Barracks at Parris Island, South Carolina, or Mare Island, California. He also introduced the so-called "Swedish System" of drills that emphasized both cardio-vascular and upper body training for all recruits.
22. Millett, *Semper Fidelis*, p. 161.
23. Marines killed in the siege included Privates C.B. King, R.E. Thomas, R. Turner and Fischer of the USS *Oregon*, while Sergeant J. Fanning and Privates J.W. Tutcher and J. Kennedy of the USS *Newark* were killed in the fighting. Private J.H. Schroeder of the *Newark* later died of his wounds at the U.S. Naval Hospital at the Cavite Naval Station in the Philippines on 10 September. See Upham Diary, p. 64.
24. Ellsworth, *One and Eighty Landings of United States Marines, 1800–1934*

(Washington, D.C.: History and Museums Division, 1974), pp. 38–9.
25. Daggett, *America in the China Relief Expedition*, p. 261.
26. *Ibid.*, p. 262.
27. Mr. B.F. Barnes, Acting Secretary to the President, memorandum to Mr. Alvey A. Adee, 31 July 1905, Washington, D.C., National Archives, RG 127, Correspondence of the United States Marine Corps, Adjutant and Inspector's Office, 1913–1933, Accession No. 1645-20, Marine Guards, Subject Folder, "Peking."
28. Brigadier General Commandant George F. Elliott, *Annual Report to the Secretary of the Navy for 1905* (Washington, D.C.: Government Printing Office, 1906), pp. 1233–4.
29. *Ibid.*, p. 1234.
30. *Ibid.*
31. Ellsworth, *One Hundred Eighty Landings*, p. 40.
32. Major General Commandant William P. Biddle, *Annual Report to the Secretary of the Navy for 1912* (Washington, D.C.: Government Printing Office, 1913), p. 590.
33. Ellsworth, *One Hundred and Eighty Landings*, p. 41.
34. *Oral History Transcript of Lieutenant General Edward A. Craig*, interviewed by Major L.E. Tatum, Washington, D.C., History and Museums Division, HQMC, 1968, pp. 48–9.
35. *Ibid.*, p. 49.
36. *Ibid.*, p. 54.
37. Millett, *Semper Fidelis*, p. 229.
38. James S. Santelli, *A Brief History of the 4th Marines*, Washington, D.C., Historical Division, HQMC, 1970, p. 18.
39. *Ibid.*, pp. 18–19.
40. Master Sergeant Russell A. Bowers served in Peking with the 'Horse Marines' as an embassy guard from 1935 to 1937. He later served throughout World War II and during the Korean War with the 1st Marine Division. See Technical Sergeant John A. Bangs, USAF, "Information on Relative: Master Sergeant Russell A. Bowers, MSgt., USMC," e-mail to Captain Phillip J. Smith, Assistant Operations Officer, Marine Security Guard Battalion, State Department, MCCDC, Quantico, Va., March 14, 2000, pp. 1–2.
41. "Comments made by Corporal William H. Chittenden, USMC, at Marine Security Guard Battalion honoring the North China Marines, 16 November 2001," at the Marine Security Guard Battalion School, MCCDC, Quantico, Va. Transcript of the speech can be found in the MSG Bn.'s S-3 Archives.
42. Allan R. Millett, *In Many A Strife: General Gerald C. Thomas and the U.S. Marine Corps, 1917–1956* (Annapolis, Md.: Naval Institute Press, 1993), pp. 117–18.
43. *Ibid.*, pp. 118–19.

44. 8 December 1941 in China was 7 December 1941 at Pearl Harbor, given the crossing of the international dateline.
45. Colonel R.D. Camp, Jr., "End of An Era: Surrender of the North China Marines," *Leatherneck*, December 1999, Vol. 82, No. 12, pp. 17–18.
46. See biographic sketch of Brigadier General William W. Ashurst, 1 December 1955, Washington, D.C., Reference Section, "Brigadier General William W. Ashurst, USMC," History and Museums Division, U.S. Marine Corps Historical Center, p. 3.
47. Nalty, *United States Marines in Nicaragua*, pp. 4–5.
48. *Ibid.*, p. 5.
49. The Dawson Agreement, negotiated by presidential envoy Thomas C. Dawson with President Estrada as a means of improving Nicaragua's financial stability, gave the United States de facto control over Nicaragua's collection of customs in order to reassure European investors of Nicaragua's solvency and its ability to repay the loans to foreign banks. See Nalty, *United States Marines in Nicaragua*, pp. 5–6.
50. *Ibid.*, p.7.
51. U.S. Department of State, *Papers Relating to the Foreign Relations of the United States (1912)* (Washington, D.C.: Government Printing Office, 1919), p. 1039.
52. *Ibid.*, pp. 1039–40.
53. Luis Mena was a Conservative Party official appointed by Zeledon who, shortly after the revolution broke out, switched sides and took up the anti-American cause of the Liberals. See Nalty, *United States Marines in Nicaragua*, pp. 6–7.
54. Ellsworth, *One Hundred and Eighty Landings*, p. 127.
55. Robert F. Zissa, "Nicaragua — 1912," *Leatherneck*, July 1984, Vol. 67, No. 7, p. 26.
56. *Ibid.*
57. Major Edwin H. McClellan, "American Marines in Nicaragua," Washington, D.C., History & Museums Division, Reference Section, "Nicaragua, Geographic Folder," pp. 17–18. Also found in Washington, D.C., National Archives, Record Group 45, Box 639, No. 40/938.
58. William Kamman, *A Search for Stability: United States Diplomacy Toward Nicaragua, 1927–1933* (South Bend, Ind.: Notre Dame University Press, 1968), pp. 16–17.
59. Millett, *Semper Fidelis*, p. 240.
60. *Ibid.*, pp. 240–1.
61. President Solorzano's letter to Secretary of State Frank B. Kellogg, 7 January 1925, in U.S. Department of State, *Papers Relating to the Foreign Relations of the United States 1925, Vol. II* (Washington, D.C.: Government Printing Office, 1940), p. 621.
62. *Ibid.*, p. 622.

63. *Ibid.*, p. 624.

64. *Ibid.*, p. 625.

65. Richard D. Millett, "The History of the Guardia Nacional De Nicaragua, 1925–1965," Ph.D. dissertation, University of New Mexico, Albuquerque, 1966, p. 77.

66. Nalty, *United States Marines in Nicaragua*, p. 12.

67. *Ibid.*, pp. 12–13.

68. Nalty, *United States Marines in Nicaragua*, pp. 14–34; Millett, *Semper Fidelis*, pp. 236–63.

69. Major General John A. Lejeune, *Annual Reports of the Navy Department for 1928* (Washington, D.C.: Government Printing Office, 1929), p. 1242.

70. Metcalf, *History of the United States Marine Corps*, p. 445.

71. Ellsworth, *One Hundred Eighty Landings*, pp. 30–1.

Chapter 3

1. Ellsworth, *One and Eighty Landings of United States Marines, 1800–1934* (Washington, D.C.: History and Museums Division, 1974), p. 66.

2. *Ibid.*, p. 1.

3. *Ibid.*

4. *Ibid.*, p. 2.

5. *Ibid.*, p. 8.

6. Major (Lieutenant General) James Carson Breckinridge was born on 13 September 1877 in Memphis, Tennessee, and appointed a second lieutenant in the Marine Corps on 11 July 1898. He rose through the ranks to the grade of lieutenant general (on the retired list). He retired from the Marine Corps on 1 October 1941. He died on 2 March 1942 and was buried in the family cemetery in Lexington, Kentucky. See biography sheet, "Lieutenant General James Carson Breckinridge, USMC," in the Lieutenant General James C. Breckinridge USMC Papers located at the Marine Corps University Archives, Marine Corps University, MCCDC, Quantico, Va. The biographic sketch was taken from the *Quarterly Bulletin of the Frontier Nursing Service*, Vol. 17, Number 4, Spring 1942.

7. Petrograd was the wartime name for the city for St. Petersburg, Russia. At the end of the World War the Bolsheviks renamed it Leningrad. In 1991 the city regained its imperial name, St. Petersburg.

8. Tsarcoy Selo (Tsarskoe Selo or "Tsar's Village") was located fifteen miles south of Petrograd; it was where the czar and his family had been living for safety.

9. Lieutenant James C. Breckinridge, letter to his mother, 6 May 1916, American Embassy, Petrograd, Russia, 478 in the Lieutenant General James C. Breckinridge USMC Papers, Marine Corps University Archives, Marine Corps University, MCCDC, Quantico, Va., p. 1.

10. There were two revolutions in Russia. The first occurred in March 1917 when Czar Nicholas II was forced to abdicate the throne; the second occurred in October 1917 (November on the western calendar) with Lenin and the Bolsheviks seizing power from Kerensky. See Basil Dmytryshyn, *USSR: A Concise History*. Third Edition (New York: Charles Scribner's Sons, 1978), pp. 38–87.

11. Major James Carson Breckinridge to his mother, 14 April 1917, Lieutenant General James C. Breckinridge Papers, Marine Corps University Archives, Marine Corps University, MCCDC, Quantico, Va., Correspondence File 1916–1917, Letter No. 505, pp. 1–2.

12. "Lieutenant General James Carson Breckinridge, USMC," biographic sketch, p. 1.

13. Brigadier General John A. Lejeune letter to Commander Edward McCauley, Jr., Office of Naval Intelligence, Navy Department, Washington, D.C., 24 August 1917, Washington, D.C., National Archives, RG 127, General Correspondence of the United States Marine Corps 1913–33, A/1, Accession No. 1645-1910-27, Box 177.

14. Secretary of State Robert Landing letter to Secretary of the Navy Josephus Daniels, 31 August 1917, Washington, D.C., National Archives, Record Group 127, Adjutant and Inspector's Office, General Correspondence of the United States Marine Corps 1913–33, Accession No. 1645-1910-1927, Subject Folder "Guard," Box 177.

15. Secretary of the Navy Josephus Daniels letter to Secretary of State Robert Lansing, 6 September 1917, Washington, D.C., National Archives, RG 127, General Correspondence of the United States Marine Corps 1913–33, Adjutant and Inspector's Office, Accession No. 1645-1910-27, Subject File, "Guards," Box 177.

16. Gunnery Sergeant William O'Grady, "Marines as Diplomatic Couriers: A Story of Stirring Experiences of War Days," unpublished monograph, History and Museums Division, U.S. Marine Corps Historical Center, Washington, D.C., Reference Section, Marine Security Guard Folder: "Historical Articles." pp. 1–2.

17. *Ibid.*, p. 2.

18. Memorandum of Brigadier General John A. Lejeune to Secretary of State, 22 October 1917, Washington, D.C., National Archives, Record Group 127, General Correspondence of the United States Marine Corps 1913–1933, Adjutant and Inspector's Office, Accession No. 1645-1910-1927, Subject File, "Guards," Box 177, p. 2.

19. *Ibid.*, p. 1.

20. *Ibid.*, p. 5.

21. *Ibid.*, pp. 6–7.

22. *Ibid.*, p. 7.

23. Gunnery Sergeant William O'Grady, "Marines as Diplomatic Couriers," p. 10.

24. *Ibid.*

25. Ambassador David R. Francis to Secretary of State Robert Lansing, telegram, sent from Petrograd, November 24, 1917, Telegram No. 861.00/722, in *Foreign Relations of the United States, 1918, Russia, Vol. 1* (Washington, D.C.: Government Printing Office, 1931), pp. 265–6.

26. *Ibid.*, p. 357.

27. David R. Francis, *Russia, From the American Embassy*. April 1916–November 1918 (New York: Charles Scribner's Sons, 1921), p. 210.

28. Hon. David R. Francis, U.S. Ambassador to Russia, to Secretary of State, 17 March 1918, in Washington, D.C., National Archives, Record Group 127, Records of the United States Marine Corps, Adjutant and Inspector's Office, Accession No. 1975-50, Box 240 Folder, No. 53729, Subject: "Guards, 1917–1918."

29. J. Butler Wright was the embassy counselor; Norman Armour was the second secretary of the embassy in Russia. See Ambassador David R. Francis letter to Secretary of State, 17 March 1918, Washington, D.C., National Archives, RG 127, General Correspondence of the United States Marine Corps 1913–33, A/I, Accession No. 1645-1910-1927, Subject, "Guards," Box 177.

30. Ambassador David R. Francis telegram to Secretary of State Robert Lansing, No. 2410, File No. 861.77/311, 24 February 1918, in *Foreign Relations of the United States, 1918*, p. 387.

31. *Ibid.*; Secretary of State to U.S. Minister to Sweden, Ira N. Morris, telegram, February 25, 1918, in *Foreign Relations of the United States, 1918*, p. 387.

32. Sergeant Thomas Baisden, "Marines As Diplomatic Couriers: Second of a Series of War Time Adventures," unpublished manuscript, Reference Section, Marine Security Guard Folder, Historical Articles: History and Museums Division, U.S. Marine Corps Historical Division, MCCDC, Quantico, Va., p. 34.

33. *Ibid.*, p. 34.

34. Admiral William S. Sims, USN, to Major General Commandant, memorandum, 19 February 1918, Washington, D.C., National Archives, RG 127, General Correspondence of the United States Marine Corps, A/I, Accession No., 1645-1910-1927, Subject "Guards," Box 177.

35. Admiral William S. Sims, USN, to Major General Commandant George Barnett, Headquarters Marine Corps, 3 March 1919, Washington, D.C., National Archives, Record Group 127,

Adjutant and Inspector, Correspondence of the United States Marine Corps, Accession No. 1645-20, "Guards," Box 177.

36. General J.C. Harbord letter to Major General Commandant, 13 April 1920, Washington, D.C., National Archives, RG 127, General Correspondence of the United States Marine Corps 1913–33, A/I, Accession No. 1645-1910-1927, Subject "Guards," Box 177.

37. Acting Secretary of State letter to Secretary of the Navy, 22 December 1920, Washington, D.C., National Archives, RG 127, General Correspondence of the United States Marine Corps 1913–1933, A/I.

38. The USS *Brooklyn* was the flagship of the U.S. Asiatic Fleet.

39. E.T. Fryer letter to Major E.H. McClellan, 6 January 1920, Washington, D.C., History and Museums Division, Marine Corps Historical Center, Reference Section, "Marines in Siberia" Reference Folder.

40. McClellan, *One Hundred and Eighty Landings*, p. 143.

41. Allan R. Millett, *"In Many A Strife:" General Gerald C. Thomas and the U.S. Marine Corps, 1917–1956* (Annapolis, Md.: Naval Institute Press, 1993), pp. 88–9.

42. The Oral History Transcript of General Lemuel C. Shepherd, Interviewed by Benis M. Frank, Washington, D.C., Historical Division, HQMC, 1967, pp. 354 and 356–7 respectively.

43. *Ibid.*, p. 357.

44. *Ibid.*

45. Secretary of State Charles Evans Hughes to Secretary of the Navy, 3 October 1923, Subject: "Appointments," Washington, D.C., History and Museums Division, Marine Corps Historical Center, Reference Section, Marine Security Guard Folder, "General Historical 1900–1947."

46. Allan R. Millett, *Semper Fidelis: The History of the United States Marine Corps* (New York: Macmillan, 1980), p. 207.

47. McClellan, *A History of the United States Marine Corps*, p. 403.

48. Millett, *Semper Fidelis*, p. 210.

49. Lieutenant Colonel Frank O. Hough, Major Verle E. Ludwig, and Henry I. Shaw, *Pearl Harbor to Guadalcanal: History of U.S. Marine Corps Operations in World War II, Vol. I* (Washington, D.C.: G-3 Division, Headquarters Marine Corps, 1958), pp. 11–15.

50. For one of the best accounts of General del Valle's time as an observer with the Italian Army see *Oral History Transcript of Lieutenant General Pedro A. del Valle*, USMC, Washington, D.C., History and Museums Division, 1973, pp. 94–6. Also see General del Valle's memoir *Roman Eagles over Ethiopia* (Harrisburg, Pa.: Military Service Pub-

lishing, 1940); and Lieutenant General del Valle's *Semper Fidelis: An Autobiography* (Hawthorne, Calif.: Christian Book Club of America, 1976). The original citation for the *Order of the Crown of Italy*, signed by Mussolini himself, can be found in General del Valle's personal papers on repository at the Marine Corps University Archives, Marine Corps University, MCCDC, Quantico, Va.

51. Harry W. Edwards, *A Different War: Marines in Europe and North Africa* (Washington, D.C.: History and Museums Division, HQMC, 1994), pp. 3–4.

52. *Ibid.*, pp. 4–5.

53. *Ibid.*, p. 5.

54. *Ibid.*

55.

56. Gunnery Sergeant Kimball enlisted in the Marine Corps Reserves in the summer of 1939 at age seventeen and drilled in Rockville, Md., with the 5th Marine Reserve Battalion. After being called to active duty in October 1940, GySgt. Kimball, now part of the newly formed 1st Provisional Marine Brigade, embarked with the division for Guantanamo Bay, Cuba. Later, the 1st Marine Division reported to the New River, N.C., Marine Barracks (later Camp Lejeune), which by this time was undergoing considerable growth. Living in a tent, GySgt. Kimball was assigned to the 1st Anti-Aircraft Machine Gun Battery .50-caliber water-cooled machine guns on tripods. With the division split into two elements, the 1st Marine Division sailed and entrained to San Francisco and embarked on the Swedish liner *John Ericsson*, and sailed for Wellington, New Zealand, in June 1942. After a brief period on New Zealand, Kimball and his fellow Marines headed for the first U.S. ground offensive of World War II on Guadalcanal. He remained on Guadalcanal with the 1st Marine Division until they were relieved by elements of the U.S. Army. Kimball, who did not leave Guadalcanal until January 10, 1943, spent a period in Finchaven, New Guinea, and later participated in the campaign on New Britain at Cape Gloucester. He returned to the United States in the summer of 1944 and reported to the Marine Barracks at 8th and I, where he remained until the summer of 1945. He volunteered for courier duty with the State Department and remained there until October 1945, when he was honorably discharged from the Marine Corps. Oral history interview with Gunnery Sergeant Robert E. Kimball, by Master Sergeant Leo J. Daugherty III, 23 September 2006, Silver Springs, Md., Side A, Part 1.

57. Kimball interview, Part 1, Side A.

58. Kimball interview, Part 1, Side B.

59. *Ibid.*

60. *Ibid.*

61. *Ibid.*

62. J.C. Holmes, Assistant Secretary of State, to Mr. Robert E. Kimball, 30 June 1945. Subject: "Per Diem and Travel Regulations." Copy in possession of the author from GySgt. Robert E. Kimball's original document.

63. Kimball Interview, Part 2, Side A.

64. *Ibid.*; See also Gunnery Sergeant Robert E. Kimball to the Commanding Officer, Marine Barracks Detachment, Washington, D.C., 21 August 1945, Subject: "Report of Courier Trip from New York to Natal, Brasil, via Lisbon, Portugal and Return." Copy in possession of the author.

65. Holmes to Kimball, 30 June 1945.

66. Known today as Guinea-Bissau.

67. Kimball interview, Part 2, Side A.

68. General Thomas Holcomb's and Colonel William A. Eddy's personal papers can be found at the Marine Corps University Archives, MCU, MCCDC, Quantico, Va. Colonel Eddy's papers contain a separate box of papers, documents and clippings on his career as a scholar and Marine officer.

Chapter 4

1. "Growth and Development of the Marine Security Guard Program: Highlights of the First Ten Years, 1947–1957," Marine Security Guard Historical File, 1947–1968, Marine Security Guard Battalion School, Marine Corps Combat Development Center, Quantico, Va., p. 1.

2. *Ibid.*

3. *Ibid.*

4. *Ibid.*

5. *Ibid.*, pp. 1–2.

6. Danny Crawford, "Chronology of Marines and the State Department," Washington, D.C., History and Museums Division, Headquarters Marine Corps, Marine Corps Historical Center, Reference Section, Marine Security Guard Folder, p. 4.

7. *Ibid.*, pp. 203.

8. This figure is in 1948 dollars. *Ibid.*, p. 3.

9. *Ibid.*, pp. 2–3. See also Under Secretary of State Robert Lovett letter to the Secretary of the Navy, 3 January 1949, Subject: "Memorandum of Agreement, Amendments To." Washington, D.C., History and Museums Division, Marine Corps Historical Center, Marine Security Guard Reference Folder, Historical Folder, p. 1.

10. *Ibid.*

11. U.S. Department of State, "Memorandum of Agreement Between the State Department and the Department of the Navy Pertaining to the Use of Marine Corps Personnel in Foreign Service Establishments," 16 December 1948, Washington, D.C., History and Museums Division, Marine Corps Historical Center, Marine Security Guard

Battalion Historical Folder 1947–1970, p. 2.

12. *Ibid.*, p. 7.
13. *Ibid.*, p. 8.
14. *Ibid.*, p. 12.
15. *Ibid.*, p. 8.
16. *Ibid.*
17. *Ibid.*, p. 9.
18. *Ibid.*, p. 10.
19. Warrant Officer–1 George Lampman, phone interview with author, 31 October 1998, Subject: "Marine Security Guard Program During the Korean War, 1949–1951."
20. "Growth and Development of the Marine Security Guard Program," pp. 4–5.
21. *Ibid.*, p. 5.
22. *Ibid.*
23. *Ibid.*, p. 6.
24. *Ibid.*
25. *Ibid.*, p. 8.
26. Master Sergeant George A. Bader letter to Leo J. Daugherty III, 15 October 1998, Subject: "Marine Security Guard Duty," in possession of author.
27. *Ibid.*, p. 7. See Commandant of the Marine Corps to Commanding Officer, Headquarters Battalion, U.S. Marine Corps, 28 September 1954, Subject: "Marine Security Guard School, Establishment of Training Syllabus," Quantico, Va., Marine Security Guard Bn. School, Historical Files, Folder 1947–1968.
28. *Ibid.*, p. 1.
29. *Ibid.*, p. 2.

Chapter 5

1. "Growth and Development of the Marine Security Guard Program: Highlights of the First Ten Years, 1947–1957," Marine Security Guard Historical File, 1947–1968, Marine Security Guard Battalion School, Marine Corps Combat Development Center, Quantico, Va., p. 4.
2. Warrant Officer–1 George Lampman, USMC (Ret)., "The Marine Security Section and Evacuation from Seoul," located in Korean War Binder, Marine Security Battalion, S-3A, Historical Collection, Quantico, Va., MSG Battalion, MCCDC, p. 1.
3. WO-1 George V. Lampman and LCDR Barry A. Zulauf, USN, "'Without So Much as a Bloody Nose:' The Evacuation of the American Embassy in Seoul, Korea," *Leatherneck*, June 2000, Vol. 83, No. 6, p. 16.
4. *Ibid.*, p. 17.
5. Sergeant Paul Dupras' comments in Lampman, "Marine Security Section and Evacuation from Seoul," 50th Anniversary Commemorative Binder, MSG Bn., MCCDC, Quantico, Va.
6. Lampman, "Marine Security Section and Evacuation from Seoul," p. 1.
7. Sergeant Glenn A. Green, com-ments in Lampman, "Marine Security Section and Evacuation From Seoul."
8. Lampman, "Marine Security Section and Evacuation From Seoul," p. 3; Lampman and Zulauf, "'Without So Much as a Bloody Nose,'" p. 19.
9. Bruce Cumings, *The Origins of the Korean War, Vol. II: The Roaring of the Cataract, 1947–1950* (Princeton, N.J.: Princeton University Press, 1990), p. 585.
10. Lampman and Zulauf, "'Without So Much as a Bloody Nose,'" p. 19.
11. Lampman, "Marine Security Section and Evacuation from Seoul," p. 5.
12. Lampman and Zulauf, "'Without So Much as a Bloody Nose,'" p. 20.
13. Sergeant Charles E. Goff, "Comments," 10 April 1999 in Lampman, "Marine Security Section and Evacuation from Seoul," p. 1.
14. Lampman and Zulauf, "'Without so Much as a Bloody Nose,'" p. 20.
15. Lampman, "Comment*s*," in "Marine Security Section and Evacuation from Seoul," pp. 8–9.
16. Sergeant Lloyd O. Henderson, "My Remembrance of 25–27 June 1950," in Lampman, "Marine Security Section and Evacuation from Seoul," p. 2.
17. Lampman, "Comments," p. 10; Lampman and Zulauf, "'Without so Much as a Bloody Nose,'" pp. 22–3.
18. Lampman, "Comments," p. 12.
19. Goff, "Comments," p. 2.
20. Technical Sergeant Jac Edwards, "Comments," 5 April 1999, in "Marine Security Section and Evacuation from Seoul," p. 6.
21. Master Sergeant George Bader letter to Leo J. Daugherty III, 15 October 1998, pp. 3–4.
22. Robert Jones Shafer, *A History of Latin America* (Lexington, Mass.: D.C. Heath, 1978), pp. 784–6; J. Fred Rippy, *Latin America: A Modern History* (Ann Arbor: University of Michigan Press, 1958), p. 440–2.
23. Shafer, *History of Latin America*, p. 785.
24. Sydney Nettleton Fisher, *The Middle East: A History*. Third Edition (New York: Alfred A. Knopf, 1979), pp. 723–4.
25. *Ibid.*
26. Sergeant Ronnell Harwood's comments to Richard@McLaughlin.net, Embassy Duty Adventures, Marine Security Guard Association MEGA Web Page, 24 September 1998, in possession of author.
27. *Ibid.*
28. This was the Thompson submachine gun. *Ibid.*, p. 1.
29. *Ibid.*
30. "Marine Security Guards in Life Threatening Situations," Washington, D.C., History and Museums Division, Marine Corps Historical Center, Reference Section, MSG Drawer, HQMC, nd., p. 1.
31. Fisher, *The Middle East*, p. 655.
32. Dr. (Captain) William D. Steeves, Jr., letter to Leo J. Daugherty III, 10 October 1998, in possession of author, p. 1.
33. *Ibid.*, p. 2.
34. *Ibid.*
35. Ed Vasgerdsian, "Cairo: An Old City, a Familiar Face, a New Outlook," *Leatherneck*, April 1999, Vol. 82, No. 4, pp. 22–8.
36. *Ibid.*, p. 25.
37. *Ibid.*
38. *Ibid.*, p. 3.
39. The political arrangement of 1926 (amended in 1943) in Lebanon divided the country along religious and ethnic lines of Maronite Christians who held the presidency, Sunni Moslems who held the premiership, and a Shiite Moslem as speaker of the parliament. See Fisher, *The Middle East*, pp. 628–30. Also see Jack Shulimson, *Marines in Lebanon 1958*, Washington, D.C., History and Museums Division, 1983, p. 2.
40. Steeves letter, p. 3.
41. Master Sergeant Rolland L. May letter to author, 20 October 1998, p. 2.
42. *Ibid.*, p. 2.
43. Tom Stevens letter to GySgt. Leo J. Daugherty III, 28 August 1999, p. 1.
44. *Ibid.*, p. 2.
45. "Marine Security Guards in Life-Threatening Situations," p. 1.
46. Staff Sergeant Lloyd E. Shank to Master Sergeant Earl J. Payne, American Embassy, Tegucigalpa, Honduras, Central America, 3 August 1956, Subject: "Detail Report of the Duty Stood on 31 July 1956 by Sergeant Shank at This Embassy," copy in possession of author, p. 1. Also Sergeant Shank to Leo J. Daugherty, letter dated 17 December 1998.
47. *Ibid.*, pp. 2–3.
48. Hon. John C. Pool, Chargéé d'Affaires, U.S. Embassy, Tegucigalpa, Honduras, to General Randolph McC. Pate, Commandant of the Marine Corps, HQMC, 13 August 1956. Copy in possession of the author, provided by Staff Sergeant Shank.
49. Honorable Geoffrey H.S. Jackson, British Minister to Honduras, British Legation, to the Hon. John C. Pool, U.S. Chargéé d'Affaires, U.S. Embassy, Tegucigalpa, Honduras, 2 August 1956. Copy in possession of the author, provided by Staff Sergeant Shank.
50. General Randolph McC. Pate, Commandant of the Marine Corps, to Staff Sergeant Lloyd E. Shank, F Company, HQMC, Washington, D.C, 12 September 1956. Subject: "Complimentary Letters." Copy in possession of the author, provided by Staff Sergeant Shank.
51. Master Sergeant W.V. "Bill" East letter to Leo J. Daugherty III, 11 February 2002, p. 1.
52. *Ibid.*

53. "ROK" refers to Republic of Korea.

54. For one of the best accounts of the South Korean coup see Peer de Silva, *Sub Rosa: The CIA and the Uses of Intelligence* (New York: New York Times Book Company, 1978), p. 176.

55. *Ibid.*, p. 177.

56. Master Sergeant Wiliam V. "Bill" East, letter to GySgt. Leo J. Daugherty, 3 January 1999.

57. Basil Dmytryshyn, *USSR: A Concise History*. Third Edition (New York: Charles Scribner's Sons, 1978), p. 295.

58. *Ibid.*, p. 301.

59. *Ibid.*, p. 302.

60. In a three-pronged assault British and French military forces attempted to seize the strategic Suez Canal from Egyptian leader Gamel Abdul Nasser, who had nationalized the international waterway while Israeli forces launched a surprise attack on Egyptian forces in Sinai Peninsula. President Dwight D. Eisenhower, who denounced the actions by Britain and France and had been in the middle of his re-election campaign in 1956, refused to send paratroopers to help the Hungarian freedom fighters. See Fisher, *Middle East: A History*, pp. 736–40.

61. Chief Warrant Officer Gary J. Bolick, "Hungarian Revolution of 1956: Observations and Comments," 2000, unpublished reminiscences, p. 1. Copy in possession of author. Original document, "Hungarian Revolution: 1956," is located in the S-3 Historical Collection, Drawer 2, Historical Files, Marine Security Guard Bn., MCCDC, Quantico, Va.

62. *Ibid.*, p. 2.

63. *Ibid.*, p. 3.

64. *Ibid.*

65. Sergeant Edward R. Parauka letter to Leo J. Daugherty III, 17 January 1999, pp. 2–3.

66. *Ibid.*, p. 4.

67. *Ibid.*, p. 5.

68. Bolick, "Hungarian Revolution of 1956," p. 4.

69. *Ibid.*, p. 5.

70. *Ibid.*

71. *Ibid.*, pp. 5–6. Today, in Berkeley Springs, West Virginia, a monument testifies to the bravery and sufferings of the Hungarian freedom fighters during the 1956 uprising. Constructed and dedicated by the Hungarian Freedom Fighters Federation on 6 October 1996, the memorial stands as a reminder that freedom from Soviet rule came to Hungary for a few days in 1956.

72. Along with Sergeant Owens, the other Marines at the U.S. Embassy in Brussels, Belgium, were Andrew Conrad, George E. Neito, Charles Dawson, Joseph Whalen, and Thomas Wittig. Unpublished manuscript by Sergeant William Owens, "Embassy Pioneers," October 1998, p. 5, in possession of author.

73. *Ibid.*, p. 5.

74. *Ibid.*, pp. 5–6.

75. *Ibid.*, p. 6.

76. *Ibid.*, p. 7.

77. Owens, "Embassy Pioneers," p. 8.

78. Joel Woldman, "Diplomatic Security: The Marine Security Guard Program at Missions Abroad," Congressional Research Service Report for Congress, No. 87-602 F, 8 July 1987, copy at Marine Security Guard Battalion, State Department, MCCDC, Quantico, Va., S-3, Historical Files, Drawer 4, Folder "1987 Congressional Hearings," p. 17; also in Thomas Palmer, "Where the U.S. Marines Went Wrong," *Boston Globe*, 12 April 1987, p. A-21.

79. Lieutenant Colonel William C. Curtis letter to GySgt. Leo J. Daugherty III, 28 October 1998.

80. *Ibid.*, p. 8.

81. The Burmese opposition group known as the AFPFL stands for "Anti-Fascist People's Freedom League."

82. "Anti-American Demonstration Leads to Ugly Riot, Precaution at U.S. Embassy," *The Guardian* (Rangoon), 22 February 1961, Vol. 5, No. 354. See Staff Sergeant J.H. Ward, Folder, "U.S. Marine Security Guard Detachment, Rangoon, Burma, Report on Military Takeover, 1961–1969," Marine Security Guard Battalion, S-3A, Historical Files, MCCDC, Quantico, Va.

83. Frank N. Trager, *Burma: From Kingdom to Republic: A Historical and Political Analysis* (New York: Frederick A. Praeger, 1966), pp. 195–6, 242–9.

84. "Precautions at U.S. Embassy," *The Guardian*, p. 1.

85. Sergeant George H. Morrow letter to Leo J. Daugherty III, nd., Subject: "American Consulate General, Stuttgart, West Germany." In possession of author, p. 1.

86. *Ibid.*, pp. 1–2.

87. Shank letter, 17 December 1998.

88. "An Old Team: Marines and the Foreign Service," 11 September 1956, Information Sheet, Washington, D.C., History and Museums Division, Marine Corps Historical Center, Reference Section, Marine Security Guard Folder "General History Folder 1948–1970," p. 9.

89. *Ibid.*

90. *Ibid.*, p. 5.

91. See "Civilian Clothing to be Furnished by the Department of State; Memorandum of Agreement— Amended 1955."

92. Mr. William O. Boswell, Director, Office of Security, U.S. Department of State, letter to Lieutenant Colonel Eugene H. Haffey, Commanding Officer, Company F, HQMC, Washington, D.C., 4 January 1962, attached to letter from Chief, Division of Physical Security, Office of Security, Department of State, Washington, D.C., 2 January 1962. Both letters can be found at Marine Security Guard Battalion, S-3 Historical Files, File "1947–1968," MSG Battalion, MCCDC, Quantico, Va., p. 2.

93. Colonel M.J. Dunbar, Commanding Officer, Company F, to Commanding Officer, Headquarters Battalion, HQMC, 30 October 1964, Subject: "Commanding Officer, Company F/Director, Marine Security Guard School: 'This is My Job.'" At Marine Security Guard Battalion, S-3 Historical Archives, Folder No. 1, Historical Folder, "1947 to 1968," MCCDC, Quantico, Va., pp. 1–2.

94. *Ibid.*, p. 2.

Chapter 6

1. Mr. Robert Acqualina of the Marine Corps Historical Section provided information on this landing. See Stanley Karnow, *Vietnam: A History* (New York: Penguin Books, 1984), p. 69; and Jack Hilliard and Richard Long, "The First Time," *Naval Institute Proceedings*, February 1969, Vol. 95, No. 2, Whole No. 792, pp. 147–9.

2. Elements of the 9th Marine Expeditionary Brigade landed on 8 May 1965 across the very same beaches at Da Nang that Percival's force did in 1845. See Hilliard and Long, "The First Time," p. 149.

3. Hon. Harris M. Cookingham's comments in Ronald H. Spector's *United States Army in Vietnam, Advice and Support: The Early Years, 1941–1960* (Washington, D.C., Center of Military History, U.S. Army, 1985), p. 7.

4. *Ibid.*, p. 96.

5. Peter Dunn, *The First Vietnam War* (New York: St. Martin's Press, 1985), p. 355.

6. Master Sergeant William V. "Bill" East letter to Leo J. Daugherty III, 11 February 2002.

7. *Ibid.*, pp. 2–3.

8. Sergeant Bob Bowen, "Post of the Corps: Saigon," *Leatherneck*, July 1966, Vol. 49, No. 7, p. 28.

9. Jack Shulimson, *U.S. Marines in Vietnam: The Landing and Buildup, 1965* (Washington, D.C.: History and Museums Division, HQMC, 1978), p. 211.

10. *Ibid.*, p. 28.

11. *Ibid.*, pp. 28–9.

12. Peer de Silva was the Central Intelligence Agency station chief. For his version of the attack see Peer de Silva, *Sub Rosa: The CIA and the Uses of Intelligence* (New York: Quadrangle Books, 1978), pp. 265–73.

13. See Ambassador Johnson's recollections in U. Alexis Johnson with Jef Olivarius McAllister, *The Right Hand of Power* (Englewood Cliffs, N.J.: Prentice-Hall, 1984), pp. 432–5.

14. *Ibid.*, p. 433.

15. *Ibid.*, pp. 433–4.

16. General William C. Westmoreland, *A Soldier Reports*. Second Printing (New York: Dell Publishing, 1980), p. 167.

17. De Silva, *Sub Rosa*, p. 266.

18. Shulimson, *U.S. Marines in Vietnam ... 1965*, p. 211.

19. Johnson, *Right Hand of Power*, p. 435.

20. Ambassador Maxwell Taylor to Secretary of State Dean Rusk, telegram dated 28 April 1965, in David C. Humphrey, Ronald D. Landa, Louis J. Smith, and Glenn W. LaFantasie, *Foreign Relations of the United States, 1964–1968; Vol. II: Vietnam, January–June 1965* (Washington, D.C.: United States Government Printing Office, 1996), pp. 612–13.

21. Shulimson, *U.S. Marines in Vietnam ... 1965*, p. 435.

22. Bowen, "Post of the Corps: Saigon," pp. 29–30.

23. *Ibid.*, p. 31.

24. *Ibid.*

25. *Ibid.*

26. East letter, p. 3.

27. *Ibid.*, pp. 32–3.

28. Shulimson, *U.S. Marines in Vietnam: An Expanding War, 1966* (Washington, D.C.: History and Museums Division, Headquarters, Marine Corps, 1982), p. 308.

29. Major Gary L. Telfer, Lieutenant Colonel Lane Rogers, and V. Keith Fleming, Jr., *U.S. Marines in Vietnam: Fighting the North Vietnamese, 1967* (Washington, D.C., History and Museums Division, Headquarters, U.S. Marine Corps, 1984), p. 244.

30. *Ibid.*

31. According to Lieutenant Colonel Philip E. Tucker, "A 1966 test of some of the world's available submachine guns resulted in the selection of the Beretta because of its accuracy, reliability, and light weight." The weapons tested included the older World War II–era Thompson submachine gun (.45-caliber), the Swedish K, the Israeli Uzi, and the Baretta. See Telfer, Rogers, and Fleming, *U.S. Marines in Vietnam ... 1967*, p. 244.

32. McGeorge Bundy to the President in "Memorandum from the President's Special Assistant for National Security Affairs (Bundy) to President Johnson," 23 March 1965, in Humphrey, et al., *Foreign Relations of the United States*, p. 470.

33. British Foreign Secretary Sir Michael Stewart and Ambassador Sir Michael Stewart were not related.

34. *Ibid.*, p. 471.

35. *Ibid.*

36. *Ibid.*

37. *Ibid.*

38. Jack Shulimson, Lieutenant Colonel Leonard A. Blaisol, Charles R. Smith, and Captain David L. Dawson, *U.S. Marines in Vietnam: The Defining Year, 1968* (Washington, D.C.: History

and Museums Division, HQMC, 1997), p. 642.

39. *Ibid.*

40. Sergeant Ronald W. Harper, "After Action Report (Enclosure 5)," in Captain Robert J. O'Brien, Officer in Charge, to Commanding Officer, Marine Security Guards, American Embassy, Saigon, Vietnam, to Commanding Officer, Marine Security Guard Battalion, State Department, Headquarters, U.S. Marine Corps, Henderson Hall, Arlington, Va., via Commanding Officer, Company C, Marine Security Guard Battalion, State Department, American Embassy, Manila, R.P. Subject: "Incident/Information/Occurrence Report, Number 1-68 Viet Cong Attack on American Embassy, 31 January 1968," 23 February 1968. Copy in possession of author; original can be found at Washington, D.C., History and Museums Division, Archives, Command Chronology, Marine Corps Historical Center, pp. 6–8.

41. Corporal George B. Zahuranic letter to Gunnery Sergeant Leo J. Daugherty III, 31 October 1998.

42. Shulimson, et al., *U.S. Marines in Vietnam ... 1968*, p. 643.

43. Sergeant Rudy A. Soto, "After Action Report, Enclosure (10)," in O'Brien, "After Action Report, Viet Cong Attack on American Embassy, 31 January 1968," pp. 1–3.

44. The original "Great Seal of the United States" taken from the Saigon Embassy is on display in the main display case at the entrance to Marshall Hall at Marine Corps Base, Quantico, Va.

45. *Ibid.*; O'Brien, "After Action Report, Viet Cong Attack on American Embassy, 31 January 1968," pp. 1–3.

46. *Ibid.*, pp. 2–3.

47. Shulimson, *U.S. Marines in Vietnam ... 1968*, p. 643.

48. Corporal James C. Marshall (1946–1968) enlisted in the Marine Corps in 1964. After he completed recruit training at Marine Corps Recruit Depot, Parris Island, South Carolina, in September 1964, the Marine Corps assigned him to the 2nd FSR as a basic supply administration and operations man. In February 1966, Corporal Marshall applied for and was accepted into the Marine Security Guard program. After completing the authorized training at Henderson Hall in April 1966, Corporal Marshall was assigned to his first and only posting at the U.S. Embassy, Saigon, Republic of Vietnam. During the fighting at the U.S. Embassy in Saigon, Corporal Marshall was killed in the early morning hours of 31 January 1968 as he held off and killed several Viet Cong attackers while atop the Norodom Compound. He was posthumously awarded a Bronze Star for his heroic actions during this engagement with the enemy. In June of 1980, the

newly constructed Marine Security Guard School Building at Marine Corps Base, Quantico, Va., was renamed in his honor in recognition of him being the first Marine Security Guard killed in action in defense of a U.S. embassy or consulate. See biographic information in "File of Corporal James C. Marshall, USMC, Dedication of Marshall Hall, June 1980," Marine Security Guard Battalion, State Department, MCCDC, Quantico, Va., S-3, Historical Files, Drawer 4, 1980.

49. O'Brien, "After Action Report, Viet Cong Attack on American Embassy, 31 January 1968," p. 5.

50. Colonel George Jacobsen was the mission coordinator for the U.S. Embassy in Saigon. *Ibid.*; Harper, "After Action Report, Enclosure 5," p. 5.

51. O'Brien, "After Action Report, The Viet Cong Attack on the U.S. Embassy, 31 January 1968," p. 5.

52. Shulimson, *U.S. Marines in Vietnam ... 1968*, pp. 642–4.

53. Dean Rusk, Address of Hon. Dean Rusk, Secretary of State, at the Marine Security Guard School graduation ceremony on 16 February 1968 in the Post Theater, Henderson Hall, Headquarters, U.S. Marine Corps, Arlington, Va., in Historical Files, Marine Security Guard Battalion, State Department, Quantico, Va., S-3, Drawer 4, Folder "1947–1968," pp. 3–6.

54. *Ibid.*, pp. 7–8.

55. C.J. Del Grosso, Commanding Officer, Marine Security Guard State Department Battalion, memorandum to Major General Carl E. Mundy, Jr., Director of Operations, Headquarters Marine Corps, 31 August 1987. Quantico, Va., Marine Security Guard Battalion, State Department, Historical Files, S-3, Drawer 3, Folder, "Marine Security Guard Issues, 1987."

56. Commandant of the Marine Corps General Leonard F. Chapman to G. Marvin Gentile, Deputy Assistant Secretary of State, letter, 1 October 1971, Headquarters United States Marine Corps, attached to Personal Security Unit Manual, U.S. Embassy, Saigon, RVN, Washington, D.C., U.S. Government Printing Office, Department of State, 1971, 27 pages, in Historical Files, Marine Security Guard Battalion, S-3, Drawer 3, Folder, "Personal Security Unit Manual, RVN."

57. Charles R. Smith, *United States Marines in Vietnam: High Mobility and Standdown, 1969* (Washington, D.C.: History and Museums Division, Headquarters Marine Corps, 1988), p. 318.

58. Graham A. Cosmas and Lieutenant Colonel Terence P. Murray, *U.S. Marines in Vietnam: Vietnamization and Redeployment, 1970–1971*. Washington, D.C., History and Museums Division, Headquarters Marine Corps, 1986, p. 390.

59. *Ibid.*

60. Cosmas and Murray, *U.S. Marines in Vietnam*, p. 390.

61. Lieutenant Colonel C. Fimian, Command Chronologies, 3d Military Police Battalion, Fleet Logistics Command, Fleet Marine Force, Pacific, 1–31 March 1971 (pp. 3–4), 5 April 1971, 1–31 May 1971 (2 June 1971), 1–30 June 1970 (3 July 1970), p. 3, and 1–31 August 1971, 23 August 1970 to 15 October 1970 (15 October 1970), all located at Washington D.C., History and Museums Division, Archives, Vietnam Records Collection, "1970," Headquarters Marine Corps, Marine Corps Historical Center, Washington Navy Yard.

62. *Ibid.*, pp. 390–1.

63. *Ibid.*, p. 391.

64. Major Charles D. Melson and Lieutenant Colonel Curtis G. Arnold, *U.S. Marines in Vietnam: The War That Would Not End, 1971–1973*. Washington, D.C., History and Museums Division, 1991, p. 10.

65. *Ibid.*

66. According to Colonel Boyette S. Hasty, who was NCOI of the Can Tho Detachment during the fall of Saigon, there were "3 Marine Houses. These included Marshall Hall, which housed the Interior Guard of whom all were Marine Security Guards; the Exterior Guards' Marine House; and the Personal Security Unit (PSU) located at the Ambassador's residence." Colonel Hasty added that the exterior guards were Marine infantrymen or "grunts" assigned to this duty. None of them were school-trained Marine Security Guards. Comments by Colonel Boyette S. Hasty, on Chapter VI of the draft of this book, September 2002.

67. *Ibid.*, pp. 10–11.

68. *Ibid.*

69. *Ibid.*

70. Karnow, *Vietnam: A History*, pp. 603–4.

71. Major George R. Dunham and Colonel David A. Quinlan, *U.S. Marines in Vietnam: The Bitter End, 1973–1975* (Washington, D.C.: History and Museums Division, HQMC, 1990), p. 5.

72. *Ibid.*, pp. 38–9.

73. This occurred on 20 May 1974.

74. Dunham and Quinlan, *U.S. Marines in Vietnam ... 1973–1975*, p. 39.

75. Ambassador Graham Martin, U.S. Embassy, Saigon, Republic of Vietnam, to Commanding Officer, Company E, Marine Security Guard Battalion, State Department, 20 May 1974. S-3 Operations, Drawer 4, "Awards and Letters of Appreciation Folder," Historical Files, Marine Security Guard Battalion, State Department, S-3 Archives, MCCDC, Quantico, Va.

76. *Ibid.*; "Facts Concerning Relocation of Company E from Saigon, Vietnam, to Addis Ababa, Ethiopia," nd., Document No. 26, Drawer 4, S-3 Historical Archives, Marine Corps Security Guard Bn., State Department, MCCDC, Quantico, Va., p. 1.; also Colonel C.J. Del Grosso, Commanding Officer, Marine Security Guard Battalion, to Major General Carl E. Mundy, Jr., Director of Operations, Headquarters Marine Corps, via Colonel J. Lloyd, 31 August 1987, Subject: "Expansion to the MSG Program Organization Structure: An Exploratory Overview," pp. 1–3. Copy in Drawer 4, Folder labeled "1987: Marine Security Guard Issues," Historical Files, S-3 Archives, Marine Security Guard Bn., State Department, MCCDC, Quantico, Va.

77. Dunham and Quinlan, *U.S. Marines in Vietnam: 1973–1975*, p. 39.

78. *Ibid.*; Captain James H. Kean was a major-selectee at the time.

79. Staff Sergeant (later Colonel) Hasty would later be commissioned and assume command of the Marine Security Guard Battalion at Quantico, Va. (2001–2003). Prior to his arrival at Can Tho, Colonel Hasty served as a Marine Security Guard from March 1972 through July 1973 at the U.S. Embassy in Saigon before transferring to the U.S. Embassy in Bangkok, Thailand. Hasty, manuscript comments, p. 284.

80. *Ibid.*, p. 38.

81. Colonel Sydney H. Batchelder, Jr., and Major D.A. Quinlan, "Operation Eagle Pull," in Brigadier General Edwin H. Simmons, et al., *The Marines in Vietnam, 1954–1973: An Anthology and Annotated Bibliography*. Second Edition (Washington, D.C.: History and Museums Division, HQMC, 1985), pp. 203–4. Also see Dunham and Quinlan, *U.S. Marines in Vietnam ... 1973–1975*. (Washington, D.C., History and Museums Division, HQMC, 1990), pp. 40–66.

82. Batchelder and Quinlan, "Operation Eagle Pull," p. 206.

83. *Ibid.*

84. As the official history of Operation *Eagle Pull* recounted, "On 15 April 1975, Major General Michel P. Ryan, III MAF commander, ordered the 31st MAU to provide the reinforced rifle company from its ground combat element, 1st Battalion, 4th Marines. A standing III MAF operation order directed the 31st MAU to develop very specific guidance as to the organization of the reinforced rifle company. It directed that besides a headquarters detachment, the command element would include medical and communications elements, a flamethrower section, an 81mm mortar section, and a 106mm recoilless rifle section. The rifle company would also be supported by a sizeable logistics support element. The complexity of the reinforced rifle company meant that more than just a routine mission was expected for this evacuation." See Dunham and Quinlan, *U.S. Marines in Vietnam ... 1973–1975*, pp. 55–6.

85. Batchelder and Quinlan, "Operation Eagle Pull," pp. 208–9.

86. *Ibid.*, p. 209.

87. Gerald R. Ford had been appointed vice president by President Richard M. Nixon on 6 December 1973 in response to the resignation of Spiro T. Agnew in early October 1973. When President Nixon resigned in August 1974 due to the Watergate scandal, Ford became president. See Richard Nixon, *RN: The Memoirs of Richard Nixon* (New York: Grosset and Dunlap, 1978), pp. 924–7; Gerald R. Ford, *A Time to Heal: The Autobiography of Gerald R. Ford* (New York: Harper and Row, 1979), pp. 100–18.

88. Captain Larry R. Zinser, "The BLT in Evacuation Operations," *Marine Corps Gazette*, December 1973, Vol. 57, No. 12, pp. 23–30; Major W. Hay Parks, "Evacuation by Military Force," *Marine Corps Gazette*, September 1978, Vol. 62, No. 9, pp. 24–33.

89. See oral history transcript of Staff Sergeant Thomas J. Sabanski, "It Was a Good Career," 7 March 1988, pp. 72–3. Interview done at Camp Joseph H. Pendleton, Calif. Manuscript in possession of the author.

90. Ford, *Time to Heal*.

91. Sabanski, oral history.

92. *Ibid.*, pp. 73–4.

93. Ford, *Time to Heal*, pp. 255–6; *U.S. Marines in Vietnam ... 1973–1975*, pp. 119–21.

94. Dunham and Quinlan, *U.S. Marines in Vietnam ... 1973–1975*, p. 143.

95. These included An Loc, which fell on 18 March; Quang Tri City and Province on 19 March; Quang Ngai and Tam Ky on 24 March; Hue and Hoi An on 26 March; Chu Lai on 27 March; and finally Da Nang itself on 29 March 1975. See Brigadier General Richard F. Carey and Major D.A. Quinlan, "Frequent Wind: Organization and Assembly," in Brigadier General Edwin H. Simmons, et al., *The Marines in Vietnam, 1954–1973: An Anthology and Annotated Bibliography* (Washington, D.C.: History and Museums Division, HQMC, 1985), pp. 218–19.

96. Dunham and Quinlan, *U.S. Marines in Vietnam ... 1973–1975*, p. 127.

97. One of the best histories written on the evacuation from South Vietnam during the last months of the Vietnam War can be found in Lieutenant Colonel A.J.C. LaValle, USAF, et al., *Last Flight From Saigon*. U.S. Air Force, Southeast Asia Monograph Series, Vol. 4, No. 6 (Washington, D.C.: Government Printing Office, 1978), pp. 17–19.

98. Dunham and Quinlan, *U.S. Marines in Vietnam ... 1973–1975*, p. 127.

99. *Ibid.*

100. *Ibid.*

101. *Ibid.*

102. *Ibid.*, pp. 127–8.

103. *Ibid.*, p. 128.

104. *Ibid.*

105. *Ibid.*, pp. 128–9.

106. *Ibid.*, p. 129.

107. Dunham and Quinlan, *U.S. Marines in Vietnam … 1973–1975*, p. 88.

108. *Ibid.*, p. 89.

109. *Ibid.*, p. 88.

110. The Marine Security Guard Detachment at Nha Trang also consisted of Sergeant M.A. McCormick, and Corporals R. L. Anderson, L. L. Brown, J. D. Sneed, and J. G. Moya. See Master Sergeant Juan J. Valdez, "The Last to Leave," *Leatherneck*, September 1975, Vol. 58, No. 9, p. 42.

111. Dunham and Quinlan, *U.S. Marines in Vietnam … 1973–1975*, p. 148.

112. *Ibid.*, p. 149–50.

113. Carey and Quinlan, "Frequent Wind: Organization and Assembly," p. 225.

114. Dunham and Quinlan, *U.S. Marines in Vietnam … 1973–1975*, p. 173.

115. Besides Staff Sergeant Hasty, the other Marines at Can Tho included Sergeants J.S. Moore, T. D. Pate, and J.W. Kirchner, and Corporals L.J. Johnson and L.B. Killens. See Valdez, "The Last to Leave," p. 42.

116. "Statement of Sergeant John S. Moore, USMC," Marine Security Guard Detachment, American Consulate General, Can Tho, Vietnam, 13 April 1975. Statement attached to Noncommissioned Officer in Charge to Commanding Officer, Marine Security Guard Battalion, State Department, HQMC, Henderson Hall, Arlington, Va., via Commanding Officer, Company C, Marine Se[RTF bookmark start: }Editing[RTF bookmark end: }Editingcurity Guard Battalion, State Department, American Consulate General, Hong Kong, BCC, Box 30, FPO, San Francisco, Calif., 15 April 1975, Subject: "Marine Security Guard Major Incident Report 1-75." Historical Files, Drawer 4, Folder, "1975: Saigon Reports, etc.," S-3, Marine Security Guard Battalion, State Department, MCCDC, Quantico, Va.

117. Staff Sergeant Boyette S. Hasty, from Noncommissioned Officer in Charge to Commanding Officer, Marine Security Guard Battalion, State Department, Headquarters Marine Corps, Henderson Hall, Arlington, Va., via Company C, Marine Security Guard Battalion, State Department, American Consulate General, Hong Kong, BCC, FPO San Francisco, Calif., MSG Bn. Historical Files, S-3, Drawer 4, Folder "1975: Saigon Evacuation Reports," MCCDC, Quantico, Va.

118. According to Colonel Hasty, "This was a purely CIA operation done without the knowledge or approval of the Consul General." Hasty, comments on manuscript, p. 315.

119. Sergeant John Moore, Marine Security Guard, Can Tho, RVN, to Mr. Francis T. McNamara, Consul General, 4 May 1975, Subject: "Evacuation of Can Tho by Congen Staff," Marine Security Guard Bn., State Department, S-3, Historical Files, Drawer 4, Folder "1975: Saigon Evacuation Reports," MCCDC, Quantico, Va., p. 1.

120. Colonel Hasty commented that he had married a Vietnamese woman on April 21 and had been able to evacuate her through Thon Son Nhut. This was, as he wrote, "the only way to save her and her family." Hasty manuscript comments, p. 316.

121. Lance Corporal Lawrence B. Killens, Marine Security Guard, Can Tho, Vietnam, to Mr. Francis Terry McNamara, Consul General, 29 April 1975, Marine Security Guard Battalion, State Department, S-3 Historical Files, Drawer 4, Folder, "1975: Saigon Evacuation Reports," MCCDC, Quantico, Va.

122. *Ibid.*, p. 2.

123. Sergeant John W. Kirchner, Marine Security Guard, U.S. Consulate, Can Tho, RVN, to Mr. Francis T. McNamara, Consul General, Can Tho, 4 May 1975, Subject: "Evacuation of Can Tho, RCV by Consul General Staff," Marine Security Guard Battalion, State Department, Historical Files, S-3, Drawer 4, Folder: "1975: Saigon Evacuation Reports," MCCDC, Quantico, Va., p. 2.

124. Staff Sergeant Boyette S. Hasty to Consul General, 1 May 1975, Subject: "Evacuation of Consulate General, Can Tho, Vietnam," Marine Security Guard Battalion, State Department, S-3 Historical Files, Drawer 4, Folder "1975: Saigon Evacuation Reports," p. 3.

125. *Ibid.*

126. Hasty, manuscript comments, p. 318.

127. Staff Sergeant Hasty recalled that this was the first cold drink the Marines had had in three days. Hasty, "Evacuation of Consulate General, Can Tho, Vietnam," p. 5.

128. For an excellent account of the evacuation from Can Tho from the State Department's point of view see Francis Terry McNamara with Adrian Hill, *Escape With Honor: My Last Hours in Vietnam* (Washington, D.C., Brassey's, 1997), pp. 75–6.

129. *Ibid.*, p. 194.

130. Staff Sergeant Sabanski oral history, p. 78.

131. Carey and Quinlan, "Frequent Wind: Organization and Assembly," p. 239.

132. Dunham and Quinlan, *U.S. Marines in Vietnam … 1973–1975*, p. 191.

133. Sergeant Potratz commented that the bodies were eventually recovered by Senator Edward A. Kennedy (D-Mass.) from the North Vietnamese. Sergeant (Warrant Officer) Doug Potratz, e-mail to Captain J.P. Valencia, 27 March 2000, Subject: "Judge Memorial," Historical Files, S-3, Drawer 4, Subject Folder, "1975: Saigon Evacuation Reports," p. 1. Marine Security Guard Battalion, State Department, MCCDC, Quantico, Va.

134. Major Guilmartin's comments in Dunham and Quinlan, *U.S. Marines in Vietnam … 1973–1975*, p. 194.

135. Arnold R. Isaacs, *Without Honor: Defeat in Vietnam and Cambodia* (Baltimore, Md.: Johns Hopkins University Press, 1983), pp. 448–9.

136. Carey and Quinlan, "Frequent Wind: Organization and Assembly," p. 236.

137. Dunham and Quinlan, *U.S. Marines in Vietnam … 1973–1975*, pp. 195–6.

138. Staff Sergeant Colin Broussard, who would carry the flag and Great Seal of the United States on him in a helicopter, had to literally pick up the ambassador out of his desk chair and escort him to the roof of the embassy. The flag carried by SSgt. Broussard is now in a glass case at Marshall Hall, MSG Bn., at Quantico. See Isaacs, *Without Honor*, pp. 474–5; and Dunham and Quinlan, *U.S. Marines in Vietnam … 1973–1975*, pp. 200–1.

139. Report of Staff Sergeant Colin D. Broussard to Major Jim Kean, Commanding Officer, Company C, Marine Security Guard Battalion, State Department, 20 May 1975, Subject: "Your Request for My After Action Report of 29 April 1975," S-3, Historical Files, Drawer 4, Subject Folder, "1975: Saigon Evacuation Reports," Marine Security Guard Battalion, State Department, MCCDC, Quantico, Va.

140. Dr. Kissinger had passed the word that no more South Vietnamese were to be evacuated from Saigon.

141. Dunham and Quinlan, *U.S. Marines in Vietnam … 1973–1975*, pp. 200–1; See Colonel John H. Madison, Jr., memorandum for Dr. Roger E. Shields, OASD-ISA (POW/MIA Affairs), U.S. Delegation Four Party Joint Military Team, 5 May 1975, Subject: "USDEL FPJMT Withdrawal from RVN," S-3, Historical Files, Drawer 4, Folder, "1975: The Evacuation From Saigon," Marine Security Guard Bn., State Department, MCCDC, Quantico, Va., pp. 10–11.

142. Valdez, "The Last to Leave," p. 41.

143. *Ibid.*

144. Major Jim Kean, Commanding Officer, Company C, Marine Security Guard Battalion, to Commanding Officer, Marine Security Guard Battalion, 14 May 1975, Subject: "Addendum

to Command Chronology Special Report from CO Company C dated May 8, 1975," S-3, Historical Files, Drawer 4, Subject Folder, "Saigon Evacuation Reports," MCCDC, Quantico, Va., pp. 1–2.

145. *Ibid.*, p. 1.

146. Carey and Quinlan, "Frequent Wind: Organization and Assembly," p. 239.

147. Sergeant E.L. Wagner, NCOIC, Vientiane, Laos, MSG Detachment, to Commanding Officer, Company C, 31 July 1975, Subject: "After Action Report of Takeover of USAID Compound, Vientiane, Laos," in Marine Security Guard Battalion, State Department, S-3, Historical Files, Subject Folder: "1975: Saigon Evacuation Reports," pp. 3–6.

148. *Ibid.*, pp. 6–7.

Chapter 7

1. David N. Gibbs, *The Political Economy of Third World Intervention: Mines, Money, and U.S. Policy in the Congo Crisis* (Chicago: University of Chicago Press, 1991), p. 95.

2. Leopoldsville is now called Kinshasa.

3. For background on the Congo Crisis and U.S. response see Ms. Elizabeth Anne Weber, "Changing With the Times: Afro-American Response to the United States' Congo Policy, 1960–1963," master's thesis, Ohio State University, Columbus, Ohio, 1991, pp. 21–5.

4. Shortly after President Kennedy entered office, Cuban exiles living in Miami and in Central America launched an abortive *coup d'état*, planned in the last few months of the Eisenhower administration, against Cuban leader Fidel Castro. The coup, known as the Bay of Pigs Affair, was a disaster from the outset. The attackers were defeated as they landed in Cuba by Castro's forces while the promised U.S. military support never materialized.

5. U.S. Department of State, Statement on the Situation in the Congo, U.S. Department of State Press Release No. 888, 17 December 1961, U.S. Department of State Bulletin, Vol. 46, No. 1175, Publication 7319, Washington, D.C., Government Printing Office, 1 January 1962, p. 11.

6. Weber, "Changing With the Times," pp. 69–70. For a full account of the violence and negotiations to end the fighting see Ambassador Edmund A. Gullion to Department of State, telegram, dated December 19, 1961, DOS, Central Files, 7706.00/12-1961, Confidential (Declassified), as reprinted in Harriet Dashnell Schwar, et al., *Foreign Relations of the United States: 1961–1963, Vol. XX: Congo Crisis* (Washington, D.C.: Government Printing Office, 1994), pp. 329–30.

7. Formerly a British colony, Rhodesia was named after Cecil J. Rhodes, a British explorer and entrepreneur in Africa at the turn of the 20th century. The country today is known as Zimbabwe.

8. E-mail from Larry A. Bell to GySgt. Leo J. Daugherty, 29 September 2003, Subject: "More Information on a Congo Incident," in possession of the author. For an excellent account of MSG Detachment in Leopoldsville during this period see Larry A. Bell, *Dead Horses in the Sun* (Bloomington, Ind.: 1st Books Library, 2003), pp. 18–64.

9. For an excellent account of the 1964 *coup d'état* in the Congo see Major Thomas P. Odom, U.S. Army, *Dragon Operations: Hostage Rescue in the Congo, 1964–1965*, Leavenworth Papers, No. 14. Fort Leavenworth, Kan., U.S. Army Command and General Staff College, 1988, pp. 17–23.

10. *Ibid.*, p. 145.

11. Bell, *Dead Horses in the Sun*, p. 22.

12. *Ibid.*, pp. 22–3.

13. *Ibid.*, pp. 31–2.

14. *Ibid.*, pp. 33–45.

15. *Ibid.*, p. 46.

16. *Ibid.*, p. 48. Corporal Bell listed his real name as Victor Hedgeman, a veteran intelligence officer who had served in the Army during World War II.

17. *Ibid.*, pp. 48–52.

18. *Ibid.*, p. 64.

19. See Vice President Hubert H. Humphrey's report to President Johnson in "The Vice President's Trip to Africa, 30 December 1967–January 11, 1968," U.S. Department of State Central Files POL 7 US/Humphrey/Secret (Declassified), in Nina-Davis Howland et al., *Foreign Relations of the United States: 1964–1968, Vol. 24: Africa* (Washington, D.C.: Government Printing Office, 1999), p. 394.

20. *Ibid.*, p. 394.

21. Howard J. Wiarda and Michael J. Kryzanek, *The Dominican Republic: A Caribbean Crucible* (Boulder, Colo.: Westview Press, 1982), pp. 92–3. For an excellent analysis of the military operations by the U.S. Marines see Major Jack K. Ringler and Henry I. Shaw, Jr., *U.S. Marine Corps Operations in the Dominican Republic, April–June 1965* (Washington, D.C.: History and Museums Division, HQMC, 1970; Reprinted in 1992 as an Occasional Paper), pp. 5–7.

22. Ringler and Shaw, *U.S. Marine Corps Operations in the Dominican Republic*, p. 5.

23. *Ibid.*, p. 5.

24. *Ibid.*; Wiarda and Kryzanek, *The Dominican Republic*, p. 92.

25. Lawrence A. Yates, *Power Pack: U.S. Intervention in the Dominican Republic, 1965–1966* (Fort Leavenworth, Kan.: Combat Studies Institute, Command and General Staff College, 1988), pp. 34–5.

26. The ambassador, William Tapley Bennett, had been on leave in Georgia visiting his sick mother. Yates, *Power Pack*, p. 24.

27. *Ibid.*, p. 37.

28. Major General R. McC. Tompkins' "Ubique," *Marine Corps Gazette*, September 1965, Vol. 49, No. 9, pp. 32–9. Also, "Tables of Organization–965," MSG Company F, Folder 3, S-3, Historical Files, Drawer 4, "Tables of Organization — USMC T/O No. 5152," Marine Security Guard Battalion, State Department, MCCDC, Quantico, Va., p. 13.

29. Lieutenant General William K. Jones, *A Brief History of the 6th Marines* (Washington, D.C.: History and Museums Division, HQMC, 1987), pp. 133–4.

30. Ringler and Shaw, *U.S. Marine Corps Operations in the Dominican Republic*, p. 17.

31. *Ibid.*

32. Jones, *A Brief History of the 6th Marines*, p. 134.

33. Ringler and Shaw, *U.S. Marine Corps Operations in the Dominican Republic*, pp. 16–17.

34. *Ibid.*, pp. 18–19.

35. Tompkins, "Ubique," p. 35.

36. Ringler and Shaw, *U.S. Marine Corps Operations in the Dominican Republic*, p. 19.

37. Tompkins, "Ubique," p. 35.

38. Second Lieutenant Phil Tucker, "Embassy Beachhead," as told to Gunnery Sergeant Paul A. Berger, *Leatherneck*, August 1965, Vol. 46, No. 8, pp. 68–9. Nancy Lee Hoffman, deputy editor of *Leatherneck*, assisted in providing this account. Permission has been given to reprint whole portions of the interview.

39. *Ibid.*, p. 68.

40. *Ibid.*, p. 69.

41. *Ibid.*

42. *Ibid.*

43. Jones, *A Brief History of the 6th Marines*, pp. 134–5; Major Lawrence M. Greenberg, *United States Army Unilateral and Coalition Operations in the 1965 Dominican Republic Intervention* (Washington, D.C.: U.S. Army Center for Military History, 1987), pp. 24, 38–40.

44. Jones, *Brief History of the 6th Marines*, p. 135.

45. *Ibid.*, p. 136.

46. James S. Santelli, *A Brief History of the 8th Marines* (Washington, D.C.: History and Museums Division, HQMC, 1976), pp. 78–80.

47. Secretary of the Navy Paul H. Nitze, "Navy Unit Commendation Citation," Dominican Republic, 26–30 April 1965, S-3 Archives, Rm. 225, Historical Files, Drawer 2, Marine Security Guard Battalion, State Department, MCCDC, Quantico, Va., p. II-3-49.

48. Dayton Mak and Charles Stuart

Kennedy, *American Ambassadors in a Troubled World: Interviews with Senior Diplomats* (Westport, Conn.: Greenwood Press, 1992), pp. 120–1.

49. Sergeant Major Oates, "Reminiscences of a Marine Security Guard in Libya," June 1999, in possession of author.

50. Interview of SSgt. Thomas Okeson, with MSgt. Leo J. Daugherty III at the MCU Gray Research Center, 26 June 2006. Interview in possession of the author. Special Security Detail 1, U.S. Marines Sworn in as Special Agents of the Office of Protective Security, Office of Security, U.S. Department of State, Washington, D.C., June 1966 through September 1967, in possession of author.

51. *Ibid.*

52. MSgt. Michael Keller, interview by MSgt. Leo J. Daugherty III, Gray Research Center, MCCDC, Quantico, Va., 26 June 2006.

53. Interviews of GySgt. Jeptha Turner, GySgt. Ed Robbs, SSgt. Virgil Melton, and GySgt. Ron Trottier by MSgt. Leo J. Daugherty III, 27 June 2006, Crossroads, MCCDC, Quantico, Va.

54. Interview of Special Agent Richard Heckman, Office of Protective Security, U.S. Department of State, conducted at the Crossroads, MCCDC, Quantico, Va., 28 June 2006. Interview in possession of the author.

55. Keller interview.

56. Tim Niblock, "The Foreign Policy of Libya," in Raymond Hinnebusch and Anoushiravan Ehteshami, *The Foreign Policies of Middle East States* (Boulder, Colo.: Lynne Reinner, 2002), pp. 222–3.

57. Commanding Officer, Company E, "Command Chronology, for the period 1 January–30 June 1970," 15 July 1970, Marine Security Guard Bn., State Department, S-3 Historical Archives, Binder 1, Drawer 3, "Command Chronologies," p. 4.

58. "Citation from Meritorious Unit Commendation, Marine Security Guard Detachment, Aden, Southern Yemen," nd., S-3 Historical Archives, Drawer 3, Folder 9, "Meritorious Unit Citations and Supporting Documentation," Marine Security Guard Battalion, State Department, MCCDC, Quantico, Va.

59. George Lenczowski, *The Middle East in World Affairs*. Fourth Edition (New York: Cornell University Press, 1980), pp. 494–5.

60. "Command Chronology, 1 January–30 June 1970," 15 July 1970, p. 4.

61. Secretary of the Navy John H. Chafee, "Citation for Meritorious Unit Commendation to Marine Security Guard Detachment, Amman, Jordan," S-3 Historical Archives, Drawer 3, Folder 9, "Meritorious Unit Citations and Supporting Documentation," Marine Security Guard Battalion, MCCDC, Quantico, Va.

62. Ralph E. Pierce, Letters to the Editor, "MSG Jerusalem, 1969–1971," *Leatherneck*, February 2004, Vol. 87, No. 2, pp. 56–8.

63. Commanding Officer, Company B, Marine Security Guard Battalion, Karachi, Pakistan, to Commanding Officer, Marine Security Guard Battalion, for the period 1 July–31 December 1978, 8 January 1979, S-3 Historical Archives, Marine Security Guard Battalion, State Department, MCCDC, Quantico, Va., Drawer 3, "Command Chronology: 1978," p. 1.

64. General Robert E. Cushman, Commandant of the Marine Corps, "Citation for Meritorious Unit Commendation to MSG Detachment, American Embassy, Khartoum, Sudan," S-3 Historical Archives, Drawer 3, Folder 9, "Meritorious Unit Citations and Supporting Documentation," Marine Security Guard Battalion, State Department, MCCDC, Quantico, Va.

65. *Ibid.*

66. See comments of Ambassador Jack Bloom Kubisch in Mak and Kennedy's *American Ambassadors in a Troubled World*, pp. 156–7.

67. Walter Laqueur, *Europe Since Hitler: The Rebirth of Europe*. Revised edition (New York: Penguin Books, 1982), pp. 489–90.

68. Department of Defense, *Terrorist Group Profiles* (Washington, D.C.: Government Printing Office, November 1988), pp. 71–2.

69. The last U.S. ambassador, Philip J. Talbot, resigned immediately after the election of Richard M. Nixon in November 1968. The ambassador's post had been vacant since January 1969. As a sign of displeasure with the military junta's suspension of basic civil liberties, President Nixon refused to immediately appoint a U.S. ambassador to Greece.

70. Al Verrier, a former Marine, provided the background on Mr. Frank Durfey, the regional security officer in Athens during this time. "Envoy Arrives to Fill Athens Post After Year," *New York Times*, 10 January 1970; Department of State Telegram, Athens, Action, NEA-15, 5 January 70, 1545 (3:45 p.m.), American Embassy, Athens to Secretary of State, Immediate #8848, Athens, Greece File, 30, 1-5-70, Subject File POL 23-8 "Greece." National Archives, College Park, Md., p. 1.

71. Staff Sergeant Johnnie P. Hirst, NCOIC, Marine Security Guard Detachment, American Embassy, Athens, Greece, to Commanding Officer, Marine Security Guard Battalion, HQMC, Henderson Hall, Arlington, Va., Special Incident Report Number 1-70, 15 September 1970, Marine Security Guard Battalion, S-3, Historical Archives, Rm. 225, Folder "Command Chronologies 1970–1975," Drawer 3, MCCDC, Quantico, Va., p. 1.

72. *Ibid.*, pp. 2–3.

73. Henry Kissinger, *Years of Upheaval* (Boston: Little, Brown, 1982), pp. 1188–9. Also see Mak and Kennedy, *American Ambassadors*, pp. 141–57.

74. *Ibid.*, p. 1189.

75. Lieutenant Colonel Joseph L. Allred, U.S. Army (Ret.), "The Impact on U.S. Military Organizations in Turkey as a Result of the 1974 Turkish-Greece Conflict over Cyprus," typed manuscript in possession of the author, pp. 1–2.

76. As Dr. Kissinger wrote, the population at the time on Cyprus was 80 percent ethnic Greek and 20 percent of Turkish descent. Kissinger, *Years of Upheaval*, pp. 1189–90.

77. *Ibid.*, p. 1190.

78. Allred, "The Impact on U.S. Military Organizations in Turkey," p. 2.

79. According to Lance Corporal Lynn, "Enosist" refers to one who is in favor of a "union with Greece." Lance Corporal Robert A. Lynn to GySgt. Leo J. Daugherty, a 7-page handwritten, untitled account of the Turkish invasion of Cyprus as seen by a Marine Security Guard, and accompanying letter to author, 1 February 1999, p. 2. Letter and account in possession of author.

80. *Ibid.*, p. 4; Kissinger, *Years of Upheaval*, p. 1191.

81. Lance Corporal Robert A. Lynn account, pp. 4–6.

82. Major W. Hays Parks, "Evacuation by Military Force," *Marine Corps Gazette*, September 1978, Vol. 62, No. 9, pp. 28–9.

83. Lance Corporal Robert A. Lynn account, pp. 6–7.

84. Secretary of the Navy, "Meritorious Unit Commendation to Marine Security Guard Detachment, Nicosia, Cyprus," Marine Security Guard Battalion, State Department, S-3, Historical Archives, Drawer 3, Folder, "Unit Citations and Awards," p. 1.

85. "President Ford and Secretary Kissinger Lead Mourners at Davies Ceremony," *Department of State Newsletter*, September 1974, No. 160, p. 3.

86. "Text of Secretary Kissinger's Remarks," *Ibid.*

87. Mak and Kennedy, *American Ambassadors in A Troubled World*, pp. 156–7.

88. *Ibid.*, p. 157.

89. "State Lauds Athens MSGs," Marine Security Guard Battalion Information Bulletin, 1 May 1975, S-3, Archives, Drawer 4, Marine Security Guard Battalion, State Department, MCCDC, Quantico, Va., Folder, "1975 Historical Documents," p. 6.

90. *Ibid.*

91. Message, Foreign Broadcast Information Service to FBIS, Washington, D.C., via Department of State, Washington, D.C., 4 October 1975, Subject: "NEA Attacks Security Measures Outside U.S. Embassy, Nicosia, Cyprus," in S-3 Archives, Marine Security Guard

Battalion, State Department, MCCDC, Quantico, Va., Drawer 4, Folder "1975 Saigon Evac Reports." MSG Bn., Bulletins "Msg. From U.S. Embassy in Nicosia, Cyprus, Pictures of U.S. Embassy Guards in Nicosia, Cyprus, AGHON," p. 1.

92. Lieutenant Colonel Allred recalled that as late as 1976, "there was an obvious feeling of concern by both the Turkish people and Turkish military that their long-standing support of America's defense was not being reciprocated by support to Turkey over Cyprus. They felt that this was a double standard and that one day the US would ask for help from Turkey and Turkey would not be there." Allred, "The Impact on U.S. Military Organizations in Turkey," p. 4.

93. Robert A. Creedon, NCOIC, Marine Security Guard Detachment, U.S. Embassy, New Delhi, to Commanding Officer, Marine Security Guard Battalion, State Department, HQMC, Henderson Hall, Arlington, Va., 14 July 1971, Subject: "Special Incident Report, 2-71," S-3 Historical Archives, Drawer 4, Folder "1947–1968," MCCDC, Quantico, Va., p. 1.

94. "Kissinger Gets Noisy Welcome," *The Times of India* (New Delhi), 7 July 1971, Vol. 133, No. 187. Copy found in S-3 Archives, Drawer 4, Historical Folder, Marine Security Guard Bn., State Department, MCCDC, Quantico, Va., Folder "Awards and Policy Documents."

95. "BlackFlags Greet Kissinger," *The Statesman*, (New) Delhi, July 7, 1971, Late City Edition, in S-3 Historical Archives, Drawer 4, Folder "Awards and Policy Documents," Marine Security Guard Bn., State Department, MCCDC, Quantico, Va.

96. *Ibid.*; "Kissinger Gets Noisy Welcome," p. 13. Also see "Red Flag in U.S. Embassy Compound," *National Herald*, New Delhi, Wednesday, July 7, 1971, Vol. 4, No. 124, in S-3 Archives, Drawer 4, Folder "Awards and Policy Documents," Marine Security Guard Bn., State Department, MCCDC, Quantico, Va.

97. According to SSgt. Creedon, Dr. Kissinger and his party were scheduled to stay at the official guest residence of the Indian government — the Ashoka Hotel, located in downtown New Delhi. See SSgt. Creedon, "Special Incident Report 2-71," p. 2.

98. *Ibid.*, pp. 2–3.
99. *Ibid.*, p. 3.
100. *Ibid.*, pp. 1–2.
101. "Marine Security Guard Detachment, Peking," 24 May 1973. Typed manuscript. S-3 Archives, Marine Security Guard Battalion, State Department, Drawer 4, Folder "Awards and Policy Documents," MCCDC, Quantico, Va.
102. One of the best accounts of the Marines in China is by Chester M. Biggs, Jr., *The United States Marines in*

North China, 1894–1942 (Jefferson, N.C.: McFarland, 2003).
103. "Marine Security Guard Detachment, Peking," p. 2.
104. *Ibid.*, p. 3.
105. *Ibid.*, pp. 3–4.
106. See Chapter 1 for details on these landings. Harry Allanson Ellsworth, *One Hundred and Eighty Landings of United States Marines, 1800–1934* (Washington, D.C.: History and Museums Division, HQMC, 1974), pp. 56 and 90; and Clyde H. Metcalf, *A History of the United States Marine Corps* (New York: G.P. Putnam's Sons, 1939), pp. 243–4.
107. One of the most detailed examinations of the life and career of this extraordinary Chinese leader is Keiji Furuya's *Chiang Kai-Shek: His Life and Times* (New York: St. John's University, 1981). Madame Chiang died in October 2003 at the age of 105. See Seth Faison's excellent article, "Madame Chiang Kaishek, a Power in Husband's China and Abroad, Dies at 105," *New York Times*, Saturday, 25 October 2003, p. A-29.
108. Captain R.C. Lewis, Commanding Officer (Acting), Company C, Marine Security Guard Battalion, American Consulate General, Hong Kong, to Commanding Officer, Marine Security Guard Battalion, 1 May 1975, Command Chronology, Special Report, in S-3 Archives, Drawer 4, Folder "1975, Saigon Evacuation Reports, *Post One Gazettes*, Ethiopia Photos, and *MSG Bn Infor Bulletins*," p. 3.
109. Major David P. Martin, Commanding Officer, Company C, Marine Security Guard Battalion, State Department, American Consulate General, Command Chronology, for the Period 1 July–31 December 1978, 22 January 1979, Marine Security Guard Battalion, State Department, HQMC, Henderson Hall, Arlington, Va., S-3 Archives, Command Chronology 1978, Marine Security Guard Battalion, State Department, MCCDC, Quantico, Va., p. 5.
110. *Ibid.*
111. Secretary of the Navy W. Graham Claytor, Jr., "Meritorious Commendation Unit Citation, Marine Security Guard Detachment, Taipei, Taiwan, 16–21 December 1978," in S-3 Archives, Drawer 3, Folder "Awards and Meritorious Unit Commendation Citations," Marine Security Guard Battalion, State Department, MCCDC, Quantico, Va.
112. Department of Defense, *Terrorist Group Profiles*, pp. 118–9.
113. General Louis Wilson, Commandant of the Marine Corps, "Certificate of Commendation," to Marine Security Guard Detachment, Tokyo, Japan, 28 July 1975, in S-3 Historical Archives, Drawer 3, Folder 9, "Awards and Meritorious Unit Commendation Citations," Marine Security Guard Battalion, State Department, MCCDC, Quantico, Va.

114. Colonel F.R. Koethe letter to Henri G. Grignon, Acting Deputy Assistant Secretary for Security, Department of State, 16 August 1974, via Commandant of the Marine Corps, 13 August 1974, Subject: "Meritorious Commendation Award for Marine Security Guards for the Period 1 January 1968 to 30 June 1974," in S-3 Archives, Marine Security Guard Battalion, State Department, MCCDC, Quantico, Va., Drawer 4, Folder "Policy and Procedures," p. 3.
115. Colonel Tom D. Parsons, Commanding Officer, to Secretary of the Navy, via the Commandant of the Marine Corps, Headquarters, Marine Security Guard Battalion, HQMC, Henderson Hall, Arlington, Va., 9 November 1972, in S-3 Archives, Marine Security Guard Battalion, State Department, Drawer 4, "Policy and Procedures," pp. 1–2.
116. *Ibid.*, p. 3.
117. Department of Defense, *Terrorist Group Profiles*, pp. 85–7.
118. Koethe letter, p. 4.
119. Parsons letter, p. 3.
120. , "D Company, El Salvador," in *Marine Security Guard Battalion Newsletter*, 1 April 1980, p. 3, in S-3 Historical Files, Folder "1980 El Salvador," Drawer 4, Marine Security Guard Battalion, State Department, MCCDC, Quantico, Va.
121. Lt. Col. Knapp, XO, MSG Bn., "Attack on American Embassy, El Salvador," R.J. Craig, Marine Corps Command Center message, 30 October 1979, S-3 Archives, Drawer 4, Folder "1979: El Salvador," MSG Bn., State Department, MCCDC, Quantico, Va.; "Marines Injured as Leftist Mob Storms U.S. Embassy," *New York Post*, 31 October 1979; "300 Raid U.S. Embassy in Salvador but are Repulsed," *The New York Times*, 31 October 1979, p. A-3; "Marines Wound 2 Salvadorans," *Atlanta Constitution*, 31 October 1979, p. 11-A.
122. "Marines Rescue U.S. Envoy from Mob in Salvador," *New York Daily News*, 13 May 1980, p. 2.
123. Secretary of the Navy E. Hidalgo, "Citation for Marine Security Guard Detachment, Managua, Nicaragua," S-3 Historical Archives, Drawer 3, Folder 9, "Meritorious Unit Citations and Supporting Documentation," Marine Security Guard Battalion, State Department, MCCDC, Quantico, Va.
124. Frank E. Juni, Regional Security Officer, American Embassy, Managua, to Chief, Office of Security, Department of State, Washington, D.C., 5 December 1979, Subject: "Detention and Release of Sgt. Steven T. Hughes, USMC, DET Managua, 11-29-79," pp. 1–5; also Sergeant Steven T. Hughes, "Incident Report," pp. 1–3, both in S-3 Archives, Drawer 4, Folder, "Deten-

tion and Release of Sgt. Steven T. Hughes, USMC, DET Managua, 5 December 1979," MCCDC, Quantico, Va.

125. Koethe letter, p. 3; Parsons letter, p. 2.

126. Colonel Tom D. Parsons, Commanding Officer, Marine Security Guard Battalion, State Department, to Secretary of the Navy, 26 December 1972, S-3 Historical Archives, Folder 9, "Awards and Meritorious Unit Commendations and Supporting Documents," MSG Bn., State Department, MCCDC, Quantico, Va., p. 1.

127. In the palace *coup d'état*, Daoud, his brother, and several other government officials were killed by forces loyal to Mohammed Nur Taraki. See Mark Urban, *The War in Afghanistan*. Second Edition (London: Macmillan, 1990), pp. 7–8.

128. Secretary of the Navy E. Hidalgo, "Citation for the Meritorious Unit Commendation to Marine Security Guard Detachment, American Embassy, Kabul, Afghanistan," in S-3 Historical Archives, Drawer 3, Folder 9, "Meritorious Unit Citations and Supporting Documents," Marine Security Guard Battalion, State Department, MCCDC, Quantico, Va.

129. See President Carter's and Secretary of State Vance's comments in "U.S. Ambassador Killed in Afghanistan," *Department of State Bulletin*, Vol. 79, April 1979, No. 2025, p. 49.

130. *Ibid.*

131. *Ibid.*

Chapter 8

1. The White Revolution, launched by Shah Mohammed Reza Pahlavi and financed by Iran's increased intake of petro-dollars in 1961, set out to re-distribute land to landless peasants, as well as bring Iran into the modern era through increased industrialization. These reforms soon came under attack as being either half-hearted or incomplete. In time, the reforms, enacted with charges of widespread fraud and corruption, led to a severe socio-economic dislocation that fueled further discontent with the monarchy. See D.R. Denman's "Land Reforms of Shah and People," in George Lenczowski, *Iran Under the Pahlavis* (Stanford, Calif.: Hoover Institution Press, 1978), pp. 253–301; Sandra Mackey, *The Iranians, Persia, Islam, and the Soul of a Nation* (New York: Plume/Penguin Press, 1998), pp. 239–68; Yahya Armajani and Thomas M. Ricks, *Middle East: Past and Present* (Englewood Cliffs, N.J.: Prentice-Hall, 1986), pp. 434–42.

2. Mackey, *The Iranians*, pp. 250–3.

3. *Ibid.*, pp. 252–3.

4. Sergeant Joseph R. Svinth served on Marine Security Guard duty from 1977 to 1980. The U.S. Embassy in Tehran was his first posting. Sergeant Joseph R. Svinth, letter to GySgt. Leo J. Daugherty III, 28 August 1999, pp. 1–3.

5. *Ibid.*, p. 3.

6. *Ibid.*

7. *Ibid.*, pp. 4–5.

8. *Ibid.*, p. 5; also see Mackey, *The Iranians*, p. 251.

9. The first attempt to force the shah to flee Iran occurred in 1951 when Mohammed Mossadeq, an Iranian nationalist and opponent of the monarchy, became prime minister. Upon taking office, Mossadeq nationalized Iran's budding oil industries. This in turn led the shah's supporters to claim that Mossadeq was a communist sympathizer. With help of the Eisenhower Administration, the CIA successfully engineered a coup against Mossadeq and restored the shah to power. Mackey, *The Iranians*, pp. 199–203. Lenczowski, "Political Process and Institutions in Iran: The Second Pahlavi Kingship," in Lenczowski, *Iran Under the Pahlavis*, pp. 442–51.

10. *Ibid.*, pp. 283–93; Jimmy Carter, *Keeping Faith: Memoirs of a President* (New York: Bantam Books, 1982), pp. 438–52.

11. Commanding Officer, Company B, Marine Security Guard Battalion, to Commanding Officer, Marine Security Guard Battalion, State Department, MCCDC, Quantico, Va., "Command Chronology, for the Period 1 January 1980–30 June 1980," 23 September 1980, History and Museums Division, Marine Corps Historical Center, HQMC, Washington, D.C., Annex A to Tab B, Report on Events of 14 February 1979.

12. *Ibid.*, p. 1.

13. Mackey, *The Iranians*, pp. 289–93; Carter, *Keeping Faith*, pp. 450–2.

14. *Ibid.*, pp. 293–5.

15. Carter, *Keeping Faith*, p. 448.

16. "Command Chronology, for the Period 1 January 1980–30 June 1980," pp. 1–2.

17. *Ibid.*, pp. 2–3.

18. The MSG Detachment in Tehran in February 1979 included the non-commissioned officer-in-charge, Gunnery Sergeant Willie M. Sutton, Jr. Watchstanders included Sergeant Gary N. Downey, Sergeant Steward D. Hill, Sergeant Jack M. Hinojos, Sergeant Donald R. Knapp, Sergeant Kenneth L. Kraus, Sergeant Ronald L. Miller, Sergeant Glenn C. Parsons, Sergeant Larry A. Pennamon, Corporal Roarke L. Anderson, Corporal Theodore Avery, Jr., Corporal E.D. Garcia, Corporal Wade S. Jeffries, Corporal Michael C. Laurent, Corporal Henry C. Lojkuc, Corporal Leonard A. Moten, Corporal Michael Rayfield, Corporal Fred J. Schmidt, Lance Corporal William M. Carey, Jr., and Lance Corporal Edwin C. Falcon. "Command Chronology, for the Period 1 January 1980–30 June 1980," p. 2.

19. William Branigin, "Iranian Leftists Battle Way into U.S. Embassy," *Washington Post*, 15 February 1979, p. A-1, in S-3 Historical Archives, Drawer 4, "1979 Iranian Hostage Crisis, Folder 1," Marine Security Guard Bn., State Department, MCCDC, Quantico, Va.

20. *Ibid.*, pp. 3–5.

21. Branigin, "Iranian leftists Battle Way into U.S. Embassy."

22. "Command Chronology, for the Period 1 January 1980–30 June 1980," pp. 6–7.

23. *Ibid.*, pp. 7–8.

24. *Ibid.*, p. 8.

25. Sergeant Glenn C. Parsons, MSG Det., Tehran, "Debriefing Notes," S-3 Archives, Drawer 4, Folder "Debriefing of Sergeant Glenn Parsons, MSG Det. Tehran, Iran, February 1979," p. 4.

26. Sajid Rizvi, "Communist Guerrillas Captured the U.S. Embassy," United Press International, 14 February 1979, S-3 Historical Archives, Drawer 4, Folder "1979 Iranian Hostage Crisis," Marine Security Guard Bn., State Department, MCCDC, Quantico, Va., pp. 1–2.

27. William Branigin, "Iran Frees Marine It Secretly Seized," *Washington Post*, 27 February 1979, p. A-1.

28. Pfc. Julie Roegner, "Wounded Marine Confides, 'I Was Just Doing My Job,'" *SAM*, July 1979; "A Brave Young Leatherneck Escapes Death in Iran," *People*; copies in S-3 Archives, Drawer 4, Folder "Articles on Sergeant Kenneth L. Kraus," 17 February 1979, "1979: Iranian Hostage Crisis Attack on U.S. Embassy," Marine Security Guard Battalion, State Department, MCCDC, Quantico, Va.

29. "Marines Cited for Heroism," in S-3 Archives, Drawer 4, Folder, "Articles on Sgt. Kenneth Kraus, USMC," loc. cit.

30. Carter, *Keeping Faith*, pp. 451–2.

31. Mackey, *The Iranians*, pp. 291–5.

32. Parsons, "Debriefing Notes," p. 4.

33. Carter, *Keeping Faith*, p. 453.

34. *Ibid.*

35. Mackey, *The Iranians*, pp. 292–3.

36. The supreme religious figure in Shi'a Islam, a branch of the Islamic faith of which over 99 percent of all Iranians follow. In this case, the students were referring to the Ayatollah Khomeini.

37. A chador is a black veil worn by most Muslim women to cover almost all of the head and body.

38. J.T. Roland, "Debriefing Report on Tehran Hostages," Commanding Officer, Company B, to Commanding Officer, Marine Security Guard Bn., 29 January 1980, Subject: "Command Chronology for the period 1 July to 31 December 1979," S-3 Historical Ar-

chives, Drawer 4, Marine Security Guard Bn., State Department, MCCDC, Quantico, Va., pp. 1–2.

39. *Ibid.*, pp. 2–3.

40. Jonathan C. Randal, "Four Women, Six Blacks in Group," *The Washington Post*, 20 November 1979, p. A-1; Michael Getler, "10 Freed Hostages Join Colleagues in Wiesbaden," *The Washington Post*, 21 November 1979, p. A-15; John Vincour, "10 Hostages Released in Iran Hold Reunion With 3 in West Germany," *New York Times*, 21 November 1979, A-12. Gerald Kessler and Michael Daly, "Through the Awful Static Came the Happiest of Words: 'I'm Fine,'" *New York Daily News*, 21 November 1979, p. 3; Toni House, "Freed Hostages to be Home for Holiday," *The Washington Star*, 21 November 1979, p. A-5.

41. The names on the letters were blotted out by Marine Security Guard Battalion to protect the authors. Anonymous to Commandant of the Marine Corps, 17 November 1979. S-3 Archives, Drawer 4, Folder "1979: Iranian Hostage Crisis, MSGs," Marine Security Guard Battalion, State Department, MCCDC, Quantico, Va.

42. "Line Corporal USMC 1945" to Commandant, United States Marine Corps, 19 November 1979, S-3 Archives, Drawer 4, Folder, "Iranian Hostage Crisis, MSGs," Marine Security Guard Bn., State Department, MCCDC, Quantico, Va.

43. Anonymous to the Commandant of the Marine Corps, 19 November 1979, S-3 Archives, Drawer 4, Folder, "1979: Iranian Hostage Crisis, MSGs," Marine Security Guard Bn., State Department, MCCDC, Quantico, Va.

44. Anonymous to the Commandant of the Marine Corps, 23 November 1979, S-3, Drawer 4, "1979: Iranian Hostage Crisis, MSGs," Marine Security Guard Bn., State Department, MCCDC, Quantico, Va.

45. Homer B. Petti to General Robert Barrow, 19 November 1979, S-3 Archives, Drawer 4, "1979: Iranian Hostage Crisis, MSGs," Marine Security Guard Bn., State Department, MCCDC, Quantico, Va.

46. Anonymous "Colonel, USMCR," to Commandant of the Marine Corps, mailgram, 24 November 1979, S-3 Archives, Drawer 4, Folder "1979: Iranian Hostage Crisis, MSGs," Marine Security Guard Bn., State Department, MCCDC, Quantico, Va.

47. James Conway, "Iranians Thronged in After Embassy Aide Ordered Door Open," unattributed newspaper article in S-3 Archives, Drawer 4, Folder "1979: Iranian Hostage Crisis, MSGs," Marine Security Guard Bn., State Department, MCCDC, Quantico, Va.

48. "Bound for Hours, Facing the Walls," *Time*, 3 December 1979, p. 36.

49. Roland, "Debriefing Report on Tehran Hostages," p. 3.

50. *Ibid.*, p. 4.

51. The shah died on 27 July 1980 and was buried in Cairo, Egypt, next to his father, who also died in exile, in South Africa. See Carter, *Keeping Faith*; Mackey, *The Iranians*, p. 299; and Lenczowski, *Iran Under the Pahlavis*, p. 371.

52. Carter, *Keeping Faith*, pp. 511–21; Mackey, *The Iranians*, pp. 297–8.

53. Barbara Honegger, "Silent Hero," *Marines*, March 1999, p. 32.

54. *Ibid.*, p. 33.

55. Lieutenant Colonel W.B. Clark, Coordinator, Marine Corps Iranian Hostage Task Force, 24 March 1980, memorandum for DC/S Manpower, Subject: "Hostage Information," in S-3 Historical Archives, Drawer 4, Folder "1980: Iranian Hostage Crisis," Marine Security Guard Bn., State Department, MCCDC, Quantico, Va.

56. "An Iranian Charges Hostage Fathered His Sister's Child," United Press International, 29 March 1980, S-3 Historical Files, Drawer 4, Folder "MSG Program and Iranian Hostage Crisis, November 1979," Marine Security Guard Bn., State Department, MCCDC, Quantico, Va.

57. Maureen Dowd and Suzanne Bilello, "Hostages Tell of Abuses; Carter Decries Barbarism," *Washington Star*, 22 January 1981, pp. A-1 and A-7. Copies in S-3 Archives, Drawer 4, Folder "1981: Hostage Release Articles, Misc. Hostage Information," Marine Security Guard Bn., State Department, MCCDC, Quantico, Va.

58. Roland, "Debriefing Report on Tehran Hostages," pp. 5–6; Henry Allen, "Semper Fi: The Guardian Elite; Tehran on Their Minds at the Marine Security Guard School," *Washington Post*, 15 February 1979, p. C-1, copy in S-3 Historical Archives, Drawer 4, Folder "1979: Iranian Hostage Crisis, MSGs," Marine Security Guard Bn., State Department, MCCDC, Quantico, Va.

59. Chargéé d'Affaires Bruce Laingen to Mrs. Lisa Moeller, 26 January 1980, in S-3 Archives, Drawer 4 "1980: Hostage Up-dates and Newsclippings, Desert One Reports and Newsclippings, etc." Marine Security Guard Bn., State Department, MCCDC, Quantico, Va.

60. "Chronology of Events (Islamabad, Pakistan), November 21, 1979."

61. Sergeant S.A. Segobiano, "Statements," in Commanding Officer, Captain Robert E. Lee, Company B, Commanding Officer, Marine Security Guard Bn., S-3, Historical Files, Drawer 4, Folder "After Action Reports: Attack on the U.S. Embassy, Islamaband, Pakistan, 21 November 1979," Marine Security Guard Bn., State Department, MCCDC, Quantico, Va., Enclosure 5, p. 1.

62. Master Sergeant Loyd G. Miller,

"Statement of Master Sergeant Loyd G. Miller," Enclosure No. 2 in "After Action Reports: Attack on the U.S. Embassy, Islamabad, Pakistan, 21 November 1979," loc. cit., p. 1.

63. Marcia Gauger, "You Could Die in Here," *Time*, 3 December 1979, p. 26.

64. *Ibid.*

65. Statements of Sergeant Michael J. Sirois and Lance Corporal Robert C. Bledsoe in "After Action Reports: Islamabad," loc. cit., Enclosures 3 and 7 respectively.

66. Gauger, "You Could in Die Here," p. 26.

67. Sergeant Sirois statement, "After Action Reports: Islamabad, Pakistan," loc. cit., Enclosure 4, p. 1.

68. Corporal Paul M. Sima, "Statement of Corporal Paul M. Sima, USMC," 25 November 1979, in "After Action Report: Islamabad Pakistan," loc. cit., Enclosure 6, p. 1.

69. *Ibid.*

70. *Ibid.*, p. 2.

71. Miller, "After Action Statement: Islamabad, Pakistan," loc. cit., pp. 1–2.

72. Randy K. Sayles, "After Action Report: Islamabad, Pakistan," loc. cit., Enclosure 9, p. 1.

73. C. William Powers, "Statement of C. William Powers, Special Agent, Drug Enforcement Agency," in "After Action Reports: Islamabad, Pakistan," loc. cit., Enclosure 8, p. 1.

74. Andrew Koritko, "Statement of Andrew Koritko, Regional Security Officer," in "After Action Report: Islamabad, Pakistan," loc. cit., Enclosure 10, p. 1.

75. Gauger, "You Could Die in Here," *Time*, 3 December 1979, p. 27.

76. Bledsoe, "After Action Reports: Islamabad, Pakistan," loc. cit., p. 1.

77. Koritko, "After Action Reports: Islamabad, Pakistan," loc. cit., p. 2.

78. Major Jeffrey T. Roland, "After Action Report," 27 November 1979, loc. cit., p. 4.

79. *Ibid.*

80. Master Sergeant Miller, "After Action Reports: Islamabad, Pakistan," loc. cit., p. 3.

81. Carter, *Keeping Faith*, p. 465.

82. Secretary of the Navy E. Hidalgo, "Meritorious Unit Commendation for Marine Security Guard Detachment, Islamabad, Pakistan," in S-3 Historical Archives, Drawer 3, Folder 9, "Meritorious Unit Citations and Supporting Documents," Marine Security Guard Bn., State Department, MCCDC, Quantico, Va.

83. MSgt. Bruce Martin, "Crowley Defended Embassy," *Quantico Sentry*, 30 November 1979, in S-3 Archives, Drawer 4, Folder "Articles on Iranian Hostage Crisis, 1979–1980," Marine Security Guard Bn., State Department, MCCDC, Quantico, Va.

84. Karen DeYoung, "Mob Invades

U.S. Embassy in Tripoli," *Washington Post*, 3 December 1979, p. 1, in S-3 Archives, Drawer 4, Folder "Articles on Marine Security Guards Released by Iranian Hostage Crisis, November 1979," Marine Security Guard Bn., State Department, MCCDC, Quantico, Va.

85. *Ibid.*, p. 3.

86. Message from American Consulate, Casablanca, to Commanding Officer, Marine Security Guard Bn., State Department, Quantico, Va., 9 June 1983, in S-3 Archives, Drawer 4, Folder "1983: Beirut Embassy Bombing," Marine Security Guard Bn., State Department, MCCDC, Quantico, Va., p. 1.

87. *Ibid.*, p. 2.

88. Chaim Herzog, *The Arab-Israeli Wars: War and Peace in the Middle East from the War of Independence through Lebanon*. Revised (New York: Vintage Press, 1984), pp. 341–3.

89. *Ibid.*, pp. 354–7.

90. Message from American Consulate, Casablanca, "Beirut Embassy Bombing," p. 2.

91. *Ibid.*

92. American Consulate, Casablanca, to Commanding Officer, Marine Security Guard Bn., State Department, 9 June 1983, Subject: "Meritorious Unit Citation: Recommendation of MSG DET Beirut," S-3 Archives, Drawer 4, File "1983: Beirut Embassy Bombing," Marine Security Guard Bn., State Department, MCCDC, Quantico, Va., p. 1.

93. Benis M. Frank, *U.S. Marines in Lebanon: 1982–1984* (Washington, D.C.: History and Museums Division, HQMC, 1987), pp. 22–3.

94. *Ibid.*, p. 59.

95. *Ibid.*, p. 60; American Consulate, Casablanca, to Commanding Officer, "Meritorious Unit Citation."

96. American Consulate, Casablanca, to Commanding Officer, "Meritorious Unit Citation," p. 11; Frank, *U.S. Marines in Lebanon*, p. 60.

97. Frank, *U.S. Marines in Lebanon*, pp. 60–1.

98. *Ibid.*, p. 61.

99. *Ibid.*, p. 62.

100. As Marines continued to guard the U.S. Embassy amid the violence spawned by the Lebanese civil war that would last until 1989, additional Marine Security Guards arrived in Beirut. Among the leathernecks who arrived that May was Sergeant Jimmie Brown, whom the Marine Corps promoted to staff sergeant the month he arrived in Beirut. While in Beirut, Staff Sergeant Brown assisted the Marine Security Guards in the day-to-day functions in protecting the U.S. Embassy against further terrorist attacks. Leaving Beirut, Staff Sergeant Brown served in various billets with the Fleet Marine Force and as a drill instructor, as well as in inspec-

tor and instructor duty with the Marine Reserve Forces. He later served as the 19th sergeant major of the Marine Security Guard Battalion.

101. Secretary of the Navy John Lehman, "Citation for the Navy Unit Commendation: MSG Detachment, Beirut, Lebanon," Drawer 3, Folder 9, "Meritorious Unit Citations and Supporting Documentation," S-3, Historical Archives, Marine Security Guard Bn., State Department, MCCDC, Quantico, Va.

102. Mel Jones, "Bombing in Beirut Kills Sailor, Soldier; Four Marines Wounded," *Navy Times*, 25 April 1984.

103. "Four Embassy Guards killed in San Salvador," Quantico *Sentry*, 28 June 1985, p. A-1, copy in S-3 Archives, Drawer 4, Folder "1985: El Salvador Attacks," Marine Security Guard Bn., State Department, MCCDC, Quantico, Va.

104. *Ibid.*; Robert J. McCartney, "Gunmen Seen Singling Out U.S. Marines," 20 June 1985, *Washington Post*, copy in S-3 Archives, Drawer 4, Folder "1985: El Salvador Attacks," Marine Security Guard Bn., State Department, MCCDC, Quantico, Va., p. A-1.

105. President Ronald Reagan, "President Reagan's Remarks on the Slayings," Quantico *Sentry*, 28 June 1985, copy in S-3 Archives, Folder "1985: El Salvador Attacks," MCCDC, Quantico, Va.

106. *Ibid.*

107. Commanding Officer R.G. Napier, Company F, Marine Security Guard Battalion, Nairobi, Kenya, to Commandant of the Marine Corps, Headquarters, Marine Corps, 29 August 1986, Subject: "Meritorious Unit Citation for Operation Kampala, and After Action Report," via Commanding Officer, MSG Bn., in S-3 Archives, Drawer 2, Folder "Operation Kampala," Marine Security Guard Bn., State Department, MCCDC, Quantico, Va.

108. *Ibid.*, p. 11.

109. For the best overall view of the Clayton Lonetree espionage case see Rodney Barker, *Dancing with the Devil: Sex, Espionage and the U.S. Marines; The Clayton Lonetree Story* (New York: Ivy Books, 1996). For the official unclassified investigations see Hon. Daniel Mica and Hon. Olympia J. Snowe, "Security at the U.S. Embassy in Moscow," 12 May 1987. Letter from Hon. Daniel A. Mica, Richard McBride, Kenneth Peele, Robert Boyer, Thomas Bruce, and Robert Jenkins to Hon. Daniel A. Mica and Hon. Olympia J. Snowe, 2 June 1987, Subject: "Summary Report of Trip to Vienna, Budapest, Bucarest [*sic*], and London, May 21–30, 1987"; Statement of Major General Carl E. Mundy, Jr., Director of Operations, Headquarters, U.S. Marine Corps, Before the Defense Policy Panel and Subcommittee on Mil-

itary Personnel and Compensation, Committee on Armed Services, House of Representatives on 5 August 1987 Concerning Marine Security Guard Program, Senators Clairborne Pell, Jesse Helms, John C. Stennis, and Mark O. Hatfield, 29 April 1987, Senate Select Committee on Intelligence, "Report on Security at the United States Missions in Moscow and Other Areas of High Risk"; U.S. House of Representatives International Operations Subcommittee (Chmn. Mica, D-Fla.), Committee on Foreign Affairs (Chmn. Fascell, D-Fla.), Report, 3 April 1987, Subject: "Marine Corps Security Guard/Training and Selection"; David C. Williams, Director, U.S. General Accounting Office, to Hon. Daniel Mica and Hon Olympia J. Snowe, 28 October 1988, Subject: "Suspected Espionage in Moscow by Marine Security Guards."

110. Barker, *Dancing with the Devil*, pp. 99–102.

111. *Ibid.*, pp. 102–3; See Sergeant Clayton J. Lonetree, School Record Book of Sgt. C.J. Lonetree, Class 5-84, in Schools and Operations, Marine Security Guard Battalion, State Department, MCCDC, Quantico, Va. Major Michael C. Dugan, Commanding Officer, Schools and Operations, gave permission to reprint portions of Sgt. Lonetree's class record, which is on permanent retention by MSG Bn. due to the nature of the case.

112. Barker, *Dancing with the Devil*, pp. 235–59.

113. *Ibid.*, pp. 1–6.

114. *Ibid.*, pp. 107–10 and 131–3.

115. See the charges on Staff Sergeant Stufflebeam and other Marine Security Guards in the Sergeant Clayton J. Lonetree Collection, S-3, Historical Archives, Marine Security Guard Battalion, State Department, MCCDC, Quantico, Va.

116. Lieutenant General Frank E. Petersen, "Charge Sheet of Sergeant Clayton J. Lonetree," 15 May 1987, in S-3, Drawer 4, Folder "1987: Post-Espionage Congressional Investigation/ Findings — II," Marine Security Guard Battalion, State Department, MCCDC, Quantico, Va., pp. 2–5. Also see Pete Early, "Spy Fiasco," *Washington Post Magazine*, 7 February 1988, pp. 21–8 and 48.

117. Barker, *Dancing with the Devil*, p. 139.

118. *Ibid.*, pp. 294–5.

119. Williams, "Suspected Espionage in Moscow by Marine Security Guards," pp. 23–4; Adjutant@adj@msg bn.usmc.mil, to g2pa2@mqgmccdc@ ggsnador, 28 October 1993, Subject: "Lonetree Lessons Learned," S-3, Drawer 4, Archives, Folder "1987: Post-Espionage Congressional Investigations–II," Marine Security Guard Bn., State Department, MCCDC, Quantico, Va., p. 1.

120. Adjutant, "Lonetree Lessons Learned," pp. 1–2.

121. Williams, "Suspected Espionage in Moscow by Marine Security Guards," pp. 23–4.

122. *Ibid.*, p. 24.

123. Barker, *Dancing with the Devil*, p. 294.

124. Lieutenant Colonel Nicholas E. Reynolds, *Just Cause: Marine Operations in Panama, 1988–1990* (Washington, D.C.: History and Museums Division, HQMC, 1996), p. 1.

125. *Ibid.*

126. *Ibid.*; Carter, *Keeping Faith*, pp. 152–85.

127. Reynolds, *Just Cause: Marine Operations in Panama*, pp. 2–6.

128. G.G. Robinson, Commanding Officer, Company D, Marine Security Guard Battalion, to Commanding Officer, Marine Security Guard Battalion, Quantico, Va., 13 March 1990, Subject: "Navy Unit Commendation," in S-3, Historical Archives, Drawer 4, Folder "1989: Panama," Marine Security Guard Bn., State Department, MCCDC, Quantico, Va. Enclosure 1, p. 3.

129. *Ibid.*, pp. 13–14.

130. Reynolds, *Just Cause: Marine Operations in Panama*, pp. 2–6; Major R.B. Neller, "Marines in Panama: 1988–1990," Marine Corps Command and Staff College, Research Paper, 1990–1991, in Marine Corps Archives, Marine Corps Research Center, MCCDC, Quantico, Va., p. 7.

131. Reynolds, *Just Cause: Marine Operations in Panama*, p. 14.

132. Robinson, "Navy Unit Commendation," p. 4.

133. *Ibid.*, p. 53.

134. Reynolds, *Just Cause: Marine Operations in Panama*, pp. 24–5.

135. Marine Security Guard Detachment in Panama, December 1989, included Staff Sergeant Michael Pellow, NCOIC; Staff Sergeant Raymond Boretti, Ass't. Detachment Commander; and Watchstanders Sergeant James Dorsey, Sergeant Jeffrey Staples, Sergeant Robert Palmer, Corporal David Davis, Corporal Richard Krout, and Corporal Eric T. Howe.

136. *Ibid.*; Robinson, "Navy Unit Commendation," pp 53–4.

137. See log book entries in "Notes from Post #1, Panama, Dec. 19 and 20, 1989," S-3, Drawer 4, Folder "1989: Panama: Operation Just Cause," Marine Security Guard Bn., State Department, MCCDC, Quantico, Va., pp. 1–4.

138. Staff Sergeant Eric T. Howe letter to GySgt. Leo J. Daugherty III, 13 October 1998, p. 2.

139. *Ibid.*, pp. 2–3.

140. Reynolds, *Just Cause: Marine Operations in Panama*, p. 25.

141. "U.S. Embassy Lowers Flag, Quits Kabul," *Washington Times*, 31 Jan-uary 1989, p. A-10; see also Don Oberdorfer, "U.S. Embassy in Kabul to be Evacuated, Closed," *Washington Post*, 31 January 1989, articles in S-3 Historical Archives, Drawer 4, Folder "1989: U.S. Embassy in Kabul Closes," Marine Security Guard Battalion, State Department, MCCDC, Quantico, Va.

142. "U.S. Embassy Lowers Flag, Quits Kabul," p. A-10.

143. Richard M. Weintraub, "U.S. Closes its Embassy in Kabul," *The Washington Post*, 31 January 1989, p. A-1. In S-3 Historical Archives, Drawer 4, Folder "1989, Articles," Marine Security Guard Battalion, State Department, MCCDC, Quantico, Va.

144. For the Marine Corps' role in the 1990–1991 Gulf War see Lieutenant Colonel Charles H. Cureton, *U.S. Marines in the Persian Gulf, 1990–1991: With the 1st Marine Division in Desert Shield and Desert Storm* (1993); Lieutenant Colonel Dennis P. Mroczkowski, *U.S. Marines in the Persian Gulf, 1990–1991: With the 2d Marine Division in Desert Shield and Desert Storm* (1993); Major Charles D. Melson, et al., *U.S. Marines in the Persian Gulf, 1990–1991: Anthology and Annotated Bibliography* (1992); Lieutenant Colonel Ronald J. Brown, *U.S. Marines in the Persian Gulf, 1990–1991, With Marine Forces Afloat in Desert Shield and Desert Storm* (1998); Lieutenant Colonel LeRoy D. Stearns, *U.S. Marines in the Persian Gulf, 1990–1991: The 3d Marine Aircraft Wing in Desert Shield and Desert Storm* (1999); Major Steven M. Zimmeck, *U.S. Marines in the Persian Gulf, 1990–1991: Combat Service Support in Desert Shield and Desert Storm* (1999); and Colonel Charles J. Quilter II, *U.S. Marines in the Persian Gulf, 1990–1991: With the I Marine Expeditionary Force in Desert Shield and Desert Storm* (1993). All published in Washington, D.C., History and Museums Division, HQMC.

145. Members of Marine Security Guard Detachment, U.S. Embassy, Kuwait, August 1990, consisted of Staff Sergeant J.B. Smith, Detachment Commander, and Watchstanders Sergeant Paul G. Rodriguez, Sergeant David K. Hudson, Sergeant Ward, Sergeant Andre, and Corporal Mark E. Royer. See Sergeant Paul G. Rodriguez, "After Action Report: Iraq's Invasion of Kuwait," S-3, Archives, Drawer 4, Folder "1990–1991: Desert Shield/Desert Storm," Marine Security Guard Battalion, State Department, MCCDC, Quantico, Va.

146. *Ibid.*; Staff Sergeant J.B. Smith, USMC, "After Action Report," S-3 Historical Files, Marine Security Guard Battalion, Drawer 1, Folder "1990," MCCDC, Quantico, Va.

147. *Ibid.*, pp. 1–4.

148. *Ibid.*, p. 4.

149. Smith, "After Action Report, MSGDET Kuwait," pp. 1–2.

150. Rodriguez, "After Action Report … Kuwait," pp. 5–6.

151. Smith, "After Action Report, MSGDET Kuwait," p. 2.

152. Corporal Mark E. Royer, "After Action Report, MSGDET Kuwait," S-3 Archives, Drawer 4, Folder "1990–1991 Desert Shield/Desert Storm," Marine Security Guard Battalion, State Department, MCCDC, Quantico, Va., p. 2.

153. Smith, "After-Action Report, MSGDET Kuwait," p. 3.

154. Commanding Officer, Marine Security Guard Battalion, to Major Larkin, Headquarters Marine Corps, 27 August 1990, Subject: "Time Line: Sequence of Events in Kuwait and Baghdad," in S-3 Archives, Drawer 4, Folder "1990–1991: Desert Shield/Desert Storm," Marine Security Guard Bn., State Department, MCCDC, Quantico, Va.

155. Smith, "After Action Report, MSGDET Kuwait," p. 4.

156. *Ibid.*

157. *Ibid.*, p. 5.

158. *Ibid.*

159. Sergeant David K. Hudson, "After-Action Report, MSGDET Kuwait," p. 2. S-3 Archives, Drawer 4, Folder "1990–1991: Desert Shield/Desert Storm," Marine Security Guard Battalion, State Department, MCCDC, Quantico, Va.

160. Smith, "After-Action Report, MSGDET Kuwait," p. 5.

161. Quilter, *U.S. Marines in the Persian Gulf, 1990–1991: With the I Marine Expeditionary Force in Desert Shield and Desert Storm*, p. 103.

Chapter 9

1. One of the best books dealing with the political instability in Africa is Howard W. French's *A Continent for the Taking: The Tragedy and Hope of Africa* (New York: Alfred A. Knopf, 2004).

2. Lt. Col. Glen R. Sachtleben, "Operation Sharp Edge: The Corps' MEU(SOC) Program in Action," *Marine Corps Gazette*, November 1991, Vol. 75, No. 11, pp. 77–86.

3. *Ibid.*, pp. 78–9.

4. *Ibid.*, p. 77. Liberia was one of the more important listening posts for U.S. intelligence gathering in the region during the Cold War era (1960–1980s).

5. *Ibid.*, pp. 78–9.

6. George J. Dunham and David A. Quinlan, *U.S. Marines in Vietnam: The Bitter End, 1973–1975* (Washington, D.C.: History and Museums Division, HQMC, 1990), pp. 40–51 and 100–24.

7. BLT 2/4 Summary: Operation Sharp Edge, observed 05 Aug. 1990, Lesson I.D. 80367–00141, U.S. Marine Corps Small Wars, *http://www.small-wars.usmc.mil*, U.S. Marine Corps

Expeditionary Warfare School, "Operation Sharp Edge."

8. Sachtleben, "Operation Sharp Edge," p. 79.

9. *Ibid.*, p. 81.

10. *Ibid.*, p. 84.

11. *Ibid.*

12. *Ibid.*, p. 85.

13. *Ibid.*

14. Lieutenant Colonel Ronald J. Brown, *U.S. Marines in the Persian Gulf, 1990–1991: With Marine Forces Afloat in Desert Shield and Desert Storm* (Washington, D.C.: History and Museums Division, HQMC, 1998), p. 80.

15. *Ibid.*, pp. 81–2. Vice Admiral Stanley R. Arthur, Commander, U.S. Navy, Central Command, during Desert Shield/Desert Storm, was a strong supporter of the Marine amphibious forces during the First Persian Gulf War (1990–91).

16. Brown, *U.S. Marines in the Persian Gulf*, pp. 82–4; Adam B. Siegel, "Eastern Exit: The Noncombatant Evacuation Operation (NEO) from Mogadishu, Somalia, in January 1991." Professional paper, 512.09, September 1991, Alexandria, Va., Center for Naval Analyses, pp. 16–17.

17. Siegel, "Eastern Exit," p. 3; Brown, *U.S. Marines in the Persian Gulf*, p. 87.

18. Brown, *U.S. Marines in the Persian Gulf*, p. 86.

19. Siegel, "Eastern Exit," pp. 7–12.

20. Brown, *U.S. Marines in the Persian Gulf*, p. 87.

21. *Ibid.*, p. 91.

22. *Ibid.*; Siegel, "Eastern Exit," p. 31.

23. Siegel, "Eastern Exit," p. 29.

24. *Ibid.*, pp. 28–9.

25. *Ibid.*, pp. 29–31.

26. *Ibid.*, p. 31.

27. Brown, *U.S. Marines in the Persian Gulf*, pp. 92–4; Siegel, "Eastern Exit," p. 31.

28. Brown, *U.S. Marines in the Persian Gulf*, p. 94.

29. Brown, *U.S. Marines in the Persian Gulf*, p. 95.

30. John A. Terrell to Thomas E. Dunkelberger, facsimile, information paper, 25 March 1994, Subject: "Fleet Antiterrorism Security (FAST) Team Platoon in Somalia"; M.C. Paulovich, Commanding Officer, Fleet Anti-Terrorism Security Team Company, Marine Corps Security Force Battalion, to Commanding Officer, Marine Corps Security Force Battalion, 5 July 1993, Subject: "Post Validation Study for the U.S. Liaison Office (USLO), Somalia." Both documents in S-3 Archives, Folder "Reopening Somalia: MSG DET Mogadishu," Marine Security Guard Battalion, State Department, MCCDC, Quantico, Va.

31. Corporal C.J. Noble to GySgt. Leo J. Daugherty III, "Fleet Antiterrorism Security Team," unpublished manuscript, 9 June 2003, pp. 1–2. Ohio State University, Lima, Ohio. Manuscript in possession of author.

32. *Ibid.*, p. 4.

33. Mark E. Mulvey, Director, Diplomatic Security Service, letter to Lieutenant General Norman E. Ehlert, Deputy Chief of Staff, Plans, Policies, and Operations Department, HQMC, 26 July 1993, in S-3 Historical Archives, Drawer 3, Folder "MSG DET Mogadishu," Marine Security Guard Battalion, State Department, MCCDC, Quantico, Va.

34. *Ibid.*

35. *Ibid.*

36. Chief Warrant Officer 2 Felix M. Arnold, Supply Officer, to Commanding Officer, Marine Security Guard Battalion, "After-Action Report," 21 July 1993, S-3 Historical Archives, File "MSG DET Mogadishu: Reopening Somalia," Marine Security Guard Battalion, State Department, MCCDC, Quantico, Va., pp. 1–3.

37. *Ibid.*, p. 3.

38. Two of the more notorious groups in Chile that aimed at driving out the U.S. and ending its support for General Pinochet were the Manuel Rodriguez Front (FPMR), and the Movement of the Revolutionary Left (MIR). See State Department, *Terrorist Group Profiles* (Washington, D.C.: Government Printing Office, November 1988), pp. 94–8.

39. "Santiago Marine Awarded Purple Heart," *Post One*, newsletter of the Marine Security Guard Battalion, November 1991, p. 1. In S-3 Historical Archives, Drawer 4, Folder "1991, News, Clippings, and Articles," Marine Security Guard Battalion, State Department, MCCDC, Quantico, Va.

40. *Ibid.*

41. Lt. Col. Richard W. Roan, Commanding Officer, Company D, Marine Security Guard Battalion, to Commanding Officer, Marine Security Guard Battalion, 20 January 1994, Subject: "Command Chronology for the Period 1 July–31 December 1993," S-3 Historical Archives, Drawer 3, Marine Security Guard Battalion, State Department, MCCDC, Quantico, Va., p. 2.

42. Deborah Schmidt, "Violence Brings Aid From Congo, Zaire Marine Guards," *Navy Times*, 16 December 1991, in S-3, Drawer 4, Folder "1991: Kuwait After Action Reports, Liberia Articles," Marine Security Guard Battalion, State Department, MCCDC, Quantico, Va.

43. *Ibid.*

44. *Ibid.*

45. French, *A Continent for the Taking*, pp. 125–7.

46. SSgt. Mike Stroup, "Operation Distant Runner Rescues Americans," *Leatherneck*, August 1994, Vol. 77, No. 8, pp. 40–1.

47. *Ibid.*, pp. 40–1.

48. SSgt. Mike Stroup, "Bringing Help in Kenya," *Leatherneck*, August 1994, Vol. 77, No. 8, p. 41.

49. Stroup, "Operation Distant Runner Rescues Americans," p. 41.

50. *Ibid.*

51. P.T. Chisolm, Commanding Officer, Company G, to Commanding Officer, Marine Security Guard Battalion, 27 August 1996, Subject: "Company Command Chronology," in Commanding Officer, Marine Security Guard Bn., to the Commandant of the Marine Corps, 11 December 1996, Subject: "Command Chronology for the period 1 January to 30 June 1996." Copy in S-3, Historical Archives, Marine Security Guard Bn., State Department, MCCDC, Quantico, Va.

52. *Ibid.*; U.S. Ambassador in Monrovia to RUEHAB/ American Embassy, Abidjan, 13 April 1996, Subject: "Operational Incident Report OIR #2-96," pp. 1–2.

53. Staff Sergeant Phil Mehringer and Sergeant R.A. Smith, "On High Alert in Monrovia," *Leatherneck*, August 1996, Vol. 76, No. 8, p. 18.

54. *Ibid.*

55. *Ibid.*

56. French, *Africa: A Continent for the Taking*, p. 183.

57. Staff Sergeant Phil Mehringer and Sergeant R.A. Smith, "Working Amid Chaos and Death," *Leatherneck*, August 1996, Vol. 76, No. 8, pp. 18–9.

58. *Ibid.*, p. 19.

59. *Ibid.*

60. In September 2003, President Taylor was forced into exile and left Liberia as a coalition force of West African peacekeepers and U.S. Marines once again landed in Monrovia to restore order.

61. Gunnery Sergeant W.E. Walters, Detachment Commander, to Commanding Officer, Company E, Marine Security Guard Battalion, 1 August 1997, Subject: "After Action Report, Military Mutiny/Coup De Etat in Freetown, Sierra Leone," in S-3 Archives, Drawer 2, Folder "After Action Report, Military Mutiny/Coup de Etat in Freetown/Sierra Leone," Marine Security Guard Battalion, State Department, MCCDC, Quantico, Va.

62. Sergeant Joseph R. Arnold, "Oral History Transcript of Sergeant Joseph R. Arnold," 5 June 1997, conducted by Major James Antel, U.S. Marine Corps, Archives Section, History and Museums Division, Marine Corps Historical Center, HQMC, p. 28.

63. Walters, "After Action Report ... Sierra Leone"; *Ibid.*, p. 2.

64. "Oral History Transcript of Sergeant Joseph R. Arnold," p. 29.

65. Walters: "After Action Report ... Sierra Leone"; *Ibid.*, p. 4.

66. *Ibid.*

67. "Oral History Transcript of Sergeant Joseph R. Arnold," p. 44.

68. *Ibid.*, p. 45.

69. Walters, "After Action Report ... Sierra Leone," p. 4.

70. *Ibid.*, pp. 4–5.

71. *Ibid.*, p. 3.

72. French, *A Continent for the Taking*, pp. 72–3.

73. *Ibid.*, p. 73.

74. Sergeant Thomas A. Ring letter to GySgt. Leo J. Daugherty III, 22 October 1998.

75. French, *A Continent for the Taking*, p. 76.

76. *Ibid.*, p. 77.

77. Gunnery Sergeant Frederick A. Upchurch, "After Action Report: Evacuation of Brazzaville," In S-3 Archives, Drawer 2, Folder "After Action Report: Evacuation of Brazzaville," Marine Security Guard Bn., State Department, MCCDC, Quantico, Va., p. 2.

78. *Ibid.*, p. 2.

79. *Ibid.*, p. 3; French, *A Continent for the Taking*, p. 74.

80. *Ibid.*, pp. 8–11.

81. A "REACT" is an emergency defensive procedure whereby the Marines don flak jackets and helmets and man their weapons. A REACT room inside the U.S. Embassy contains this equipment.

82. Upchurch, "After Action Report: Evacuation of Brazzaville," p. 11.

83. *Ibid.*, pp. 12–13.

84. French, *A Continent for the Taking*, pp. 77–9, 189–228.

85. *Ibid.*, pp. 229–58.

86. *Ibid.*, pp. 250–1.

87. *Ibid.*, p. 251.

88. Staff Sergeant T. Richardson, "After Action Report to the Commanding Officer," Marine Security Guard Battalion, State Department, 1 September 1998, S-3, Archives, Drawer 2, Folder, "After Action Report on the Evacuation of U.S. Embassy Kinshasa, Democratic Republic of the Congo," p. 1.

89. *Ibid.*, p. 2.

90. *Ibid.*

91. *Ibid.*, p. 3.

92. *Ibid.*, p. 4.

93. *Ibid.*

94. *Ibid.*

95. Osama Bin Laden, the 17th child of Mohammed Bin Laden, a Yemeni construction magnate, born "around 1957" in Saudi Arabia, emerged as one of several radical Muslim leaders who subscribed to driving the Soviets out of Afghanistan during the 1980s. At the conclusion of that war in 1989, Bin Laden returned to Saudi Arabia, where he soon took up a new crusade, this time against the United States, which had sent 540,000 troops to Saudi Arabia to defend the kingdom against an expected Iraqi attack in 1990. After the conclusion of Desert Storm, Bin Laden became an outspoken opponent of the kingdom's dependence on foreigners ("infidels") to defend itself. Eventually declared persona non grata by the Saudi government and stripped of his Saudi citizenship, Bin Laden took up a new jihad, this time against the United States and the Saudi royal family. Bin Laden's group, known "Al-Qaida" or "the Base," made up from his supporters during the Soviet-Afghan War (1979–1989), including the Makhtab al Khidmat or Services Center, became the center of radical Islamic groups in the Middle East and Africa that helped carry out the first bombings of the World Trade Center in New York in 1993. With Al-Qaida's support, the Makhtab became the prime suspects behind the bombings of the U.S. embassies in Nairobi, Kenya, and Dar es Salaam in Tanzania in 1998. See Ahmed Rashid, *Taliban: Militant Islam, Oil, and Fundamentalism in Central Asia* (New Haven, Conn.: Yale University Press, 2001), pp. 131–2.

96. *Ibid.*, p. 134.

97. Lieutenant Colonel Dennis G. Sabal, Commanding Officer, Fox Company, e-mail to Colonel David S. Burgess, Commanding Officer, Marine Security Guard Battalion, 12 August 1998, via Lieutenant Colonel David W. Berkman, Executive Officer, MSG Bn., Folder "Bombings at Nairobi, Kenya and Dar es Salaam," S-3 Archives, Drawer 2, Marine Security Guard Battalion, State Department, MCCDC, Quantico, Va.

98. Lucien Vandenbroucke, "Tragedy and Inspiration in Nairobi: When Uncommon Valor Became Commonplace," *State*, October 1988, p. 16.

99. *Ibid.*, p. 2.

100. *Ibid.*, p. 2.

101. *Ibid.*; John E. Lange, "Dar es Salaam: Confronting the Crisis," October 1988, *State*, pp. 21–5.

102. *Ibid.*

103. Sergeant Brian P. Johnson to Gunnery Sergeant Leo J. Daugherty III, e-mail, "After-Action Report of Events at Dar es Salaam," nd.

104. Corporal Cody McCabe e-mail to Gunnery Sergeant Leo J. Daugherty III.

105. Madeline Albright, *Madam Secretary: A Memoir* (New York: Miramax Books, 2003), pp. 364–5.

106. Vandenbroucke, "Tragedy and Inspiration in Nairobi," pp. 17–18.

107. Carl Goodman, "Playing Tribute to Fallen Heroes," *State*, October 1998, pp. 10–14.

108. Albright, *Madam Secretary*, p. 365; For a complete assessment of the tragedy see Admiral William J. Crowe, USN (Ret)., "Report of the Accountability Review Boards: The Bombings of the U.S. Embassies in Nairobi, Kenya and Dar es Salaam, Tanzania, on August 7, 1998," Washington, D.C., U.S. Department of State, January 1999, in S-3 Archives, Drawer 2, Folder "Report of the Accountability Review Boards: The Bombings of the U.S. Embassies in Nairobi, Kenya, and Dar es Salaam, Tanzania, on August 7, 1998," Marine Security Guard Bn., State Department, MCCDC, Quantico, Va.

109. Sabal e-mail to Burgess, p. 3.

110. *Ibid.*

111. *Ibid.*

112. Autumn Gray, "A Mother's Tearful Goodbye," *Potomac News*, 13 August 1998, p. A-2.

113. Gunnery Sergeant Cross's statements in Detachment Commander to Commanding Officer, B Company, Marine Security Guard Battalion, "Command Chronology for the Period of 1 January to 30 June 1998," 10 January 1999. Copies can be found in S-3 Files, Marine Security Guard Bn., MCCDC, Quantico, Va., and the Marine Corps University Archives, Alfred M. Gray Research Center, Marine Corps University, MCCDC, Quantico, Va., "Command Chronology for 1 January–30 June 1998," pp. 3 and in Enclosure 1 of the same report.

114. Albright, *Madam Secretary*, p. 286; As a footnote to the tragedies in Nairobi and Dar es Salaam, Pakistani security forces captured Ahmed Khalfan Ghailiani, who is wanted for complicity in the twin embassy bombings in East Africa on 25 July 2004, after a ferocious gun battle near the town of Gujrat. His capture is considered a major blow to the Al-Qaida terrorist network. Presently, Mr. Ghailiani is awaiting extradition to the United States on charges of mass murder. See Munir Ahmad, "Al Qaeda Claims Murder Attempt: Warns of More 'Painful Strikes,'" *Washington Times*, 1 August 2004.

115. Albright, *Madam Secretary*, p. 286.

116. Master Sergeant Reed, the Detachment Commander at the U.S. Embassy in Prague, Czech Republic, had been temporarily assigned to the U.S. Embassy in Damascus, Syria. See Operational Incident Report #4-98, American Embassy, Damascus, Syria, to Commanding Officer, Marine Security Guard Bn., State Department, Quantico, Va., 21 December 1998, in Detachment Commander, Gunnery Sergeant Donald D. Downey, Jr., to Commanding Officer, Company B, Marine Security Guard Battalion, 1 January 1999, Subject: "Command Chronology for the Period 01 July to 31 December 1998," in S-3 Historical Archives, Marine Security Guard Battalion, State Department, MCCDC, Quantico, Va., p. 1.

117. Sergeant Bryan Paxton Oral History, interviewed by Gunnery Sergeant Leo J. Daugherty III, 8 December 2000, at Marine Security Guard Bn., MCCDC, Quantico, Va., in possession of the author.

118. Operational Incident Report #4–98, p. 2.

119. *Ibid.*, p. 3.

120. Sergeant Bryan Paxton Oral History.

121. Gunnery Sergeant Wheeler, Marine Security Guard Detachment, Islamabad, Pakistan, letter to Marine Security Guard Battalion, 15 November 1998, Subject: "Photograph for *Leatherneck*, *The State*, and the [*Marine Corps*] *Gazette*," in S-3 Archives, Drawer 3, Folder 21, "Cancellation of Marine Corps Ball in Islamabad, November 1998," Marine Security Guard Bn., State Department, MCCDC, Quantico, Va.

122. Jon Anderson, "Embassy in Albania on Alert: Marines and SEALS on Guard Amid Terrorist Fears," *Stars and Stripes*, 17 August 1998, Vol. 57, pp. 1–2.

123. Jon Anderson, "Marines Hunker Down at Embassy in Albania," *Stars and Stripes*, 22 August 1998, copy in S-3 Historical Archives, in Commanding Officer, Marine Security Guard Detachment, Tirana, Albania, to Commanding Officer, Company A, Commanding Officer to Commandant of the Marine Corps, 1 April 1999, Subject: "Battalion Command Chronology 1 January to 30 June 1998," Marine Security Guard Battalion, State Department, MCCDC, Quantico, Va., Drawer 5.

124. Captain Marius L. Harrison to Captain William J. Gibbons, 7 March 2002, Subject: "R290830Z Oct. 01 CG MCCDC Quantico V MXBUL 5400; Activation of the Fourth Marine Expeditionary (Unclassified)"; Colonel Boyette Hasty to Lieutenant Colonel Roger M. Strauss, 9 June 2002, Subject: "Command of Marine Security Guard (MSG) Bn.; 4th Marine Expeditionary Brigade (AT), 4th MEB (AT) at BN Mission and METLs," 11 January 2002. Power Point slide presentation.

125. Brigadier General D.V. O'Dell, Commanding General, 4th Marine Expeditionary Brigade (AT), 10 January 2002, Subject: "AT Battalion T/O Brief," in S-3 Archives, Drawer 3, Folder "4th MEB (AT) Organizational Documents," Marine Security Guard Battalion, State Department, MCCDC, Quantico, Va.

126. "4th Marine Expeditionary Brigade (AT)," Mission Statement, Power Point slide presentation, in S-3 Archives, Drawer 3, Folder, "4th MEB (AT) Organizational Documents."

127. Lt. James D. Jarvis, "Marines Reclaim Post 1, Kabul," *Leatherneck*, February 2002, Vol. 85, No. 2, pp. 16–18.

128. *Ibid.*, p. 16.

129. *Ibid.*, p. 18.

130. The last Marine detachment served there until February 1989, when the embassy was ordered closed due to the increasing violence from the Afghan civil war (1989–1997) that brought the Taliban (and Al-Qaida) to power. See Rashid, *Taliban*, pp. 40–79.

131. Corporal Matthew B. Roberson, "Afghanistan: Kabul; 4th MEB Mans Embassy," *Leatherneck*, March 2002, Vol. 85, No. 3, p. 19.

132. *Ibid.*

133. *Ibid.*

134. Commanding Officer, Marine Security Guard Bn., to Head, Homeland Defense Branch, Security Division, Plans, Policies and Operations Department, HQMC, 8 December 2003, Subject: "Site Visit for Potential Detachment Activation, American Embassy, Kabul, Afghanistan (1–2 November 2003)"; Commanding Officer, Bravo Company, to Commanding Officer, Marine Security Guard Bn., 4 November 2003, Subject: "Site Visit for Potential Detachment Activation, American Embassy, Kabul, Afghanistan (1–2 November 2003); Inspecting Officer, Captain Robert J. Pleak, to Commanding Officer, Marine Security Guard Bn., 2 November 2003, Subject: "Site Visit for Potential Detachment Activation, American Embassy, Kabul, Afghanistan (1–2 November 2003)"; American Embassy, Kabul, Afghanistan to RUEHC/ Secretary of State, Washington, D.C., 11 December 2002, Subject: "Country Clearance for Captain Robert J. Peak; Projected Integration Plan for Marine Security Guards into Kabul," working paper; James A. McWhirter to Mr. Anthony G. Moore, 28 January 2002, Subject: "Return of MSG Detachment to Kabul, Afghanistan." All in S-3, Bravo Company, SAI Binder "Kabul, Afghanistan," Marine Security Guard Bn., State Department, MCCDC, Quantico, Va.

135. On December 31, 2006, Saddam Hussein was executed by the Iraqis after being convicted for the murder of 181 innocent Iraqis after a failed assassination attempt.

136. Phone conversation between Gunnery Sergeant Edward J. Burke, S-3 Operations Chief, and author, 30 June 2004, at Marine Security Guard Battalion, State Department, MCCDC, Quantico, Va.

137. Comments by Gunnery Sergeant Richard K. Prather to author on "MSG Lessons Learned from Enduring Freedom and Operation Iraqi Freedom," Marine Security Guard Battalion, MCCDC, Quantico, Va., on 16 November 2004.

138. Commanding Officer, Marine Security Guard Bn., to Commandant of the Marine Corps, 29 July 1969, Subject: "Predeployment Training: Request for Waiver," S-3, Historical Archives, Drawer 4, Folder "Policy and Training Issues, 1969–1974," Marine Security Guard Bn., State Department, MCCDC, Quantico, Va.

139. Interview of Sergeant Jose Martinez by author, at Marine Security Guard Battalion, 15 November 2004, MCCDC, Quantico, Va. A copy is on file with the S-3 Historical Files, Drawer 3, MSG Bn., State Department, MCCDC, Quantico, Va.

140. *Ibid.*

141. *Ibid.*

142. Rowan Scarborough, "Assault Force to Position 2,000 Marines off Monrovia," *Washington Times*, 26 July 2003, p. A-1 and A-4.

143. *Ibid.*

144. *Ibid.*, p. A-4.

145. *Ibid.*

146. Alexandra Zavis, "Liberia in Chaos: Marines Help Evacuate U.S. Embassy as Dozens Die," *Daily Press*, Hampton Roads, Va., 22 July 2003, pp. A-1 and A-9.

147. Glenn Kessler, "U.S. Role in Liberia is Outlined," *The Washington Post*, 26 July 2003, pp. A-1 and A-14.

148. "A Warm Welcome from Weary Liberians: 26th MEU Marines 'Just Here to Help the People,'" *Marine Corps Times*, 25 August 2003, Vol. 5, No. 33, p. 10.

149. *Ibid.*

150. Sergeant Jason R. Scamlin, "An Overview and Lessons Learned from the 2003 Liberian Civil War," S-3 Archives, Drawer 3, Folder 20, "Lessons Learned from the 2003 Liberian Civil War," Marine Security Guard Battalion, State Department, MCCDC, Quantico, Va., pp. 5–20.

151. *Ibid.*, pp. 20–8.

152. For the Marine Corps' response to the crises in Haiti during the 1990s see Colonel Nicholas E. Reynolds, *A Skillful Show of Strength: U.S. Marines in the Caribbean, 1991–1996* (Washington, D.C.: History and Museums Division, HQMC, 2003).

153. "Yorktown Marines Land in Haiti, Anti-Terror Unit to Provide Security as Rebels Move Toward Capital," *Virginian-Pilot*, 24 February 2004, pp. A-1 and A-12. Tim Weiner and Lydia Polgreen, "Haitian Rebels Stake Claim to Power," *Virginian-Pilot*, 2 March 2004, p. A-10.

154. "Yorktown Marines Land in Haiti," p. A-12.

155. C. Mark Brinkley, "Marines Lead the Way for U.N. in War-torn Haiti," *Marine Corps Times*, 15 March 2004, Vol. 6, No. 10, p. 10.

156. Mark Stevenson and Paisley Dodds, "Haitians Show Indifference to U.S. Marines' Presence," *Virginian-Pilot*, Friday, 5 March 2004; Paisley Dodds and Ian James, "Aristide Escapes into Exile: U.S. Marines, Vanguard of U.N.-approved Forces, Sent to Quell Haitian Uprising," *The Daily Press*, Hampton Roads, 1 March 2004, A-1, A-5.

157. Stevenson and Dodds, "Haitians Show Indifference to U.S. Marines' Presence," *Virginian-Pilot*, 5 March 2004.

158. Weiner and Polgreen, "Haitian Rebels Stake Claim to Power," p. A-10.

Also see Drew Brown, "Marines Expect to Have Limited Role in Haiti," *Virginian-Pilot*, 2 March 2004, p. A-10.

159. Syed Mohsin Naqvi and Elise Labott, "Karachi Bombs Near U.S. Offices," 26 May 2004, www.CNN.com, in S-3 Historical Archives, Folder 18, "Bomb Blasts in Karachi, Pakistan, 27 May 2004," Marine Security Guard Battalion, State Department, MCCDC, Quantico, Va., pp. 1–2.

160. The other Marine Security Guards at the U.S. Consulate in Karachi, Pakistan, included Staff Sergant Michael B. Polendey, Sergeants Christopher J. Beillo, Victor S. Hurd, Ruben H. Felipecarde, Elizar Andrade, and Corporal Richard Weber. See Marine Security Guard Battalion to Commandant of the Marine Corps, 27 May 2004, Subject: "/OPER-3SIR/54050/003/Mar/-/-." In S-3, Historical Archives, Drawer 3, Folder 18, "Bomb Blasts in Karachi, Pakistan, 26 May 2004," Marine Security Guard Battalion, State Department, MCCDC, Quantico, Va.

161. *Ibid.*

162. American Consulate, Karachi, Pakistan, to Commanding Officer, Marine Security Guard Battalion, 26 May 2004, Subject: "Operational Incident Report #6-04." In S-3 Archives, Drawer 3, Folder 18, "Bomb Blasts in Karachi, Pakistan, 26 May 2004," Marine Security Guard Battalion, State Department, MCCDC, Quantico, Va.

163. "Terrorists Attack U.S. Consulate in Jiddah," Associated Press, 6 December 2004, Fox News, http//www.foxnews.com/story/0,2933,140574,000.html.

164. "U.S. Consulate Stormed: Al-Qaida Blamed for Daring Raid on Heavily Guarded U.S. Compound," *The Virginian-Pilot*, 7 December 2004, p. A-14.

165. *Ibid.*, p. A-14.

166. Corky Siemaszko, "Marines Saved 'em from Qaeda," *New York Daily News*, 8 December 2004.

167. The reference here is to the name of the Iraqi city Fallujah, which had become a haven for terrorists and had been taken by U.S. Marines and soldiers in November 2004 in some of the heaviest fighting to occur in Operation Iraqi Freedom.

168. "Terrorists Attack U.S. Consulate in Jiddah."

169. *Ibid.*

170. www.msg-history.com/historical items/ H_Dos_ SECSTATE_BirthdayMsg.h.

171. Lieutenant Colonel James G. Kyser, "United States Marine Corps Year in Review 2005," *Faircount's Special Operations*, p. 36.

172. Greg Jaffe, "Rumsfeld Pushes Major Revamping of U.S. Military," *Wall Street Journal*, 11 March 2005, pp. A-1, A-8; Sean D. Naylor, "Corps Commandos," *Marine Corps Times*, 20 June 2005; Sue A. Lackey, "The SOCOM Dilemma: Defense Secretary Rumsfeld Wants More Marine Involvement in the Command, But There is a Deep Divide Over How that Will be Accomplished," Navy League of the United States, 7 April 2005, www.navyleague.org/sea_power/apr_05_30.php.

173. General Bryan D. Brown, U.S. Army Special Operations Command, and General Michael W. Hagee, USMC, Memorandum of Agreement Between the United States Marine Corps and United States Special Operations Command (draft), in Marine Special Operations Component Binder, Chief Historian, Marine Corps Historical Division, Marine Corps University, MCCDC, Quantico, Va.

174. Formed to better respond to terrorist threats and natural disasters, the Expeditionary Strike Groups — amphibious warships and their embarked Marine Expeditionary Unit (a reinforced battalion), surface warships, submarines, and advanced airborne surveillance platforms — have increased the response time and operational reach of the Navy–Marine Corps Team to quickly respond to either a terrorist attack or natural disaster. ESGs combine the traditional multi-mission capabilities of the MEU (SOC) and Amphibious Ready Groups with enhanced organic air defense, undersea warfare, and strike capability. See United States Marine Corps, *Marine Corps Concepts and Programs* (Washington, D.C.: Headquarters Marine Corps, 2004), p. 28.

175. Terry L. Love, "LTC Terry Love's Account of Working with the Marines During Operation Lifeline, Disaster Assistance Center — Pakistan," 25 January 2008, Hampton, Va. Manuscript in possession of the author and reprinted with permission, p. 1.

176. *Ibid.*

177. *Ibid.*, p. 2.

178. Lieutenant Colonel Franklin D. Baker to Captain Debra R. Gomez, 21 March 2007, Subject: "Name Change for Marine Security Guard Battalion," S-3 Historical Files, MSG Battalion, State Department, MCCDC, Quantico, Va.

179. *Ibid.*, p. 4.

Chapter 10

1. Deborah Schmidt, "Women Security Guards Finding Gradual Acceptance," *Navy Times*, 16 December 1991, p. 15; Captain S.J. Conboy, Policy Paper No. 2, "Women Marines on the Program," 17 August 1992, Policy Statement Reference Almar 221–92, p. 1. S-3 Archives, Drawer 4, Folder "1992: News Articles and Clippings: 1992, Women Marines, etc."

2. Schmidt, "Women Security Guards," p. 15.

3. Conboy, "Women Marines on the Program," p. 1.

4. Major W.T. Tucker, Commanding Officer, Company C, to Commanding Officer, Marine Security Guard Battalion, 3 April 1980, Subject: "Evaluation of Women Marine (WM) Security Guards," in S-3 Archives, Folder: "1980: MSG Bn. Newsletter; Evaluation of WM MSGs in Mid-East, Updates/Newsclippings," p. 1; Commanding Officer, Company A, to Commanding Officer, Marine Security Guard Battalion, 8 April 1980, "Evaluation of Women Marine Security Guards," S-3 Archives, Drawer 4, Folder "1980: MSGBn Newsletter, Evaluation of WM MSGs in Mid-East Hostage Up-Dates/News Clippings." Marine Security Guard Bn., State Department, MCCDC, Quantico, Va.

5. *Ibid.*, p. 2.

6. *Ibid.*, p. 3.

7. Major R.H. Kayser, Commanding Officer, Company D, Marine Security Guard Battalion, to Commanding Officer, Marine Security Guard Battalion, State Department, 6 April 1980, in S-3 Archives, Drawer 4, in Tucker, "Evaluation of Women MSGs," Enclosure 5, p. 1.

8. *Ibid.*, pp. 1–2.

9. Major R.G. Richard, Commanding Officer, Company F, Nairobi, Kenya, to Commanding Officer, Marine Security Guard Battalion, State Department, 19 March 1980, Subject: "Evaluation of Women Marine Security Guards Assigned to Company F," in Tucker, "Evaluation of Women MSGs," Enclosure 6, p. 2.

10. *Ibid.*

11. Message, American Consulate, Frankfurt, to Commanding Officer, Marine Security Guard Bn., 2 May 1980, in Tucker, "Evaluation of Women MSGs," Enclosure 7, pp. 1–3.

12. Mel Jones, "Corps Eyes Moslems are WM Pullouts," *Navy Times*, 10 December 1979, in S-3 Archives, Drawer 4, Folder "1980: Articles on Iranian Hostage Crisis," Marine Security Guard Battalion, State Department, MCCDC, Quantico, Va.

13. Conboy, "Women Marines on the Program," p. 1.

14. *Ibid.*

15. Schmidt, "Women Security Guards," p. 15.

16. *Ibid.*

17. *Ibid.* Company B is now headquartered in Nicosia, Cyprus.

18. Lieutenant Colonel Mary V. "Ginger" Jacocks letter to Gunnery Sergeant Leo J. Daugherty III, 6 June 2002.

19. Comments on manuscript by Lieutenant Colonel Mary V. Jacocks, July 2004, to author.

20. *Ibid.*, p. 2.

21. *Ibid.*, p. 3.
22. *Ibid.*
23. Jacocks' comments on manuscript.
24. Staff Sergeant Becki Wass, "Soldier Trains at MSG School," *The Sentry*, Quantico, Va., 25 February 1983.
25. *Ibid.*
26. *Ibid.*
27. Sergeant Carlos Simonetti letter to GySgt. Leo J. Daugherty III, 19 October 1998.
28. Congressman Samuel S. Stratton, Chairman, Subcommittee of the House Armed Services Committee, to Brigadier General Albert E. Brewster, Legislative Assistant to the Commandant, 7 November 1979, in S-3 Archives, Drawer 4, Folder "1979 Iranian Hostage Crisis." Marine Security Guard Battalion, State Department, MCCDC, Quantico, Va.
29. Henry Allen, "The Guardian Elite: Tehran on Their Minds at the Marine Security Guard School," *Washington Post*, 15 February 1979, p. C-1.
30. "Marine Security Guards: Upholding Traditional Standards of Discipline," *Marine Security Guard Battalion Newsletter*, January 1980, pp. 1–2. In S-3 Archives, Drawer 4, "1980: Iranian Hostage Crisis," Marine Security Guard Bn., State Department, MCCDC, Quantico, Va.
31. Allen, "The Guardian Elite."
32. Dan Epstein, "Training Future Embassy Guards," *Quantico Sentry*, 29 November 1979, p. 1. In S-3 Archives, Drawer 4, Folder "1979: Hostage Crisis, Articles, Newsletters, etc.," Marine Security Guard Bn., State Department; R.T. Wolfertz, Operations and Training Officer, to S-3 Files, 18 January 1980, Subject: "Hostage Situation Training," S-3 Archives, Drawer 4, Folder: "1980 MSG Bn. Newsletter Evaluation of WM Marine Security Guards in Mid-East, Hostage Up-Dates/NewsClipping," Marine Security Guard Battalion, State Department, MCCDC, Quantico, Va.
33. "Marine Guards are Trained for Limited Missions," *New York Times*, 11 November 1979, p. 12. In S-3 Archives, Drawer 4, Folder "Articles on Iranian Hostage Crisis," Marine Security Guard Bn., State Department, MCCDC, Quantico, Va.
34. "Hostage Training Instituted," *Daily Pilot*, Orange County, Calif., 10 December 1979, S-3 Archives, Drawer 4, Folder "Articles on the Iranian Hostage Crisis, 1979–1980," Marine Security Guard Battalion, State Department, MCCDC, Quantico, Va.
35. "MSG Graduate Ready for True Test of Confidence," *Quantico Sentry*, 14 Friday 1979, p. 3. In S-3 Archives,

Drawer 4, Folder "Newspaper Articles on the Hostage Crisis in Iran, 1979," Marine Security Guard Battalion, State Department, MCCDC, Quantico, Va.
36. General P.X. Kelley, memorandum to the Secretary of the Navy, 22 April 1987, Subject: "Marine Security Guard Matters," p. 1. In S-3 Archives, Drawer 4, Folder "1987: Congressional Investigations Post–Lonetree Espionage Affair," Marine Security Guard Battalion, State Department, MCCDC, Quantico, Va.
37. General Alfred M. Gray, CMC, letter to Hon. Secretary of State George P. Schultz, nd.; Colonel C.J. Del Gross, Commanding Officer, MSG Bn., to Major General Carl E. Mundy, Jr., Director of Operations, HQMC, 31 August 1987, Subject: "Expansion to the MSG Program, Organization Structure: An Exploratory Overview"; Commanding Officer, Marine Security Guard Battalion, to Major General Carl E. Mundy, Jr., Director of Operations, HQMC, 4 June 1987, Subject: "Comments on Brown Report." All in S-3 Archives, Drawer 4, Folder "1987: Post–Lonetree Investigations," Marine Security Guard Battalion, State Department, MCCDC, Quantico, Va.
38. Kelley, memorandum to the Secretary of the Navy, p. 2.
39. Major General Carl E. Mundy, Jr., Deputy Chief of Staff for Operations, "Testimony Before the Defense Policy Panel and Subcommittee on Armed Services and House of Representatives on 3 April 1987, Concerning the Marine Security Guard Program." In S-3 Archives, Drawer 4, Folder "1987: Lonetree Investigations: Congressional Hearings and Testimony," p. 4. Marine Security Guard Battalion, State Department, MCCDC, Quantico, Va.
40. *Ibid.*, p. 5.
41. "MSG Graduate Ready for True Test of Confidence," p. 3.
42. Lieutenant Colonel Arthur P. Brill, Jr., "From Tripoli to the 21st Century: Corps' MSG Detachments, A Growth Industry," *Seapower*, April 1998, pp. 77–81.
43. Paul Koscak, "School Screens Marines for Coveted Overseas Guard Duty," *State*, U.S. Department of State, May 2003, No. 468, pp. 17–19.
44. Hampton Sides, "First to Die," *Reader's Digest*, February 2004, pp. 155–9.
45. Gordon Lubold, "3 Years … 3 Embassies," *Marine Corps Times*, 3 May 2004, Vol. 6, No. 17, p. 10.
46. Brill, "From Tripoli to the 21st Century," p. 78.
47. *Ibid.*
48. Koscak, "School Screens Marines," p. 19.

49. The Chemical, Biological Incidence Response Force or CBIRF was created in 1996 at Camp Lejeune, N.C., and is now located at Indianhead, Md. CBIRF, like MSG Bn., State Department, is a part of the 4th MEB Anti-Terrorism Force. CWO2 J.A. Pcola was one of the original members.
50. Conversation with CWO2 J.A. Pcola, NBC Officer, with author, 17 November 2004, at Marine Security Guard Battalion, State Department, MCCDC, Quantico, Va.
51. Gunnery Sergeant Upchurch, "After Action Report: Evacuation of Brazzaville," Marine Security Battalion S-3 Historical Folder "1996," MCCDC, Drawer 1, Quantico, Va., pp. 12–13.
52. Commanding Officer, Marine Security Guard Battalion, "Command Chronology for the Period of 1 January to 30 June 2003," 4 December 2003, MSG Bn., State Department, MCCDC, Quantico, Va., S-3 Historical Archives, Drawer 4, p. 5.
53. Gunnery Sergeant Steve E. Rice, SNCOIC of the Recruiting and Advertising Team, conversation with author, 17 November 2004, MSG Battalion, State Department, MCCDC, Quantico, Va.

Chapter 11

1. "MSG Det Kampala," *Marines*, August 1986, pp. 18–21.
2. Remarks by Hon. George P. Schultz, Secretary of State, at an American Legion ceremony honoring U.S. Marine Security Guards, Washington, D.C., 11 May 1984, in S-3 Archives, Drawer 4, Folder "1984, News Clippings and Articles on MSG Marines," Marine Security Guard Battalion, State Department, MCCDC, Quantico, Va.
3. Hon. Madeline K. Albright, Secretary of State, "Remarks to Department of State Employees on the East Africa Bombings," Washington, D.C., 10 August 1998, Office of the Spokesman, U.S. Department of State, http://seccretary.state.gov/www/statement/1998, copy in S-3 Archives, Drawer 4, Folder "1998: Bombings in Nairobi, Kenya, and Dar es Salaam, Tanzania," Marine Security Guard Battalion, State Department, MCCDC, Quantico, Va.
4. Lubold, "3 Years … 3 Embassies," *Marine Corps Times*, 3 May 2004, p. 10.
5. Danny J. Crawford, "Two Centuries of Teamwork: U.S. Marines and the Foreign Service," *Shipmate*, November 1980, pp. 23–7.
6. *Ibid.*, p. 27.

Bibliography

Primary Sources

Official Records

Marine Security Guard Battalion Command Chronologies for the years 1979 through 2006, S-3, Marine Corps Combat Development Center (MCCDC), Marine Corps Base, Quantico, Va.

Historical Document Files, Marine Corps Embassy Security Guard Command (MCESGC) for the years 1947 through 1998, S-3, Marine Corps Embassy Security Guard Command, Quantico, Va. Row 2, Drawers 1, 2 and 3.

Marine Security Guard Reference Folders, U.S. Marine Corps Historical Division, Marine Corps University, MCCDC, Quantico, Va.

Marine Corps University Archives, Marine Corps University, MCCDC, Quantico, Va.

Personal Papers

Lieutenant General James Carson Breckinridge, USMC (Deceased)

Major General Smedley D. Butler, USMC (Deceased)

Lieutenant General Pedro del Valle, USMC (Deceased)

Colonel William A. Eddy, USMC (Deceased)

General Wallace M. Greene, USMC (Deceased)

General Thomas Holcomb, USMC (Deceased)

Lieutenant General John H. Russell, USMC (Deceased)

Collection

The Boxer Rebellion Collection, 1899–1900.

U.S. National Archives (Washington, D.C.)

U.S. Marine Legation Guard, Managua, Nicaragua, 1909–1925, Record Group 127, Series 18, 43, and 1975–70/5–2.

U.S. Marine Corps, Records of Overseas Brigades, Battalions, and Regiments, 1889–1914. RG 127, Series 43.

Records Relating to the Correspondence of the Adjutant and Inspector's Office, Headquarters United States Marine Corps, 1913–1933, RG 127.

Records Relating to the Activities of the 3d Brigade, U.S. Marine Corps, and the Legation and Consular Guard Detachments in China, RG 127.

Headquarters U.S. Marine Corps

Annual Reports to the Secretary of the Navy for the Years 1867–1930 by the Commandant of the Marine Corps.

United States Department of State

Foreign Relations of the United States: Diplomatic Papers, 1932. Volume IV: The Far East. Washington, D.C.: Government Printing Office, 1948.

Foreign Relations of the United States: Diplomatic Papers, 1938. Volume IV: The Far East. Washington, D.C.: Government Printing Office, 1955.

Foreign Relations of the United States, 1958–1960. Volume XII: Near East Region; Iraq, Iran, Arabian Peninsula. Edited by Edward C. Keefer and Glenn W. LaFantasie. Washington, D.C.: Government Printing Office, 1993.

Foreign Relations of the United States, 1958–1960. Volume XI: Lebanon and Jordan. Edited by John P. Glennon and Louis J. Smith. Washington, D.C.: Government Printing Office, 1992.

Foreign Relations of the United States, 1961–1963. Volume XX: Congo Crisis. Edited by Harriet Dashnell Schwar. Washington, D.C.: Government Printing Office, 1994.

Foreign Relations of the United States, 1964–1968. Volume 24: Africa. Edited by Nina-Davis Howland and David S. Patterson. Washington, D.C.: Government Printing Office, 1999.

Foreign Relations of the United States, 1964 -1968. Volume II: Vietnam. January–June 1965. Edited by David C. Humphrey, Ronald D. Landa, Louis J. Smith, and Glenn LaFantasie. Washington, D.C.: United States Government Printing Office, 1996.

Papers Relating to the Foreign Policy of the United States: 1900; With the Annual Message of the President, December 3, 1900. Washington, D.C.: Government Printing Office, 1902.

Papers Relating to the Foreign Relations of the United States: 1912. Washington, D.C.: Government Printing Office, 1919.

Papers Relating to the Foreign Relations of the United States: 1918. Volume III: Russia. Washington, D.C.: Government Printing Office, 1932.

Papers Relating to the Foreign Relations of the United States: 1925. Volume II. Washington, D.C.: Government Printing Office, 1940.

U.S. Department of Defense

Terrorist Group Profiles. Washington, D.C.: Government Printing Office, November 1988.

United States Senate

U.S. Senate Select Committee on Intelligence, "Report on Security at the United States Missions in Moscow and Other Areas of High Risk." Washington, D.C.: Government Printing Office, April 29, 1987.

U.S. Marine Corps Official Histories

Brown, Ronald J. *U.S. Marines in the Persian Gulf, 1990–1991: With Marine Forces Afloat in Desert Shield and Desert Storm.* Washington, D.C.: History and Museums Division, 1998.

Cosmas, Graham A., and Terence Murray. *U.S. Marines in Vietnam: Vietnamization and Redeployment, 1970–1971.* Washington, D.C.: History and Museums Division, HQMC, 1986.

Cureton, Charles H. *U.S. Marines in the Persian Gulf, 1990–1991: With the 1st Marine Division in Desert Shield/Desert Desert Storm.* Washington, D.C.: History and Museums Division, HQMC, 1991.

Dunham, George J., and David A. Quinlan. *U.S. Marines in Vietnam: The Bitter End, 1973–1975.* Washington, D.C.: History and Museums Division, HQMC, 1990.

Edwards, Harry W. *A Different Kind of War: Marines in Europe and North Africa.* Washington, D.C.: History and Museums Division, HQMC 1994.

Ellsworth, Harry Allanson. *One Hundred and Eighty Landings of United States Marines 1800–1934.* Washington, D.C.: History and Museums Division, HQMC, 1974.

Frank, Benis M. *U.S. Marines in Lebanon, 1982–1984.* Washington, D.C.: History and Museums Division, HQMC, 1987.

Fuller, Stephen M., and Graham A. Cosmas. *Marines in the Dominican Republic: 1916–1924.* Washington, D.C.: History and Museums Division, HQMC, 1974.

Hough, Frank O., Verle E. Ludwig, and Henry I. Shaw. *Pearl Harbor to Guadalcanal: History of U.S. Marine Corps Operations in World War II, Volume I.* Washington, D.C.: G-3, Historical Division, HQMC, 1958.

Jones, William K. *A Brief History of the 6th Marines.* Washington, D.C.: History and Museums Division, HQMC, 1987.

Melson, Charles D., and Curtis G. Arnold. *U.S. Marines in Vietnam: The War that Would Not End, 1971–1973.* Washington, D.C.: History and Museums Division, HQMC, 1991.

Melson, Charles D., Evelyn A. Englander, and David A. Dawson. *U.S. Marines in the Persian Gulf, 1990–1991: Anthology and Annotated Bibliography.* Washington, D.C.: History and Museums Division, HQMC, 1992.

Mroczkowski, Dennis, P. *U.S. Marines in the Persian Gulf, 1990–1991: With the 2d Marine Division in Desert Shield and Desert Storm.* Washington, D.C.: History and Museum Division, HQMC, 1993.

Nalty, Bernard C. *The Barrier Forts: A Battle, A Monument, and A Mythical Marine.* Washington, D.C.: Historical Branch, G-3 Division, HQMC, 1962.

_____. *The United States Marines in Nicaragua,* 4th Edition. Washington, D.C.: Historical Branch, G-3 Division, HQMC, 1968.

Quilter, Charles J. *U.S. Marines in the Persian Gulf, 1990–1991: With the I Marine Expeditionary Force in Desert Shield and Desert Storm.* Washington, D.C.: History and Museums Division, HQMC, 1993.

Reynolds, Nicholas E. *Just Cause: Marine Operations in Panama, 1988–1990.* Washington, D.C.: History and Museums Division, HQMC, 1996, 50 pages.

_____. *"A Skillful Show of Strength": U.S. Marines in the Caribbean, 1991–1996.* Washington, D.C.: History and Museums Division, HQMC, 2003.

Ringler, Jack K., Jr., USMC, and Henry I. Shaw, Jr. *U.S. Marine Corps Operations in the Dominican Republic, April–June 1965,* Occasional Paper. Washington, D.C.: History and Museums Division, HQMC, 1970.

Santelli, James S. *A Brief History of the 4th Marines.* Washington, D.C.: History and Museums Division, HQMC, 1970.

_____. *A Brief History of the 8th Marines.* Washington, D.C.: History and Museums Division, HQMC, 1976.

Shulimson, Jack. *Marines in Lebanon 1958.* Washington, D.C.: History and Museums Division, HQMC, 1983.

_____. *U.S. Marines in Vietnam: An Expanding War, 1966.* Washington, D.C.: History and Museums Division, HQMC, 1982.

_____. *U.S. Marines in Vietnam: The Landing and Buildup, 1965.* Washington, D.C.: History and Museums Division, HQMC, 1978.

Shulimson, Jack, Leonard A. Blaisol, Charles R. Smith, and David A. Dawson. *U.S. Marines in Vietnam: The Defining Year, 1968.* Washington, D.C.: History and Museums Division, HQMC, 1997.

Simmons, Edwin H., et al. *The Marines in Vietnam, 1954–1973: An Anthology and Annotated Bibliography.* Washington, D.C.: History and Museums Division, HQMC, 1985.

Smith, Charles R. *U.S. Marines in Vietnam: High Mobility and Standdown, 1969.* Washington, D.C.: History and Museums Division, HQMC, 1988.

Stearns, LeRoy D. *U.S. Marines in the Persian Gulf, 1990–1991: 3d Marne Aircraft Wing in Desert Shield and Desert Storm.* Washington, D.C.: History and Museums Division, HQMC, 1999.

Tefler, Gary L., Lane Rogers, and V. Keith Fleming. *U.S. Marines in Vietnam: Fighting the North Vietnamese, 1967.* Washington, D.C.: History and Museums Division, HQMC, 1984.

Zimmeck, Steven M. *U.S. Marines in the Persian Gulf,*

1990–1991: Combat Service Support in Desert Shield and Desert Storm. Washington, D.C.: History and Museums Division, HQMC, 1999.

U.S. Army Publications

Greenberg, Lawrence M. *United States Army Unilateral and Coalition Operations in the 1965 Dominican Republic Intervention.* Washington, D.C.: U.S. Army Center for Military History, 1987.

Odom, Thomas P. *Dragon Operations: Hostage Rescues in the Congo, 1964–1965.* Leavenworth Papers, No. 14. Fort Leavenworth, Kan., U.S. Army Command and General Staff College, Combat Studies Institute, July 1988.

Spector, Ronald H. *United States Army in Vietnam: Advice and Support; The Early Years, 1941–1960.* Washington, D.C.: Center for Military History, 1985.

Spiller, Roger J. *"Not War But Like War," The American Intervention in Lebanon.* Fort Leavenworth, Kan., U.S. Army Command and General Staff College, Combat Studies Institute, January 1981.

Yates, Lawrence A. *Power Pack: The American Intervention in the Dominican Republic, 1965–1966.* Leavenworth Papers, No. 15. Fort Leavenworth, Kan., U.S. Army Command and General Staff College, Combat Studies Institute, July 1988.

U.S. Air Force Publications

LaValle, A.J.C. *Last Flight From Saigon.* U.S. Air Force, Southeast Asia Monograph Series, Volume IV, No. 6. Washington, D.C.: Government Printing Office, 1978.

Oral Histories

Oral History Transcript of Sergeant Joseph R. Arnold, USMC, conducted by Major James C. Antel, USMC, U.S. Marine Corps Historical Center, Archives Section, History and Museums Division, HQMC, 5 June 1997.

Oral History Transcript of Lieutenant General Edward A. Craig, U.S. Marine Corps (Deceased) by Major L.E. Tatem. Washington, D.C.: Historical Division, HQMC, 1968.

Oral History Transcript of General Lemuel C. Shepherd, USMC (Deceased), by Benis M. Frank (Deceased).

Interviews and Reminiscences

Lieutenant Colonel Joseph L. Allred, U.S. Army (Ret.)

Master Sergeant George A. Bader, U.S. Marine Corps (Ret.)

Master Sergeant John A. Bangs, U.S. Air Force (March 2000)

William H. Chittenden (Quantico, Va., November 2001)

Lieutenant Colonel William C. Curtis, USMC (Ret.) (October 1998)

Master Sergeant William V. "Bill" East, USMC (February 2002)

Sergeant Ronnell Harwood, USMC (October 1998)

Lieutenant Colonel Mary V. Jacocks, USMC (June 2002)

Sergeant Brian P. Johnson, USMC

WO-1 George Lampman, USMC (Ret.) (October 1998)

Lieutenant Colonel Terry Love, U.S. Army (January 2008)

Sergeant Robert A. Lynn, USMC

Master Sergeant Rolland May, USMC

Corporal Cody McCabe, USMC

Sergeant George H. Morrow, USMC

Corporal C.J. Noble

Sergeant Major W.C. Oates, Jr., USMC (June 1999)

Major General D.V. O'Dell, USMC

Sergeant Edward R. Paruka, USMC (January 1999)

Sergeant Bryan Paxton, USMC (December 2000)

Staff Sergeant Thomas J. Sabanski, USMC (March 1988)

Staff Sergeant Lloyd E. Shank, USMC (December 1998)

Sergeant Carlos Simonetti, USMC (October 1998)

Captain William D. Steeves, Jr. (October 1998)

Tom Stevens (August 1999)

Sergeant Joseph R. Svinth, USMC (August 1999)

Corporal George B.B. Zahuranic, USMC (October 1998)

Diaries and Log Books

Althouse, Adelbert, Log of the USS *Brooklyn* (Copy). Washington, D.C.: Reference Section, History and Museums Division, Subject Folder: "Marines in Siberia, 1918–1920," Marine Corps Historical Center, Marine Corps University Archives, MCCDC, Quantico, Va.

The Diary of Private Oscar J. Upham, USMC. Special Collections, Marine Corps University Archives, Marine Corps University, Alfred M. Gray Research Center, MCCDC, Quantico, Va.

Memoirs

Albright, Madeline, with Bill Woodward. *Madam Secretary: A Memoir.* New York: Miramax Books, 2003.

Baker, James A., III, with Thomas M. DeFrank. *The Politics of Diplomacy: Revolution, War and Peace, 1989–1992.* New York: G. Putnam, 1995.

Bell, Larry A. *Dead Horses in the Sun.* Bloomington, Indiana: 1st Books, 2003.

Carter, Jimmy. *Keeping Faith: Memoirs of a President.* New York: Bantam Books, 1982.

Clinton, William J. *My Life.* New York: Vintage Publishing, 2005.

De Silva, Peer. *Sub Rosa: The CIA and the Uses of Intelligence.* New York: New York Times Book Company, 1978.

Del Valle, Pedro A. *Roman Eagles Over Ethiopia.* Harrisburg, Pa.: Military Service Publishing Co., 1940.

_____. *Semper Fidelis: An Autobiography.* Hawthorne, Calif.: Christian Book Club of America, 1976.

Ford, Gerald R. *A Time to Heal: The Autobiography of Gerald R. Ford.* New York: Harper and Row, 1979.

Francis, David R. *Russia: From the American Embassy, April 1916–November 1918.* New York: Charles Scribner's Sons, 1921.

Johnson, U. Alexis, with Jef Olivarius McAllister. *The Right Hand of Power.* Englewood Cliffs, N.J.: Prentice-Hall, 1984.

Kissinger, Henry. *White House Years.* Boston: Little, Brown, 1979.

_____. *Years of Upheaval.* Boston: Little, Brown, 1982.

Mak, Dayton, and Charles Stuart Kennedy. *American Ambassadors in a Troubled World: Interviews with Senior Diplomats.* Westport, Conn.: Greenwood Press, 1992.

McNamara, Francis Terry. *Escape with Honor: My Last Hours in Vietnam.* Washington, D.C.: Brassey's, 1997.

Morris, Charles N. "The Autobiography of Commodore Charles N. Morris, USN," *U.S. Naval Institute Proceedings,* 1880, Vol. 6, No. 12.

Nixon, Richard M. *RN: The Memoirs of Richard Nixon.* New York: Grosset and Dunlap, 1978.

Perry, Matthew C. *The Personal Journal of Commodore Matthew C. Perry.* Edited by Roger Pireau with an introduction by Samuel Eliot Morison. Washington, D.C.: Smithsonian Institution, 1968.

Rusk, Dean, as told to Richard Rusk. *As I Saw It.* Edited by Daniel S. Papp. New York: W.W. Norton, 1990.

Vandegrift, Alexander A., as told to Robert B. Asprey. *Once a Marine: The Memoirs of General A.A. Vandegrift, USMC.* New York: W.W. Norton, 1964.

Westmoreland, William C. *A Soldier Reports.* New York: Dell Publishing, 1980.

Unpublished Manuscripts

Baisden, Thomas. "Marines as Diplomatic Couriers: The Stirring Experiences of War Days," Part 2, unpublished monograph, Reference Section, Marine Security Guard Folder, Historical Articles: History and Museums Division, U.S. Marine Corps Historical Division, MCCDC, Quantico, Va.

Bolick, Gary J. "Hungarian Revolution of 1956: Observations and Comments," dtd. 2000, unpublished reminiscences, S-3 Historical Collection, Drawer 2, Historical Files, Marine Corps Embassy Security Guard Command, MCCDC, Quantico, Va.

Lampman, George. "Evacuation from Seoul," 50th Anniversary Commemorative Binder, Marine Corps Embassy Security Guard Command, MCCDC, Quantico, Va.

_____. "The Marine Security Section and Evacuation from Seoul," unpublished manuscript located in Korean War Binder, Marine Security Guard Battalion, S3-A, Historical Collection, Marine Corps Embassy Security Guard Command, MCCDC, Quantico, Va.

"Marine Security Guards in Life Threatening Situations." Quantico, Va.: History and Museums Division, USMC, Reference Section, MSG Drawer, HQMC, nd.

McClellan, Edwin H. "American Marines in Nicaragua." Washington, D.C.: History and Museums Division, Reference Section, "Nicaragua," Geographic Folder.

_____. "History of the United States Marine Corps." Unpublished draft history. Washington, D.C.: Historical Section, HQMC, July 1925, p. 23. The manuscript is in the possession of the author.

_____. "Marines in Siberia." Reference Folder, Unpublished Draft History. Washington, D.C.: Historical Section, HQMC.

O'Grady, William. "Marines as Diplomatic Couriers: The Stirring Experiences of War Days," Part 1, unpublished monograph, Reference Section, Marine Security Guard Folder, Historical Articles, History and Museums Division, U.S. Marine Corps Historical Division, MCCC, Quantico, Va.

Owens, William. "Embassy Pioneers," October 1998, Manuscript found in Historical Drawers, S-3, Marine Corps Embassy Security Guard Command, MCCDC, Quantico, Va.

Sabanski, Thomas J. "It Was a Good Career," March 1988, Marine Corps Base, Camp Joseph H. Pendleton, Calif., Manuscript in possession of the author.

Ward, J.H., Staff Sergeant. "U.S. Marine Security Guard Detachment, Rangoon, Burma, Report on Military Takeover, 1961–1969," unpublished report, S-3, Historical Files, Marine Corps Embassy Security Guard Command, MCCDC, Quantico, Va.

Published Reports

Crowe, William J. *Report of the Accountability Review Boards: The Bombings of the U.S. Embassies in Nairobi, Kenya and Dar Es Salaam, Tanzania on August 7, 1998.* Washington, D.C.: U.S. Department of State, January 1999.

Siegel, Adam B. "Eastern Exit: The Noncombatant Evacuation Operation (NEO) from Mogadishu, Somalia in January 1991," Professional Paper, No. 512.09, September 1991, Alexandria, Va., Center for Naval Analyses.

Woldman, Joel. "Diplomatic Security: The Marine Security Guard Program and Missions Abroad," Congressional Research Report for Congress, No. 87–602 F, dtd. 8 July 1987.

SECONDARY SOURCES

Dissertations and Theses

Millett, Richard D. "The History of the Guardia Nacional De Nicaragua." Ph.D. Dissertation, University of New Mexico, Albuquerque, 1966.

Weber, Elizabeth Anne. "Changing with the Times: Afro-American Response to the United States' Congo Policy, 1960–63." M.A. Thesis, Ohio State University, Columbus, Ohio, 1991.

Articles

Ahmad, Munir. "Al Qaeda Claims Murder Attempt: Warns of More 'Painful Strikes.'" *Washington Times,* August 1, 2004.

"Anti-American Demonstration Leads to Ugly Riot, Precaution at U.S. Embassy." *The Guardian* (Rangoon), February 22, 1961, Vol. 5, No. 354.

Allen, Henry. "Semper Fi! The Guardian Elite: Tehran on Their Minds at the Marine Security Guard School." *Washington Post,* February 15, 1979.

Anderson, Jon. "Embassy in Albania on Alert: Marines and seals on Guard Amid Terrorist Fears." *Stars and Stripes*, August 17, 1998.

_____. "Marines Hunker Down at Embassy in Albania." *Stars and Stripes*, August 22, 1998.

"Black Flags Greet Kissinger." *The Statesman* (New Delhi), July 7, 1971.

"Bound for Hours, Facing the Walls." *Time*, December 3, 1979.

Bowen, Bob. "Posts of the Corps: Saigon." *Leatherneck*, July 1966, Vol. 49, No. 7.

Branigin, William. "Iranian Leftists Battle Way into U.S. Embassy." *Washington Post*, February 15, 1979.

"A Brave Young Leatherneck Escapes Death in Iran." *People*, February 17, 1979.

Brill, Arthur P., Jr., "From Tripoli to the 21st Century, Corps' MSG Detachments: A Growth Industry." *Seapower*, April 1998.

Brinkley, C. Mark. "Marines Lead the Way for U.N., in War-torn Haiti." *Marine Corps Times*, March 15, 2004, Vol. 6, No. 10.

Brown, Drew. "Marines Expect to Have Limited Role in Haiti." *The Virginia-Pilot*, March 2, 2004.

Camp, Richard D. "End of an Era: Surrender of the North China Marines." *Leatherneck*, December 1999, Vol. 82, No. 12.

Carlson, Evans Ford. "Marines as Aid to Diplomacy in China." *Marine Corps Gazette*, February 1936, Vol. 20, No. 1.

Conway, James. "Iranians Thronged in After Embassy Aide Ordered Door Open." Unattributed newspaper article in Marine Security Guard Files, S-3, Drawer 4, Folder "1979."

Crawford, Danny. "Chronology of Marines and the State Department," Washington, D.C., History and Museums Division, HQMC, Marine Corps Historical Center, Reference Section, Marine Security Guard Folder.

_____. "Two Centuries of Teamwork: U.S. Marines and the Foreign Service." *Shipmate*, November 1980.

DeYoung, Karen. "Mob Invades U.S. Embassy in Tripoli." *Washington Post*, December 3, 1979.

Dodds, Paisley, and Ian James. "Aristide Escapes into Exile: U.S. Marines Vanguard of U.N.-approved Forces Sent to Quell Haitian Uprising." *The Daily Press*, March 1, 2004.

Dowd, Maureen, and Suzanne Bilello. "Hostages Tell of Abuses; Carter Decries Barbarism." *Washington Star*, January 22, 1981.

Early, Pete. "Spy Fiasco." *Washington Post Magazine*, February 7, 1988.

"Envoy Arrives to Fill Athens Post After Year." *New York Times*, January 10, 1970.

Epstein, Dan. "Training Future Embassy Guards." *The Sentry*, Quantico, Va., November 29, 1979.

Faison, Seth. "Madame Chiang Kai-shek, a Power in Husband's China and Abroad, Dies at 105." *New York Times*, October 25, 2003.

Ferry, Brenda W., and Leo J. Daugherty. "Ambassadors in Blue." *State Magazine*, February 1999, No. 422.

Gauger, Marcia. "You Could Die Here." *Time*, December 3, 1979.

Getler, Michael. "10 Freed Hostages Released in Iran Hold Reunion with 3 in West Germany." *New York Times*, November 12, 1979.

Goodman, Carl. "Tragedy and Inspiration in Nairobi." *State Magazine*, October 1998.

Hilliard, Jack, and Richard Long. "The First Time." *U.S. Naval Institute Proceedings*, February 1969, Vol. 95, No. 2, Whole No. 792.

Honegger, Barbara. "Silent Hero." *Marines*, March 1999.

"Hostage Training Instituted." *Daily Pilot* (Orange County, Calif.), December 10, 1979.

House, Toni. "Freed Hostages to be Home for Holiday." *The Washington Star*, November 21, 1979.

"An Iranian Charges Hostage Fathered His Sister's Child." United Press International, March 29, 1980.

Jarvis, James D. "Marines Reclaim Post 1, Kabul." *Leatherneck*, February 2002, Vol. 85, No. 2.

Jones, Mel. "Bombing in Beirut Kills Sailor, Soldier; Four Marines Wounded." *Navy Times*, April 25, 1984.

_____. "Corps Eyes Moslems are WM Pullouts." *Navy Times*, December 10, 1979.

Keene, R.R. "Samoa: Marines Intercede in Bloody Power Struggle." *Leatherneck*, April 1999, Vol. 82, No. 4.

Kessler, Gerald, and Michael Daly. "Through the Awful Static Came the Happiest of Words, 'I'm Fine.'" *New York Daily News*, November 21, 1979.

Kessler, Glenn. "U.S. Role in Liberia is Outlined." *Washington Post*, July 26, 2003.

"Kissinger Gets Noisy Welcome." *The Times of India* (New Delhi), July 7, 1971, Vol. 133, No. 187.

Koscak, Paul. "School Screens Marines for Coveted Overseas Guard Duty." *State Magazine*, U.S. Department of State, May 2003.

Krout, Mary H. "Perry's Expedition to Japan." *U.S. Naval Institute Proceedings*, February 1921, Vol. 47, No. 2.

Lampman, George, with Barry A. Zulauf. "Without So Much as a Bloody Nose: The Evacuation of the American Embassy in Seoul, Korea." *Leatherneck*, June 2000, Vol. 83, No. 6.

Lange, John E. "Dar es Salaam: Confronting the Crisis." October 1998, *State Magazine*.

Lubold, Gordon. "3 Years ... 3 Embassies." *Marine Corps Times*, May 3, 2004.

"Marine Guards are Trained for Limited Missions." *New York Times*, November 1979.

"Marine Security Guards: Upholding Traditional Standards of Discipline." *Marine Security Guard Newsletter*, January 1980.

"Marines Rescue U.S. Envoy from Mob in Salvador." *New York Daily News*, May 13, 1980.

Martin, Bruce. "Crowley Defended Embassy." *Quantico Sentry*, November 30, 1979.

McCartney, Robert J. "Gunmen Seen Singling Out U.S. Marines." *Washington Post*, June 20, 1985.

McClellan, Edwin H. "The Capture of the Barrier Forts in the Canton River, China." *Marine Corps Gazette*, September 1920, Vol. 5, No. 3.

_____. "The Naval War with France." *Marine Corps Gazette*, December 1922, Vol. 7, No. 4.

Mehringer, Phil, and R.A. Smith. "Working Amidst Chaos." *Leatherneck*, August 1996, Volume 76, No. 8.

"MSG Det Kampala." *Marines*, August 1986.

"MSG Graduate Ready for True Test of Confidence." *The Sentry*, Quantico, Va., Friday, April 14, 1979.

Oberdorfer, Don. "U.S. Embassy in Kabul to be Evacuated, Closed," *Washington Post*, January 31, 1989.

Palmer, Thomas. "Where the US Marines Went Wrong." *Boston Globe*, April 12, 1987.

Parks, W. Hay. "Evacuation by Military Force." *Marine Corps Gazette*, September 1978, Vol. 62, No. 9.

"President Ford and Secretary Kissinger Lead Mourners at Davies Ceremony." *Department of State Newsletter*, September 1974.

Randal, Jonathan. "Four Women, Six Blacks in Group." *Washington Post*, November 20, 1979.

Reagan, Ronald. "President Reagan's Remarks on the Slayings." Quantico *Sentry*, June 28, 1985.

Roberson, Matthew B. "Afghanistan: Kabul: 4th MEB Mans Embassy." *Leatherneck*, March 2002, Vol. 85, No. 3.

Roegner, Julie. "Wounded Marine Confides, 'I was just doing my job.'" *SAM Magazine*, July 1979.

Sachtleben, Glen. "Operation Sharp Edge: The Corps' MEU(SOC) Program in Action." *Marine Corps Gazette*, November 1991, Vol. 75, No. 11.

Scarborough, Rowan. "Assault Force to Position 2,000 Marines off Monrovia." *Washington Times*, July 26, 2003.

Schmidt, Deborah. "Violence Brings Aid from Congo, Zaire Marine Guards." *Navy Times*, December 16, 1991.

_____. "Women Security Guards Finding Gradual Acceptance." *Navy Times,* December 16, 1991.

Sides, Hampton. "The First to Die." *Reader's Digest*, February 2004.

"State Lauds Athens MSGs." *Marine Security Guard Information Bulletin*, May 1, 1975.

Stevenson, Mark, and Paisley Dodds. "Haitians Show Indifference to U.S. Marines' Presence." *The Virginia-Pilot*, March 5, 2004.

Stroup, Mike. "Bringing Help in Kenya." *Leatherneck*, August 1994, Vol. 77, No. 8.

_____. "Operation Distant Runner Rescues Americans." *Leatherneck,* August 1994, Vol. 77, No. 8.

Tompkins, R. McC. "Ubique," *Marine Corps Gazette*, September 1965, Vol. 49, No. 9.

Tucker, Phillip. "Embassy Beachhead." *Leatherneck*, August 1965, Volume 46, No. 8.

"U.S. Ambassador Killed in Afghanistan." *Department of State Bulletin*, Vol. 79, April 1979, No. 2025.

"U.S. Embassy Lowers Flag, Quits Kabul." *Washington Times*, January 31, 1989.

Valdez, Juan J. "The Last to Leave." *Leatherneck*, September 1975, Vol. 58, No. 9.

Vandenbroucke, Lucien. "Tragedy and Inspiration in Nairobi: When Uncommon Valor Became Commonplace." *State Magazine*, October 1998.

Vasgerdsian, Ed. "Cairo: An Old City, a Familiar Face, a New Outlook." *Leatherneck*, April 1999, Vol. 82, No. 4.

"A Warm Welcome from Weary Liberians: 26th MEU Marines 'just here to help the people.'" *Marine Corps Times*, August 25, 2003.

Wass, Becki. "Soldier Trains at MSG School." *The Sentry*, Quantico, Va., February 25, 1983.

Weiner, Tim, and Lydia Polgreen. "Haitian Rebels Stake Claim to Power." *The Virginia-Pilot*, March 2, 2004.

Weintraub, Richard M. "U.S. Closes its Embassy in Kabul." *Washington Post*, January 31, 1989.

"Yorktown Marines Land in Haiti, Anti-Terror Unit to Provide Security as Rebels Move Toward Capital." *The Virginia-Pilot*, February 24, 2004.

Zavis, Alexandra. "Liberia in Chaos: Marines Help Evacuate U.S. Embassy as Dozens Die." *Daily Press* (Hampton Roads, Va.), July 22, 2003.

Zinser, Larry R. "The BLT in Evacuation Operations," *Marine Corps Gazette*, December 1973, Vol. 57, No. 12.

BOOKS

Armajani, Yahya, and Thomas M. Ricks. *The Middle East: Past and Present*. Englewood Cliffs, N.J.: Prentice-Hall, 1986.

Bailey, Thomas A. *A Diplomatic History of the American People*, Ninth Edition. Englewood Cliffs, N.J.: Prentice-Hall, 1974.

Barker, Rodney. *Dancing with the Devil: Sex, Espionage and the U.S. Marines: The Clayton Lonetree Story*. New York: Ivy Books, 1996.

Biggs, Chester M. *The United States Marines in North China, 1894–1942*. Jefferson, N.C.: McFarland, 2003.

Clubb, O. Edmund. *20th Century China*. New York: Columbia University Press, 1966.

Collum, Richard S. *History of the United States Marine Corps*. Philadelphia: L.R. Hamersly, 1890.

Cumings, Bruce. *The Origins of the Korean War, Volume II: The Roaring of the Cataract, 1947–1950*. Princeton, N.J.: Princeton University Press, 1990.

Daggett, A.S. *America in the China Relief Expedition*. Nashville, Tenn.: The Battery Press, 1903, Reprinted 1997.

Dmytryshyn, Basil. *The USSR: A Concise History*. New York: Charles Scribner's Sons, 1978.

Dunn, Peter. *The First Vietnam War*. New York: St. Martin's Press, 1985.

Ehteshami, Anoushirivan, et al. *The Foreign Policies of Middle East States*. Boulder, Co.: Lynne Reinner, 2002.

Fisher, Sydney Nettleton. *The Middle East: A History*, Third Edition. New York: Alfred A. Knopf, 1979.

French, Howard W. *A Continent for the Taking: The Tragedy and Hope of Africa*. New York: Alfred A. Knopf, 2004.

Furuya, Keiji. *Chiang Kai-Shek: His Life and Times*. New York: St. John's University, 1981.

Gibbs, David N. *The Political Economy of Third World Intervention: Mines, Money, and U.S. Policy in the Congo Crisis*. Chicago: University of Chicago Press, 1991.

Graebner, Norman A., et al. *An Uncertain Tradition: American Secretaries of State in the Twentieth Century*. New York: McGraw Hill, 1961.

Hane, Miksio. *Modern Japan: A Historical Survey*, Second Edition. Boulder, Colo.: Westview Press, 1992.

Heinl, Robert Debs, and Nancy A. Heinl. *Written in Blood: The Story of the Haitian People, 1492–1971*. Boston: Houghton Mifflin, 1978.

Herzog, Chaim. *Arab-Israeli Wars: War and Peace in the Middle East from the War of Independence through Lebanon*, Revised Edition. New York: Vintage Press, 1984.

Howe, Russell Warren. *Black Africa: Africa South of the*

Sahara from Pre-History to Independence, Volume I: From Pre-History to the Eve of the Colonial Era. New York: Walker and Co., 1966.

Hsu, Immanuel C.Y. *The Rise of Modern China*, Fourth Edition. New York: Oxford University Press, 1990.

Isaac, Arnold R. *Without Honor: Defeat in Vietnam and Cambodia.* Baltimore, Md.: Johns Hopkins University Press, 1983.

Kamman, William. *A Search for Stability: United States Diplomacy Toward Nicaragua, 1927–1933.* South Bend, Indiana: Notre Dame University Press, 1968.

Karnow, Stanley. *Vietnam: A History.* New York: Penguin Books, 1984.

Kennan, George F. *Soviet-American Relations, 1917–1920: Volume II, The Decision to Intervene.* Princeton, N.J.: Princeton University Press, 1989.

Laqueur, Walter. *Europe Since Hitler: The Rebirth of Europe*, Revised Edition. New York: Penguin Books, 1982.

Lenczowski, George. *Iran Under the Pahlavis.* Stanford, Calif.: Hoover Institution Press, 1978.

_____. *The Middle East in World Affairs.* Fourth Edition. New York: Cornell University Press, 1980.

Mackey, Sandra. *The Iranians, Persia, Islam, and the Soul of a Nation.* New York: Plume/Penguin Press, 1998.

Makers of Modern Africa: Profiles in History. London: African Journal, 1981.

Metcalf, Clyde H. *A History of the United States Marine Corps.* New York: G.P. Putnam's Sons, 1939.

Millett, Allan R. *In Many A Strife: General Gerald C. Thomas and the U.S. Marine Corps, 1917–1956.* Annapolis, Md.: Naval Institute Press, 1993.

_____. *Semper Fidelis: The History of the United States Marine Corps.* New York: Macmillan Publishing Company, 1980.

Preston, Diana. *The Boxer Rebellion: The Dramatic Story of China's War on Foreigners that Shook the World in the Summer of 1900.* New York: Berkley Books, 2000.

Quirk, Robert E. *An Affair of Honor: Woodrow Wilson and the Occupation of Vera Cruz.* New York: W.W. Norton and Company, 1962.

Rapoport, David C. *Inside Terrorist Organizations.* New York: Columbia University Press, 1988.

Rashid, Ahmed. *Taliban: Militant Islam, Oil, and Fundamentalism in Central Asia.* New Haven: Yale Nota Bene/Yale University Press, 2001.

Rippy, J. Fred. *Latin America: A Modern History.* Ann Arbor: University of Michigan Press, 1958.

Schmidt, Hans. *Maverick Marine: General Smedley D. Butler and the Contradictions of American Military History.* Lexington: University Press of Kentucky, 1987.

Shafer, Robert Jones. *A History of Latin America.* Lexington, Mass.: D.C. Hath and Co., 1978.

Takekoshi, Yosaburo. *Japanese Rule in Formosa.* Preface by Baron Shimpei Goto, translated by George Braithwaite. London: Longmans, Green and Co., 1907.

Tan, Chester C. *The Boxer Catastrophe.* New York: W.W. Norton, 1967.

Thomson, James C., Peter W. Staley, and John Curtis Perry. *Sentimental Imperialists: The American Experience in East Asia.* New York: Harper and Row, 1985.

Trager, Frank N. *Burma, From Kingdom to Republic: A Historical and Political Analysis.* New York: Frederick A. Praeger, 1966.

Urban, Mark. *The War in Afghanistan*, Second Edition. London: Macmillan, 1990.

Wakeman, Frederic, Jr. *The Fall of Imperial China.* New York: The Free Press, 1975.

Wheelan, Joseph. *Jefferson's War: America's First War on Terror, 1801–1805.* New York: Carroll and Graf, 2003.

Wiarda, Howard J., and Michael J. Kryzanek. *The Dominican Republic: A Caribbean Crucible.* Boulder, Co.: Westview Press, 1982.

Index

383